Statistics for Social Data Analysis

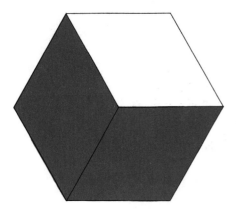

Statistics for Social Data Analysis

THIRD EDITION

GEORGE W. BOHRNSTEDT
American Institutes for Research

DAVID KNOKE
University of Minnesota

F. E. PEACOCK PUBLISHERS, INC.   ITASCA, ILLINOIS

For our teachers, Edgar F. Borgatta and David R. Segal

Abbreviated Contents

Contents

Preface

The third edition of *Statistics for Social Data Analysis* is a major revision of the two earlier editions. It attempts to keep pace with new developments and recent practices in applied statistics in several social science disciplines, especially sociology, political science, and education. In particular, new chapters have been added that deal with nonlinear and logistic regression, log-linear models, and structural equation systems. Our approach emphasizes statistics as a tool for solving research problems, rather than as an end in and of itself. Hence, we constantly stress formulating important substantive hypotheses as the essential prelude to quantitative data analysis. We also underscore the importance of estimating intervals within which population parameters may be found and of measuring the magnitude of association between variables. We believe this approach offers students superior insights into the ways social scientists actually conduct research than did the older convention of hypothesis tests about point estimates.

At least four distinctive features characterize this book:

1. A focus on the *continuous-discrete distinction* when considering the level at which a variable is measured
2. An emphasis on establishing whether meaningful *substantive relationships* exist between and among variables
3. The use of *real data in examples* whenever possible
4. The *opportunity for the student to analyze real data sets* using a standard, widely available computer package—Statistical Package for the Social Sciences (SPSS).[1]

---

1. SPSS is a trademark of SPSS Inc. (Chicago) for its proprietary computer software. No materials describing such software may be produced or distributed without the written permission of SPSS Inc.

None of our editions emphasizes the conventional levels of measurement (nominal, ordinal, interval, and ratio) that were popularized a generation ago. Instead, we present statistics for analyzing continuous and discrete variables separately and in combination. Although debates continue in the social science methodology journals about the best choices among statistical techniques, even a cursory examination of the leading journals indicates that the continuous-discrete distinction is widely applied by current practitioners. Most researchers use either covariational techniques (variations of the general linear model) or analyses of crosstabulated categoric variables.

Many, if not most, statistics texts begin with univariate statistics, followed by chapters on inference and hypothesis testing, before finally examining bivariate and multivariate relationships. As a result, for most of a semester the student may not realize that scientists are rarely if ever interested in describing and making inferences about a single variable. For this reason we make a special effort to explain to the student that social scientists are interested in establishing relationships between and among variables. We begin this emphasis in the first chapter, in which we describe the research process in general, and continue with it to the end of the book. Even in chapter 2, on frequency distributions and their description, examples are given to illustrate that social scientists are rarely interested in a single frequency distribution and its description (e.g., its mean and standard deviation).

We used real data sets when constructing most examples in the book, and in some places we developed mini-theories that are then tested with actual data sets. Our purpose is to show how the substance of social science is tied to statistics in the research cycle, rather than focusing solely on technique. By studying propositions and hypotheses and methods for evaluating them, the student learns to appreciate the entire research process.

Our hands-on approach emphasizes learning-by-doing that uses realistic examples. One strength of the text is that many problems at the ends of chapters are designed to require only pencil and paper or hand-held calculators to find a solution, while other problems allow students to work with computers using prepared data files of actual social data. This combination of problems permits the student to learn the step-by-step computations needed for calculating each statistic, and also to experience the excitement and frustration of testing hunches and hypotheses with real data. Two data sets serve as illustrations within the text and for chapter problems: the 1991 General Social Survey and the U.S. States Data Set. They have been created as SPSS files for personal computer and copies are available on 3.5-inch floppy diskettes from the publisher. Our *Instructor's Manual* describes how to install the data sets and also gives some basic instruction in using SPSS programs.

Other special features of the book should facilitate student mastery of social statistics as well. We avoid excessive proofs and theorems, often relegating them to boxes set off from the main text. All key concepts introduced in the text are also reproduced in the margins. This feature not only underscores the key concepts but also makes it easy for the student to review them. Lists of all key concepts and statistical symbols appear at the end of each chapter, in order of presentation in the text, to indicate the material the student should have mastered in the chapter. An alphabetical list of all key terms and their definitions is presented in a glossary at the end of the book. Thus, a student can easily find the definition of a key concept or statistical symbol without having to know where it is first used. All major formulas are printed between colored horizontal bars for emphasis and easy review.

Implicit in this text is our conviction that the culture of the classroom should foster cooperation. However, we do not believe that cooperation precludes conflict and critique. We would be grateful for comments from instructors and students about the text, the problems, and the general approach, as well as suggestions for additional problems or other material that would enhance its use. We also would be happy to distribute such suggestions to instructors who have adopted the text. David Knoke can be contacted through electronic mail as follows:

knoke001@maroon.tc.umn.edu

We are indebted to A. Hald for reprinting the Area Under the Normal Curve and E. S. Pearson and H. O. Hartley for the reprint of the *F*-Distribution Table. We are also grateful to the literary executor of the late Ronald A. Fisher, F. R. S., to Dr. Frank Yates, F. R. S., and to the Longman Group Ltd. of London, for permission to reprint Tables III and IV from their book *Statistical Tables for Biological, Agricultural, and Medical Research* (6th ed., 1974).

We acknowledge permission from SPSS Inc. to use their software package SPSS™ throughout the book to illustrate the analysis of survey data with the computer. We also acknowledge cooperation of the National Opinion Research Center and the Roper Opinion Research Center for making available the General Social Surveys.

Any book with technical materials will have some errors. In spite of our best attempt to prevent them, we are certain some will be found. We ask instructors and students to notify us or the publisher if you find errors. We will attempt to correct them in future printings of the book.

We are grateful for the fine editorial help provided by Caryl Wenzel and the production staff of Publishers Services, Inc. We are grateful to Karl Krohn for assistance with data preparation. We thank our publisher F. Edward Peacock for his steadfast sustenance over the years. The second author is particularly grateful for support to the Center for Advanced Study in the Behavioral Sciences (CASBS) in Palo Alto, California. He was a fellow at the center during the 1992–93 academic year (supported by National Science Foundation grant SES-9022192).

Finally, we thank our wives and children for their continuing support.

George W. Bohrnstedt
David Knoke
Palo Alto, California

Statistics for Social Data Analysis

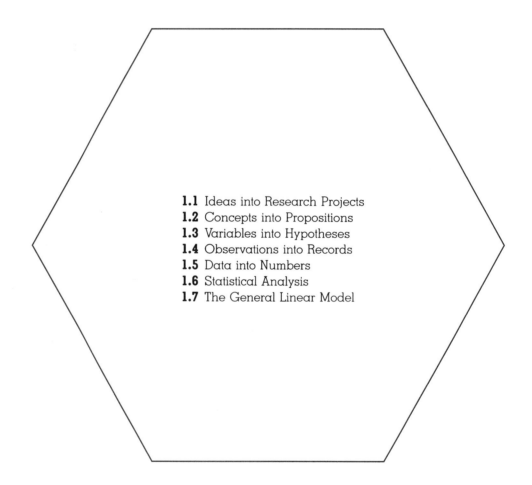

Statistics in the Research Process

Our emphasis throughout this book is on how to use statistics as a tool to analyze social data. Statistical methods are means to answer substantive questions about social relations, whether the primary motivation comes from theoretical issues or from practical concerns. Our central interest is in reducing uncertainty, or put more positively, increasing knowledge about how humans behave in a variety of social situations. As a general principle, we believe that explaining variation is the central task shared by all social scientists: How do people, groups, communities, or nations differ from one another and what are the consequences of such variation? The particular behaviors to be explained may differ from discipline to discipline and from researcher to researcher, but the general approach remains universal. All social and behavioral scientists seek to account for the differences they observe among social actors by examining the patterns of variation in their characteristics, activities, and attitudes.

For example, can we explain differences in the annual incomes that people earn by measuring their differences in years of education, work experience, supervisory responsibilities, and work ethics? Or should we also take into consideration their companies' market positions, union bargaining contracts, and racial and sex discrimination practices? Another example, can we understand why some people vote for the Republican presidential candidate, others for the Democrat, and others stay home on Election Day? Are different electoral behaviors attributable to the variation in voters' attitudes towards the candidates, the political parties, the election issues, and to their social group memberships? If so, which factors are most important in shaping the voters' decisions? The large and sophisticated body of statistical techniques available to social researchers offers them a variety of ways to answer such questions. Properly and cautiously applied, the goal of social statistics is to permit researchers to reach tentative conclusions about the existence and strength of social relationships.

Our approach to statistics stems directly from the conviction that adequately explaining any human behavior is equivalent to showing how variations in that behavior are related to multiple, measured causes. As a tool, statistical analysis occupies a key position within the larger set of activities that make up the social research process. Although every research project follows a unique course, enough similarities occur to describe this process as a succession of steps from initial design through final conclusion.

1. Researchers formulate what are often initially vague ideas into more concrete, researchable problems.
2. The relationships among abstract concepts are translated into rigorous hypotheses containing variables that can be observed.
3. Instruments are created or borrowed to measure the variables specified by the research hypotheses.
4. Observations on a representatively selected sample of social units (e.g., persons, organizations, communities) are systematically recorded.
5. Observational data are reduced to a set of numbers and entered into a storage device, typically a personal computer, for later analysis.
6. Appropriate statistical methods are applied to key variables in the data set to determine whether evidence can be garnered in support of the hypothesized relations.
7. The researcher reaches a conclusion about the relative importance of the sources of variation initially believed to explain the social phenomena of interest. The typical result is an incremental improvement in our collective understanding of the social worlds in which we live.

This chapter fills in some of the details of the social research process. Because social statistics is an integral part of that design, they cannot be studied in isolation from the larger issues of hypothesis formation, operationalization, sampling, and measurement. These issues will rise again and again as you proceed through this book and learn the variety of statistical techniques available to the modern social researcher. Nothing can substitute for a thorough grasp of the larger research enterprise in which statistical methods play a central role. To help you acquire a feel for the research experience, we illustrate statistical procedures with many examples taken from two social data sets, described in Boxes 1.1 and 1.2. Moreover, at the end of every chapter, we provide problems for you to apply your newly gained knowledge of social statistics. Ultimately, our desire is for students to acquire sufficient statistical skill to design and carry out their own projects. The most rewarding (although sometimes frustrating!) way to comprehend the beauty of social research is to grapple directly with the

---

BOX 1.1   General Social Survey Samples

Beginning in 1972, the National Opinion Research Center has conducted annual (except 1979, 1981, and 1992) General Social Surveys of the U.S. adult population. With an average of about 1,500 personal interviews lasting 90 minutes or more, the first 18 GSS data files have a cumulative 27,782 cases. The topics covered range from abortion attitudes to military spending to work experiences. Many examples and chapter problems in this text use GSS data. We have created an SPSS system file containing more than 450 variables from the 1991 GSS. It is available on a floppy diskette for classroom use on request to the publisher. Many chapter problems require these measures and the data set is ideal for student paper assignments.

Although the GSS follows a complex sampling procedure that violates simple random sampling assumptions, the principal investigators advise applying statistical tests in the conventional manner. Because our main use of GSS samples is to illustrate how social statistics can be applied to large data sets, we apply the various statistical tests without modification.

BOX 1.2   The U.S. States Data Set

The U.S. States Data Set comprises a small-N data set useful for illustrating relationships among variables pertinent to highly aggregated units of analysis. The District of Columbia is also included, for a total of 51 cases. The federal government, through such agencies as the Bureau of the Census and the National Center for Health Statistics, collects voluminous data on many social and economic conditions. We extracted some 225 variables from the state portion of the 1987 *City-County Data Book* and added a few from other sources. Most measures apply to 1982–1986, although some assess changes over longer periods. These data were compiled as an SPSS computer system file, available on a floppy diskette for classroom use on request to the publisher.

Analyses of the U.S. States Data Set should be done cautiously. Given the demographic and economic flow connections among them, the states are not independent cases; they are not a simple random sample, but a complete population of states. Thus, what the results of a statistical inference generalize to is unclear. However, we apply statistical methods both to illustrate small-N procedures and to assess the magnitudes of relations among state-level variables.

A further word of caution: The U.S. States Data Set treats large and small states equally, with each contributing 1/51st of the cases. Thus, these variables *cannot* be used to calculate a correct mean or proportion for the U.S. population as a whole. Rather, the values represent the mean or proportion of the states' scores. For example, the mean percentage of women in the states' labor forces in 1986 was 56.8%. To obtain the correct value for the U.S. population requires *weighting* every state's score to its population size before calculation. Thus, the weighted average of U.S. women in the labor force was 55.4%. This figure is lower than the states' average because women living in the smaller states tended to enter the labor force at higher rates than women in the more populated states. Because we are mainly interested in characterizing the variables that apply to the states, we use the unweighted measures and interpret them accordingly.

numerous dilemmas and decisions that researchers must confront and resolve at every step in the research cycle.

1.1   Ideas into Research Projects

Scientific research is the effort to reduce uncertainty about some aspect of the world by systematically examining the relationships among its parts. Every research project builds on the current state of knowledge, but seeks to extend understanding into previously unknown areas. If inquiry were simply confined to demonstrating again what is already known, it would not be called research. Scientific activity differs from other types of scholarship—such as philosophy, theology, literature, and even pure mathematics—by insisting that its explanations be limited to the real world of observable entities. The existence of the soul, the number of angels dancing on a pinhead, and the essence of the good are all questions of faith and assumption, irrelevant to the conduct of scientific inquiry. In other words, research restricts itself to aspects of the empirical world whose properties can be verified through observation and manipulation. In the sense that the state of reality ultimately defines what information a researcher can learn, the laboratory experiment of a chemist differs little from the consumer attitude survey of a market analyst.

scientific research—the effort to reduce uncertainty about some aspect of the world by systematically examining the relationships among its parts

Given that all science continually seeks to improve its explanation of some observable phenomena, where do the ideas for research projects come from? At any time, disciplinary specialists stake out particular topics as ripe for debate and analysis. For example, some recent vogues in sociology include organizational births and deaths, the origins of the welfare state, the ecological concentration of the urban underclass, the role of biological maturation in shaping the life course, and the relationship of age to criminal activity. Within each topical specialty, an active community of research scholars (which may be scattered across international boundaries) communicates its current findings, new ideas, and proposals for new research projects through a variety of media: journal publications, conferences, working papers, guest lectures, retreats, electronic mail, and foundation review panels. From this constant flood of information, both established and novice researchers can extract suggestions for further investigations that could lead to new insights about the phenomenon of interest.

applied research— research that attempts to explain social phenomena with immediate public policy implications

Some research projects are generated by practical concerns about the impact or effectiveness of specific social programs and policies. **Applied research** attempts to explain social phenomena with immediate public policy implications. For example, does the Head Start preschool program increase the scholastic performance of children from backgrounds of poverty? How can drug addicts be persuaded to stop sharing needles that spread AIDS? Can the error rates of airline pilots be reduced by redesigning instrumental panel layouts? Do work-release experiences and halfway houses lower the amount of recidivism among former prisoners? Policymakers and administrators who grapple day-to-day with serious social problems urgently need answers to such questions. They demand practical solutions through applied social science knowledge. Many applied research projects are initiated by state and federal funding agencies through so-called "requests for proposals" (RFPs) that very rigidly specify the design and analysis requirements that must be met by the applicants. Whether the project findings have relevance beyond the confines of a particular study generally has little importance for both funders and principal investigators.

basic research— research that examines the validity of general statements about relationships involving fundamental social processes

Other research projects arise primarily from investigators' theoretical interests, without concern for immediate applications of the results. Rather, **basic research** examines the validity of general statements about relationships involving fundamental social processes. Basic researchers develop knowledge about general principles of social behavior that may account for a wide range of specific activities. For example, is the division of household labor between husbands and wives best conceptualized as an exchange process or as a symbolic interaction involving self-conceptualizations? Do neo-Marxist ideas of capitalist exploitation of labor better predict companies' job training practices than neoclassical economists' notions of human capital formation? Are voters' presidential choices influenced mainly by mass media messages or by their local social networks? In answering these questions researchers are mainly concerned with verifying or disproving assertions embedded in general theories of human behavior, even if the practical policy implications are not obvious. Indeed, the substance of the project is typically secondary to its ability to illustrate abstract analytic relations. Basic research projects are usually initiated by academic investigators who have devoted a substantial portion of their careers to mastering the theoretical background. The National

Science Foundation, a federal agency whose mission is to support all sciences, is the major funding source for basic social science research in the United States. It seldom solicits proposals, but relies on investigator-initiated proposals from research grants, which are evaluated and approved by "peer review" panels of senior scientists who consider each proposal's basic scientific merits. Other federal agencies that fund basic social research, in specific areas, include the National Institute of Mental Health, the National Institute for Drug Abuse, and the National Institute on Aging.

Whether applied or basic research drives a project, a researcher's dominant goal is to account accurately for the observed variation in the phenomena under investigation. In practice reaching this goal requires the researcher to identify as many as possible of the major factors creating differences among the persons, objects, or events of interest. For example, in an applied study of why some elderly people require nursing home care and others are able to remain in their own homes, an investigator would want to include such factors as the individual's physical health and mobility, mental alertness, retirement income and savings, care-providing relatives, availability of a personal automobile or mass transit, vacancy rates in nursing homes, and so on. Or, to explain participation in social movement protests, a basic researcher ought to consider factors such as potential participants' benefit-harm calculations, distributive justice and equity norms, public good valuations, solidary social attachments, perceptions of probable state repression, and so on. The key point is that almost all social behaviors are caused by many factors with differing impacts. (Basic features of causal analysis are discussed in detail in chapter 11.) These diverse causes must be explicitly included in the analysis if an accurate account of the sources of variation is to be achieved. The process of examining the causal forces producing social behaviors begins with specifying testable hypotheses, as described in the following section.

1.2 Concepts into Propositions

The core component of a social research project is a formal **proposition,** a statement about the relationship between abstract concepts. Many propositions take an implied "If . . . , then . . ." form, where the element in the first clause is usually assumed to be

proposition— a statement about the relationship between abstract concepts

a cause of the element in the second clause. For example, here is a common proposition in organizational research, numbered here for reference:

P1: The more centralized the decision making, the lower the employee commitment to the organization.

Many of us have a general feeling from personal experience that this proposition states a plausible causal relationship between these two concepts, at least in modern industrial societies. Certainly, we would doubt the truth of a statement relating centralized decision making to higher commitment to the organization. But what exactly do the concepts *decision making* and *employee commitment* mean? A **concept** entails a precisely defined object, behavior, perception (of self or others), or phenomenon that is relevant to the particular theoretical concerns at hand. Thus, the full meaning of the proposition above requires definitions of these two abstract concepts, which are not to be confused with their everyday language meanings.

concept— a precisely defined object, behavior, perception (of self or others), or phenomenon that is relevant to the particular theoretical concerns at hand

Concepts are usually defined according to widely accepted meanings of the term already held by the scientific audience with whom one wishes to communicate. Definitions generally consist of lists of attributes or characteristics that are necessary and sufficient for a particular real entity to qualify unambiguously as an instance of the concept. Thus, an organizational researcher might define "centralized decision making" as "the ratio of supervisors to workers choosing among alternative actions affecting organizational performance." Or, "employee commitment" could be defined as "expressed intentions to continue as an employee of an organization." Other definitions may offer narrower and more precise criteria that could serve better in a particular research project. Much of the debate in social theory centers on the most appropriate way to define abstract concepts.

When a sequence of propositions is connected through common concepts, the resulting set may comprise a social theory for research purposes. More formally, a **social theory** is a set of two or more propositions in which concepts referring to certain social phenomena are assumed to be causally related. To continue the organization example, a second proposition might be as follows:

social theory— a set of two or more propositions in which concepts referring to certain social phenomena are assumed to be causally related

P2: The lower the employee commitment to the organization, the higher the rate of job turnover.

To make P2 fully comprehensible, we would need a formal definition of the "job turnover" concept, presumably one emphasizing
vacancies due to employee decisions rather than actions by the
firm (i.e., quitting employment rather than layoff or firing). To
produce a minimal social theory, P1 can be linked to P2 through the
common concept of "employee commitment." The logical deduction
that connects the two concepts unique to both propositions is as
follows:

P3: The more centralized the decision making, the higher
the rate of job turnover.

Again, our commonsense notions of these terms suggest this
relationship fits with our personal experiences. A more elaborate
theory of alienation in formal organizations might be constructed by
adding propositions that causally link the three concepts to others,
such as employee earnings and organizational values.

The three propositions above did not state the explicit forms of
their relationships. In the absence of contrary assertions, **linearity**
is assumed. That is, the amount of change (increase or decrease) in
one concept caused by a change in another concept is constant
across its range. The linearity assumption is widespread in the
social sciences, where nonlinear conceptualization (e.g., exponential, power, and logarithmic curves) have not penetrated into
theoretical thinking. An extended discussion of the plausibility of
linear relations and their application to statistical techniques appears in section 1.7.

linearity—the amount of change (increase or decrease) in one concept caused by a change in another concept is constant across its range

Very few theoretical propositions claim to be universally true,
applying at all times and places without exception. Most are
created to explain observed variations in fairly restricted circumstances, although subsequent research may show them to have
broader applications. Nevertheless, during their initial stages of
development and testing, theories should identify the **scope** or
boundary conditions—the times, places, or activities—under
which its propositions are expected to be valid. For example, a
theoretical proposition about the father's roles in the socializing of
male children may be irrelevant to societies where the mother's

scope (boundary conditions)—the times, places, or activities under which the propositions of a social theory are expected to be valid

brother takes over many of these functions. Or, the importance of social network ties for occupational mobility may be quite different in market and state socialist economies. By specifying the apparent limits of their propositions, theorists can help researchers to avoid unsuitable tests as well as to probe the boundaries of situations where theories may pertain.

1.3   Variables into Hypotheses

variable— any characteristic or attribute of persons, objects, or events that can take on different numerical values

The term **variable** refers to any characteristic or attribute of persons, objects, or events that can take on different numerical values. Thus, the number of voluntary job quits each month may range from zero to the entire work force. Variables can be classified in several ways. One of the most important ways is to distinguish between latent variables and manifest variables. **Latent variables** are not observable and can only be measured indirectly. Examples of latent variables include concepts such as the degree of centralization in decision making and the degree of employee commitment—concepts used in illustrating propositions in the immediately preceding section. **Manifest variables,** logically enough, can be observed. Examples of manifest variables include the ratio of supervisors to line workers and the number of absences an organization has per month (i.e., phenomena that can be directly observed and counted).

latent variable— a variable that cannot be observed and can only be measured indirectly

manifest variable— a variable that can be observed

Theoretical propositions are necessarily stated in abstract terms, using concepts that cannot be directly observed. To be useful for scientific research, therefore, the concepts must be restated in terms that allow measurement and testing of the relationships. In effect, propositions are translated into **operational hypotheses** by replacing the abstract concepts with observable, concrete referents or terms. For example, P1 can be turned into H1 by substituting for both concepts:

operational hypothesis— a proposition restated with observable, concrete referents or terms replacing abstract concepts

> H1: The larger the number of task assignments made only by supervisors, the lower the percentage of workers expressing desires to continue working for the organization.

Centralization is operationalized by counting the number of task assignments made exclusively by supervisors; employee commitment is operationalized by verbal expressions of desires to continue their employment. Similarly, if we substitute "voluntary job quits per month" for the abstract concept "the rate of job turnover," P2 can be rewritten as H2:

H2: The lower the percentage of workers expressing desires to continue working for the organization, the greater the number of voluntary job quits per month.

In each instance, a concept was replaced by an indicator that, in principle, can be observed for a set of social units, in this example, work organizations. That is, latent concepts or variables are replaced with manifest variables.

A variable can be contrasted to a **constant** which has an unchanging value. "State of residence" is a variable because it differs across the U.S. population, but "Minnesota" is a constant that is invariant for all persons living there. Note that constants may be the values comprising a variable: "Male" and "female" are constants for individuals that constitute the variable *gender*.

Variables can also be classified by the roles they play in a hypothesis that states or implies a causal relationship. An **independent variable** has an antecedent or causal role, usually appearing first in the hypothesis. The **dependent variable** plays a consequent, or affected, role in relation to the independent variable. That is, its values depend on the values taken by the independent variable. It usually comes second in the hypothesis. No ambiguity is present in a statement such as "An increase in unemployment causes a decrease in consumer confidence." Note that some variables may be both independent and dependent variables, even within the same theory. The workers' expressed desires to continue working for the organization is a dependent variable in H1 and an independent variable in H2. The distinguishing criterion is whether its change produces changes in the values of other variables or whether its change is the result of other variables' changes.

Some variables cannot be manipulated; they are called **status variables.** Examples include race, gender, and, for most people, religious affiliation. Even though status variables cannot be manipulated, they nevertheless are often treated as independent variables in researchers' propositions and hypotheses. The outcomes associated with status variables are not usually thought of as due

constant— a value that does not change

independent variable— a variable that has an antecedent or causal role, usually appearing first in the hypothesis

dependent variable— a variable that has a consequent, or affected, role in relation to the independent variable

status variable— a variable whose outcomes cannot be manipulated to causal processes. Instead, they are assumed to be noncausal associations that must be explained by other variables. Observed associations involving status variables are very important in social and behavioral research because they stimulate researchers to search for causal processes that can explain these relationships. For example, the observation that African Americans and Latinos on average have lower incomes than Asian Americans and Caucasians is a noncausal association, but this observation should stimulate researchers to identify causal variables that explain racial differences in incomes (e.g., education, values, family structures, discrimination).

When translating theoretical propositions into operational hypotheses, care must be taken to preserve a fairly rigorous correspondence between the latent and observed variables. Too loose a fit between both systems can result in empirical tests using indicators having little relevance to the ideas motivating the research project. A variable's **validity** refers to the degree to which its operationalization accurately reflects the concept it is intended to measure. For example, the abstract concept *attitude towards sexual permissiveness* would appear much better operationalized by asking people whether they agree that "the only moral standard of sexual conduct is that in the Bible," than by asking "the number of different sex partners you had in the past year," since the former measure is attitudinal and the latter is behavioral. Researchers should strive to create as strong as possible an **epistemic relationship** connecting abstract concepts to operational variables, so that results of empirical tests will permit meaningful conclusions about theoretical propositions. Weak concept-variable linkages only render the empirical findings ambiguous as a test of the theory. More detailed treatments of how to establish validity can be found in various research methodology textbooks.

A closely related consideration in selecting appropriate variables for operational hypotheses is whether they are reliable indicators of the intended concepts. **Reliability** refers to the extent to which different operationalizations of the same concept produce consistent results. High reliability means that two procedures yield the same outcome, or the same procedure reapplied over time shows high agreement. For example, we could alternatively operationalize the concept *industrialization* with such variables measured at the national level as "kilowatt hours of electricity per capita" and "proportion of gross national product in manufactur-

validity—the degree to which a variable's operationalization accurately reflects the concept it is intended to measure

epistemic relationship—the relationship between abstract, theoretical (unobserved) concepts and their corresponding operational (observed) measurements

reliability—the extent to which different operationalizations of the same concept produce consistent results

ing." Both variables will tend to rank the same countries as high or low, and thus be judged highly reliable measures of industrialization. But few social scientists would argue that "frequency of church attendance" and "tons of wheat harvested" are very reliable indicators of industrialization. Extensive discussion of ways to assess reliability can also be found in most methodology texts.

Recent years have seen the rapid development of statistical techniques that combine both unobserved concepts and observed variables into a unified framework. These methods permit simultaneous estimation of the causal relationships among concepts and of the epistemic relationships connecting variables to concepts. We examine some of these procedures in chapter 12.

1.4   Observations into Records

Once theoretical propositions have been translated into research hypotheses involving variables, procedures can be developed for making observations necessary to determine the fit of the data to the hypotheses. The general term **data collection** applies to all manner of activities by which researchers construct a project's primary data records. Although some projects actually involve prolonged periods in natural settings (such as participant observation in communities or household personal interviews), for many researchers the data collection period consists of short, intense bursts of work in confined settings: experimental manipulations in human subjects laboratories, telephone interviews, mail questionnaires, computer simulations, content analyses of historical documents, and transcriptions of verbal exchanges. Each data collection method involves complex routines with unique requirements and its own limitations. These issues can be fully addressed only in texts devoted to explicating the nuances of various research methodologies.

A common concern for all types of research projects is the selection of objects for observation, or **units of analysis.** Depending on how the research hypotheses are stated, the level of social phenomena from which data are to be collected may range from nations to communities to groups to individuals and on down to highly specific actions such as conversational greetings. The entire set of persons, objects, or events that have at least one common characteristic of interest to a researcher constitutes the **population**

data collection— the activity of constructing primary data records for a given sample or population of observations

unit of analysis— an object for observation

population— the entire set of persons, objects, or events that have at least one common characteristic of interest to a researcher

sample— a subset of cases or elements selected from a population

representativeness— the selection of units of analysis whose characteristics accurately stand for the larger population from which the sample was drawn

random sample — a sample whose cases or elements are selected at random from a population

systematic sampling interval — the number of cases between sample elements in a list used for a systematic random sample

under investigation. Except for censuses that attempt to collect data from every unit in a population, observations can usually be made on only a **sample,** a subset of cases or elements selected from a population. Time and money constraints prevent enumeration and investigation of an entire population. But properly conducted sampling procedures can ensure cost-efficient conclusions that correctly reflect what is going on in a population. The key to sampling is **representativeness**—the selection of units of analysis whose characteristics accurately stand for the larger population from which the sample was drawn. Representative sampling is critical for statistical data analysis because many tests allow a researcher to generalize findings about samples to the parent population only if the probability of a unit's selection is known. The only way to guarantee representativeness is to draw a **random sample** of units from a list that completely enumerates all members of the population. Each population unit is given an equal chance of being included in the sample. The actual choices are made either by a "simple random selection" of every sample element (typically using a table of random numbers or a "random number generator" computer routine) or by a "systematic random selection" that takes every kth case from the list beginning with a randomly chosen start. When k is small, the sample will be larger and vice versa. For example, in a state university of 30,000 students, selecting every 50th case produces a sample of 600 students, while setting $k = 200$ yields a sample of only 150 cases. An investigator can decide the sample size—the number of cases to be selected (which also determines the **systematic sampling interval** width, k)—according to the required accuracy of statistical estimates, as discussed in chapter 3.

When complete population listings are either not available or too costly to create, more complicated sampling procedures can be used to try to ensure representativeness. Details of these methods are available in specialized textbooks. Because the statistics discussed in this book assume simple random samples, we will not bother to describe these other sampling designs. Instead, we will simply assume that the distortions created by treating complex samples as though they were generated by simple random sampling are minimal, as noted in Box 1.1.

Whenever living human beings are the subjects of social and medical research, questions of ethical treatment must be answered before proceeding with data collection. Research funding agencies usually require prior approval of investigators' plans for protecting their subjects' integrity before they will release grants. Most universities maintain internal human subjects committees, composed of diverse faculty members who certify that proposals pass muster. Many professional societies also have formal codes of research ethics to which they encourage their members to adhere. These criteria typically include no risk of harm to subjects (physical or psychological); informed consent to participate, especially from underage or mentally impaired subjects; confidential protection of subjects' identities from parties outside the project; and responsible representation of research findings. Social researchers have an obligation to put the well-being of those whom they study ahead of whatever personal or disciplinary benefits the project may produce. Abuse and fraud in social research can only harm the fragile trust and credibility that scientists must preserve with the society that supports their activities.

1.5 Data into Numbers

The process of assigning numbers to observations according to a set of rules is **measurement.** Often the numerical codes for each variable have been set up long before the first interview or content analyses begin. For example, for 50 years a Gallup poll question—"How well is the President doing his job?"—has used a standard four-category response: 1 = Poor, 2 = Fair, 3 = Good, and 4 = Excellent. For such forced-response items, coding merely requires transferring the number next to a checkmark on the interview schedule into a storage device, typically directly onto a computer file. Other types of field records—particularly historical documents and verbal transcripts but also open-ended survey questions—require more elaborate coding procedures to extract information and reduce it to numerical values. Sometimes the coding categories can be anticipated in advance of data collection, but more often the codes are inductively generated in the process of examining each case. New categories are created and assigned unique numbers as different responses are encountered. Some variables may have dozens or hundreds of categories, depending on how varied the sample's responses are and how much detail the investigator wishes to preserve.

measurement—the process of assigning numbers to observations according to a set of rules

A special problem experienced in every data collection is **missing data.** With few exceptions, all projects encounter cases

missing data—no meaningful information for a given observation on a particular variable

from which no meaningful information for a particular variable is forthcoming. Some items are skipped because they do not apply to a given subject, such as asking a single person how happy she is with her marriage. Sometimes a subject refuses to answer a very personal question, such as his annual income or whether she ever had an abortion. Another subject simply may not know the answer to a difficult question, such as her maternal grandfather's occupation when her mother was 16 years old. Occasionally, a field worker fails to record information properly and a call-back proves impossible. To cover such instances, special codes must be designated to indicate the data values that are missing. Sometimes several missing values should be created for a given variable; for example, one might use 8 = Does Not Know, 9 = No Answer, −1 = Refused to Answer, 0 = Inappropriate Question (Skipped). Missing data codes enable analysts to omit these cases from later statistical analyses.

The end result of coding is to assign a unique value to every case for each variable. In other words, good coding schemes must be **mutually exclusive** (each observation receives one and only one code on a given variable) and **exhaustive** (every case must receive a code for each variable, even if only a missing value can be assigned). Coding instructions that allow more than one numerical value to be assigned to a particular case for a given variable violate the mutual exclusivity criterion. For example, when ethnic origins are measured, a code of 1 = Chinese and 2 = Asian is clearly flawed; the analyst must decide whether countries or continents are desired. Note that if greater detail is initially recorded, variables may be later **recoded** to produce grosser classifications. Thus, Chinese, Japanese, Korean, Indian, Vietnamese, and other nationalities could be collapsed into a single "Asian origin" category. But, if only the broader category "Asian" is initially recorded, recovering the finer detail will be impossible.

The coding process produces two products: the **codebook,** a complete record of all coding decisions, and a **data file,** containing the entire set of numerical values for each variable for every case. A codebook should contain information about the sampling and field operations: interviewer and coder instructions, verbatim question wording for every variable, numerical codes of all valid responses and missing data, column locations of each item in the data file, and other miscellaneous information likely to be useful for future users. A codebook usually exists physically on printed pages, and often is also stored as a file on a computer diskette or tape that can

mutually exclusive— each observation must receive one and only one code on a given variable

exhaustive— every case must receive a code for each variable, even if only a missing value can be assigned

recode— the process of changing the codes established for a variable

codebook— a complete record of all coding decisions

data file— the entire set of numerical values for each variable for every case

be distributed together with the data file. The data file itself initially consists of a rectangular array of numbers. Each line (row) in the array contains all the information for a particular case; thus, for a project with N subjects, the data file will have N lines. Each column in the array contains the numerical codes of a specific variable for the N cases. (Such forms are still sometimes called "card image records" in a reference to an earlier era when data were physically stored as holes punched into 80-column cards.) With increasing frequency, a data file is stored as a **system file** that has been created by a computer software statistics package such as SPSS, SAS, or STATA. A system file contains not only the numerical records, but also includes the names of every variable, their value labels, and the missing data codes. Such files can be accessed directly by the statistical and data management programs in the package, saving substantial time when the data are analyzed repeatedly. For our use in writing this book, we created both the 1991 General Social Survey (GSS) and U.S. States Data Set files as SPSS system files for the personal computer. As Boxes 1.1 and 1.2 indicate, these data sets are both available for your own use if you have access to the SPSS package either on personal or mainframe computer. Box 1.3 explains more about the SPSS package.

system file— a data file created by a computer software statistics package

A final task in data set preparation is dissemination to the wider use community. Most federally funded projects require that data collected with taxpayer funds ultimately become publicly available. Various archiving services—such as the Interuniversity Consortium for Political and Social Research (ICPSR) at Ann Arbor, Michigan, and the Roper Center at Storrs, Connecticut—receive numerous data files from projects around the world. These files are archived and cataloged for eventual redistribution to secondary users. We obtained both the 1991 GSS and the U.S. States Data Set from these archives.

1.6 Statistical Analysis

With a data set in hand, statistical analysis to evaluate the operational hypotheses can now begin. How to choose statistical procedures that are most appropriate for particular measures and hypotheses is the subject of the remainder of this book. The basic principle is to select procedures that retain the maximum amount of information available in the data. An important consideration is

---

BOX 1.3   SPSS—Statistical Package for the Social Sciences

Over the past 25 years, SPSS mainframe and personal computer software programs have become one of the most comprehensive and widely available data management and analysis packages. All statistical tests described in this book can be done using such SPSS routines as FREQUENCIES, CORRELATION, REGRESSION, MEANS, T-TEST, ONEWAY, ANOVA, CROSSTABS, LOGLINEAR, LOGISTIC REGRESSION, and LISREL. Because of its simplified syntax, SPSS is easy to learn and apply, requiring about two hours of classroom instruction using the brief expository materials in the *Instructors' Manual* for this text. Consequently, we have built the computer exercises in each chapter around SPSS analyses of the 1991 General Social Survey and U.S. States Data Set. As described in Boxes 1.1 and 1.2, both files are available in an SPSS EXPORT format on request to the publisher. Using IMPORT instructions, these system files can be installed either in mainframe or personal computer hard disks for students' use as homework and laboratory assignments.

---

whether the variables to be analyzed are discrete or continuous measures, because certain types of analyses are suitable only to particular kinds of variables. Thus, log-linear models (chapter 10) require discrete variables, regression analysis (chapter 6) uses primarily continuous measures, while analysis of covariance (chapter 8) combines both types.

discrete variable—a variable that classifies persons, objects, or events according to the kind or quality of their attributes

A **discrete variable** classifies persons, objects, or events according to the kind or quality of their attributes. A small number of distinct categories contain all the cases, including a separate category for the cases with missing values. For example, U.S. citizens could be classified into four regions, "North," "South," "East," and "West," with a fifth category "Other" for persons living in the territories and overseas. No intrinsic order from high to low can be imposed on these labels, so the variable is **nonorderable discrete.** But, if the categories can be meaningfully arranged into

nonorderable discrete variable— a discrete measure in which the sequence of categories cannot be meaningfully ordered

an ascending or descending sequence, then it is an **orderable discrete variable.** Many attitude variables have such formats, for example, recording responses to statements in Likert-type scales such as "strongly agree," "agree," "neither agree nor disagree," "disagree," and "strongly disagree." Similarly, asking respondents' self-placements as "upper, middle, working, or lower class" produces an ordered discrete measure. A special type of discrete variable is the **dichotomous variable,** which may either be ordered or not. A dichotomy (literally "two-cut") classifies cases into two mutually exclusive categories (exhaustiveness is assured by providing codes for missing values). Gender is a fundamentally nonorderable dichotomous variable: Female or male are the only meaningful categories (assuming that hermaphrodites do not occur). An ordered dichotomy is exemplified by a supervisor-subordinate classification of employees.

> **orderable discrete variable**— a discrete measure that can be meaningfully arranged into an ascending or descending sequence

> **dichotomous variable**— a discrete measure with two categories that may or may not be ordered

In contrast to discrete measures, **continuous variables** can, at least in theory, take on all possible numerical values in a given interval. Social science measures lack the precision of natural sciences' instruments that can record time, weight, and length to millionths and billionths of a unit. Still, many variables contain large numbers of ordered categories that effectively represent points along an intended continuum. Most importantly, they can be treated as though they were continuous variables, for use in statistical analyses that require continuous measures. Age is a continuous variable, even though most projects record only the years at the respondents' last birthdays. However, a child development study might record age to the nearest month or even day. Other variables commonly treated as continuous are the number of years people attended school, the number of children ever born, occupational prestige, and annual earned income. If the units of analysis are not individuals but collectivities such as organizations, cities, or nations, many measures will have continuous properties: the number of employees, the average burglaries per 100,000 population, the percentage of substandard houses, and so on.

> **continuous variable**— a variable that, in theory, can take on all possible numerical values in a given interval

You should be alert to a common practice by social scientists of treating many ordered discrete variables as continuous measures. Although agreement with attitude items offering five or seven response categories is technically a discrete ordered variable, an analyst can make use of very powerful statistical techniques by assuming that these categories have continuous properties. The rationale behind this assumption is that "strength of attitude" is fundamentally a continuous property that our measuring devices only crudely tap. Our major concern should be whether treating ordered categories as continuous results in distorted conclusions from statistical analyses. So far, most evidence suggests that statistical techniques are fairly "robust" under such circumstances. The one clearly inappropriate treatment is the use of nonordered discrete measures in analyses that require continuous variables. In no meaningful way can the code numbers for respondents' religious affiliations, states of residence, or preferred leisure activity be analyzed and interpreted as though they formed continuous measures.

scale construction—the creation of new variables from multiple items

In addition to analyzing single measures taken directly from data sets, new variables may be created using multiple items. Such **scale construction** is very often performed with attitude items that were designed to capture beliefs and opinions about a certain domain, for example, political alienation, marital happiness, and interracial tolerance. Often a "battery" of items tapping related facets of some unobserved attitude are presented to respondents. Their responses can be analyzed using such techniques as factor analysis, latent structure analysis, or Guttman scaling to determine whether they form a single-dimensional multi-item scale with high reliability. Most of these methods are beyond the scope of this book. However, the increasing importance of models combining measurement and structural relations requires that you learn some basics of the factor analytic approach. Chapter 12 provides a general introduction to these issues.

descriptive statistics— statistics concerned with summarizing the properties of a sample of observations

inferential statistics— statistics that apply the mathematical theory of probability to make decisions about the likely properties of populations based on sample evidence

inference— a generalization or conclusion about some attribute of a population based on the data in a sample

statistical significance test— a test of inference that conclusions based on a sample of observations also hold true for the population from which the sample was selected

Statistical analysis consists of two broad branches with divergent aims. **Descriptive statistics** are concerned with summarizing the properties of a sample of observations. Chapter 2 presents many basic sample statistics for describing the typical values and the amount of variation in a variable's values. These summary statistics do not directly reveal very much about the population from which the sample was drawn. For that purpose, **inferential statistics** apply the mathematical theory of probability to make decisions about the likely properties of populations based on sample evidence. An **inference** is a generalization or conclusion about some attribute of a population based on the data in a sample. If a sample is highly representative of the population, as random sampling assures, then inferences about the parent population can be made with a high level of confidence (although not with complete certainty). **Statistical significance tests** thus are designed to allow us to make statements about the probability that hypothesized relationships actually occur. We can decide to minimize the risk of being incorrect when making statements about a population on the basis of a particular sample's results. Further, as investigators in charge of the analysis, we can control the level of risk or error that we wish to incur when making such inferences from sample to population. Inferential statistics comprise the major portion of this text, beginning with chapter 3.

We view statistical significance testing as an adjunct to the most essential goal of social data analysis: estimating the strength of relationships among variables. A variable whose relationship with another is weak may be statistically significant only because a large sample size enables us to detect this marginal connection. For example, during the presidential elections of the 1980s, several analysts argued that a "gender gap" in voting existed with men more likely than women to vote for Republican candidates. However, while a statistically significant difference did occur in some political opinion polls, the difference rarely amounted to more than 5%, certainly a very weak effect although perhaps enough to swing a tight race. To assess the magnitude of relations among variables, various statistical **measures of association** have been developed. This book devotes considerable attention to methods for measuring the size, direction, and strengths of independent variables in explaining variation in dependent measures.

measures of association— statistics that show the direction and/or magnitude of a relationship between variables

By the end of statistical analysis an investigator is usually in a good position to reach a conclusion about the propositions or informed hunches that originally motivated the project. Both the probabilistic decisions regarding the operational hypotheses and the measures of strengths of relationships among causal variables should reveal whether previous knowledge about some social phenomenon has been challenged or supported. The conventional strategy is to assume that the current state of knowledge is correct unless compelling evidence indicates the falsity of its claims. This requirement of disproof is a conservative stance that places the burden on challengers to show where and how prior beliefs are incorrect. A theory whose propositions have withstood many attempts to refute them holds a strong position in any science. But, it is never "proven" to be true, just "not disproven." Future research may uncover evidence, perhaps under specialized conditions, that cast doubt on the truth value of the theory. By testing hypotheses that can be rejected, we permit social knowledge to grow incrementally as the limits of its applicability are probed. Thus, any outcome from a well-designed and carefully conducted research project is potentially useful. Results will either reinforce existing knowledge, thereby giving greater confidence that we understand the way the world operates, or they will cast doubt on what we think we already know, and thus force us to revise our understanding of social reality. In either event the stage is set for the next cycle through the neverending research process.

1.7   The General Linear Model

In learning about the diverse statistical methods in the following chapters you may become bewildered by the apparent dissimilarities among them. Be reassured that substantially greater unity exists than is first apparent. For example, several statistical techniques are special instances of an approach known in mathematical statistics as the **general linear model.** Without going into technical details, the general linear model assumes the relationships among independent and dependent measures basically vary according to straight-line patterns. You are likely to be familiar with such lines from algebra where a plot of the general equation $Y = a + bX$ produces a straight line with positive or negative slope depending on the sign of b. All that is required are numerical values for a and b to fix the line precisely on a set of Cartesian coordinates (i.e., graph paper).

general linear model— a model that assumes the relationships among independent and dependent measures basically vary according to straight-line patterns

An assumption of linear relationships among variables is generally compatible with the research hypotheses that typically abound in the social sciences: "The greater the X, the greater (or lesser) the Y." The implication is that a measured change in X creates a predictable change in Y, a linear expectation. Social scientists seldom express hypotheses about the numerical values of the slope b and intercept a, but leave these values to be estimated from observational data. Indeed, many empirical patterns of joint variations among pairs of variables suggest reasonably linear approximations, for example, the percentage of children in a state born to teenage mothers and the percentage of persons living in poverty, as shown in Figure 1.1.

Statistical methods based on linearity assumptions among variables offer a powerful way to analyze social data consistent with the way most social scientists conceptualize and interpret these relations. The general linear model is a highly flexible tool that can

FIGURE 1.1
Graph of Poverty and Teenage Births, U.S. States

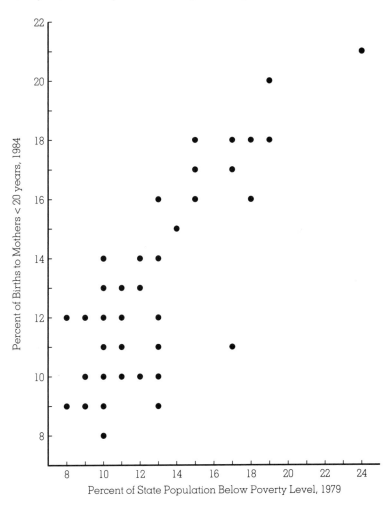

Source: U.S. States Data Set

be modified to suit specific combinations of discrete and continuous measures available for testing hypotheses. Thus, where all variables are continuous, regression analysis is appropriate (chapters 6 and 8). If the dependent variable is continuous but the independent variables are discrete, the analysis of variance is the appropriate technique (chapter 4). A dichotomous dependent variable with continuous independent variables points to logistic regression (chapter 9). A combination of continuous and discrete independent variables suggests the analysis of covariance (chapter 8). And the integrated measurement-structural equation models in chapter 12 present a presumption of linearity among observed and unobserved variables. These convergences among seemingly disparate techniques through the underlying general linear model mean that statistical analysis is really not as complicated as it appears. We hope to demonstrate this assertion in the following chapters.

Review of Key Concepts

These key concepts are listed in the order of appearance in this chapter. Combined with the definitions in the margins, they will help you to review the material and can serve as a self-test for mastery of the concepts.

scientific research
applied research
basic research
proposition
concept
social theory
linearity
scope (boundary conditions)
variable
latent variable
manifest variable
operational hypothesis
constant
independent variable
dependent variable
status variable
validity
epistemic relationship
reliability
data collection
unit of analysis
population
sample

representativeness
random sample
systematic sampling interval
measurement
missing data
mutually exclusive
exhaustive
recode
codebook
data file
system file
discrete variable
nonorderable discrete variable
orderable discrete variable
dichotomous variable
continuous variable
scale construction
descriptive statistics
inferential statistics
inference
statistical significance test
measures of association
general linear model

PROBLEMS

General Problems

1. Give a formal definition of the concept *downsizing* that could be used in a theory of organizational change.

2. Use these concepts to form two bivariate propositions: divorce rate, female labor force participation, family income, and number of children.

3. What theoretical scope [boundary condition(s)] is implied by the following statement: "Latin American peasantries have access to mass media, urban markets, and consumer goods that have eroded their differences with urban dwellers."

4. Translate the following proposition into an operational hypothesis: "People are less likely to perceive themselves as acting altruistically if the normative expectations to help are made salient."

5. Identify the independent and dependent variables in the following propositions:
   a. Annual earnings of college-educated black women are significantly higher than among white women.
   b. The stiffer the international competition an industry faces, the more likely it is to experience falling profit levels.
   c. The increase in homelessness primarily resulted from deinstitutionalization of the mentally ill.

6. Which of the following are variables and which are constants?
   a. Grade point average.   d. Eye color.
   b. Left-handed.   e. Size of workplace.
   c. Aggressiveness.   f. Lake Winnebago.

7. Port Town has a population of 150,000 persons, two thirds of whom are old enough to vote. City Opinions, Inc., wants to draw a sample of 500 voting-age residents to find out how many plan to vote in the city council elections and for whom. Assuming the company can obtain a complete listing of all residents, how large should the systematic sampling interval, k, be in order to assure the required sample?

8. a. What measurement criteria are violated if only the following categories are used to record U.S. survey respondents' current place of residence?

    (1). Texas.   (4). New England.

    (2). Ohio.   (5). Connecticut.

    (3). Reno.   (6). Bridgeport.

    b. What changes would you suggest?

9. Indicate whether the following variables are nonorderable discrete, orderable discrete, dichotomous, or continuous:

    a. Suicide rate: annual percentage.

    b. Self-employment: owns a business or not.

    c. Presidential job rating: excellent, good, fair, poor.

    d. Hourly wage: to nearest cent.

    e. College status: graduate or nongraduate.

    f. High school sport played: hockey, basketball, football, swimming.

    g. TV viewing: average amount of time spent watching per week.

    h. Liking of country music: 7-point scale from "strongly like" to "strongly dislike."

10. Finish these statements:

    a. _____ is the effort to reduce uncertainty by examining relationships among some aspects of the world.

    b. _____ address questions of immediate policy relevance.

    c. A variable is _____ to the degree that it measures the intended concept.

    d. The stronger the _____, the tighter the connection between abstract concepts and operational variables.

    e. One way to assure that the results of a sample analysis will be _____, is to select its units of analysis _____.

    f. _____ is the process of assigning numbers to observations according to a set of rules.

    g. The assumption that relationships between measures form a straight line is _____.

Statistics for Social Data Analysis

Describing Variables

2

T his chapter introduces methods for describing the distributions of discrete and continuous variables for a set of observations. As noted in chapter 1, discrete variables classify persons, objects, or events according to the *quality* of their attributes, while continuous variables classify them according to their *quantities*. First, we show how to represent compactly the full distribution of a single variable for a given set of observations. Then, we show how to summarize a variable's distribution using just two values, its average or central tendency and its dispersion or variance. These statistics describe a distribution's basic features and form the foundation for inquiries into the joint distributions of two or more variables examined in later chapters.

2.1 Frequency Distributions for Discrete and Continuous Variables

The first step in constructing a distribution is to determine how many observations occur in each response category of the variable. Suppose we want to find out how satisfied American workers are with their jobs. The 1991 General Social Survey (GSS; see Box 1.1) asked a sample of 1,517 American adults, "On the whole, how satisfied are you with the work you do—would you say you are very satisfied, moderately satisfied, a little dissatisfied, or very dissatisfied?" By offering respondents only four responses, this item forms a distribution with four ordered categories. However, 368 people either were not working or would not answer the question

tally—a count of the frequency of outcomes observed for a variable or the frequency of joint outcomes of several variables

frequency distribution—a table of the outcomes, or response categories, of a variable and the number of times each outcome is observed

outcome—a response category of a variable

relative frequency distribution—a distribution of outcomes of a variable in which the number of times each outcome is observed has been divided by the total number of cases

percentage distribution—a distribution of relative frequencies or proportions in which each entry has been multiplied by 100

relative frequency (proportion)—the number of cases in an outcome divided by the total number of cases

percentage—a number created by multiplying a proportion by 100

about their job satisfaction. We combine both types of nonresponse into a "not appropriate" category. Next, we make a **tally** of the number of GSS respondents recorded in each of these five categories. (We used a personal computer to tally the data stored in a permanent file and to print out the number of observations or cases in each category.) From the tally results we construct a **frequency distribution,** which is a table of the **outcomes,** or response categories, of a variable and the number of times each outcome is observed. The first column of Table 2.1 shows that there are 510 very satisfied respondents, 482 moderately satisfied, 108 a little dissatisfied, and 49 very dissatisfied, while 368 people either were not working or gave no answer. We conclude that most Americans are satisfied with their jobs.

These counts can be transformed into familiar **relative frequency distributions** and **percentage distributions,** as shown in the second and third columns of Table 2.1. To form **relative frequencies,** or **proportions,** we divide the number of cases in each outcome by the total number of cases. In the 1991 GSS the proportion of very satisfied workers is 510/1,517 = 0.336; of moderately satisfied is 482/1,517 = 0.318; of a little dissatisfied is 108/1,517 = 0.071; and so on. We again conclude that a majority of people are satisfied with their jobs. However, comparisons to other frequency distributions based on different total numbers of cases are now easier to make and more meaningful with relative proportions. Proportions are transformed into **percentages** by multiplying each by 100. For example, in the third column in Table 2.1 the percentage

TABLE 2.1

Job Satisfaction of Working Respondents

Job Satisfaction	Frequency (f)	Proportion (p)	Percent (%)	Cumulative frequency (cf)	Cumulative percent (c%)
Very Satisfied	510	.336	33.6	510	33.6
Moderately Satisfied	482	.318	31.8	992	65.4
A Little Dissatisfied	108	.071	7.1	1,100	72.5
Very Dissatisfied	49	.032	3.2	1,149	75.7
Not Appropriate	368	.243	24.3	1,517	100.0
Total	1,517	1.000	100.0	1,517	100.0

Source: 1991 General Social Survey

of workers who are very dissatisfied is (.032)(100) = 3.2%. Percentages *standardize* a sample size by indicating the number of observations that would fall into each outcome of a variable if the total number of cases were 100.

Percentages are usually presented to the nearest tenth. Because speaking about tenths of a person is awkward, we could round our results up or down to the nearest whole percent. Generally, values of 0.1 to 0.4 are rounded down to the next whole number, and values of 0.5 to 0.9 are rounded up. (Rules for **rounding** appear in Box 2.1.) Thus, we conclude that 34 of every 100 persons in the GSS are very satisfied. Alternatively, we could multiply each percentage by 10 and say that *if* we had observed 1,000 persons, we would expect 336 to be very satisfied, 318 moderately satisfied, and so on. Either procedure makes an important point clear: *Whenever data are summarized, some distortion almost always occurs.* The trade-off in comprehension and interpretation usually makes small distortions worthwhile. For this reason social researchers who use percentages become accustomed to dealing with fractions of cases.

rounding—expressing digits in more convenient and interpretable units, such as tens, hundreds, or thousands, by applying an explicit rule

We use a shorthand notation for frequencies and relative frequencies. N denotes the total sample size (in the 1991 GSS, N = 1,517). And f_i denotes the frequency associated with the ith outcome (category) of a variable. The subscript i can take values from 1 to the number of response categories (K) into which the variable is coded. For Table 2.1, $K = 5$. If we code very satisfied = 1, moderately satisfied = 2, a little dissatisfied = 3, very dissatisfied = 4, and not appropriate = 5, then $f_1 = 510$ (there are 510 very satisfied in the distribution), $f_2 = 482$, $f_3 = 108$, $f_4 = 49$, and $f_5 = 368$. The first column of Table 2.1, labeled f, gives the number of cases in each job-satisfaction category. The sum of the frequencies for each outcome equals the total sample size:

$$f_1 + f_2 + f_3 + \ldots + f_K = N$$

In the 1991 GSS

$$510 + 482 + 108 + 49 + 368 = 1,517$$

The *proportion* of cases in the ith outcome of a variable is p_i. Its formula is:

$$p_i = \frac{f_i}{N}$$

As shown in the second column of Table 2.1, the proportion very satisfied in the GSS data is $p_1 = f_1/N = 510/1{,}517 = 0.336$.

The sum of all the proportions in a frequency distribution always equals 1.00 (except for any rounding error). In the case where $K = 5$,

$$
\begin{aligned}
p_1 + p_2 + p_3 + p_4 + p_5 &= \frac{f_1}{N} + \frac{f_2}{N} + \frac{f_3}{N} + \frac{f_4}{N} + \frac{f_5}{N} \\
&= \frac{(f_1 + f_2 + f_3 + f_4 + f_5)}{N} \\
&= \frac{N}{N} = 1.00
\end{aligned}
$$

Because a percentage is simply a proportion multiplied by 100, the sum of the percentages associated with all the categories in a frequency distribution always equals 100.0%. The total of the third column in Table 2.1 verifies this summation.

BOX 2.1   Rules of Thumb for Recoding and Rounding

Recoding Rules

1. The greater the measurement precision, the better.
2. Choose an interval width that is narrow enough not to distort the original distribution of observations, but wide enough to avoid too many categories concealing the underlying distribution shape.
3. The number of intervals should be somewhere between 6 and 20. A larger number of categories generally cannot be easily grasped by the reader.

BOX 2.1 *(continued)*

Rounding Rules

1. Round digits 1 to 4 down by leaving the digit to the left unchanged.
2. Round digits 6 to 9 up by increasing the digit to the left by 1.
3. Numbers ending in 5 are rounded alternately; the first number ending in 5 is rounded down, the second is rounded up, the third is rounded down, and so forth.
4. Never round past the original measurement interval.

Several examples of rounding are given below for data originally recorded to the nearest tenth of a year:

Unit of Measurement	Original Number (in years)	Rounded Number
Years	36.6	37
Years	433.3	433
Decades	36.6	4
Decades	433.3	43
Centuries	36.6	0
Centuries	433.3	4

Table 2.2 shows the relative frequency distributions for three other *discrete variables*. The genders of the 1,517 GSS respondents were determined visually by the interviewer at the beginning of the interview. Region of residence uses the Census Bureau's classification of states into four major categories. To measure the number of children ever born, respondents were asked, "How many children have you ever had? Please count all that were born alive at any time (including any you had from a previous marriage)." Nine categories of increasing frequency were offered for their responses (the GSS combined eight or more children into a single category). Respondents were not explicitly offered "no answer" as a choice:

TABLE 2.2

Percentage Distributions of Gender, Region of Residence, and Number of Children

Gender		Region of Residence		Number of Children	
Male	41.9%	Northeast	19.7%	None	27.6%
Female	58.1	Midwest	25.0	One	16.8
Total	100.0%	South	35.9	Two	24.7
(N = 1,517)		Far West	19.4	Three	14.2
		Total	100.0%	Four	8.4
		(N = 1,517)		Five	3.6
				Six	1.6
				Seven	1.5
				Eight or More	1.1
				No Answer	0.5
				Total	100.0%
				(N = 1,517)	

Source: 1991 General Social Survey

The interviewer recorded that response only when a respondent did not give a number.

The response categories associated with gender and region of residence clearly are *not* continuous variables, because they do not classify respondents according to magnitude or *quantity* of the response. Instead, they are *nonordered discrete variables*, because the sequence of their categories has no intrinsic order. However, number of children is an *ordered discrete variable*, because only one sequence of categories is meaningful. (It is not a continuous variable because fractional numbers of children are not possible.) A variable having only two categories is a **dichotomous variable,** or **dichotomy** (literally, "cut in two"). Gender—male or female—is an example of a dichotomy.

dichotomous variable (dichotomy)— a variable having only two categories

2.2   Grouped and Cumulative Distributions

Building frequency distributions is easy for discrete variables. Tallying the numbers of men and women poses little difficulty, as does counting the numbers of children ever born. However, constructing a frequency distribution for a *continuous* variable first requires **grouped data.** That is, a researcher must decide how to collapse together observations having different values.

grouped data— data that have been collapsed into a smaller number of categories

In principle any two coded values of a continuous variable can be subdivided infinitely. For example, suppose someone's weight is recorded with a pointer on a bathroom scale, as in the illustration below:

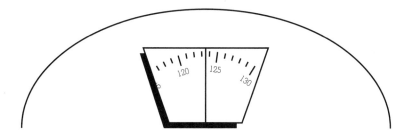

This person's weight is 123.4625 pounds, to be precise. But usually we do not require this much precision. In everyday conversation we would round to the nearest whole number and say that the person weighs 123 pounds. For some scientific work that value might be too imprecise. A scientist might decide that a measurement in tenths of a pound is precise enough, in which case the person's weight would be recorded as 123-and-a-half pounds, or 123.5 pounds.

For continuous variables, measurement precision can be as accurate as the measuring instrument will allow. But, a decision on how to group observations having different values must ultimately be made. In other words, a **measurement interval** or **measurement class** must be selected within which observations will be treated as having equal value. For some variables the measurement interval is obvious. The year of birth is probably sufficiently accurate in a study of adult voters. But, for a study of infants' social learning, age to the nearest month is essential because many important changes occur in short time spans. For many social analyses measurement units are less clear since standard, well-investigated scales have not been developed. Most attitude scales, which typically record responses to statements in ordered sequences from "strongly disagree" to "strongly agree," have this characteristic. Clearly, continuous variables require researchers to decide in detail the degree of measurement precision.

measurement interval (measurement class)— a grouping of observations that is treated equally

The process of grouping continuous variables from many initial values into fewer categories is called **recoding.** For example, an age distribution for the U.S. population cannot easily display the hundred or more reported values. Instead, we might recode annual ages into nine decade-wide categories:

recoding—the process of grouping continuous variables from many initial values into fewer categories

> 10 years or less
> 11–19 years
> 20–29 years
> 30–39 years
> 40–49 years
> 50–59 years
> 60–69 years
> 70–79 years
> 80 years or more

The intervals above do not overlap the categories' endpoints as in the following:

> 10 years or less
> 10–20 years
> 20–30 years
> 30–40 years
> and so on

Overlapping violates the mutual exclusiveness principle discussed in section 1.5. Persons aged 10, 20, 30, 40, 50, 60, 70, or 80 years could be placed in two categories rather than in a single measurement class.[1] Box 2.1 summarizes some basic principles for grouping or recoding measures.

How wide should measurement intervals be for continuous variables? The rule of thumb is that measurement intervals should be narrow enough not to distort the original distribution but wide enough to avoid too many categories that conceal the underlying distribution. Generally, between 6 and 20 intervals should be used to present data in a frequency distribution. Sometimes fewer than six intervals will not seriously distort the shape of the distribution. Readers often find that more than 20 categories are difficult to interpret. Common sense indicates that eight 10-year intervals may be practical for a study of all Americans' ages, but not sufficient for

---

1. The RECODE procedure in SPSS accepts statements such as RECODE AGE (1 THRU 9=1)(9 THRU 19=2)(19 THRU 29=3), even though the mutual exclusion principle seems to be violated. However, SPSS actually follows these instructions sequentially, so that when it finds cases with 9 years it recodes them to 1. At that point no cases remain in the data with values of 9 to be recoded to 2 according the next part of the instruction. Thus, the statement above is identical to the command RECODE AGE (1 THRU 9=1)(10 THRU 19=2)(20 THRU 29=3). To avoid confusion all SPSS users should write mutually exclusive RECODE commands.

a survey of elementary schoolchildren because only the first two categories would apply.

Researchers often need to know a specific outcome's *relative* position in a distribution of continuous scores. If 5.8% of Minnesota's labor force is unemployed, is that rate high or low relative to other states? This question can be answered by a cumulative frequency distribution or cumulative percentage distribution. The **cumulative frequency** at a given score is the total number of observations at or below that score. Every GSS asks respondents, "What is the highest grade in elementary school or high school that you finished and got credit for?" High school graduates are also asked, "Did you complete one or more years of college for credit?" and "Do you have any college degrees?" These responses are used to determine the numbers of years of formal education (from 0 to 20). Table 2.3 reports four distributions for these data. In the third column the

cumulative frequency— for a given score or outcome of a variable, the total number of cases in a distribution at or below that value

TABLE 2.3

Cumulative Distributions of Respondent Education in Years

Education	f	%	cf	c%
None	2	0.1	2	0.1
1	0	0.0	2	0.1
2	0	0.0	2	0.1
3	5	0.3	7	0.5
4	5	0.3	12	0.8
5	6	0.4	18	1.2
6	12	0.8	30	2.0
7	25	1.6	55	3.6
8	68	4.5	123	8.1
9	56	3.7	179	11.9
10	73	4.8	252	16.7
11	85	5.6	337	22.3
12	461	30.4	798	52.8
13	130	18.6	928	61.5
14	175	11.5	1,103	73.0
15	73	4.8	1,176	77.9
16	194	12.8	1,370	90.7
17	43	2.8	1,413	93.6
18	45	3.0	1,458	96.6
19	22	1.5	1,480	98.0
20	30	2.0	1,510	100.0

No Answer = 7
Source: 1991 General Social Survey

cumulative frequency
distribution—a
distribution of scores
showing the number of
cases at or below each
outcome of the variable
being displayed in the
distribution

cumulative percentage—
for a given score or
outcome of a variable, the
percentage of cases in a
distribution at or below
that value

cumulative percentage
distribution—a
distribution of scores
showing the percentage of
cases at or below each
outcome of the variable
being displayed in the
distribution

statistical table—a
numerical display that
either summarizes data or
presents the results of a
data analysis

diagram (graph)—a
visual representation of a
set of data

bar chart—a type of
diagram for discrete
variables in which the
numbers or percentages of
cases in each outcome are
displayed

cumulative frequency distribution (denoted *cf*) is the distribution of responses at or below each year of education. The cumulative frequency to 8 years (grade school graduate) is 123, to 12 years (high school graduate) is 798, to 16 years (college graduate) is 1,370, and so on. To produce each *cf*, simply start with the frequency in the lowest category (f_1), add to it the frequency in the next highest category (f_2), then add to that sum the frequency in the third highest category (f_3), and so on.

Easier to interpret is a **cumulative percentage** of responses, denoted *c%* in the fourth column of Table 2.3. The percentages in the second column were summed to form this **cumulative percentage distribution.** The procedure is similar to calculating the values of the *cf*, except that the percentages at each category, instead of the frequencies, are cumulated. Both the percentage distribution and the cumulative percentage distribution make clear the standing of a given observation *relative* to others. Cumulative percentage distributions are commonly used in calculating percentiles, for example, in showing the relative achievement test scores of schoolchildren. The calculation of percentiles is presented in section 2.6.

2.3   Graphing Frequency Distributions

Frequency distribution tables are one way to communicate quantitative information in a clear, precise manner. We give some principles of **statistical table** construction in Box 2.2. Other ways to display single variable distributions are **diagrams** or **graphs,** such as bar charts and histograms. This section describes some elementary features of data graphs, whose choice depends on whether the variables are discrete or continuous.

For nonordered discrete variables a **bar chart** offers effective visual images. First, categories of the discrete variable are arrayed along a horizontal axis. Then, equally spaced vertical bars are erected above each category label to heights proportional to the frequency of the observations in each category (either the actual case counts or the percentages). The frequencies or the percentages are sometimes printed above each bar. Figure 2.1 is a bar chart illustrating the region of residence in the 1991 GSS, using the data in Table 2.2. Importantly, whenever discrete variable categories have no inherent order, the bars should not touch one another but should stand apart. A bar chart adds no information beyond

BOX 2.2 Statistical Tables

Statistical tables are a basic tool of the social scientist's trade. The art of constructing, reading, and interpreting tables can best be learned, as are all crafts, by much practice. Some basic pointers on how to communicate findings through tables are given here.*

Tables come in two basic forms: those that display "raw data" and those that present analyses. Raw-data tables contain frequencies or counts of observations classified in various ways, such as the number of burglaries reported in each of 50 neighborhoods last year, or the number of homicides classified according to familiarity between murderer and victim in each of eight regions of the United States. Analytic tables display the consequences of some manipulation of the data by a researcher that claims to give an interpretation of the process producing the raw data. Such tables are highly varied and may range from simple percenting of raw data all the way to systems of nonlinear simultaneous equations for complex mathematical models.

Each table begins with a heading, usually the word *Table*, an identifying number, and a brief phrase describing its central contents. Examples from a recent issue of the *American Sociological Review* include the following:

Table 1. Percentages: Males and Females to Whom Each Disorder Occurred in the Preceding Six Months

Table 2. Logistic Regression Coefficients for Senior Academic Track Enrollment and Selected Student Characteristics by Ethnicity: High School and Beyond Sample, 1980 and 1982

Table 3. Standardized Regression Coefficients: Per Capita Townsend Clubs and Selected Independent Measures for Full Models, 48 States

Under the heading, usually below a rule, are subheadings that label the various columns in the main body of the

(continued on next page)

BOX 2.2   *(continued)*

table. These subheadings most often are either variable names and categories or summary statistics such as column marginals (*N*s). To save space, short labels are preferred; if further clarification is required, subheadings can be footnoted, with the expanded explanations appearing at the bottom of the table.

Additional information, as in a cross-tabulation between two or more variables, appears in the column farthest to the left (sometimes called the *stub*). Each entry in this column describes the content of one of the rows forming the body of the table. For example, if attitude responses appear in the rows, the labels or response categories in the first column, from top to bottom might be: "Very Strongly Agree," "Strongly Agree," "Agree," "Neither Agree Nor Disagree," "Disagree," "Strongly Disagree," and "Very Strongly Disagree."

The main body of the table consists of the intersections of the entries under column and row headings. It displays the appropriate data in either raw or analyzed form. If the table contents are percentages, the preferable way to arrange them is so that they total to 100% down each column. A percentage total is usually the next to last row entry. The last row, labeled *N* at the left, gives the base frequencies on which the percentages were calculated. An example of a percentage table in this chapter is Table 2.2.

The number of cases with missing data (observations that could not be used in the main body of the table due to lack of information) may be reported directly below the body of the table. Any additional information about the data (such as its source) or about the analyses performed should be included in notes below the table.

---

*An extended discussion of table construction and interpretation appears in the article by James A. Davis, & Ann M. Jacobs. 1968. Tabular Presentation. In David L. Sills (Ed.), *International Encyclopedia of the Social Sciences* (Vol. 15, pp. 497–509). New York: Macmillan.

FIGURE 2.1
Bar Chart Showing Region of Residence

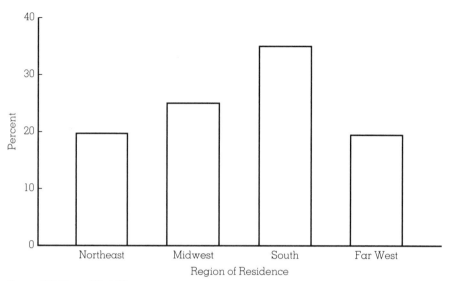

Source: 1991 General Social Survey

that found in a table displaying the same data. In fact, it communicates less information if the sample sizes on which categories are based are omitted and only the percentages are shown. Diagrams can be constructed only after the information for a table has been assembled.

For ordered discrete and grouped continuous variables **histograms** can display the distributions. The vertical bars of a histogram touch one another, indicating an underlying order among categories that is absent from the nonordered variables in bar charts. Figure 2.2 shows a histogram for the number of children ever born to GSS respondents, using the data in Table 2.2. If the midpoints of each category are connected by a line, rather than drawn as vertical bars, the resulting diagram is a **polygon.** Figure 2.3 shows a polygon for the children-ever-born variable. As with bar charts, constructing histograms or polygons requires frequency or percentage distributions of a variable.

For an elegant discussion of the principles of graphic display for social science data, with many stunning examples of both good and bad usage, see Edward Tufte's *The Visual Display of Quantitative Information* (1983).

histogram—a type of diagram that uses bars to represent the frequency, proportion, or percentage of cases associated with each outcome or interval of outcomes of a variable

polygon—a diagram constructed by connecting the midpoints of a histogram with a straight line

FIGURE 2.2

Histogram Showing Number of Children Ever Born

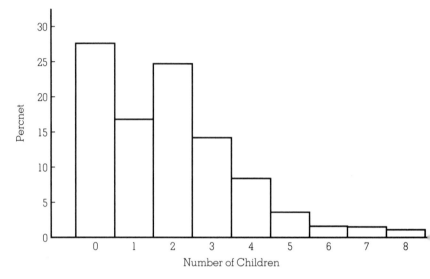

Source: 1991 General Social Survey

2.4   Measures of Central Tendency

central tendency—
average value of a set of
scores

variation—the spread or
dispersion of a set of
scores around some
central value

Two broad purposes are served by two descriptive statistics that summarize a frequency distribution. First, a single number summarizes the **central tendency** or average value of a set of scores (e.g., "The median income of persons with bachelors' degrees is . . ."; "The modal political party preference in Germany is . . ."). Second, a single number summarizes the amount of **variation** or dispersion in a distribution, because a central tendency statistic does not reveal how typical that number is of the other sample observations. For example, most scores may be close to the central tendency score or spread widely away from it. If most scores are near the average value, that statistic describes the distribution much better than if the scores are widely dispersed.

The mode, the median, and the mean are the commonly used central tendency statistics. We illustrate their calculation with two frequency distributions. Table 2.3 displays the GSS respondents' years of education. Table 2.4 shows the number of deaths from motor vehicles in 1986 for the 50 U.S. states and the District of Columbia. These two examples exemplify how to calculate descrip-

FIGURE 2.3

Polygon Showing Number of Children Ever Born

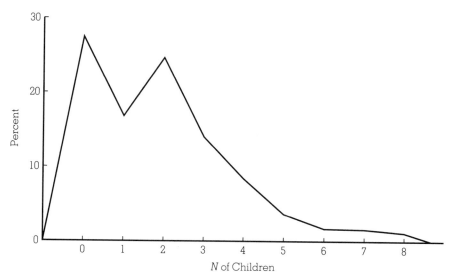

Source: 1991 General Social Survey

tive statistics for both grouped and ungrouped distributions, respectively.

2.4.1. Mode

The **mode** is that single *category* among the K categories in a distribution with the largest number (or highest percentage) of observations. For example, if 18 people say that their favorite snack is pretzels, 8 say potato chips, and 23 say popcorn, then the modal category is "popcorn." Do not confuse the *modal frequency* (number of cases) with the *modal category*. A modal category is not required to contain a majority of the cases, only *more* than any other single category. Some distributions are said to be *bimodal* (i.e., to have *two* modes). Strictly speaking, in a bimodal distribution the largest two categories must each have exactly the same number of observations. But in practice this equality very rarely occurs, and scientists use the term *bimodal* to describe any distribution where two categories are roughly equal and contain the greatest number of cases.

mode — the single category among the K categories in a distribution with the largest number (or highest percentage) of observations

TABLE 2.4

Number of Deaths from Motor Vehicle Accidents in 1986

State	Deaths	State	Deaths
District of Columbia	86	Oklahoma	725
Alaska	98	Washington	763
Vermont	105	Wisconsin	769
North Dakota	120	Massachusetts	773
Hawaii	124	Mississippi	785
South Dakota	152	Maryland	796
Rhode Island	155	Kentucky	829
Delaware	160	Louisiana	987
Wyoming	163	New Jersey	1,059
New Hampshire	181	Arizona	1,073
Maine	218	South Carolina	1,077
Montana	240	Indiana	1,077
Idaho	273	Virginia	1,141
Nevada	274	Alabama	1,180
Nebraska	311	Missouri	1,205
Utah	370	Tennessee	1,372
Iowa	446	Georgia	1,604
Connecticut	448	Ohio	1,609
West Virginia	470	Illinois	1,633
Kansas	519	Michigan	1,666
New Mexico	539	North Carolina	1,727
Minnesota	608	Pennsylvania	1,968
Arkansas	624	New York	2,183
Oregon	649	Florida	2,925
Colorado	657	Texas	3,701
		California	5,523

Source: U.S. States Data Set

Any statistic describing discrete measures can also describe continuous measures. Thus, the mode is a central tendency statistic applicable to both types of variables.

2.4.2. Median

median—the outcome that divides an ordered distribution exactly into halves

The **median** (Mdn) applies only to variables whose categories can be ordered from lowest to highest. The median is the outcome that divides an ordered distribution exactly into halves. That is, half the cases will have scores above the median value and half will have scores below the median. Whether any case exists that has the median value depends on whether the number of observations is odd or even. Consider three example distributions:

Distribution X: 2, 3, 6, 7, 10, 12, 45
Distribution Y: 2, 3, 6, 7, 10, 12, 45, 51
Distribution Z: 5, 7, 12, 12, 13, 19

Distribution X has an odd number of cases (seven). Its median is the score of the fourth observation, or 7. Distribution Y has an even number of cases (8), so its median falls halfway between the scores of the fourth and fifth cases. Its value is the average of the values of these two cases, $(7 + 10)/2 = 8.5$. Although the values surrounding the median case in distribution Z are both 12, the rule still applies that the median is either the score of the middle case (for an odd number of observations), or the average of the scores for two cases (for an even number of cases). Hence the median value of Z is $(12 + 12)/2 = 12$. The median is easy to calculate in distributions with small number of observations.

For grouped frequency distributions many statistics textbooks recommend the complex formula on page 62 in section 2.6 to calculate the median value as the 50th percentile. We offer a simpler and more accurate approach to finding the median: For any grouped frequency distribution the median is the value of that category at which the cumulative percentage reaches 50.0%. In general, median values calculated using ungrouped data will not precisely equal medians when the same data are grouped. The grouping process loses information about the individual scores. However, researchers often have only the grouped data displays, for example, from published census tables and newspaper charts. Seldom does one category exactly cumulate to 50.0%. In such instances, the median value is the first category in the cumulative distribution to exceed 50.0%. (The SPSS FREQUENCIES program also calculates medians this way.) The modal education category of GSS respondents can be calculated from the data displayed in Table 2.3. Given 1,510 responses, the median value must fall between the 755th and 756th cases, which surround 50.0% in the cumulative percentage distribution. As shown by the *cf* and *c%* in the third and fourth columns, these two cases both occur in the response category "12 years," hence, this value is the median of that distribution (high school graduate).

2.4.3.   Mean

mean—the arithmetic average of a set of data in which the values of all observations are added together and divided by the number of observations

The arithmetic **mean,** often called the *average*, is the most common measure of central tendency. It can be calculated only for continuous distributions. The values of all observations are added together and divided by the number of observations. The formula for the mean statistic is as follows:

$$\overline{Y} = \sum_{i=1}^{N} \frac{Y_i}{N}$$

The Greek capital letter sigma (Σ) symbolizes the summation operation. Appendix A, "The Use of Summations," gives basic rules on its use. The formula for the mean tells us to add all the scores in the Y distribution from the first to the Nth observation, then divide that sum by the number of cases, N. Because a constant can be moved from inside to outside a summation sign, an equivalent formula for the mean is:

$$\overline{Y} = \left(\frac{1}{N}\right)\Sigma Y_i = \frac{\Sigma Y_i}{N}$$

The incompletely labeled sum sign is understood to mean summation occurs over all observations of Y from the first to the Nth case.

To illustrate computation of the mean, apply the formula to the states' motor vehicle deaths in Table 2.4:

$$\overline{Y} = (86 + 98 + \ldots + 3701 + 5523)/51$$
$$= (48{,}140)/51$$
$$= 943.92157, \text{ or, rounding to the nearest tenth, } 943.9$$

The formula above cannot be used to calculate the mean of a grouped frequency distribution. A slightly more complex formula for the mean of grouped data is as follows:

$$\overline{Y} = \sum_{i=1}^{K} \frac{(f_i Y_i)}{N}$$

where

f_i = The frequency of cases with score Y_i.

K = The number of categories in the distribution.

Each score is "weighted" by the number of times it appears in the distribution. Then the K weighted products are added together and divided by the total number of cases in the distribution.

Applied to the group education data in Table 2.3, the mean is as follows:

$$\overline{Y} = [0(2) + 1(0) + 2(0) + 3(5) + 4(5) + 5(6) + 6(12) + 7(25)$$
$$+ 8(68) + 9(56) + 10(73) + 11(85) + 12(461) + 13(130) + 14(175)$$
$$+ 15(73) + 16(194) + 17(43) + 18(45) + 19(22) + 20(30)]/1,510$$
$$= 12.9 \text{ years of schooling}$$

One would use this formula for grouped data only in situations where the raw data are not available.

The mean of a dichotomous variable is a special case of the grouped frequency mean. Coding the first category "0" and the second category "1," a dichotomous variable's mean is simply the proportion of cases with the score "1."

$$\overline{Y} = \frac{\Sigma f_i Y_i}{N}$$

$$= \frac{(f_0)(0) + (f_1)(1)}{N} = \frac{(f_1)(1)}{N} = \frac{f_1}{N}$$

$$= p_1$$

where

f_0 = The number of cases coded 0.

f_1 = The number of cases coded 1.

p_1 = The proportion of cases coded 1.

The gender distribution in Table 2.2 has 881 women and 636 men. If women are coded 1 and men coded 0, the mean score is $[((636)(0) + (881)(1))/1,517] = 0.581$, which is the proportion of women in the sample. (Although the proportion of women in the U.S. adult population is actually about 0.525, the GSS has a higher level because men tend to be less available for interviews [e.g., in the armed forces, in prison, traveling on work] and because women are more likely than men to grant interviews.)

2.5 Measures of Dispersion

The choice of a measure to describe the dispersion among a set of scores depends on whether the variable is discrete or continuous. In this section we discuss the indices of diversity and qualitative variation, range, average absolute deviation, variance, and standard deviation. We also describe how to measure skewness, another aspect of a frequency distribution's shape.

2.5.1 Indices of Diversity and Qualitative Variation

index of diversity— measures whether two observations selected randomly from a population are likely to fall into the same or into different categories

Statistics describing discrete variable variation can be applied to ordered and to nonordered measures. The **index of diversity,** D, measures whether two observations selected randomly from a population are likely to fall into the same or into different categories. To calculate D, we simply square the proportion of cases in each of the K discrete categories, sum these squares, and subtract from 1.

$$D = 1 - \sum_{i=1}^{K} p_i^2$$

where

p_i = The proportion of observations in the ith category.

The higher the value of D, the more equally dispersed are the cases among the variable's K categories. The minimum possible value of D is 0, when all cases fall into a single category. The maximum value of D occurs when the proportions in every category are equal. However, the number of categories limits the maximum possible value. The more categories a discrete variable has, the larger the maximum value D can attain. For example, D for a 4-category variable (each p_i = 0.25) cannot be larger than 0.75, while D for a 10-category variable (each p_i = 0.10) can attain a maximum value of 0.90. *Thus, values of D for discrete variables with different numbers of categories cannot be compared directly.*

index of qualitative variation— a measure of variation for discrete variables; a standardized version of the index of diversity

Instead, a second dispersion statistic describing discrete variables, the **index of qualitative variation** (IQV), standardizes the diversity index for the number of categories.

$$IQV = \frac{(1 - \sum_{i=1}^{K} p_i^2)}{(K - 1)/K}$$

$$= \frac{K}{K - 1}(D)$$

The maximum IQV value is always 1.0 whenever cases are equally spread over all K categories, that is, when $p_i = 1/K$ for every p_i. Thus, direct comparisons are possible of the dispersion among discrete variables with differing numbers of categories.

For example, consider both the region of residence and number of children in Table 2.2 as discrete variables. The values of D for these measures are:

$$D_{residence} = 1 - (0.197^2 + 0.359^2 + 0.250^2 + 0.194^2) = 0.73$$

and

$$D_{children} = 1 - (0.276^2 + 0.168^2 + 0.247^2 + 0.142^2 + 0.084^2 + 0.036^2 + 0.016^2 + 0.015^2 + 0.011^2 + 0.005^2) = 0.81$$

When adjusted for the differing numbers of categories (four versus nine), their IQV values are

$$IQV_{residence} = \frac{0.73}{3/4} = 0.97$$

and

$$IQV_{children} = \frac{0.81}{9/10} = 0.90$$

suggesting a more equal distribution for the regional measure than for the children-ever-born variable.

2.5.2. Range

The simplest statistic describing dispersion for both ordered discrete and continuous variables is the **range.** A distribution's range is

range—the difference between the largest and smallest scores in a distribution

defined as the difference between the largest and smallest scores. The range of education shown in Table 2.3 is from 0 to 20 years, or $20 - 0 = 20$. Because it uses only the two extreme scores, the range provides almost no information about the other $N - 2$ observations in the sample. It cannot reveal how spread out or clustered these cases are between the highest and lowest scores. Only small proportions of respondents in Table 2.3 have fewer than 9 years or more than 16 years of schooling, indicating that most cases are bunched around the center of the distribution. Other dispersion statistics better summarize the spread among *all* the scores.

2.5.3. Average Absolute Deviation

As a measure of central tendency, the mean uses information about every observation in a continuous variable's distribution. A good measure of variation should also summarize how much each observation deviates from central tendency, that is, how close or far each is from the mean. The deviation, or distance, of a score, Y_i, from the mean, $\overline{Y}$, is commonly calculated as:

$$d_i = Y_i - \overline{Y}$$

In any distribution where the scores are not all identical, some deviations are positive (above the mean) and some are negative (below the mean). However, the mean of all N deviations is always 0, because the arithmetic mean equalizes the sum of deviations in both positive and negative directions. (Try this exercise on Table 2.4.) Therefore, the average deviation is an unsuitable measure of dispersion because its value is always zero.

One solution is to remove negative signs by taking absolute values of the deviations before averaging them. The formula for the **average absolute deviation** (AAD) uses vertical bars to indicate the absolute values of d_i:

average absolute deviation—the mean of the absolute values of the difference between a set of continuous measures and their mean

$$\text{AAD} = \frac{\Sigma |d_i|}{N}$$

AAD is larger than zero, except when all N observations have exactly the same score.

Unfortunately, the AAD cannot fulfill an important requirement for a measure of dispersion—the spread of scores around the mean is a minimum. If the median is used as the central tendency measure when computing deviations (that is, if $d_i = Y_i - \text{Mdn}$), then the formula for AAD gives a smaller numerical value than when deviations are computed using the mean. To illustrate the problem, consider the education data in Table 2.3, which has a mean of 12.9 years and a median of 12 years (i.e., the cumulation to 50.0% falls into this category). The average absolute deviation about the median (2.23) is smaller than the average absolute deviation about the mean, (2.28), which is always the case. The AAD fails to meet an important criterion for an acceptable dispersion statistic; therefore, it is never used in social data analysis.

2.5.4. Variance and Standard Deviation

Another procedure for eliminating the negative signs from a distribution of deviations is squaring. The arithmetic mean, defined in section 2.4.3, minimizes the average squared deviation of all scores in a distribution. That is, no other number (including the median) produces a smaller value when we calculate the deviations from the mean, square them, and average them over all observations. This desirable feature of the mean is built into a very important dispersion statistic for a continuous distribution—the **variance.** The formula for the variance—the mean squared deviation, s_Y^2—can be expressed in two equivalent ways:

variance—the mean square deviation of a continuous distribution

$$s_Y^2 = \frac{\displaystyle\sum_{i=1}^{N} d_i^2}{N-1}$$

$$s_Y^2 = \frac{\displaystyle\sum_{i=1}^{N} (Y_i - \overline{Y})^2}{N-1}$$

If the mean, $\overline{Y}$, is replaced in these formulas by any other number (such as Mdn), a larger value for s_Y^2 will always result. Unlike the mean formula that has N in the denominator, both variance formulas divide the numerator by $(N-1)$. This divisor produces an *unbiased* estimate of the population variance, a highly desirable property for any statistic (see section 3.10).

Table 2.5 shows the step-by-step calculation of the variance for the motor vehicle fatality data in Table 2.4, using a mean of 943.92. Because of the squaring, the variance is always a nonnegative number and is generally much larger than the original scores. The vehicular death variable $s_Y^2 = 976,819$ on a scale whose highest score is only 5,523. The unit of measure for this variance is not a fatality but "squared fatality," which makes an intuitively meaningful interpretation practically impossible.

standard deviation—the positive square root of the variance

To restore the original measurement intervals, we take the positive square root of the variance, called the **standard deviation.** Its formula is simply:

$$s_Y = \sqrt{s_Y^2}$$

For the state data the standard deviation is $\sqrt{976,819} = 988.3$ deaths. Looked at in isolation, the standard deviation lacks intuitive meaning. However, some valuable applications of the standard deviation will be presented in chapter 3.

The variance and standard deviation formulas are tedious to apply to large numbers of cases. The procedures are simplified in following the *computation formula* for s_Y^2.

$$s_Y^2 = \left(\frac{\Sigma Y_i^2}{N-1}\right) - \left(\frac{N}{N-1}\right)(\bar{Y})^2$$

Table 2.6 applies this computing formula to the motor vehicle death data.

For grouped data, such as Table 2.3, the variance formula requires weighting by the relative frequency in each category:

$$s_Y^2 = \frac{\sum\limits_{i=1}^{K} d_i^2 f_i}{N-1} = \frac{\Sigma (Y_i - \bar{Y})^2 f_i}{N-1}$$

Each deviation is first squared and then multiplied by the number of cases having score Y_i. Then, the weighted squared deviations for

TABLE 2.5
Calculation of Variance for Vehicle Deaths in Table 2.4

$(Y_i - \bar{Y})$		d_i	d_i^2	$(Y_i - \bar{Y})$		d_i	d_i^2
86 − 943.92	=	−857.92	736,026.7	725 − 943.92	=	−218.92	47,926.0
98 − 943.92	=	−845.92	715,580.6	763 − 943.92	=	−180.92	32,732.1
105 − 943.92	=	−838.92	703,786.8	769 − 943.92	=	−174.92	30,597.0
120 − 943.92	=	−823.92	678,844.2	773 − 943.92	=	−170.92	29,213.7
124 − 943.92	=	−819.92	672,268.8	785 − 943.92	=	−158.92	25,255.6
152 − 943.92	=	−791.92	627,137.3	796 − 943.92	=	−147.92	21,880.3
155 − 943.92	=	−788.92	622,394.8	829 − 943.92	=	−114.92	13,206.6
160 − 943.92	=	−783.92	614,530.6	987 − 943.92	=	43.08	1,855.9
163 − 943.92	=	−780.92	609,836.0	1,059 − 943.92	=	115.08	13,243.4
181 − 943.92	=	−762.92	582,046.9	1,073 − 943.92	=	129.08	16,661.7
218 − 943.92	=	−725.92	526,959.8	1,077 − 943.92	=	133.08	17,710.3
240 − 943.92	=	−703.92	495,503.4	1,077 − 943.92	=	133.08	17,710.3
273 − 943.92	=	−670.92	450,133.6	1,141 − 943.92	=	197.08	38,840.5
274 − 943.92	=	−669.92	448,792.8	1,180 − 943.92	=	236.08	55,733.8
311 − 943.92	=	−632.92	400,587.7	1,205 − 943.92	=	261.08	68,162.8
370 − 943.92	=	−573.92	329,384.2	1,372 − 943.92	=	428.08	183,252.5
446 − 943.92	=	−497.92	247,924.3	1,604 − 943.92	=	660.08	435,705.6
448 − 943.92	=	−495.92	245,936.6	1,609 − 943.92	=	665.08	442,331.4
470 − 943.92	=	−473.92	224,600.2	1,633 − 943.92	=	689.08	474,831.2
519 − 943.92	=	−424.92	180,557.0	1,666 − 943.92	=	722.08	521,399.5
539 − 943.92	=	−404.92	163,960.2	1,727 − 943.92	=	783.08	613,214.3
608 − 943.92	=	−335.92	112,842.2	1,968 − 943.92	=	1,024.08	1,048,740.0
624 − 943.92	=	−319.92	102,348.8	2,183 − 943.92	=	1,239.08	1,535,319.0
649 − 943.92	=	−294.92	86,977.8	2,925 − 943.92	=	1,981.08	3,924,678.0
657 − 943.92	=	−286.92	82,323.1	3,701 − 943.92	=	2,757.08	7,601,490.0
				5,523 − 943.92	=	4,579.08	20,967,974.0

$$\Sigma d_i^2 = 48,840,949.7$$

$$s_Y^2 = \frac{\Sigma \, d_i^2}{N - 1}$$

$$= \frac{48,840,949.7}{50}$$

$$= 976,819$$

$$\text{and } s_Y = \sqrt{976,819} = 988.3$$

TABLE 2.6

Computing Formula Calculation of Vehicle Deaths Variance

Y_i	Y_i^2	Y_i	Y_i^2
86	7,396	725	525,625
98	9,604	763	582,169
105	11,025	769	591,361
120	14,400	773	597,529
124	15,376	785	616,225
152	23,104	796	633,616
155	24,025	829	687,241
160	25,600	987	974,169
163	26,569	1,059	1,121,481
181	32,761	1,073	1,151,329
218	47,524	1,077	1,159,929
240	57,600	1,077	1,159,929
273	74,529	1,141	1,301,881
274	75,076	1,180	1,392,400
311	96,721	1,205	1,452,025
370	136,900	1,372	1,882,384
446	198,916	1,604	2,572,816
448	200,704	1,609	2,588,881
470	220,900	1,633	2,666,689
519	269,361	1,666	2,775,556
539	290,521	1,727	2,982,529
608	369,664	1,968	3,873,024
624	389,376	2,183	4,765,489
649	421,201	2,925	8,555,625
657	431,649	3,701	13,697,401
		5,523	30,503,529

$$\Sigma Y_i^2 = 94,281,334$$

$$\frac{\Sigma Y_i^2}{N - 1} = \frac{94,281,334}{50} = 1,885,626.7$$

$$\overline{Y} = 943.92157$$

$$\left(\frac{N}{N - 1}\right) (\overline{Y})^2 = \left(\frac{51}{50}\right) (890,987.93) = 908,807.7$$

$$s_Y^2 = 1,885,626.7 - 908,807.7 = 976,819$$

the K outcomes of Y are summed and divided by $(N - 1)$. Table 2.7 shows the calculations for the education data, yielding a variance of 8.90; the standard deviation is 2.98 years of schooling.

A more convenient computing formula also exists for grouped frequency distributions:

$$s_Y^2 = \left(\frac{N}{N - 1} \right) \left(\frac{\Sigma Y_i^2 f_i}{N} - \left(\frac{\Sigma Y_i f_i}{N} \right)^2 \right)$$

TABLE 2.7

Calculation of Variance for Education in Table 2.3

$(Y_i - \bar{Y})$	d_i	d_i^2	f_i	$d_i^2 f_i$
$(0 - 12.884)$	-12.884	165.997	2	331.994
$(3 - 12.884)$	-9.884	97.693	5	488.465
$(4 - 12.884)$	-8.884	78.925	5	394.625
$(5 - 12.884)$	-7.884	62.157	6	372.942
$(6 - 12.884)$	-6.884	47.389	12	568.668
$(7 - 12.884)$	-5.884	34.621	25	865.525
$(8 - 12.884)$	-4.884	23.853	68	1,622.004
$(9 - 12.884)$	-3.884	15.085	56	844.760
$(10 - 12.884)$	-2.884	8.317	73	607.141
$(11 - 12.884)$	-1.884	3.549	85	301.665
$(12 - 12.884)$	-0.884	0.781	461	360.041
$(13 - 12.884)$	0.116	0.013	130	1.690
$(14 - 12.884)$	1.116	1.245	175	217.875
$(15 - 12.884)$	2.116	4.477	73	326.821
$(16 - 12.884)$	3.116	9.709	194	1,883.546
$(17 - 12.884)$	4.116	16.941	43	728.463
$(18 - 12.884)$	5.116	26.173	45	1,177.785
$(19 - 12.884)$	6.116	37.405	22	822.910
$(20 - 12.884)$	7.116	50.637	30	1,519.110

$$\Sigma d_i^2 f_i = 13{,}436.03$$

$$s_Y^2 = \frac{\Sigma d_i^2 f_i}{N - 1} = \frac{13436.03}{1{,}509} = 8.90$$

$$s_Y = \sqrt{s_Y^2} = 2.98$$

The adjustment ratio, $N/(N-1)$, removes bias in the sample variance. Table 2.8 illustrates this formula's application to the grouped education data.

Dichotomous grouped frequency distributions are a special case. The computing formula for the variance of a 1-0 dichotomy reduces to:

TABLE 2.8
Computing Formula Calculation of Education Variance

Y_i	f_i	$Y_i f_i$	Y_i^2	$Y_i^2 f_i$
0	2	0	0	0
3	5	15	9	45
4	5	20	16	80
5	6	30	25	125
6	12	72	36	432
7	25	175	49	1,225
8	68	544	64	4,352
9	56	504	81	4,536
10	73	730	100	7,300
11	85	935	121	10,285
12	461	5,532	144	66,384
13	130	1,690	169	21,970
14	175	2,450	196	34,300
15	73	1,095	225	16,425
16	194	3,104	256	49,664
17	43	731	289	12,427
18	45	810	324	14,580
19	22	418	361	7,942
20	30	600	400	12,000
Total	1,510	19,455		264,072

$$s_Y^2 = \left(\frac{N}{N-1}\right)\left(\left(\frac{\sum Y_i^2 f_i}{N}\right) - \left(\frac{\sum f_i Y_i}{N}\right)^2\right)$$

$$= \left(\frac{1,510}{1,509}\right)\left(\left(\frac{264,072}{1,510}\right) - \left(\frac{19,455}{1,510}\right)^2\right) = 8.89$$

$$s_Y = 2.98$$

$$s_Y^2 = (p_0)(p_1)$$

where

p_0 = The proportion of cases coded 0.

p_1 = The proportion of cases coded 1.

Thus, 636 women and 881 women in the 1991 GSS give a gender variance of $(636/1,517)(881/1,517) = (.42)(.58) = 0.24$ and a standard deviation of 0.49. A dichotomy's variance always has a smaller numerical value than its standard deviation, because the product of two proportions is less than 1.00, and the square root of a number less than 1.00 is always a larger value. To demonstrate that the variance formula for a dichotomy equals the variance of any grouped frequency distribution, you should also calculate the gender variance with the standard formula on page 54.

2.5.5. Skewness

When the distribution of a continuous variable is graphed, the plot may be nonsymmetric about its median value. That is, there may be more categories with small numbers of observations on one side of the median than on the other side. Whenever this condition occurs, and one end of the distribution has a long "tail" (i.e., there are many categories with small frequencies), the result is said to be a **skewed distribution.** Thus, the distribution of education, using data from Table 2.3, is skewed. When distributions are skewed, the mean and the median differ, as they do in this example (mean = 12.9, Mdn = 12). When the long tail is to the right of the median (toward the high-valued categories), the distribution is said to have **positive skew;** when the tail is to the left of the median (toward the low-valued categories), the distribution has **negative skew.** (Put another way, a positively skewed distribution has a mean that is higher than its median, while a negatively skewed distribution has a median that is higher than its mean.) Years of schooling in Table 2.3 has a positive skew.

One measure of skewness in a distribution is:

$$\text{Skewness} = \frac{3(\overline{Y} - \text{Mdn})}{s_Y}$$

skewed distribution—a distribution that is nonsymmetric about its median value, having many categories with small frequencies at one end

positive skew—the tail of a skewed distribution is to the right of the median (mean greater than median)

negative skew—the tail of a skewed distribution is to the left of the median (median greater than mean)

If the mean and median are identical, then skewness equals zero. But, as the mean and median differ by large amounts relative to the distribution's standard deviation, skewness takes on either large positive or negative values. The skewness for education is [(3)(12.9 − 12)]/2.98 = 0.91, indicating a slightly positive skew.

When a distribution is relatively symmetric, its mean and median will be very close to one another. However, when the distribution is highly skewed, they can differ rather sharply. As the skewness formula shows, the mean is higher than the median for distributions with a positive skew. The opposite ordering holds for distributions with a negative skew. The mean and median differ because the mean is a weighted average—extreme values affect it—whereas the median is not. Consequently, many social scientists favor using the median as a central tendency measure for distributions that are highly skewed, such as distributions of personal income. For example, the U.S. Census Bureau's analyses of earnings by Americans of different races, genders, ages, or regions typically report median values for people in these categories, to avoid distortions that the use of means would create.

2.6   Percentiles and Quantiles

percentile—the outcome or score below which a given percentage of the observations in a distribution falls

A useful statistic that can be derived from cumulative distributions is the **percentile,** which is the outcome or score below which a given percentage of the observations falls. For example, in Table 2.3, 14 years of education is at the 73rd percentile. That is, 73% of the respondents have 14 or fewer years of education. The median is the 50th percentile. The median is the outcome that divides the distribution in two halves. In Table 2.3 the median is 12 years of education; the 90th percentile is 16 years of education.

When data are grouped in categories of more than unit width, the computation of percentiles can be quite tedious. Their computation requires a knowledge of true limits and midpoints, topics to which we now turn.

2.6.1.   True Limits and Midpoints

Grouping data in measurement classes raises problems of determining the true limits and midpoints of the intervals. For the purpose of instruction only, the data in Table 2.5 on motor vehicle deaths have been recoded into wider intervals in Table 2.9. The width is 800 deaths as can be seen in the first column of the table. The interval limits are defined by whole numbers—such as 1–800 deaths—but the **true limits** of the interval are 0.5–800.5. These numbers are the exact lower and upper bounds of numerical values that could be rounded into the category. Note that true limits cover the entire interval so as to ensure that there are no gaps or holes in the distribution. The second column of Table 2.9 shows the true limits for the seven measurement intervals created for this example.

true limits—the exact lower and upper bounds of numerical values that could be rounded into the category

The **midpoint** of an interval is figured by adding the true limits of each measured category and dividing by 2. The midpoint of the interval 0.5–800.5 for example, is (0.5 + 800.5)/2 = 400.5. The midpoints for all the other intervals are shown in the third column of Table 2.9. *The midpoint is the single number that best represents the entire measurement interval.*

midpoint—a number exactly halfway between the true upper and lower limits of a measurement class or interval, obtained by adding the upper to the lower limits and dividing by 2

Once we have selected the measurement interval, we tally the frequency (*f*), or the number of cases, in each interval, as shown in the fourth column of Table 2.9. These frequencies are next converted to proportions and cumulative frequencies as shown in the last two columns of the table.

2.6.2 Computing Percentiles

When the data are grouped such as they are in Table 2.9, percentiles are computed using the following formula:

TABLE 2.9
Distribution of Deaths from Motor Vehicle Accidents

Deaths	True Limits	Midpoint	f	p	cf
1–800	0.5–800.5	400.5	31	.61	31
801–1600	800.5–1600.5	1200.5	10	.20	41
1601–2400	1600.5–2400.5	2000.5	7	.14	48
2401–3200	2400.5–3200.5	2800.5	1	.02	49
3201–4000	3200.5–4000.5	3600.5	1	.02	50
4001–4800	4000.5–4800.5	4400.5	0	.00	50
4801–5600	4800.5–5600.5	5200.5	1	.02	51

Source: U.S. States Data Set

$$P_i = L_p + \left(\frac{(p_i)\ (N) - cf_p}{f_p} \right) (W_i)$$

where

P_i = The score of the *i*th percentile.

L_p = The true lower limit of the interval containing the *i*th percentile.

p_i = The *i*th percentile written as a proportion (e.g., the 75th percentile becomes 0.75 in the formula).

N = The total number of observations.

cf_p = The cumulative frequency up to *but not including* the interval containing P_i.

f_p = The frequency in the interval containing the *i*th percentile.

W_i = The width of the interval containing P_i; $W_i = U_p - L_p$.

where U_p and L_p are the upper and lower true limits of the interval containing P_i.

In Table 2.5 the 90th percentile is given by:

$$P_{90} = 1600.5 + \left(\frac{(.90)\ (51) - 41}{7} \right) (800) = 2160.5$$

since $i = 90$, $L_p = 1600.5$, $N = 51$, $cf_p = 41$, $f_p = 7$, and $W_i = 800$.

The median number of deaths from motor accidents in Table 2.4 is 725, the value of the 26th case. By contrast the median number of deaths for the data in Table 2.9, where the data have been more coarsely grouped, is the 50th percentile:

$$P_{50} = 0.50 + \left(\frac{(.40)\ (51) - 0}{31} \right) (800) = 526.95$$

As this example makes clear, grouping the data can create nontrivial errors in the description, especially where the ungrouped distribution is highly skewed. When computing descriptive statistics such as the mean, median, or variance, it is always preferable to use the data in their most disaggregated form.

2.6.3 Quantiles

Percentiles are special cases of **quantiles** that divide a set of observations into groups with known proportions in each group. Other special cases of quantiles are quartiles, quintiles, and deciles.

Quartiles are the values of a number scale that divide the observations into *four equal groups of equal size*. Q_1 is that point below which one-fourth of the observations lie, Q_2 is the point below which one-half of the observations lie, and so on. **Quintiles** divide the observations into *5 equal groups*, and **deciles,** into *10 equal groups*. As we saw above, *percentiles* divide observations into *100 equal groups*.

P_i is used to designate the *i*th percentile, D_i the *i*th decile, K_i the *i*th quintile, and Q_i the *i*th quartile. In this notation, $Q_1 = P_{25}$—the first quartile is exactly the same as the 25th percentile. Similarly, $K_1 = D_2$—the first quintile is the same as the second decile. Box 2.3 shows the relationship of the various quantiles to percentiles in tabular form.

Using the data in Table 2.3 on respondent's years of education, the third quartile, Q_3, is 15 years of education; that is, 75 percent of the respondents have 15 or fewer years of education. Alternatively, fewer than 25% of the respondents have 15 or more years of education.

2.7 Standardized Scores (*Z* Scores)

Researchers often compare scores across two or more distributions with different means and standard deviations. But, an identical score can mean something quite different in each sample. For example, an annual income of $80,000 is quite unusual in a sample of schoolteachers, but not in a sample of physicians. To compare scores across distributions, taking their different means and standard deviations into account, we can transform the original distribution to **standardized scores** (*Z* **scores** as they are more

quantile—a division of observations into groups with known proportions in each group

quartiles—the values of a number scale that divide a set of observations into four groups of equal size

quintiles—the values of a number scale that divide a set of observations into five groups of equal size

deciles—the values of a number scale that divide a set of observations into 10 groups of equal size

standard scores (*Z* scores)—a transformation of the scores of a continuous frequency distribution by subtracting the mean from each outcome and dividing by the standard deviation

---

BOX 2.3   Relationships of Quartiles, Quintiles, and Deciles to Percentiles

Of all the quantiles, the percentile provides the largest number of equal-sized groups—100 of them. The relationships of quartiles, quintiles, and deciles to percentiles is therefore easily shown, as in the following table:

Quartile	Percentile	Quintile	Percentile	Decile	Percentile
Q_1	P_{25}	K_1	P_{20}	D_1	P_{10}
Q_2	P_{50}	K_2	P_{40}	D_2	P_{20}
Q_3	P_{75}	K_3	P_{60}	D_3	P_{30}
		K_4	P_{80}	D_4	P_{40}
				D_5	P_{50}
				D_6	P_{60}
				D_7	P_{70}
				D_8	P_{80}
				D_9	P_{90}

---

commonly called). Using a distribution's mean and standard deviation, the Z transformation puts all the scores in each distribution onto the same scale, one where the unit of measurement is the standard deviation. The Z score formula for the ith case in a distribution is:

$$Z_i = \frac{d_i}{s_Y} = \frac{(Y_i - \bar{Y})}{s_Y}$$

The Z_i score corresponding to a given Y_i score is the number of standard deviations in which case i lies above or below the mean of its distribution. The larger the Z score in the positive or negative direction, the further away that case falls from the sample mean. A Z score of 0 occurs when an observation falls exactly at the distribution's mean.

Table 2.10 shows the calculation of Z scores for states' vehicle fatalities. For example, the Z scores for Maine (-0.73) is as many standard deviation units below the mean percentage as Michigan's Z score ($+0.73$) is above the mean. All but five states' Z scores fall within ± 1.00 standard deviations of the mean (943.9). The five noteworthy Z scores all occur at the upper end of the range, reflecting the distribution's positive skew. Those states

TABLE 2.10

Z Scores for Motor Vehicle Accident Deaths in 50 States

State	Y_i	$\dfrac{Y_i - \bar{Y}}{s_Y}$	Z_i
District of Columbia	86	(86 − 943.9) / 988.3	−0.87
Alaska	98	(98 − 943.9) / 988.3	−0.86
Vermont	105	(105 − 943.9) / 988.3	−0.85
North Dakota	120	(120 − 943.9) / 988.3	−0.83
Hawaii	124	(124 − 943.9) / 988.3	−0.83
South Dakota	152	(152 − 943.9) / 988.3	−0.80
Rhode Island	155	(155 − 943.9) / 988.3	−0.80
Delaware	160	(160 − 943.9) / 988.3	−0.79
Wyoming	163	(163 − 943.9) / 988.3	−0.79
New Hampshire	181	(181 − 943.9) / 988.3	−0.77
Maine	218	(218 − 943.9) / 988.3	−0.73
Montana	240	(240 − 943.9) / 988.3	−0.71
Idaho	273	(273 − 943.9) / 988.3	−0.68
Nevada	274	(274 − 943.9) / 988.3	−0.68
Nebraska	311	(311 − 943.9) / 988.3	−0.64
Utah	370	(370 − 943.9) / 988.3	−0.58
Iowa	446	(446 − 943.9) / 988.3	−0.50
Connecticut	448	(448 − 943.9) / 988.3	−0.50
West Virginia	470	(470 − 943.9) / 988.3	−0.48
Kansas	519	(519 − 943.9) / 988.3	−0.43
New Mexico	539	(539 − 943.9) / 988.3	−0.41
Minnesota	608	(608 − 943.9) / 988.3	−0.34
Arkansas	624	(624 − 943.9) / 988.3	−0.32
Oregon	649	(649 − 943.9) / 988.3	−0.30
Colorado	657	(657 − 943.9) / 988.3	−0.29
Oklahoma	725	(725 − 943.9) / 988.3	−0.22
Washington	763	(763 − 943.9) / 988.3	−0.18
Wisconsin	769	(769 − 943.9) / 988.3	−0.18
Massachusetts	773	(773 − 943.9) / 988.3	−0.17
Mississippi	785	(785 − 943.9) / 988.3	−0.16
Maryland	796	(796 − 943.9) / 988.3	−0.15

(Continued next page)

TABLE 2.10 *(continued)*

Z Scores for Motor Vehicle Accident Deaths in 50 States

State	Y_i	$\dfrac{Y_i - \bar{Y}}{s_Y}$	Z_i
Kentucky	829	(829 − 943.9) / 988.3	−0.12
Louisiana	987	(987 − 943.9) / 988.3	+0.04
New Jersey	1,059	(1,059 − 943.9) / 988.3	+0.12
Arizona	1,073	(1,073 − 943.9) / 988.3	+0.13
South Carolina	1,077	(1,077 − 943.9) / 988.3	+0.13
Indiana	1,077	(1,077 − 943.9) / 988.3	+0.13
Virginia	1,141	(1,141 − 943.9) / 988.3	+0.20
Alabama	1,180	(1,180 − 943.9) / 988.3	+0.24
Missouri	1,205	(1,205 − 943.9) / 988.3	+0.26
Tennessee	1,372	(1,372 − 943.9) / 988.3	+0.43
Georgia	1,604	(1,604 − 943.9) / 988.3	+0.67
Ohio	1,609	(1,609 − 943.9) / 988.3	+0.67
Illinois	1,633	(1,633 − 943.9) / 988.3	+0.70
Michigan	1,666	(1,666 − 943.9) / 988.3	+0.73
North Carolina	1,727	(1,727 − 943.9) / 988.3	+0.79
Pennsylvania	1,968	(1,968 − 943.9) / 988.3	+1.04
New York	2,183	(2,183 − 943.9) / 988.3	+1.25
Florida	2,925	(2,925 − 943.9) / 988.3	+2.00
Texas	3,701	(3,701 − 943.9) / 988.3	+2.79
California	5,523	(5,523 − 943.9) / 988.3	+4.63

each have very large populations, hence more drivers and more fatalities.

Because the Z transformation standardizes a distribution of scores, not surprisingly every distribution of Z scores has the *same* mean, variance, and standard deviation. Specifically, the mean of a Z score distribution is always zero, and its variance and standard deviation always equal 1. Box 2.4 gives proofs of the mean and variance for a standardized distribution. Z scores are easy to compute in the ungrouped data in Table 2.10. If you transform the grouped education data in Table 2.3 to Z scores, using that distribution's mean and standard deviation, and apply the mean and variance formulas for grouped data, you will also see that the Z score mean is 0 and the variance is 1 (within rounding error limits). Because we use Z scores *very* often in this text, you should be sure that you thoroughly understand this section.

BOX 2.4   The Mean and Variance of a Z-Score Distribution

Any numerical distribution that is transformed to Z scores remains a distribution having a specific mean and variance. Hence, using the formula for the mean, we can calculate the mean of a Z-score distribution by substituting Z in place of Y:

$\bar{Z} = \sum\limits_{i=1}^{N} \dfrac{Z_i}{N}$. But, the numerator (ΣZ_i) is equal to $\Sigma(Y_i - \bar{Y})$, which

is always zero (see section 2.5.3). Hence $\bar{Z} = 0$.

A Z score's variance is $s_Z^2 = \dfrac{\Sigma(Z_i - \bar{Z})^2}{N - 1}$. However, because

the mean of Z scores is 0, the variance reduces to:

$$s_Z^2 = \frac{\Sigma(Z_i - 0)^2}{N - 1} = \frac{\Sigma Z_i^2}{N - 1}$$

To find the numerical value of the Z-score distribution's variance, we must convert from the standard score back into the original Y values. The Z score in its original Y-score form is $Z_i = (Y_i - \bar{Y})/s_Y$. Substitute this quantity in the equation for the variance of Z:

$$s_Z^2 = \frac{\Sigma Z_i^2}{N - 1} = \frac{\Sigma[(Y_i - \bar{Y})/s_Y]^2}{N - 1}$$

Simplify the right-hand side by squaring the fraction in the numerator and dividing both the top and bottom by $(N - 1)$:

$$s_Z^2 = \frac{\Sigma(Y_i - \bar{Y})^2}{(s_Y^2)(N - 1)}$$

$$= s_Y^2/s_Y^2 = 1.00$$

since in the second to last step, the term $\Sigma(Y_i - \bar{Y})^2/(N - 1)$ is the definition of s_Y^2.

2.8   Exploratory Data Analysis Methods for Displaying
           Continuous Data

In this section we provide a brief introduction to some techniques
for displaying continuous data called **exploratory data analysis**
(EDA). One EDA method for displaying frequency distributions of
grouped continuous data is called a **stem-and-leaf diagram.**
Figure 2.4 shows a stem-and-leaf diagram for the U.S. States Data
Set voter turnout in the 1988 congressional election. The variable is
the percentage of eligible voters casting ballots in that election. To
construct a stem-and-leaf display, one takes the following steps:

**exploratory data
analysis**—methods for
displaying distributions of
continuous variables

**stem-and-leaf
diagram**—a type of
graph that displays the
observed values and
frequency counts of a
frequency distribution

1. Order the data values from lowest to highest.
2. Decide on the *leading digit* and the *trailing digit* in
   the display. Ordinarily one keeps the number of
   leading digits to no more than $N/3$ so that the display
   is interpretable.
3. For each observation write down each leading digit
   from lowest to highest under a column labeled
   "stem," and for each stem write the relevant trailing
   digit, which are called "leaves."

In this example the 51 congressional voting turnout values
range from 6.5% to 62.3%. We chose the 10s place (the decile) as the
leading digit and the 1s place as the trailing digit. Any digits after
the decimal point were simply ignored by rounding to the nearest
whole percent. For example, in Louisiana's turnout of 6.5%, the
leading digit is "0" (there is no 10s place) and its trailing digit, after
rounding up, is "7." For Minnesota and Montana, with the highest
turnouts at 62.3%, the leading digit is "6" and the trailing digit is "2."

A stem-and-leaf diagram somewhat resembles a histogram
turned on its side. The stem of Figure 2.4 consists of the leading
digits of the turnout data. To the right of each stem are its leaves,
consisting of the next digit of the relevant data points. Thus, in the
"0" stem, Lousiana's "7" appears as a leaf value. There are no
leaves in the "1" and "2" stems, indicating that no states had 1988
turnouts between 10% and 29%. In the "6" stem, representing
observed turnouts of 60–69%, Minnesota's and Montana's "2"
values each appear as leaves, along with two other states' "2"
values, and a fifth entry of "1" for a state with a 61% turnout.
Importantly, each entry on the leaf stands for one observation.

FIGURE 2.4

Stem-and-Leaf Diagram of 1988 Voter Turnout

Stems	Leaves	(*N*)
0	7	(1)
1		(0)
2		(0)
3	224568999	(9)
4	001111234556789	(15)
5	001111112222344678888	(21)
6	12222	(5)

Source: U.S. States Data Set

Thus, each leaf total can be written in parentheses at the extreme right of the diagram, as we have done to facilitate interpretation. Figure 2.4 makes clear that the distribution of 1988 voter turnout was slightly negatively skewed, that is, more states had lower than higher turnout (the exact mean was 47.3% and the median was 49.9%). A virtue of stem-and-leaf diagrams over histograms is the reader's ability to recover more precise information about the individual data points comprising the distribution. For example, how many states had turnouts of 52%?

A second EDA technique for displaying and interpreting data is called a **box-and-whisker** diagram or more simply a **boxplot.** A box-and-whisker diagram shows the central tendency, variability, and shape of a distribution of observed data. To construct box-and-whisker diagrams you must know the range, the median, and the "hinges" of a distribution. We illustrate with the motor vehicle fatality data in Table 2.4.

The **lower hinge** is the value of the observation that divides the lower quartile from the upper three-quarters of an ordered distribution and is signified by H_1. The data in Table 2.4 consist of 51 observations, making the 13th case in the distribution the lower quartile. This observation is Idaho, with a value of 273 fatalities. Hence, $H_1 = 273$. The **upper hinge** is the value of the observation that divides the upper quartile from the lower three-quarters of an

box-and-whisker (boxplot)— a type of graph for discrete and continuous variables in which boxes and lines represent central tendency, variability, and shape of a distribution of observed data

lower hinge— the value of the observation that divides the lower quartile from the upper three-quarters of an ordered distribution. Symbolized by H_1

upper hinge— the value of the observation that divides the upper quartile from the lower three-quarters of an ordered distribution. Symbolized by H_2

ordered distribution and is signified by H_2. In Table 2.4 the 39th case marks the upper quartile; it is Alabama, with an annual motor vehicle fatality of 1,180. Therefore, $H_2 = 1,180$.

In distributions with a large number of cases, Q_1 and Q_3 (see section 2.6) can be used to identify H_1 and H_2, respectively.

To construct the boxplot, draw a rectangular box between the two hinges, H_1 and H_2, as shown in Figure 2.5. Next determine whether the distribution contains any **outliers.** An outlier is any value that is so extreme (either large or small) that it seems to stand far apart from the rest of the distribution. One way to identify outliers is to calculate whether any observations lie below the **lower inner fence** (LIF) or above the **upper inner fence** (UIF). To compute the LIF and UIF, we must first determine the **_H_-spread** (short for **hinge spread**) of the distribution, which is merely the difference between the upper and lower hinges.

outlier— an observed value that is so extreme (either large or small) that it seems to stand apart from the rest of the distribution

lower inner fence— that part of an ordered distribution below which an observation is considered an outlier. Symbolized by LIF

upper inner fence— that part of an ordered distribution above which an observation is considered to be an outlier. Symbolized by UIF

hinge spread (_H_-spread)— the difference between the upper and lower hinges, i.e., $H_2 - H_1$. Symbolized by HS

$$HS = H_2 - H_1$$

where HS is H-spread

In the U.S. States Data Set on motor vehicle accidents, $HS = 1,180 - 273 = 907$. With this information we can now determine the two inner fences and see whether the distribution contains any outliers.

$$\text{LIF} = H_1 - (1.5)(HS)$$
$$\text{and}$$
$$\text{UIF} = H_2 + (1.5)(HS)$$

For the data in Table 2.4, LIF = $273 - (1.5)(907) = -1087.5$ and UIF = $1,180 + (1.5)(907) = 2,540.5$. Quite clearly the LIF is smaller than any admissible value since no state can have a negative number of accidents! Hence there are no outliers in the lower end of the distribution. But, notice that the deaths for Florida, Texas, and California are all outliers at the upper end of the distribution. An outlier is given special attention in a box-and-whisker plot by identifying it as a point with a label, as shown in Figure 2.5.

The diagram is completed by drawing a whisker (dotted line) from H_2 (the upper hinge) to the largest value in the distribution that is not an outlier, 2,183 in this example. The second whisker is drawn

FIGURE 2.5

Box-and-Whisker Plot of Motor Vehicle Fatalities

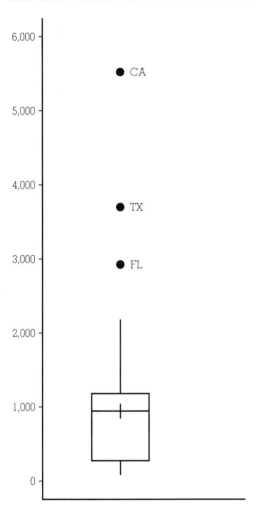

from H_1 (the lower hinge) to the smallest value in the distribution that is not an outlier, 86 in this case.

The box-and-whisker diagram for motor vehicle deaths makes clear that (1) the distribution is positively skewed since the absolute distance from the median to the upper hinge (H_2) is substantially greater than the absolute distance from the median to the lower hinge (H_l), and (2) Florida, Texas, and California clearly are outliers.

This section gave only a brief overview of how exploratory data analysis techniques can usefully describe distributions. Chapter 4 presents a second example comparing two distributions using stem-and-leaf and boxplot diagrams.

Review of Key Concepts and Symbols

These key concepts and symbols are listed in the order of appearance in this chapter. Combined with the definitions in the margins, they will help you to review the material and can serve as a self-test for mastery of the concepts.

tally	central tendency
frequency distribution	variation
outcome	mode
relative frequency distribution	median
percentage distribution	mean
relative frequency (proportion)	index of diversity
percentage	index of qualitative variation
rounding	range
dichotomous variable	average absolute deviation
(dichotomy)	variance
grouped data	standard deviation
measurement interval	skewed distribution
(measurement class)	positive skew
recoding	negative skew
cumulative frequency	percentile
cumulative frequency	true limits
distribution	midpoint
cumulative percentage	quantile
cumulative percentage	quartiles
distribution	quintiles
statistical table	deciles
diagram (graph)	standardized scores (Z scores)
bar chart	exploratory data analysis (EDA)
histogram	stem-and-leaf diagram
polygon	box-and-whisker (boxplot)

lower hinge	d_i
upper hinge	AAD
outlier	s_Y^2
lower inner fence	s_Y
upper inner fence	P_i
hinge spread (H-spread)	D_i
N	K_i
f_i	Q_i
p_i	Z_i
cf	H_1
$c\%$	H_2
Mdn	LIF
$\bar{Y}$	UIF
D	HS
IQV	

PROBLEMS

General Problems

1. Construct a frequency distribution for the following set of outcomes:

```
0   2   0   2   3
1   3   4   5   4
3   0   2   5   3
0   2   1   3   4
```

2. Construct a table of relative frequencies and a percentage distribution for the following set of European national origins, where F = French, G = German, E = English, I = Italian, R = Russian, and O = Other:

F E F E I G I R O R I F E O E F E G I R

3. Construct cumulative frequency and cumulative percentage distributions for the following men's suit prices, using measurement intervals "$99 and under"; $100–199; $200–299; and $300–399:

$99.42	$199.51	$299.95	$399.24	$199.87	$199.50
$99.62	$399.12	$199.33	$99.72	$199.50	

4. Round the following numbers to the units of measurement shown:

	Original	Rounded Units
a.	$7.42	Dollars
b.	$6.87	Dollars
c.	$233.12	Hundreds
d.	$350.01	Hundreds
e.	$14,499.62	Thousands
f.	$6,743.58	Thousands

5. Construct a histogram and a polygon for the following data on frequency of movie attendance: Never = 0; Seldom = 15; Often = 20; Regularly = 5.

6. In 10 games the hockey team scored the following number of points: 2, 0, 4, 1, 6, 3, 1, 2, 2, 0. Compute the (a) mean, (b) median, and (c) mode of this distribution.

7. Compute the (a) range, (b) average deviation, (c) variance, and (d) standard deviation for the following data: 2, 5, 8, 11, 14.

8. The population (to the nearest 100,000 inhabitants) of a state's eight largest cities is 5, 11, 3, 9, 6, 9, 6, 7. Find the (a) mean, (b) mode, (c) median, (d) variance, (e) standard deviation, and (f) skewness.

9. During the last election for mayor the Republican candidate got 55% of the votes and the Democratic candidate got 45%. What was the variance of this distribution?

10. On a 100-point scale of approval of the president, a sample of 2,000 voters has a mean of 60 and a standard deviation of 15. What are the Z scores for voters giving approval ratings of (a) 90, (b) 55, and (c) 85?

Problems Requiring the 1991 General Social Survey

11. Describe the frequency distribution of respondents' brothers and sisters (SIBS), using the central tendency and dispersion statistics discussed in this chapter.

12. For the ideal number of children (CHLDIDEL) reported by respondents, give the (*a*) mode, (*b*) median, (*c*) range, (*d*) mean, (*e*) variance, (*f*) standard deviation, and (*g*) the *Z* score for having four children.

13. Compare respondents' perceptions of their current family incomes (FINRELA) with their recollections of their families' incomes when they were 16 years old (INCOM16). What are the modal categories of each variable and which has the higher median value?

14. Compare respondents' confidence in the American press (CONPRESS) with their confidence in the executive branch of the federal government (CONFED), using whatever statistics you think appropriate.

Problems Requiring Use of the U.S. States Data Set

15. For the percentage of state population change from 1980–1986 (POPPC), find the (*a*) range, (*b*) mode, (*c*) median, (*d*) mean, and (*e*) standard deviation.

16. For the percentage of the state electorates casting votes in 1988 (TURN88), give the (*a*) mode, (*b*) median, (*c*) range, (*d*) mean, (*e*) variance, (*f*) standard deviation, and (*g*) the *Z* score for a turnout of 43%.

17. Find the mean and standard deviation for serious crimes per 100,000 state residents (CRIMEPC), and calculate whether New York with a score of 5,555 is less typical than Iowa with a score of 3,943.

Statistics for Social Data Analysis

Making Statistical Inferences

3

Social scientists seldom study a sample because they are only interested in describing that sample's central tendency and dispersion. Rather, they also wish to draw inferences about the population from which the sample was selected. Because assessing the entire population is often too costly, some method is required for *generalizing* from the sample results to the larger population. Reasonably accurate conclusions can be reached using elementary principles of probability theory. This chapter introduces some basic concepts necessary for understanding the topic of statistical inference. It explains both estimation and hypothesis testing for single-sample estimates of population values from sample data and shows how to apply some fundamental probability distributions.

3.1 Drawing Inferences About Populations from Samples

A statistical significance test permits one to make a reasonable **inference** that conclusions drawn from a sample of observations are true for the population from which that sample came. Absolute certainty is never possible, for by chance one might have selected an unusually deviant set of sample cases. But, if the sample is drawn randomly, an inference about the population can be made with a calculable probability that the conclusion cannot be rejected.

Random sampling, introduced in chapter 1, requires that each observation (i.e., a person, an object, or an event) in a population has an equal chance of being selected for the sample. That is, if the

inference—the process of making generalizations or drawing conclusions about the attributes of a population from evidence contained in a sample

random sampling—a procedure for selecting a set of representative observations from a population, in which each observation has an equal chance of being selected for the sample

77

population consists of N units, each unit has a probability of exactly $1/N$ of being chosen for the sample. The 1991 General Social Survey sampled 1,517 American adults, only a tiny fraction of the nearly 180 million people age 18 and over.[1] Each person had less than one chance in 118,000—or a probability smaller than .000009—of being interviewed. Furthermore, literally trillions of unique samples of 1,517 persons might have been drawn by the National Opinion Research Center. Given that only one of these possible samples was actually selected, how likely is it that these results accurately reflect some attribute of interest in the entire population? Probability theory and hypothesis-testing procedures help to ensure that the chances of mistaken conclusions are small.

3.2   Some Basic Probability Concepts

probability distribution
— a set of outcomes, each of which has an associated probability of occurrence

The observations in a population have an associated **probability distribution.** For example, in a randomly shuffled deck of 52 playing cards, the chance that the first card dealt is the ace of spades is 1/52. Similarly, the chance of randomly drawing a card from the heart suit is 13/52 or 1/4. Probabilities are usually expressed not as fractions but as proportions; thus, the probability of drawing the ace of spades is .019 and the probability of a heart is .25. The sum of the probabilities for all observations in the population must add to 1.00. Thus, the sum of the probabilities for the heart, diamond, club, and spade suits is .25 + .25 + .25 + .25 = 1.00. If an outcome cannot occur, such as a joker card excluded from the deck, it has a probability of .00.

3.2.1.   Continuous Probability Distributions

The simple examples above show how easy probabilities are to calculate for a small population with discrete outcomes. They are simply relative frequencies or proportions (see section 2.1, page 32). As noted in chapter 1, many social measures are continuous, classifying observations by the quantity of an attribute: annual income, achievement test scores, rates of AIDS infection. In princi-

---

1. A U.S. national sample cannot be selected by simple random sampling, which requires a complete listing of every person in the population. Survey research organizations use more cost-efficient sampling techniques that we cannot describe here. We analyze the GSS data as though they had been drawn using simple random procedures, which causes only minor errors in statistical inference.

ple, a **continuous probability distribution** means that no interruptions occur between a variable's outcomes. Probabilities attached to various outcomes of a continuous variable can be connected by a single continuous line, as in the hypothetical example in Figure 3.1. A very precisely measured continuous variable (such as an income of $27,463.18) means that few cases will have identical outcomes; hence, the probability of observing any outcome approaches zero in a large sample with continuous measures. For this reason probabilities for continuous variables are measured as the interval between two outcomes, a and b. The probability of observing an outcome of variable Y lying between points a and b is labeled alpha (α); that is, $p(a \leq Y \leq b) = \alpha$. This expression is read, "The probability that outcome Y is greater than or equal to a and less than or equal to b is alpha," where alpha is a probability expressed as a decimal between .00 and 1.00. In general, the probability of a variable Y can simply be denoted as $p(Y)$.

continuous probability distribution—a probability distribution for a continuous variable, with no interruptions or spaces between the outcomes of the variable

3.2.2. Describing Discrete Probability Distributions

In the same way that researchers can describe and summarize a sample with statistics such as the mean, they also can describe and summarize population distributions. The three major population descriptors are the mean, standard deviation, and variance. These descriptors are called **population parameters** because they are

population parameter— a descriptive characteristic of a population, such as a mean, standard deviation, or variance. Symbolized by θ

FIGURE 3.1
A Continuous Probability Distribution

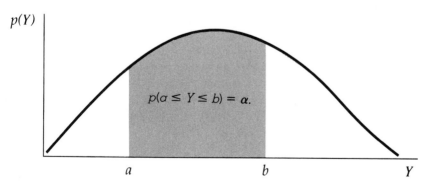

Source: David Knoke and George W. Bohrnstedt, *Basic Social Statistics* (Itasca, IL: F. E. Peacock Publishers, Inc., 1991), 153.

constants in the populations. By contrast, the sample mean, standard deviation and variance are *variables*, because their numerical values vary from sample to sample. For this reason statistics are used as estimators of parameters.

The single number that best describes a probability distribution of discrete scores is its **expected value,** labeled $E(Y)$ and given by

expected value—the single number that best describes a probability distribution of discrete scores

$$E(Y) = \sum_{i=1}^{K} Y_i p(Y_i)$$

In computing the expected value of a probability distribution, we simply weight each of the K outcomes by its probability of occurrence and add up the resulting terms. That is, the score of the observations in the ith category is multiplied by the probability of a case falling into that category, then these products are summed across all K categories in the distribution.

mean of a probability distribution—the expected value of a population of scores

The **mean of a probability distribution,** labeled μ_Y (Greek letter *mu*) is defined the same way as the expected value, that is:

$$\mu_Y = \sum_{i=1}^{K} Y_i p(Y_i)$$

For example, the mean of the distribution of outcomes of a die toss is computed as the sum of the products of the die face value times the (equal) probability of that face value: $\mu_Y = 1(1/6) + 2(1/6) + 3(1/6) + 4(1/6) + 5(1/6) + 6(1/6) = (1 + 2 + 3 + 4 + 5 + 6)(1/6) = 21/6 = 3.5$.

We can also compute the expected value of other functions of Y, which are represented by a very general function, call it $g(Y)$.

$$E[g(Y)] = \sum_{i=1}^{K} g(Y_i) p(Y_i)$$

variance of a probability distribution—the expected spread or dispersion of a population of scores

One application of this general formulation for expected values is provided by the definition of the **variance of a probability distribution,** which is labeled σ_Y^2 (Greek letter *sigma*). First, let $g(Y) = (Y - \mu_Y)^2$. Then it follows that

$$\sigma_Y^2 = E(Y - \mu_Y)^2$$

$$= \sum_{i=1}^{K}(Y_i - \mu_Y)^2 p(Y_i)$$

As in a sample, the variance of a probability distribution measures the spread or dispersion in the population.

The square root of the population variance is called the standard deviation, as it is with sample statistics (see chapter 2). For a population it is symbolized σ_Y and is given by

$$\sigma_Y = \sqrt{\sigma_Y^2}$$

Using die tosses as an example (recall that $\mu_Y = 3.5$), we can calculate that $\sigma_Y^2 = (1 - 3.5)^2(1/6) + (2 - 3.5)^2(1/6) + (3 - 3.5)^2(1/6) + (4 - 3.5)^2(1/6) + (5 - 3.5)^2(1/6) + (6 - 3.5)^2(1/6) = 17.5/6 = 2.92$, and $\sigma_Y = \sqrt{2.92} = 1.71$.

Because researchers ordinarily cannot observe entire populations, the parameters μ_Y and σ_Y^2 are of largely theoretical interest. You need to understand the concept of expected value, however, in order to understand the discussion of inference in the sections and chapters that follow.[2] Box 3.1 provides a summary of symbols used for the sample statistics introduced in chapter 2 and the population parameters used thus far in this chapter.

The following sections introduce some theorems that can be used to estimate the probability of observing a given outcome in a distribution having a known mean and standard deviation. These preliminaries will be useful in thinking about how rare a given sample mean is in a population of sample means generated by taking all possible samples of size N. In drawing an inference we first hypothesize that a population has a mean equal to some value, μ_Y. If the discrepancy between the *observed* sample mean and the *hypothesized* population mean is too large—that is, if it is too "deviant" to have come from a population with a mean of μ_Y—we reject the hypothesis about the value of the population mean, μ_Y.

---

2. We have not discussed the expected value, mean, and variance for continuous probability distributions because integral calculus is needed to do so. However, the definitions of the mean and variance for continuous probability distributions are identical to those for discrete probability distributions.

BOX 3.1   Population Parameter and Sample Statistic Symbols

Statistical formulas may apply either to an entire population of observations or to a sample drawn from a population. While the formulas are often the same or similar, the symbolic notation differs. Roman letters are used for *sample statistics* calculated on sample data, while Greek letters stand for the *population parameters*. For some basic statistics and parameters, the symbols are:

Name	Sample Statistic	Population Parameter
Mean	$\overline{Y}$	μ_Y (mu)
Variance	s_Y^2	σ_Y^2 (sigma-squared)
Standard Deviation	s_Y	σ_Y (sigma)

3.3   Chebycheff's Inequality Theorem

A close connection exists between the distance of an observation from the mean of a distribution and the probability of that observation: On average observations far from the mean occur less often than those close to the mean. Thus, a score that is one-half standard deviation above the mean ($Z = +.50$; see chapter 2) has a higher probability of occurring than a score that is two standard deviations below the mean ($Z = -2.00$). In general, the more distant an outcome is from its mean, the lower the probability of observing it.

The Russian mathematician Pafnuty Chebycheff first proved a theorem about the relationship between the size of a deviation and the probability of observing it. His result refers to the outcomes in a population, not in a sample, and it holds for any shape of distribution, no matter how skewed. **Chebycheff's inequality theorem** states that the probability a variable differs absolutely

Chebycheff's inequality theorem—the probability a variable differs absolutely from the mean by k or more standard deviations is *always* less than or equal to the ratio of 1 to k^2 (for all k greater than 1.0)

from the mean by k or more standard deviations is *always* less than or equal to the ratio of 1 to k^2 (for all k greater than 1.0):

$$p(|Z| \geq k) \leq \frac{1}{k^2}$$

This equation says that the probability that the absolute value of an observation's Z score is k or more standard deviations from the mean is equal to or less than 1 divided by the square of k standard deviations. Clearly, as k gets larger in the positive or negative direction, the probability decreases; hence, according to Chebycheff, extreme scores are unlikely.

For example, consider a student scoring two standard deviations above the class mean on a midterm exam. The theorem states that the probability of observing a score this far above or below the mean is $1/(2^2)$ or less (i.e., $p \leq .25$). And an observed $Z = \pm 3$ or greater has a probability of $1/(3^2) = .11$ or less. Chebycheff's inequality theorem applies regardless of the underlying shape of a population distribution. Importantly, the theorem is a claim about *probability*, not about certainty. It does not guarantee that any given outcome will be rarer than another that is closer to the mean. It only asserts that, without information about the shape of a distribution, the probability of an observation decreases the farther it lies from the mean.

More precise probability statements can be made if we have some knowledge of the distribution's shape. If a population distribution is unimodal (has one mode) and is symmetric about its mean, a derivation of Chebycheff's inequality theorem states:

$$p(|Z| \geq k) \leq \left(\frac{4}{9}\right)\left(\frac{1}{k^2}\right)$$

Thus, outcomes in a unimodal symmetric distribution that are two or more standard deviations from the mean will be observed with probability $(.444)(1/2)^2 = (.444)(.25) = .111$ or less. Compare this probability to .25 when no assumptions can be made about the shape of the distribution. Chebycheff's inequality shows how knowledge about a distribution's shape affects the probability of observing deviant cases, a point relevant to the next section.

3.4   The Normal Distribution

A very important family of unimodal, symmetric distributions in inferential statistics are Gaussian distributions, after the German mathematician Carl Friedrich Gauss. Unfortunately, today they are exclusively called **normal distributions,** because they were originally believed to be useful in establishing social norms for many kinds of variables. Although we now know that almost no social data take such shapes, the term continues in wide use today. All normal distributions are described by a rather formidable equation:

normal distribution—a smooth, bell-shaped theoretical probability distribution for continuous variables that can be generated from a formula

$$p(Y) = \frac{e^{-(Y - \mu_Y)^2/2\sigma_Y^2}}{\sqrt{2\pi\sigma_Y^2}}$$

A particular normal curve's shape is determined by only two values, the population mean, μ_Y, and its variance, σ_Y^2. Figure 3.2 shows two normal curves one with $\sigma_Y^2 = 10$ and the other with $\sigma_Y^2 = 15$, and both with $\mu_Y = 0$. The smaller the population variance, the closer on average are its observations to the mean, and hence the "thinner" the tails of that normal distribution. Although the normal curve tails seem to touch the horizontal axis, the theoretical distribution of values actually ranges from $-\infty$ to $+\infty$. Thus, the tails approach but never actually reach the horizontal axis in each direction.

Calculating probabilities of outcomes for normal distributions with differing means and variances would be tedious and time-consuming. But every distribution of scores can easily be converted to standardized (Z) scores (see section 2.7, pages 63–64). The formula for a population is $Z_i = (Y_i - \mu_Y)/\sigma_Y$. Thus, only one table of probabilities associated with distributions is necessary—the standardized normal distribution table in Appendix C, "Area Under the Normal Curve." A schematic appears in Figure 3.3.

The total area under a normal curve is unity (1.00). We noted above that the probabilities of all the cases in a distribution must sum to 1.00. Half the area in a normal curve lies to the right of the mean (which is .00, because the mean of Z scores is always zero; see Box 2.4, page 67). All the Z scores in this portion are positive numbers. The other half of the area under the normal curve lies to the left of the mean, corresponding to negative Z scores. In Figure 3.3 Z_a refers to a specific Z whose probability of occurrence we seek.

FIGURE 3.2

Two Examples of Normal Distributions

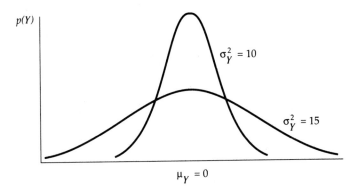

Source: David Knoke and George W. Bohrnstedt, *Basic Social Statistics* (Itasca, IL: F. E. Peacock Publishers, Inc., 1991), 157.

The shaded area refers to the probability of a value between $Z = 0$ and Z_α.

For example, suppose that we want to determine the probability that an outcome is least 1.55 standard deviations above the mean of a normal distribution. Then $Z_\alpha = (+1.55)(\sigma_Z) = +1.55$, because the standard deviation of Z scores (σ_Z) is always 1 (see Box 2.4). Turn to

FIGURE 3.3

Example of the Probability of Observing an Outcome in a Standardized Normal Distribution

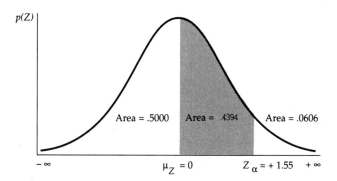

Source: David Knoke and George W. Bohrnstedt, *Basic Social Statistics* (Itasca, IL: F. E. Peacock Publishers, Inc., 1991), 159.

Appendix C to find the probability that this particular value occurs. First, look *down* the left column of the table until you find 1.5. Then look *across* this row to the column labeled .05. (The sum of these two headings is the 1.55 Z score of interest.) The number in this cell is .4394, the probability of an outcome lying *between* $Z = 0$ and $Z_a =$ 1.55. The probability that $Z_a \geq +1.55$ lies in the *unshaded* area in the right tail of the normal distribution. This probability is .5000 − .4394 = .0606, since the probability for the entire half of the distribution equals .5000. Because a normal distribution is symmetric, it should be clear that the probability of an observation −1.55 or more standard deviations (i.e., to the left of the mean) also equals .0606. Probabilities from both halves of the normal curve can be added. Thus, .8788 of the area lies between $Z_a = -1.55$ and $Z_a =$ +1.55, while only .1212 of the area lies in the two tails beyond Z_a scores of −1.55 and +1.55 (i.e., $p(|Z_a| \geq 1.55) = .1212$).

3.4.1.   The Alpha Area

The area in the tail of a normal distribution that is cut off by a given Z_a is called the **alpha area,** or simply α. It is defined as

$$p(|Z| \geq |Z_a|) = \alpha$$

This expression is read, "The probability that the absolute value of an observed Z score is equal to or greater than Z_a absolute standard deviations equals alpha." Because an α area might also be located in the left tail, the formula above uses absolute values of Z and Z_a. Z_a is called a **critical value** because it is the minimum value of Z necessary to designate an alpha area.

We illustrate an α area in Figure 3.4, where the portion of the normal distribution between Z_a and $+\infty$ is labeled α. When we discuss hypothesis testing in section 3.8, in some cases we will split α equally between the left and right tails of the normal distribution. In such instances the probability located in the right tail is $\alpha/2$, and the probability in the left tail is also $\alpha/2$. The two critical Z scores cutting off these areas are labeled $Z_{\alpha/2}$ and $-Z_{\alpha/2}$, respectively. Figure 3.5 illustrates these critical values, as do the following examples.

Assume that using the normal curve is appropriate and that we choose to concentrate $\alpha = .05$ entirely in the right tail, as in Figure 3.4. What value of Z_a will exactly cut off the upper 5% of the normal

alpha area—the area in the tail of a normal distribution that is cut off by a given Z_a

critical value—the minimum value of Z necessary to designate an alpha area

FIGURE 3.4

Probability Distribution for a Type I Error in the Right Tail

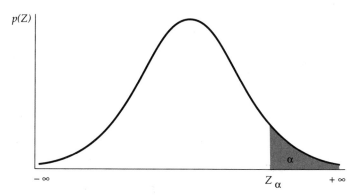

Source: David Knoke and George W. Bohrnstedt, *Basic Social Statistics* (Itasca, IL: F. E. Peacock Publishers, Inc., 1991), 160.

curve? We look up .4500 in the body of Appendix C, because .5000 − .4500 = .0500. The two tabled entries closest to .4500 are .4495 and .4505, respectively corresponding to Z = 1.64 and Z = 1.65. Averaging these two values, we conclude that Z scores that are +1.645 standard deviations or larger occur for only 5% of the

FIGURE 3.5

Areas Under the Normal Curve for Various Z Scores

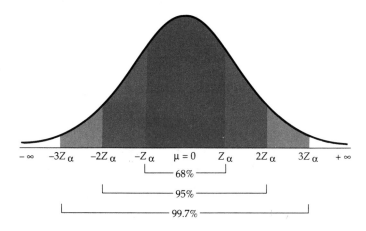

Source: David Knoke and George W. Bohrnstedt, *Basic Social Statistics* (Itasca, IL: F. E. Peacock Publishers, Inc., 1991), 161.

observations in a normally distributed population. Therefore, $Z_\alpha =$ $+1.645$ for this problem. What Z_α cuts off .01 in the left tail of a normal distribution?

Suppose we decide to split α between both tails, as in Figure 3.5. If we set $\alpha = .05$, then $\alpha/2 = .025$. To determine the pair of $Z_{\alpha/2}$ values that will put 2.5% of the area into each tail, we first calculate that $.5000 - .0250 = .4750$. Next, using Appendix C, we determine that the $+Z_{\alpha/2}$ associated with .4750 is $+1.96$. Because a normal curve is symmetric, $-Z_{\alpha/2} = -1.96$. Thus, 95% of the area under the standardized normal distribution lies between $-Z_{\alpha/2} = -1.96$ and $+Z_{\alpha/2} = +1.96$. A total of 5% of the scores are located farther from the mean in the two tails. You should be able to demonstrate that about 68% of the outcomes in a normal curve fall between standard deviations of -1 and $+1$. What proportion of the scores fall outside the range from -3 to $+3$ standard deviations? Assuming a normal distribution any observation that is three or more standard deviations from the mean is rare indeed. Figure 3.5 graphically summarizes this information.

3.5   The Central Limit Theorem

central limit theorem—if all possible random samples of N observations are drawn from any population with mean μ_Y and variance σ^2_Y, then as N grows large, these sample means approach a normal distribution, with mean μ_Y and variance σ^2_Y/N

A very important use of the normal curve depends on the **central limit theorem,** which states:

If all possible random samples of N observations are drawn from any population with mean μ_Y and variance σ^2_Y, then as N grows large, these sample means approach a normal distribution, with mean μ_Y and variance σ^2_Y/N; that is:

$$\mu_{\bar{Y}} = \mu_Y$$

$$\sigma^2_{\bar{Y}} = \sigma^2_Y/N$$

The central limit theorem says that, for samples of the same size N, the mean of all sample means equals the mean of the population from which these samples were randomly drawn. Furthermore, the variance of this new hypothetical distribution is smaller than the original population variance by a factor of $1/N$. No assumptions need to be made about the shape of the population.

The hypothetical distribution of all possible means for samples of size N is called the **sampling distribution of sample means.** A sampling distribution for means involves the mean of every sample of size N that could be formed from a given population. Because any large population contains billions and trillions of unique samples, no one can actually compute the means making up a sampling distribution. It remains a purely theoretical construct. Yet, because the central limit theorem relates two population parameters (μ_Y and σ_Y^2) to the sampling distribution's mean and variance, its shape is completely determined by just these two parameters. The central limit theorem guarantees that a sample mean comes closer to the population mean as the sample size (N) increases, because the sampling distribution's variance becomes smaller as N increases. The standard deviation of a sampling distribution is called the **standard error.** Its formula is the square root of the sampling distribution variance:

sampling distribution of sample means— a distribution consisting of the means of all samples of size N that could be formed from a given population

standard error—the standard deviation of a sampling distribution

$$\sigma_{\bar{Y}} = \sigma_Y / \sqrt{N}$$

Knowing that sample means are normally distributed, regardless of the population from which the samples came, and assuming that N is large, we can reach some important conclusions. Suppose we draw a random sample of $N = 400$ observations from a population with $\mu_Y = 100$ and $\sigma_Y = 15$. The standard error of the sampling distribution of means for a sample size of 400 can be calculated as follows:

$$\sigma_{\bar{Y}} = 15 / \sqrt{400} = 0.75$$

From our understanding of the normal curve, we know that 95% of all sample means fall within ±1.96 standard errors of the population mean. Therefore, in this example 95% of the sample means fall in the interval between 98.53 and 101.47—that is, $100 \pm (1.96)(.75)$. The central limit theorem assures us, first, that the mean of a random sample should equal the population mean (100), and second, that only 5% of these samples have means that lie outside the interval from 98.53 to 101.47. Suppose we increase the sample size from 400 to 1,000. The standard error now becomes even smaller; specifically, $\sigma_{\bar{Y}} = 15 / \sqrt{1000} = .47$. Thus, 95% of this sampling distribution's means occur between 99.08 and 100.92; that is, inside the interval bounded by $100 \pm (1.96)(.47)$. Thus, on average one sample mean in 20 will fall outside this interval. We can have considerable confidence that *any* random sample of size 1,000 would give us a very accurate estimate of the mean of the population from which it was drawn.

Although the central limit theorem requires a large N to be applicable, we cannot say precisely how large a sample must be. Some textbooks say 30 observations, others suggest 100. On the basis of experience, we suggest that when the sample size is 100 or more, the sampling distribution of means closely approximates a normal distribution. But for samples with 30 or fewer cases, we would hesitate to assume a normal sampling distribution. For samples sizes between 30 and 100 cases, one may cautiously assume the central limit theorem applies unless the underlying population has an extremely odd shape.

3.6   Sample Point Estimates and Confidence Intervals

The central limit theorem has an important corollary: The mean of a random sample $(\overline{Y})$ is the best single estimate of the mean of the population mean, μ_Y, from which the sample was drawn. The sample mean is a **point estimate** of the population mean, because only a single value is estimated. We can also construct a **confidence interval** around this estimate, allowing us to express the degree to which we believe this interval contains the true population mean. (An interval either does or does not contain the population parameter, but because we do not know with certainty what that value is, we can only form a judgment regarding our best guess as to where the parameter occurs.)

Again, the central limit theorem allows us to use the normal curve to construct a confidence interval having a specific probability, α. The formula for calculating the upper and lower limits of a α-level confidence interval is as follows:

$$\overline{Y} \pm (Z_{\alpha/2})(\sigma_{\overline{Y}})$$

To find the **upper confidence limit** (or UCL), add the product of the critical value $(Z_{\alpha/2})$ times the standard error to the sample mean. The **lower confidence limit** (or LCL) subtracts this product from the sample mean. For example, if we choose $\alpha = .05$, the critical values

point estimate—a sample statistic used to estimate a population parameter

confidence interval—a range of values constructed around a point estimate that makes it possible to state the probability that an interval contains the population parameter between its upper and lower confidence limits

upper confidence limit—the highest value of a confidence interval

lower confidence limit—the lowest value of a confidence interval

of $Z_{\alpha/2}$ that put .025 of the area into each tail of the normal distribution are -1.96 and $+1.96$. We can expect that 95% of the intervals bounded by 1.96 standard errors above and below the sample mean will contain the population mean, μ_Y. For a 95% confidence interval, the lower confidence limit is $\overline{Y} - 1.96\ \sigma_{\overline{Y}}$ and the upper confidence limit is $\overline{Y} + 1.96\ \sigma_{\overline{Y}}$. Similarly, the LCL and UCL for a 68.26% confidence interval are $\overline{Y} - \sigma_{\overline{Y}}$ and $\overline{Y} + \sigma_{\overline{Y}}$, respectively. And for a 99% confidence interval, the LCL is $\overline{Y} - 2.58\ \sigma_{\overline{Y}}$ and the UCL is $\overline{Y} + 2.58\ \sigma_{\overline{Y}}$. The smaller the α, the wider the confidence interval.

The symbol $Z_{\alpha/2}$ introduced above can now be more precisely defined. In Appendix C $Z_{\alpha/2}$ is the value that cuts off an area on the right tail of the normal curve equal to $\alpha/2$. To be 95% confident that a given interval contains μ_Y, then $\alpha = .05$ by implication, and $\alpha/2 = .025$. As section 3.5 shows, $Z_{\alpha/2} = \pm 1.96$ gives the correct interval for a specific $\sigma_{\overline{Y}}$.

Caution is in order when interpreting confidence intervals. A great temptation is to conclude that one can be 95% confident that a given interval contains the population mean. In fact, after an interval has been constructed, the probability that it contains the population mean is either 1.00 or 0.00, depending on whether the population mean is actually inside or outside the interval. What we can conclude is that, with repeated construction of confidence intervals, 95% of such intervals will contain the population mean.

Figure 3.6 illustrates the concept of a confidence interval. The solid vertical line represents the true population mean, a constant ($\mu_Y = 50.5$ in this example). The horizontal lines represent the confidence intervals constructed around the means of 15 different random samples. All but two (the 6th and 14th intervals from the top) contain the population mean, $\mu_Y = 50.5$. The point estimates (i.e., the sample means) appear next to each interval. If we were able to construct confidence intervals for every possible sample of size N, we would find that $1 - \alpha$ of them contain the population mean and only α of them do not.

In general, for a given confidence interval, larger sample sizes produce smaller intervals around the sample mean. Suppose we know that $\sigma_Y = 15$ and we observe $\overline{Y} = 51.0$ for a random sample of $N = 100$. To be 95% confident that a particular interval contains the population mean, the interval is bounded by LCL $= 51.0 - 1.96\ (15/\sqrt{100}) = 48.06$ and UCL $= 51.0 + 1.96\ (15/\sqrt{100}) = 53.94$. Suppose

FIGURE 3.6

Example Illustrating the Concept of a Confidence Interval

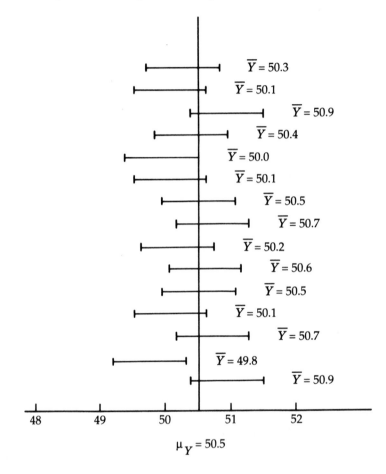

Source: David Knoke and George W. Bohrnstedt, *Basic Social Statistics* (Itasca, IL: F. E. Peacock Publishers, Inc., 1991), 167.

we observe $\overline{Y} = 51.0$ for a random sample of $N = 500$. The 95% interval for such samples is bounded by LCL = $51.0 - 1.96\,(15/\sqrt{500})$ = 49.69 and UCL = $51.0 + 1.96\,(14/\sqrt{500}) = 52.31$. Thus, for a given α, increasing N decreases the confidence interval's width.

To construct a confidence interval around a sample mean, three assumptions are necessary: (1) that the sample for estimating μ_Y is drawn randomly; (2) that N is "large" (at least > 30); and (3) that we know the population variance (σ_Y^2), so that the standard error ($\sigma_{\overline{Y}}$)

~~can be~~ computed. Most often the third assumption is violated. Clearly, if we knew (σ_Y^2), we would not need to analyze sample data. But, most of the time we do not know the population parameters and thus must estimate their probable values from sample evidence. When N is large, a good estimate of the standard error of the sampling distribution can be made by using the sample standard deviation, s_Y. Putting a caret ($\hat{}$) above $\hat{\sigma}_{\overline{Y}}$ signifies that it is an estimated value:

$$\hat{\sigma}_{\overline{Y}} = s_Y/\sqrt{N}$$

The GSS sample data in Table 2.3 on page 39 provided a sample estimate of mean education = 12.9 years, with a standard deviation = 2.98. The sample size on which these statistics were calculated was 1,510 respondents. Applying these sample statistics to the formula above yields an estimated standard error of $\hat{\sigma}_{\overline{Y}} = 2.98/\sqrt{1510} = 2.98/38.86 = 0.077$. We can be 95% confident that the population mean schooling is contained in the interval defined by $12.9 \pm (1.96)(.077)$. This computes to a LCL of 12.75 years and a UCL of 13.05 years. What are the limits defining the 99% confidence interval? This very large sample produced a confidence interval that is small relative to the size of the sample standard deviation, underscoring the importance of N in making inferences. Although this example uses the 1991 GSS sample data, we can consult the 1990 U.S. Census to check whether the confidence interval does in fact contain the population mean. For persons aged 25 years and older, the census found the mean years of schooling was 12.8, which falls within the interval estimated from GSS data. For most variables of interest to social researchers, such population data do not exist for comparison to sample estimates. To increase your confidence that your interval contains the population parameter, all you can realistically do is to increase the interval width by setting a smaller α-level.

Another important application of the central limit theorem is to determine the size of a sample necessary for attaining a particular level of accuracy in estimating the population mean. For a large sample, assuming a normally distributed population,

$$p\left(\left|\frac{\overline{Y} - \mu_Y}{\sigma_{\overline{Y}}}\right| \leq Z_{\alpha/2}\right) = p\left(\left|\frac{k\sigma_Y}{\sigma_{\overline{Y}}}\right| \leq Z_{\alpha/2}\right) = 1 - \alpha$$

This expression states that the probability is approximately $1 - \alpha$ that the difference between the sample mean and the population mean falls within k standard deviations. Suppose we desire an accuracy of no more than .25 standard deviation at $\alpha = .05$ (hence $Z_{\alpha/2} = \pm 1.96$). Solving the formula above for N yields:

$$\frac{k\sigma_Y}{\sigma_{\bar{Y}}} = Z_{\alpha/2}$$

$$\frac{.25\sigma_Y}{\sigma_Y/\sqrt{N}} = 1.96$$

$$.25\sqrt{N} = 1.96$$

$$N = \left(\frac{1.96}{.25}\right)^2 = 61.47 \text{ cases}$$

That is, at least 62 cases are required. To improve accuracy to within .10 standard deviation, N must be increased to at least 385 observations.

3.7 The t Distribution

t distribution—one of a family of test statistics used with small samples selected from a normally distributed population or, for large samples, drawn from a population with any shape

The examples above assume that the standard error of the sampling distribution ($\sigma_{\bar{Y}}$) is known. Fortunately, another family of theoretical distributions, the **t distributions,** does not require us to know the standard error. They are sometimes called "Student's t" because W. S. Gossett, who first applied them to an important problem, signed his 1908 article "Student." The formula for a **t variable,** or **t score,** is

t variable (*t* score)—a transformation of the scores of a continuous frequency distribution derived by subtracting the mean and dividing by the estimated standard error

$$t = \frac{Y - \mu_Y}{s_Y/\sqrt{N}}$$

where

$s_Y/\sqrt{N}$ estimates the sampling distribution's standard error from the sample standard deviation and size.

The similarity of t scores to Z scores for drawing inferences is evident. The only difference is that t involves the sample standard deviation (s_Y), whereas Z assumes a knowledge of the population standard deviation (σ_Y) that, as we noted above, is usually not available.

The shape of each t distribution varies with sample size and sample standard deviation. As with Z-transformed normal distributions, all t distributions are symmetrical, bell-shaped, and have a mean of zero. But a normal distribution and a t distribution differ in two important ways. First, using a t distribution to test hypotheses requires the sample to be drawn from a normally distributed population. However, violating this assumption has only minor effects on t score computation. Therefore, unless we are certain that the underlying population from which the sample is drawn is grossly nonnormal, we can use a t distribution even when N is small.

Second, a t distribution for a given sample size has a larger variance than a normal Z distribution. Thus, the standard errors of the family of t distributions are all larger than the standard error of a standardized normal distribution or Z curve (see Figure 3.7). This assumption also must be qualified. As the sample N grows larger (i.e., in the range of 30 to 100 cases or more), t distributions increasingly approach the normalized Z distribution in shape. For a very large N, the probabilities associated with outcomes in both distributions are almost identical. You can verify their convergence

FIGURE 3.7

Comparing a t Distribution with Four Degrees of Freedom with the Standardized Normal Distribution

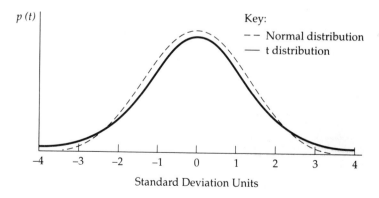

Source: David Knoke and George W. Bohrnstedt, *Basic Social Statistics* (Itasca, IL: F. E. Peacock Publishers, Inc., 1991), 169.

by comparing probabilities for Z values in Appendix C with t values for $N = \infty$ in Appendix D. But, for a small sample N, more cases fall into the extreme sections of the tails of a t compared to a Z distribution, as Figure 3.7 makes clear. In other words, t distributions have "thicker" tails than Z distributions. Thus, at given values of α such as .01, t_α will always be larger than Z_α (or $t_{\alpha/2}$ will be greater than $Z_{\alpha/2}$).

degrees of freedom—the number of values free to vary when computing a statistic

As noted in Section 2.5.4, the denominator of the sample variance (s_Y^2) involves the constant $N - 1$. This numerical value is therefore a parameter in each t distribution. It is called the **degrees of freedom,** and is symbolized by df and also by ν (lower case Greek *nu*). The concept of degrees of freedom comes from the restriction that the sum of all deviations about the mean must equal zero (see Section 2.5.3 on page 52). Although you could arbitrarily assign values to $N - 1$ of the deviations, the value of the last deviation then would be completely determined by your other choices; that is, this final score is *not* free to vary. For example, if you know that the mean of four observations is 8 and three of these scores are 4, 7, and 9, then the fourth value must be 12. Once the mean and $N - 1$ values are fixed, the Nth value is completely constrained. In a given set of N deviations from the mean, $N - 1$ of them may assume any values, but the Nth score has no freedom to vary for a given mean. Hence, there are $N - 1$ df in a t distribution for a sample of N observations.

t distributions are bell-shaped, symmetric curves having zero means and standard errors that vary with both the population standard deviation and the degrees of freedom. The smaller the df, the flatter the curve. Figure 3.7 compares a t distribution with four degrees of freedom to a standard normal distribution. Because t distribution values are nearly identical to Z-normal values when N is very large (well over 100 cases), they can always be used to make inferences from a sample mean to a population mean. Inferences about means reported in published research are almost always made using a t distribution. If N is small, applying a t distribution requires that a normal population be randomly sampled. However, unless the population is grossly nonnormal, violating this assumption does not cause serious inferential problems.

A confidence interval around the sample mean point estimate can be constructed with confidence $1 - \alpha$ by applying the formula

$$\overline{Y} \pm (t_{\alpha/2})(s_Y/\sqrt{N})$$

Begin by choosing a desired degree of confidence, which specifies α. For example, for a 99% confidence interval $\alpha = .01$. Next, find the entry in the row in Appendix D labeled "Two-tailed test" that contains the specified α level (in this example, .01 above the fifth column). Go down this column until it intersects the row listing the correct *df* for your sample; the entry is the critical value of *t* that defines the α-level confidence interval. Insert this critical value, sample standard deviation, and sample size into the confidence interval formula just above, then calculate both the upper- and lower-confidence limits. Suppose that the sample point estimate of the mean $\overline{Y} = 46$; the sample standard deviation $s_Y = 12$; the sample size $N = 23$; and you choose $\alpha = .05$. For $df = 23 - 1 = 22$, Appendix D gives the critical value of *t* as 2.074. The UCL = 46 + $(2.074)(12/\sqrt{23}) = 51.2$ and the LCL = $46 - (2.074)(12/\sqrt{23}) = 40.8$.

Caution is in order when interpreting confidence intervals. The temptation is great to make statements suggesting that one can be 95% confident that a given interval contains the population mean. In fact, of course, after an interval is constructed, the probability that it contains the true population mean is either zero or one, depending on whether it actually does or does not contain the population mean. What we can say, however, is that, *in the long run*, 95% of such intervals will contain the population mean.

3.8   Hypothesis Testing

3.8.1.   Null Hypotheses

Suppose that we draw a sample of observations and find that two variables are related. We want to know whether we are justified in concluding that this relationship also occurs in the population from which the sample data came. The basic question of statistical inference is this: What is the probability that the relationship observed in the sample data could come from a population in which there is *no* relationship between the two variables? If we can show that this probability is very high, then even though a relationship occurs in the sample, we would be extremely hesitant to conclude that the two variables are related in the population. If the chance were small (perhaps less than 1 in 20 or less than 1 in 100) that the sample relationship could have been created by randomly sampling observations from a population in which no relationship exists, we would decide that the hypothesis should be accepted.

When samples are small, the probability of observing a relationship in the sample where none exists in the population is higher than when samples are large. For example, suppose that in a population of 1,000 no relationship exists between a pair of variables. If we choose a sample of 900 observations, the probability that we would find sample results indicating a relationship among two variables is much smaller than if we draw a sample of only 50 observations. Conversely, if a relationship *does* exist in a population, the probability is much greater in a larger sample than in a smaller sample that we would observe a sample outcome that indicates a relationship.

Suppose we have an hypothesis that two variables (for example, voting and years of education) are related in a population of interest (e.g., adult Americans). One way to determine if two variables are related in the population is to test the hypothesis that they are *unrelated* using the sample observations (as we noted in chapter 1). The way to make this test is to state a **null hypothesis** that *no* relationship between the variables exists in the population. This statement is contrary to the **research hypothesis** stating an expected relationship between variables, either based on theory or past research. Although as social scientists we firmly believe that the research hypothesis is correct, we actually perform the statistical inference test on the null hypothesis, because we hope to show that it is a false statement about the situation. In other words, we expect to "nullify" that hypothesis. The basic question of inference arises: What is the probability that the relationship found in the sample data could have come from a population in which there is no relationship between the two variables? The research hypothesis can be restated as a null hypothesis, using the symbol H_0 (where the subscript zero stands for "null"):

null hypothesis— a statistical hypothesis that one usually expects to reject. Symbolized H_0

research hypothesis— a substantive hypothesis that one usually does not expect to reject

H_0: Voting is not related to years of education.

We really expect to show that this null hypothesis is an untrue statement about the population of adult Americans. If the probability is small—less than .05 (that is, less than 1 chance in 20)—that the sample evidence could have arisen as the outcome of a random sampling from such a population, then we reject the null hypothesis. In concluding that H_0 is false, we accept its alternative—the research hypothesis, H_1, stating that the two variables do in fact covary in the population:

H_1: Voting is related to years of education.

From a scientific point of view the acceptance of an **alternative hypothesis** is conditional, because the truth about social relationships can only be assessed indirectly, through the rejection of false hypotheses.

As another example of a null hypothesis, consider research on the relationship between social class and alienation. If you suspect that a relationship exists between these two variables—for example, that working-class people are more alienated than middleclass people—then you might formulate a research hypothesis in these terms:

H_1: The higher the social class, the lower the alienation.

However, in testing this relationship with a random sample of observations drawn from some population, you would restate the research hypothesis as a null relationship in which the two variables do not covary:

H_0: Social class is unrelated to alienation.

Notice that the research and null hypotheses are consistent with your real expectation of finding evidence that social classes differ in their levels of alienation. You hope to reject the null hypothesis, thus lending weight to the original social relationship that you believe exists between class and alienation.

If the research hypothesis is correct, then you should find evidence in the sample that will allow you to reject the null hypothesis. On the other hand, if social class and alienation really *are* unrelated—as some studies indicate—then your sample data should turn up insufficient evidence to reject this H_0. You would then conclude that your original research hypothesis is probably not true. That conclusion, however, always carries a probability of

alternative hypothesis—
a secondary hypothesis about the value of a population parameter that often reverses the research or operational hypothesis. Symbolized H_1

being incorrect. We turn next to procedures for deciding the level of probability of reaching a false conclusion.

3.8.2. Type I and Type II Errors

Whenever we deal with probabilities, we run the risk making an incorrect decision. Otherwise we would be dealing with certainties, which is never the case. A **probability (α, or alpha) level** for rejection of a null hypothesis is usually set at .05 (that is, one chance in 20) or lower. By setting this α level before beginning to examine the data, we deliberately choose to run a given risk of incorrect inference from a sample relationship to a population relationship.

In making inferences we might make two different types of judgment error. First, based on the significance test results, we might reject a null hypothesis that in fact is true; that is, we might reject the hypothesis that two variables are unrelated, based on the sample results, when in the population they are in fact unrelated. In other words, if we had known the truth about the population, we would not have rejected the H_0, but unfortunately we did reject the H_0 and thus made an error. Such an error occurs when, simply by chance, the sample we draw contains many of the most deviant observations in the population from which it was selected. Even when sampling is done randomly, there is always some chance that one will select a sample whose variables show a relationship that is quite different from the population relationship. Concluding that H_0 is false when in the population it is really true leads to a **Type I error, or false rejection error.** The chance of making this mistake is the same as the probability level that we set for rejection of the null hypothesis (α). Thus, Type I error is often called α-error, or *alpha error.*

The second type of error, **Type II error,** may also be called a **false acceptance error.** This error occurs in the opposite fashion: Although the null hypothesis is actually false, we fail to reject it on the basis of the sample data. This type of decision-making error is also called β-error or (*beta-error*). Box 3.2 offers some help in keeping the two types of error distinct.

The probability of making a Type II error is not simply 1.0 minus the probability of a Type I error; that is, if α is .05, β is *not* just $1.00 - .05 = .95$. It is more complicated than that. A complete account of how to find the probability of a Type II error would take us into a long discussion of the "power" of statistical tests and lead us away

probability (alpha) level—the probability selected for rejection of a null hypothesis, which is the likelihood of making a Type I error

Type I error (false rejection error)— a statistical decision error that occurs when a true null hypothesis is rejected; its probability is alpha

Type II error (false acceptance error)— a statistical decision error that occurs when a false null hypothesis is not rejected; its probability is beta

---

BOX 3.2.   Remembering Type I and Type II Errors

Type I and Type II errors are often confused. One way to keep them apart is to memorize this table.

		Based on the sample results, the decision made is	
		Reject null hypothesis	*Do not reject null hypothesis*
In the population from which the sample is drawn, the null hypothesis is	*True*	Type I or false rejection error (α)	Correct decision
	False	Correct decision	Type II or false acceptance error (β)

---

from our immediate goal, which is to present the basis of significance tests.

Although no simple mathematical relationship exists between Type I and Type II errors, it is important to note that they are related to one another. Reducing the potential probability of making a false rejection error—setting α at a very low level, such as .001—tends to increase the risk of making a false acceptance error. Standard methods for offsetting false acceptance error are (1) to increase the sample size, thus reducing sampling error in making inferences about population relationships from sample data; or (2) to repeat the study using another independently drawn sample so that consistent results strengthen our belief in the findings.

3.9   Testing Hypotheses About Single Means

3.9.1.   An Example of a Hypothesis Test About a Single Mean with Exact Hypotheses

We use a rather contrived example to show hypothesis testing about a single mean. The example is contrived because social science theory is ordinarily not precise enough to suggest two exact alternatives. However, the example helps to make clear some of the important features about hypothesis testing that cannot otherwise easily be shown. Suppose we have two competing hypotheses based on two previous surveys, suggesting somewhat different estimates of the number of hours that Americans watch television each day. Suppose that the results of one poll suggest that Americans spend 2.9 hours per day and a second, unrelated poll, suggests that the daily average is 3.2 hours. The null hypothesis and its alternative can then be stated as:

$$H_0: \mu_Y = 2.9$$
$$H_1: \mu_Y = 3.2$$

(Which result is chosen to be the null and which the alternative hypothesis is clearly arbitrary in this example.) We now use the 1991 GSS data to determine whether H_0 can be rejected. We will use a t test to evaluate H_0.

Suppose we set $\alpha = .05$. Using Appendix D and employing a one-tailed test, the observed t must be about 1.65 or larger to reject H_0. We can use this information to see how large the observed mean would have to be in order to reject H_0. In general, to test a hypothesis about a single mean we use the formula

$$t = \frac{\overline{Y} - \mu_{Y_0}}{s_Y / \sqrt{N}}$$

where μ_{Y_0} is the hypothesized population mean under H_0.

Using the 1991 GSS data we find that $s_Y = 2.32$, for $N = 1,014$. Therefore, the estimated standard error of the sampling distribution of means is $s_Y / \sqrt{N} = .073$. To determine how large $\overline{Y}$ would have to be in order to reject H_0 at $\alpha = .05$, we can substitute these numbers in the formula above as follows:

$$1.65 = \frac{\overline{Y} - 2.9}{.073}$$

Solving for $\overline{Y}$, we obtain $\overline{Y} = 3.02$, which is the critical value (c.v.) for the null hypothesis test. That is, if $\overline{Y} \geq 3.02$, we will reject H_0 in favor of H_1. This situation is depicted in Figure 3.8.

FIGURE 3.8

An Example of Testing Hypotheses About a Single Mean About Hours of Television Watching per Day

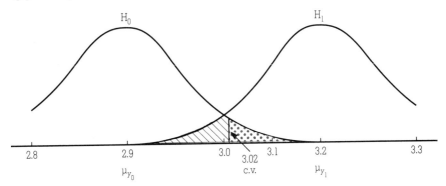

Note that there are two separate sampling distributions, the left one under the assumption that H_0 is true and the right one under the assumption that H_1 is true. The shaded area is the tail of the distribution under H_0 is $\alpha = .05$, or the probability of falsely rejecting the null hypothesis (see Box 3.2). But there is also a probability of making a Type II, or false acceptance, error that can now be calculated. It is the cross-hatched area in the left tail of the sampling distribution under the assumption that H_1 is true. This is the probability of falsely accepting H_0 when H_1 is true. The formula for calculating this probability is as follows:

$$t = \frac{\text{c.v.} - \mu_{Y_1}}{s_Y/\sqrt{N}}$$

where μ_{Y_1} is the hypothesized population mean under H_1.

To compute t in this example, we insert the c.v. = 3.02, $\mu_{Y_1} = 3.20$, and the estimated standard error, .073, into the formula for t:

$$t = \frac{3.02 - 3.20}{.073} = -2.47$$

We next consult Appendix C, which shows that the probability from $-\infty$ to -2.47 is $.5000 - .4932 = .0068$. That is, roughly 7 times in 1,000 one would fail to reject the null hypothesis, H_0, when in fact the alternative hypothesis, H_1, is true. The probability $1 - \beta$ is called the

power of the test—the probability of correctly rejecting H_0 when H_0 is false

power of the test. It is the probability of correctly rejecting H_0 when H_0 is false. In our example the power of the test is $1 - .0068 = .9932$. That is, if H_1 is true we would correctly reject H_0 more than 99% of the time.

We will not hold you in suspense any longer. The 1,014 respondents in the 1991 GSS reported watching an average of 3.11 hours of television per day. Therefore, since the c.v. is 3.02, we reject the null hypothesis that the mean television watching is 2.9 hours per day. Instead, we accept the alternative hypothesis that Americans watch 3.2 hours of television per day.

As stated above, this example is somewhat contrived in that it assumes either the null hypothesis or the alterative hypothesis is true. In all likelihood, of course, neither is true. Indeed, another option, is that of **suspending judgment** pending further research. But, the example above does demonstrate that one can compute the probability of a Type II error and the power of the test if one is able to specify two exact alternative hypotheses. Box 3.3 summarizes the steps for testing a single mean with two exact hypotheses.

suspending judgment—a position taken by a researcher when the results of a statistical test permit neither clear rejection nor clear acceptance of the null hypothesis or alternative hypothesis

Our example can also be used to illustrate another important point: The power of the test can be increased or decreased just by increasing or decreasing the sample size. For example, suppose that $N = 40$ instead of 1,014. Then the standard error increases from .073 to $2.32/\sqrt{40} = .367$. You can easily demonstrate for yourself that, in this case, the critical value for the observed mean $\bar{Y} = 3.51$. Under H_1 this generates a t value of 0.84 for which the value of β is calculated using Appendix C to be $.5000 - .2995 = .2005$. Hence, by decreasing the sample size from 1,014 to 40, the power of the test, $1 - \beta$, decreases from .9932 to .7995. That is, in a sample of 40 one would correctly reject the null hypothesis when it is false only 80 times out of 100. Furthermore, if the alternative is true, one would fail to reject the null hypothesis about 20 times out of 100 (Type II error). This example should make it very clear that using a large sample size substantially improves the power of the test and reduces the likelihood of making a false acceptance error.

3.9.2.   One-Tailed Test About a Single Mean

Suppose we are interested in how urbanized American states were in 1986, the most recent year for which data are available. The U.S. Census Bureau classifies a "metropolitan area population" as

---

BOX 3.3   Summary of Steps in Testing Between Two Exact Hypotheses About Means

Step 1. Choose an α level (probability of a Type I or false rejection error) for the null hypothesis.

Step 2. Examine Appendix D to determine how large the t value must be under H_0 in order to reject the null hypothesis.

Step 3. Estimate the standard error of the sampling distribution from the data using $s_Y/\sqrt{N}$ and use μ_0 in the formula for the t statistic to determine the critical value for rejecting H_0.

Step 4. Calculate β (the probability of a Type II or false acceptance error) using the estimated standard error and the mean hypothesized to be true under H_1 in the formula for the test statistic.

Step 5. Compare the observed sample mean with the critical value and either reject H_0 or not.

---

those persons living in 281 designated metropolitan statistical and consolidated areas. In 1970 the U.S. states had on average (mean) 64.4% of their residents living in such locations. (In computing this average each state is weighted equally; for the U.S. as a whole, 76.7% of its populace lived in metro areas.) But, natural population growth and migration trends in the intervening years might have brought more people into rural communities, perhaps reducing the metropolitan proportion. Because we surmise that the 1986 urbanization level may be lower than that of 1970, our null and alternative hypotheses are:

$$H_0: \mu_Y \geq 64.4\%$$
$$H_1: \mu_Y < 64.4\%$$

We can test the null hypothesis with the U.S. States Data Set to determine whether H_0 can be rejected in favor of H_1. Table 3.1 shows the percentages living in metropolitan areas for all 51 cases in 1986

TABLE 3.1

Percentage of State Population Living in Metropolitan Areas in 1986

State	Percent	State	Percent
District of Columbia	100.0	Delaware	66.0
New Jersey	100.0	Missouri	65.9
California	95.7	Minnesota	65.8
Maryland	92.9	Georgia	64.3
Connecticut	92.6	Alabama	64.1
Rhode Island	92.5	South Carolina	60.2
Florida	90.9	Oklahoma	58.5
Massachusetts	90.8	New Hampshire	56.4
New York	90.5	North Carolina	55.0
Pennsylvania	84.6	Kansas	52.0
Nevada	82.5	New Mexico	47.6
Illinois	82.4	Nebraska	46.9
Colorado	81.6	Kentucky	45.5
Washington	81.0	Alaska	44.0
Texas	80.7	Iowa	42.9
Michigan	80.2	Arkansas	39.3
Ohio	78.8	North Dakota	37.3
Utah	77.0	West Virginia	36.6
Hawaii	76.9	Maine	36.1
Arizona	75.4	Mississippi	30.0
Virginia	71.5	Wyoming	28.8
Louisiana	69.1	South Dakota	28.2
Indiana	68.0	Montana	24.4
Oregon	67.4	Vermont	23.1
Tennessee	66.8	Idaho	19.4
Wisconsin	66.5		

t test—a test of significance for continuous variables where the population variance is unknown and the sample is assumed to have been drawn from a normally distributed population

one-tailed hypothesis test — a hypothesis test in which the alternative is stated in such a way that the probability of making a Type I error is entirely in one tail of a probability distribution

(recall that the District of Columbia is included). We evaluate H_0 with a **t test.** The degrees of freedom for this test are $N - 1 = 51 - 1 = 50$. Because the alternative hypothesis is inexact in one direction, the only grounds for rejecting the null hypothesis is when the sample mean is less than the hypothesized parameter of 64.4%. This alternative concentrates the entire region of rejection (alpha) into one tail of the sampling distribution. Hence, a test with this form of H_1 is called a **one-tailed hypothesis test.**

Suppose we set $\alpha = .05$. With α located entirely in the sampling distribution's left tail, the critical value of t for 50 df is -1.684 (using the row for 40 df in Appendix D as an approximation). The test statistic calculated from sample data must be smaller than -1.684 (i.e., greater in the negative direction) in order to reject H_0. The general formula to test a hypothesis about a single mean is as follows:

$$t = \frac{\overline{Y} - \mu_{Y_0}}{s_Y / \sqrt{N}}$$

where

$\overline{Y}$ is the sample mean.

μ_{Y_0} is the hypothesized mean under H_0.

$s_Y / \sqrt{N}$ is the estimated standard error of the sampling distribution.

For 1986 the mean percent living in metropolitan areas is $\overline{Y} = 64.2\%$ with $s_Y = 22.4$. Therefore, the t for the test is:

$$t_{50} = \frac{64.2 - 64.4}{22.4 / \sqrt{51}} = -0.06$$

We have subscripted the t with its degrees of freedom. Although the average state urbanization fell 0.2% in 16 years, the amount of change was not sufficiently large to reject the null hypothesis in favor of the alternative. Hence, we conclude that the mean state metropolitan population in 1986 was not significantly lower than the 64.4% level of 1970.

Box 3.4 shows the steps in performing a statistical test of a null hypothesis about a single mean with an inexact directional alternative. The procedures for testing statistical significance are basically similar for all the statistics employed in this text. *Thus, you should memorize the steps in this box.*

As mentioned in section 3.9, exact hypotheses can rarely be stated as compelling tests of theory in the social sciences. Therefore, hypothesis testing usually offers only a weak analysis of one's substantive hypotheses. By choosing a very large N, a researcher can reduce the estimated standard error of the sampling distribution to a very small size (recall that $\hat{\sigma}_{\overline{Y}} = s_Y / \sqrt{N}$). Thus, almost any null hypothesis can be rejected, hardly an encouraging foundation for erecting a sophisticated science. Given the weakness of statistical significance tests, we emphasize the importance of *estimation* in

---

BOX 3.4   Statistical Significance Testing Steps

Step 1. State the research hypothesis believed to be true in the form of a statistical alternative hypothesis (H_1).

Step 2. State the statistical null hypothesis (H_0) that is expected to be rejected.

Step 3. Choose an α level (probability of a Type I or false rejection error) for the null hypothesis.

Step 4. Examine the tabled values of the test statistic to see how large it must be in order to reject the null hypothesis at α. This is the critical value for that test statistic.

Step 5. Calculate the test statistic, entering the sample descriptive statistics into the appropriate formula.

Step 6. Compare the test statistic to the critical value. If the test statistic is as large or larger than the critical value, then reject the null hypothesis, with an α-probability of a Type I (false rejection) error. If it is smaller than the critical value, then do not reject the null hypothesis, with a β-probability of a Type II (false acceptance) error.

---

making inferences from sample statistics to population parameters. After testing an hypothesis, we recommend using the sample mean as a point estimate around which to construct a confidence interval. Given $\overline{Y} = 64.2\%$ and $s_Y = 22.4$ for $N = 51$, the 99% confidence interval is $64.2 \pm (2.704)(22.4/\sqrt{51})$ or LCL = 55.7% and UCL = 72.7%. On average 99 out of 100 samples with confidence limits so derived will contain the parameter for the U.S. states' mean urban percentage.

3.9.3.   Two-Tailed Test About a Single Mean

Often social researchers have only vague ideas about their alternative hypotheses. Although the null hypothesis is clearly stated, H_0 might be rejected by either a larger *or* a smaller sample mean. A **two-tailed hypothesis test** is a suitable procedure. In two-tailed tests the alternative hypothesis is inexact and without a specific direction. This form of H_1 admits that one does not know whether the population parameter is smaller or larger than the exact value in H_0.

two-tailed hypothesis test— a hypothesis test in which the region of rejection falls equally within both tails of the sampling distribution

Suppose we are uncertain about how much satisfaction people get from the city or place where they live. The 1991 GSS recorded responses to such a question on a seven-point scale, from "none" (coded 7) to "a very great deal" (coded 1). Without prior knowledge we might guess that respondents tend to choose the scale midpoint, "a fair amount" (coded 4). But, we really do not know whether the population response is more likely to be higher or lower. Hence, our best alternative is simply that the mean population parameter is something other than 4.00. Stated more formally, these two statistical hypotheses are as follows:

$$H_0: \mu_Y = 4.00$$

$$H_1: \mu_Y \neq 4.00$$

The statistical test is two-tailed because the probability of a Type I error must be equally distributed between the upper and lower tails of the sampling distribution. In this sense a two-tailed test parallels constructing a confidence interval around the mean hypothesized under H_0. (Of course, a confidence interval is built around a sample mean, *not* a population parameter.)

As in all significance testing, one first chooses an α level, say .001 in this case. Then the critical value of the test statistic is located in the appropriate appendix table. Two critical values exist for two-tailed hypothesis tests—one in the negative tail and the other in the positive tail of the sampling distribution. Figure 3.9 shows this relationship for the general case. For our test of mean residential satisfaction, $N = 1,015$, and thus $df = 1,014$. The sample standard deviation is 1.45, so the estimated standard error is $1.45/\sqrt{1015} = .045$. Appendix D shows that the critical value necessary to reject the null hypothesis in favor of the two-tailed alternative is ± 3.291. (Box 3.5 explains how Appendix D is used for both one- and two-tailed hypothesis tests.) Because H_0 specifies that $\mu_Y = 4.00$, the two critical values defining the regions of rejection are $LCL = 4.00 - (3.291)(.045)$ and $UCL = 4.00 + (3.291)(.045)$, or 3.85 and 4.15, respectively. That is, if the observed sample mean is either less than 3.85 or greater than 4.15, H_0 must be rejected in favor of H_1. Because the 1991 GSS

FIGURE 3.9

The *t* Distribution for Two-Tailed Hypothesis Tests About a Single Mean

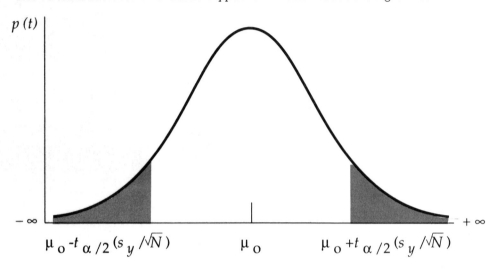

Source: David Knoke and George W. Bohrnstedt, *Basic Social Statistics,* (Itasca, IL: F. E. Peacock Publishers, Inc., 1991), 184.

sample mean is 2.91, the null hypothesis that residence satisfaction falls at the scale midpoint must be rejected. Instead, the most likely population parameter is the same as the sample value, 2.91, which is close to "quite a bit" of satisfaction with city or place of residence.

Although hypothesis testing has a long tradition in the social sciences, we strongly believe that *estimation is much more useful and important than hypothesis testing*, because virtually any statistical hypothesis can be rejected by simply choosing a large enough sample size. For this reason, even though hypothesis testing is very common, we urge that confidence intervals always be estimated.

The 99.9% confidence interval around the GSS sample mean of 2.91 for residential satisfaction is bounded by LCL = 2.91 − (3.291)(.045) = 2.76 and UCL = 2.91 + (3.291)(.045) = 3.06. We hope you agree that knowing with 99.9% confidence that the true population mean probably lies between 2.76 and 3.06 is more informative than the outcome of the hypothesis test (i.e., knowing only that our initial hypothesis that the population mean is 4.00 must be rejected).

BOX 3.5   Using Appendix D for One-or Two-tailed Hypothesis Testing

Appendix D can be used to place the probability of a Type I error (α) all in one tail or to divide it between the left and the right tails of a t-distribution. To place the probability entirely into the right tail, look along the row labeled "One-tailed" until you reach the value you chose for α. Then look down the column under that α-level to find the critical value corresponding to the df in the stub on the left. For example, for $\alpha =$ .05 and $N = 31$, the critical value of t is found by looking across the row labeled "one-tailed test" until you come to .05; then look down that column until you come to the row for $df = 31 - 1 = 30$. Thus, the critical value of $t = 1.697$. Recall that for $\alpha = .05$, the critical value of $Z = 1.645$. This difference in critical values illustrates that when N is small, a larger critical value is necessary to be able to reject the null hypothesis than when N is very large.

Appendix D can also be used to divide the probability of a Type I error equally into both tails of a t distribution. This division is especially useful for computing confidence intervals, as well as in computing two-tailed hypothesis tests. For example, for $\alpha = .05$ and $df = 30$, look across the row labeled "Two-tailed test" until you come to .05. Then look down this column until you come to the row labeled 30. In this example the critical value $= 2.042$.

3.9.4.   One-Tailed Versus Two-Tailed Tests

If current knowledge allows a directional alternative hypothesis, then a one-tailed significance test should be used. A one-tailed H_1 permits a more powerful statistical test than does a two-tailed alternative, except when the observed sample mean falls into the tail of the test statistic opposite from that predicted. A one-tailed hypothesis test rewards you with powerful tests for correctly anticipating into which tail of the t-distribution the mean falls. But, you are penalized if your expectation turns out to be wrong. Nevertheless, if you have a directional alternative, then a one-tailed test should be used. Many researchers and applied statisticians would contest this principle because one-tailed tests require a smaller critical value to reject H_0, thus stacking the deck in favor of rejection. If previous research results were mixed, or if research is purely exploratory, or if good notions about the population parameter are absent, then a two-tailed test is preferable. But, most importantly, population parameters should always be estimated along with hypothesis testing when making inferences about population parameters from sample data.

The hypothesis tests discussed in this chapter involve single means. Most social researchers wish to compare statistics across several groups. For example, do liberal arts, engineering, or agricultural graduates earn higher starting salaries? Are rates of AIDS infection lower for persons using condoms, other prophylactic methods, or no method at all? Such questions require comparing *two or more* sample values and asking whether they probably differ significantly from one another in the population. Evaluating this type of question is the topic of subsequent chapters.

3.10 Properties of Estimators

Chance factors operate even in random sampling to ensure that a particular sample's point estimates of means and variances will not be identical to the population values. The basic goal of inferential statistics is to use the sample values as *estimators* of corresponding population parameters. To be a good estimator of population parameter θ, a sample statistic $\hat{\theta}$ should be unbiased, consistent, efficient, and sufficient.

unbiased estimator—an estimator of a population parameter whose expected value equals the parameter

An **unbiased estimator** equals, on average, the population parameter. That is,

$$E(\theta) = \theta$$

The expected value (i.e., the mean) of the estimator for all possible samples of size N from the same population equals the population parameter. For example, the central limit theorem in section 3.5 indicates that $E(\overline{Y}) = \mu_Y$. Thus, the sample mean, $\overline{Y}$, is an unbiased estimate of the population mean, μ_Y. Similarly, if we take all possible random samples of size N from a population and compute each sample's variance,

$$s_Y^2 = \frac{\Sigma(Y_i - \overline{Y})^2}{N - 1}$$

then the mean of this sampling distribution will equal the population variance, that is:

$$E(s_Y^2) = \frac{\Sigma(Y_i - \overline{Y})^2}{N} = \sigma_Y^2$$

The difference in the denominators of the sample statistic $(N - 1)$ and the population parameter (N) is required to produce an unbiased estimate. Because $E(s_Y^2) = \sigma_Y^2$, we conclude that the sample variance is an unbiased estimator of the population variance.

A **consistent estimator** approximates the population parameter more closely as N gets larger. A sample statistic $\hat{\theta}$ is a consistent estimator if, as $N \rightarrow \infty$, then $E(\hat{\theta} - \theta)^2 \rightarrow 0$. That is, as N approaches infinity, the expected variance of the difference between a sample statistic and a population parameter gets closer to zero. Both the sample mean and the median are consistent estimators of the population mean, μ_Y. As N increases, the variance of each sampling distribution gets smaller.

> **consistent estimator**—an estimator of a population parameter that approximates the parameter more closely as N gets large

An **efficient estimator** has a sampling distribution whose standard error, at a given N, is smaller than any other estimator. That is, the variance of the difference between a sample statistic and a population parameter, $E(\hat{\theta} - \theta)^2$, is as small as possible. We previously showed that the variance of the sampling distribution for the mean is σ_Y^2/N. The sampling distribution variance for the median is $(\pi/2)(\sigma_Y^2/N)$ for a large N. Thus, the mean is roughly $\pi/2$ more efficient than the median as an estimator of μ_Y, and hence, it is preferred as the more efficient estimator of μ_Y.

> **efficient estimator**—the estimator of a population parameter among all possible estimators that has the smallest sampling variance

Finally, an estimator is **sufficient** if it cannot be improved by adding information. The sample value contains all the information available about the population parameter. For a normally distributed variable the sample mean is sufficient to estimate the population mean.

> **sufficient estimator**—an estimator of a population parameter that cannot be improved by adding information

The sample mean ($\overline{Y}$) and sample variance (s_Y^2) are unbiased, consistent, efficient, and sufficient estimators, respectively, of the population mean (μ_Y) and variance (σ_Y^2). These properties make them indispensable statistics in inferential analysis.

3.11   The Chi-Square and *F* Distributions

With an understanding of the standardized normal distribution (section 3.4), we can now introduce two theoretical probability distributions that are very valuable for the statistical significance tests to be presented in subsequent chapters. Both make use of the normal distribution in their construction.

chi-square distribution
—a family of distributions, each of which has different degrees of freedom, on which the chi-square test statistic is based

Like the normal curve, the **chi-square distribution** (χ^2) is actually a family of distributions. Each family member varies in the number of degrees of freedom used in its creation. To construct a χ^2 variable, begin with a normally distributed population of observations, having mean μ_Y and variance σ_Y^2. Then take a random sample of N cases, transform every observation into standardized (Z score) form, and square it. For the ith case

$$Z_i^2 = \frac{(Y_i - \mu_Y)^2}{\sigma_Y^2}$$

The distribution of the sum of these squared Z scores is called a chi-square distribution with N degrees of freedom. To form a χ^2 with one degree of freedom, cases are sampled from the normal distribution one at a time. A χ^2 with one *df* is shown in Figure 3.10. As a result of the squaring, a χ^2 distribution has no negative values but is very skewed, ranging between 0 to positive infinity. Because most of the values in the standardized normal distribution lie between -1.00 and $+1.00$, so most of the values for χ^2 with one degree of freedom fall below 1.00.

To find the chi-square distribution for two degrees of freedom (χ_ν^2, where the subscript ν indicates the *df*), two observations (Y_1 and Y_2) are independently and randomly drawn from the normal distribution. Again, they are transformed to Z scores, squared, and then added together. Thus, the score of the first plus the second case is

$$\frac{(Y_1 - \mu_Y)^2}{\sigma_Y^2} + \frac{(Y_2 - \mu_Y)^2}{\sigma_Y^2} = Z_1^2 + Z_2^2$$

As shown in Figure 3.10, this chi-square distribution is somewhat less skewed, with a lower probability that values fall between zero and 1.00.

FIGURE 3.10

χ^2 Distributions with 1, 2, 8, and 22 Degrees of Freedom

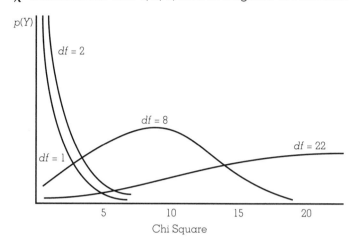

Suppose we continue to generate chi-square distributions with ν degrees of freedom by adding ν independently sampled, squared Z scores. As these new probability distributions are created, they become progressively less skewed and more bell-shaped, as shown in Figure 3.10 for χ^2 distributions with 8 and 22 *df.* The exact shape and location of each member of this family of distributions depends only on the degrees of freedom involved in creating it from an underlying standardized normal distribution. The mean of each chi-square distribution is the product of its degrees of freedom times the variance of Z (which is always 1; see Box 2.4, page 67). In other words, the mean of a chi-square for a distribution based on ν independent observations is ν, its *df.* Further, the variance of a chi-square distribution with ν *df* is always 2ν. Thus, knowledge of the degrees of freedom is sufficient to specify completely a given chi-square distribution. Chapter 5 shows how to use tabled values of chi-square to reach conclusions about the probable independence of variables in a population from which a sample has been randomly drawn.

The second very important theoretical distribution is the ***F* distribution,** named after Sir Ronald Fisher who developed many important applications. Research hypotheses often involve inferences from sample data about the equality of the variances of two populations. The F distribution provides a suitable test statistic for such questions. It requires that random, independent samples be

F **distribution**—a theoretical probability distribution for one of a family of F ratios having ν_1 and ν_2 *df* in the numerator and denominator, respectively drawn from two normal populations that have the same variance (i.e., $\sigma^2_{Y_1} = \sigma^2_{Y_2}$). Then the F variable is formed as the ratio of two chi-squares, each divided by its degrees of freedom, ν_1 and ν_2:

$$F = \frac{(\chi^2_{\nu_1}/\nu_1)}{(\chi^2_{\nu_2}/\nu_2)}$$

The F ratio distribution is nonsymmetric, ranges across the nonnegative numbers (because of the two chi-squares), and its shape depends on the degrees of freedom associated with the numerator (ν_1) and denominator (ν_2). Chapter 4 demonstrates how to use the tabled values of F to make decisions regarding the probable equality of population variances, based on sample estimates.

Review of Key Concepts and Symbols

These key concepts and symbols are listed in the order of appearance in this chapter. Combined with the definitions in the margins, they will help you review the material and can serve as a self-test for mastery of the concepts.

inference	point estimate
random sampling	confidence interval
probability distribution	upper confidence limit
continuous probability distribution	lower confidence limit
	t distribution
population parameter	t variable (t score)
expected value	degrees of freedom
mean of a probability distribution	null hypothesis
	research hypothesis
variance of a probability distribution	alternative hypothesis
	probability (alpha) level
Chebycheff's inequality theorem	Type I error (false rejection error)
normal distribution	Type II error (false acceptance error)
alpha area	
critical value	power of the test
central limit theorem	suspending judgment
sampling distribution of sample means	t test
	one-tailed hypothesis test
standard error	two-tailed hypothesis test

unbiased estimator	$\mu_{\bar{Y}}$
unbiased estimator	$\sigma^2_{\bar{Y}}$
consistent estimator	$\hat{\sigma}_{\bar{Y}}$
efficient estimator	
sufficient estimator	t
chi-square distribution	ν
F distribution	df
N	$t_{\alpha/2}$
$p(Y_i)$	H_0
$E(Y)$	H_1
μ_Y	α
$g(Y)$	β
σ^2_Y	θ
σ_Y	$1 - \beta$
α	χ^2
$\alpha/2$	F
Z_α	ν_1
$Z_{\alpha/2}$	ν_2

PROBLEMS

General Problems

1. Find the expected values of the following probability distributions:

(a)	Y_i	$p(Y_i)$	(b)	Y_i	$p(Y_i)$
	10	.05		10	.05
	20	.20		20	.05
	30	.50		30	.15
	40	.20		40	.60
	50	.05		50	.15

2. In a population of test scores not known to be normally distributed, the mean is 50 and the standard deviation is 15. What proportion of the observations will fall into the interval from 20 to 80?

3. What is the standard error in a population with $\sigma_Y = 100$ and (a) $N = 25$; (b) $N = 100$; (c) $N = 625$.

4. Find the Z scores for the normal distribution that correspond to the following alphas:

   a. $\alpha = .03$, one-tailed.   d. $\alpha = .02$, two-tailed.
   b. $\alpha = .15$, one-tailed.   e. $\alpha = .20$, two-tailed.
   c. $\alpha = .02$, one-tailed.   f. $\alpha = .001$, two-tailed.

5. Using the central limit theorem, find the mean and standard error of sampling distributions with the following characteristics:

	μ_Y	σ_Y^2	N
a.	12.5	40	50
b.	40	100	100
c.	0	100	500
d.	14	160	80
e.	200	200	200

6. For $\mu_Y = 30$ and $\sigma_Y = 12$ and $N = 30$, find the critical values for (a) $\alpha = .05$, one-tailed; and (b) $\alpha = .01$, two-tailed.

7. For a sample of $N = 64$ with $\sigma_Y = 16$ and $\overline{Y} = 20$, find (a) the LCL and UCL for the 95% confidence interval; and (b) the LCL and UCL for the 99% confidence interval.

8. Test the null hypothesis that $\mu_Y = 80$ for a sample of 25 subjects in which $\overline{Y} = 71$ and $s_Y = 20$ for a one-tailed test in which $\alpha = .01$. State the (a) critical value; (b) degrees of freedom; (c) test statistic; and (d) your decision.

9. Test the null hypothesis that $\mu_Y = 60$ for a sample where $N = 49$, $\overline{Y} = 62.5$ and $s_Y = 7$ using a two-tailed test in which $\alpha = .05$. State the (a) critical value; (b) degrees of freedom; (c) test statistic; and (d) your decision.

10. After a kindergarten class spends eight months with a new curriculum, the 15 pupils are tested for reading readiness. The mean score is 15, with a variance of 9. If the minimum score for entry into the first grade is 12, can we conclude that the new curriculum produces reading readiness significantly above the minimum? (Use $\alpha = .01$.)

GET FILE / KEEP   [handwritten]

Problems Requiring the 1991 General Social Survey

11. Find the empirical probability distribution for GSS respondents' ages at first marriage (AGEWED) and determine the probability that an ever-married person was first wed after age 30.

12. Test the hypothesis that respondents were drawn from a population where the mean preference for spending a social evening with friends (SOCFREND) is 3.50 or higher on a seven-point scale. Use $\alpha = .01$.

    FREQUENCY VARIABLES [handwritten]

13. Using the SPSS selection procedures to select only black respondents (RACE = 2), test the null hypothesis that they agree with both statements "the government should do more to help blacks" and "blacks should get no special treatment" (HELPBLK = 3). Use $\alpha = .05$.

    TEMPORARY SELECT IF [handwritten]
    RACE = 2 [handwritten]
    FORMAT = ONEPAGE [handwritten]

14. Selecting only women (SEX = 2) who worked part-time during the previous week (WRKSTAT = 2), test the null hypothesis that the mean number of hours they worked (HRS1) was 20 or fewer, setting $\alpha = .01$.

    TEMPORARY SELECT IF [handwritten]
    SEX = 2 AND [handwritten]
    WRKSTAT = 2 [handwritten]

Problems Requiring Use of the U.S. States Data Set

15. In 1979–1981 the average female life expectancy for the 50 states and Washington D.C. was 77.86 years. Test the null hypothesis that the mean male life expectancy (LIFEXPM) was not significantly different, using $\alpha = .001$.

16. Using the distribution on average number of persons per household (NPERHH), what is the expected probability that any state would have an average of more than 3.00 persons per household?

17. Between 1977 and 1982, the percentage of the U.S. labor force working in manufacturing industries fell in some states, but it increased in others. Use MFGECHNG to test the hypothesis that on average, the percentage employed in manufacturing fell by −5% or more, using $\alpha = .001$.

Statistics for Social Data Analysis

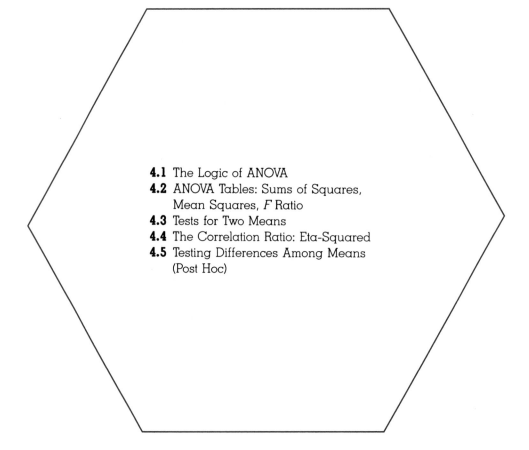

Analysis of Variance

4

T his chapter considers a special version of the general linear
model, in which the independent variable is a set of discrete
categories and the dependent variable is a continuous measure.
This technique is called the **analysis of variance,** or ANOVA for
short. We show how to test an hypothesis that the sample means of
several groups—*J* groups in general—come from the same rather
than different populations. We also present a special case of
ANOVA in which differences in the means of only two groups are
analyzed. We consider only ANOVA models in which a single
variable classifies observations into groups; hence, they are sometimes called *one-way* analyses of variance. More advanced
ANOVA techniques that simultaneously categorize observations
according to two or more variables are too complex for treatment
here.

analysis of variance— a
statistical test of the
difference of means for
two or more groups

4.1   The Logic of ANOVA

4.1.1.   An Example of Regional Crime Rates

An example illustrates the logic of the analysis of variance. We are
interested in the perennial question of whether states located in
different regions of the country have different crime rates. Specifically, we wondered whether the South and West experience more
serious crimes, allegedly due to a "culture of violence" in these two
regions. To test this hypothesis, we used the U.S. States Data Set,
classifying each according to the Census Bureau's four major

regional categories. (For this analysis we omitted Washington, DC, which is a city with one of the highest murder rates in the nation.) To compensate for different state population sizes, the dependent variable was the rate of serious crimes known to the police per 1,000 population in 1985.

Our initial research hypothesis is that serious crime rates are highest among states in the South *(S)*, followed in order by the West *(W)*, the Northeast *(N)*, and the Midwest *(M)*. The null hypothesis is that these four population means—labeled μ_S, μ_W, μ_N, and μ_M— equal one another. Hence, the four regional means also equal the overall, or the **grand mean,** of the 50-state population, μ. However, if the alternative hypothesis is true and the null hypothesis rejected, we then expect to find that $\mu_S > \mu_W > \mu_N > \mu_M$.

grand mean—in analysis of variance, the mean of all observations

An ANOVA model offers techniques to test the null hypothesis that all *J* sample means come from the same population and, therefore, all equal one another. Formally, the null hypothesis for every ANOVA is:

$$H_0: \mu_1 = \mu_2 = \ldots = \mu_J$$

The alternative hypothesis is that at least one sample mean comes from a population whose mean differs from the other population means. Rejecting the null hypothesis implies one of several alternative possibilities.

1. Each population mean differs from every other mean, i.e.,

$$H_1: \mu_1 \neq \mu_2 \neq \ldots \neq \mu_J.$$

2. Some subsets among the population means differ from one another (e.g., μ_1 differs from μ_2 but equals μ_3 and μ_4).
3. Some combinations of means differ either from a single mean or from another combination of means (e.g., μ_2 differs from the average of μ_3 and μ_4).

ANOVA is a test of the null hypothesis about equal population means. If the results compel rejection of the null, we still must determine which observed means differ from the others.

4.1.2.   Effects of Variables

To examine the impact of a group classification on a continuous dependent variable in an ANOVA, consider a single population having mean μ for the dependent measure. If, as H_0 states,

> The J group means all equal one another, then they also all equal this population's grand mean, μ.

This fact is used to measure the **effects** of the classification variable on the dependent variable. The effect of the jth group, labeled α_j, is defined as the difference between that group's mean and the grand mean:[1]

effect—the impact of the classification variable on the dependent variable

$$\alpha_j = \mu_j - \mu$$

If group j has no effect on the dependent variable, then $\alpha_j = 0$; that is, $\mu_j = \mu$. But, whenever a group effect occurs, α_j will be either positive or negative, depending on whether that group's mean is above or below the grand mean, μ.

In the U.S. States Data Set, the mean serious crime rate was 4.77 crimes per 1,000 population in 1985. The regional rates are as follows: South, $\mu_S = 4.59$; $\mu_W = 5.80$; $\mu_N = 4.36$; and $\mu_M = 4.21$. Thus, the region effects are as follows: $\alpha_S = -0.18$; $\alpha_W = +1.03$; $\alpha_N = -0.41$; and $\alpha_M = -0.56$. We can see already that the South and West have higher crime rates than the other two regions, although the West's effect is unexpectedly much greater than the South's effect. Indeed, the South's mean is below the grand mean. We still need to determine whether these differences are statistically significant, in the sense that the observed 1985 data reflect a relationship probably occurring in the population of repeated observations of the regional crime rates.

4.1.3.   The ANOVA Model

An ANOVA asks what proportion of the total variation in dependent variable Y can be attributed to individual i's membership in the jth

---

1. The use of alpha with a subscript (α_j) is not to be confused with α without a subscript, which refers to the probability of a Type I error (see section 3.8.2 on page 100).

group classification. The general model for an ANOVA with one independent variable decomposes an observed score into three components:

$$Y_{ij} = \mu + \alpha_j + e_{ij}$$

where

Y_{ij} = The score of the ith observation in the jth group.

μ = The grand mean, common to all cases in the population.

α_j = The effect of group j, common to every case in that group.

e_{ij} = The error score, unique to the ith case in the jth group.

error term—in ANOVA, that part of an observed score that cannot be attributed to either the common component or the group component

By rearranging this formula we see that the **error term,** or residual, is that part of an observed score that cannot be attributed to either the common component or the group component:

$$e_{ij} = Y_{ij} - \mu - \alpha_j$$

The error terms in ANOVA can be viewed as discrepancies between observed scores and those predicted by membership in a group. ANOVA error terms take into account the fact that every case i in group j does not have the identical observed Y_j score. For example, every state in the South does not have exactly 4.59 serious crimes per 1,000 population; some have higher rates, while others are lower. The error term, e_{ij}, reflects this fact.

4.2   ANOVA Tables: Sums of Squares, Mean Squares, *F* Ratio

4.2.1   Sums of Squares

To determine the proportion of variance in Y_{ij} attributable to the group effects (the α_j) and the proportion due to error (e_{ij}), begin with the numerator of the sample variance:

$$\sum_{i=1}^{N} (Y_i - \overline{Y})^2$$

Each of the N observations in a sample is a member of one of the J groups. If n_j is the number of cases in the jth group, then $n_1 + n_2 + \ldots + n_J = N$. That is, the sum of observations across the J subgroups equals the total sample size, N. Thus, by attaching to each case both an individual (i) and group (j) subscript, the variance numerator can also be written using a double summation operator (see Appendix A):

$$\sum_{i=1}^{N}(Y_i - \overline{Y})^2 = \sum_{j=1}^{J}\sum_{i=1}^{n_j}(Y_{ij} - \overline{Y})^2$$

The term $\sum_{j=1}^{J}\sum_{i=1}^{n_j}(Y_{ij} - \overline{Y})^2$ is the **total sum of squares,** or SS_{TOTAL}. It shows the sum of squared deviations of each score from the grand mean of all groups, ($\overline{Y}$).

total sum of squares— a number obtained by subtracting the scores of a distribution from their mean, squaring, and summing these values

For example, suppose there are $N = 5$ observations, each belonging either to group 1 or group 2 (i.e., $J = 2$), with the number of observations in each group $n_1 = 3$ and $n_2 = 2$. Then, expanding the terms on the right:

$$\sum_{j=1}^{J}\sum_{i=1}^{n_j}(Y_{ij} - \overline{Y})^2 = [(Y_{11} - \overline{Y})^2 + (Y_{21} - \overline{Y})^2 + (Y_{31} - \overline{Y})^2]$$
$$+ [(Y_{12} - \overline{Y})^2 + (Y_{22} - \overline{Y})^2]$$

The first line contains the sum for group $j = 1$, and the second line contains the sum for group $j = 2$.

A one-way ANOVA partitions the total sum of squares into two components: (1) the sum of squares lying between the means of the group categories, the **between sum of squares,** or SS_{BETWEEN}; and (2) the sum of squared deviations from the group means, the **within sum of squares,** or SS_{WITHIN}. In forming this partition the same value can be simultaneously added to and subtracted from any expression without changing its value. Therefore, subtract and add $\overline{Y}_j$ (the mean of the jth group to which case i belongs) to that case's deviation from the grand mean:

between sum of squares— a value obtained by subtracting the grand mean from each group mean, squaring these differences for all individuals, and summing them

within sum of squares— a value obtained by subtracting each subgroup mean from each observed score, squaring and summing

$$Y_{ij} - \overline{Y} = Y_{ij} + (\overline{Y}_j - \overline{Y}_j) - \overline{Y}$$

Rearrange the four terms on the right to create two deviations:

$$Y_{ij} - \overline{Y} = (Y_{ij} - \overline{Y}_j) + (\overline{Y}_j - \overline{Y})$$

The first term on the right, $(Y_{ij} - \overline{Y}_j)$, is the deviation of the ith individual's score from the mean of the jth group, to which it belongs. It is the sample estimate of the error term, e_{ij}. The second term on the right, $(\overline{Y}_j - \overline{Y})$, is the deviation of the jth group's mean from the grand mean of all groups. It is the sample estimate of the jth group's effect, $\alpha_j = \mu_j - \mu$. Squaring both sides of this equation and summing across all scores yields:

$$\sum_{j=1}^{J} \sum_{i=1}^{n_j} (Y_{ij} - \overline{Y})^2 = \sum_{j=1}^{J} \sum_{i=1}^{n_j} (Y_{ij} - \overline{Y}_j)^2 + \sum_{j=1}^{J} n_j (\overline{Y}_j - \overline{Y})^2$$

This equality demonstrates that the total sum of squares can always be partitioned into

$$SS_{WITHIN} = \sum_{j=1}^{J} \sum_{i=1}^{n_j} (Y_{ij} - \overline{Y}_j)^2$$

and

$$SS_{BETWEEN} = \sum_{j=1}^{J} n_j (\overline{Y}_j - \overline{Y})^2$$

Therefore:

$$SS_{TOTAL} = SS_{WITHIN} + SS_{BETWEEN}$$

Except where all observations in a sample have identical scores, their variance is greater than zero. Some proportion of this variation may be attributable to the effects of the groups to which the observations belong. In other words, the *between*-group sum of squares summarizes the effects of the independent classification variable under study. But, within a specific group, cases may still differ among themselves because of random factors such as sampling variation or from the effects of unobserved causal variables. Thus, the *within*-group sum of squares reflects the operation of unmeasured factors. To treat every group member as having the same score would result in errors.

4.2.2. Sums of Squares in the Regional Effects Example

If the null hypothesis about regional differences in states' serious crime rates were true, then we would observe equal means in all groups; that is, $\mu_S = \mu_W = \mu_N = \mu_M$. The SS_{BETWEEN} would equal zero, and hence $SS_{\text{TOTAL}} = SS_{\text{WITHIN}}$. That is, all the observed variation in state crime rates would be random error variance. In instances where the independent variable has no effect, the general ANOVA model for sample data reduces to

$$Y_{ij} = \overline{Y} + e_{ij}$$

Suppose, however, that state region were related to crime, that is, $\mu_S > \mu_W > \mu_N > \mu_M$. And further assume that each state *within* a particular region experiences an identical level of serious crime; that is, no deviations occur around each group mean. Then, for sample data the crime rates for the four regions would equal:

$$Y_{i,S} = \overline{Y} + a_S$$
$$Y_{i,W} = \overline{Y} + a_W$$
$$Y_{i,N} = \overline{Y} + a_N$$
$$Y_{i,M} = \overline{Y} + a_M$$

where these four a_j sample effects estimate the α_j population effects.

In this case $SS_{\text{TOTAL}} = SS_{\text{BETWEEN}}$, meaning that *all* the variation in serious crime is attributable to the region in which a state is located. In reality, of course, one discrete variable can never explain *all* the variation in a dependent variable. First, unmeasured *systematic* factors might affect the dependent variable. For example, different urbanization, racial and ethnic composition, or extent of policing might each affect a particular state's crime rate. These factors are not controlled in a one-way ANOVA. Second, *random* factors, such as an unusual spurt in prison escapes or parole violations, could also affect a state's crime rate. Because variation in the dependent variable may arise from both unmeasured systematic and random factors, the set of equations for sample data must include both effects and error terms:

$$Y_{i,S} = \overline{Y} + a_S + e_{i,S}$$

$$Y_{i,W} = \overline{Y} + a_W + e_{i,W}$$

$$Y_{i,N} = \overline{Y} + a_N + e_{i,N}$$

$$Y_{i,M} = \overline{Y} + a_M + e_{i,M}$$

Table 4.1 shows that substantial within-group variation (error) occurs among the states in all four regions. And the fact that the four regional means are clearly not equal suggests that between-group variation also occurs. Thus, the variation in crime scores (SS_{TOTAL}) seems to be attributable to both $SS_{BETWEEN}$ and SS_{WITHIN}. To determine whether these apparent differences are statistically significant requires calculating several ANOVA quantities, including the sums of squares, the mean squares, and an F-ratio, as shown below.

To compute SS_{TOTAL}, subtract each observation from the grand mean, square it, and sum: $SS_{TOTAL} = (7.56 - 4.77)^2 - (6.57 - 4.77)^2 + \ldots + (2.69 - 4.77)^2 = 80.13$. $SS_{BETWEEN}$ is directly calculated by subtracting each group mean from the grand mean, multiplying by group size, and summing, according to the formula:

$$SS_{BETWEEN} = \sum_{j=1}^{J} n_j(\overline{Y}_j - \overline{Y})^2$$

which in this example is simply: $(16)(4.59 - 4.77)^2 + (13)(5.80 - 4.77)^2 + (9)(4.36 - 4.77)^2 + (12)(4.21 - 4.77)^2 = 19.38$.

Finally, SS_{WITHIN} can be computed by direct calculation, where each observation is subtracted from its *group* mean, squared, and then added:

$$SS_{WITHIN} = \sum_{j=1}^{J} \sum_{i=1}^{n_j} (Y_{ij} - \overline{Y}_j)^2$$

Thus, $SS_{WITHIN} = (7.56 - 4.59)^2 + (6.57 - 4.59)^2 + \ldots + (2.69 - 4.21)^2 = 60.75$. An alternative procedure uses the fact that $SS_{TOTAL} = SS_{BETWEEN} + SS_{WITHIN}$ to compute by simple subtraction from the two previous quantities:

$$SS_{WITHIN} = SS_{TOTAL} - SS_{BETWEEN}$$

Thus, $SS_{WITHIN} = 80.13 - 19.38 = 60.75$.

TABLE 4.1

Serious Crimes per 1,000 State Population by Region in 1985

Observation	Y_{ij}	Observation	Y_{ij}
SOUTH:		*WEST:*	
Florida	7.56	Colorado	6.92
Texas	6.57	Arizona	6.90
Louisiana	5.71	Oregon	6.73
Oklahoma	5.42	Nevada	6.68
Maryland	5.38	New Mexico	6.54
Delaware	4.96	Washington	6.53
Georgia	4.89	California	6.52
South Carolina	4.83	Alaska	5.82
Tennessee	4.32	Utah	5.31
North Carolina	4.11	Hawaii	5.20
Alabama	3.92	Montana	4.33
Virginia	3.78	Wyoming	4.01
Arkansas	3.58	Idaho	3.86
Mississippi	3.27		
Kentucky	2.95		
West Virginia	2.23		
$\Sigma Y_{ij} = 73.49$		$\Sigma Y_{ij} = 75.34$	
$\overline{Y}_S = 4.59$		$\overline{Y}_W = 5.80$	
$S_S = 1.37$		$S_W = 1.13$	
NORTHEAST:		*MIDWEST:*	
New York	5.56	Michigan	6.36
Connecticut	5.42	Illinois	5.27
New Jersey	5.10	Missouri	4.65
Massachusetts	4.72	Kansas	4.35
Rhode Island	4.71	Ohio	4.26
Vermont	3.87	Indiana	4.16
Maine	3.67	Minnesota	4.13
New Hampshire	3.23	Wisconsin	3.98
Pennsylvania	2.99	Iowa	3.94
		Nebraska	3.78
		South Dakota	2.98
		North Dakota	2.69
$\Sigma Y_{ij} = 39.26$		$\Sigma Y_{ij} = 50.56$	
$\overline{Y}_N = 4.36$		$\overline{Y}_M = 4.21$	
$S_N = 0.95$		$S_M = 0.96$	

$\overline{Y} = 4.77$

$s_Y = 1.28$

4.2.3.   Mean Squares

The next step in an ANOVA is to compute the mean squares corresponding to SS_{BETWEEN} and SS_{WITHIN}. The two **mean squares** each estimate a variance—the first due to group effects and the second due to error. If no group effects exist, the two estimates should be identical. If a significant group effect exists, the between-group variance, called the **mean square between** (MS_{BETWEEN}), will be larger than the within-group variance, called the **mean square within** (MS_{WITHIN}).

mean square—estimate of variance used in the analysis of variance

mean square between— a value in ANOVA obtained by dividing the between sum of squares by its degrees of freedom

mean square within— a value in ANOVA obtained by dividing the within sum of squares by its degrees of freedom

Mean squares are averages computed by dividing each sum of squares by its appropriate degrees of freedom (df). (See section 3.7 for a discussion of degrees of freedom.) The degrees of freedom associated with the between-group variance are simply $J - 1$, because once we know the grand mean, $(\overline{Y})$, and the means of $J - 1$ of the groups, $(\overline{Y}_j)$, then the mean of the Jth group is automatically determined. Thus, to compute MS_{BETWEEN}, simply divide SS_{BETWEEN} by $J - 1$:

$$MS_{\text{BETWEEN}} = \frac{\sum_{j=1}^{J} n_j (\overline{Y}_j - \overline{Y})^2}{J - 1}$$

$$= \frac{SS_{\text{BETWEEN}}}{J - 1}$$

Therefore in the regional crime rate example

$$MS_{\text{BETWEEN}} = 19.38/(4 - 1) = 6.46$$

The degrees of freedom associated with the within-group variance is $N - J$. Each group has $n_j - 1$ degrees of freedom, so adding across all J groups gives:

$$(n_1 - 1) + (n_2 - 1) + \ldots + (n_J - 1)$$

$$= (n_1 + n_2 + \ldots + n_J) - (1 + 1 + \ldots + 1)$$

$$\underbrace{\qquad N \text{ cases} \qquad}\qquad \underbrace{\qquad J \text{ of these} \qquad}$$

$$= N - J$$

Therefore, to compute MS_{WITHIN}, divide SS_{WITHIN} by $N - J$:

$$MS_{\text{WITHIN}} = \frac{\sum\limits_{j=1}^{J} \sum\limits_{i=1}^{n_j} (Y_{ij} - \overline{Y}_j)^2}{N - J}$$

$$= \frac{SS_{\text{WITHIN}}}{N - J}$$

For the crime example $MS_{\text{WITHIN}} = 60.75/(50 - 4) = 1.32$.

The estimated variance due to group membership is much larger than the estimated variance due to error (6.46 vs. 1.32). Such a difference would occur if a regional effect on serious crime exists. The next step in ANOVA is to determine how much larger MS_{BETWEEN} must be relative to MS_{WITHIN} before the hypothesis of no group effect can be rejected.

4.2.4. The *F* Ratio

The family of *F* distributions was introduced in section 3.11. In ANOVA an *F* test statistic is computed simply as the ratio of the two mean squares. Its two degrees of freedom, ν_1 and ν_2, are the *df* for these two *MS*:

$$F_{J-1, N-J} = \frac{MS_{\text{BETWEEN}}}{MS_{\text{WITHIN}}}$$

The sampling distribution of *F* can be used to test the null hypothesis that none of the variance in the dependent variable is due to group effects. Two assumptions are required:

1. The *J* groups are independently drawn from a normally distributed population;
2. The population variance is identical to the variances of the *J* groups.

This latter assumption is called **homoscedasticity.** When the *J* population variances differ, they are *heteroscedastic*.

If both assumptions hold, the computed *F* ratio statistic is distributed according to a theoretical *F* distribution with $J - 1$ *df* in the numerator and $N - J$ *df* in the denominator. Because the

homoscedasticity— a condition in which the variances of two or more population distributions are equal

alternative hypothesis in ANOVA typically expects the between-group estimate of the variance to be larger than the within-group variance estimate *in the population,* the significance test requires only one tail of the distribution. (Recall from chapter 3 that each F distribution is formed as a ratio of two chi-square distributions.) If the computed F ratio is larger than the critical value associated with a chosen α level, we reject the null hypothesis and conclude that group effects occur.

For $\alpha = .05$, .01, and .001, Appendix E provides three sets of tables of critical values for many F distributions. The numerator *dfs*, (ν_1), run across the column headings of each table, while the denominator *dfs*, (ν_2), are found in the rows. The entry in the intersection of a row and column is the critical value of F necessary to reject the null hypothesis at the α-level for that table.

We can apply the F test to the regional crime data. Given $MS_{BETWEEN} = 6.46$ and $MS_{WITHIN} = 1.32$,

$$F_{3,46} = \frac{6.46}{1.32} = 4.89$$

Because $J = 4$ and $N = 50$ in this example, this F ratio has $4 - 1 = 3$ *df* in the numerator and $50 - 4 = 46$ *df* in the denominator. Setting $\alpha = .01$, turn to the second F table in Appendix E and find the entry where $\nu_1 = 3$ and $\nu_2 = 46$. In this case no row for $\nu_2 = 46$ exists. The two nearest tabled denominator *dfs* are 40 and 60. Hence to approximate the critical value, simply average the critical values for 40 and 60: $(4.31 + 4.13)/2 = 4.22$. Because the computed F ratio is 4.89, we can reject the null hypothesis of no group effects with only a .01 chance of making a Type I error. We conclude that serious crimes per 1,000 state population in 1985 differed significantly among the four regions. Exactly where the differences occur remains to be determined. Section 4.5 provides some procedures.

ANOVA summary table—a tabular display summarizing the results of an analysis of variance

The results of a one-way analysis of variance are commonly presented in an **ANOVA summary table,** as illustrated by Table 4.2. It provides easy access to all the relevant information needed to interpret the hypothesis test—the sums of squares, degrees of freedom, mean squares, F ratio, and probability level.

TABLE 4.2

Summary of ANOVA for Regional Crime Rates

Source	SS	df	MS	F
Regression	19.38	3	6.46	4.89*
Error	60.75	46	1.32	
Total	80.13	49		

* Significant at $\alpha = .01$

4.3   Tests for Two Means

Analyses of variance are usually performed when a classification results in three or more groups. However, ANOVA is perfectly possible with just two groups. The Z and the t distributions (both discussed in chapter 3) are also available to test the statistical significance of differences in two population means. After presenting these tests, we show that they are special cases of the more general ANOVA and thus give the same results. We apply these tests to an example from the 1991 GSS in which the null hypothesis is that the political views of men and women do not differ significantly. This variable is operationalized by asking survey respondents to rate themselves on a seven-point scale from "extremely liberal" (1) to "extremely conservative" (7), with "moderate, middle of the road" as the scale midpoint (4). Our alternative hypothesis is that men and women hold different political views, but we do not have compelling grounds to assert which gender is more conservative. Hence, a two-tailed alternative hypothesis is plausible:

$$H_0: \mu_F = \mu_M$$
$$H_1: \mu_F \neq \mu_M$$

4.3.1.   *Z* Test Procedures

The central limit theorem (see section 3.5) guarantees that for large samples the distribution of all sample means (i.e., the sampling distribution) will be normal, and its mean is an unbiased estimate of the mean of the population from which the samples were selected. To test the difference between the means of two populations, a corollary of the central limit theorem is relevant:

> The distribution of the difference between two sample means, from random samples of N_1 and N_2 with population means μ_1 and μ_2 and variances σ_1^2 and σ_2^2, follows a normal distribution that has mean $\mu_1 - \mu_2$ and standard deviation (standard error) $\sqrt{\sigma_1^2/N_1 + \sigma_2^2/N_2}$. No assumptions are required about the shape of the original population distributions.

When the population parameters are unknown, the sampling distribution's values can be computed as

$$\mu_{(\bar{Y}_1 - \bar{Y}_2)} = \mu_1 - \mu_2$$
$$\sigma_{(\bar{Y}_1 - \bar{Y}_2)} = \sqrt{\sigma_1^2/N_1 + \sigma_2^2/N_2}$$

mean difference hypothesis test— a statistical test of a hypothesis about the difference between two population means

The table of probabilities associated with the normal distribution allow us to perform a **mean difference hypothesis test** about two population means. It only requires that N_1 and N_2 are large (that is, $N_1 + N_2$ should be *at least* 60 and preferably 100 or more) and that the variances of both populations (σ_1^2 and σ_2^2) are known. Because these population parameters are seldom known, they are usually estimated from the sample statistics. If $N_1 + N_2$ is large, the known sample variances, s_1^2 and s_2^2, can be substituted for the unknown population variances, σ_1^2 and σ_2^2, to estimate the standard error:

$$\hat{\sigma}_{(\bar{Y}_1 - \bar{Y}_2)} = \sqrt{s_1^2/N_1 + s_2^2/N_2}$$

To test the null hypothesis that $\mu_1 = \mu_2$, which implies that $\mu_1 - \mu_2 = 0$, refer to the summary of steps in Box 3.4 on page 108. Choose an α level (the probability of making a Type I error) and calculate the test statistic. Next, determine the critical value and compare it to the observed test statistic. Finally, decide whether to reject the null hypothesis in favor of the alternative.

For our analysis of male-female political views in the 1991 GSS, we choose $\alpha = .01$. Given the large number of cases of each gender ($N_1 = 621$ men; $N_2 = 838$ women), the standardized or Z score is the appropriate theoretical distribution. The Z test statistic for the difference in means has $(\overline{Y}_1 - \overline{Y}_2) - (\mu_1 - \mu_2)$ in the numerator and $\sigma_{(\overline{Y}_1 - \overline{Y}_2)}$ in the denominator. Appendix C shows that the critical values for a two-tailed test at $\alpha = .01$ are $-Z_{\alpha/2} = -2.58$ and $+Z_{\alpha/2} = +2.58$.

Under the null hypothesis, H_0: $\mu_1 - \mu_2 = 0$, the mean of the first population equals the mean of the second population. We test whether the observed difference in the two sample means $(\overline{Y}_1 - \overline{Y}_2)$ could have occurred if the true difference in population means were exactly zero; that is, $(\mu_1 - \mu_2) = 0$. Thus, this term drops out of the numerator of the Z score used to test H_0:

$$Z_{(\overline{Y}_1 - \overline{Y}_2)} = \frac{(\overline{Y}_1 - \overline{Y}_2) - (\mu_1 - \mu_2)}{\sigma_{(\overline{Y}_1 - \overline{Y}_2)}}$$

$$= \frac{\overline{Y}_1 - \overline{Y}_2}{\sqrt{\sigma_1^2/N_1 + \sigma_2^2/N_2}}$$

Or, using our large sample estimate for $\sigma_{(\overline{Y}_1 - \overline{Y}_2)}$:

$$Z_{(\overline{Y}_1 - \overline{Y}_2)} = \frac{(\overline{Y}_1 - \overline{Y}_2)}{\hat{\sigma}_{(\overline{Y}_1 - \overline{Y}_2)}}$$

$$= \frac{\overline{Y}_1 - \overline{Y}_2}{\sqrt{s_1^2/N_1 + s_2^2/N_2}}$$

Figure 4.1 diagrams two situations for a sampling distribution where H_0: $\mu_2 - \mu_1 = 0$ is true. In Panel A the difference in sample means, $(\overline{Y}_1 - \overline{Y}_2)$, is a small positive value lying close to the hypothesized population difference of zero. We would not reject the null hypothesis at conventional levels of α because this small difference is highly probable in a population where $\mu_1 - \mu_2 = 0$. The observed sample difference in Panel B is substantial. We most probably would reject the null hypothesis that the two samples came from populations where $\mu_1 - \mu_2 = 0$, as this outcome is very unlikely in the sampling distribution (it occurs in the far right tail). These two sample means probably came from populations where $\mu_1 > \mu_2$.

FIGURE 4.1
Two Examples of Outcomes When the Null Hypothesis About Mean Differences is True

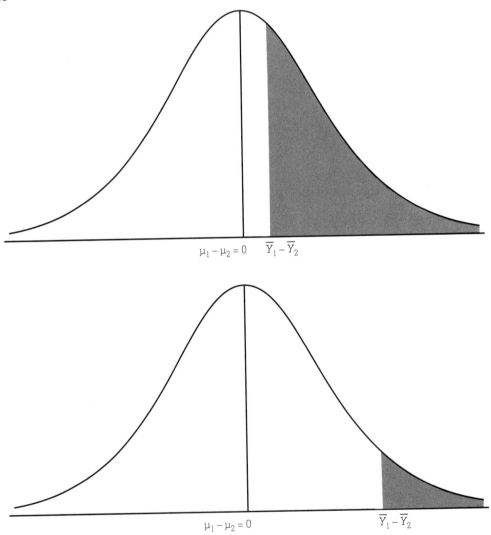

Source: Adapted from David Knoke and George W. Bohrnstedt. Basic Social Statistics (Itasca, IL: F. E. Peacock Publishers, Inc., 1991), 202.

The mean political views for the 621 men is 4.14, while the mean for the 838 women is 4.04. The two sample variances are 1.90 and 1.66, respectively. Hence the test statistic is computed as

$$Z_{(\bar{Y}_1 - \bar{Y}_2)} = \frac{4.14 - 4.04}{\sqrt{\dfrac{1.90}{621} + \dfrac{1.66}{838}}}$$

$$= \frac{.100}{.071} = +1.41$$

Because this computed Z value does not exceed the critical value ($+2.58$), we cannot reject the null hypothesis in favor of the alternative that men and women differ in their political views. We conclude that men and women probably hold similar political views.

4.3.2.   Hypothesis Testing with Proportions

Chapter 2 defined a proportion as the frequency of cases of a specific type, divided by the total number of cases. The sample mean is given by $\bar{Y} = \Sigma Y_i / N$. But, when Y_i has only values of 1 and 0, the numerator term, ΣY_i, equals f_1. Thus, as section 2.4.3 (page 49) showed, the mean of a dichotomous variable is the proportion of cases having the value 1, that is, p_1. For example, 1,078 of 1,414 GSS respondents agreed that they were "in favor of the death penalty for persons convicted of murder." Hence, $p_1 = 1,078/1,414 = 0.762$, or 76.2%.

The same formulas used in section 4.3.1 to test hypotheses about mean differences can be applied to dichotomous dependent variables, to perform **significance testing with proportions.** The variance of a dichotomy is simply pq, where $q = 1 - p$. Thus, in the capital punishment example, the sample variance is $s_Y^2 = (0.762)(1 - 0.762) = (0.762)(0.238) = 0.181$. And the standard error of a sampling distribution of proportions, s_p, is

significance testing with proportions—using statistical tests to determine whether the observed difference between sample proportions could occur by chance in the populations from which the samples were selected

$$s_p = \sqrt{pq/N}$$

In this example $s_p = \sqrt{(.762)(.238)/1414} = 0.011$.

Suppose we hypothesize that Republicans, who are conventionally considered more conservative, more strongly favor the death penalty than do Democrats. Then the two hypotheses are

$$H_0: p_R = p_D$$

$$H_1: p_R > p_D$$

where p_R is the proportion of Republicans favoring the death penalty and p_D is the proportion of Democrats. In the 1991 GSS of the 611 Republicans (including Independents leaning towards the Republican party) with opinions, 86.1% supported capital punishment; while only 67.0% of the 622 Democrats (including Democrat-leaning Independents) favored the death penalty. Hence, $p_R = 0.861$ and $p_D = 0.670$. Setting $\alpha = .05$, we can calculate the test statistic for the difference between two means:

$$Z_{(p_R - p_D)} = \frac{.861 - .670}{\sqrt{\dfrac{(.861)(.139)}{611} + \dfrac{(.670)(.330)}{622}}}$$

$$= \frac{.191}{.023} = +8.30$$

Because the critical value of Z_α for a one-tailed alternative is $+1.645$, we reject the null hypothesis. We conclude that Republicans support the death penalty at a higher level than do Democrats.

The formula for the standard error used in the test statistic clearly shows that, as N_1 and N_2 get large, the standard error grows smaller. If N_1 and N_2 are sufficiently large, almost *any* difference in $\overline{Y}_1$ and $\overline{Y}_2$ will become significant. For this reason, more cautious strategies of hypothesis testing should be adopted. For example, unless the mean difference is at least one-quarter standard deviation, it could be considered unimportant regardless of statistical significance. An even better approach would be to estimate the strength of a relationship among variables. How large a relationship should be depends on the specific research problem, so a general principle is impossible to state. Most importantly, mere statistical significance cannot reveal the entire story.

4.3.3. *t* Test Procedures

When data consist of two small samples—usually where $N_1 + N_2 < 100$ and certainly where fewer than 60 cases are available—the assumptions necessary for the Z test of mean differences are untenable. However, the family of t distributions may be used instead, if two key assumptions can be made: (1) both samples are drawn randomly from two independent, normally distributed populations; and (2) the two population variances are homoscedastic, that is, $\sigma_1^2 = \sigma_2^2 = \sigma^2$. Unlike the Z test discussed above, the shapes of the population distributions are important to using the t test. However, in practice, violating this assumption may have only a small impact on the results.

To make a single estimate of the population variance, the two sample variances are pooled, using the following formula:

$$s^2 = \frac{(N_1 - 1)(s_1^2) + (N_2 - 1)(s_2^2)}{N_1 + N_2 - 2}$$

where
$N_1 + N_2 - 2$ is the df associated with the pooled estimate.

The degrees of freedom equal the sum of the dfs associated with s_1^2 and s_2^2. Specifically, $df_1 + df_2 = (N_1 - 1) + (N_2 - 1) = N_1 + N_2 - 2$.

For small samples the test statistic for the difference between two means is

$$t_{(N_1 + N_2 - 2)} = \frac{(\bar{Y}_1 - \bar{Y}_2) - (\mu_1 - \mu_2)}{s_{(\bar{Y}_1 - \bar{Y}_2)}}$$

$$= \frac{\bar{Y}_1 - \bar{Y}_2}{\sqrt{s^2/N_1 + s^2/N_2}}$$

$$= \frac{\bar{Y}_1 - \bar{Y}_2}{s\sqrt{\dfrac{1}{N_1} + \dfrac{1}{N_2}}}$$

where
$s_{(\bar{Y}_1 - \bar{Y}_2)}$ is the estimated standard error of the mean difference.

To illustrate this procedure, we examine whether unionization rates are lower in states with so-called "right to work" laws (which ban closed shops) than in states without such laws. Table 4.3 shows the data. Because the two groups are small (21 and 30 states, respectively), a *t* test is appropriate, on assumption that the data are independent samples drawn randomly from two normally distributed populations.

The null and alternative hypotheses, where group 1 is the right-to-work states, and group 2 is the other states, are

$$H_0: \mu_1 - \mu_2 = 0$$

$$H_1: \mu_1 - \mu_2 < 0$$

Setting $\alpha = .01$ for $df = 21 + 30 - 2 = 49$ gives a critical value in Appendix D of -2.704 for a one-tailed test to reject the null. Calculating s^2 and taking its square root to obtain s:

$$s = \sqrt{\frac{(21 - 1)(3.70)^2 + (30 - 1)(6.73)^2}{21 + 30 - 2}} = 5.69$$

Thus, *t* is calculated as:

$$t_{49} = \frac{13.58 - 23.10}{(5.69)\sqrt{1/21 + 1/30}} = \frac{-9.52}{1.62} = -5.88$$

Therefore, the alternative hypothesis that right-to-work states have less-unionized labor forces than other states is supported.

Researchers almost exclusively use *t* tests rather than *Z* tests for analyzing differences in two means. As *N* increases, the *t* and *Z* distributions converge to the latter's critical values. In Appendix D (the *t* distribution) look across the row where *df* equals infinity (∞) to the *t* entry under column headed by a given α. Compare it to the *Z* value in Appendix C for the same α; they are identical. Also, as *N* increases (beyond 100 or more), the central limit theorem renders the assumption that the samples come from normally distributed populations increasingly unimportant (see section 3.5). Finally, because researchers almost never know the standard error of the population, a *t* test is preferable. Although you should know the difference between a *Z* and a *t* distribution, in practice one always uses *t* tests.

TABLE 4.3

Percentage of Unionized State Labor Forces by Right-to-Work Status

Right-to-Work States		*Non–Right-to-Work States*	
State	*Percent*	*State*	*Percent*
Iowa	20.5	New York	35.6
Alabama	18.2	Michigan	33.7
Alaska	18.2	District of Columbia	33.4
Tennessee	17.3	Washington	32.9
Utah	16.8	Hawaii	31.5
Nevada	16.3	West Virginia	28.9
Nebraska	16.3	Illinois	27.5
Wyoming	15.6	Oregon	27.5
North Dakota	14.2	Ohio	27.4
Louisiana	13.8	Pennsylvania	27.0
Arkansas	13.2	Missouri	26.6
Arizona	12.8	California	25.4
Georgia	12.7	Indiana	25.1
Texas	12.5	Wisconsin	24.5
Kansas	12.0	Minnesota	24.5
Virginia	10.9	Montana	21.7
South Dakota	10.3	Kentucky	20.4
Florida	9.6	Delaware	20.3
Mississippi	9.3	New Jersey	19.9
North Carolina	8.9	Massachusetts	19.7
South Carolina	5.8	Rhode Island	19.4
		Connecticut	18.9
		Maryland	18.6
		Maine	18.5
		Colorado	18.0
		Idaho	16.1
		Oklahoma	12.9
		New Mexico	12.8
		New Hampshire	12.3
		Vermont	11.9
$N_1 = 21$		$N_2 = 30$	
$\overline{Y}_1 = 13.58\%$		$\overline{Y}_2 = 23.10\%$	
$s_1 = 3.70$		$s_2 = 6.73$	

4.3.4.   Comparing Two Distributions with Stem-and-Leaf Diagrams and Boxplots

In section 2.8 we showed how to construct stem-and-leaf diagrams and box-and-whisker plots for a single distribution. In this section we show how these same tools can be used to compare two distributions.

Using the data from Table 4.3, Figure 4.2 shows two stem-and-leaf diagrams of the percentage of unionized state workers in states with and without right-to-work laws. Figure 4.3 shows the boxplots for the right-to-work states and non–right-to-work states separately. The median for the right-to-work states is the 11th observation, which has the value $Mdn_R = 13.2$. Since there are 11 observations from the observation at the lowest end of the distribution, and since 11 is an odd number, the lower hinge is the 6th observation. Hence $H_1 = 10.9$. Similarly, there are 11 observations from Mdn_R to the largest observation (20.5) and hence the upper hinge is the 16th

FIGURE 4.2

Stem-and-Leaf Diagrams for Percent Unionized Labor Force

Stems	Leaves	(**N**)
	Right-to-Work States	
0	699	(3)
1	00123333446667788	(17)
2	1	(1)
	Non–Right-to-Work States	
0		
1	223368999	(9)
2	000025555777889	(15)
3	23346	(5)

Source: U.S. States Data Set

FIGURE 4.3

Box-and-Whisker Plots for Percent Unionized Labor Force

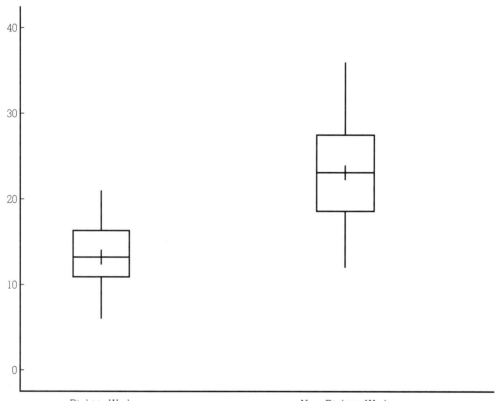

Right to Work   Non-Right to Work

Source: U.S. States Data Set

observation, or $H_2 = 16.3$. And the hinge spread $HS_R = H_2 - H_1 = 5.4$. To check for outliers we compute the lower and upper inner fences:

$$LIF_R = 10.9 - (1.5)(5.4) = 2.8$$

and

$$UIF_R = 16.3 + (1.5)(5.4) = 24.4$$

Since no value is smaller than 2.8 and none larger than 24.4, we conclude that there are no outliers in the right-to-work states' data. The boxplot for these data is shown on the left side of Figure 4.3.

Since the non–right-to-work data have 30 observations, the median, Mdn_N, lies between the 15th and 16th observations, for $Mdn_N = (21.7 + 24.5)/2 = 23.1$. Verify for yourself that $H_1 = 18.6$, $H_2 = 27.5$, and $HS_N = 8.9$. Hence $LIF_N = 5.25$ and $UIF_N = 40.85$. Because no observation is smaller than 5.25 and none is larger than 40.85, there are also no outliers in the non–right-to-work states' data.

Figure 4.3 visually confirms that states with right-to-work laws have significantly lower rates of unionization than do states without such laws. Furthermore, the figure confirms that states without right-to-work laws have much greater variation in unionization than do states with such laws.

4.3.5. Confidence Intervals and Point Estimates

confidence interval for mean differences— an interval constructed around the point estimate of the difference between two means

A **confidence interval for mean differences** can be constructed around the point estimate of the difference between two means, just as we showed for a single mean in section 3.6. For any desired level of confidence, such as $1 - \alpha$, the formula is:

$$(\overline{Y}_1 - \overline{Y}_2) \pm t_{\alpha/2} s_{(\overline{Y}_1 - \overline{Y}_2)}$$

point estimate for mean differences— the difference between the sample means used to estimate the difference between two population means

To compute a 95% confidence interval around the sample estimate of difference in percent unionized change between right-to-work and other states, start with the **point estimate for mean differences,** $\overline{Y}_1 - \overline{Y}_2 = -9.52\%$. The estimated standard error is $s_{(\overline{Y}_1 - \overline{Y}_2)} = 1.62$. Appendix D shows that for a 95% confidence level with $N_1 + N_2 - 2 = 49$ df, $t_{\alpha/2}$ is approximately 2.00. Therefore, the upper confidence limit (UCL) is $-9.52\% + (2.00)(1.62) = -6.28\%$ and the lower confidence limit (LCL) is $-9.52 - (2.00)(1.62) = -12.76\%$. In other words, we can be 95% confident that the interval bounded by -12.76% and -6.28% contains the true difference in percent unionized between the two groups of states.

A confidence interval around the difference in proportions is given by

$$(p_1 - p_2) \pm t_{\alpha/2} s_{(p_1 - p_2)}$$

The data in section 4.3.2 on Republican and Democrat support of the death penalty was $p_R - p_D = 0.191$ and $s_{p_R - p_D} = 0.023$. Sample sizes were $N_R = 611$ and $N_R = 622$, for $df = 611 + 622 - 2 = 1{,}231$. From Appendix D a 99% confidence interval requires $t_{\alpha/2} = \pm 2.58$. Thus, the LCL is $.191 - (2.58)(.023) = 0.132$ and the UCL is $.191 + (2.58)(.023) = 0.250$. We can be 99% confident that the true difference between the proportions of Republicans and Democrats favoring capital punishment lies between .132 and .250. Furthermore, our best estimate of the true population difference is the point estimate, $p_R - p_D = .191$. In other words, on the death penalty question, the difference between Republicans and Democrats is substantially greater than zero.

4.3.6. Relationship of t to F

The t test and the F test for testing the differences in means are intimately related. When only two groups are compared, that is, when $J = 2$, both ANOVA and the t test give identical results. In fact, applied to the same data, the square root of an F ratio with 1 and v_2 degrees of freedom equals a t value with v_2 degrees of freedom. Hence:

$$t_{v_2} = \sqrt{F_{1,v_2}}$$

Usually when $J = 2$ the researcher reports only a t test, while when $J > 2$, the results of an ANOVA are always reported.

4.4 The Correlation Ratio: Eta-Squared

If a Z test, t test, or an analysis of variance allows the null hypothesis to be rejected, the next question is: How strong is the relationship between the variables? Because a sufficiently large N allows almost any difference among means to be significant, the results of a statistical test are no guide to the importance of a relationship. Therefore, after rejecting a null hypothesis the strength of the relationship should be assessed by computing the **correlation ratio** or **eta-squared,** or η^2 (Greek letter *eta*).

In section 4.2.1 we showed that $SS_{TOTAL} = SS_{BETWEEN} + SS_{WITHIN}$. Dividing both sides of that equation by SS_{TOTAL}, it becomes:

correlation ratio (eta-squared)— a measure of nonlinear covariation between a discrete and a continuous variable, the ratio of $SS_{BETWEEN}$ to SS_{TOTAL}

$$1.00 = \frac{SS_{\text{BETWEEN}}}{SS_{\text{TOTAL}}} + \frac{SS_{\text{WITHIN}}}{SS_{\text{TOTAL}}}$$

$$= \text{"Explained } SS\text{"} + \text{"Unexplained } SS\text{"}$$

The ratio of SS_{BETWEEN} to SS_{TOTAL} represents the proportion of the total sum of squares that is explained (in a statistical sense) by the independent or group variable. Similarly, the ratio of SS_{WITHIN} to SS_{TOTAL} can be thought of as the unexplained proportion of the total sum of squares. These two components add to 1.00. Therefore, the proportion of variance in the dependent variable attributable to the group variable is defined as

$$\eta^2 = \frac{SS_{\text{BETWEEN}}}{SS_{\text{TOTAL}}}$$

Because η^2 is a population parameter notation, its sample estimate is designated with a caret (i.e., $\hat{\eta}^2$). Eta-squared always ranges between zero and 1.00. The more the sample means differ from one another and the smaller the sample variances, the relatively larger the SS_{BETWEEN}, and thus the closer $\hat{\eta}^2$ comes to 1.00.

Using the statistics from the ANOVA in Table 4.2,

$$\hat{\eta}^2 = \frac{19.38}{80.13} = 0.242$$

That is, 24.2% of the variation in states' serious crime rates can be accounted for by the region in which they are located. As social science analyses go, this is a substantial proportion of variance explained, but should not be taken as a guideline against which to gauge the strength of findings in general. Typically, a single independent variable in social research seldom accounts for more than 25% to 30% of the variance in a dependent variable, and often for as little as 2% to 5%.

4.5   Testing Differences Among Means (Post Hoc)

The alternative hypothesis for an ANOVA can take several forms, as noted in section 4.1. Three possibilities are as follows:

1. All the population means differ from one another;
2. Some subsets of the population means differ from one another; or
3. Some combination of the means differs from some single mean or from some other combination of means.

The F value itself is uninformative about which of these alternatives is true in a given situation. Using a series of t tests to examine all possible pairs of means is not legitimate, because not all $J^2 - J$ comparisons among the J group means are independent of one another. A method is required that is guided by the researcher's ideas about where differences among the groups may occur.

Two basic approaches to comparing means are available. The first, called *a priori* or **planned comparison,** unfortunately requires more mathematical treatment than we can assume for this book. The second approach, called *a posteriori* or **post hoc comparison,** is less statistically powerful but still useful in social science research. This section briefly introduces one form of post hoc comparison, the **Scheffé test.**

To make multiple comparisons among J means, a contrast can be formed. A **contrast,** labeled Ψ (Greek letter *psi*), among J population means is defined as

$$\Psi = c_1\mu_1 + c_2\mu_2 + \ldots + c_J\mu_J$$

where

The c_j are weights under the constraint that $c_1 + c_2 + \ldots + c_J = 0$; that is, the c_j sum to zero.

Using the regional crime example we hypothesize that the South and West regions have higher rates than the Northeast and Midwest. Thus, we need to form contrasts of the two former regions with the two latter regions, as follows: $c_S = c_W = -1/2$ and $c_N = c_M = 1/2$. By using plus and minus signs, the c_js add to zero: $c_S + c_W + c_N = c_M = -1/2 - 1/2 + 1/2 + 1/2 = 0$. The contrast for this hypothesis, call it Ψ_1, is given by

planned comparison— hypothesis test of differences between and among population means carried out before doing an analysis of variance

post hoc comparison— hypothesis test of the differences among population means carried out following an analysis of variance

Scheffé test— one form of post hoc comparison of differences in group means

contrast— a set of weighted population means that sum to zero, used in making post hoc comparisons of treatment groups

$$\Psi_1 = (-1/2)\mu_s + (-1/2)\mu_W + (1/2)\mu_N + (1/2)\mu_M$$

$$= \frac{-\mu_S - \mu_W}{2} + \frac{\mu_N + \mu_M}{2}$$

The *average* of the South and West is contrasted to the *average* of the Northeast and Midwest. Other contrasts consistent with the hypothesis are possible. For example, we could have let $c_S = 1$, $c_W = 1$, $c_N = -1$ and $c_M = -1$, which also sum to zero.[2] Once we form a contrast using sample means, we must compare its size to its standard error, much as a t test does. If the ratio is sufficiently large, we conclude that the comparison between the means is significant. If not, we cannot reject the null hypothesis that the true difference among means is zero. An unbiased estimate of a contrast using sample data is given by

$$\hat{\Psi} = c_1\overline{Y}_1 + c_2\overline{Y}_2 + \ldots + c_J\overline{Y}_J$$

And the estimated variance of a contrast is given by

$$\hat{\sigma}^2_{\hat{\psi}} = MS_{\text{WITHIN}} \left(\frac{c_1^2}{n_1} + \frac{c_2^2}{n_2} + \ldots + \frac{c_J^2}{n_J} \right)$$

where

MS_{WITHIN} = The mean square within obtained from the ANOVA.

n_j = The number of observations in the jth group.

The test statistic for a post hoc comparison is formed by the ratio of the absolute value of $\hat{\Psi}$ to its standard error:

$$t = \frac{|\hat{\Psi}|}{\hat{\sigma}_{\hat{\psi}}}$$

2. Many ANOVA computer packages, such as SPSS, require either integer contrasts or single decimal-place contrasts. Thus, 0.5 and -0.5 are permissible, but contrasts such as 0.25 would be rounded incorrectly to 0.3.

The critical value against which to evaluate this test statistic is given by

$$\text{c.v.} = \sqrt{(J - 1)(F_{J - 1, N - J})}$$

where

$F_{J-1,N-J}$ = The critical value for the α level chosen to test the null hypothesis in the ANOVA.

Therefore, whenever $|\hat{\Psi}|/\hat{\sigma}_{\hat{\psi}} \geq \sqrt{(J - 1)(F_{J - 1, N - J})}$, we reject the null hypothesis. There are $N - J$ degrees of freedom associated with this t test.

The regional crime rate example illustrates how to perform a multiple mean comparison. The hypothesized contrast is

$$\hat{\Psi}_1 = \frac{(4.36 + 4.21)}{2} + \frac{(-4.59 + -5.80)}{2}$$

and

$$\hat{\sigma}^2_{\hat{\psi}_1} = (6.46)\left[\frac{(1/2)^2}{16} + \frac{(1/2)^2}{13} + \frac{(-1/2)^2}{9} + \frac{(-1/2)^2}{12}\right] = 0.539$$

Taking the square root,

$$\hat{\sigma}_{\hat{\psi}_1} = \sqrt{0.539} = .73$$

Therefore, the test statistic is $t = |-0.91|/.73 = 1.25$. The critical value for $\alpha = .01$ is $\sqrt{(4 - 1)(4.22)} = 3.56$. Because 3.56 is larger than 1.25, we conclude that the hypothesized paired regional differences cannot be rejected. Since we know from the ANOVA above that the four means are not equal, the next plausible contrast is the western states versus the other three regions. What weights should be assigned to form this contrast?

You should now know how to do an ANOVA for multiple groups, a t test for two groups, and to make post hoc comparisons among means. Thus, you should be able to undertake meaningful tests of hypotheses involving two or more means.

Review of Key Concepts and Symbols

These key concepts and symbols are listed in the order of appearance in this chapter. Combined with the definitions in the margins, they will help you to review the material and can serve as a self-test for mastery of the concepts.

analysis of variance (ANOVA)	post hoc comparison
grand mean	Scheffé test
effect	contrast
error term	α_j
total sum of squares	e_{ij}
between sum of squares	SS_{TOTAL}
within sum of squares	$SS_{BETWEEN}$
mean square	SS_{WITHIN}
mean square between	$MS_{BETWEEN}$
mean square within	MS_{WITHIN}
homoscedasticity	$\mu_{(\bar{Y}_1 - \bar{Y}_2)}$
ANOVA summary table	$\sigma_{(\bar{Y}_1 - \bar{Y}_2)}$
mean difference hypothesis test	$\hat{\sigma}_{(\bar{Y}_1 - \bar{Y}_2)}$
significance testing with	s_p
proportions	s^2
confidence interval for mean	η^2
differences	$\hat{\eta}^2$
point estimate for mean	Ψ
differences	c_j
correlation ratio (eta-squared)	$\hat{\sigma}_{\hat{\Psi}}^2$
planned comparison	

PROBLEMS

General Problems

1. A voting analyst hypothesizes that support for the Clinton-Gore ticket in 1992 was highest among self-identified Democrats, next strongest among Independents, and least among Republicans.

Write the null and alternative forms of the hypothesis in symbolic form.

2. Using a cultural-capital scale, a family sociologist finds that the overall mean of a random sample of families is 26.8. If the mean scores for city-dwelling families is 18.3, for rural families is 22.6, and for suburban families is 37.4, what are the effects (a_j) for being a family in each area?

3. A social psychologist administers an intellectual flexibility test to a sample of 75 undergraduates at a large state university. She obtains means of 8.65 from 30 education students, 11.42 from 20 art majors, and 9.26 from 25 engineering students. What are the effects (a_j) for each type of major, using the weighted sample mean as an estimate of the population mean?

4. Find the degrees of freedom and critical values of F for the following:
   a. $\alpha = .05$, 2 groups, 30 subjects.
   b. $\alpha = .01$, 2 groups, 300 subjects.
   c. $\alpha = .001$, 6 groups, 60 subjects.
   d. $\alpha = .001$, 20 groups, 600 subjects.

5. Find the degrees of freedom and critical values of F for the following:
   a. $\alpha = .05$, $n_1 = 8$, $n_2 = 9$.
   b. $\alpha = .01$, $n_1 = 12$, $n_2 = 10$, $n_3 = 11$.
   c. $\alpha = .001$, $n_1 = 22$, $n_2 = 18$, $n_3 = 20$.
   d. $\alpha = .001$, $n_1 = 15$, $n_2 = 15$, $n_3 = 15$, $n_4 = 15$.

6. An experimenter divides 200 subjects into three groups, two of which have the same size and the third of which is as large as the other two combined. If the mean problem-solving times of the two smaller groups are 8 minutes and 10 minutes, what is the mean solution-time of the third group, if the grand mean is 11 minutes?

7. A total of 45 subjects, divided equally into three groups, yields a total sum of squares = 284.25 and an error sum of squares = 239.75. What is the $MS_{BETWEEN}$?

8. A team of business analysts draws random samples of workers from four automobile plants in the Midwest, with sample sizes of 13, 15, 12, and 11. On a 10-point scale of plans for starting their own businesses, the $SS_{TOTAL} = 186.33$, and the $SS_{BETWEEN} = 24.22$.

What is the value of eta squared? Is the probability less than $\alpha = .05$ that the population means differ significantly across the four plants? Report the observed F ratio and critical value.

9. Listed below are the statistics quiz scores from a class of 15 students who were assigned to three study methods: (1) no preparation; (2) studied alone; and (3) studied with a classmate:

No Preparation	Studied Alone	Studied Together
4	4	5
5	6	6
6	7	8
6	7	9
8	8	9

Compute the effect parameters (a_j) for each treatment condition. Then calculate the total sum of squares, the between sum of squares, and the within sum of squares. Determine the mean squares and the F ratio and evaluate it against the null hypothesis that the three population means are equal. Display these results in an ANOVA summary table. Finally, compute $\hat{\eta}^2$ and interpret the results.

10. Test the post hoc hypothesis in Problem 9 that studying with a classmate is superior to the other two methods. Set $\alpha = .05$. Report $\hat{\Psi}$ and $\hat{\sigma}_{\hat{\Psi}}^2$.

Problems Requiring the 1991 General Social Survey

11. Test the hypothesis that "most people can be trusted" (TRUST) is related to region of residence (REGION) by performing an analysis of variance. Set $\alpha = .001$. Compute $\hat{\eta}^2$ and interpret the results. (Eliminate all "other, depends" responses to the TRUST measure.)

12. What is the relationship between a person's age and the number of children ever born? Recode AGE into six roughly decade-wide categories [i.e., RECODE AGE (LO THRU 29=1)(30 thru 39=2) . . . (70 THRU HI=6)]. Then perform an ANOVA with

CHILDS as the dependent variable. Set $\alpha = .001$. Compute $\hat{\eta}^2$ and interpret the results.

13. Do beliefs that more money should be spent to solve the problems of cities vary with size of the place in which people live? Use the six SRCBELT codes as the independent variable in an ANOVA of NATCITY. Set $\alpha = .05$. Compute $\hat{\eta}^2$ and interpret the results.

Problems Requiring Use of the U.S. States Data Set

14. Determine if the rate of 1980–1986 population growth (POPPC) in the Mountain and Pacific states was higher than in the rest of the country. [Recode as follows: RECODE REGION (1 THRU 7=1)(8,9=2)]. Set $\alpha = .05$. Compute $\hat{\eta}^2$ and interpret the results.

15. Test the hypothesis that per-capita welfare rolls (AFDC) are higher in the richer states (INCRANK) than in the poorer states. Set $\alpha = .05$. Compute $\hat{\eta}^2$ and interpret the results. [Recode the rank order of states' per capita incomes at the median: RECODE INCRANK (LO THRU 25=1)(26 THRU HI=2)].

Statistics for Social Data Analysis

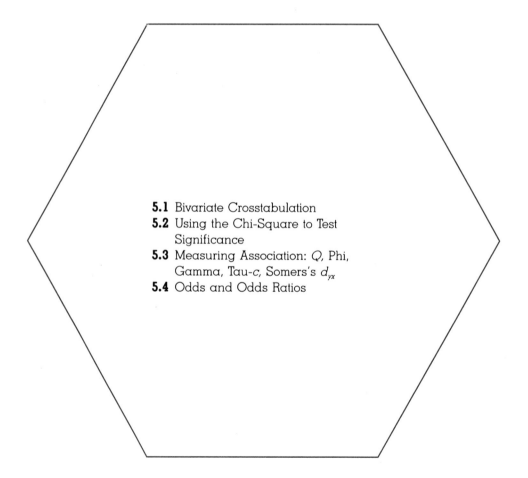

Analyzing Categoric Data

5

Analysis of variance reveals the relationship between two variables by examining means on a continuous dependent variable for the categories of a discrete independent variable. But, there are other techniques for finding how two variables are related. One is crosstabulation, described in this chapter; another is bivariate regression, introduced in chapter 7.

In this chapter we explain the logic of bivariate crosstabulation, a method for detecting statistical significance as well as ways to estimate the strength of the relationships between two discrete variables.

5.1. Bivariate Crosstabulation

The **bivariate crosstabulation** or *joint contingency table* displays the simultaneous outcomes of observations on two discrete variables. The categories of either variable may be orderable or nonorderable. The inferential and descriptive statistics discussed in this chapter can be applied to crosstabulations (or "crosstabs" as they are often called) of either type, although some measures of association can be meaningfully interpreted only when the variables' categories are orderable in a sequence from lowest to highest.

Suppose we are interested in the relationship between level of education and attitude towards women's roles outside the home, taking sex-role attitude as the dependent variable. Respondents in

bivariate crosstabulation (joint contingency table)— a tabular display of the simultaneous outcomes of observations on two discrete variables

the 1991 GSS were asked whether they strongly agreed, agreed, disagreed, or strongly disagreed with the statement: "It is better for everyone involved if the man is the achiever outside the home and the woman takes care of the home and family." Respondents' highest degree earned in school was coded into one of five ordered categories: less than high school, high school diploma, junior college (associate degree), bachelor degree, graduate degree. Crossing the 4 sex-role categories with the 5 degree categories results in 20 combinations. Because we treat sex-role attitude as a dependent variable with education as a predictor, we display their joint distribution as a four-row, five-column crosstabulation (or a 4 × 5 table—read as "four by five"—for short). As shown in the frequency crosstab in Table 5.1, the column values increase from left to right, and the row values go from disagreement at the bottom to agreement at the top. Hence, even though many computer programs print their crosstabs with the lowest categories in the top row, you should reorder pairs of joint table variables in this sequence. When presented in this manner, the categories of orderable variables conforms to an $X \times Y$ coordinate system, such as used for graphing two continuous variables (see chapter 6).

cell—the intersection of a row and a column in a crosstabulation of two or more variables. Numerical values contained within cells may be cell frequencies, cell proportions, or cell percentages

marginal distributions —the frequency distributions of each of two crosstabulated variables

row marginals—the frequency distribution of the variable shown across the rows of a crosstabulation

column marginals—the frequency distribution of the variable shown across the columns of a crosstabulation

The **cells** making up the body of a crosstab contain the number of cases having particular joint values of the two variables. The **marginal distributions** (or as they are more simply called, *the marginals*) are the row totals (**row marginals**) shown on the right and the column totals (**column marginals**) shown at the bottom of

TABLE 5.1

Frequency Crosstabulation of Sex Roles by Degree

Man Achieves Outside Home, Woman Takes Care of Home and Family	Highest Education					
	Less than High School	High School	Junior College	Bachelor Degree	Graduate Degree	Total
Strongly Agree	25	38	5	5	2	75
Agree	106	179	17	34	5	341
Disagree	58	231	24	67	24	404
Strongly Disagree	14	90	10	38	19	171
Total	203	538	56	144	50	991

Missing Data: 526 cases
Source: 1991 General Social Survey

the table. The grand total of all cases, N, appears in the lower right cell (991 persons). The missing data frequency, reflecting cases with no information on one or both variables, is reported in a footnote to the table (526 cases in this example, because one-third of the GSS sample was not asked the sex-role item).

A frequency crosstabulation is seldom useful for deciding whether two variables covary and, if so, how. When a frequency distribution has unequal marginals, direct comparisons of cell frequencies are difficult to make. We need some way to standardize the joint frequency table to a common denominator, so that the pattern of covariation is more apparent. A *percentage crosstabulation* allows such a pattern to emerge. *Percentages should always be calculated within categories of the independent variable.* For our example, we chose formal education degree as the independent variable, on the assumption that such a condition is lifelong, while sex-role attitude is a more contemporary state. To percentagize within each of the five degree categories, we first locate the column total for "less than high school" (203), in the last row of Table 5.1. We then divide this total into each of the four cell frequencies in that column and multiply by 100 to change those proportions to percentages. Thus, among respondents with less than a high school degree, the percentage strongly agreeing that men should achieve outside the home while women take care of home and family is $(25/203)(100) = 12.3\%$; the percentage agreeing is $(106/203)(100) = 52.2\%$; while 28.6% disagree and 6.9% strongly disagree. Similar computations were performed on the other columns, including the total column, as shown in Table 5.2.

Now we can quite clearly see that a gradient of increasing disagreement with the sex-role statement occurs from the less educated to the more educated. The percentage strongly disagreeing is more than 30% higher among those respondents with graduate degrees than among those without a high school diploma. Persons with intermediate degrees have percentages that fall in between. The opposite pattern appears across the columns within the "strongly agree" row: The percentage of less-educated respondents is 8% larger than the percentage of strongly agreeing graduates. Later, we discuss some descriptive statistics that summarize how strongly two variables are related in a crosstabulation. But, first we show how to test whether a pattern observed in sample data is likely to reflect covariation in the population from which the sample was drawn.

TABLE 5.2

Percentage Crosstabulation of Sex Roles by Degree

Man Achieves Outside Home, Woman Takes Care of Home and Family	Highest Education					
	Less than High School	High School	Junior College	Bachelor Degree	Graduate Degree	Total
Strongly Agree	12.3	7.1	8.9	3.5	4.0	7.6
Agree	52.2	33.3	30.4	23.6	10.0	34.4
Disagree	28.6	42.9	42.9	46.5	48.0	40.8
Strongly Disagree	6.9	16.7	17.9	26.4	38.0	17.3
Total	100.0%	100.0%	100.1%*	100.0%	100.0%	100.1%*
(N)	(203)	(538)	(56)	(144)	(50)	(991)

* Does not total to 100.0% due to rounding.
Missing Data: 526 cases
Source: 1991 General Social Survey and Table 5.1

5.2   Using the Chi-Square to Test Significance

In section 3.11 we discussed some properties of the chi-square (χ^2) family of sampling distributions, which is based on the normal curve. When the sample N of a bivariate crosstabulation is large (e.g., 100 or more observations), a **chi-square test** of statistical significance can be used to determine the likelihood that the two variables are unrelated in the population. That is, the null hypothesis is that no covariation exists between the two variables in the population. The alternative hypothesis is that the two variables are related in the population and in the same manner as in the sample crosstab. The chi-square test compares the observed cell frequencies of the sample crosstabulation table with the frequencies that one would expect to observe *if* the null hypothesis were true. Determining these expected frequencies holds the key to calculating the value of the chi-square for a crosstab.

If no relationship exists between two crossed variables, we say that they are **statistically independent.** This condition implies that, for the population, identical percentages of the dependent variable will be found within each category of the independent variable. Similarly, within each category of the dependent variable, the same percentages of the independent responses would occur. For example, if the GSS respondents' sex-role attitudes were

chi-square test— a test of statistical significance based on a comparison of the observed cell frequencies of a joint contingency table with frequencies that would be expected under the null hypothesis of no relationship

statistically independent — a condition of no relationship between variables in a population

unrelated to their education, except for sampling error, we would expect to find the percentages within the five columns of Table 5.2 to equal one another and thus to equal the percentages in the row marginals. That is, because 7.6% of all 991 respondents strongly agreed, we would expect that 7.6% in each of the five degree groups would also strongly agree. Similarly, 34.4% would agree, 40.8% would disagree, and 17.3% would strongly disagree within each column. Only two of the five columns ("high school" and "junior college") come close to this distribution, suggesting that statistical independence does not occur.

We can calculate what the bivariate crosstab frequencies would be *if* the two variables were statistically independent, that is, as if the H_0 of no relationship were true. Panel A of Table 5.3 displays an

TABLE 5.3

Expected Frequencies for Crosstabulation of Sex Roles by Degree, Under Null Hypothesis of Independence

Man Achieves Outside Home, Woman Takes Care of Home and Family	Highest Education						
	Less than High School	High School	Junior College	Bachelor Degree	Graduate Degree	Total	(N)
A. Expected Frequencies							
Strongly Agree	15.36	40.72	4.24	10.90	3.78	75	
Agree	69.85	185.12	19.27	49.55	17.20	341	
Disagree	82.76	219.33	22.83	58.70	20.38	404	
Strongly Disagree	35.03	92.83	9.66	24.85	8.63	171	
Total	203	538	56	144	50	991	
B. Column Percentages							
Strongly Agree	7.57	7.57	7.57	7.57	7.57	7.57	
Agree	34.41	34.41	34.41	34.41	34.41	34.41	
Disagree	40.77	40.77	40.77	40.77	40.77	40.77	
Strongly Disagree	17.26	17.26	17.26	17.26	17.26	17.26	
Total*	100.01%	100.01%	100.01%	100.01%	100.01%	100.01%	
(N)	(203)	(538)	(56)	(144)	(50)	(991)	
C. Row Percentages							
Strongly Agree	20.48	54.29	5.65	14.53	5.05	100.0%	(75)
Agree	20.48	54.29	5.65	14.53	5.05	100.0%	(341)
Disagree	20.48	54.29	5.65	14.53	5.05	100.0%	(404)
Strongly Disagree	20.48	54.29	5.65	14.53	5.05	100.0%	(171)
Total	20.48	54.29	5.65	14.53	5.05	100.0%	(991)

* Percentages do not total to 100.0% due to rounding.

independence relationship for the sex-role attitude and degree crosstab in Table 5.1. These cell entries, carried out to two decimal places for accuracy, are the **expected frequencies** under the null hypothesis of independence. Panel B reveals that the percentages within each column of these expected frequencies are identical, while panel C discloses that the percentages within each row are also identical. Calculated either way, these percentage distributions are identical to either the row marginals (last column in panel B) or the column marginals (bottom row in panel C).

The row and column marginal frequencies in Table 5.1 were used to calculate the 20 expected frequencies in the cells of Panel A in Table 5.3. If the two variables in any crosstabulation are independent, the formula for the expected frequency in row i and column j is:

$$\hat{f}_{ij} = \frac{(f_{i.})(f_{.j})}{N}$$

where

$\hat{f}_{ij}$ = The expected frequency of the cell in the ith row and the jth column.

$f_{i.}$ = The total in the ith row marginal.

$f_{.j}$ = The total in the jth column marginal.

N = The grand total, or sample size for the entire table.

For example, the expected frequency under the null hypothesis of independence for strongly disagreeing graduates (row 4, column 5) is:

$$\hat{f}_{45} = \frac{f_4.f_5}{N} = \frac{(171)(50)}{991} = 8.63$$

The χ^2 test statistic summarizes the differences across the 20 pairs of cells between the observed frequencies in Table 5.1 and the expected frequencies in Table 5.3. (Because the row and column marginals of both tables are identical, these values are not used.) If $\hat{f}_{ij}$ is the expected frequency under the null hypothesis and f_{ij} is the observed frequency for the same cell, then the chi-square for the table is calculated by the formula:

expected frequency—in a chi-square test, the value that cell frequencies are expected to take, given the hypothesis under study (ordinarily, the null hypothesis)

$$\chi^2 = \sum_{i=1}^{R} \sum_{j=1}^{C} \frac{(\hat{f}_{ij} - f_{ij})^2}{\hat{f}_{ij}}$$

where:

$\hat{f}_{ij}$ = The expected frequency of the cell in the ith row and the jth column.

f_{ij} = The observed frequency in the corresponding cell.

C = The number of columns in the crosstabulation.

R = The number of rows in the crosstabulation.

A version of the formula somewhat easier to remember is as follows:

$$\chi^2 = \sum_{i=1}^{R} \sum_{j=1}^{C} \frac{(E_{ij} - O_{ij})^2}{E_{ij}}$$

where

E_{ij} = The expected frequency in the ith row, jth column under independence.

O_{ij} = The observed frequency in the corresponding cell.

The difference between an observed and expected frequency in a given cell is first squared (to remove plus and minus signs) and then divided by the expected frequency for that cell. The 20 chi-square components in our example are arranged in the cells of Table 5.4. The larger the value, the greater the relative difference between observed and expected frequencies for that cell. The nine largest differences in Table 5.4 are underscored to highlight where the major deviations from the null hypothesis of independence occur. Both Tables 5.1 and 5.3 must be inspected to determine where the excesses and deficits occur, because the squaring masks the directions of these differences. The discrepancies are very small within both the high school and junior college columns, but the independence model greatly overestimates the observed frequencies in four cells (bachelor and graduate degree holders who strongly disagree and respondents without high school diplomas who agree and strongly agree). The independence model also

TABLE 5.4

Chi-Square Components for Crosstabulation of Sex Roles by
Degree

Man Achieves Outside Home, Woman Takes Care of Home and Family	Highest Education				
	Less than High School	High School	Junior College	Bachelor Degree	Graduate Degree
Strongly Agree	6.05	0.18	0.14	3.19	0.84
Agree	18.71	0.20	0.27	4.88	8.65
Disagree	7.41	0.62	0.06	1.17	0.64
Strongly Disagree	12.63	0.09	0.01	6.96	12.46

greatly underestimates the observed frequencies in five cells
(bachelors who strongly agree and agree, graduates who agree,
and respondents without high school diplomas who disagree and
strongly disagree). In other words, the independence hypotheses
fails to capture the tendency for the least-educated to endorse the
sex-role item and for graduates and bachelors to reject it.

The sum of the 20 components in Table 5.4 is 85.16. Thus, we say
that $\chi^2 = 85.16$ for the independence (null) hypothesis in this
crosstabulation. To understand the meaning of this number in
making a decision about whether or not to reject the null hypothesis, we must compare it to the critical value for the chi-square under
the null hypothesis. The chi-square test statistic for a large N follows
a chi-square distribution for a specific degrees of freedom, as
discussed in section 3.11. For a bivariate crosstabulation the
degrees of freedom depend on the number of rows and columns.
For a table with R rows, if we know the total in a given column and
the frequencies within $R - 1$ cells of that column, then the
frequency in the Rth row of that column is determined by subtraction. Hence, each column has only $R - 1$ degrees of freedom.
Similarly, within a given row, there are only $C - 1$ degrees of
freedom because the row marginals are fixed. For *every* bivariate
crosstab, the total degrees of freedom equals the product of the
number of rows less 1, times the number of columns less 1.

$$df = (R - 1)(C - 1)$$

Table 5.1 has $(4 - 1)(5 - 1) = 12$ *df*. Thus, the sampling distribution appropriate to evaluating the chi-square of 85.16 obtained for Table 5.4 is the χ^2 sampling distribution with 12 degrees of freedom. Using the tabled values of chi-square distributions in Appendix B, we find that the critical value for rejecting H_0 at $\alpha = .001$ is 32.909 for $df = 12$. Clearly, the covariation in Table 5.1 is very unlikely to be observed in a population in which the sex-role attitude and education variables are unrelated. We therefore reject the null hypothesis of independence with only a very small probability of making a Type I error and conclude that not only are attitude and degree related in the 1991 GSS sample, but this relationship is statistically significant; that is, these two variables are very probably related in the population as well.

One reason why the χ^2 test statistic was so large is that chi-square values are directly proportional to the sample size. For example, tripling every cell frequency in a crosstab will triple the calculated value of the chi-square but leave its *df* unchanged. This sensitivity of χ^2 to sample size in a crosstab underscores the important difference between statistical significance and substantive importance. A large sample size provides a good basis for drawing an inference about the population from which the sample came. But, the magnitude of the population relationship might not have much substantive importance, in the sense of exhibiting little covariation. Thus, although a large sample *N* allows us more easily to reject the null hypothesis, that decision fails to give us much information about the strength, or magnitude, of the population relationship. Statistical significance is only the first part of an answer to the question, "How are two social variables related?" If a statistical significance test reveals that the variables are probably related in the population, we can then turn to the second part of the answer, which requires us to find out how strongly the variables are related. The next section discusses suitable measures of the magnitude of association.

5.3   Measuring Association: Q, Phi, Gamma, Tau-*c*, Somers's d_{yx}

This section examines four **measures of association,** statistics that describe the strength of the covariation between pairs of discrete variables. All good measures of association use a *proportionate reduction in error* (*PRE*) approach. The PRE family of statistics is based on comparing the errors made in predicting the dependent

measures of association
—statistics that show the direction and/or magnitude of a relationship between pairs of discrete variables

variable with knowledge of the independent variable, to the errors made without information about the independent variable. Thus, every PRE statistic reflects how well knowledge of one variable improves prediction of the second variable. The general formula for any PRE statistic is given in terms of decision rules about expected values of one variable, Y, conditioned on the values of a second variable, X. A general PRE formula involves the ratio between two decision rules:

$$\text{PRE statistic} = \frac{\begin{array}{c}\text{Error without} \\ \text{decision rule}\end{array} - \begin{array}{c}\text{Error with} \\ \text{decision rule}\end{array}}{\text{Error without decision rule}}$$

When variables Y and X are unrelated, we are unable to use any of our knowledge about the first variable to reduce errors when we try to estimate values of the second variable. Thus, the PRE statistic's value is zero. In the opposite case when a perfect prediction from one variable to the other is possible, we make no errors, and the PRE statistic takes its maximum value of 1.00. Intermediate values of the PRE measure show that we have greater or lesser degrees of predictability.

2 × 2 table— a crosstabulation of a pair of dichotomies

To illustrate measures of association, we use a **2 × 2 table** (read "two by two"), crosstabulating a pair of dichotomies. Table 5.5 displays both the frequency and percentage crosstabs for two nonorderable dichotomies—smoking by gender—among 1,016 GSS respondents. Men are almost 9% more likely than women to say that they smoke.

The first four italic letters designate for the four cells of a 2 × 2 table, as follows:

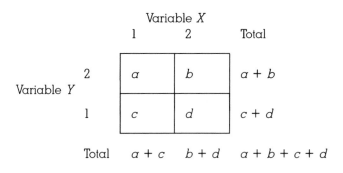

TABLE 5.5

Frequency and Percentage Crosstabulations of Smoking by Gender

| | Gender | | |
Smoking	Male	Female	Total
Frequency Crosstabulation:			
Yes	152	167	319
No	266	431	697
Total	418	598	1,016
Percentage Crosstabulation:			
Yes	36.4	27.9	31.4
No	63.6	72.1	68.6
Total	100.0%	100.0%	100.0%
(N)	(418)	(598)	(1,016)

Missing Data: 501 cases
Source: 1991 General Social Survey

By definition the categories of nonorderable dichotomies have no intrinsic sequence, so their sequence in a tabular display is arbitrary. We chose to arrange Table 5.5 with the "male" heading the left column and "female" in the right column, thus treating women as the higher gender. Hence, measures of association calculated on these data must be interpreted consistently with this arbitrary category sequence. Had we instead organized the table so that "male" appeared in the right column, then any measure of association would have the reverse interpretation.

Using conventional cell notation, an approximate formula for χ^2 in a 2 × 2 table is as follows:

$$\chi^2 = \frac{N(bc - ad)^2}{(a + b)(a + c)(b + d)(c + d)}$$

A 2 × 2 table has only 1 degree of freedom, because $(R - 1)(C - 1) = (2 - 1)(2 - 1) = 1$. Cells b and c are called the *main diagonal* cells, while a and d are the *off-diagonal* cells. Thus, the numerator of χ^2 involves the *cross-product differences* between the main and off-diagonal cells. These values reappear below in the formulas for several measures of association. For the smoking-gender crosstab in Table 5.5,

$$\chi^2 = \frac{1016((167)(266) - (152)(431))^2}{(319)(418)(598)(697)} = 8.13$$

Because the critical value for χ^2 at $\alpha = .01$ with $df = 1$ is 6.63, the calculated value of χ^2 is significant at $p < .01$. We reject the null hypothesis that no gender difference in smoking exists in the population, with less than one chance in 100 of making a Type I error.

5.3.1.   Yule's Q

Yule's Q—a symmetric measure of association for 2 × 2 cross tabulations

Yule's Q is a measure of association that uses the cross-product difference of a 2 × 2 table, that is,

$$Q = \frac{bc - ad}{bc + ad}$$

Yule's Q ranges between -1.00 to $+1.00$, with $Q = 0.00$ indicating no relationship between the dichotomies. A positive value means that the two high categories are associated, as are the two low categories. A negative sign indicates an inverse relationship, meaning that the high category on one variable is associated with the low category on the other variable. For Table 5.5 where "female" and "yes" are considered the high categories, the value of Q is:

$$Q = \frac{(167)(266) - (152)(431)}{(167)(266) + (152)(431)} = \frac{-21,090}{109,934} = -0.19$$

Thus, the negative sign means that women are *less* likely than men to smoke, a direction that is evident in the percentage differences between the two gender columns.

Interpreting the magnitudes of Yule's Q is somewhat arbitrary. We suggest the following verbal labels be applied to the *absolute values* of Q that fall into these intervals:

.00 to .24 "virtually no relationship"

.25 to .49 "weak relationship"

.50 to .74 "moderate relationship"

.75 to 1.00 "strong relationship"

Thus, the Q of -0.19 really represents virtually no covariation between gender and smoking, despite the significant chi-square. This example underscores once again the difference between statistical significance and substantive importance. The large N (1,016 cases) gives a substantial boost to the value of the chi-square (recall that χ^2 is proportional to sample size). However, the magnitude of the smoking-gender relationship is so small that we might as well consider it to be nonexistent.

Yule's Q gives misleading information when one of the four cells has a zero frequency. In such cases Q is either -1.00 or $+1.00$ (convince yourself of this by computing a simple example). Yet less than a "perfect" relationship may exist between the two dichotomies. By *perfect,* we mean that all cases fall either only into the two main diagonal cells or only into the two off-diagonal cells. The cells of a 2 × 2 table should always be examined for the presence of zero frequencies. If a zero cell is present, then some alternative measure of association should be chosen.

5.3.2. Phi

Phi (φ) also measures association in a 2 × 2 table. As with Yule's Q, phi ranges between -1.00 and $+1.00$, with 0.00 indicating no relationship. Phi's value is sensitive to the row and column marginals of the table, as shown by the denominator of its formula:

$$\phi = \frac{bc - ad}{\sqrt{(a + b)(c + d)(a + c)(b + d)}}$$

For any 2 × 2 table with a given set of row and column totals, phi can attain a maximum or minimum value that may be considerably short of the hypothetical range between -1.00 and $+1.00$. Some researchers prefer to adjust phi to remove this limitation. The value of **phi adjusted (ϕ_{adj})** involves dividing the observed value of phi by the maximum absolute value, **phi maximum (ϕ_{max}):**

phi— a symmetric measure of association for 2 × 2 crosstabulations

phi adjusted— a symmetric measure of association for a 2 × 2 crosstabulation in which phi is divided by phi maximum to take into account the largest covariation possible, given the marginals

phi maximum— the largest value that phi can attain for a given 2 × 2 crosstabulation; used in adjusting phi for its marginals.

$$\phi_{adj} = \frac{\phi}{|\phi_{max}|}$$

The parallel bars around phi maximum indicate absolute value.

To calculate ϕ_{max} for a given set of 2 × 2 table marginals, you first must find the proportions in the row and column marginals. That is, divide the four row and column totals by the sample N. Next, identify the row and the column with the smallest proportions (if one or both marginal proportions exactly equal 0.50, either may be chosen). Compare these two proportions, calling the smaller of the two p_j and the larger of the two p_i (this step finds the proportion of cases having the rarest occurrence, sometimes called "item difficulty" in attitude research). Then estimate ϕ_{max} for the table as:

$$\phi_{max} = \frac{\sqrt{p_j - p_j p_i}}{\sqrt{p_i - p_i p_j}}$$

Table 5.6 illustrates this procedure for the smoking and gender crosstab. The value of phi calculated from the observed frequencies in the top panel is −0.192. The proportions in the bottom panel show that the smallest row marginal is 0.314 (for smokers) and the smallest column marginal is 0.411 (for men). Hence, $p_j = 0.314$ and $p_i = 0.411$. The estimated value of $\phi_{max} = (\sqrt{.314} - (.314)(.411))/(\sqrt{.411} - (.411)(.314)) = 0.810$. Finally, the adjusted value is $\phi_{adj} = (-0.192)/|.810| = -0.237$. This adjustment indicates a slightly stronger inverse relationship than suggested in the observed data, although not quite high enough to consider smoking and gender to be even weakly related. Although ϕ_{adj} is sometimes reported in analyses of a 2 × 2 table, we recommend reporting both the actual and the adjusted values. However, ϕ_{adj} is preferable to reporting only the actual values of ϕ.

5.3.3.   Gamma

gamma—a symmetric measure of association suitable not only to crosstabs of two dichotomies, but also to tables whose variables are both ordered discrete measures with more than two categories

The **gamma (G)** measure of association is suitable not only to crosstabs of two dichotomies, but also to tables whose variables are both ordered discrete measures with more than two categories. Gamma is a *symmetric* PRE measure of association; that is, the same gamma value is obtained whether the first variable predicts

TABLE 5.6

Calculation of Phi Adjusted for the Smoking by Gender
Crosstabulation

Smoking	Gender		Total
	Male	*Female*	*Total*
Observed Values:			
Yes	152	167	319
No	266	431	697
Total	418	598	1,016
	$\phi = -0.192$		
Proportions:			
Yes	.149	.164	.314*
No	.262	.424	.686
Total	.411	.589*	1.000
	$\phi_{max} = 0.810$	$\phi_{adj} = -0.237$	

* Proportions do not total due to rounding.
Source: Table 5.5

the second variable or vice versa. Gamma ranges between -1.00 and $+1.00$, with zero indicating no relationship. Unlike ϕ, it is a "margin-free" measure of association, meaning that its value does not depend on the row or column marginals.

The crosstab in Table 5.7 shows a 3 × 3 joint frequency distribution of two ordered variables. GSS respondents were presented with a list of nine national institutions and asked, "As far as the people running these institutions are concerned, would you say you have a great deal of confidence, only some confidence, or hardly any confidence at all?" Among those institutions were "major companies" and "organized labor." If respondents' support for one institution were unrelated to their support for the other, the percentage distributions within columns would be identical (save for sampling error). As the bottom panel in Table 5.7 shows, persons with great confidence in organized labor tend to have higher confidence in major companies (59.7%), while those with some or hardly any confidence in labor are likely to have only some confidence in business (53.0% and 55.0%, respectively). This modest positive covariation in the sample is sufficient to reject the null

TABLE 5.7

Frequency and Percentage Crosstabulations of Confidence in Business by Confidence in Labor

| Confidence in Major Companies | Confidence in Organized Labor | | | |
	Hardly Any	Only Some	A Great Deal	Total
Frequency Crosstabulation:				
A Great Deal	52	140	163	355
Only Some	131	219	53	403
Hardly Any	55	54	57	166
Total	238	413	273	924
Percentage Crosstabulation:				
A Great Deal	21.8	33.9	59.7	38.4
Only Some	55.0	53.0	19.4	43.6
Hardly Any	23.1	13.1	20.9	18.0
Total	99.9%*	100.0%	100.0%	100.0%
(N)	(273)	(413)	(238)	(924)

Missing Data: 593 cases
* Does not total to 100.0% due to rounding.
Source: 1991 General Social Survey

hypothesis that the two measures are unrelated in the population ($\chi^2 = 113.9$, $df = 4$, $p < .001$). However, the relationship is far from one of perfect predictability, since some respondents with great confidence in one institution have hardly any confidence in the other.

Gamma measures the strength of association between pairs of ordered variables such as those displayed in Table 5.7. Its calculation requires systematically evaluating *all* pairs of observations in a crosstabulation, counting the total number that are untied concordant pairs and the total number that are untied discordant pairs. In a **concordant pair,** one observation has a higher rank on both variables than does the other member of the pair. For example, a person who has great confidence in both business and labor has higher rank than someone with hardly any confidence in both institutions. In a **discordant pair,** one member of a pair of observations ranks higher than the other member on one variable, but ranks lower on the second variable. For example, compare one

concordant pair—in a crosstabulation of two orderable discrete variables, one observation has a higher rank on both variables than does the other member of the pair

discordant pair—in a crosstabulation of two orderable discrete variables, one member of a pair of observations ranks higher than the other member on one variable, but ranks lower on the second variable

respondent with great confidence in labor and hardly any in confidence in business to a second person who has some confidence in both institutions. In this pair the first respondent ranks higher in labor confidence than the second person, but ranks lower in business confidence.

To obtain the total number of concordant pairs (n_s) in a crosstab, we must systematically count pairs of observations having consistent rank orderings in the table. The observations in a given cell form concordant pairs with the sum of cases in all the cells in rows below and to the left. For example, in Table 5.7 the 163 observations in the *upper-right* cell (top row and right column) form concordant pairs with the 459 (= 131 + 219 + 55 + 54) respondents in the four cells below and to its left. That is, (163)(459) = 74,817 concordant pairs involve the upper-right cell. Still within the top row, proceed to the 140 observations in the middle column. These cases rank consistently higher on both variables than the 186 cases (= 131 + 55) in the two cells below and to the left. Thus, another (140)(186) = 26,040 concordant pairs are added to the cumulative total. Within the second row of the table, the 53 observations in the right column have higher ranks than the 109 (= 54 + 55) cases below and to its right, for (53)(109) = 5,777 concordant pairs. Finally, in the second row, middle column, 219 cases ranking higher than 55 below and to the right contribute (219)(55) = 12,045. Summing, Table 5.7 contains 74,817 + 26,040 + 5,777 + 12,045 = 118,679 concordant pairs.

To calculate the total number of untied discordant pairs (n_d), proceed across the crosstab in the opposite direction: Observations in a given cell form discordant pairs with the sum of cases in all cells in rows below and to the right. In Table 5.7 the 52 observations in the *upper-left* cell have higher rank on the row variable (confidence in major companies) but lower rank on the column variable (confidence in organized labor) compared to the 383 cases (= 219 + 53 + 54 + 57) in the four cells below and to its right. Thus, (52)(383) = 19,916 discordant pairs involve the upper-left cell. Still within the top row, the 140 cases in the middle column form discordant pairs with the 110 (= 53 + 57) observations in the two cells below and to the right, for an additional (140)(110) = 15,400 discordant pairs. Switching to the second row, we find (131)(111) = 14,541 and (219)(57) = 12,483 discordant pairs. Thus, Table 5.7 contains 62,340 discordant pairs.

The formula for gamma uses the total number of untied pairs of both types:

$$G = \frac{n_s - n_d}{n_s + n_d}$$

The formula clearly shows gamma's PRE character. If we randomly draw any pair of observations from a crosstab and try to predict whether they have consistent ranks or inconsistent ranks, the chances of a correct prediction depend on the numbers of concordant and discordant pairs in the table. When $n_s = n_d$, prediction is no better than chance and gamma equals zero. But if n_s is far larger than n_d, gamma will be positive, and we will be more successful in predicting that the respondent with the higher value on one variable will also have the higher value on the second variable, compared to the second member of the pair. Note especially that when $n_d = 0$ (i.e., there are no discordant pairs), $G = 1.00$. Prediction error is also reduced when n_d is substantially larger than n_s. In this case gamma is negative, meaning that we predict that when one member of a pair ranks higher than the other member on one variable, then reverse rank order occurs for that pair on the other variable. The maximum negative value, $G = -1.00$, occurs whenever $n_s = 0$ (i.e., there are no concordant pairs).

Applying the formula for gamma to the data in Table 5.7, the association between confidence in major companies and in organized labor is as follows:

$$G = \frac{118{,}679 - 62{,}340}{118{,}679 + 62{,}340} = \frac{56{,}339}{181{,}019} = +0.31$$

Given that gamma's maximum positive value is $+1.00$, this value suggests only a weak positive association between the two confidence measures.

The population parameter that G estimates is labeled γ (Greek lowercase gamma). If we have a simple random sample of cases, the sampling distribution of G approaches normality as N becomes large (50 or more). The test statistic is approximated by

$$Z = (G - \gamma) \sqrt{\frac{n_s + n_d}{N(1 - G^2)}}$$

where

γ = The population value of gamma under the null hypothesis.

Since the formula gives a rather conservative estimate of Z, there may be circumstances where the absolute value of Z is in fact larger than that computed this way. The exact calculations are given elsewhere.[1]

In this example the null and alternative hypotheses are H_0: $\gamma = 0$ and H_1: $\gamma > 0$. To test the null hypothesis we choose $\alpha = .01$. Appendix C shows that the critical value is $Z = +2.33$. Now, using the sample value of G calculated above, the standard score (that is, the test statistic) is:

$$Z = (0.31 - 0) \sqrt{\frac{118,679 + 62,340}{924 (1 - 0.31^2)}}$$

$$= 4.56$$

Since 4.56 exceeds $+2.33$, we reject the null hypothesis and instead conclude that confidence in major companies and confidence in organized labor have a weak positive association.

When the formula for G is applied to a 2 × 2 table, its value is identical to Yule's Q, showing that Yule's Q is a special case of the more general gamma measure of association.

5.3.4. Tau *c*

Although it is not a PRE-type measure of association, **tau *c* (τ_c)** uses information about the number of concordant and discordant untied pairs in a crosstab of two discrete ordered variables. It also counts the number of **tied pairs** of observations in the table. A tied pair is one in which both cases have the same value on at least one of the

tau *c*— a non–PRE-type measure of association that uses information about the number of concordant and discordant untied pairs in a crosstab of two discrete ordered variables

tied pair— a pair in which both cases have the same value on at least one of the variables

---

1. See H. T. Reynolds, *The Analysis of Cross-Classification* (New York: Free Press, 1977), pp. 85–88.

two variables. For example, if one case has hardly any confidence in labor and some confidence in business while the second case has some confidence in both institutions, they form a tied pair. The number of rows and columns in a table do not have to be same (i.e., a nonsquare table can be analyzed). Tau c ranges in value from -1.00 to $+1.00$ and equals zero when the two variables are unrelated. The formula for tau c is as follows:

$$\tau_c = \frac{2m(n_s - n_d)}{N^2(m - 1)}$$

where

m = The smaller of R rows or C columns.

Unlike gamma, whose denominator counts only the number of concordant and discordant pairs, τ_c's denominator counts *all* pairs including the pairs of tied observations. Thus, tau c for a given table always has a smaller value than gamma. If many tied pairs occur in a crosstab, gamma's value will be much larger than tau c's value. Neither statistic is preferred to the other. Each simply conceptualizes the meaning of an association between two discrete ordered variables in different terms.

Applied to the square crosstab in Table 5.7, and based on the knowledge from computing G that $n_s = 118{,}679$ and $n_d = 62{,}340$, the positive association between confidence in major companies and organized labor again appears:

$$\tau_c = \frac{(2)(3)(118{,}679 - 62{,}340)}{(924)^2(3 - 1)} = \frac{338{,}034}{1{,}707{,}552} = +0.198$$

The standard error of the sampling distribution for tau c is very complex and will not be presented here. However, a quick and not-too-dirty estimate has been developed by Somers.[2]

---

2. Somers, R. (1980). Simple Approximations to Null Sampling Variances: Goodman and Kruskal's Gamma, Kendall's Tau, and Somers's d_{yx}. *Sociological Methods and Research, 9,* 115–126.

$$\hat{\sigma}_{\tau_c} = \sqrt{\frac{4(R + 1)(C + 1)}{9NRC}}$$

This formula can only be used as an approximation when there is simple random sampling, and the null hypothesis states that $\tau_c = 0$ in the population.

To test whether $\tau_c = 0.198$ differs significantly from zero, we choose $\alpha = .01$. The critical value is then $+2.33$ for a one-tailed test (see Appendix C). The test statistic is as follows:

$$Z = \frac{\tau_c}{\hat{\sigma}_{\tau_c}}$$

In this example the test statistic is calculated as follows:

$$Z = \frac{0.198}{\sqrt{\dfrac{4(3 + 1)(3 + 1)}{9(924)(3)(3)}}}$$

$$= \frac{0.198}{0.029}$$

$$= 6.83$$

Because this value is greater than $+2.33$, we reject the null hypothesis and again conclude that confidence in organizations and organized labor are weakly related in the population.

5.3.5.   Somers's d_{yx}

Somers's d_{yx} is an *asymmetric* PRE measure of association for discrete ordered variables that counts not only the number of concordant and discordant untied pairs, but also the number of tied pairs of a certain type. Unlike gamma and tau c, the value of Somers's d_{yx} depends on which variable is considered independent and which dependent. In trying to predict variable Y from knowledge of variable X, we take into account only the pairs of observations that are tied on variable Y, the dependent variable.

Somers's d_{yx}— an asymmetric PRE measure of association for discrete ordered variables that counts not only the number of concordant and discordant untied pairs, but also the number of tied pairs of a certain type

But, we ignore any pairs on which both observations are tied on the independent variable, X. Somers's d_{yx} for predicting variable Y from variable X (assuming that Y is the row variable and X is the column variable) is given by the formula:

$$d_{yx} = \frac{n_s - n_d}{n_s + n_d + T_r}$$

where

T_r = The number of ties associated with the row variable.

To count the number of ties associated with the row variable in Table 5.7, simply begin at the upper-left cell, that is, where the first row and first column join. Multiply the frequency of cases (52) in that cell by the sum of the cases in the cells to the right within that row (140 + 163 = 303). This product is (52)(303) = 15,756. Next, move to the cell to the right in that row and multiply its frequency by the total observations in cells to the right (i.e., (140)(163) = 22,820). Because no observations are found to the right of the final column in the first row (the row marginals are ignored), the process continues by moving to the next row. Again, multiply a given cell's frequency by the sum of frequencies in cells to the right within that row. For the second row in Table 5.7, these products are (131)(272) = 35,632 and (219)(53) = 11,607. For the third row, the two products are (55)(111) = 6,105 and (54)(57) = 3,078. The sum of all these terms forms T_r = 15,756 + 22,820 + 35,632 + 11,607 + 6,105 + 3,078 = 94,998, which is entered into the denominator of Somers's d_{yx}:

$$d_{yx} = \frac{118{,}679 - 62{,}340}{118{,}679 + 62{,}340 + 94{,}998} = \frac{56{,}339}{276{,}017} = +0.204$$

The presence of numerous tied pairs means the value of Somers's d_{yx} will be much smaller than the value of gamma for the same crosstab. (It is only a coincidence that d_{yx} nearly equals τ_c in this example.)

Somers presents an approximation to the standard error of the sampling distribution that can be used to test for the significance of $\hat{d}_{yx}$.[3]

---

3. Somers, "Simple Approximations to Null Sampling Variances."

$$\hat{\sigma}_{d_{yx}} = \frac{2}{3R} \sqrt{\frac{(R^2 - 1)(C + 1)}{N(C - 1)}}$$

Then the test statistic for $\hat{d}_{yx}$ is

$$Z = \frac{\hat{d}_{yx}}{\hat{\sigma}_{d_{yx}}}$$

If we again choose $\alpha = .01$, Appendix C reveals that the critical value is +2.33 for a one-tailed test. We compute:

$$Z = \frac{0.204}{\frac{2}{(3)(3)} \sqrt{\frac{(3^2 - 1)(3 + 1)}{924(3 - 1)}}}$$

$$= 6.98$$

Since 6.98 is larger than +2.33, we must reject the null hypothesis that confidence in major companies and confidence in organized labor are unrelated.

The asymmetric nature of Somers's d_{yx} means that two different values are likely to be found in any table larger than 2 × 2. For d_{xy} the T_r is replaced in the denominator by T_c, the number of ties associated with the column variable. A procedure identical to that described above is used to calculate T_c. Verify that Somers's d_{xy} for Table 5.7 is +0.21, treating confidence in labor at the dependent variable. Although the two statistics have very similar values in this example, you should always clearly state the dependent variable when reporting this measure of association, since they will not always have similar magnitudes.

As the reader has most certainly discerned, the calculation of concordant and discordant pairs can be quite tedious, especially in larger tables. Although a more general algorithm for the computations could be presented, computers carry out such calculations with great ease, allowing the analyst to concentrate on other tasks.

5.4   Odds and Odds Ratios

odds—the frequency of being in one category relative to the frequency of not being in that category

In current statistical practice the most important measure of association for crosstabulations is the odds ratio, which is the foundation for the techniques presented in Chapter 10. Games of chance have familiarized most people with the concept of odds. An **odds** is the frequency of being in one category relative to the frequency of not being in that category. For example, in poker the odds that the first card dealt is the queen of hearts is 1/51 (pronounced "one to fifty-one"). This odds expressed as a decimal is .01961. Contrast an odds with a probability, which is the ratio between a category of interest to all categories. The probability of drawing the queen of hearts is 1/52 (pronounced "one fifty-second"). This ratio expressed as a decimal is .01923, a lower value than the equivalent odds. The contrast between odds and probability is even sharper when relatively larger proportions of cases per category are involved. For example, in poker the odds that a first card dealt is a club is 13/39 (which reduces to 1/3), whereas the probability of a club is 13/52 (which reduces to 1/4). Expressed as decimals, the odds (0.333) is much higher value than the probability (0.250). Another important difference in these descriptive statistics are their ranges. Probabilities are constrained within the range between 0.00 (i.e., a zero chance of occurrence) and 1.00 (i.e., certainty of occurrence). But, because an odds is the ratio between occurrence and nonoccurrence, it ranges between zero to positive infinity. That is, whenever the chance of a category occurring is greater than the chance it will not occur, its odds exceeds 1.00. For example, the odds that the queen of hearts will *not* be drawn is 51/1, or 51.00 as a decimal. Note that when an outcome is as likely to occur as not to occur, its odds reduce to 1/1 or 1.00 as a decimal. But, in probability terms, equally likely outcomes have a probability of 0.50.

A probability is easily translated to an odds by dividing the proportion corresponding to a category of interest (p_i) by the proportion obtained after subtracting it from 1.00:

$$\text{odds}_i = \frac{p_i}{1 - p_i}$$

The odds for empirical events can easily be computed from the numbers and percentages reported in various media. For example, among Americans ages 20–24 who die, cancer is the principal cause of death for 4.5%. Therefore, the odds of a person in that age group dying from cancer is 4.5/95.5 = 0.047 or slightly less than one to twenty. In comparison, in 1980 Americans drove their motor vehicles a total of about 1,476,200,000,000 miles resulting in 39,126 passenger fatalities. Thus, the odds that a mile of driving produced a fatality is 39,126/1,476,200,000,000 or 1 to 37,729,387 = 0.000000265.

The concept of a simple odds can be extended to the **conditional odds** within the cells of a crosstabulation, analogous to the percentages discussed earlier in section 5.1. A conditional odds is the chance of being in one category of a variable relative to the remaining categories of that variable, within a specific category of a second variable. Thus, separate conditional odds may be calculated for the different categories of the second measure. Consider again the 2 × 2 crosstab of gender and smoking in Table 5.5. In the total column at the right the simple odds of smoking is the ratio of that row's total (319 observations) to total in the second row (697). Thus, the odds that a respondent smokes is 319/697 = 0.46. However, this simple odds is not the same as the conditional odds found within columns for the second variable, gender. Among women, the conditional odds of smoking is only 167/431 = 0.39, while men yield a higher conditional odds of 152/266 = 0.57. In other words, the respondents' gender *conditions* their smoking behavior. The more information we have about a person's gender, the more accurately we can predict that person's chances of being a smoker.

conditional odds—the chance of being in one category of a variable relative to the remaining categories of that variable, within a specific category of a second variable

When variables in a crosstab are related (as shown by both a chi-square significance test and a descriptive measure of association), their conditional odds are not equal. To compare directly two conditional odds, a single descriptive statistic called the **odds ratio** (OR) can be formed by dividing one conditional odds by another. In terms of the standard symbols designating the cell frequencies of a 2 × 2 table, the formula for the odds ratio of variables X and Y is as follows:

odds ratio (cross-product ratio)—the ratio formed by dividing one conditional odds by another conditional odds

$$OR^{XY} = \frac{b/d}{a/c} = \frac{bc}{ad}$$

Note that the simplified OR formula on the right multiplies the main diagonal cell frequencies and divides this product by the product of the off-diagonal cell frequencies. The odds ratio is thus sometimes called the **cross-product ratio.** The odds ratio for smoking (S) by gender (G) in Table 5.5 is $OR^{SG} = (167)(266)/(152)(431) = 0.68$, which indicates that the odds of smoking for women is only about two-thirds the odds of smoking for men. If the gender columns had been switched while the row order remained the same, we appear to find a different OR^{SG}: $(152)(431)/(167)(266) = 1.47$. But, this apparent inconsistency is resolved by recognizing that our substantive interpretation of the relationship between the two variables must also be reversed: men are 1.47 times more likely than women to smoke. If either of these ORs is inverted, the other value is revealed: $1/1.47 = .68$ and $1/.68 = 1.47$. Thus, each combination of four cells yields odds ratios having a consistent interpretation, as long as we keep track of the reference categories.

If two variables are unrelated, their conditional odds are identical and, therefore, the OR = 1.00. Odds ratios greater than 1.00 indicate a positive covariation of the variables (i.e., a tendency for the "high" categories of both variables to be associated), while ORs lower than 1.00 indicate a negative or inverse covariation (i.e., a tendency for the "high" category of one variable to be associated with the "low" category of the other variable). Because an odds is undefined when its denominator is zero, an OR cannot be calculated whenever a zero cell occurs. This problem exists as well with Yule's Q for 2×2 tables. Note that Yule's Q is a simple function of the odds ratio:

$$Q = \frac{\text{odds ratio} - 1}{\text{odds ratio} + 1} = \frac{bc/ad - 1}{bc/ad + 1} = \frac{bc - ad}{bc + ad}$$

In other words, Q is simply an OR that has been "normed" to be symmetrical with a range constrained between -1.00 and $+1.00$. Note that when OR = 1 (no relationship), $Q = 0.00$ (also no relationship).

Odds ratios can also be computed for large crosstabulations. The requirements are four cells identified by two columns and two rows. Table 5.8 is a 2×7 crosstab of 1988 presidential vote (P) by political views (V). This relationship is highly significant as indicated by $\chi^2 = 103.8$ for $df = 6$, $p < .001$ (gamma $= +0.47$, tau $c = +0.36$, and Somers's $d_{yx} = +0.34$ with vote as the dependent variable). Many OR^{PV}s can be calculated with the frequencies in this crosstab. For example, the OR of having voted for Bush versus Dukakis among extreme conservatives relative to

TABLE 5.8

Frequency and Percentage Crosstabulations of 1988 Presidential Vote by Political Views

Presidential Vote in 1988	Political Views							
	Extremely Liberal	Liberal	Slightly Liberal	Moderate	Slightly Conservative	Conservative	Extremely Conservative	Total
Frequency Crosstabulation:								
Voted for Bush	5	29	51	221	112	110	28	551
Voted for Dukakis	13	63	83	136	43	28	5	371
Total	18	92	134	357	155	138	33	922
Percentage Crosstabulation:								
Voted for Bush	27.8	31.5	38.1	61.9	72.3	79.7	82.1	59.8
Voted for Dukakis	72.2	68.5	61.9	38.1	27.7	20.3	17.9	40.2
Total	100.0	100.0	100.0	100.0	100.0	100.0	100.0	100.0
(N)	(18)	(92)	(134)	(357)	(155)	(138)	(33)	(922)

Missing Data: 595 cases

Source: 1991 General Social Survey

conservatives is $(28)(28)/(110)(5) = 1.43$. Similarly, the OR of having voted for Bush among conservatives versus slight conservatives is $(110)(43)/(28)(112) = 1.51$, not much different. In this table, 21 such odds ratios can be computed involving pairs of categories of the independent variable (political views). Obviously, all of these relations are not independent. Indeed, given that only six degrees of freedom are available in this table, we can have only six unique odds ratios. Once these six ORs have been determined, the remaining ORs are constrained to particular values. In chapter 10 you will learn about log-linear models, methods based on the odds ratio measure of association, that permit very elaborate hypotheses about relationships among tabulated variables to be tested for statistical significance.

Review of Key Concepts and Symbols

These key concepts and symbols are listed in the order of appearance in this chapter. Combined with the definitions in the margins, they will help you to review the material and can serve as a self-test for mastery of the concepts.

bivariate crosstabulation (joint contingency table)	f_{ij}
	PRE
cell	Q
marginal distributions	ϕ
row marginals	ϕ_{adj}
column marginals	ϕ_{max}
chi-square test	G
statistically independent	γ
expected frequency	n_s
measures of association	n_d
2 × 2 table	τ_c
Yule's Q	m
phi	$\hat{\sigma}_{\tau_c}$
phi adjusted	d_{yx}
phi maximum	T_r
gamma	$\hat{\sigma}_{d_{yx}}$
concordant pair	OR^{XY}
discordant pair	
tau c	
tied pair	
Somers's d_{yx}	
odds	
conditional odds	
odds ratio (cross-product ratio)	

PROBLEMS

General Problems

1. In several presidential elections researchers have observed a "gender gap" in which men and women vote for candidates in different proportions. Test this hypothesis by calculating χ^2 and Yule's Q for these frequencies from the 1991 General Social Survey:

Vote by Gender		
	Gender	
Did you vote for Dukakis or Bush?	Women	Men
Bush	288	269
Dukakis	242	139

Missing data = 579
Source: 1991 General Social Survey

2. Do men and women differ in their expectations that the United States will go to war in the future? Here is a crosstabulation from the 1991 GSS. Calculate χ^2 and Yule's Q to determine how strongly gender is related to war expectations.

War Expectations by Gender		
	Gender	
Do you expect the U.S. to fight in another war in the next 10 years?	Women	Men
Yes	307	158
No	257	248

Missing data = 547
Source: 1991 General Social Survey

3. Who are more likely to abstain from drinking alcoholic beverages—the more educated or the less educated? Using this crosstabulation from the 1991 GSS, calculate χ^2, ϕ, ϕ_{adj}, and ϕ_{max}.

	Drinking by Education	
	Education	
Do you ever have occasion to use any alcoholic beverages such as liquor, wine, or beer, or are you a total abstainer?	Less than College	Some College
Yes	320	379
No	206	107

Missing data = 505
Source: 1991 General Social Survey

4. Is education related to internationalism? Shown are frequencies from the 1991 GSS showing how respondents at three levels of education answered a question about the U.S. role in world affairs. What are the conditional odds in favor of an active part for each level of education?

	Internationalism by Education		
	Education		
Do you think it is best for the future of this country if we take an active part in world affairs, or if we stay out of world affairs?	Less than High School Graduate	High School Graduate and Some College	College Graduate
Active Part	130	436	183
Stay Out	93	119	34

Missing data = 522
Source: 1991 General Social Survey

5. The 1991 GSS asked, "There are always some people whose ideas are considered bad or dangerous by other people. For instance, somebody who is against all churches and religion ... If such a person wanted to make a speech in your (city/town/community) against churches and religion, should he be allowed to speak, or not?" Among the male GSS respondents 339 said they would allow the speech and 87 would not allow it. Among the female respondents 374 would allow and 179 would not allow the speech. What are the conditional odds in favor of allowing an atheist to speak, and what is the odds ratio?

6. Now consider whether tolerance for civil liberties is a function of education. For this table from the 1991 GSS calculate the conditional odds in favor of allowing an atheist to speak in public for both levels of education, and the odds ratio for the table.

Atheist Speech by Education

If such a person wanted to make a speech . . . against churches and religion, should he be allowed to speak, or not?	Education	
	Less than College	**Some College**
Yes	310	400
No	204	62

Missing data = 541
Source: 1991 General Social Survey

7. Does exposure to television weaken or strengthen one's confidence in the press? Calculate chi-square, gamma, and tau *c* for this crosstabulation from the 1991 GSS.

Confidence in the Press by Television Viewing

As far as the people running the press, would you say you have . . .	Hours of TV Watching on an Average Day		
	0–1 Hour	**2–4 Hours**	**5 or More**
A Good Deal of Confidence	276	41	17
Only Some Confidence	196	174	47
Hardly Any Confidence	130	97	15

Missing data = 524
Source: 1991 General Social Survey

8. Does childbearing have any relationship to traditional sex role attitudes? Apply chi-square, gamma, and tau *c* to this table from the 1991 GSS.

Expected Children by Sex-Role Attitude

Do you expect to have any more children?	Women should take care of running their homes and leave running the country up to men.			
	Strongly Disagree	Disagree	Agree	Strongly Agree
Yes	66	110	33	7
No	127	360	225	23

Missing data = 566
Source: 1991 General Social Survey

9. How strongly related are traditional sex-role attitudes and sexual morality, according to χ^2 and Somers's d_{yx} applied to this table from the 1991, using premarital sexual relations as the dependent variable?

Premarital Sex by Sex-Role Attitude

If a man and a woman have sex relations before marriage, do you think it is . . .	Women should take care of running their homes and leave running the country up to men.			
	Strongly Disagree	Disagree	Agree	Strongly Agree
Always wrong	20	117	116	15
Almost always wrong	10	56	29	2
Sometimes wrong	42	91	45	3
Not wrong at all	127	223	63	12

Missing data = 546
Source: 1991 General Social Survey

10. Are more-educated people more tolerant of homosexuality? Apply χ^2 and Somers's d_{yx} to this table from the 1991 GSS, using homosexuality as the dependent variable.

Homosexuality Attitude by Education			
	Education		
What about sexual relations between two adults of the same sex— do you think it is . . .	**Less than High School Graduate**	**High School Graduate and Some College**	**College Graduate**
Always wrong	188	395	113
Almost always wrong	4	21	13
Sometimes wrong	4	21	16
Not wrong at all	17	73	58

Missing data = 522
Source: 1991 General Social Survey

Problems Requiring the 1991 General Social Survey

11. Which race—African-American or Caucasian—is more tolerant of allowing an atheist to speak in public? Crosstabulate SPKATH by RACE, after omitting "other" race, and compute chi-square and phi. What do you conclude?

12. Are less-educated people more or less likely than more-educated people to smoke? Find this relationship by crosstabulating SMOKE with EDUC recoded into three categories (0–11 years, 12–15 years, 16 or more years). Calculate chi-square, gamma, tau c, and Somers's d_{yx}. What do you conclude?

13. Does the three-category education measure in Problem 12 have the same pattern with DRINK? Calculate chi-square, gamma, tau c, and Somers's d_{yx}. What do you conclude?

Problems Requiring Use of the U.S. States Data Set

14. Dichotomize states per-capita income ranks (INCRANK) into a bottom third and an upper two-thirds, crosstabulate with female labor force participation rate (FEMLFP) dichotomized at the median. Calculate chi-square, gamma, tau c, and Somers's d_{yx}. What do you conclude? [Use RECODE INCRANK (LO THRU 17 = 1)(18 THRU HI = 2) and RECODE FEMLFP (LO THRU 58 = 1)(58 THRU HI = 2)]

15. Dichotomize percentage turnout for the 1988 U.S. representatives election (TURN88) at the median and crosstabulate with REGION dichotomized into South and non-South. Calculate chi-square, gamma, tau c, and Somers's d_{yx}. What do you conclude? [Use RECODE TURN88 (LO THRU 49 = 1)(49 THRU HI = 2) and RECODE REGION (5,6,7 = 1)(ELSE = 2)]

Statistics for Social Data Analysis

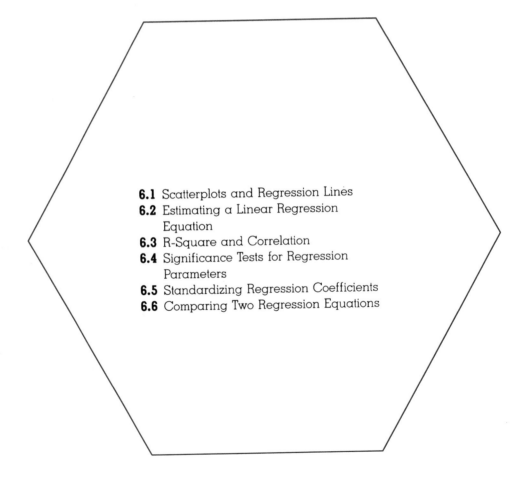

Bivariate Regression and Correlation

6

T he crosstabulations discussed in chapter 5 reveal the covariation between pairs of discrete variables in a sample of observations. This chapter examines relationships among pairs of continuous variables. The bivariate regression and correlation procedures assume that the *form* of the relationship between Y and X is *linear* and that the dependent variable is distributed normally at every level of the independent variable. But, even when data violate these assumptions, the methods may still be quite **robust;** that is, we will seldom be wrong when making a conclusion about statistically significant or insignificant results.

robust — methods used in which violating assumptions will seldom produce wrong conclusions

6.1 Scatterplots and Regression Lines

Displaying the relationship between pairs of continuous measures requires different graphic display techniques than previously described. The **scatterplot** is a useful method for visualizing how two continuous variables covary. To construct a scatterplot, begin with a set of Cartesian coordinates, such as you used in high school algebra. Values of the independent variable (X) are located on the horizontal axis, while the dependent variable (Y) values are situated on the vertical axis. Then the position of the ith observation is plotted as a data point on the graph at its X, Y coordinates. The scatter of all points reveals how the pair of variables covaries. Figure 6.1 graphs four idealized patterns of bivariate relationships.

scatterplot — a type of diagram that displays the covariation of two continuous variables as a set of points on a Cartesian coordinate system

FIGURE 6.1

Scatterplots of Four Idealized Bivariate Relationships

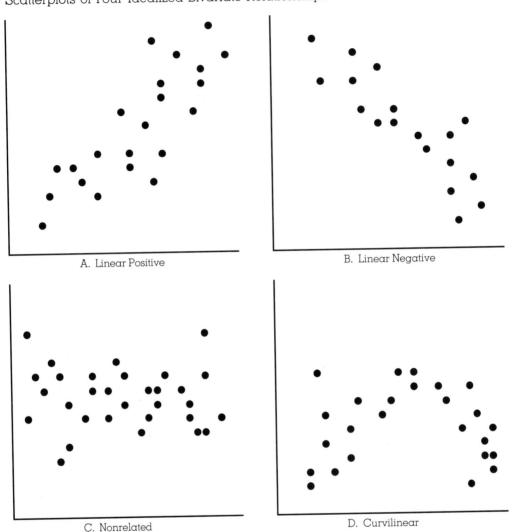

A. Linear Positive

B. Linear Negative

C. Nonrelated

D. Curvilinear

Suppose we hypothesize that personal income in the United States covaries with citizens' educational levels:

H1: The higher the percentage of a state's population with a college degree, the higher its per capita annual income.

Figure 6.2 plots the 51 states' per capita annual incomes (in 1985) against the percent with at least 16 years of education (in 1980). Positive covariation is evident in the scatter of points from the lower left to the upper right. Low values of one variable tend to be found with low values of the other, and high values of both tend to be associated. This figure provides visual evidence supporting our hypothesis.

Expressing an hypothesized relationship in statistical form requires a specific notation system to designate both variables and observations. Consistent with the scatterplot notation, a dependent variable in a regression analysis is designated Y, while the independent variable (sometimes called the **predictor variable**) is X. To indicate a specific individual observation—such as a person, city, or a state—a subscript represents the case number (from 1 to N, the sample size). In general, X_i stands for the score of the ith observation on variable X. By replacing the general subscript with a specific number, we indicate the score of a specific observation. In the state example X_{37} denotes the value of education for the 37th state on the alphabetic list (Oregon), which has a value of 17.9% college educated. Similarly, Y_{37} represents Oregon's annual per capita income, $9,925.

> **predictor variable**—independent variable in a regression analysis

Estimating the **linear relationship** between a dependent variable (Y) and an independent variable (X), we "regress Y on X," producing a **bivariate linear relationship,** or more simply, **bivariate regression.** The general form of a linear equation in algebraic form is written as

$$Y = a + bX$$

The ordinate, or Y value, equals the sum of a constant, a, (the point at which the line intercepts the Y-axis) plus the product of the slope, b, times the X value. The line's intercept with the Y-axis (a) shows the Y value when $X = 0$. The line's slope (b) shows the amount of change in Y units for a one-unit change in X.

> **linear relationship**—covariation in which the value of the dependent variable is proportional to the value of the independent variable
>
> **bivariate linear relationship (bivariate regression)**—a regression of Y on X

Social researchers typically assume that two variables are linearly related unless they have strong initial reasons to believe that a nonlinear form, such as an exponential or logarithmic function, is more accurate. A linear relationship is the most elementary form and hence a reasonable first approximation. Because *parsimony* (simplicity) is a major aim of all science, determining whether a linear function best describes the relation-

FIGURE 6.2

Scatterplot of State Per Capita Income in 1985 by Percentage with 16 or More Years of Education in 1980

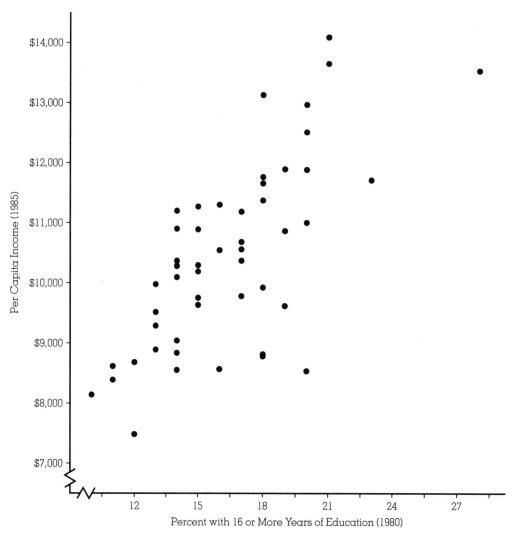

Source: U.S. States Data Set

ship between two variables makes sense as a first step. Only after a straight line is clearly found not to describe a relationship should more complex functional forms be examined. Chapter 9 discusses several nonlinear forms, including logistic regression.

If states' annual per capita incomes had a perfect linear relationship with college education levels, then all the data points would fall on a straight line, showing how each percent of educated populace leads to dollars of income. The scatterplot in Figure 6.2 obviously falls considerably short of such perfect linearity, but is not so far away as to be a completely random pattern. The figure does *not* suggest that a curvilinear function would better describe the data. Therefore, we proceed to techniques that measure how well a straight line approximates the covariation of two continuous variables.

We begin with a **prediction equation** in which the *i*th observation's value on the dependent variable is an exact linear function of its independent variable value:

$$\hat{Y}_i = a + b_{YX}X_i$$

The subscript of the *b* indicates the order of the regression, with the dependent variable followed by the independent variable. The "hat" ($\hat{\ }$) over the Y_i indicates it is a predicted (or "expected") value, which may or may not equal the observed value for that case (Y_i without a hat). But, actual social data never follow a perfect linear relationship, just as we saw in Figure 6.2. Consequently, we must take deviations from the linear prediction into account, through the **linear regression model:**

$$Y_i = a + b_{YX}X_i + e_i$$

The absence of the caret over the dependent variable means that it is the observed rather than the predicted score of *Y*. The **error term** (e_i) represents that portion of the *i*th observation's score on variable *Y* that is not predicted from its linear relation to *X*. Thus, e_i measures the discrepancy in making a prediction by using a linear regression equation. Across *N* observations, some prediction errors will be positive (>0), some will be negative (<0), and some may be exactly zero (i.e., when the predicted score exactly equals the observed

prediction equation—a regression equation without the error term, useful for predicting the score on the dependent variable from the independent variable(s)

linear regression model—a model that takes into account deviations from the linear prediction by showing the linear relationship between a continuous dependent variable and one or more independent variables, plus an error term

error term—the difference between an observed score and a score predicted by the model

score). Just as with deviations from the mean of a distribution, the sum of the errors (Σe_i) equals zero because the positive and negative values exactly cancel one another.

residual—the amount that remains after subtracting the prediction equation from the linear regression model

A regression error term is also called a **residual,** because it is the amount that remains after subtracting the prediction equation from the linear regression model:

$$Y_i - \hat{Y}_i = [a + b_{YX} X_i + e_i] - [a + b_{YX} X_i]$$
$$= e_i$$

A basic task of regression analysis is to estimate the values for the two regression coefficients based on the observed data. The estimates a and b_{YX} must minimize the residuals, that is, make the prediction errors using that equation smaller than the errors made with any other linear relationship.

regression line—a line that is the best fit to the points in a scatterplot, computed by ordinary least squares regression

A **regression line** can be superimposed on the scatterplot of data points. This line has the useful property that, for each value of X_i, a precise $\hat{Y}_i$ value is predicted on the assumption of that linear relationship. Then, the location of the data points can be compared to their values predicted by the regression line to determine how large are the errors for all observations. The next section presents a method for estimating the two parameters of the linear regression model from sample data, for fitting a regression line through the scatterplot, and for determining how closely the predicted scores are to the observed scores.

6.2 Estimating a Linear Regression Equation

6.2.1. The Least Squares Criterion

All N sample observations on two variables are used to estimate a bivariate regression equation. Estimators for the two coefficients (a and b_{YX}) comply with a minimum *least squares error sum* criterion. Because the sum of the residuals (Σe_i) is always zero, squaring removes the negative signs so that the sum of these squared errors is greater than zero. Consequently, summing of squared differences between each observed score (Y_i) and its score predicted by the regression equation $\hat{Y}_i$ produces a quantity smaller than that obtained by using any other straight line equation. That is,

$$\sum_{i=1}^{N}(Y_i - \hat{Y}_i)^2 = \sum_{i=1}^{N}e_i^2$$

is a minimum.

Estimators having this minimum error property produce **ordinary least squares (OLS)** estimates of a and b_{YX}. OLS regression procedures resemble the calculation of the arithmetic mean. Section 2.5.4 (page 53) showed that the mean has the desirable property of minimizing the sum of all the squared deviations for a set of scores. Similarly, the regression line minimizes the sum of squared prediction errors.

ordinary least squares — a method for obtaining estimates of regression equation coefficients that minimizes the error sum of squares

The OLS estimator of the **bivariate regression coefficient,** or regression slope (b_{YX}), from the observed X and Y scores is as follows:

bivariate regression coefficient — a parameter estimate of a bivariate regression equation that measures the amount of increase or decrease in the dependent variable for a one-unit difference in the independent variable

$$b_{YX} = \frac{\Sigma(Y_i - \overline{Y})(X_i - \overline{X})}{\Sigma(X_i - \overline{X})^2}$$

(Box 8.2 on page 286 shows how this OLS estimate is derived for multivariate regression equations.) The numerator in the formula is the sum of the product of the deviations of the X and Y variables around their means. When this term is divided by $N - 1$, it is called the **covariance,** labeled s_{YX}. That is,

covariance — the sum of the product of deviations of the Xs and Ys about their respective means, divided by $N - 1$ in the sample and N in the population

$$s_{YX} = \frac{\Sigma(Y_i - \overline{Y})(X_i - \overline{X})}{N - 1}$$

Its computing formula is:

$$s_{YX} = \frac{N\Sigma X_i Y_i - \Sigma X_i \Sigma Y_i}{N(N - 1)}$$

The denominator of the formula for b_{YX} is the sum of squared deviations around the mean of the independent variable, $\overline{X}$. As shown in chapter 3, dividing this term by $N - 1$ forms the sample *variance:*

$$s_X^2 = \frac{\sum_{i=1}^{N}(X_i - \overline{X})^2}{N - 1}$$

Because $N - 1$ appears in both the denominator of the covariance and the sample variance, that term cancels out of their ratio. Therefore, the OLS estimator of the bivariate regression coefficient can be estimated by the ratio

$$b_{YX} = \frac{s_{YX}}{s_X^2}$$

computing formula for b —easy-to-use formula for calculating the bivariate regression coefficient

Although the two formulas for b_{YX} given above are conceptually accurate, they are difficult to calculate without a computer. The following **computing formula for b,** which requires no deviations, gives identical numerical results and can be done with only a hand calculator:

$$b_{YX} = \frac{N\Sigma Y_i X_i - \Sigma Y_i \Sigma X_i}{N\Sigma X_i^2 - (\Sigma X_i)^2}$$

intercept—a constant value in a regression equation showing the point at which the regression line crosses the Y axis when values of X equal zero

The OLS estimator of the **intercept** (a) is simply:

$$a = \overline{Y} - b\overline{X}$$

This formula assures that the coordinate pair $(\overline{X}, \overline{Y})$ always falls on the regression line, regardless of the specific value of a and b. Hence, to calculate the intercept, the bivariate regression coefficient is computed first, then entered into the preceding formula along with the means of both variables.

conditional mean—the expected average score on the dependent variable, Y, for a given value of the independent variable, X

A linear regression equation estimates a **conditional mean** for Y, that is, one predicted value of the dependent variable $(\hat{Y}_i)$ for each specific value of the independent value (X_i). If no linear relationship exists between Y and X, then the slope b_{YX} equals zero. As shown in Figure 6.3, in such a situation the regression line parallels the X-axis at a distance exactly $\overline{Y}$-units from the origin (recall that all regression lines pass through the means of both variables). All predicted values equal a, because $\hat{Y}_i = a + 0X_i$ implies that $\hat{Y}_i = a$ and thus $\hat{Y}_i = \overline{Y}$. When the regression slope is zero, knowledge of a specific X_i value does not produce a predicted value of Y that differs from the mean of all observations. However,

FIGURE 6.3
The Regression Line When $b = 0$

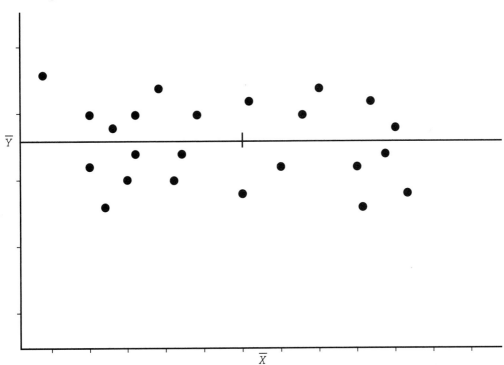

when Y and X are indeed linearly related, then the conditional mean of Y depends on the specific value of X_i. Furthermore, these conditional means fall precisely on the straight line determined by the regression slope and intercept.

6.2.2.   Linear Regression Applied to State Per Capita Incomes

To apply the OLS computing formulas for b_{YX} and a to the state example data, Table 6.1 displays the individual states' values and their sums. Other relevant statistics appear at the bottom the table. Given these values,

TABLE 6.1

Calculation of Means, Variances, Correlation Coefficients, and
Regression Coefficients for Per Capita Income (Y) and
Percentage with 16 or More Years of Education (X_1)

(1) State	(2) Y	(3) X	(4) X²	(5) YX	(6) Y²
Alabama	8,681	12.2	148.84	105,908.2	75,359,761
Alaska	13,650	21.1	445.21	288,015.0	186,322,500
Arizona	10,561	17.4	302.76	183,761.4	111,534,721
Arkansas	8,389	10.8	116.64	90,601.2	70,375,321
California	11,885	19.6	384.16	232,946.0	141,253,225
Colorado	11,713	23.0	529.00	269,399.0	137,194,369
Connecticut	14,090	20.7	428.49	291,663.0	198,528,100
Delaware	11,375	17.5	306.25	199,062.5	129,390,625
Florida	11,271	14.9	222.01	167,937.9	127,035,441
Georgia	10,191	14.6	213.16	148,788.6	103,856,481
Hawaii	11,003	20.3	412.09	223,360.9	121,066,009
Idaho	8,567	15.8	249.64	135,358.6	73,393,489
Illinois	11,302	16.2	262.44	183,092.4	127,735,204
Indiana	9,978	12.5	156.25	124,725.0	99,560,484
Iowa	10,096	13.9	193.21	140,334.4	101,929,216
Kansas	10,684	17.0	289.00	181,628.0	114,147,856
Kentucky	8,614	11.1	123.21	95,615.4	74,200,996
Louisiana	8,836	13.9	193.21	122,820.4	78,074,896
Maine	9,042	14.4	207.36	130,204.8	81,757,764
Maryland	12,967	20.4	416.16	264,526.8	168,143,089
Massachusetts	12,510	20.0	400.00	250,200.0	156,500,100
Michigan	10,902	14.3	204.49	155,898.6	118,853,604
Minnesota	11,186	17.4	302.76	194,636.4	125,126,596
Mississippi	7,483	12.3	151.29	92,040.9	55,995,289
Missouri	10,283	13.9	193.21	142,933.7	105,740,089
Montana	8,781	17.5	306.25	153,667.5	77,105,961
Nebraska	10,546	15.5	240.25	163,463.0	111,218,116
Nevada	11,200	14.4	207.36	161,280.0	125,440,000

(continued on next page)

TABLE 6.1   *(continued)*

(1) State	(2) Y	(3) X	(4) X²	(5) YX	(6) Y²
New Hampshire	11,659	18.2	331.24	212,193.8	135,932,281
New Jersey	13,129	18.3	334.89	240,260.7	172,370,641
New Mexico	8,814	17.6	309.76	155,126.4	77,686,596
New York	11,765	17.9	320.41	210,593.5	138,415,225
North Carolina	9,517	13.2	174.24	125,624.4	90,573,289
North Dakota	9,635	14.8	219.04	142,598.0	92,833,225
Ohio	10,371	13.7	187.69	142,082.7	107,557,641
Oklahoma	9,754	15.1	228.01	147,285.4	95,140,516
Oregon	9,925	17.9	320.41	177,657.5	98,505,625
Pennsylvania	10,288	13.6	184.96	139,916.8	105,842,944
Rhode Island	10,892	15.4	237.16	167,736.8	118,635,664
South Carolina	8,890	13.4	179.56	119,126.0	79,032,100
South Dakota	8,553	14.0	196.00	119,742.0	73,153,809
Tennessee	9,290	12.6	158.76	117,054.0	86,304,100
Texas	10,373	16.9	285.61	175,303.7	107,599,129
Utah	8,535	19.9	396.01	169,846.5	72,846,225
Vermont	9,619	19.0	361.00	182,761.0	92,525,161
Virginia	11,894	19.1	364.81	227,175.4	141,467,236
Washington	10,866	19.0	361.00	206,454.0	118,069,956
Washington D.C.	13,530	27.5	756.25	372,075.0	183,060,900
West Virginia	8,141	10.4	108.16	84,666.4	66,275,881
Wisconsin	10,298	14.8	219.04	152,410.4	106,048,804
Wyoming	9,782	17.2	295.84	168,250.4	95,687,524
Sums (Σs)	531,306	832.1	14,134.55	8,849,810	5,652,405,000

$$\overline{Y} = 531,306/51 = 10417.8$$

$$\overline{X} = 832.1/51 = 16.3$$

$$s_Y^2 = \frac{(51)(5,652,405,000) - (531,306)^2}{(51)(50)} = 2,347,682.10$$

$$s_X^2 = \frac{(51)(14,134.55) - (832.1)^2}{(51)(50)} = 11.165$$

$$s_{XY} = \frac{(51)(8,849,810) - (531,306)(832.1)}{(51)(50)} = 3,623.8$$

$$b_{YX} = \frac{(51)(8,849,810) - (531,306)(832.1)}{(51)(14,134.6) - 692,390.4} = 324.5$$

Or alternatively, $b_{YX} = s_{XY}/s_X^2 = 3623.76/11.165 = 324.6$. (The slight discrepancies arise from rounding.)

A bivariate regression coefficient measures the amount of change in a dependent variable for a one-unit difference in an independent variable. Thus, a 1% increase in a state's college-educated population is associated with an expected increase in annual per capita income of $324.6.

Given $\overline{X} = 16.3\%$, $\overline{Y} = \$10,417.8$ and $b_{YX} = \$324.6$, we easily compute $a = \$10,417.8 - (\$324.6)(16.3) = \$5,126.8$. Thus, the complete bivariate regression equation is

$$\hat{Y}_i = \$5,126.8 + \$324.6X_i$$

Figure 6.4 shows the regression line drawn through the scatterplot of the 51 data points. If the education percentage scale were extended far enough to the left, the line would intercept the Y-axis at $5,126.8. If a state had no one who was college educated, the predicted income for that state would be $5,126.8—the value of the intercept. The regression equation has a positive slope of $324.6. Although the line comes close to a few observations, none of the 51 data points falls exactly on the line. A regression line always passes through the means of both Y and X. In this example that point has coordinates $10,417.8 income and 16.3% education.

Figure 6.5 illustrates the concept of residuals, or *errors in prediction*. As noted in section 6.1, a residual is simply the difference between an observed value and the value predicted using the regression equation, that is, $e_i = Y_i - \hat{Y}_i$. Figure 6.5 illustrates two errors in prediction, one positive (observation X_7, Connecticut) and one negative (case X_{24}, Mississippi). Residuals provide a way to measure the magnitude of the linear relationship between two continuous variables, as the next section explains.

FIGURE 6.4

Scatterplot of Per Capita Income by College Educated Percentage, with Regression Line

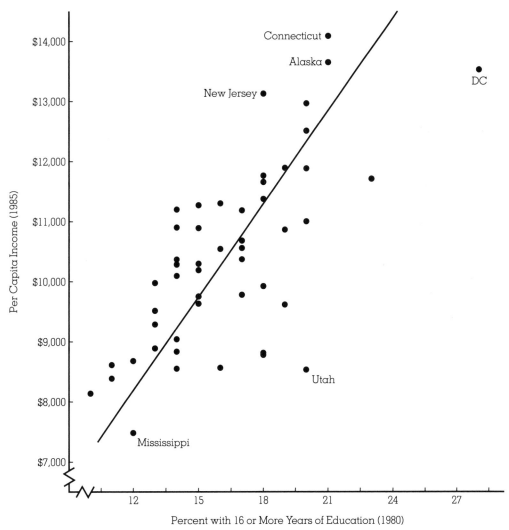

Source: U.S. States Data Set

FIGURE 6.5
Method of Accounting for an Observation by the Regression Line and an Error Component

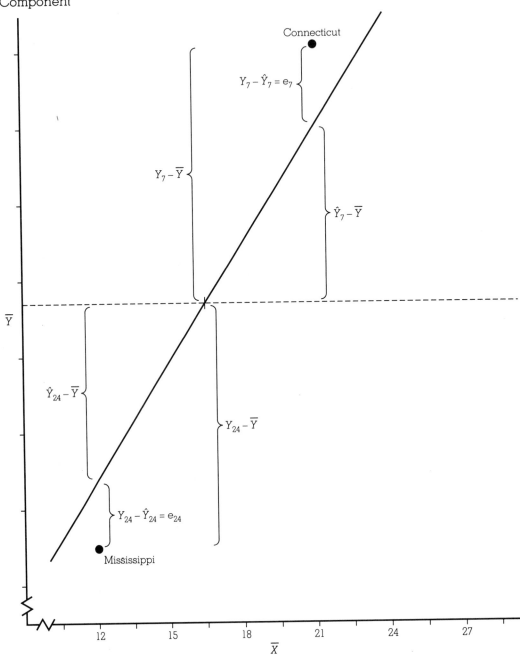

6.3 R-Square and Correlation

6.3.1. Partitioning the Sum of Squares

One way to determine how strongly two variables covary is to measure how closely the values of the observations come to the regression line. In the ideal situation where all observations fall exactly on the regression line, the N $\hat{Y}_i$ scores predicted from X_i would have no errors (i.e., $\hat{Y}_i - Y_i = 0$). But perfect prediction simply is not possible with actual social data. Greater or lesser amounts of error are always present in any regression. Our realistic goal is to determine the relative contributions of both prediction and error to the variation that we observe in the dependent variable. Because Y's variation is due both to the effects of X and to random error, we can partition the total sum of squares in a distribution of scores into a systematic component and a random component.

Create a deviation by subtracting the mean from observation Y_i. Then both add and subtract the expected score (due to linear regression) from this deviation, producing the following identity:

$$(Y_i - \overline{Y}) = (Y_i - \hat{Y}_i) + (\hat{Y}_i - \overline{Y})$$

Every observation thus has two components:

1. $Y_i - \hat{Y}_i$ indicates the discrepancy between an observation and its predicted value; this discrepancy is the error term e_i.
2. $\hat{Y}_i - \overline{Y}$ indicates that portion of an observed score that is due to the linear relationship between Y and X.

Squaring both sides of the identity above and summing across all N sample observations results in the **regression sum of squares** and the **error sum of squares.** (This method works because the sum of the cross-multiplied components on the right side of the equation is zero.) If we rearrange these terms, it turns out that

$$\sum_{i=1}^{N}(Y_i - \overline{Y})^2 = \sum_{i=1}^{N}(\hat{Y}_i - \overline{Y})^2 + \sum_{i=1}^{N}(Y_i - \hat{Y}_i)^2$$

regression sum of squares—a number obtained in linear regression by subtracting the mean of a set of scores from the value predicted by linear regression, squaring, and summing these values

error sum of squares—a numerical value obtained in linear regression by subtracting the regression sum of squares from the total sum of squares

total sum of squares
— the total of regression
and error sums of squares

The term to the left of the equal sign is called the **total sum of squares,** or SS_{TOTAL}, and is recognizable from Section 2.5.4 (page 53) as the numerator of the variance. The two terms to the right of the equal sign represent, respectively, the regression sum of squares and the error sum of squares. Thus, the simplified accounting identity is

$$SS_{TOTAL} = SS_{REGRESSION} + SS_{ERROR}$$

This accounting equation shows that, assuming Y and X are linearly related, all the variation observed in a dependent variable (SS_{TOTAL}) can be allocated to a portion due to its linear relation with the independent variable and to a portion due to errors of prediction.

6.3.2.   The Coefficient of Determination

How much prediction error might be eliminated by using a regression model? If we lacked all knowledge of how two variables are related, our best guess about Y_i for each X_i would be simply the sample mean $\overline{Y}$ (see section 6.2.1 and Figure 6.3). That is, the sum of squared errors $\Sigma(Y_i - \hat{Y}_i)^2$ would be reduced to $\Sigma(Y_i - \overline{Y})^2$ because the mean would be substituted for the predicted value in every case. But then SS_{ERROR} would be identical to SS_{TOTAL}, hence $SS_{REGRESSION}$ would equal zero. To the extent that we can use information about X_i to improve our prediction of Y_i, we eliminate errors up to but not exceeding the total sum of squares.

Because SS_{TOTAL} depends on sample size, a procedure to standardize the partitioned values is necessary in order to make comparisons across a variety of distributions. The sum of the squared errors for regression ($SS_{REGRESSION}$) and the sum of the squared errors about the mean (SS_{TOTAL}) contain the information necessary to construct a standardized *proportional reduction in error* (PRE) measure of the partitioning in linear regression. As discussed in section 5.3, all PRE measures have the general form

$$\text{PRE statistic} = \frac{\text{Error without decision rule} - \text{Error with decision rule}}{\text{Error without decision rule}}$$

If the application of a decision rule leaves an error as large as the one occurring when no decision rule is used, then the PRE value is 0. That is, none of the error is reduced by the decision rule. In contrast, if no error remains after applying the decision rule, then the PRE value reaches its maximum of 1.00, meaning that *all* of the error was eliminated by the decision rule. Hence, a PRE statistic standardizes a partition between 0 and 1.00, with higher values indicating the proportion of variation "explained" by the decision rule.

Thus, linear regression can be viewed as a decision rule about expected mean values $\hat{Y}_i$, conditional on observed X_i values. If any linear relation exists between Y and X, the regression equation produces a proportionally smaller prediction error than occurs when only the mean is used as the decision rule.

The regression PRE statistic is called the **coefficient of determination,** because it indicates the proportion of total variation in Y "determined" by its linear relationship to X. Its symbol, R^2_{YX} (read "R-square"), is derived by substituting two of the partition components into the general PRE formula:

coefficient of determination—a PRE statistic for linear regression that expresses the amount of variation in the dependent variable explained or accounted for by the independent variable(s) in a regression equation

$$R^2_{YX} = \frac{\Sigma(Y_i - \overline{Y})^2 - \Sigma(Y_i - \hat{Y}_i)^2}{\Sigma(Y_i - \overline{Y})^2}$$

Or

$$R^2_{YX} = \frac{SS_{\text{TOTAL}} - SS_{\text{ERROR}}}{SS_{\text{TOTAL}}}$$

$$= 1 - \frac{SS_{\text{ERROR}}}{SS_{\text{TOTAL}}}$$

Thus R-square equals 1 minus the ratio of the error sum of squares to the total sum of squares. The squaring confines the range of R^2_{YX} between 0.0 and 1.00. Whenever SS_{ERROR} is zero (perfect prediction occurs), $R^2_{YX} = 1.0$, and whenever $SS_{\text{ERROR}} = SS_{\text{TOTAL}}$ (i.e., all variation is due to error) $R^2_{YX} = 0.0$. Because $SS_{\text{REGRESSION}} = SS_{\text{TOTAL}} - SS_{\text{ERROR}}$, it follows that a fourth formula for R-square is

$$R^2_{YX} = \frac{SS_{\text{REGRESSION}}}{SS_{\text{TOTAL}}}$$

The coefficient of determination is clearly the proportion of the total sum of squares attributable to a least squares regression line fitted to the data.

A computing formula for the bivariate coefficient of determination involves the ratio of the square covariance to the product of both variances:

$$R^2_{YX} = \frac{s^2_{YX}}{s^2_X s^2_Y}$$

Applying the calculating formula for the covariance in section 6.2.1 to the data in Table 6.1, we find

$$s_{YX} = \frac{(51)(8,849,810) - (531,306)(832.1)}{(51)(50)}$$

$$= 3,623.8$$

Using the column sums in Table 6.1, we compute $s^2_X = 11.165$ and $s^2_Y = 2,347,682.10$. The R-square formula yields

$$R^2_{YX} = \frac{(3,623.8)^2}{(11.165)(2,347,682.10)} = 0.501$$

Thus 50.1% of the variation in state per capita annual income is "explained" (statistically) by the percentage of state citizens with at least a college degree. A bivariate association of this magnitude is quite substantial by social science standards.

The quantity $1 - R^2_{YX}$ is the amount of variance in the variable Y that *cannot* be attributed to its linear relationship with by X. Hence it is called the **coefficient of nondetermination.** In our example its numerical value is $1 - 0.501 = 0.499$. That is, the linear relationship of Y to X cannot account for 49.9% of the variance in Y. In chapter 9 we discuss how adding predictors to create a multiple regression equation may further reduce the proportion of unexplained variation in a dependent variable.

coefficient of nondetermination—a statistic that expresses the amount of variation in a dependent variable that is left *unexplained* by the independent variable(s) in a regression equation

6.3.3. The Correlation Coefficient

The square root of R^2_{YX}, which summarizes the linear relationship between two continuous variables, is called the Pearson product-moment **correlation coefficient,** after the statistician Karl Pearson. Its formula is

correlation coefficient—a measure of association between two continuous variables that estimates the direction and strength of linear relationship

$$r_{YX} = \sqrt{R^2_{YX}}$$
$$= \frac{s_{XY}}{s_Y s_X}$$

The correlation coefficient's usefulness lies in showing the direction of the relationship between X and Y. Whereas R^2_{YX} conceals whether the two variables are directly or inversely related, a positive or a negative sign is attached to r_{YX} to indicate the direction of the covariation. This sign must agree with the sign of the regression coefficient (b_{YX}). In our example the correlation between income and education at the state level is $+0.708$. Unlike R^2_{YX}, r_{YX} can range between -1.00 for a perfect inverse association to $+1.00$ for a perfect direct association. An $r_{YX} = 0$ means Y and X are unrelated.

From the definition of R-square, it follows that the correlation coefficient is *symmetric;* that is, $r_{YX} = r_{XY}$:

$$r_{YX} = \frac{s_{YX}}{s_Y s_X}$$

$$= \frac{\Sigma(Y_i - \overline{Y})(X_i - \overline{X})/(N - 1)}{s_Y s_X}$$

$$= \frac{\Sigma(X_i - \overline{X})(Y_i - \overline{Y})/(N - 1)}{s_X s_Y}$$

$$= \frac{s_{XY}}{s_X s_Y}$$

$$= r_{XY}$$

Although the correlation coefficient is symmetric, you should convince yourself that the bivariate coefficient b_{YX} from regressing Y on

X does *not* equal the coefficient b_{YX} from regressing X on Y. Section 6.3.5 discusses how these two different regression coefficients *are* related to R-square.

6.3.4.   Correlating Z Scores

Standardizing two variables (that is, changing them from Y and X to Z_Y and Z_X) and then correlating them produces some interesting results. Recall from Box 2.4 (page 67) that a distribution of Z scores always has a variance and standard deviation = 1.00. Given that $r_{YX} = s_{YX}/(s_Y s_X)$, the formula for the correlation of two Z scores is as follows:

$$r_{Z_Y Z_X} = \frac{s_{Z_Y Z_X}}{s_{Z_Y} s_{Z_X}} = \frac{s_{Z_Y Z_X}}{(1)(1)} = s_{Z_Y Z_X}$$

Thus, the correlation of two Z scores equals their covariance! Furthermore, because the mean of a Z score is zero (i.e, $\bar{Z}_X = \bar{Z}_Y = 0$), and because $s_{Z_Y Z_X} = \Sigma(Z_{Y_i} - \bar{Z}_Y)(Z_{X_i} - \bar{Z}_X)/(N - 1)$, the correlation coefficient can be expressed entirely in terms of Z scores:

$$r_{Z_Y Z_X} = s_{Z_Y Z_X} = \frac{\Sigma Z_Y Z_X}{N - 1}$$

Furthermore, given the definition of both Z scores in terms of the original Y and X variables—$Z_{Y_i} = (Y_i - \bar{Y})/s_Y$ and $Z_{X_i} = (X_i - \bar{X})/s_X$—it follows that

$$
\begin{aligned}
r_{Z_Y Z_X} &= \frac{\Sigma Z_Y Z_X}{N - 1} \\
&= \frac{\Sigma[(Y_i - \bar{Y})/s_Y]\,[(X_i - \bar{X})/s_X]}{N - 1} \\
&\quad \frac{\Sigma(Y_i - \bar{Y})(X_i - \bar{X})/(N - 1)}{s_Y s_X} \\
&= \frac{s_{YX}}{s_Y s_X} \\
&= r_{YX}
\end{aligned}
$$

That is, the correlation of two Z-transformed variables, Z_Y and Z_X, equals the correlation of their original variables, X and Y. Importantly, the correlation coefficient remains unchanged whether the variables are measured in their original metrics or transformed to standardized scores.

6.3.5. The Relationship Between Regression and Correlation

The relationships between a bivariate correlation coefficient and a regression coefficient are functions of both variables' standard deviations. First, recall that b_{YX} can be expressed as the ratio of covariance to variance: $b_{YX} = s_{YX}/s_X^2$. Rearranging these terms to isolate the covariance gives $s_{YX} = b_{YX}s_X^2$. Next, substituting $(b_{YX})(s_X^2)$ for s_{YX} in the equation for the correlation $r_{YX} = s_{YX}/s_Ys_X$ yields $r_{YX} = (b_{YX})(s_X^2)/(s_Ys_X)$. Thus, a correlation coefficient can be expressed in terms of a bivariate regression coefficient:

$$r_{YX} = b_{YX}\frac{s_X}{s_Y}$$

and conversely

$$b_{YX} = r_{YX}\frac{s_Y}{s_X}$$

Knowing the values for b_{YX}, s_Y, and s_X allows the calculation of r_{YX}. Or knowing r_{YX}, s_Y, and s_X allows b_{YX} to be determined. In the state data example

$$r_{YX} = b_{YX}\frac{s_X}{s_Y} = (324.6)\left(\frac{3.34}{1{,}532.21}\right) = +0.7076$$

$$b_{YX} = r_{YX}\frac{s_Y}{s_X} = (.7076)\left(\frac{1{,}532.21}{3.34}\right) = 324.6$$

These relationships hold only in the bivariate regression case. The multiple regression coefficients discussed in chapter 8 do not have such simple relations to the correlation coefficients.

6.4   Significance Tests for Regression Parameters

As with other descriptive statistics, researchers typically use sample data to estimate bivariate regression and correlation coefficients. Corresponding to each statistic—b_{YX}, a, R^2_{YX}, and r_{YX}—are population parameters—β_{YX}, α, ρ^2_{YX}, and ρ_{YX}. To draw inferences about these population parameters from sample data requires test statistics having known distributions, as described in the following subsections.

6.4.1.   Testing the Coefficient of Determination

For the coefficient of determination, the basic null hypothesis is that, in the population, none of the dependent variable's variance can be attributed to its linear relation with the independent variable:

$$\text{H}_0\text{: } \rho^2_{YX} = 0$$

where ρ^2_{YX} (Greek letter *rho*) refers to the population parameter.

The alternative hypothesis is that R-square in the population is greater than zero: $\text{H}_1\text{: } \rho^2_{YX} > 0$. The statistical significance test for the sample R^2_{YX} uses the F distribution discussed in chapter 3. In a regression analysis the SS_{TOTAL} has $N - 1$ degrees of freedom associated with it. Because the $SS_{\text{REGRESSION}}$ (defined in section 6.3.1) is estimated from b_{YX} (which is a single function of the Xs), it has only one degree of freedom. Just as the total sum of squares can be partitioned into two mutually exclusive components (see section 6.3.1), degrees of freedom can also be partitioned:

$$df_{\text{TOTAL}} = df_{\text{REGRESSION}} + df_{\text{ERROR}}$$
$$N - 1 = 1 + df_{\text{ERROR}}$$
$$N - 2 = df_{\text{ERROR}}$$

mean squares—estimates of variance in a linear regression

mean square regression—a value in linear regression obtained by dividing the regression sum of squares by its degrees of freedom

The next step is to compute the mean squares associated with $SS_{\text{REGRESSION}}$ and SS_{ERROR}. In computing **mean squares** we are calculating two variances, one due to the effect of the independent variable on the dependent variable and one due to error. If a nonzero regression effect exists, then the **mean square regression**

($MS_{\text{REGRESSION}}$) will be significantly larger than the **mean square error** (MS_{ERROR}). Both terms are calculated by dividing the appropriate sum of squares by its associated degrees of freedom.

mean square error—a value in linear regression obtained by dividing the error sum of squares by its degrees of freedom

$$MS_{\text{REGRESSION}} = \frac{SS_{\text{REGRESSION}}}{1}$$

$$MS_{\text{ERROR}} = \frac{SS_{\text{ERROR}}}{N-2}$$

If the null hypothesis about the population coefficient of determination (H_0: $\rho^2_{YX} = 0$) is true, then both $MS_{\text{REGRESSION}}$ and MS_{ERROR} will be unbiased estimates of σ^2_e, the variance of prediction errors (i.e., the e_i). However, if the true population parameter is greater than zero (H_1: $\rho^2_{YX} > 0$), then we also expect $MS_{\text{REGRESSION}} > MS_{\text{ERROR}}$ in the sample. Because F is simply the ratio of two estimates of the same σ^2_e, the null hypothesis can be tested by calculating

$$F_{1,N-2} = \frac{MS_{\text{REGRESSION}}}{MS_{\text{ERROR}}}$$

where the two degrees of freedom are $\nu_1 = 1$, and $\nu_2 = N - 2$, respectively.

If the calculated value of F is as large or larger than the critical value for the chosen α probability level, then we reject the null hypothesis and conclude that ρ^2_{YX} is greater than zero (with an α chance of Type I error). If the F ratio is less than the critical value, we cannot reject the null hypothesis that $\rho^2_{YX} = 0$ in the population.

The simplest way to compute $SS_{\text{REGRESSION}}$ follows from the fact that $R^2_{YX} = SS_{\text{REGRESSION}}/SS_{\text{TOTAL}}$, as shown in section 6.3.2. Therefore,

$$SS_{\text{REGRESSION}} = (R^2_{YX})(SS_{\text{TOTAL}})$$

Combining the definition of variance in section 2.5.4 (page 53), ($s^2_Y = \Sigma(Y_i - \overline{Y})^2/(N - 1)$) with the expression $SS_{\text{TOTAL}} = \Sigma(Y_i - \overline{Y})^2$, the total sum of squares can be calculated.

$$SS_{\text{TOTAL}} = (s_Y^2)(N - 1)$$

Hence, calculate $SS_{\text{REGRESSION}} = (R_{YX}^2)(s_Y^2)(N - 1)$. Finally, from the accounting equation for partitioning sums of squares, we obtain the last component we need by subtraction:

$$SS_{\text{ERROR}} = SS_{\text{TOTAL}} - SS_{\text{REGRESSION}}$$

From the data in Table 6.1, $s_Y^2 = 2,347,682.10$, $R_{YX}^2 = 0.501$, and $N = 51$. Therefore,

$$SS_{\text{TOTAL}} = (2,347,682.10)(50) = 117,384,105$$
$$SS_{\text{REGRESSION}} = (0.501)(117,384,105) = 58,809,437$$

And

$$SS_{\text{ERROR}} = 117,384,105 - 58,809,437 = 58,574,668$$

Furthermore,

$$MS_{\text{REGRESSION}} = 58,809,437/1 = 58,809,437$$

and

$$MS_{\text{ERROR}} = 58,574,668/(51 - 2) = 1,195,401.4$$

If we set $\alpha = .001$, we see from Appendix E that the critical value for an F with 1 and 60 degrees of freedom is 11.97. But our test statistic is $F_{1,49} = 58,809,437/1,195,401.4 = 49.2$. Hence, we can easily reject the null hypothesis that $\rho_{YX}^2 = 0$ in the population in favor of the alternative that $\rho_{YX}^2 > 0$. Table 6.2 summarizes these computations in a conventional format which, for reasons explained in chapter 5, is called an analysis of variance table.

6.4.2. Testing the Correlation Coefficient

Because the sample correlation coefficient, r_{XY}, is simply the square root of the coefficient of determination, R_{YX}^2, the significance test for the latter also serves for the former. However, a second statistical significance test exists for the correlation coefficient. The standard-

TABLE 6.2

Summary of Per Capita Income Analysis

Source	SS	df	MS	F
Regression	58,809,437	1	58,809,437	49.2*
Error	58,574,668	49	1,195,401.4	
Total	117,384,105	50		

* Significant at $\alpha = .001$

ized normal distribution (Z) is used to find the probability of observing a given r_{XY} under the null hypothesis H_0: $\rho_{XY} = 0$. The **r-to-Z transformation,** developed by the English statistician Ronald Fisher, uses the natural logarithm function

$$Z = \left(\frac{1}{2}\right) \ln \left(\frac{1 + r_{XY}}{1 - r_{XY}}\right)$$

For persons whose hand calculators lack a natural log key, Fisher's r-to-Z table in Appendix F gives values for virtually all possible correlation coefficients (for negative correlations, just attach a negative sign to the tabled values, because the normal distribution is symmetrical).

This Z score's variance is inverse to sample size:

$$\hat{\sigma}_Z^2 = \frac{1}{N - 3}$$

The test statistic involves the difference between Z scores and is also distributed as a standardized normal variate:

$$Z = \frac{Z_r - Z_\rho}{\hat{\sigma}_Z}$$

Under the null hypothesis that the population correlation is zero, $Z_\rho = 0$.

r-to-Z transformation—a natural logarithm transformation in the value of the correlation coefficient to a Z score, to test the probability of observing r under the null hypothesis

For the state data we already know that $r_{YX} = 0.501$ is significantly different from zero, so let us instead test a different null hypothesis. For example, what is the probability that $\rho_{XY} = 0.60$, given that the sample correlation is 0.501 and $N = 51$? Suppose we set $\alpha = .05$ (i.e., the critical value for a one-tailed test is -1.645). The r-to-Z transformations in Appendix F for those two correlations are 0.693 and 0.549, respectively, while $\sigma_Z^2 = 1/(51 - 3) = 0.021$. Hence the test statistic, distributed approximately as a Z score following the normal distribution, is computed as follows:

$$\frac{0.549 - 0.693}{\sqrt{0.021}} = -0.99$$

This Z value falls considerably short of the critical value necessary to reject the hypothesis. Therefore, we conclude that we cannot reject the hypothesis that the true population correlation is 0.60. Of course, many other values in the same vicinity as the sample point estimate of 0.501 also cannot be rejected as highly unlikely values for the parameter.

6.4.3. Testing b and a

Throughout this chapter we have written the bivariate regression equation in Roman letters, implying that it is estimated with sample data:

$$\hat{Y}_i = a + b_{YX} X_i$$

population regression equation—a regression equation for a population rather than a sample

The corresponding **population regression equation** is written using Greek letters for the parameters:

$$\hat{Y}_i = \alpha + \beta_{YX} X_i$$

The population parameters, α and β_{YX}, are estimated by a and b_{YX} in the sample data. Do not confuse these α and β parameters with other uses of the same Greek symbols, such as the α probability level and the β probability of a Type II error. Unfortunately, modern statistics makes limited use of the Greek alphabet, with several symbols serving multiple purposes.

The typical null hypothesis about the population regression parameter is that it equals zero: H_0: $\beta_{YX} = 0$. Selecting an alternative hypothesis, hence choosing a one- or two-tailed test, depends on our knowledge of the relationship between X and Y. If we really have no idea whether X's effect is to increase or decrease Y, then the alternative H_1: $\beta_{YX} \neq 0$ implies a two-tailed region of rejection. But, if we believe that only a positive effect is plausible, then the alternative H_1: $\beta_{YX} > 0$ puts the entire region of rejection in the right tail of the test statistic's sampling distribution. Conversely, if only a negative relationship is credible, then the one-tailed alternative H_1: $\beta_{YX} < 0$ locates the region of rejection all in the left tail.

To test whether the sample regression estimate, b_{YX}, differs significantly from the hypothesized population parameter, the t sampling distribution is used to estimate the probability of making a Type I error in rejecting the null hypothesis. The t test for the null hypothesis that $\beta_{YX} = 0$ is as follows:

$$t = \frac{b_{YX} - \beta_{YX}}{s_b}$$

$$= \frac{b_{YX} - 0}{s_b}$$

where s_b is the estimate of σ_b, the standard error of the regression coefficient.

Here the *standard error*, a concept introduced in section 3.5 (page 89), is the standard deviation of the sampling distribution of the regression coefficient. To test the hypothesis that β_{YX} differs from zero, two assumptions are necessary:

1. Y is normally distributed for every outcome of X in the population; and
2. The variances of the prediction errors are identical at every outcome of X, a condition known as **homoscedasticity.**

homoscedasticity—a condition in which the variances of the prediction errors are equal at every outcome of the predictor variable

Then, according to the central limit theorem, the sampling distribution of b_{YX} will be normally distributed as N gets large. The mean of this sampling distribution equals the population regression parameter β_{YX}, and its variance is

$$\sigma^2_b = \frac{\sigma^2_e}{\Sigma(X_i - \bar{X})^2}$$

An estimate of the denominator can be obtained from the sample variance of the X_is by $\Sigma(X_i - \bar{X})^2 = (s^2_X)(N - 1)$. An estimate of the numerator, σ^2_e (the variance of the prediction errors), is the MS_{ERROR} from the R-square significance test:

$$\hat{\sigma}^2_e = \sqrt{MS_{ERROR}}$$

Because the MS_{ERROR} has $N - 2$ degrees of freedom, the t test for the regression coefficient also has $N - 2$ df. Thus, its t ratio, with the df indicated in the subscript, is

$$t_{N-2} = \frac{b_{YX} - \beta_{YX}}{\sqrt{\dfrac{MS_{ERROR}}{\Sigma(X_i - \bar{X})^2}}}$$

$$= \frac{b_{YX} - 0}{\sqrt{\dfrac{MS_{ERROR}}{(s^2_X)(N - 1)}}}$$

For the states' income-education data, a one-tailed alternative (H_1: $\beta_{YX} > 0$) is plausible, since we expect income to go up with education. For $\alpha = .001$ and $df = 49$, the critical value of t in Appendix D is less than 3.46 (using the last column and $df = 60$ as approximations). We compute:

$$t_{49} = \frac{324.6}{\sqrt{\dfrac{1,195,401.4}{(11.165)(50)}}} = \frac{324.6}{46.27} = 7.02$$

Because we will need this information in section 6.4.4, note that $s_b = 46.27$. Since $t_{49} = 7.02$ far exceeds the critical value of 3.46, we easily reject the null hypothesis that $\beta_{YX} = 0$ in the population. With little chance of being wrong, we conclude that per capita annual income and the percent with at least a college degree significantly covary in a positive direction in the United States. Note that the t-value of 7.02 when squared equals 49.2, the value of the F when the R^2_{YX} was tested for significance. This correspondence is no coincidence. In the bivariate case there is an intimate relationship between r_{YX} (and hence R^2_{YX}) and b_{YX}, as was shown in section 6.3.5. When one is significant, the other will also be significant. Furthermore, $t^2_{\nu_2} = F_{1,\nu_2}$ for the t and F involved in the two tests of significance. Hence, only one of these tests needs to be conducted.

A t test can also be applied to the significance of the population regression intercept, α. Its formula is

$$t_{N-2} = \frac{a - \alpha}{\sqrt{\dfrac{MS_{\text{ERROR}}}{N}}}$$

In the states' income-education example, where the sample $a =$ 5,126.8 and $N = 51$ states, if we set the probability of rejection at $\alpha =$ .001, a two-tailed test of the null hypothesis H_1: $\alpha = 0$ yields the following:

$$t_{49} = \frac{5,126.8 - 0}{\sqrt{\dfrac{1,195,401.4}{51}}} = 33.49$$

Because the critical value is 3.46, the null hypothesis can also be rejected with only a .001 probability of Type I error. As pointed out previously, the intercept in this example is the expected annual income per capita for a state whose citizens have no college degrees. The absurdity of such a condition makes the intercept a relatively uninformative parameter estimate in this case. This result underscores the point that social researchers must think about their statistical analyses and not just mechanically apply the formulas.

6.4.4. Confidence Intervals

As we stress throughout this book, confidence intervals built around point estimates are more important than tests designed to reject the hypothesis that a parameter is zero in the population. The estimated standard error of the regression coefficient, s_b, can be used to construct a confidence interval around the sample point estimate, b_{YX}. In general, the upper and lower confidence intervals for a given α-level are $b_{YX} \pm (s_b)$(c.v.). First, decide on a probability level for a two-tailed test (because the interval must be symmetric around the sample point estimate of b_{YX}). For example, setting $\alpha = .05$ for $df = 49$ designates critical t values equal to ± 2.00. Therefore, the upper and lower 95% confidence interval are $b + s_b$ (2.00) and $b - s_b$ (2.00).

For large samples (with more than 100 cases), the critical values for t at $\alpha = .05$ are ± 1.96 (i.e., the Z scores for a two-tailed significance test). Because these values are very close to 2.00, a statistical rule-of-thumb asserts that if a regression coefficient is twice its standard error in size, then b_{YX} is significant at the .05 level. Remember the correct interpretation is that across repeated samples of size N, the confidence interval on average will contain the β_{YX} population parameter only $(1 - \alpha)$ of the time. But, as pointed out in section 3.6 (page 91), to say that the population parameter has a 95% chance of being inside a particular interval is *not correct*: it is either inside that specific interval or it is not.

In the income-education equation the confidence interval around the b_{YX} regression estimate is bounded by LCL = 324.6 − (46.27)(2.00) = 232.06 and UCL = 324.6 + (46.27)(2.00) = 417.14. Therefore, the confidence interval is from $232.06 to $417.14, a fairly wide range but one that still does not include zero. Does the confidence interval for $\alpha = .001$ include zero?

6.5 Standardizing Regression Coefficients

The meaning of a regression coefficient is clear when both independent and dependent variables have obvious units of measurement. Thus, a year of schooling or a dollar of income are well-understood scales whose units make intuitive sense. However, many social variables lack intrinsically interpretable scales. For example, religiosity might be measured by the frequency of agreement with seven items such as "The Bible is God's Word," and "There is a life after death." Or, workers may be asked to rate their job satisfaction on a 1 to 10 scale. Regression coefficients estimated for such arbitrary scales do not have an obvious meaning. Consequently, many researchers prefer to standardize their regression coefficients.

The symbol for a standardized bivariate regression coefficient, usually called a **beta coefficient,** or **beta weight,** is β^*.[1] Standardization involves rescaling both the independent and dependent variables in terms of their standard deviations. A simple way to do this is first to convert both the Y and X variables to Z scores, then estimate the regression equation as before. The same result is reached by first multiplying b_{YX} by the standard deviation of the independent variable and then dividing by the standard deviation of the dependent variable:

beta coefficient (beta weight)—a standardized regression coefficient indicating the amount of net change, in standard deviation units, of the dependent variable for an independent variable change of one standard deviation

$$\beta^*_{YX} = (b_{YX}) \left(\frac{s_X}{s_Y} \right)$$

But, the preceding section showed that this transformation is also the correlation between X and Y. Hence, in the bivariate case only, a standardized regression coefficient equals its correlation coefficient: $\beta^*_{YX} = r_{YX}$.

β^*_{YX} is interpreted in standard deviation units. For a one standard deviation difference in X, the expected difference in Y is β^*_{YX} standard deviation units, either larger or smaller depending on the sign of the coefficient. In the income-education example the correlation coefficient of 0.501 indicates that each standard deviation increase in percent college-educated predicts a $+0.501$ standard deviation increase in per capita annual income. In actual dollars this expected increase is $(0.501)(10,417.8) = 5,219.32$, recalling that 10,417.8 is the standard deviation of Y. Given that actual range of state per capita incomes is only \$6,607 (the difference between Mississippi and Connecticut), the effect of education on per capita income seems to be quite substantial.

Because the mean of a standardized variable equals zero, the intercept in a standardized regression equation is also zero. This result is demonstrated by inserting zeros for the means of X and Y in the formula for the intercept of the nonstandardized equation: $a = \bar{Y} - b_{YX}\bar{X}$, (i.e., $a = 0 - b0 = 0$). Therefore, the prediction

---

1. Once again, we encounter the practice in statistics of using a few Greek symbols for many purposes. Here we star (*) the beta coefficient (β^*) to distinguish it from the population parameter β, introduced in the preceding section.

equation expressing the linear relation between two Z-score variables has no intercept term:

$$\hat{Z}_Y = \beta^*_{YX} Z_X$$
$$= r_{YX} Z_X$$

In our income-education example the standardized prediction
equation is $\hat{Z}_Y = 0.501\ Z_X$.

Finally, we note that everything stated above about the regression of Y on X could be restated for the regression of X on Y.
Although it is always true that $r_{YX} = r_{XY}$ (i.e., the correlation
coefficient is symmetric), it is *not* generally the case that the
unstandardized $b_{YX} = b_{XY}$. (If this is not apparent to you, reread
section 6.3.5.) However, the product of two standardized bivariate
regression coefficients is the same as the product of their correla-
tion coefficients: $(\beta^*_{YX})(\beta^*_{XY}) = (r_{YX})(r_{XY})$. But, the right-hand side of the
equation is the same as squaring the correlation coefficient, which
is the coefficient of determination: $(r_{YX})(r_{XY}) = r^2_{YX} = R^2_{YX}$. Hence,
multiplying the complementary bivariate regression parameters
reveals the proportion of variance in either variable explained
statistically by its linear association with the other variable, regardless of which one is assumed to be the independent and which the
dependent variable. Examining R^2_{YX} to determine the proportion of
variance explained is obviously much more straightforward.

6.5.1.   Regression Toward the Mean

The standardized form of the prediction equation is useful for
understanding how the term *regression* came to be applied to this
form of analysis. Suppose we are interested in the relationship
between mothers' and daughters' weights. We sample 500 mothers,
match them to their oldest daughters, and weigh both pairs. We find
that $\bar{X} = \bar{Y} = 135$ pounds, $s_Y = s_X = 15$, and $r_{XY} = 0.70$, where X and
Y refer to mothers' and daughters' weights, respectively.

Now if we standardize the two variables, our prediction is:

$$\hat{Z}_Y = 0.70\ Z_X$$

Notice that mothers whose weight is one standard deviation above
the mean (i.e. $Z_X = 1$) are predicted to have daughters whose
weights on average are only $+0.70$ standard deviations above the

mean. In contrast, mothers whose weights place them one standard deviation below the mean (i.e. $Z_X = -1$) are predicted to have daughters who are only -0.70 standard deviations below the mean. That is, a daughter's weight exhibits **regression toward the mean;** or, on average, daughters are predicted to be closer to the mean in weight than their mothers are.

This regression can be seen clearly by examining Table 6.3, which gives examples of observed and predicted values for mothers' and daughters' weights (both standardized and unstandardized). On average, mothers who are above the mean are predicted to have daughters who weigh less than they do, and mothers below the mean are predicted to have daughters who are heavier than they are. This seems to imply that the population of women is becoming more homogeneous with respect to weight across time. Indeed there is less variability in the *predicted* weight of the daughters (compare second and fourth columns in Table 6.3). But, the fact that the predicted scores are closer to the mean and have less variance should *not* lead you to an erroneous conclusion. Since we found in our sample that s_Y and s_X were identical, there is as much variance in the *observed* weight of the daughters as there is in the observed weight of the mothers.

regression toward the mean—a condition demonstrated when the predicted scores on the dependent variable show less variability about the mean than the observed scores do, due to the imperfect correlation between two variables

TABLE 6.3

Illustration of Regression Toward the Mean, Using the Prediction of Daughter's Weight from Mother's Weight

Standardized Weight		Unstandardized Weight	
Observed Mother's Weight	Predicted Daughter's Weight	Observed Mother's Weight	Predicted Daughter's Weight
+3	+2.1	180	166.5
+2	+1.4	165	156.0
+1	+0.7	150	145.5
0	0.0	135	135.0
−1	−0.7	120	124.5
−2	−1.4	105	114.0
−3	−2.1	90	103.5

Prediction Equation	Prediction Equation
$\hat{Z}_Y = 0.7\, Z_Y$	$\hat{Y} = 40.5 + 0.7\, X$

Imperfect correlation is the cause of regression toward the mean. Notice that when two variables are perfectly correlated, $\hat{Z}_Y$ = (1.00) Z_X, then no regression toward the mean will occur. But if r_{XY} = 0.2, the amount of regression will be substantial. These examples reaffirm that the weaker the relationship between two variables, the more the regression towards the mean, or alternatively, the more the mean becomes the best predicted outcome for Y for any value of X. Furthermore, the smaller the correlation between X and Y, the smaller the variance of $\hat{Y}$ (the predicted dependent variable). We state without proof:

$$s^2_{Z_Y} = r^2_{XY}$$

As the relationship between X and Y approaches zero, the variance of $\hat{Y}$ approaches zero as well, thereby accounting for the *apparent* homogenization of observations.

6.6 Comparing Two Regression Equations

Sometimes researchers are interested in whether the correlations and regressions between two variables, X and Y, are the same for two populations, 1 and 2. To find out, two statistical tests are available—a correlation difference test and a regression difference test. These tests will not necessarily give the same results, so both should be done.

Assuming that two independent random samples of size N_1 and N_2 are drawn from the two populations, the **correlation difference test** tests the null hypothesis that the correlations are equal in the populations, H_0: $\rho_1 = \rho_2$, against a two-tailed alternative, H_1: $\rho_1 \neq \rho_2$. First, both the *sample* correlations, r_1 and r_2, are transformed to Z scores using Fisher's r-to-Z transformation table in Appendix F. Following these transformations an α level is chosen and the test statistic is computed as follows:

correlation difference test—a statistical test to determine whether two correlation coefficients differ in the population

$$Z = \frac{Z_{r_1} - Z_{r_2}}{\sqrt{\dfrac{1}{N_1 - 3} + \dfrac{1}{N_2 - 3}}}$$

The **regression difference test** tests the null hypothesis that the unstandardized population regression coefficients are equal, H_0: $\beta_{Y_1X_1} = \beta_{Y_2X_2}$, against a two-tailed alternative, H_1: $\beta_{Y_1X_1} \neq \beta_{Y_2X_2}$. First, a pooled variance is estimated from the two *sample* error sums of squares:

regression difference test—a statistical test to determine whether two regression coefficients differ in the population

$$s_{YX}^2 = \frac{SS_{\text{ERROR}_1} + SS_{\text{ERROR}_2}}{N_1 + N_2 - 4}$$

Then, the standard error of the difference in regression coefficients is estimated:

$$s_{b_1 - b_2} = \sqrt{s_{YX}^2 \left(\frac{1}{N_1 s_{Y_1}^2} + \frac{1}{N_2 s_{Y_2}^2} \right)}$$

where N_1 and N_2 are the respective sample sizes, and $s_{Y_1}^2$ and $s_{Y_2}^2$ are the variances of Y in the two samples. Finally, a t test statistic with $N_1 + N_2 - 4$ degrees of freedom is computed with the following formula:

$$t = \frac{(b_1 - b_2) - (\beta_1 - \beta_2)}{s_{b_1 - b_2}}$$

In the 1991 GSS the correlation between respondents' years of education (X) and income (Y) for 449 men is $r_M = 0.399$, while the same correlation for 462 women is $r_W = 0.375$. Appendix F indicates that $Z_{r_M} = 0.424$ and $Z_{r_W} = 0.394$. Therefore,

$$Z = \frac{0.424 - 0.394}{\sqrt{\dfrac{1}{449 - 3} + \dfrac{1}{462 - 3}}} = 0.45$$

Because the critical value of Z at $\alpha = .05$ is ± 1.96, we cannot reject the null hypothesis. That is, the education-income correlations seem to be the same for both genders.

However, the regression of income on education produces quite different results for the two sexes. The men's equation is:

$$\hat{Y}_{1i} = -3.70 + 2.45\, X_{1i}$$

while the women's equation is:

$$\hat{Y}_{2i} = -4.43 + 1.61\, X_{2i}$$

where income is measured in thousands of dollars. Each additional year of education increases men's expected annual incomes by $2,450, but only increases women's predicted incomes by $1,610. The research question is whether this observed difference in sample regression coefficients is highly unlikely if the two gender populations' regression coefficients were equal (i.e., if $\beta_1 - \beta_2 = 0$).

The sample error sums of squares are 140,860.33 for men and 58,698.56 for women, while the sample variances of Y are 373.80 and 148.21, respectively. The estimated pooled variance is

$$s_{YX}^2 = \frac{140,860.33 + 58,698.56}{449 + 462 - 4} = 220.02$$

and the estimated standard error is

$$s_{b_1 - b_2} = \sqrt{220.02 \left(\frac{1}{(449)(373.80)} + \frac{1}{(462)(148.21)} \right)} = 0.067$$

Therefore, the test statistic is

$$t_{907} = \frac{2.45 - 1.61}{0.067} = 12.54$$

Because the critical value at $\alpha = .001$ for a two-tailed t with 907 df is ± 3.29, we can easily reject the null hypothesis. That is, a year of education yields significantly higher annual income to men than does a year of education for women. The finding that the correlations are essentially identical for men and women means that the scatter of the data around these two regression lines is roughly the same. In other words, education explains approximately as much of the variance in income for men ($r_M^2 = 0.159$) as for women ($r_W^2 = 0.141$).

Review of Key Concepts and Symbols

These key concepts and symbols are listed in the order of appearance in this chapter. Combined with the definitions in the margins, they will help you to review the material and can serve as a self-test for mastery of the concepts.

robust	
scatterplot	a
predictor variable	b_{YX}
linear relationship	e_i
bivariate linear relationship	$\hat{Y}_i$
(bivariate regression)	s_{YX}
prediction equation	SS_{TOTAL}
linear regression model	$SS_{\text{REGRESSION}}$
error term	SS_{ERROR}
residual	R^2_{YX}
regression line	r_{YX}
ordinary least squares	$r_{Z_Y Z_X}$
bivariate regression coefficient	α
covariance	β_{YX}
computing formula for b	ρ_{YX}
intercept	ρ^2_{YX}
conditional mean	df_{TOTAL}
regression sum of squares	$df_{\text{REGRESSION}}$
error sum of squares	df_{ERROR}
total sum of squares	$MS_{\text{REGRESSION}}$
coefficient of determination	MS_{ERROR}
coefficient of nondetermination	$\hat{\sigma}^2_Z$
correlation coefficient	s_b
mean squares	σ^2_b
mean square regression	σ^2_e
mean square error	$\hat{\sigma}^2_e$
r-to-Z transformation	β^*_{YX}
population regression equation	$\hat{Z}_Y$
homoscedasticity	$s^2_{\hat{Z}_Y}$
beta coefficient (beta weight)	$s_{b_1 - b_2}$
regression toward the mean	
correlation difference test	
regression difference test	

PROBLEMS

General Problems

1. For the following data on 10 persons, construct a scatterplot showing the relationship between education and interest in politics, and describe the relationship in verbal terms:

Person (i)	Education (Years X_i)	Interest in Politics (Y_i)
1	18	23
2	16	25
3	14	20
4	12	19
5	12	21
6	12	15
7	11	11
8	10	12
9	10	9
10	9	10

2. Using data from 73 industrial nations, a development economist wants to estimate an equation for the linear relationship between per capita income (Y) in U.S. dollars, and export-sector dependency (X) in percentage. He has the following statistics: $\bar{X} = 24\%$, $s_X^2 = 225$, $\bar{Y} = \$750$, $s_Y^2 = 202{,}500$, $s_{XY} = -4{,}500$. Estimate both the unstandardized regression equation and report the coefficient of determination. Give a substantive interpretation of the economist's finding.

3. The American Chemical Association hires you to forecast the number of new jobs for chemistry teachers next year. Using data from the past 25 years, you discover that the best single predictor of next year's faculty vacancies is the previous year's undergraduate course enrollments for the entire nation. You estimate the following regression equation:

$$\hat{Y}_i = 154.6 + .37\, X_i$$

where $\hat{Y}_i$ is the predicted number of chemistry vacancies next year and X_i is last year's undergraduate enrollments (in thousands of students). Using this equation

a. How many job openings occur for each 10,000 enrolled students?

b. If last year's enrollments were 700,000 students nationwide, what is your forecast for the number of job vacancies to occur this year?

c. How many students must enroll this year for 500 chemistry vacancies to occur next year?

$$\hat{Y}_i = 154.6 + .37 X_i$$

Exam

4. Fill in the missing values in the table below:

	SS_{TOTAL}	$SS_{REGRESSION}$	SS_{ERROR}
a.	————	2,785	14,347
b.	83.46	————	57.21
c.	1,193	384.3	————
d.	472.49	54.22	————

5. A family sociologist hypothesizes that part of the variance in wives' marital happiness can be attributed to its linear regression on husbands' participation in household chores. Data from 58 wives produced $SS_{ERROR} = 6,500$ and $s_{YX}^2 = 150$ for the dependent variable. Compute R_{YX}^2 for this bivariate equation and test whether this value is statistically different from zero at $\alpha = .001$. Display your findings in an ANOVA-type format and state your decision.

6. If $b_{YX} = 1.2$, $s_X = .5$, and $s_Y = .8$, what do r_{XY} and R_{XY}^2 equal?

7. If $N = 32$, $b_{YX} = 1.7$, and $s_b = .75$, test the null hypothesis that $b = 0$ in the population, using a one-tailed test with $\alpha = .05$.

8. Test the following R-squares for significant difference from zero at the stated α level:

	R_{YX}^2	N	SS_{TOTAL}	α
a.	0.10	30	212.0	.05
b.	0.30	61	132.5	.01
c.	0.05	100	4,587	.001

Report the F ratio, df, and your decision about the null hypothesis.

9. If $b_{YX} = 2.00$, $s_b = .80$, and $N = 20$, construct a 95% confidence interval around b.

10. Find β^* for the following:

$\beta = b \frac{s_x}{s_y}$

	b_{YX}	s_Y	s_X
a.	2.75	4.25	.30
b.	−5.00	90	10
c.	0.22	3.50	5.55

Problems Requiring the 1991 General Social Survey

11. Are older people more conservative than younger people? Regress POLVIEWS on AGE and report the equation. Test whether the b coefficient is significantly different from zero in the population at $\alpha = .05$, one-tailed.

12. Does the strength of religious belief explain variation in the rate of church attendance? Regress ATTEND on RELITEN and report both R^2_{YX} and the F ratio for the test that H_0: $\rho_{YX} = 0$, at $\alpha = .01$.

13. Do more-educated people prefer fewer children than less-educated people? Regress CHLDIDEL on EDUC, report the standardized regression equation, the t test for β^*_{YX}, and whether you can reject H_0: $\beta^*_{YX} = 0$ at $\alpha = .001$.

14. Do people living in larger communities feel that the government is spending too little on cities? Regress NATCITY on XNORCSIZ and report the unstandardized regression equation, F test for the R-square, and whether the sample b differs significantly from zero in the population at $\alpha = .01$.

Problems Requiring Use of the U.S. States Data Set

15. Does the extent of unionization of a state's labor force increase its voting participation? Regress TURN84 on UNION and test whether the b coefficient differs significantly from zero in the population at $\alpha = .05$, one-tailed.

16. Is crime linked to urbanization at the state level? Regress SERCRIME on URBAN86 and report both R^2_{YX} and the F ratio for the test that H_0: $\rho^2_{YX} = 0$, at $\alpha = .01$.

17. Do states with more physicians per capita spend more on health care? Regress HEALTHEX on DOCSPC and report the unstandardized regression equation, F test for the R-square, and whether the sample b differs significantly from zero in the population at $\alpha = .05$.

Statistics for
Social Data
Analysis

The Logic of Multivariate Contingency Analysis

7

In our examination of various aspects of the relationship between two variables in preceding chapters, we have discussed measures of association and tests of significance for both discrete and continuous variables. Tools have been presented to help you determine whether two variables systematically covary, and whether the sample relationship is likely to reflect the population from which the sample was drawn.

For some research purposes, establishing that two variables significantly covary may be sufficient. In most instances the fact that, for example, on average men have higher earned incomes than women, even in the same occupation, hardly needs to be verified again with a new set of data. But the researcher may want to explore the income difference as a consequence of other social factors, such as amount of education, work experience, employment status (full- or part-time), and employer discrimination. In such cases the research problem changes from the examination of a two-variable relationship to a consideration of three or more variables, as their relationships bear upon some theoretical issue. In this chapter we present some of the basic procedures for conducting **multivariate contingency analysis,** or statistical analysis of data on three (or more) variables, using both discrete and continuous variables.

multivariate contingency analysis— statistical techniques for analyzing relationships among three or more discrete variables

7.1   Controlling Additional Variables

A basic reason for bringing additional variables into the analysis of the relationship between an independent and a dependent variable is to clarify the true relationship between them. **Covariation** between two variables can arise because of the confounding effects of other factors. To establish the true amount of covariation between two variables, we need to remove the part that is due to other factors.

covariation—joint variation, or association, between a pair of variables

In laboratory-type experiments the removal of the effects of other factors is accomplished by application of the experimental design. Some additional variables can literally be "held constant" by making sure they apply uniformly to all subjects under experimental and control conditions. For example, in studying the effects of different amounts of fertilizer on the productivity of seed crops, we hold constant the effects of soil, water, and sunlight by making sure that all experimental plots contain the same type of soil, receive the same amounts of water, and have the same exposure to sunlight. Then we can be fairly sure that any plant growth differences we find would not be due to differences in these rival factors that are known to affect crop growth. In a social experiment we might hold constant the manner in which stimuli are presented to subjects and their responses are recorded.

random assignment—in an experiment the assignment of subjects to treatment levels on a chance basis

Variables that might disturb a bivariate relationship can be controlled in experiments by **random assignment** of subjects to the different experimental treatments. For example, to study the effects of marijuana on driving ability, we must try to eliminate such possible confounding effects as intelligence and motor skills. Clearly, the results of the experiment would not be credible if all the better drivers had been exposed to low dosages and all the worst drivers to high dosage conditions. Since it would be very hard to obtain subjects who had identical IQ and manual dexterity scores, the preferred solution is to assign persons at random to smoke different amounts of marijuana before taking the driving test (including a control group that would smoke no marijuana). Random assignment to a treatment group might be made by flipping coins or by consulting a table of random numbers. The purpose of this procedure is to ensure that no experimental group differs, *on average,* from the others in driving abilities before subjects ingest different levels of the drug.

The technique of random assignment of subjects to experimental treatment groups helps to eliminate the confounding effect of rival factors. Thus, it helps isolate the true impact of the independent variable on the dependent measure. Unfortunately, all social behavior cannot be studied experimentally. In naturally occurring data such as that collected through sample surveys, other techniques for eliminating rival factors must be used. These techniques consist of identifying the additional variables likely to affect a relationship, measuring these factors, and "holding constant" their effects through statistical manipulation of the data.

Statistical control of rival factors differs from experimental control in that the researcher has no direct physical ability to shape the attributes of the persons or objects studied. The methods for controlling additional variables statistically adjust the data in an attempt to render the respondents equivalent on the rival factors, thereby eliminating their impact on the bivariate relationship of interest. Statistical controls are less powerful than randomization in eliminating the confounding effects of other variables for two reasons:

1. Measurement error, which is always present to some degree, reduces the precision with which statistical adjustments can be made.
2. Identification or inclusion of all potential rival factors may be impossible.

The second of these limitations suggests the extreme importance of theory in guiding social research. The decision to select some variables to be controlled statistically and not to consider others among the many possible candidates depends on our understanding of the role such variables play in the theory under investigation. For example, in studying the impact of religiosity on teenage premarital sexual behavior, we would be guided by theory and past research to control such factors as degree of parental supervision, academic ability, participation in school sex education programs, and peer group attitudes. But we would not try to adjust for the effects of physical appearance and food preferences.

The basic purpose of statistical controls is to eliminate, or at least reduce, the effect of confounding factors on a bivariate relationship.

It is possible to distinguish three special applications, which provide various means to control spuriousness, interpretation, and multiple causes.

7.1.1.   Spuriousness

An important point in controlling additional variables is that *establishing covariation between two variables is not equivalent to proving causation.* Even if the independent variable is shown to change in time prior to a change in the dependent variable, the conditions for inferring a causal relationship are not complete. Besides time order and covariation, a causal inference must eliminate the possibility of **spuriousness** in the observed relationship. (See chapter 11 for a more-detailed discussion on causal interference.) Two variables are spuriously related when the only reason they correlate is that both are caused by one or more other variables.

spuriousness—covariation between two variables due only to the effect of a third variable

A classic illustration of a spurious relationship is the observation that, in Holland, communities where many storks nest in chimneys have higher birth rates than communities where fewer storks nest. While covariation and (probably) temporal-order conditions can be reasonably met, we should not conclude that storks cause babies, even if we have no knowledge of human reproduction, because we have not ruled out the possibility that the observed pattern is a spurious consequence of one or more rival factors that are simultaneously affecting both the number of babies and the number of storks. Storks and babies are more prevalent in rural than in urban areas. Pollution and sanitation levels, community attitudes toward human and animal life, and historical patterns of selective migration may all combine to create a spurious correlation between these two variables.

Take another classic case: The number of fire trucks called to a fire and the subsequent amount of damage done to buildings covary together. Can you figure out what rival factor(s) makes this a spurious, noncausal relationship?

These examples present clear-cut cases of spurious relationships that disappear when the appropriate common cause of both variables is held constant (by techniques described later). Less obvious cases of spurious relationships may occur in social behavior.

Where a covariation results because two variables have a common cause but are causally unrelated themselves, statistically holding constant the common factor (also called *partialling out* the effects due to other variables) eliminates the covariation observed in the data. If successive statistical controls for alleged, common causes fail to alter the observed covariation, there are much firmer grounds than existed in the simple bivariate relationship for asserting the establishment of a causal relationship.

The variables chosen to control in these cases, of course, must be realistic candidates as causes of spuriousness. Social theory and past empirical research are indispensable sources of information about appropriate factors to control when examining covariation for spuriousness.

7.1.2. Explanation

Another reason for bringing additional variables into the analysis of bivariate relationships is to attempt an **explanation** (or **interpretation) of** an observed **association.** Two variables may be causally related, but the process may be more complex than the simple correlation implies. Controlling the relationship for variables representing the *intervening process* connecting the independent and dependent variable can deepen our understanding of the bivariate relationship.

> **explanation (interpretation) of association** — covariation between two variables due to an intervening third variable

For example, an inverse relationship between age and liberalism in personal morality is widely known to exist. That is, older persons tend to adhere to less permissive attitudes concerning child-rearing, sexuality, drug usage, and the like. One possible explanation for this relationship might be the degree of religiosity. Traditional religious values are more often found among older persons, both because they were raised in an era when such beliefs were strongly socialized (a generational or period process) and because as people age they may become more concerned about ultimate values (an aging process). Traditional religious doctrines contain many injunctions and prescriptions for belief and behavior in nonreligious matters. Hence, one reason older people may support less permissive morality is their greater religiosity, compared to younger people. (This explanation is commonly accepted by both religious leaders and social scientists.) By holding constant the level of religiosity, we might expect to reduce some or all of the observed covariation between age and personal morality beliefs.

Such an outcome would not imply that the two variables were spuriously related, but rather that the explanation for their covariation can be interpreted—at least in part—by a process in which greater age induces greater religiosity, which in turn restricts permissiveness in other areas. In a statistical sense both spuriousness and explanation are similar in that holding constant other variables eliminates or reduces the original bivariate association. But in a substantive sense the spuriousness and the interpretive analyses are quite different.

> A *spurious relationship* exists where the two original variables have no causal connection but are only dependent on a common cause. An *explanatory or interpretive relationship* exists where the two original variables have a causal connection and additional intervening variables elaborate the understanding of that connection.

Figure 7.1 illustrates the conceptual difference played by a third factor that completely accounts for the observed covariation between variables A and B according to the two types of effects, spuriousness and explanation. In the case of spuriousness, C is a common cause of both variables, while in the case of explanation, C is an intervening factor that shows in greater detail how the causal effect of A is transmitted to B. An understanding of the role a third variable plays in explicating the covariation between two others is not revealed by the statistical pattern. *The proper understanding of whether spuriousness or explanation is implied by an analysis depends on the researcher's ability to draw on past research and theory to conceptualize the roles that third variables play.*

7.1.3. Multiple Causes

multiple causation—the view that social behavior is caused by more than one factor

Very few social theories, at least since the 19th century, have posited that human behavior is due to a single factor. Instead, many suggest **multiple causation;** that is, they identify several variables

FIGURE 7.1

Two Roles Played by a Third Variable in the Analysis of
Bivariate Covariation

A. SPURIOUSNESS   B. EXPLANATION

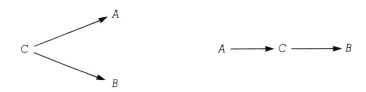

as causally important in the explanation of the variation of some
dependent variable. Some factors may carry important policy
implications because their values may be subject to manipulation,
as through training programs or funding of services.

In this type of research the emphasis is not on the relationship
between a single independent variable and the dependent measure, but on discovering the multiple, simultaneous relationship of
several independent variables to the dependent measure(s) of
interest. For example, in the study of social stratification, several
researchers have developed and tested quite elaborate models of
the status attainment process. An individual's earnings may be
depicted as a consequence of the interplay of social background,
education, occupation, industry, and other career variables. *By
statistically controlling for several causal factors at the same time,
the analyst can make some inferences about the relative importance of each factor for earnings, with spurious and explanatory
relationships controlled.*

This chapter lays the groundwork by investigating the basic
techniques for statistically controlling a single, third variable in
two-variable systems of categoric measures. The extension to more
than three variables is straightforward but is not covered in this text.

7.2   Controlling for a Third Variable in 2 × 2 Tables

As we noted in chapter 5, the simplest bivariate relationship can be
examined by the crosstabulation of two dichotomous variables.
Similarly, the basic principles of examining a bivariate relationship

for the effects of other variables utilize a *three-variable crosstabula-tion*. To present these principles, we will describe the possible results of controlling for a third variable, illustrating different outcomes with purely hypothetical data.

7.2.1. A Hypothetical Example: Family Religiosity and Teenagers' Sex Activity

To make the hypothetical example more meaningful, we will assume a relationship between family religiosity (X) and premarital sexual intercourse among teenagers (Y). The hypothetical data in Table 7.1 classify 192 responses by whether or not teenagers said they belonged to a "highly religious family" and whether or not they admitted to ever having sexual relations. Table 7.1 can be called a **zero-order table,** where *order* refers to the number of other variables held constant.

zero-order table—a crosstabulation of two variables in which no additional variables have been controlled

In this example family religiosity is the independent variable and premarital sex is the dependent variable. For this reason we have percentaged the table on family religiosity, that is, the column percentages add to 100. As might be expected, nonreligious teenagers are considerably more likely to admit to premarital sex, at more than twice the rate of those who classify their families as religious. The correlation for this table is -0.26, indicating a

TABLE 7.1

Crosstabulation of Family Religiosity and Teenagers' Premarital Intercourse Variables, Hypothetical Data

| | | Family Highly Religious? | | |
		No	Yes	Total
	Yes	42.9% (36)	16.0% (160)	27.1% (52)
Ever Premarital Sex?	No	57.1% (56)	84.0% (84)	72.9% (140)
	Total	100.0% (92)	100.0% (100)	100.0% (192)

$$r_{XY} = -0.26$$

moderate inverse relationship. To compute this and other correlations in this chapter we have coded yes = 1 and no = 0.

We will consider whether this apparent causal relationship might be explained by the effects of other social processes that intervene between family religiosity and teenagers' premarital sexual experience. Suppose the provision of frequent opportunities to have sex is an important factor in determining whether a teenager actually has such an experience. Perhaps teenagers in more religiously oriented households have their activities restricted more by their parents. If this causal sequence exists, we would expect that when opportunity is statistically controlled, the relationship between religiosity and premarital sex might change.

Other possible outcomes could occur if the data in Table 7.1 were further crosstabulated by another dichotomy. In this hypothetical case, the control variable is whether or not the teenager has regular use of an automobile (*W*). Tables 7.2 to 7.5 illustrate four possible statistical patterns that might be found among these responses. Each result suggests a different interpretation about

TABLE 7.2

Example of No Effect of a Third Variable, Hypothetical Data

		Access to a Car						
		No				**Yes**		
		Family Highly Religious?				**Family Highly Religious?**		
		No	**Yes**	**Total**		**No**	**Yes**	**Total**
Ever Premarital Sex?	**Yes**	39.7% (25)	15.9% (11)	27.3% (36)	**Yes**	37.9% (11)	16.1% (5)	26.7% (16)
	No	60.3% (38)	84.1% (58)	72.7% (96)	**No**	62.1% (18)	83.9% (26)	73.3% (44)
	Total	100.0% (63)	100.0% (69)	100.0% (132)	**Total**	100.0% (29)	100.0% (31)	100.0% (60)
		$r_{XY} = -0.27$				$r_{XY} = -0.25$		

TABLE 7.3

Example of Partial Effect of a Third Variable, Hypothetical Data

		Access to a Car							
		No				**Yes**			
		Family Highly Religious?				Family Highly Religious?			
		No	Yes	Total		No	Yes	Total
Ever Premarital Sex?	Yes	25.5% (12)	12.9% (11)	17.4% (23)	Yes	53.3% (24)	33.3% (5)	48.3% (29)
	No	74.5% (35)	87.1% (74)	82.6% (132)	No	46.7% (21)	66.7% (10)	51.7% (60)
	Total	100.0% (47)	100.0% (85)	100.0% (132)	Total	100.0% (45)	100.0% (15)	100.0% (60)
		$r_{XY} = -0.16$				$r_{XY} = -0.17$		

TABLE 7.4

Example of Complete Explanation by a Third Variable, Hypothetical Data

		Access to a Car							
		No				**Yes**			
		Family Highly Religious?				Family Highly Religious?			
		No	Yes	Total		No	Yes	Total
Ever Premarital Sex?	Yes	11.1% (4)	11.1% (8)	11.1% (12)	Yes	66.7% (32)	66.7% (8)	66.7% (40)
	No	88.9% (40)	88.9% (80)	88.9% (120)	No	33.3% (16)	33.3% (4)	33.3% (20)
	Total	100.0% (44)	100.0% (88)	100.0% (132)	Total	100.0% (48)	100.0% (12)	100.0% (60)
		$r_{XY} = 0.00$				$r_{XY} = 0.00$		

TABLE 7.5

Example of Interaction Effect of a Third Variable, Hypothetical Data

		Access to a Car						
		No				*Yes*		
		Family Highly Religious?				*Family Highly Religious?*		
		No	*Yes*	*Total*		*No*	*Yes*	*Total*
	Yes	50.0% (26)	11.8% (8)	28.3% (34)	*Yes*	25.0% (10)	25.0% (8)	25.0% (18)
Ever Premarital Sex?	*No*	50.0% (26)	88.2% (60)	71.7% (86)	*No*	75.0% (30)	75.0% (24)	75.0% (54)
	Total	100.0% (52)	100.0% (68)	100.0% (120)	*Total*	100.0% (40)	100.0% (32)	100.0% (72)
		$r_{XY} = -0.42$				$r_{XY} = 0.00$		

the original relationship. Each pair of tables is called a **first-order table,** since the number of other variables held constant is one.

first-order table—a subtable containing the crosstabulation or covariation between two variables, given a single outcome of a third, control variable

7.2.2. No Effect of a Third Variable

In Table 7.2 the original 2 × 2 table has been split into two *subtables,* each resembling the original table in general form but with different cell frequencies. We now have a 2 × 2 × 2 table. Notice that the cell and marginal frequencies of the two subtables, when added pairwise, must exactly equal the frequencies in the original 2 × 2 table. As the total *N*s for both subtables show, about two-thirds of the teenage sample do not have regular use of an automobile. All respondents within the same subtable have the same level on the car access variable; that is, all 132 persons in the first subtable have no regular access and all 60 in the second subtable do have regular access. Thus, each subtable "holds constant" the variation in the third factor, permitting us to observe what happens to the covariation between the other two variables.

Note that in the example introduced with Table 7.1, the relationship between religiosity and sexual experience remains unchanged in Table 7.2. Both subtables of Table 7.2 show teens from highly religious families reported having sexual intercourse less than half as often as the other teenagers queried. The percentages are not noticeably different across the two subtables. Among persons without cars, $r_{XY} = -0.27$, and among persons with cars, $r_{XY} = -0.25$. These values are called **conditional correlation coefficients** because they refer to correlations under certain conditions of the third variable.

conditional correlation coefficients—correlation coefficients calculated between two crosstabulated continuous variables within each category of a third variable

If both first-order relationships in the two subtables are the same magnitude in the original zero-order relationship, we would conclude that opportunity—at least as operationalized by use of a car—has *no effect* on the original covariation. When such patterns are found, attention must be directed elsewhere for an explanation of why religiosity and premarital sex are related.

An alternative way to analyze the data is to compute odds ratios for the data in Table 7.1 and 7.2. If access to a car has no effect on the relationship between premarital sex and religiosity, we would expect the odds ratios (see section 5.4 on page 178) in the subtables of Table 7.2 to be approximately equal to the odds ratios for Table 7.1. The odds ratio for Table 7.1 is $(36)(84)/(16)(56) = 3.38$ and the odds ratio for the subtable associated with no access to a car in Table 7.2 is $(25)(58)/(11)(38) = 3.47$ and the odds ratio for those with access to a car is $(11)(26)/(5)(18) = 3.18$. *Regardless of access to a car*, those who come from irreligious families are over three times as likely to engage in premarital sex as those who come from highly religious families.

7.2.3.   Partial Effect of a Third Variable

Table 7.3 demonstrates another possible result when a third variable is held constant. In this case we can see that the magnitude of the association between religiosity and premarital sexual experience is the same in both subtables, but it is somewhat weaker than in the original 2 × 2 table. The conditional correlation coefficients are -0.16 and -0.17, respectively, for no regular access and regular access to a car. We can conclude that opportunity, as measured by regular use of an automobile, partially accounts for the association observed originally between the other two variables.

To understand what this partial explanation means, consider the percentages within each subtable. Among persons who are *not* from highly religious families, those able to use a car regularly are twice as likely to have had sex as those without access to a car (53.3% to 25.5%). Similarly, among teenagers from highly religious homes, those with access to a car are more than twice as likely to have had sex as those lacking such access (33.3% to 12.9%). However, the opportunity to use a car does not eliminate all the differences in sexual experience between the religious- and non-religious-background teens. Teens from nonreligious families are still more likely to have had sex than teens from religious families, regardless of access to a car, but the differences have been diminished somewhat from that found in Table 7.1, where opportunity was not held constant. Hence, if these results were found, we would conclude that opportunity explains *part* of the association between religiosity and premarital sex, but considerable covariation still remains to be accounted for by other factors not yet held constant.

7.2.4.   Complete Explanation by a Third Variable

Table 7.4 shows what the data might look like if the third variable *completely accounts for the association* observed in the zero-order table. The correlations in both subtables (which you should check for yourself) are exactly zero, indicating that with each opportunity level held constant, no differences in sexual experience occur between the teens from highly religious and nonreligious families. Without regular access to a car, only 11.1% of the teenagers manage to have premarital intercourse, whereas among those with regular use of the car, two-thirds have had intercourse. The reason that the strong inverse relationship between family religiosity and sex appeared in the zero-order table is apparent from the marginal distributions in the two subtables: more than half the nonreligious-background youths regularly use a car, but only one out of eight religious-background teenagers have regular access to a car. If we found such clear-cut patterns in real data, we would probably conclude that opportunity does explain the association. That is, a teenager's family religiosity determines the access he or she has to the family car (an opportunity process, in the sense that more religious parents are stricter about letting their children go on unchaperoned dates). In turn, the opportunity that use of a car permits is the major determinant of having premarital sexual intercourse.

As an alternative to computing the correlations in the subtables, one can easily compute the odds ratios (see section 5.4 on page 178), which both equal 1.00, as they should, since access to a car explains the relationship between religiosity and premarital sex.

What is the reason that holding access to automobiles constant explains the relationship of family religiosity to teenagers' premarital sex in Table 7.4 but not in Table 7.2? To find the answer, consider how access is related to the other two measures. As an exercise, form two tables, one showing the covariation between access and religiosity, the other showing the covariation between access and premarital sex. (Use the marginal totals in the columns and the rows of the subtables.) You will find that in the "no effects" situation (Table 7.2), access is virtually uncorrelated with both other variables. Holding access constant can do nothing to alter the relationship between religiosity and premarital sex. But in the "explanation" situation (Table 7.4), access (W) is strongly correlated with both variables, positively with premarital sex $(r_{WY} = 0.60)$ and inversely with family religiosity $(r_{WX} = -0.43)$.

Thus, by holding constant the level of automobile use, the inverse covariation between the other two variables is reduced to zero. This situation is of greatest importance in trying to find statistical explanations for observed associations among pairs of variables. *A third variable can produce an explanation for the covariation between two others only if it has nonzero relationships with both the other variables.* If the original bivariate association is positive, the control variable must be positively associated with both the independent and dependent variables. If the original bivariate association is inverse, the control variable must be positively associated with one and inversely associated with the other, as in the example in Table 7.4.

Notice that the pattern in the first-order tables in Table 7.4 is the same that would be found if the covariation of the original two variables were spurious. That is, in both explanation and spuriousness, when the rival factor is held constant, the first-order associations between the two variables fall to zero. Whether you should regard such statistical results as indicating an explanation of the original association or as revealing a spurious original association depends on your understanding of the causal role of the factor that is held constant. In the hypothetical example we regarded opportunity as an intervening process, that is, as a consequence of religiosity in the household and as a cause itself of premarital sexual experience. A different substantive variable that had a similar statistical effect of reducing the first-order correlations to zero might lead to an evaluation of the religiosity-sex association as spurious. For example, if we had achieved the same results as Table 7.4, where the variable held constant was family structure (such as, whether the teenager lived in an intact family or a so-called broken home), we probably would be inclined to describe the relationship as spurious. Intact families would tend to be more strict in all kinds of personal behavior—religious, sexual, educational—than would families lacking two parents. Hence, the association of religiosity with premarital sex would reflect not a causal relationship but a more general pattern of morality stemming from the family condition.

Our discussion of the differences between explanation and spuriousness in bivariate associations controlled for the effects of third variables should alert you to the fact that the finding is not determined by the statistical outcome. As with most situations, an understanding of social behavior requires thinking carefully about the meaning behind statistical relationships. A good grasp of basic social theory and previous empirical research, plus a little common sense, is helpful in this task.

7.2.5. Interaction Effect of a Third Variable

Table 7.5 shows another result from controlling a 2 × 2 table that occurs with some frequency. The first-order associations differ substantially in the two subtables. In the example the correlation between family religiosity and premarital sex for teens from highly religious families is zero, but the correlation is −0.42 among those from nonreligious families. The use of odds ratios makes the interpretation of the interaction effect clear. For those who have access to a car, coming from a less than highly religious family has no effect on the likelihood of engaging in premarital sex; that is, the odds ratio equals 1.00, as it must whenever a correlation is zero. By contrast the odds ratio, if one does not have access to a car, is 7.5. That is, if one does not have access to a car and comes from a less than highly religious family, one is 7.5 times as likely to engage in premarital sex compared to someone who does not have access to a car and comes from a highly religious family. Holding constant the third variable reduces the association in one subtable but increases it in another. At times we can even find conditional correlations with opposite signs.

Whenever the relationships in subtables are not the same, an **interaction effect** is present. That is, *the association between two variables in each partial table differs when controlling for a third variable.* We cannot describe the effect of the third variable, as we did in the other three examples, by reference to a single type of outcome. Instead, we must specify which subtable we are referring to in describing the effect of the controlled variable.

The discovery of an interaction is often just the beginning for further analysis. It cries out for the researcher to provide an explanation of why the variables have different covariations for different levels of the third variable.

7.2.6.   Summary of Conditional Effects

Because graphing results often makes tabled results clearer, the results found in Tables 7.2 to 7.5 are diagrammed in Figure 7.2. Panel A, for example, shows clearly that having access to a car has no effect on the relationship between family religiosity and premarital sex—the lines are virtually identical for each category of access. Panel B, however, shows that *both* family religiosity and access to a car affect the rates of premarital sex. Both variables make independent contributions to explaining premarital sex. The large difference between the lines for access and no access indicates that availability of a car affects the percentage of teenagers ever having premarital sex. But the fact that each line still has a negative slope, across religious and nonreligious family membership, shows that religiosity has an independent effect on premarital sex. Therefore, car access provides only a partial explanation. In Panel C the relationship between family religiosity and premarital sex is seen to be spurious, because, when car access is controlled for, the slope of both lines is zero across family religiosity. An interaction effect is shown in Panel D; for those with car access, no relationship occurs between family religiosity and premarital sex. In contrast, for those without such access, there is a negative relationship between family religiosity and premarital sex.

One noteworthy point illustrated in Figure 7.2 is that *if there is no interaction effect, the relationship between the independent and*

FIGURE 7.2

Examples of Conditional Effects, Hypothetical Data (Tables 7.2 to 7.5)

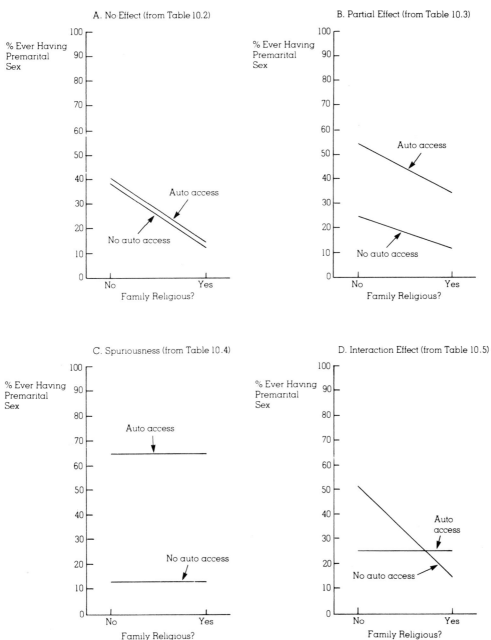

A. No Effect (from Table 10.2)

B. Partial Effect (from Table 10.3)

C. Spuriousness (from Table 10.4)

D. Interaction Effect (from Table 10.5)

dependent variables within categories of the control variables is the same. Therefore, when the relationship is graphed, it is shown by parallel lines. The relationships in Panels A, B, and C are shown by two parallel lines because there is no interaction between the independent and control variables. In contrast, the lines in Panel D are *not* parallel, indicating that an interaction effect does exist.

The four examples above were deliberately chosen to give a clear-cut picture of different outcomes that might be found when a simple 2 × 2 relationship is controlled by a third variable. These illustrations were created to show ideal conditions. We cannot caution you too strongly that such exaggerated results are not likely to be found in most real data situations. In our personal experience we have almost never discovered a situation such as that shown in Table 7.4, in which a strong bivariate relationship completely disappeared when a single third variable was held constant. Partial effects (Table 7.3) or interaction effects (Table 7.5) are more likely to be found. Social behavior is seldom so simple that controlling for a single additional variable fully accounts for the observed two-variable relationship.

We did not compute significance tests on the zero-order relationships reported in this section, but had the data been real we would have. This is done in the next section, where we show how statistical tests may be applied to three-variable crosstabulations, using examples from real GSS data.

7.3. The Partial Correlation Coefficient

Analyzing relationships of three variables together calls for computing the conditional correlation coefficients for each crosstabulation, as we did in section 7.2. When no interaction effects are present, a single coefficient that is a weighted average of the conditional correlation coefficients can be computed. This is called the **partial correlation coefficient,** which is given by

partial correlation coefficient—a measure of association for continuous variables that shows the magnitude and direction of covariation between two variables that remains after the effects of a control variable have been held constant

$$r_{XY \cdot W} = \frac{r_{XY} - r_{XW}r_{YW}}{\sqrt{1 - r_{XW}^2} \, \sqrt{1 - r_{YW}^2}}$$

Read the term $r_{XY \cdot W}$ as "The partial correlation between X and Y, controlling for (or in the presence of) W." Notice that the computation of $r_{XY \cdot W}$ requires first computing the three zero-order correlations, r_{XY}, r_{XW}, and r_{YW}.

A casual inspection of the formula for the partial correlation coefficient does not clearly reveal that it produces a correlation between two variables, controlling for a third. To clarify this measure of association we will use a visual presentation called the **Venn diagram.** In Figure 7.3 we have represented correlations of 0, 0.5, and 1.0 with three diagrams. In Panel A, where X and Y are uncorrelated, the two circles do not overlap at all. When the two are correlated $r_{XY} = 0.5$, as in Panel B, half the total area of Y overlaps with X. Perfect correlation is represented by the total overlap of X and Y in Panel C.

Venn diagram—a type of graph that uses overlapping shaded circles to demonstrate relationships or covariation among a set of variables

Now let us consider the interrelationship among three variables, W, X and Y, using the Venn diagrams in Figure 7.4. Note that the three circles in Panel A are drawn to indicate that X and Y and X and W are correlated, but W and Y are *un*correlated. This diagram suggests clearly that controlling for W should not reduce the correlation between X and Y, since W does not intersect the X-Y overlap. Now look at the numerator of the formula for the partial correlation coefficient. If Y and W are uncorrelated, as in Panel A, the numerator is $r_{XY} - (r_{XW})(0) = r_{XY}$. That is, the intuition drawn from the Venn diagram is correct: To reduce or "explain" the X-Y correlation, it is necessary for W to correlate with *both* X and Y.

Now consider Panel B in Figure 7.4. In this case the entire overlap between X and Y is also intersected by W. In correlational terms this means that the entire correlation between X and Y can be explained by taking W into account. This occurs in partial correla-

FIGURE 7.3

Venn Diagrams Showing Correlation Between Two Variables

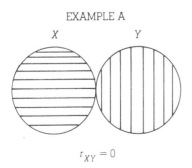

EXAMPLE A

X Y

$r_{XY} = 0$

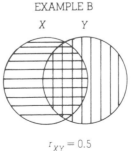

EXAMPLE B

X Y

$r_{XY} = 0.5$

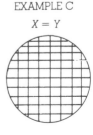

EXAMPLE C

$X = Y$

$r_{XY} = 1.0$

FIGURE 7.4

Venn Diagrams Showing Interpretation of $r_{XY \cdot W}$

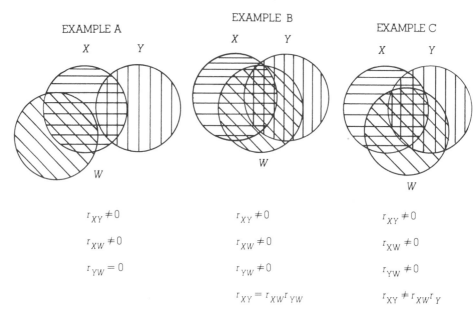

EXAMPLE A	EXAMPLE B	EXAMPLE C
$r_{XY} \neq 0$	$r_{XY} \neq 0$	$r_{XY} \neq 0$
$r_{XW} \neq 0$	$r_{XW} \neq 0$	$r_{XW} \neq 0$
$r_{YW} = 0$	$r_{YW} \neq 0$	$r_{YW} \neq 0$
	$r_{XY} = r_{XW} r_{YW}$	$r_{XY} \neq r_{XW} r_{Y}$

tion whenever $r_{XY} = r_{XW} r_{YW}$, since in this situation the numerator of the partial correlation coefficient equation, which is $r_{XY} - r_{XW} r_{YW}$, equals zero.

The typical situation is shown in Panel C in Figure 7.4. In this case one part of W intersects the X-Y crosshatch. Therefore, controlling for W does not entirely account for the correlation between X and Y. While the partial correlation, $r_{XY \cdot W}$, will be smaller than the zero-order correlation, r_{XY}, it will not be zero.

The squared partial correlation coefficient indicates the amount of variance in Y "explained" by X, controlling for W. If W is uncorrelated with either X or Y, r_{XY}^2 and $r_{XY \cdot W}^2$ will be virtually the same. If, however, W is correlated with both X and Y, $r_{XY \cdot W}^2$ will usually be smaller than r_{XY}^2. That is, the amount of variance X can explain in Y is reduced, with W being taken into account.

7.3.1.   An Example: Relationships Among Three Variables

To show how to use the partial correlation coefficient, we will consider the relationships between public drinking, premarital sexual attitudes, and gender from the 1991 GSS data set. Example A in Table 7.6 presents the zero-order relationship between visiting a public drinking place (X), such as bars and taverns, and attitude toward premarital sexual intercourse (Y). The latter, originally a four-category response, has been collapsed into a dichotomy between those who think it is "always" or "almost always" wrong and those who are more tolerant.[1]

As Table 7.6 shows, these two variables are strongly related. Suppose we set $\alpha = .05$. The zero-order correlation coefficient is $r_{XY} = -0.393$, with $t = -12.94$. Therefore, we reject the null hypothesis that in the population $\rho_{XY} = 0$ and conclude instead that those who claim never to drink in public places are considerably more likely to view premarital sex as wrong. But perhaps women are intolerant of both public drinking and premarital sex.

To test for this possibility we introduce gender (W) as a control variable. These zero-order tables are also shown in Table 7.6. In Example B the zero-order correlation of $r_{YW} = 0.122$ indicates that women are more likely than men to see premarital sex as wrong. And in Example C the zero-order correlation of $r_{XW} = -0.221$ suggests that women are less likely to visit a bar than men are. (Both of these zero-order correlations are significant at the $\alpha = .05$ level, with t values of 3.80 and -7.03.)

Now we can compute the partial correlation coefficient:

$$r_{XY \cdot W} = \frac{-0.393 - (-0.221)(0.122)}{\sqrt{1 - (-0.24)^2}\sqrt{1 - 0.122^2}} = -0.378$$

That is, controlling for gender reduces the zero-order relationship between public drinking and attitudes toward premarital sex from -0.393 to -0.378—a very small amount. Hence, we would conclude that the relationship between public drinking and attitude toward premarital sex cannot be explained by gender.

7.3.2. Testing the Partial Correlation for Significance

We have computed a partial correlation coefficient, but we have not tested whether it is statistically significant. To do this we establish

---

1. We have collapsed this variable only to simplify our illustration. In an actual analysis of these data we would not have done so, since we thereby lose some valuable information.

TABLE 7.6

Zero-Order Relationships Between Public Drinking, Premarital Sex, and Gender

---

EXAMPLE A

		Visit Bar (X)		
		Never	**Yes**	**Total**
Premarital Sex (Y)	**Wrong**	55.5% (288)	17.4% (82)	37.4% (370)
	Not Wrong	44.5% (231)	82.6% (388)	62.6% (619)
	Total	100.0% (519)	100.0% (470)	100.0% (989)

$$r_{XY} = -0.393$$

EXAMPLE B

		Gender (W)		
		Male	**Female**	**Total**
Premarital Sex (Y)	**Wrong**	30.4% (125)	42.4% (245)	37.4% (370)
	Not Wrong	69.6% (286)	57.6% (333)	62.6% (619)
	Total	100.0% (411)	100.0% (578)	100.0% (989)

$$r_{YW} = 0.122$$

EXAMPLE C

		Gender (W)		
		Male	**Female**	**Total**
Visit Bar (X)	**Wrong**	60.6% (249)	38.2% (221)	47.5% (470)
	Not Wrong	39.4% (162)	61.8% (357)	52.5% (519)
	Total	100.0% (411)	100.0% (578)	100.0% (989)

$$r_{XW} = -0.221$$

Source: 1991 General Social Survey

the null hypothesis, $H_0: \rho_{XY \cdot W} = 0$, and the alternative hypothesis, $H_1: \rho_{XY \cdot W} < 0$. Thus, we expect the relationship to be negative.

The test for the partial correlation is as follows:

$$F_{1,N-3} = \frac{r^2_{XY \cdot W}(N-3)}{1 - r^2_{XY \cdot W}}$$

Or, by taking the square root of the right side of the equation, the expression is for a t test is

$$t_{N-3} = \frac{r_{XY \cdot W} \sqrt{N-3}}{\sqrt{1 - r^2_{XY \cdot W}}}$$

Using the results from the example in Section 7.3.1 and setting $\alpha = .05$, we find

$$F_{1,986} = \frac{(-0.393)^2(989 - 3)}{1 - (-0.393)^2} = 180.10$$

or

$$t_{986} = -13.42$$

Since the critical value for the t test is -1.65 for a one-tailed test, the null hypothesis can be confidently rejected. That is, we infer that in the population, visiting bars and premarital sexual attitude are correlated, even after holding constant gender.

Review of Key Concepts and Symbols

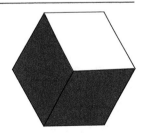

These key concepts and symbols are listed in the order of appearance in this chapter. Combined with the definitions in the margins, they will help you review the material and can serve as a self-test for mastery of the concepts.

multivariate contingency   covariation
   analysis   random assignment

spuriousness
explanation (interpretation) of
    association
multiple causation
zero-order table
first-order table

conditional correlation
    coefficients
interaction effect
partial correlation effect
Venn diagram
$r_{XY \cdot W}$

PROBLEMS

General Problems

1. These hypotheses might be found in family sociology:

    > Male children who belong to disrupted families
    > (single parents; blended families) are likely to have
    > less effective supervision than male children in
    > nondisrupted families (both biological parents pres-
    > ent).
    >   The number of illegal acts committed by male
    > juveniles decreases with the level of effective super-
    > vision.

    What kind of causal relationship is expressed by these hypothe-
    ses? Diagram the relationship.

2. Suggest how a positive covariation between a married woman's
   participation in the paid labor force and her chances of
   divorcing could be spurious due to the number of children
   present in the marriage. Show this hypothesis as a causal
   diagram. What would you expect to happen to the correlation
   coefficient between female labor force participation and divorce
   when number of children is held constant, if the spuriousness
   hypothesis is correct?

3. Suggest three interpretive relationships for a causal connection
   in which the degree to which a nation depends on a single raw
   export product leads to frequent military dictatorships. Show the
   relationships you develop as causal diagrams.

4. A three-way crosstabulation of gender, wages, and work status yields the following partial frequency tables:

		Full-Time Work				**Part-Time Work**	
		Men	**Women**			**Men**	**Women**
Wages	**High**	50	20	**High**		10	15
	Low	20	20	**Low**		10	25

Calculate the correlation coefficients and odds ratios for the zero-order relation between gender and wages. What kind of relationship is suggested by holding work status constant?

5. A sex researcher hypothesizes that men watch pornographic films more often than women because they are more likely to believe that such materials do not lead to a breakdown in moral behavior. The 1991 GSS yields the following crosstabulation:

		Do sexual materials lead to breakdown of morals?					
		Yes			**No**		
		Men	**Women**			**Men**	**Women**
Have you seen an X-rated movie in the last year?	**Yes**	46	48	**Yes**		90	46
	No	162	347	**No**		92	112

Reconstruct the zero-order X-rated movie by gender table, calculate the partial table correlations and odds ratios, and determine whether the hypothesis is correct. What kind of relationship do you find?

6. Panel A is the zero-order table for the relationship of age to attitude towards legalization of marijuana, and Panel B is the partial table of responses among highly religious persons:

		A. Zero-Order Table			B. Partial Table for Highly Religious	
		Young	Old		Young	Old
Legalize marijuana?	Yes	17	14	Yes	10	7
	No	28	31	No	25	18

Calculate the zero-order correlation coefficient and the conditional correlation coefficients as well as the odds ratios. What kind of effect is observed when religiosity is held constant?

7. To study whether interracial contacts might be a function of opportunities mediated by attitudes, white respondents in the 1991 GSS were asked whether any blacks are living in their neighborhood and whether anyone in their family had brought a friend who was black home for dinner in recent years. The zero-order relationship is

		Brought a black home for dinner?	
		No	Yes
Any blacks live close by?	Yes	95	143
	No	40	133

Upon holding constant the respondents' opinions about whether the nation is spending too much or too little on the problems of blacks, the following partial tables are observed:

		Too much spending:				Too little/about right:	
		A black to dinner?				A black to dinner?	
		No	Yes			No	Yes
Any blacks live close by?	Yes	10	26		Yes	85	117
	No	5	29		No	35	104

Do these results support the hypothesis that the relationship between proximity and behavior can be completely explained by an intervening attitude?

8. Calculate the partial correlation coefficients $r_{XY \cdot W}$ between X and Y after controlling for Z.

	r_{XY}	r_{XZ}	r_{YZ}
a.	0.30	0.40	0.70
b.	−0.45	0.20	−0.30
c.	0.15	0.20	−0.75
d.	−0.60	−0.40	−0.40

9. Assortative mating means that marriages usually take place between persons of similar social backgrounds. The degree of assortative mating may differ by social context, however. Suppose you found the following:

		Urban Origin				Rural Origin	
		Husband's Religion				Husband's Religion	
		Catholic	Protestant			Catholic	Protestant
Wife's Religion	Protestant	30	60		Protestant	10	80
	Catholic	30	20		Catholic	20	5

a. Calculate: (1) the zero-order correlation between spouses' religions; (2) the correlation between religions in the two subtables; (3) the partial correlation between religions, holding constant origin; and (4) the *t* ratio for the significance of the partial *r* at $\alpha = .001$.

b. What kind of effect does the urban-rural origin have on assortative mating?

10. The relationship between family size (number of children) and satisfaction with family life may depend on the age at which women began to have their children. Here are two partial tables, one for women who started their families while still teenagers, and the other for women who began child-bearing at a later age:

| | | Began in Teens | | | | Began Later | | |
| | | Size of Family | | | | Size of Family | | |
		Low	Medium	High		Low	Medium	High
	High	15	10	5		60	30	15
Satisfaction with Family	Medium	5	15	20		20	15	15
	Low	5	5	25		20	15	10

Analyze these data, giving (a) the zero-order correlation; (b) both first-order correlations; (c) the partial correlation between satisfaction and size of family, controlling for age at which childbearing began; and (d) the *t* ratio for the significance of the partial correlation for $\alpha = .05$. Note: In your calculations assume the categories are coded Low = 0, Medium = 1, High = 2.

Problems Requiring the 1991 General Social Survey

11. Political analysts have noted that self-described liberals tend to be concentrated among the college educated, but this phenomenon may be a recent development. Test this hypothesis by dichotomizing POLVIEWS into conservative and nonconservative (moderate plus liberal) categories, EDUC into college

graduates and nongraduates, and AGE into those 45 or younger versus older respondents. What happens to the POLVIEWS–EDUC correlation when AGE is held constant?

12. Attitudes toward abortion for poorer women (ABPOOR) covary with religiosity (RELITEN), but is the strength of association the same for Catholics as for Protestants? (Note: Control for RELIG after excluding other categories.)

13. What is the partial correlation between subjective social class (CLASS) and attitude toward working if the financial reward were unnecessary (RICHWORK), controlling for EDUC, dichotomized into college graduates and nongraduates?

Problems Requiring Use of the U.S. States Data Set

14. State welfare payments (AFDCPAY) are known to be higher in wealthier states than in poorer states (INCPC). Show this covariation by dichotomizing these variables at their medians. Then determine whether the correlation between these two variables is the same for states experiencing high population change from 1980 to 1986 and those with lower population change.

15. The rate of infant mortality (INFANTPC) is *higher* where local governments spend a larger percentage of their budgets on healthcare expenditures (HEALTHEX). Can this paradox be explained by the availability of physicians per capita (DOCSPC)? Dichotomize these variables as follows:

> RECODE DOCSPC(LO THRU 185=1)(186 THRU HI=2).
> RECODE INFANTPC(LO THRU 10.99=1)(11.00 THRU HI=2).
> RECODE HEALTHEX(LO THRU 7.99=1)(8.00 THRU HI=2).

What are the zero-order and partial correlations between INFANTPC and HEALTHEX with DOCSPC held constant?

Statistics for
Social Data
Analysis

Multiple Regression Analysis

8

Multiple regression analysis examines the joint relationship between a dependent variable and two or more independent, or predictor, variables. It is an extension of the bivariate methods introduced in chapter 6 and is the most widely applied version of the general linear model in contemporary social science. Therefore, the parameter estimation and significance testing procedures for the multiple regression model are the most important techniques in this book, forming the foundation for more advanced methods described in later chapters.

Few social scientists today hypothesize that all the variation in some measure can be completely accounted for by its covariation with a single independent variable. Single-cause explanations, such as delinquency resulting from associating with deviant companions, have been largely replaced with complex accounts in which several unique sources of variation are posited. Thus, conflict between ethnic groups might be hypothesized to arise from competition for jobs; broad cultural, religious, and linguistic differences; income inequality; and exclusion from political power. Or, children's educational attainment may be a joint function of their parents' education, number of siblings, teacher encouragement, intellectual ability, personal aspirations, and peer pressures. The value of the multiple regression approach lies in its capacity to estimate the relative importance of several hypothesized predictors of the dependent variable of interest. Before presenting the regression model and the technical details involved in using it, we will describe a substantive problem for which regression techniques are appropriate.

multiple regression analysis—a statistical technique for estimating the relationship between a continuous dependent variable and two or more continuous or discrete independent, or predictor, variables

8.1.   An Example of a Three-Variable Regression Problem

Ira Reiss, a prominent family sociologist, has developed a theory of sexual permissiveness that has been rather widely accepted among sociologists. The basic proposition of his theory is as follows:

To the extent that a particular group has an autonomous, free courtship system, the likelihood of accepting sexual permissiveness is increased.[1]

Anything that promotes autonomy from the social control institutions of society promotes higher levels of sexual permissiveness.

Two factors that Reiss examines in his work with a national adult sample are religion and education. Religions embody many of the major sexual norms against premarital and extramarital sexuality in society, so the first derived proposition we will examine is as follows:

> P1: The greater the religiosity, the less the sexual permissiveness.

Since education can lead students to challenge and explore commonly accepted values, it should encourage autonomy of thought and action. The second derived proposition, therefore, is as follows:

> P2: The higher the individual's educational attainment, the greater the sexual permissiveness.

index—a variable that is a summed composite of other variables that are assumed to reflect some underlying construct

We will test these two hypotheses using the 1991 GSS data, in which sexual permissiveness is measured by a three-item index. An **index** is a variable that is a summed composite of other variables that are assumed to reflect some underlying construct. In this case the index is the sum of each individual's responses to three items divided by three. The three items deal with attitudes toward premarital sex, extramarital sex, and homosexual relations. The actual items, along with their frequency distributions, are shown in Table 8.1.

---

1. I. L. Reiss, and B. Miller, "Heterosexual Permissiveness: A Theoretical Analysis," in W. Burr, R. Hill, I. Nye, and I. L. Reiss (Eds.), *Contemporary Theories about the Family: Research-Based Theories*, Vol. 1 (New York: Free Press, 1979); I. L. Reiss, *Family Systems in America* (3rd ed.) (New York: Holt, Rinehart & Winston, 1980), Chap. 7.

TABLE 8.1

Frequency Distributions for Three Items in Sexual Permissiveness Index

---

A. *Premarital Sexual Relations*
   . . . If a man and woman have sexual relations before marriage, do you think it is always wrong, . . . or not wrong at all?
B. *Extramarital Sexual Relations*
   What is your opinion about a *married* person having sexual relations with someone *other* than the marriage partner—is it always wrong, . . . or not wrong at all?
C. *Homosexual Relations*
   What about sexual relations between two *adults* of the *same* sex—do you think it is always wrong, . . . or not wrong at all?

		A. Premarital		B. Extramarital		C. Homosexual	
Code	Response	N	%	N	%	N	%
1	Always wrong	137	9.0	368	24.3	349	23.0
2	Almost always wrong	45	3.0	50	3.3	15	1.0
3	Wrong only sometimes	74	4.9	20	1.3	21	1.4
4	Not wrong at all	194	12.8	12	0.8	65	4.3
9	Missing*	1,067	70.3	1,067	70.3	1,067	70.3
	Total	1,517	100.0%	1,517	100.0%	1,517	100.0%

*Treated as missing data in the analysis.
Source: 1991 General Social Survey

To construct an index, we must assume that the items comprising it reflect some underlying latent, unobservable characteristic. In this case we are assuming that people who hold a sexually restrictive attitude (the latent, unobserved variable) are more likely to say that premarital sex, extramarital sex, and homosexual relations are wrong. In contrast, those who hold a permissive attitude would be expected to argue that these behaviors are not wrong. Figure 8.1 shows that we conceive the three observed variables as a function of a latent, unobserved theoretical **construct**—sexual permissiveness. Since the three observed variables, or **indicators** as they are often called, are presumed to reflect a single underlying variable, we expect them to be positively correlated with each other. Indeed they are. In the 1991 GSS data the correlation between attitudes about premarital sex and extramarital sex is 0.34, between premarital sex and homosexual relations is 0.36, and between extramarital

construct—unobserved concept used by social scientists to explain observations

indicator—observable measure of underlying unobservable theoretical construct

FIGURE 8.1

Effects of Latent, Unobserved Variable on Covariation among a Set of Observed Indicators

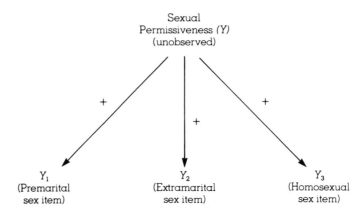

sex and homosexual relations is 0.31. These data provide some evidence for the presumption that the three items can be used as a single index of sexual permissiveness. More details on index construction of this sort are given in Box 8.1, which also introduces the concept of **Cronbach's alpha,** a measure of internal reliability.

Cronbach's alpha—a measure of internal reliability for multi-item summed indexes

Religiosity is measured by church attendance, which in the GSS data ranges from "never" (0) to "several times a week" (9). Education is coded from 0, for no formal schooling, to 20, for eight years of college. The two hypotheses drawn from P1 and P2 to be tested are as follows:

H1: The greater the church attendance, the less the sexual permissiveness.

H2: The more the years of education, the higher the sexual permissiveness.

8.2 The Three-Variable Regression Model

As in the bivariate regression model introduced in section 6.1 (beginning on page 191), the dependent variable in multiple regression is assumed to be linearly related to the independent variables. In the case of two independent variables, the three-variable *population regression equation* is as follows:

BOX 8.1   An Introduction to Index Construction

Social scientists often use indexes constructed from other variables to reflect some underlying latent unobservable variable. Perhaps the most common example is the IQ test, with which you are familiar. These test constructors assume that the responses to many individual items can be summed into a total score called IQ. Indices are often proxies for constructs, which social scientists find useful to explain observations. We do not really know if there is something called IQ, or religiosity, for example, but by positing such constructs we can account for observations in a succinct, logical, summary way.

When a set of indicators is posited to reflect an underlying construct, the items should be substantially correlated with one another. The higher the correlation among the items, the more confident we can be that the items are measuring the same construct. Furthermore, for a given level of correlation among the measures, the greater the number of indicators, the more confidence we can have in the index constructed from them. If five different people measure the length of an open field and the five observations are averaged, we will be more confident of what the true size of the field is than if a single person takes the measurement. For the same reason our confidence in an index increases with the number of independent measures taken. The assumption, however, is that *all* of the items do in fact reflect the same underlying construct. To summarize, *the quality of an index can be judged by the average intercorrelation among the indicators and the number of indicators that comprise it.*

A statistic that summarizes the reliability of an index is called Cronbach's alpha. It is a measure of the internal consistency of a set of items, and it ranges from zero (no internal consistency) to unity (perfect internal consistency). The usual computing formula is too complex to present here. But it reduces to a rather simple formula if the items to be summed into an index (and perhaps divided by the numbers of items, to create an average response across items) have equal or near-equal variances, as they will if all items use the

(Continued next page)

BOX 8.1   *(Continued)*

same response category format. This formula also can be used if all items are converted to Z scores before summing. The formula for Cronbach's alpha is as follows:

$$\alpha = \frac{k\bar{r}}{1 + (k - 1)\,\bar{r}}$$

where
k = The number of indicators in the index.
$\bar{r}$ = The average intercorrelation among the k items comprising the index.

We can show how to use alpha with the three-item sexual permissiveness index example used in the text. The $k = 3$ items intercorrelate 0.34, 0.36, and 0.31. Therefore, the average intercorrelation is $\bar{r} = (0.34 + 0.36 + 0.31)/3 = 0.337$. And

$$\hat{\alpha} = \frac{3(0.337)}{1 + (3 - 1)(0.337)} = 0.604$$

where the caret ($\hat{\ }$) is used to indicate an estimate of the underlying population parameter.

Since this index is composed of only three items, an $\hat{\alpha}$ of 0.604 is barely acceptable. We strive for indices with alphas of 0.70 or higher. If we had five or six items with an average correlation of 0.40, we could use the formula to verify that $\hat{\alpha}$ would be 0.77. This demonstrates that the number of indicators, as well as their average intercorrelation, contributes to our confidence in an index.

$$Y_i = \alpha + \beta_1 X_{1i} + \beta_2 X_{2i} + e_i$$

where
X_1 and X_2 = The two independent variables.
    e_i = The error or residual term.

Then the *population prediction equation* is

$$\hat{Y}_i = \alpha + \beta_1 X_{1i} + \beta_2 X_{2i}$$

With two independent variables the *sample regression* and *prediction equations* are given by

$$Y_i = a + b_1 X_{1i} + b_2 X_{2i} + e_i$$
$$\hat{Y}_i = a + b_1 X_{1i} + b_2 X_{2i}$$

As in bivariate regression, we use **ordinary least squares** (OLS) methods to estimate values for α, β_1, and β_2, such that Σe_i^2 is a minimum. We state without proof that the following sample values are unbiased estimates of the population parameters:

ordinary least squares —a method for obtaining estimates of regression equation coefficients that minimizes the error sum of squares

$$a = \overline{Y} - (b_1 \overline{X}_1 + b_2 \overline{X}_2)$$

$$b_1 = \left(\frac{s_Y}{s_{X_1}}\right) \frac{r_{YX_1} - r_{YX_2} r_{X_1 X_2}}{1 - r_{X_1 X_2}^2}$$

$$b_2 = \left(\frac{s_Y}{s_{X_2}}\right) \frac{r_{YX_2} - r_{YX_1} r_{X_1 X_2}}{1 - r_{X_1 X_2}^2}$$

Notice that the regression estimates can all be obtained if we simply know the sample means, standard deviations, and zero-order correlation coefficients for the three variables under investigation. Therefore, when doing regression analysis, we must always compute and report these statistics in a summary table.

We have done this for the GSS sexual permissiveness example in Table 8.2. Notice that we have tabled only half the correlations. Since $r_{XY} = r_{YX}$ for all X and Y, to show the bottom half of the matrix would be redundant. We also have tabled the sample data for age and gender of respondent. These data will be used in examples later in the chapter.

In making these and all other computations in the subsequent examples, we have used a **listwise deletion** procedure; that is, we have used an observation only if data on *all* variables being

listwise deletion —in multiple regression analysis the removal of all cases that have missing values on *any* of the variables

TABLE 8.2

Correlations, Means, and Standard Deviations among Sexual
Permissiveness, Religiosity, and Education

Variable	(Y)	(1)	(2)	Mean	Standard Deviation
Y Sexual Permissiveness	1,000	−0.399	0.296	1.854	0.778
1 Religiosity		1,000	0.004	3.887	2.653
2 Education			1.000	12.774	3.014

Note: $N = 442$
Source: 1991 General Social Survey

pairwise deletion—in
multiple regression
analysis the removal of a
case from the calculation
of a correlation coefficient
only if it has missing
values for one of the
variables

analyzed are present. The 1991 GSS has $N = 1,517$ cases. By using
a listwise procedure we have lost 1,075 cases, resulting in $N = 442$ in
Table 8.2. Most of these cases were lost because the GSS split-ballot
questionnaire asked only a third of the sample all three sexual
permissiveness items. The alternative to the listwise procedure is
pairwise deletion. Since regression analysis depends on correlations for estimating regression coefficients, and because correlations are based on pairs of observations, we can use the available
cases for each individual correlation coefficient.

There are two possible problems with the pairwise procedure.
First, since the number of cases available varies from correlation to
correlation, the N for any given problem is unclear. The N is crucial
in computing tests of significance. Second, the matrix (table) of
correlations generated by pairwise deletion is sometimes poorly
conditioned, so that the configuration of correlations observed may
not logically occur in real data. The technical details of this
condition are beyond the scope of this text. While an ill-conditioned
correlation matrix is rarely generated when pairwise procedures
are used, it can happen. When it does, the computer will not be
able to obtain a solution for the regression estimates sought.

We recommend that pairwise deletion procedures only be used
when there will be a large loss in cases (roughly 5% or more) due to
use of a listwise procedure. The danger of using a listwise
procedure in such instances is the nonrandom loss of cases, which
can provide biased estimates of population parameters. When
there is a substantial missing data problem for a variable, the
researcher needs to show whether and how the missing cases
might affect the analysis. The usual procedure is to show, using *t*

tests, that the missing observations do not differ significantly from the observations that are present on major demographic characteristics such as sex, education, race, and so on. Showing no significant differences on these variables is only partially reassuring, however, since we can never know whether the missing data have been generated for random or systematic reasons. Can you think of systematic ways that data loss can occur?

We can now use the formulas presented above to estimate the intercept and the two regression coefficients for religiosity and education, respectively, in the sexual permissiveness example. Since we need to know b_1 and b_2 to estimate the intercept, we estimate the regression coefficients, b_1 and b_2, prior to estimating a:

$$b_1 = \left(\frac{0.778}{2.653}\right) \frac{-0.399 - (0.296)(0.004)}{1 - (0.004)^2} = -0.117$$

$$b_2 = \left(\frac{0.778}{3.014}\right) \frac{0.296 - (-0.399)(0.004)}{1 - (0.004)^2} = 0.077$$

$$a = 1.854 - [(-0.117)(3.887) + (0.077)(12.774)] = 1.325$$

Therefore, the prediction equation for this example is as follows:

$$\hat{Y} = 1.325 - 0.117X_1 + 0.077X_2$$

8.2.1. Interpretation of b_1 and b_2

The regression coefficients b_1 and b_2 have the following interpretation:

> A **multiple regression coefficient** measures the amount of increase or decrease in the dependent variable for a one-unit difference in the independent variable, controlling for the other independent variable or variables in the equation.

multiple regression coefficient—a measure of association showing the amount of increase or decrease in a continuous dependent variable for a one-unit difference in the independent variable, controlling for the other independent variable(s)

In the sexual permissiveness example the dependent variable ranges from 1 = "always wrong" to 4 = "not wrong at all." Thus b_1 = -0.117 indicates that for a one-unit change on the religious attendance measure, a respondent's score on the sexual permissiveness scale is expected to drop by -0.117, on average. And for each additional year of education, the respondent's permissiveness score is expected to change an average of 0.077, since $b_2 = 0.077$.

As we noted in describing the concept of control in chapter 7, if two independent variables are uncorrelated, controlling for one of them will not affect the relationship between the other independent variable and the dependent variable. This can be seen by noting that if $r_{X_1 X_2} = 0$, then

$$
\begin{aligned}
b_1 &= \left(\frac{s_Y}{s_{X_1}} \right) \frac{r_{YX_1} - (r_{YX_2})(0)}{1 - 0^2} \\
&= \frac{s_Y}{s_{X_1}} r_{YX_1}
\end{aligned}
$$

This equals the bivariate regression coefficient, b, introduced in chapter 6. That is, when the two independent variables are uncorrelated, the relationship between one of them and the dependent variable is unchanged when controlling for the other independent variable. In the sexual permissiveness example $r_{X_1 X_2} = 0.004$, which is very close to zero. This suggests that the bivariate coefficients relating the independent variables to the dependent variable should not differ much from the multiple regression coefficients. That they do not is indicated in the table below:

Independent Variable	Bivariate Coefficients	Multiple Regression Coefficients
Religiosity	-0.117	-0.117
Education	0.077	0.077

8.2.2   Standardized Regression Coefficients (Beta Weights)

Since the measurement units of the dependent variable and religious attendance are both arbitrary, the interpretation of the regression coefficients is less clear than might be wanted. For this reason we suggest that the standardized regression (or beta) coefficients introduced in section 6.5 (on page 220) for the bivariate case should be computed as well. These are the regression coefficients, or *beta weights*, we would obtain if the three variables were converted to Z scores prior to estimating the regression equation.

Regardless of the number of independent variables, the following relationship holds between the metric coefficients and standardized regression coefficients (beta weights):

$$\beta_j^* = \left(\frac{s_{X_j}}{s_Y}\right) b_j$$

We simply multiply the metric regression coefficient by the ratio of the standard deviation of the independent variable X_j to the dependent variable Y. Hence in the case of two independent variables, X_1 and X_2:

$$\beta_1^* = \left(\frac{s_{X_1}}{s_Y}\right) b_1$$

$$\beta_2^* = \left(\frac{s_{X_2}}{s_Y}\right) b_2$$

Using the data from the sexual permissiveness example:

$$\beta_1^* = \left(\frac{2.653}{0.778}\right)(-0.117) = -0.399$$

$$\beta_2^* = \left(\frac{3.014}{0.778}\right)(0.077) = 0.298$$

Since the means of Z-transformed variables are zero, the intercept for the standardized regression equation is zero. Hence

$$\hat{Z}_Y = -0.399Z_1 + 0.298Z_2$$

The two independent variables are now in the same metric, and so we can determine their relative ability to predict sexual permissiveness by examining which of the variables is larger in absolute value. Religiosity is a more potent predictor ($\beta_1^* = -0.399$) than education ($\beta_2^* = 0.298$). For each standard deviation difference in religiosity, controlling for education, we can expect, on average, a -0.399 standard deviation change in the sexual permissiveness variable. In contrast, a standard deviation change in education, controlling for religiosity, results in a 0.298 standard deviation change, on average, in sexual permissiveness.

We still do not know how much of the variance in sexual permissiveness these two variables can account. We also do not know whether the two regression coefficients are statistically significant. The next three sections consider these issues.

8.2.3.   The Coefficient of Determination in the Three-Variable Case

The coefficient of determination ($R^2_{Y \cdot X}$) was introduced in section 6.3.2 (on page 206) as the sum of squares due to regression ($SS_{\text{REGRESSION}}$) divided by the total sum of squares (SS_{TOTAL}).

$$R^2_{Y \cdot X} = \frac{SS_{\text{REGRESSION}}}{SS_{\text{TOTAL}}}$$

We can use this same formulation to determine how much variance X_1 and X_2 can "explain" in the dependent variable Y.

An alternative formulation for the coefficient of determination is as follows:

$$R^2_{Y \cdot X} = \frac{\Sigma(Y_i - \overline{Y})^2 - \Sigma(Y_i - \hat{Y}_i)^2}{\Sigma(Y_i - \overline{Y})^2}$$

$$= \frac{SS_{\text{TOTAL}} - SS_{\text{ERROR}}}{SS_{\text{TOTAL}}}$$

since $SS_{\text{TOTAL}} = SS_{\text{REGRESSION}} + SS_{\text{ERROR}}$, and $SS_{\text{REGRESSION}} = SS_{\text{TOTAL}} - SS_{\text{ERROR}}$. In the bivariate case $\hat{Y}_i = a + bX_i$, where in the case of two independent variables, $\hat{Y}_i = a + b_1X_{1i} + b_2X_{2i}$. This latter equation, therefore, must be substituted in the formula above for $\hat{Y}_i$ in order to determine $SS_{\text{REGRESSION}}$.

Ordinarily the sum of squares due to regression will be larger in the multivariate case than in the bivariate case. It can *never* be smaller, since one reason for including additional variables is to explain additional variance in the dependent variable. There are several computational formulas for $R^2_{Y \cdot X_1 X_2}$, four of which are presented in this section. You should convince yourself that they all give the same answer.

The first two formulas for the coefficient of determination in the three-variable case are as follows:

$$R^2_{Y \cdot X_1 X_2} = \frac{r^2_{YX_1} + r^2_{YX_2} - 2r_{YX_1} r_{YX_2} r_{X_1 X_2}}{1 - r^2_{X_1 X_2}}$$

$$R^2_{Y \cdot X_1 X_2} = \beta^*_1 r_{YX_1} + \beta^*_2 r_{YX_2}$$

We have added subscripts to R^2 to clarify which independent variables are being used to predict the dependent variable. In the subscript the variable being predicted (Y) is to the left of the dot and the predictor variables, X_1 and X_2, are to the right of the dot.

We can use either of these equations to compute the amount of variance in sexual permissiveness that can be accounted for by religiosity and education. We will use the second one because it involves fewer computations. Using the GSS data in Table 8.2 and the beta weights calculated in the preceding section,

$$R^2_{Y \cdot X_1 X_2} = (-0.399)(-0.399) + (0.298)(0.296)$$

$$= 0.2474$$

Thus, these two variables together account for 24.7% of the variance in sexual permissiveness. Since 75.3% of the variance remains unexplained, a more complex theory than these two simple propositions is obviously needed.

Two other formulations of the coefficient of determination are informative, not as computational formulas, but because they shed light on the meaning of the coefficient. They are as follows:

$$R^2_{Y \cdot X_1 X_2} = r^2_{YX_1} + (r^2_{YX_2 \cdot X_1})(1 - r^2_{YX_1})$$

$$R^2_{Y \cdot X_1 X_2} = r^2_{YX_2} + (r^2_{YX_1 \cdot X_2})(1 - r^2_{YX_2})$$

These two equations indicate that with two independent variables, the coefficient of determination can be divided into two components. In the first equation the first component is the amount of variance in Y that X_1 alone can account for—$r^2_{YX_1}$. The second component is the additional amount of variance in Y that X_2 can explain, after controlling for X_1. This term, $(r^2_{YX_2 \cdot X_1})(1 - r^2_{YX_1})$, is the **part correlation** squared between Y and X_2, controlling for X_1. (Notice that the part correlation is the square of the partial correlation $(r_{YX_2 \cdot X_1})$, multiplied by the term $(1 - r^2_{YX_1})$. Hence, the part and partial correlations are intimately related.)

part correlation—a measure of the proportion of variance in a dependent variable that an independent variable can explain, when squared, after controlling for the other independent variable in a multiple regression equation

Figure 8.2 uses Venn diagrams to examine how these two components relate to the coefficient of determination. Panel A, which diagrams the first equation, shows $r^2_{YX_1}$ as the area of overlap between the Y and X_1 circles, *including* that part of the Y and X_1 overlap that also overlaps X_2. And $(r^2_{YX_2 \cdot X_1})(1 - r^2_{YX_1})$ is shown as the

FIGURE 8.2

Venn Diagrams Showing Two Different But Equivalent Decompositions of $R^2_{Y \cdot X_1 X_2}$

A. $R^2_{Y \cdot X_1 X_2} = r^2_{YX_1} + (r^2_{YX_2 \cdot X_1})(1 - r^2_{YX_1})$

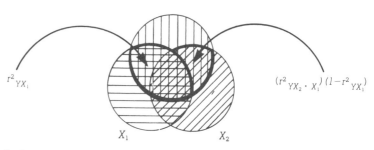

B. $R^2_{Y \cdot X_1 X_2} = r^2_{YX_2} + (r^2_{YX_1 \cdot X_2})(1 - r^2_{YX_2})$

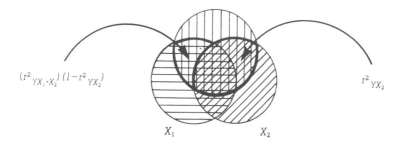

overlap between Y and X_2, *excluding* that part of the Y and X_2 overlap that also overlaps X_1. This diagram indicates that the coefficient of determination can be thought of as the amount of variance explained in Y by X_1, *plus* the amount of Y accounted for by X_2, controlling for X_1. In other words, we have first allocated to X_1 all the variance in Y that is *jointly contributed* by X_1 and X_2; then we have added on the variance in Y that is *uniquely* explained by X_2.

An alternative but equivalent decomposition is shown in the second equation above and in Panel B of Figure 8.2. This decomposition shows $r^2_{YX_2}$ as the overlap between the Y and X_2 circles, including that part of the Y and X_2 overlap that also includes X_1. As in Panel A, the coefficient of determination also includes the amount of variance in Y that can be accounted for by X_1, controlling for X_2; that is, $(r^2_{YX_1 \cdot X_2})(1 - r^2_{YX_2})$.

These two alternative but equivalent formulas for $R^2_{Y \cdot X_1 X_2}$ make an important point:

> When both X_1 and X_2 correlate with the dependent variable and are themselves intercorrelated, there is no unique way to partition the amount of variance in Y due to the two independent variables. However, when the two independent variables are uncorrelated, as they are in an experiment (or should be if the assignment of subjects to conditions has indeed been random), then we can uniquely partition the amount of variance in Y to X_1 and X_2.

This is one reason experimental research is preferred to nonexperimental research in the social sciences. When an experiment is possible and can be ethically justified, it offers a better opportunity to determine the effects of independent variables on a dependent variable.

When X_1 and X_2 are uncorrelated, the total variance in Y can be uniquely partitioned into two segments, one due to X_1 and the second due to X_2. If, in the first formula for $R^2_{Y \cdot X_1 X_2}$ presented above, $r_{X_1 X_2} = 0$, then

$$R^2_{Y \cdot X_1 X_2} = \frac{r^2_{YX_1} + r^2_{YX_2} - 2r_{YX_1}r_{YX_2}(0)}{1 - 0^2}$$

$$= r^2_{YX_1} + r^2_{YX_2}$$

That is, if X_1 and X_2 are uncorrelated, the amount of variance each explains in Y is simply $r^2_{YX_1}$ and $r^2_{YX_2}$, respectively, and these two components sum to the coefficient of determination—$R^2_{Y \cdot X_1 X_2}$. This is shown with Venn diagrams in Figure 8.3.

The square root of the coefficient of determination is called the **multiple correlation coefficient.** While $R_{Y \cdot X_1 X_2}$ is often reported in research reports, it is less useful than $R^2_{Y \cdot X_1 X_2}$ as an interpretive tool, since it has no clear meaning.

multiple correlation coefficient—the coefficient for a multiple regression equation, which, when squared, equals the ratio of the sum of squares due to regression to the total sum of squares

8.2.4. Testing the Significance of the Coefficient of Determination with Two Independent Variables

In section 6.4.1 (page 212), for the bivariate case, we tested $R^2_{Y \cdot X}$ for significance with an F test with 1 and $N - 2$ degrees of freedom. Where $\rho^2_{Y \cdot X_1 X_2}$ is the coefficient of determination in the population with two independent variables, the null hypothesis is H_0: $\rho^2_{Y \cdot X_1 X_2} = 0$. We will also test this hypothesis with an F test, though the degrees of freedom will differ from those in the bivariate case. The degrees of freedom associated with SS_{TOTAL} are $N - 1$, regardless of the number of independent variables. In the case of two independent variables, $SS_{\text{REGRESSION}}$ is estimated from the two regression coefficients and hence has 2 df associated with it. Since we know that, in general, $df_{\text{TOTAL}} = df_{\text{REGRESSION}} + df_{\text{ERROR}}$, by subtraction $df_{\text{ERROR}} = N - 3$.

FIGURE 8.3
Venn Diagrams Showing the Decomposition of $R^2_{Y \cdot X_1 X_2}$ When X_1 and X_2 Are Uncorrelated

$$R^2_{Y \cdot X_1 X_2} = r^2_{YX_1} + r^2_{YX_2}$$

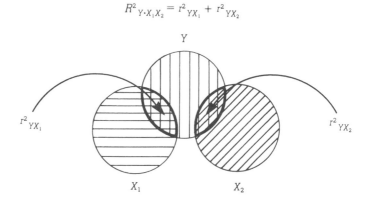

We can compute the mean squares needed for the F test by dividing the sums of squares by the appropriate degrees of freedom. That is, with two independent variables

$$MS_{\text{REGRESSION}} = \frac{SS_{\text{REGRESSION}}}{2}$$

$$MS_{\text{ERROR}} = \frac{SS_{\text{ERROR}}}{N - 3}$$

If the null hypothesis that $\rho^2_{Y \cdot X_1 X_2} = 0$ in the population is true, both $MS_{\text{REGRESSION}}$ and MS_{ERROR} are unbiased estimates of the variance of the errors of prediction, σ^2_e. If, however, $\rho^2_{Y \cdot X_1 X_2}$ is greater than zero in the population, then $MS_{\text{REGRESSION}}$ is greater than MS_{ERROR} as well. If in a given sample the ratio of $MS_{\text{REGRESSION}}$ to MS_{ERROR} is larger than some predetermined critical value, we reject the hypothesis that $\rho^2_{Y \cdot X_1 X_2} = 0$ in the population.

Specifically, we choose an alpha level and calculate the following test statistic:

$$F_{2, N-3} = \frac{MS_{\text{REGRESSION}}}{MS_{\text{ERROR}}}$$

We next look in Appendix E to determine the critical value for an F with 2 and $N - 3$ degrees of freedom. If the test statistic is as large or larger than the critical value, we reject the null hypothesis; otherwise we do not.

To calculate the mean squares, we need to know the terms in the numerators—$SS_{\text{REGRESSION}}$ and SS_{ERROR}. To calculate these sums of squares, we use the same logic as we did in the bivariate case. Therefore,

$$SS_{\text{REGRESSION}} = R^2_{Y \cdot X_1 X_2} SS_{\text{TOTAL}}$$

and

$$SS_{\text{ERROR}} = SS_{\text{TOTAL}} - SS_{\text{REGRESSION}}$$

We can now ask whether the coefficient of determination observed in section 8.2.3, 0.2474, is significantly different from zero in the population. We set $\alpha = .01$. To calculate the sums of squares, we note from Table 8.2 that $s_Y = 0.778$; therefore, the variance of variable Y in the sample, $s_Y^2 = (0.820)^2 = 0.672$, with $N = 442$. Since, in general, $SS_{\text{TOTAL}} = s_Y^2(N - 1)$, it follows that

$$SS_{\text{TOTAL}} = (0.605)(442 - 1) = 266.805$$

$$SS_{\text{REGRESSION}} = (0.247)(266.805) = 65.901$$

$$SS_{\text{ERROR}} = 266.805 - 65.901 = 200.904$$

We now can divide these figures by their degrees of freedom to determine the mean squares:

$$MS_{\text{REGRESSION}} = \frac{65.901}{2} = 32.951$$

$$MS_{\text{ERROR}} = \frac{200.904}{442 - 1} = 0.456$$

The test statistic is then

$$F_{2,439} = \frac{32.951}{0.456} = 72.261$$

An examination of Appendix E indicates that the critical value for 2 and 439 df is 4.61. Therefore, we can reject with great confidence the null hypothesis that $\rho^2_{Y \cdot X_1 X_2} = 0$ in the population.

8.2.5. Testing b_1 and b_2 for Significance

Two null hypotheses can be tested to determine whether or not the two regression coefficients are zero in the population. These hypotheses assert that the population parameters are zero: $H_0: \beta_1 = 0$ and $H_0: \beta_2 = 0$. We will show how to test whether the sample regression coefficient, b_1, is statistically significant first and return to the test of b_2 later. However, the two tests are very similar.

To test whether the observed b_1 differs statistically from zero, we construct a t variable, just as we did in the bivariate case. In the three-variable case,

$$t = \frac{b_1 - 0}{s_{b_1}}$$

To obtain the t value, we need to estimate the standard error of the regression coefficient, s_{b_1}. If we assume that in the population being sampled the dependent variable, Y, is normally distributed for any *joint outcome* of X_1 and X_2, the sampling distribution of b_1 (and of b_2 as well) is normally distributed as N gets large. Furthermore, the mean of the sampling distribution of b_1 will equal β_1; that is, $E(b_1) = \beta_1$. The variance of the sampling distribution of b_1 is as follows:

$$\sigma^2_{b_1} = \frac{\sigma^2_e}{\Sigma(X_{1i} - \overline{X}_1)^2(1 - \rho^2_{X_1 \cdot X_2})}$$

As was true for the bivariate case, we can estimate the numerator, σ^2_e, with MS_{ERROR}. The term $\rho^2_{X_1 \cdot X_2}$ is the correlation squared for predicting X_1 from X_2. It is estimated by $R^2_{X_1 \cdot X_2}$. Now that we have estimates of σ^2_e and $\rho^2_{X_1 \cdot X_2}$, we can obtain a sample estimate of $\sigma^2_{b_1}$. For the sample statistic,

$$s^2_{b_1} = \frac{MS_{ERROR}}{\Sigma(X_{1i} - \overline{X}_1)^2(1 - R^2_{X_1 \cdot X_2})}$$

The square root is used in the denominator of the t ratio. The t ratio will have $N - 3$ degrees of freedom, since there are $N - 3$ *df* associated with MS_{ERROR}. Hence, for b_1 we have

$$t_{N-3} = \frac{b_1}{s_{b_1}} = \frac{b_1}{\sqrt{\dfrac{MS_{ERROR}}{\Sigma(X_{1i} - \overline{X}_1)^2 (1 - R^2_{X_1 \cdot X_2})}}}$$

In the preceding section we determined that MS_{ERROR} is 0.456. Since $s^2_{X_1} = \Sigma(X_{1i} - \overline{X}_1)^2/(N - 1)$, we also know that $\Sigma(X_{1i} - \overline{X}_1)^2 = s^2_{X_1}(N - 1)$. And since Table 8.2 shows that $s_{X_1} = 2.653$, we can see that $s^2_{X_1} = (2.653)^2 = 7.0384$. With $N = 442$, it follows that $\Sigma(X_{1i} - \overline{X}_1)^2 = (7.0384)(442 - 1) = 3{,}103.934$. And we see from Table 8.2 that $r_{X_1 X_2} = 0.004$. Hence $R^2_{X_1 \cdot X_2} = 0.000016$.

Now we set $\alpha = .01$ and calculate t_{439}:

$$t_{439} = \frac{-0.117}{\sqrt{\dfrac{0.456}{(3,103.934)(1 - 0.000016)}}}$$

$$= \frac{-0.117}{0.0121} = -9.65$$

For $\alpha = .01$ and 439 df, we see from Appendix D that the critical value is -2.33 for a one-tailed test. Since the observed test statistic is much larger than the critical value, we reject the null hypothesis that β_1 equals zero.

The test for a b_2 regression coefficient is very similar to that for b_1. The t test for calculating the test statistic is as follows:

$$t_{N-3} = \frac{b_2}{s_{b_2}} = \frac{b_2}{\sqrt{\dfrac{MS_{\text{ERROR}}}{\Sigma(X_{2i} - \overline{X}_2)^2 \, (1 - R^2_{X_2 \cdot X_1})}}}$$

where
$$R^2_{X_2 \cdot X_1} = r^2_{X_2 X_1}$$

We know that $MS_{\text{ERROR}} = 0.456$, and from Table 8.2 we can see that $s^2_{X_2} = 3.014^2 = 9.084$, $r_{X_1 X_2} = 0.004$, with $N = 442$. Therefore, $\Sigma(X_{2i} - \overline{X}_2)^2 = s^2_{X_2}(N - 1) = (9.084)(441) = 4,006.044$. Furthermore, $R^2_{X_2 \cdot X_1} = -.004^2 = .000016$. If we set $\alpha = .01$, we can compute the test statistic:

$$t_{439} = \frac{0.077}{\sqrt{\dfrac{0.456}{(4,006.044)(1 - .000016)}}}$$

$$= \frac{0.077}{0.0107} = 7.20$$

Appendix D indicates that the critical value for a one-tailed hypothesis test with 439 degrees of freedom is 2.33. Since this test statistic is 7.11, we reject the null hypothesis.

Table 8.3, which summarizes the results for testing the two propositions about sexual permissiveness, shows support for both propositions. That is, as religiosity increases, sexual permissiveness decreases, controlling for educational attainment. And as educational attainment increases, so does sexual permissiveness.[2] Before accepting these propositions, however, we need to be certain that no other variables might account for the observed relationships. One such variable is the gender of the respondent.

8.2.6. Confidence Intervals for b_1 and b_2

As in the bivariate case, we can use the standard errors of b_1 and b_2 to construct confidence intervals around the point estimates. If we pick $\alpha = .01$, the upper and lower limits for the 99% confidence interval for the population parameter, β_1, are $b_1 + s_{b_1} 2.58$ and $b_1 - s_{b_1} 2.58$. Since we saw in Table 8.3 that $s_{b_1} = 0.0121$ and $b_1 = -0.117$, we have $-0.117 + (0.0121)(2.58) = -0.086$ and $-0.117 - (0.0121)(2.58) = -0.148$. Therefore, the 99% confidence interval for β_1 is bounded by -0.148 and -0.086.

The upper and lower limits to a 99% confidence interval for β_2 are given by $b_2 + s_{b_2}2.58$ and $b_2 - s_{b_2}2.58$. Convince yourself that in the sexual permissiveness data these limits are 0.048 and 0.104.

8.2.7. Partial Correlation in the Three-Variable Case

Partial correlation methods were introduced in chapter 7. For three variables Y, X_i, and X_j:

$$r_{YX_j \cdot X_i} = \frac{r_{YX_j} - r_{YX_i}r_{X_iX_j}}{\sqrt{1 - r_{YX_i}^2}\sqrt{1 - r_{X_iX_j}^2}}$$

---

2. It is also possible to test a, the intercept for statistical significance, but the formula for doing so is omitted here because it is too complex. Most statistics computer programs routinely calculate the t test for you.

TABLE 8.3
Results of Regression of Sexual Permissiveness Index on
Religiosity and Educational Attainment Variables

Independent Variable	B_j^*	b_j	s_{b_j}	t
Religiosity	−0.399	−0.117	0.0121	−9.65*
Educational attainment	0.298	0.077	0.0107	7.20*
Intercept		1.325		
		$R^2 = 0.247*$		

*Significant for $\alpha = .001$.

The partial correlation coefficient is an estimate of the relationship between a variable, Y, and a second variable, X_j, controlling for a third variable, X_i. And the square of the partial correlation coefficient is the amount of variance in Y that can be accounted for by X_j, controlling for (or taking into account) X_i. As we showed in sections 8.2.2 and 8.2.3, the standardized regression coefficient, β_j^*, is given by

$$\beta_j^* = \left(\frac{s_{X_j}}{s_Y} \right) b_j = \frac{r_{YX_j} - r_{YX_j}r_{X_iX_j}}{1 - r_{X_iX_j}^2}$$

Notice that the beta weight in this equation and the partial correlation coefficient given above have the same numerator. This means both will always have the same sign, and they usually are very similar in size. Their similarity has led some researchers and statisticians to refer to the regression coefficients from multiple regression analysis as **partial regression coefficients.** The similarity between β_j^* and $r_{YX_j \cdot X_i}$ can be illustrated for the example where sexual permissiveness was regressed on religious attendance and education. As we found in section 8.2.2, $\beta_1^* = -0.399$ and

$$r_{YX_1 \cdot X_2} = \frac{-0.399 - (0.298)(0.004)}{\sqrt{1 - 0.298^2}\sqrt{1 - 0.004^2}} = -0.419$$

Since the results from the regression and partial correlation analyses are very similar, one of them is superfluous. Ordinarily

partial regression coefficient—the effect of regressing a dependent variable on an independent variable, controlling for one or more other independent variables.

the regression coefficients are of greater interest, so partial correlation coefficients are usually not presented or discussed in research reports. One interesting and important application of the partial correlation coefficient will be shown in chapter 11, which describes a technique called *path analysis*.

> The tests of significance for the partial correlation coefficients are identical to those used in testing the regression coefficients. Therefore, if you test the regression coefficients for significance, you have also indirectly tested the partial correlation coefficients for significance.

8.3 Multiple Regression with *K* Independent Variables

If K independent variables are each hypothesized to affect a dependent, continuous variable in a linear, additive manner, then the general **population regression model** for the ith observation is as follows:

population regression model—a regression model for a population in which K independent variables are each hypothesized to affect a dependent, continuous variable in a linear, additive manner

$$Y_i = \alpha + \beta_1 X_{1i} + \beta_2 X_{2i} + \ldots + \beta_K X_{Ki} + \epsilon_i$$
$$= \alpha + \sum_{j=1}^{K} \beta_j X_{ji} + \epsilon_i$$

where
α = The constant or intercept.
β_j = The regression coefficient, the effect of independent variable X_j on dependent variable Y.
ϵ_i = The error term, or residual, for the ith case.

To estimate the population regression parameters with sample data, we choose an estimator that provides the **best linear and unbiased estimate (BLUE)** having minimum variance. Box 8.2 summarizes the BLUE properties desired in a multiple regression equation. The sample regression equation and the prediction equation are as follows:

best linear and unbiased estimate (BLUE)—an estimator for population regression parameters that assumes a linear relationship, no measurement error, and normally distributed error terms

$$Y_i = a + b_1 X_{1i} + b_2 X_{2i} + \ldots + b_K X_{Ki} + e_i$$
$$\hat{Y}_i = a + b_1 X_{1i} + b_2 X_{2i} + \ldots + b_K X_{Ki}$$

BOX 8.2   The BLUE Regression Criteria

Several properties comprise the best linear unbiased estimator (BLUE) characteristics traditionally sought in making inferences about population regression parameters (α and β) from estimates based on sample data (a and b). Among these assumptions are the following:

1. The relationship between the dependent variable and its predictors is linear, and no irrelevant variables are either omitted from or included in the equation.
2. All variables are measured without error.
3. The error term (e_i) for a single regression equation has the following properties:
   A. e_i is normally distributed.
   B. The expected value (mean) of the errors is zero: $\sum_{i=1}^{N} e_i = 0$
   C. The errors are independently distributed with constant variances (homoscedasticity):
   $$\frac{\sum e_i^2}{N} = \sigma_e^2$$
   D. Each predictor is uncorrelated with the equation's error term: $\rho_{X_{ji}e_i} = 0$
4. In systems of interrelated equations (see chapter 12) the error in one equation is assumed to be uncorrelated with the errors in the other equations: $\rho_{e_i e_j} = 0$

Violating the BLUE assumptions may result in ordinary least squares regression estimates that are biased or significance tests that are incorrect, although parameter estimates may be "robust" to some violations. Advanced methods for assessing how severely assumptions have been violated, for example by examining residuals, are suggested in D. Belsley et al. (1980) *Regression Diagnostics* (New York: Wiley). Alternatives to OLS estimation methods, such as weighted least squares, can be substituted where appropriate.

In the case of K independent variables, a multiple regression coefficient shows the amount of difference in the dependent variable that can be attributed to a one-unit difference in the independent variable, controlling (holding constant) the effects of the other $K - 1$ independent variables included in the equation. The intercept term shows the expected value of the dependent variable when all the independent measures equal zero.

Estimation of the population regression parameters, α and the β_K, is done with ordinary least squares (OLS) techniques, thus assuring that the sum of the squared errors in the prediction (Σe_i^2) is minimized. For those students familiar with calculus, Box 8.3 explains the principles behind OLS estimation. The basic inputs to

---

BOX 8.3   Deriving OLS Estimators of a and b for Regression Equations

The basic principle of ordinary least squares (OLS) estimation is to find values of a and b_k that make the sum of squared errors as small as possible. The situation is most easily illustrated with a two-predictor regression equation:

$$Y_i = a + b_1 X_{1i} + b_2 X_{2i} + e_i$$

The error for observation i is just the difference between that case's observed score and its value predicted by the regression equation:

$$e_i = (Y_i - \hat{Y}_i)$$

If $\hat{Y}_i$ is replaced by its regression equation estimate, squared, and summed across all N cases, the value that OLS seeks to minimize is the sum of the squared errors (Σe_i^2), or

$$\Sigma(Y_i - \hat{Y}_i)^2 = \Sigma(Y_i - a - b_1 X_{1i} - b_2 X_{2i})^2$$

According to basic calculus, any quadratic equation attains a minimum at the point where the first derivative equals 0. Therefore, taking partial derivatives of the right side of the

(Continued next page)

BOX 8.3   *(continued)*

expression above for each of the a and b_k estimates and setting them equal to zero gives:

$$-2\ \Sigma(Y_i - a - b_1 X_{1i} - b_2 X_{2i}) = 0$$

$$-2\ \Sigma X_{1i}(Y_i - a - b_1 X_{1i} - b_2 X_{2i}) = 0$$

$$-2\ \Sigma X_{2i}(Y_i - a - b_1 X_{1i} - b_2 X_{2i}) = 0$$

Simplifying and rearranging gives the usual form of three so-called normal equations (which have nothing to do with the normal distribution) for a straight line:

$$\Sigma Y_i = Na + b_1\Sigma X_{1i} + b_2\Sigma X_{2i}$$

$$\Sigma X_{1i}Y_i = a\Sigma X_{1i} + b_1\Sigma X_{1i}^2 + b_2\Sigma X_{1i}X_{2i}$$

$$\Sigma X_{2i}Y_i = a\Sigma X_{2i} + b_1\Sigma X_{1i}X_{2i} + b_2\Sigma X_{2i}^2$$

Three equations with three unknowns can be solved to give unique estimates of the unknowns. To obtain a, divide the first normal equation by N and rearrange:

$$a = \bar{Y} - b_1\bar{X}_1 - b_2\bar{X}_2$$

This equation shows that the least squares regression line always passes through the point whose coordinates are the means of all variables, $\bar{Y}, \bar{X}_1,$ and $\bar{X}_2$.

To find formulas for the bs, begin with the definition of the regression error as $e_i = Y_i - \hat{Y}_i$. Because $\hat{Y}_i = a + b_1 X_{1i} + b_2 X_{2i}$ and $a = \bar{Y} - b_1\bar{X}_1 - b_2\bar{X}_2$, we can substitute for a in the equation for the expected score:

$$\hat{Y}_i = \bar{Y} + b_1(X_{1i} - \bar{X}_1) + b_2(X_{2i} - \bar{X}_2)$$

and then substitute into the equation for the error term:

$$e_i = (Y_i - \hat{Y}_i) = Y_i - [\bar{Y} + b_1(X_{1i} - \bar{X}_1) + b_2(X_{2i} - \bar{X}_2)]$$

$$= (Y_i - \bar{Y}) - b_1(X_{1i} - \bar{X}_1) - b_2(X_{2i} - \bar{X}_2)$$

BOX 8.3   *(continued)*

Because OLS estimators of the *b*s must minimize the sum of squared error terms, the next step is to form these sums of squares:

$$\Sigma e_i^2 = \Sigma(Y_i - \hat{Y}_i)^2 = \Sigma[(Y_i - \bar{Y}) - b_1(X_{1i} - \bar{X}_1) - b_2(X_{2i} - \bar{X}_2)]^2$$

Finally, taking derivatives of the expression on the right with respect to each of the *b*s results in these estimators:

$$b_1 = \frac{(\Sigma YX_{1i})(\Sigma X_2^2) - (\Sigma YX_{2i})(\Sigma X_{1i}X_{2i})}{(\Sigma X_{1i}^2)(\Sigma X_{2i}^2) - (\Sigma X_{1i}X_{2i})}$$

and

$$b_2 = \frac{(\Sigma YX_{2i})(\Sigma X_1^2) - (\Sigma YX_{1i})(\Sigma X_{2i}X_{1i})}{(\Sigma X_{2i}^2)(\Sigma X_{1i}^2) - (\Sigma X_{2i}X_{1i})}$$

Similar procedures can be used to derive estimators of parameters for regression equations with more independent variables, but writing these becomes increasingly formidable as predictors are added to the equation. Consequently, solutions to multiple regression equations are compactly obtained through matrix algebra manipulations that are performed by computer programs.

computerized multiple regression programs are a matrix of correlations among *K* variables and vectors of their means and standard deviations. Table 8.4 illustrates such data for an example to be analyzed below. Only the lower-triangular portion of the correlation matrix is reported. Because $r_{AB} = r_{BA}$ for all pairs *A* and *B*, showing the upper half of the matrix would be redundant.

To illustrate multiple regression with more than two independent variables, we analyze the seven variables in Table 8.4 from the U.S. States Data Set (excluding Washington, DC). We attempt to explain variation in the number of infant deaths per 1,000 live births in 1984 as a linear additive function of the other six variables. Some

TABLE 8.4

Correlations, Means, and Standard Deviations for Infant Mortality Regression Analysis

Variable	(1)	(2)	(3)	(4)	(5)	(6)	(7)	*Mean*	*s*
(1) Infant Mortality/1,000 Births	1.000							10.616	1.398
(2) Births to Unwed Mothers (%)	.630	1.000						20.096	5.183
(3) Physicians/100,000 Population	−.182	.274	1.000					178.120	44.146
(4) White Population (%)	−.596	−.608	−.025	1.000				86.702	11.576
(5) Persons Below Poverty Level (%)	.514	.514	−.400	−.378	1.000			12.498	3.463
(6) Local Gov't Health Budget (%)	.598	.285	−.408	−.258	.501	1.000		7.508	4.974
(7) Cropland (1,000 acres)	−.191	−.278	−.278	.202	.016	.117	1.000	8,907.180	9,203.476

Note: $N = 50$; missing data = 1.
Source: U.S. States Data Set

nested regression equations — regression equations where independent variables are successively added to an equation to observe changes in the predictors' relationships to the dependent variable

measures represent social structural forces, others the effects of health policies, and one variable—farm cropland—we expected would be unrelated to states' infant mortality rates. We later compare the results of three **nested regression equations,** that is, where independent variables are successively added to an equation to observe changes in the predictors' relationships to the dependent variable. (All analyses reported below were performed by a computer, with calculations carried to many decimal places; hence, some results may differ due to rounding imprecision.)

Our first equation regresses infant mortality rates on three indicators of states' population composition: X_1 = percentage of state population below the poverty line; X_2 = percentage of births to unwed mothers; and X_3 = percentage white. The estimated prediction equation for this equation is as follows:

$$\hat{Y}_i = 11.012 + 0.093\,X_{1i} + 0.086\,X_{2i} - 0.038\,X_{3i}$$

As discussed in section 8.2, each *metric regression coefficient* measures the amount of increase or decrease in the dependent variable for a one-unit difference in the independent variable, controlling for the other independent variables in the equation. In this example the dependent variable measures the rate of infant deaths per 1,000 live births during the year. Therefore, $b_1 = 0.093$ means that for a 1% increase in a state's poverty population, its infant mortality is expected to increase on average by 0.093 deaths per 1,000 live births. Conversely, decreasing state poverty by 1%

would produce an average decrease of 0.093 infant deaths per 1,000 live births. Similarly, $b_2 = 0.086$ means that each percentage of births to unwed mothers is associated with an increase of 0.086 infant deaths per 1,000 live births. Finally, the $b_3 = -0.038$ coefficient indicates that states with a 1% higher white population have on average -0.038 fewer infant deaths per 1,000 live births (i.e., the more *nonwhite* its population, the higher its infant mortality).

Recall from section 8.2.2 that standardized regression coefficients (or beta weights) are formed by multiplying the metric regression coefficients by the ratio of the standard deviation of the independent variable X_j to the standard deviation of the dependent variable Y. Hence, in the case of the three-predictor regression equation, the beta weights are as follows:

$$\beta_1^* = \left(\frac{3.463}{1.398} \right) (0.093) = 0.230$$

$$\beta_2^* = \left(\frac{5.183}{1.398} \right) (0.086) = 0.319$$

$$\beta_3^* = \left(\frac{11.576}{1.398} \right) (-0.038) = -0.315$$

Because the means of Z-transformed variables are zero (see Box 2.4 on page 67), no intercept exists in a standardized regression equation. Therefore, the complete standardized multiple regression equation is

$$\hat{Z}_{Y_i} = 0.230 \, Z_{X_{1i}} + 0.319 \, Z_{X_{2i}} - 0.315 \, Z_{X_{3i}}$$

All three independent variables now share the same scale (i.e., standard deviation units), so their relative impacts on infant mortality can be compared by examining which coefficients have the largest absolute values. Both the births to unwed mothers and the percentage of white population have betas that are clearly larger than the beta for percentage in poverty. Thus, we can conclude that, net of the others' effects, poverty is a less potent predictor of state infant mortality than are racial composition and illegitimate births. Each one standard deviation difference in out-of-wedlock births produces an average 0.32 standard deviation change in infant mortality. An almost identical effect occurs in the opposite direction for percentage white. In contrast, a one standard deviation change in poverty, controlling for the other two variables, results in only a 0.23 standard deviation change in infant mortality.

8.3.1.   The Coefficient of Determination with K Independent Variables

A simple formula for the multiple regression coefficient of determination for an equation with K predictors is as follows:

$$R^2_{Y \cdot X_1 X_2 \ldots X_K} = \beta^*_1 r_{YX_1} + \beta^*_2 r_{YX_2} + \ldots + \beta^*_K r_{YX_K}$$

$$= \sum_{j=1}^{K} \beta^*_j r_{YX_j}$$

The subscripts attached to R^2 clarify which independent variables predict the dependent variable. The predicted variable (Y) appears to the left of the centered dot and all the predictor variables, X_1 through X_K, are listed to the right of the dot. Note that the value of a multiple regression coefficient of determination just sums the products of each standardized regression coefficient times that predictor variable's correlation with the dependent measure. Whenever a β^*_j is smaller than its corresponding r_{YX_j}, meaning that the predictors are correlated, then that X's net contribution to multiple R^2 is less than the full amount of its squared correlation with Y. In effect, the multiple R-squared summarizes the portion of each predictor's covariation with the dependent variable that remains after controlling for the effects jointly shared with the other predictors. For this reason multiple regression coefficients are sometimes referred to as *partial regression coefficients*.

Using the standardized regression equation above and the correlations in Table 8.4, the estimated value of R^2 for this example can be calculated as follows:

$$R^2_{Y \cdot X_1 X_2 X_3} = (0.230)(0.514) + (0.319)(0.630) + (-0.315)(-0.596)$$

$$= 0.507$$

The linear, additive combination of the three independent variables jointly account for 50.7% of the 50 states' variation in infant mortality.

Because 49.3% of the variation remains unexplained, additional predictors can be added to our initial regression equation to increase the amount of explained variance. However, the more predictors that we add to an equation, the greater the possibility that we will be unwittingly taking advantage of chance covariation to increase the R^2. Consequently, we cannot add predictors without penalty. An **adjusted coefficient of determination** (R^2_{adj}) takes into account the number of independent variables relative to the number of observations. In effect, any increase in explained variation must be paid for with the degrees of freedom required to include each predictor and the intercept a:

adjusted coefficient of determination—a coefficient of determination that takes into account the number of independent variables relative to the number of observations

$$R^2_{adj} = R^2_{Y \cdot X_1 \ldots X_K} - \left(\frac{(K)(1 - R^2_{Y \cdot X_1 \ldots X_K})}{(N - K - 1)} \right)$$

For small samples such as the U.S. States Data Set, the adjustment may quite substantially reduce the unadjusted R^2 value. In the equation with three predictors, the adjustment produces a 3.2% drop in explained variation:

$$R^2_{adj} = 0.507 - \left(\frac{(3)(1 - 0.507)}{(50 - 3 - 1)} \right) = 0.475$$

In multiple regression, as in life, there is "no free lunch."

As in the three-variable case, there is another approach to calculating multiple R-squared in the K-variable case.

$$R^2_{Y \cdot X} = \frac{\Sigma(Y_i - \bar{Y})^2 - \Sigma(Y_i - \hat{Y}_i)^2}{\Sigma(Y_i - \bar{Y})^2}$$

$$= \frac{SS_{TOTAL} - SS_{ERROR}}{SS_{TOTAL}}$$

$$= \frac{SS_{REGRESSION}}{SS_{TOTAL}}$$

because $SS_{TOTAL} = SS_{REGRESSION} + SS_{ERROR}$ and, thus, $SS_{REGRESSION} = SS_{TOTAL} - SS_{ERROR}$. Every multiple regression computer program automatically computes these sums of squares and calculates the value of both R^2 and R^2_{adj}.

8.4 Significance Tests for Parameters

8.4.1. Testing Multiple R^2 with K Independent Variables

For the three-variable case in section 8.2.4, we tested the hypothesis that the population coefficient of determination (ρ^2) differed significantly from zero, using a F test with 1 and $N - 3$ degrees of freedom. In parallel fashion a sample multiple regression R^2 can also be used to test the null hypothesis H_0: $\rho^2 = 0$ in the case of K independent variables. This null hypothesis is equivalent to a test that all K regression coefficients are zero (i.e., in the population H_0: $\beta_1 = \beta_2 = \ldots \beta_K = 0$). The degrees of freedom associated with the SS_{TOTAL} in a regression equation are always $N - 1$, regardless of the number of independent variables. If an equation has K independent variables, $SS_{\text{REGRESSION}}$ has K degrees of freedom associated with it, one for each predictor variable. Because in general, $df_{\text{TOTAL}} = df_{\text{REGRESSION}} + df_{\text{ERROR}}$, by subtraction $df_{\text{ERROR}} = N - K - 1$.

To compute the mean squares required in the F test, divide each sum of squares by its associated degrees of freedom. That is, with K independent variables

$$MS_{\text{REGRESSION}} = \frac{SS_{\text{REGRESSION}}}{K}$$

$$MS_{\text{ERROR}} = \frac{SS_{\text{ERROR}}}{N - K - 1}$$

When the null hypothesis that $\rho^2 = 0$ in the population is true, both $MS_{\text{REGRESSION}}$ and MS_{ERROR} are unbiased estimates of the variance of the errors of prediction, σ_e^2. However, if $\rho^2 > 0$ in the population, then $MS_{\text{REGRESSION}}$ will be greater than MS_{ERROR}. The F ratio test statistic is as follows:

$$F_{K, N-K-1} = \frac{MS_{\text{REGRESSION}}}{MS_{\text{ERROR}}}$$

For given levels of α use the appropriate table in Appendix E to find the critical value of F with K (column heading) and $N - K - 1$ (row heading) degrees of freedom necessary to reject the null hypothesis as probably untrue.

Calculating the mean squares for the F test requires computing both $SS_{\text{REGRESSION}}$ and SS_{ERROR} from the sample data. The procedures are identical to those followed in the bivariate regression (see section 6.4.1 on page 212) and the three-variable regression (see section 8.2.4) cases:

$$SS_{\text{TOTAL}} = (s_Y^2)(N - 1)$$
$$SS_{\text{REGRESSION}} = (R^2_{Y \cdot X_1 \ldots X_k})(SS_{\text{TOTAL}})$$
$$SS_{\text{ERROR}} = SS_{\text{TOTAL}} - SS_{\text{REGRESSION}}$$

To determine whether the coefficient of determination differs significantly from zero in the population, we set $\alpha = .001$, which fixes the critical value for $F = 6.60$ with $df = 3$ and 46. In Table 8.4 the standard deviation of infant mortality is $s_Y = 1.398$; therefore, the sample variance is 1.954. As a result,

$$SS_{\text{TOTAL}} = (1.954)(50 - 1) = 95.746$$
$$SS_{\text{REGRESSION}} = (0.507)(95.707) = 48.543$$
$$SS_{\text{ERROR}} = 95.746 - 48.543 = 47.203$$

Next divide these values by their degrees of freedom to find the mean squares:

$$MS_{\text{REGRESSION}} = \frac{48.543}{3} = 16.181$$

$$MS_{\text{ERROR}} = \frac{47.203}{46} = 1.026$$

Then the test statistic is

$$F_{3,46} = \frac{16.181}{1.026} = 15.77$$

Since the critical value is 6.60, we can reject with great confidence the null hypothesis that $\rho^2 = 0$ in the population.

An even simpler alternative way to calculate F directly using the multiple R^2 is as follows:

$$F_{K,N-K-1} = \frac{MS_{\text{REGRESSION}}}{MS_{\text{ERROR}}}$$

$$= \frac{R^2_{Y \cdot X_1 \ldots X_K}/K}{(1 - R^2_{Y \cdot X_1 \ldots X_K})/(N - K - 1)}$$

Using the results from the infant mortality example,

$$F_{3,46} = \frac{0.507/3}{(1 - 0.507)/(50 - 3 - 1)} = 15.77$$

A variation of this formulation comes in very handy in comparing coefficients of determination from nested regression equations. Box 8.4 presents the derivation of this formula.

8.4.2. Testing b_j

For the jth independent variable, X_j, the standard error of its estimated regression parameter, b_j, can be computed with this formula:

$$s_{b_j} = \sqrt{\frac{\sigma_e^2}{(s_{X_j}^2)(N-1)(1 - R^2_{X_j \cdot X_1 \ldots X_{K-1}})}}$$

The term in the numerator, the squared standard error of estimate (σ_e^2), is simply the mean square error:

$$\sigma_e^2 = MS_{\text{ERROR}} = \frac{SS_{\text{ERROR}}}{N - K - 1}$$

In the infant mortality equation with three predictors, $\sigma_e^2 = 47.203/(50 - 3 - 1) = 1.026$. For the first two terms in the denominator of the formula $((s_{X_j}^2)(N-1))$, the infant mortality example gives: for percentage poor $(3.463)^2(49) = 587.626$; for percentage unwed mothers $(5.183)^2(49) = 1,316.311$; and for percentage white $(11.576)^2(49) = 6,566.185$.

The third term in the denominator of the standard error formula is a bit more complicated. It involves regressing in turn the

---

BOX 8.4   Deriving the F Test for the Coefficient of Determination with Several Independent Variables

When the coefficient of determination is tested with two or more independent variables, $MS_{\text{REGRESSION}} = SS_{\text{REGRESSION}}/df_{\text{REGRESSION}}$ and $MS_{\text{ERROR}} = SS_{\text{ERROR}}/df_{\text{ERROR}}$. For K independent variables K degrees of freedom are associated with $SS_{\text{REGRESSION}}$ and $N - K - 1$ df with SS_{ERROR}. Therefore,

---

$$F_{K,N-K-1} = \frac{SS_{\text{REGRESSION}}/K}{SS_{\text{ERROR}}/(N - K - 1)}$$

As shown in section 6.4.1, $SS_{\text{REGRESSION}} = (R^2_{Y \cdot X})(SS_{\text{TOTAL}})$ and $1 = R^2_{Y \cdot X} + \dfrac{SS_{\text{ERROR}}}{SS_{\text{TOTAL}}}$. From the latter, it follows that: $SS_{\text{ERROR}} = (1 - R^2_{Y \cdot X})(SS_{\text{TOTAL}})$. Substituting these two results for the case of K independent variables into the equation for F yields the following:

$$F_{K,N-K-1} = \frac{(R^2_{Y \cdot X_1 \ldots X_K})(SS_{\text{TOTAL}}/K)}{(1 - R^2_{Y \cdot X_1 \ldots X_K})(SS_{\text{TOTAL}})/(N - K - 1)}$$

$$= \frac{R^2_{Y \cdot X_1 \ldots X_K}/K}{(1 - R^2_{Y \cdot X_1 \ldots X_K})/(N - K - 1)}$$

because SS_{TOTAL} cancels in both the numerator and the denominator.

---

independent variable X_j on the remaining $K - 1$ predictors in the equation, then subtracting the resulting R^2 from 1. Thus, for the infant mortality example, three additional multiple regression equations are necessary, each of which regresses one of the X_j on the other two. For example, percentage poor (X_1) is regressed on percentage unwed mothers (X_2) and percentage white (X_3). When these regressions are done, the following three R^2s result: for percentage poor $= .2707$; for percentage unwed mothers $= .4631$; and for percentage white $= .3751$. Therefore, using the formula above, the three estimated standard errors of the regression coefficients are:

$$s_{b_1} = \sqrt{\frac{1.026}{(587.626)(1 - .2707)}} = .049$$

$$s_{b_2} = \sqrt{\frac{1.026}{(1,316.311)(1 - .4631)}} = .038$$

$$s_{b_3} = \sqrt{\frac{1.026}{(6,566.185)(1 - .3751)}} = .016$$

These values are shown in parentheses in the first column of Table 8.5. In practice, of course, computer programs routinely calculate the standard errors for all multiple regression coefficients from the correlation matrix and the vector of standard errors.

TABLE 8.5
Nested Multiple Regression Equations for Infant Mortality

Independent Variables	(1)	(2)	(3)
Intercept	11.012***	11.566***	11.774***
	(1.936)	(1.732)	(1.726)
Poverty Level (%)	0.093	−0.036	−0.033
	(0.049)	(0.056)	(0.055)
Births to Unwed Mothers (%)	0.086*	0.129**	0.121**
	(0.038)	(0.042)	(0.042)
White Population (%)	−0.038*	−0.031*	−0.029*
	(0.016)	(0.014)	(0.014)
Physicians/100,000 Population	—	−0.007	−0.007
		(0.004)	(0.004)
Local Gov't Health Budget (%)	—	0.100**	0.104**
		(0.031)	(0.031)
Cropland (1,000 acres)	—	—	−.000019
			(0.000014)
R^2	.507***	.657***	.670***
R^2_{adj}	.475***	.618***	.624***

Note: Numbers in parentheses are standard errors.
$N = 50$; Missing data $= 1$.
* $p < .05$ **$p < .01$ *** $p < .001$
Source: U.S. States Data Set

The final step in testing a regression coefficient for statistical significance involves a *t* test of the null hypothesis that the population regression value is zero: H_0: $\beta_j = 0$. The alternative hypothesis may be either one-tailed, if the presumed direction of the effect is known: H_1: $\beta_j < 0$ or H_1: $\beta_j > 0$; or two-tailed, if no *a priori* information about the probable sign of the regression parameter can be stated: H_1: $\beta_j \neq 0$. Given a sample estimate of b_j from a multiple regression, the *t* test is identical to that for the bivariate regression case.

$$t_{N-K-1} = \frac{b_j - \beta_j}{s_{b_j}} = \frac{b_j - 0}{s_{b_j}} = \frac{b_j}{s_{b_j}}$$

To continue with the infant mortality example, the following *t* ratios are computed:

$$t_{46} = \frac{b_1}{s_{b_1}} = \frac{.093}{.049} = 1.90$$

$$t_{46} = \frac{b_2}{s_{b_2}} = \frac{.086}{.038} = 2.26$$

$$t_{46} = \frac{b_3}{s_{b_3}} = \frac{-.038}{.016} = -2.38$$

Appendix D shows that the critical value required to reject a null hypothesis in favor of a two-tailed alternative when $df = 46$ at $\alpha = .05$ is approximately ± 2.021. So, we conclude that a state's infant mortality varies as a function of the percentage of births to unwed mothers and the percentage white. The percentage below the poverty line is not significant at the $\alpha = .05$ level. However, if a one-tailed null hypothesis were used, which has a critical value of only 1.684, we could conclude that all three predictors differ significantly from zero.

Two cautionary notes are in order here. First, unless the *K* independent variables have correlations equal to zero with one another, the *K t* ratios used for significance testing are not independent. Thus, reported probabilities of statistical significance may be slightly biased, although the biases will generally be too small to cause any practical concern. Second, and more important,

multicollinearity—a condition of high or near perfect correlation among the independent variables in a multiple regression equation

extremely high correlations among the K predictors can seriously distort the estimates of the b_j standard errors. As can be seen from the formula presented above, a coefficient's standard error increases to the extent that it can be predicted by a linear combination of the remaining $K - 1$ predictors. Such a condition is called **multicollinearity.** Exact prediction of one predictor by the others (that is, perfect multicollinearity in which $R^2 = 1.00$) results in an inability to estimate the requested equation. Much more common is the situation where a very large proportion of the variance in an independent variable is explained by the others. Although several tests for the presence of multicollinearity exist, they are beyond the scope of this text. However, researchers should always visually inspect the correlation matrix of the variables used in their equations (such as Table 8.4). If high correlations (e.g., 0.80 or higher) occur among the predictor variables, then regressions may risk multicollinearity that produces large standard errors. In such cases one or more predictors can be eliminated from the regression and the equation reestimated.

A significance test also exists for hypotheses about the multiple regression population intercept, α. Because of the rarity with which substantive problems in social research concern this term, we do not present formulas for calculating its standard error. Rather, computer programs will generate an estimate of s_a from the sample data that can be entered into a t test:

$$t_{N-K-1} = \frac{a - \alpha}{s_a}$$

The intercept standard error for the infant mortality equation is 1.936; hence, the observed t ratio is $11.012/1.936 = 5.69$, sufficiently large to reject the null hypothesis that the population parameter is zero at $\alpha < .001$. But that null hypothesis is not meaningful, since we had no reason to believe that the states' expected infant mortality rate would be zero when the three predictors were taken into account.

The significance testing procedures described above apply only to regression coefficients in their metric form. No parallel tests are presented for the standardized regression coefficients (beta weights), because identical results would occur. Most computer programs calculate and print only the standard errors for the b_j

estimates, not for the β_j^* values. But the t ratios that apply to former also apply to the latter.

After all standard errors and t scores have been calculated for a multiple regression equation, the full set of sample descriptive and inferential statistics can be compactly displayed. Journal styles vary across the social science disciplines, but the format we find most informative consists of four lines:

1. The unstandardized regression coefficients, written in equation form, followed by the adjusted R^2
2. The standardized regression parameters, also in equation form
3. The standard errors in parentheses
4. The t ratios and F ratio in parentheses.

Thus, for the infant mortality equation

$$\hat{Y}_i = 11.012 + 0.093\ X_1 + 0.086X_2 - 0.038\ X_3 \quad R^2_{adj} = .475$$

$$\hat{Z}_{Y_i} = \quad - \quad + 0.230\ Z_1 + 0.319\ Z_2 - 0.315\ Z_3$$

$$\begin{array}{cccc} (1.936) & (.049) & (.038) & (.016) \\ (5.69) & (1.90) & (2.26) & (-2.38) \quad (F_{3,46} = 15.77) \end{array}$$

When several equations must be reported, a tabular display offers a more suitable compact format, such as Table 8.5's presentation of nested multiple regression equations.

8.4.3. Confidence Intervals for b_j

Using the regression coefficients' standard errors, confidence intervals can be constructed around each b_j point estimate, as in the three-variable regression case in section 8.2.6. For example, setting $\alpha = .05$, the lower and upper limits for the 95% confidence interval for the population parameter, β_j, are $b_j \pm (s_b)(t_{c.v.})$. Given that $b_1 = 0.093$ and $s_b = .049$, the lower confidence limit is $0.093 - (.049)(2.021) = -0.006$ and the upper confidence limit is $0.093 + (.049)(2.021) = +0.192$. Hence, the 95% confidence interval for β_1 is bounded by -0.006 and $+0.192$, which obviously includes zero (recall that the preceding two-tailed significance test was unable to reject the null hypothesis that the true population parameter is zero). Convince yourself that the 95% confidence limits for unwed mothers are .009 and .163 and for percentage white are $-.070$ and $-.006$.

8.5   Comparing Nested Equations

We mentioned above that additional independent variables can be entered into a regression equation, resulting in a nested set. Table 8.5 shows the results of two expansions of the initial equation predicting states' infant mortality rates (which appears in column 1). The equation in column 2 adds two measures of health care, the number of physicians per 100,000 state population and the percentage of local government budgets spent on health care. Adding these predictors changes the values of several estimated coefficients in the previous equation, most notably increasing the size of the unwed mothers coefficient (from 0.086 to 0.129) and making it statistically significant at a lower probability. But only one of the two new variables is significant, local health expenditures (significant at $p < .01$). Note also that adding these variables substantially increases the adjusted R^2 (which is more meaningful than the unadjusted R^2) from 47.5% in the first equation to 61.8% in the second, despite the loss of two degrees of freedom from adding the two new predictor variables. Clearly, local health expenditures are an important variable related to urban infant mortality. But, paradoxically, the estimated regression coefficient is positive, which implies that the larger the budget share a local government spends on health, the *higher* its infant mortality! Perhaps the health budget should not be considered an independent variable; rather, in states whose infant mortality is high, local governments may respond by increasing their health expenditures.

Finally, the equation in column 3 adds total state farm cropland, a variable that we do *not* hypothesize to have any relationship to infant mortality. As expected, its regression coefficient is not statistically significant, while most of the other coefficients show little or no change, and the adjusted R^2 increases by less than 1% at the cost of another degree of freedom.

The independent variables in the equation in column 1 are contained within the more inclusive set of variables in the equation in column 2, which in turn is a subset of the predictors in the equation in column 3. We can perform a test to determine whether the variables added to an equation result in a significant increase in the explained variance. Just as the test for whether R^2 is significantly greater than zero takes the *df* into account, so we must pay for the nested regression equation test with the difference in degrees of freedom used by each equation. The formula uses the *unadjusted* coefficients of determination (because an adjustment for *df*s occurs during the computation):

$$F_{(K_2-K_1),(N-K_2-1)} = \frac{(R_2^2 - R_1^2)/(K_2 - K_1)}{(1 - R_2^2)/(N - K_2 - 1)}$$

where the subscripts attached to R^2 and K indicate whether these values come from the first (less-inclusive) equation or from the second (more-inclusive) equation. For the F ratio to be significant, the difference in R-squares must be large relative to the number of independent variables added to the second equation.

To illustrate the procedure, calculate the test statistic to compare the equations in the first and second columns in Table 8.5:

$$F_{(5-3),(50-5-1)} = \frac{(.657 - .507)/(5 - 3)}{(1 - .657)/(50 - 5 - 1)} = \frac{.150/2}{.343/44} = 10.06$$

For 2 and 44 *df*, this F ratio is large enough to reject the null hypothesis H_0: $\rho_2^2 - \rho_1^2 = 0$ at $p < .001$, since the critical value for $\alpha = .001$ is roughly 8.25. On the other hand, can you demonstrate that the equation in the third column does not significantly increase the explained variance over that obtained in the second column?

8.6 Dummy Variable Regression: ANCOVA with Interactions

8.6.1. The Analysis of Covariance

To this point, our discussion of multiple regression analysis has assumed that all variables are continuous measures. But, many important social variables are discrete or categoric in nature. Chapters 5, 7, and 10 discuss how to analyze such dependent variables. This section describes methods for using discrete measures as independent variables in regressions involving continuous dependent variables. To illustrate the approach consider an hypothesis that occupational prestige—a measure of a job's "goodness"—varies according to a person's gender-race category. Using the 1991 General Social Survey to test this hypothesis, we will regress the NORC occupational prestige scores (which range from 17 [equivalent to "miscellaneous food preparation occupations"] to 86 [equivalent to "physician"]) on four categories: 1 = white women, 2 = white men, 3 = black women, and 4 = black men (we drop all cases of "other race"). Because these numbers are arbitrary, the gender-race variable cannot be entered directly into a regression equation. One way to create an interpretable classification is to use a set of J **dummy variables** as predictors. Each D_j is a separate variable that is coded 1 to indicate the presence of specific attributes for a case and 0 to indicate their absence. Thus, for the four gender-race combinations, the set of four dummy variables might be:

dummy variable—a variable coded 1 to indicate the presence of an attribute and 0 its absence

$D_{WW} = 1$ if a respondent is a white woman, 0 if not.
$D_{WM} = 1$ if a respondent is a white man, 0 if not.
$D_{BW} = 1$ if a respondent is a black woman, 0 if not.
$D_{BM} = 1$ if a respondent is a black man, 0 if not.

Any $J - 1$ of a set of J dummy variables may be entered as predictors in a regression equation. Because information about all but one of the dummies determines the value of the last category, the Jth dummy predictor is not linearly independent of the others. For example, if a respondent is coded 0 on D_{WW}, 0 on D_{WM}, and 1 on D_{BW}, then we know that person must be 0 on D_{BM}, because the person is a black woman, and hence not a "black man." Similarly, knowing that D_{WM}, D_{BW}, and D_{BM} are each scored 0 reveals a respondent to be a white woman (i.e., $D_{WW} = 1$). In general, if a discrete variable has J categories, then any $J - 1$ unique dummy variables created from it can be used in a regression equation. In particular, a dichotomous variable, such as teacher/student, is represented in regression analysis by a single 0-1 dummy variable.

Choosing white man as the omitted category, we regress occupational prestige scores of 1,415 GSS respondents on the white woman, black woman, and black man dummy variables, yielding the following equation (t ratios in parentheses):

$$\hat{Y}_i = 44.674 - 1.755D_{WW} - 5.983D_{BW} - 9.737D_{BM} \quad R^2_{adj} = 0.030$$

$$(83.35) \quad (-2.40) \quad (-4.42) \quad (-5.74) \quad F_{3,1411} = 15.61$$

The equation intercept indicates that, after controlling for gender-race, the mean prestige of respondents' occupations is 44.674, about that of insurance salespersons, plumbers, and dental assistants. All three dummy variable coefficients are significant at least at $p < .05$, and all have negative signs. That is, relative to white men, the other three gender-race groups have lower average occupational prestige. Note that the adjusted R^2 of .030 is significant at the $\alpha = .001$ level, because the critical value for 3 and 1,411 df is 5.42, as can be determined from Appendix E. However, the four race-gender combinations explain only 3% of the variation in occupational prestige.

Separate regression equations for the four gender-race categories can now be derived from the single equation above, as follows. When $D_{WW} = 1$, the predicted occupational prestige for white women is

$$\hat{Y}_{WW} = 44.674 - 1.755(1) - 5.983(0) - 9.737(0)$$
$$= 42.919$$

Similarly when $D_{BW} = 1$, the predicted occupational prestige for black women is

$$\hat{Y}_{BW} = 44.674 - 1.755(0) - 5.983(1) - 9.737(0)$$
$$= 38.691$$

And when $D_{BM} = 1$, the predicted value for black men is

$$\hat{Y}_{BM} = 44.674 - 1.755(0) - 5.983(0) - 9.737(1)$$
$$= 34.937$$

Because the dummy variable for white men was omitted from the equation, they might appear to have no equation; but as the following calculation shows, their predicted value is just the intercept:

$$\hat{Y}_{WM} = 44.674 - 1.755(0) - 5.983(0) - 9.737(0)$$
$$= 44.674$$

That is, white men on average hold occupations with prestige scores of 44.674, which is higher than the predicted scores of the other three gender-race groups.

The t test associated with a given dummy variable has a special interpretation—it is a test for the difference between two means. In particular, it tests the difference between the mean associated with a given category (e.g., white women) and that for omitted category (e.g., white men in this example). Thus the t value for D_{WW} indicates whether there is a significant difference between the mean prestige score of the white women (42.919) and that for white men (44.674). If we choose $\alpha = .05$, the t value is the ratio of the regression coefficient to its standard error: $-1.755/0.732 = -2.40$. The difference in means is significant, since the critical value is a t ratio of ± 1.96. The t values for D_{BW} and D_{BM} are -4.42 and -5.74, respectively, indicating that the mean prestige scores of black women and black men both differ significantly from that of white men.

Importantly, the value of R^2 and the predicted values of the dependent variable are invariant regardless of which of the $J - 1$ dummy variables are entered in the equation. However, the t tests for the coefficients will necessarily differ because the reference (omitted) category will differ. The implication is that one should be careful to choose as the omitted category a substantively or theoretically important group, so that meaningful statistical tests are performed.

When a multiple regression equation includes *both* a set of dummy variables and one or more continuous measures as predictors, the model is called an **analysis of covariance (ANCOVA),** reflecting this method's origins in experimental research. A continuous variable is called a **covariate,** and the dummy variables are referred to as **treatment levels.** The ANCOVA predictors each exert additive effects on the dependent variable, so that within each category of the treatment dummies, the effect of a covariate is identical. Suppose we choose education (years of formal schooling) as a covariate (X_1) and include it in the occupational prestige equation along with the three gender-race dummy predictors. The result is the following equation (t ratios in parentheses):

analysis of covariance (ANCOVA)—a multiple regression equation including one or more dummy variables, with a continuous independent variable and no interaction terms

covariate—a continuous variable in an analysis of covariance

treatment level—a term in experimental research to indicate the experimental group to which a subject has been assigned

$$\hat{Y}_i = 14.822 - 0.745 D_{WW} - 3.826 D_{BW} - 6.209 D_{BM} + 2.231 X_1$$
$$(10.43) \quad (-1.18) \quad\quad (-3.27) \quad\quad (-4.23) \quad\quad (22.22)$$
$$R^2_{adj} = 0.281 \quad\quad\quad F_{4,1410} = 139.21$$

The t ratio for education clearly reveals it to be a powerful predictor of occupational prestige. In effect, for each additional year of schooling completed, an average respondent gains almost 2¼ points on the scale. Thus, college graduates (16 years) have almost a 9-point advantage over high-school graduates (12 points). When education is in the equation, the intercept and all three gender-race dummy variable coefficients are somewhat smaller. Indeed, the coefficient for white women is no longer significant; that is, controlling for education, white women have prestige scores not significantly different from white men. But both black women and black men continue to have lower occupational standing than white men.

As mentioned above, education in the ANCOVA equation exerts an additive effect on occupational prestige. For example, the predicted prestige score for a white woman with 12 years of schooling is $\hat{Y}_i = 14.822 - (0.745)(1) + (2.231)(12) = 40.849$ points. This is exactly a 2.231-point difference from a college-attending white woman (i.e., with 13 years of education) $\hat{Y}_i = 14.822 - (0.745)(1) + (2.231)(13) = 43.080$. Identical 2.231-point differences also occur between the members of *any* gender-race group who are exactly one year apart in education. That is, the effect of education on occupational prestige is *constant* within each dummy variable category.

Researchers may want to know whether a set of dummy variables contribute significantly to the variance of a dependent variable (occupational prestige in this case) beyond that explained by a covariate (e.g., education). To answer this question, we can use the F test for the difference between coefficients of determination, introduced in section 8.5. In our example $R_2^2 = 0.283$ is the *unadjusted* coefficient of determination for the equation including both the gender-race dummies and the education covariate, while $R_1^2 = 0.270$ is the square of the correlation between education and prestige. (We used the unadjusted R-squares, instead of the adjusted values because the F test takes the degrees of freedom into account.) If the F test is significant, it means that the intercept for at least one of the groups is reliably different from that of one of the other groups. We set $\alpha = .05$; reference to Appendix E indicates that the critical value for 3 and 1,410 df is 2.60. The results are as follows:

$$F_{(4-1)(1415-4-1)} = \frac{(0.283 - 0.270)/(4 - 1)}{(1 - 0.283)/(1415 - 4 - 1)} = 8.52$$

Given an F of 8.52, we are confident that the intercept for one of the groups differs significantly from that of at least one other group. Examination of the regression coefficients for the dummies above suggests that the intercepts for both black women and black men are significantly lower than that of the omitted white males.

8.6.2. ANOVA with Dummy Variables

By now you probably realize that multiple regression and analysis of variance are special versions of the general linear model. A regression performed with only a single set of dummy variables is identical to a one-way ANOVA. Rather than deriving this fact mathematically, we demonstrate it with an example that translates dummy regression coefficients into ANOVA effects. Table 8.6 displays the coefficients produced by ANOVA and by regression when GSS respondents' political views (1 = extremely liberal to 7 = extremely conservative) are the dependent variable and the seven categories of political party identification shown in the table's rows form the independent variable. In general, the more one identifies with the Republican category, the more conservative the political

TABLE 8.6

Effects of Party Identification on Political Views, ANOVA Compared to Dummy Variable Regression

Party Categories	ANOVA α_j	Regression b_j	Mean
Grand Mean	4.09	—	—
Intercept	—	3.75	—
Strong Democrat	−.34	—[a]	3.75
Not Strong Democrat	−.26	.08	3.83
Independent, Leans Democrat	−.56	−.21	3.54
Independent	−.08	.26	4.01
Independent, Leans Republican	.27	.61	4.36
Not Strong Republican	.21	.55	4.30
Strong Republican	.76	1.10	4.85

$$\eta^2 = .085^{***} \qquad R^2 = .085^{***}$$
$$F_{6,1436} = 22.20^{***} \qquad F_{6,1436} = 22.20^{***}$$

Note: $N = 1{,}443$; Missing data $= 74$.
[a]Omitted category in dummy variable regression.
$^{***}p < .001$
Source: 1991 General Social Survey

views, although the progression is not monotonic. At first glance the two sets of effects appear contradictory. More than half of the ANOVA effect coefficients (α_j) are negative, while only one of the dummy regression coefficients (b_j) has a negative sign. Recall, however, that the reference points for each scale differ. For ANOVA the effects are calculated as deviations of each treatment category mean from the grand mean of the sample (see section 4.1.2 on page 123). For dummy regression the effects are deviations from the mean of the omitted category, the "Strong Democrats" in this example (see section 8.6.1).

Transforming the values from one scale into the second scale simply requires aligning them by an adjustment factor. For one-way ANOVA and regression with a comparable set of dummy variables, the adjustment factor involves the sample mean, $\bar{Y}$, and the sample estimate of the regression intercept, a. A dummy regression coefficient translates into an ANOVA effect: $\alpha_j = b_j + (a - \bar{Y})$. And, by rearrangement, an ANOVA effect translates into a dummy regression coefficient: $b_j = \alpha_j + (\bar{Y} - a)$.

For example, using the values in Table 8.6, the regression coefficient for Independents ($+.26$) can be changed into the ANOVA effect ($-.08$) by adding to it the difference between the intercept and the mean ($3.75 - 4.09 = -.34$). Similarly, the ANOVA effect for Strong Democrats ($-.34$) becomes the regression value (0, since it is the omitted category), by adding the difference between mean and intercept ($4.09 - 3.75 = .34$). Convince yourself that all the remaining coefficients in one method can be transformed to their corresponding values in the other procedure. If one compares the means generated for the seven categories (see the last column in Table 8.6), they are the same as the predicted means computed from the dummy variable analysis. That is, one can capture all of the information in an analysis of variance using dummy variable analysis. Thus, analysis of variance and multiple regression are fundamentally equivalent variations of a common underlying general linear model.

8.6.3. Regression Equations with Interaction Terms

Dummy variables are especially useful for estimating and testing **interaction effects,** which reflect differences in the relationship between two variables within categories of a third variable. Suppose we believe not only that gender-race affects occupational

interaction effects— differences in the relationship between two variables within categories of a third variable

prestige but also that those effects vary according to people's education. That is, the more highly educated members of one gender-race group may be more likely to achieve higher or lower occupational prestige than are the more educated members of another group. In other words, not only might the intercepts for the different gender-race groups vary, but so too might their regression slopes. To examine this hypothesis, we must enter the education variable (X_1) into the regression equation along with the dummy variables, and also include three interaction terms created by multiplying each dummy category by the continuous measure, for example, X_1D_{WW}. Consequently, each interaction term takes on values equal to the continuous measure for group members, but is 0 for nongroup members. Thus, the interaction variable for education times the white woman dummy (X_1D_{WW}) gives each white woman respondent the same score that she also has on the education variable, but it gives the black women and men and the white men respondents scores of 0.

To test a set of interactions, the R_2^2 for the equation with the multiplicative interaction terms is compared to the R_1^2 for the equation that includes only the additive effects of the variables. The test statistic for the difference in the two equations' coefficients of determination is the same F ratio used in section 8.5 to compare nested equations. Our null hypothesis is that $H_0:\rho_2^2 - \rho_1^2 = 0$ in the population. If this hypothesis can be rejected at a chosen α value, we conclude that significant interaction effects exist. For the equation with only education and the three gender-race dummies, $R^2 = 0.283$, while for the equation that also includes the three interaction terms, $R^2 = 0.289$. (Again, we use the two *unadjusted* coefficients of determination because the F ratio takes the degrees of freedom into account.) Therefore,

$$F_{(7-4)(1415-7-1)} = \frac{(0.289 - 0.283)/(7 - 4)}{(1 - 0.289)/(1415 - 7 - 1)} = 3.96$$

Thus, we conclude that at least one significant interaction effect occurs in this example. The full regression equation is (t ratios in parentheses):

$$\hat{Y}_i = 16.799 - 6.094D_{WW} - 9.782D_{BW} + 6.605D_{BM} + 2.084X_1$$
$$\quad (8.33) \quad (-2.15) \quad\quad (-1.59) \quad\quad (1.12) \quad\quad (14.20)$$
$$+ 0.409X_1D_{WW} + 0.468X_1D_{BW} - 1.106X_1D_{BM} \quad R_{adj}^2 = 0.286$$
$$\quad (1.94) \quad\quad\quad (0.97) \quad\quad\quad (-2.32) \quad\quad F_{4,1410} = 81.78$$

Although these relationships appear more complex than those in the ANCOVA equation estimated in section 8.6.1, they can be interpreted by calculating the effect of education for each specific gender-race category. The effect of education that is common to every group is +2.084 prestige points per year of schooling. The three education-dummy interaction effects apply only to that group whose dummy variable score is 1. Because there is no dummy variable for the omitted white men, their education effect is just the common coefficient, +2.084 prestige points per year of schooling. For white women their +0.409 interaction coefficient must be added to the common education coefficient, producing an increase of 2.084 + 0.409 = +2.491 prestige points per year of schooling. Similarly, black women's education effect on occupational prestige is 2.084 + 0.468 = +2.552 points, about as much as white women. However, black men do not fare as well in turning their education into occupational prestige. Their negative interaction coefficient is subtracted from the common coefficient, yielding 2.084 − 1.106 = 0.978 prestige points, which is less than half the gains experienced by the other three gender-race categories.

8.7 Comparisons Across Populations

Standardizing the coefficients in a multiple regression has the advantage of allowing interpretations that do not depend on the units in which the variables are measured (e.g., years, days, or minutes). Suppose that we are interested in comparing the coefficients from regression equations estimated for samples drawn from two different populations. For example, we might be interested in comparing the multiple regressions obtained from different historical periods, from different nations, or from different subpopulations within the same society. We have no reason to expect that the standard deviations of variables (used to compute the β^*s) will be equal across these populations. Indeed, we typically expect them to differ. For example, as years of education and annual incomes increased during the 20th century, the variability among these measures also increased. Therefore, if we standardized the b's in each equation using either the population or sample estimates of the standard deviations, we may reach misleading conclusions about the relative important of each predictor.

Table 8.7 illustrates a situation with three multiple regression equations of the 1991 GSS respondents' annual incomes (in

TABLE 8.7

Regressions of Annual Income (in $100s) for Samples of All
Respondents, Men, and Women

Independent	All	Men	Women
Intercept	−215.72[a]	−257.30	−140.59
	—	—	—
	(−6.82)[c]***	(−5.57)***	(−4.16)***
Occupational Prestige	3.23	3.15	3.07
	.25[b]	.22	.33
	(7.32)***	(4.52)***	(7.06)***
Education	14.98	18.55	9.54
	.24	.27	.20
	(6.87)***	(5.74)***	(4.16)***
Age	2.20	3.56	0.87
	.16	.23	.09
	(5.45)***	(5.71)***	(2.15)*
Black	−22.91	1.22	−16.99
	−.04	.002	−.05
	(−1.47)	(0.04)	(−1.21)
R^2_{adj}	.210***	.244***	.225***
SS_{ERROR}	22,073,544.52	12,944,100.77	5,562,424.64
(N)	(949)	(467)	(482)

Missing data = 568.
[a]Unstandardized regression coefficient
[b]Standardized regression coefficient
[c]t ratio.
* $p < .05$
*** $p < .001$
Source: 1991 General Social Survey

hundreds of dollars) on their occupational prestige scores, years of
education, current age, and a dummy variable for race (black
versus other). The equation in the first column is for all 949
respondents without missing data. The second and third columns
report the regression estimates for 467 men and 482 women,
respectively. The effect of race on income is not significantly
different from zero in all three equations, but the effects of both
education and age appear to be much stronger for men than for
women. However, the size of these differences depends on which
type of coefficient is examined. For example, the ratio of the
standardized education coefficients is about a third larger for men
(.27/.20 = 1.35), but the unstandardized coefficient ratio is almost
twice as large (18.55/9.54 = 1.94). Similar contrasts occur for the age

effects (standardized ratio = 2.55; unstandardized ratio = 4.09). And the relative occupational prestige effects are opposite (standardized ratio = .22/.33 = .67; unstandardized ratio = 3.15/3.07 = 1.03).

Given these different results, which coefficients should be emphasized? First, we urge researchers always to report both types of equations, just as we have done in Table 8.7, so that readers can compare them and draw their own conclusions. Second, we argue that each type of coefficient has a valuable but distinct use. The standardized β^*s are useful in comparing the relative importance of predictors *within* equations. Thus, by squaring each β^* in the men's equation, we see that education (.073 of the variance in income) is somewhat more important than either age (.053) or occupational prestige (.048) in predicting annual incomes net of one another. But, for the women, the most important predictor is occupation (.109) followed far behind in importance by education (.040) and age (.008).

When we seek to contrast the predictors *between* equations, the unstandardized coefficients are most meaningful. Thus, each year of education adds \$1,855 to a man's annual income (18.55 × \$100), but only \$954 to a woman's income. The gender gap in income at 12 years of schooling is \$10,812. Similarly, the expected difference in annual incomes between a man and a woman having the same age is (\$3.56 − 0.87) × 100 = \$269. The gap at age 40 is \$10,760. The main reason for the greater metric coefficient impacts lies in the substantial gender difference in income variation. Not only did men make higher mean incomes (274.73 hundreds of dollars) than did women (152.52 hundreds), but the men's income standard deviation (192.45) was more than half again as large as the women's standard deviation (122.69). Consequently, standardizing each equation resulted in a major shift in the relative ratios of the unstandardized regression coefficients.

The differences in the multiple regression coefficients estimated for a pair of identically specified equations can be tested for statistical significance using the **Chow test.** The null hypothesis is that every regression coefficient in the first population equals its corresponding regression coefficient in the second equation. That is, H_0: $\beta_{j_1} = \beta_{j_2}$ for all J pairs of predictors. The error sum of squares for each equation, reported at the bottom of Table 8.7, are entered into the formula for the F ratio:

chow test—a test of statistical significance for the differences in multiple regression coefficients for a pair of identically specified equations

$$F_{K+1, \, N_1+N_2-2K-2} = \frac{[SS_{ERROR_{TOTAL}} - (SS_{ERROR_1} + SS_{ERROR_2})]/(K+1)}{(SS_{ERROR_1} + SS_{ERROR_2})/(N_1 + N_2 - 2K - 2)}$$

where

The subscripts "1" and "2" index the two separate samples.

TOTAL indicates the combined sample.

K is the number of independent variables in one equation.

The Chow test for the data in Table 8.4 yields the following F value:

$$F_{5,939} = \frac{[22,073,544.52 - (12,944,100.77 + 5,562,424.64)]/5}{(12,944,100.77 + 5,562,424.64)/(467 + 482 - 8 - 2)}$$

$$= \frac{713,403.82}{19,708.76} = 36.20$$

which is significant at $p < .001$. Therefore, we conclude that one or more of the regression coefficients are not equal across the two samples. Because the Chow test is a global test of significant differences, we cannot further pinpoint which pairs of coefficients are not equal. However, the structural equation models in chapter 12 show how to test whether specific regression parameters are equal or different across equations.

Review of Key Concepts and Symbols

These key concepts and symbols are listed in the order of appearance in this chapter. Combined with the definitions in the margins, they will help you to review the material and can serve as a self-test for mastery of the concepts.

multiple regression analysis	multiple regression coefficient
index	part correlation
construct	multiple correlation coefficient
indicator	partial regression coefficient
Cronbach's alpha	population regression model
ordinary least squares	best linear and unbiased
listwise deletion	estimate (BLUE)
pairwise deletion	nested regression equations

adjusted coefficient of determination	β_j^*
multicollinearity	$R^2_{Y \cdot X_1 X_2}$
dummy variable	SS_{TOTAL}
analysis of covariance (ANCOVA)	$SS_{REGRESSION}$
covariate	SS_{ERROR}
treatment level	$MS_{REGRESSION}$
interaction effect	MS_{ERROR}
Chow test	$r_{YX_j \cdot X_i}$
α	$R^2_{Y \cdot X_1 X_2 \ldots X_K}$
β_j	R^2_{adj}
a	s_{b_j}
b	σ^2_e
	D

PROBLEMS

General Problems

1. Using the following information, compute the a, b_1, and b_2 coefficients for the regression of Y on X_1 and X_2:

			Correlations	
Variable	Mean	Standard Deviation	X_2	Y
X_1	4	2	0.40	0.50
X_2	16	4	—	−.30
Y	32	8	—	—

2. Compute the beta weights for the data shown in Problem 1, writing out the regression equation for standardized variables.

3. Using survey data from a sample of 65 respondents, a regression equation predicting political party preference with eight independent variables has a coefficient of determination of 0.073. Is the coefficient of determination significantly different

from zero at $\alpha = .05$? If the sample size were 650 would the coefficient of determination differ significantly from zero at the same probability level?

4. When support for a law to register handguns is regressed on size of community of residence (X_1) and number of guns owned (X_2) for $N = 400$, the following statistics are found:

$$b_1 = 2.43 \qquad s_{b_1} = 1.05$$
$$b_2 = -1.33 \qquad s_{b_2} = 0.72$$

Test both b_j's for statistical significance, using $\alpha = .01$, one-tailed tests.

5. When $N = 200$, $k = 6$, $b_1 = 3.470$, $MS_{ERROR} = 5.96$, $\Sigma(X_{1i} - \overline{X}_1)^2 = 8.38$, and $R^2_{X_1 \cdot X_2} = .327$, is b_1 significant at $\alpha = .001$ for a two-tailed test?

6. Form the 95% and 99% confidence intervals around b_1 in Problem 5.

7. Give a verbal interpretation of the following unstandardized regression equation, where Y is a seven-point scale measuring how often per month a married couple spends social evenings with their friends, X_1 is the couple's annual income in $10,000s, X_2 is how many years they have been married, and X_3 is a dummy variable for the presence of young children (1 = children, 0 = no children):

$$\hat{Y} = 3.432 + 0.161X_1 - 0.034X_2 - 0.562X_3$$

8. Construct dummy variable codes for partnership, as measured with these categories: married, living together; partner, living together; married, living apart; partner, living apart; not married, no partner; no answer.

9. Assume that D_N = North, D_S = South, D_E = East, and D_W = West, that X_1 is a measure of age, and Y is satisfaction with place of residence. Set up two equations necessary to test whether region and age interact in the prediction of satisfaction with place of residence.

10. In a sample of 637 people, the number of hours per week spent watching television sports (Y) is predicted by annual income (X_1)

(measured in thousands of dollars) and a set of two dummy variables for occupation: D_1 = white-collar and D_2 = blue collar. The results of three regression analyses are:

$$\hat{Y} = 3.471 - 0.752D_1 \qquad\qquad R^2 = 0.183$$
$$\hat{Y} = 3.773 - 0.564D_1 - 0.002X_1 \qquad\qquad R^2 = 0.245$$
$$\hat{Y} = 3.281 - 0.420D_1 - 0.003X_1 + 0.012X_1D_1 \quad R^2 = 0.263$$

a. Is there a significant interaction between collar color and TV sports watching? Set $\alpha = .001$.

b. Using the interaction equation, calculate the predicted hours of TV sports watching for a white-collar worker making $25,000 per year.

Problems Requiring the 1991 General Social Survey

11. Regress satisfaction with one's health (SATHEALT) on EDUC and AGE.
    a. Present the regression coefficients with their tests of significance and beta weights.
    b. Present the coefficient of determination with its test of significance.
    c. Interpret the results.
    Note: set $\alpha = .001$. Also recode health satisfaction so that the most satisfied category has the highest value: RECODE SATHEALT(7=1)(6=2)(5=3)(4=4)(3=5)(2=6)(1=7)(ELSE=9).

12. To the health satisfaction equation in Problem 11, add dummy variables for marital status (MARITAL), using married, widowed, divorced, and separated, with never married as the omitted category.
    a. What are the effects of marital status on SATHEALT?
    b. Is there a significant increase in R^2 above age and education when marital status is added to the equation, at $\alpha = .05$?

13. Does the effect of age on church attendance vary with religious affiliation? Using RELIG, create dummy variables for Protestant, Catholic, and Jew (using Other/None as the omitted category) and form interaction terms with AGE.
    a. Test the R^2 for an ANCOVA equation with ATTEND predicted by age and the three religious dummy variables, setting $\alpha = .05$.

b. Test the R^2 for the regression equation that includes the AGE-RELIG dummy variable interaction terms, with $\alpha = .05$.

c. Test the difference in R^2 for the two equations above, setting $\alpha = .05$.

14. Use regression and analysis of variance to determine whether respondents' political views (POLVIEWS) differ significantly across the nine U.S. census regions (REGION).

a. Report both the ANOVA effects and the dummy regression coefficients, using the Pacific region as the omitted category.

b. What is the formula for translating each regression β_j into an ANOVA α_j?

c. Present an ANOVA summary table for the results, setting the significant level at $\alpha = .05$.

Problems Requiring Use of the U.S. States Data Set

15. Estimate a regression equation that predicts states' crime rates per capita (CRIMEPC) from the percentage of population age 15–24 years (AGE3) and median household income (HHMDNINC). Test for the significance of the multiple R^2 and of each regression coefficient, using $\alpha = .05$.

16. Estimate a regression equation predicting each state's local government employment per 10,000 population (LGEMPLPC) with three predictors: poverty (POORPCT), female labor force participation (FEMLFP), and unionization (UNION). Report the 95% confidence intervals for the three unstandardized regression coefficients.

17. Estimate two regression equations predicting states' divorce rates (DIVORPC):

a. In the first equation use as predictors the percentage of urban population (URBAN86) and net 1980–1986 migration rate (MIGRATE). Test R^2 for significance for $\alpha = .05$.

b. For the second equation add state marriage rates (MARRYPC) to the equation in (a). Does the amount of explained variance increase significantly? What difference does including MARRYPC in the equation make for your conclusion about the sources of variation in DIVORPC?

Statistics for
Social Data
Analysis

Nonlinear and Logistic Regression

9

In chapter 8 all the variables used in multiple regression analyses were measured on scales having intervals of constant width. Consequently, a metric regression coefficient represents the net effect of an independent variable on a dependent variable that remains constant throughout that predictor's range. That is, an estimated β_j indicates that the dependent variable increases by equal β-amounts per unit of the independent variable. For example, if each additional year of education is estimated to produce a $950 return in a person's annual income, that effect is the same for those persons with 10 years as for those with 20 years of schooling. This chapter considers situations where the amount of change in the dependent variable *varies* according to the level of the independent variable. Although such relationships cannot be accurately represented by a straight regression line, nonlinear relationships can be converted to linear relationships by transforming the variables' scales. Relationships among the transformed variables can then be estimated with techniques presented in earlier chapters. This chapter also examines two types of multivariate analysis —logistic regression and probit analysis—in which the dependent variables may be either dichotomous or multicategory nonordered discrete variables. We will discuss the techniques required to estimate these relationships.

9.1 Nonlinear Regression

9.1.1. Comparing Linear to Nonlinear Relationships

In the absence of reasons for expecting that two continuous variables are related in a nonlinear fashion, researchers can test an hypothesis that only linearity is present. The procedure involves comparing proportions of the dependent variable's variance that can be attributed to its linear and nonlinear relationships with a predictor variable. To simplify the presentation, we examine only the bivariate case, although the procedure readily applies to multivariate equations. The null hypothesis that we seek to reject is as follows:

H_0: Y has only a linear relation to X.

The hypothesis testing procedure follows several familiar steps:

1. Collapse the independent variable into a set of ordered discrete categories that do not seriously distort the original distribution. As a rule of thumb, between 6 and 20 categories should suffice.
2. Perform a one-way analysis of variance (ANOVA; see chapter 4) on the dependent variable, using the collapsed categories created in step 1 as the independent variable.
3. Using the ANOVA sums of squares, compute η^2 (eta-square; see section 4.4 [page 145]). This statistic measures the proportion of variance in the dependent variable that is explained statistically by its *nonlinear* relationship to the predictor's categories.
4. Regress the dependent variable on the same collapsed independent variable, treating it as a continuous predictor. Compute R^2 (R-square), which measures the proportion of variance in the dependent variable that is statistically explained by its *linear* relationship to the predictor.
5. Calculate an F ratio, to test whether η^2 is significantly larger than R^2 at a chosen α level.

$$F_{K-2,N-K} = \frac{(\eta^2 - R^2_{Y\cdot X})/(K - 2)}{(1 - \eta^2)/(N - K)}$$

where

K = The number of categories associated with ANOVA.

$(K - 2)$ and $(N - K)$ = The degrees of freedom for the F ratio.

If F is significantly larger than the critical value, then reject the null hypothesis that the variables are linearly related in the population (i.e., that H_0: $\eta^2 = \rho^2_{Y\cdot X}$) in favor of the alternative, H_1: $\eta^2 > \rho^2_{Y\cdot X}$.

To illustrate, Figure 9.1 uses the 1991 GSS data to plot the mean number of children born to 721 ever-married women categorized into seven different current age intervals. The means clearly do not fall on a straight line. Women aged 30 and under have the fewest children (1.50), in part because many are still in their peak

FIGURE 9.1

Mean Number of Children Born to Ever-Married Women by Current Age

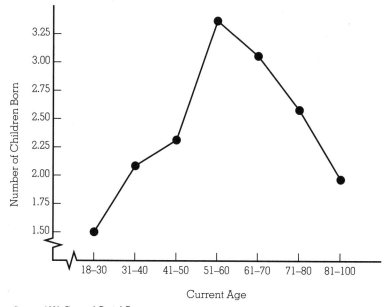

Source: 1991 General Social Survey

childbearing years. Women aged 51–60 in 1991 bore the most children (3.40 on average), while each of the three older cohorts had fewer offspring. This dynamic may be mainly historical, given that the middle cohort came of childbearing age during the baby boom era of the 1950s and 1960s, while older women had experienced the depression era's "birth dearth."

The linear regression of children born on women's ages in decades yields an estimated $R^2 = .038$, indicating that current age linearly explains less than 4% of the variance in the number of children. But a one-way ANOVA with these seven categories yields $\eta^2 = .110$, showing that, allowing for nonlinearity, current age explains 11% of the childbearing variance. For $\alpha = .001$ the critical value is $F_{5,714} = 4.10$. The test statistic's value is as follows:

$$F_{5,714} = \frac{(.110 - .038)/(7 - 2)}{(1 - .110)/(721 - 7)} = 11.55$$

Therefore, we can reject the null hypothesis in favor of the alternative that childbearing is nonlinearly related to women's current ages in the population from which the GSS sample came, with only a very small probability of a Type I error.

9.1.2. Functional Forms of Nonlinear Equations

Once nonlinearity is detected, the next step is to determine its precise functional form. In mathematical notation the expression $Y = f(X)$ merely means that the expected value of dependent variable $\hat{Y}_i$ is some (unspecified) function of the independent variable value, X_i. Ordinary least squares (OLS) regression specifies that the relationship takes a linear and additive form: $\hat{Y}_i = \alpha + \beta X_i$. But many other functional forms express various types of nonlinear relationships, as illustrated by the plots of some example equations in Figures 9.2A–D for positive values of X. In the quadratic (parabolic) function in Figure 9.2A, $\hat{Y}_i = \alpha + \beta X_i^2$, α indicates the point at which the curve crosses the Y-axis (i.e., where $X_i = 0$). At successive values on the X-axis, the amount of change in Y grows increasingly larger. If the β coefficient has a negative sign, then the parabola is inverted, indicating that successive amounts of X predict increasingly negative amounts of Y. In the reciprocal function in Figure 9.2B, $\hat{Y}_i = \alpha + \beta/X_i$, as larger values of X are divided

FIGURE 9.2A
Quadratic ($\hat{Y}_i = 2 + .25X_i^2$)

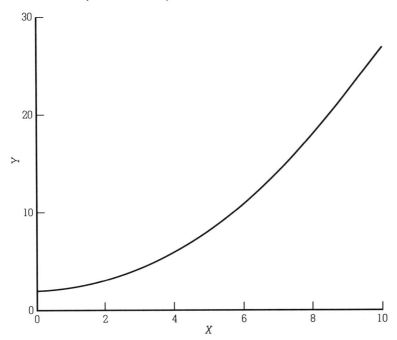

into the constant parameter β, successively smaller decreases in the predicted value of Y slowly approach a limit (asymptote) at the intercept α.

In the two natural logarithmic functions plotted in Figure 9.2C, $\hat{Y}_i = \alpha + \beta \log X_i$, successively larger values of X predict increasingly smaller changes in Y, although no ultimate limit is approached. The rapidity with which a logarithmic curve flattens out depends on the size of β (equals 1 in both examples), while the point at which the curve crosses the X-axis depends on the intercept value α (the line never intercepts the Y-axis, as the logarithm of a negative X-value is not defined). Finally, the exponential function in Figure 9.2D, $\hat{Y}_i = e^{\alpha + \beta X_i}$, resembles the parabola but the values of Y change much more rapidly as a function of changing X. (Compare X^2 to e^X for the same values of X.) The precise shape and location of an exponential curve depends on its parameters: If $\beta > 0$, the curve increases as X increases, as in Figure 9.2D; if $\beta < 0$, the curve decreases as X increases. The term e is **Euler's constant,** an

Euler's constant — an irrational number that is used as the base of natural logarithms

FIGURE 9.2B

Reciprocal ($\hat{Y}_i = 2 + 8/X_i$)

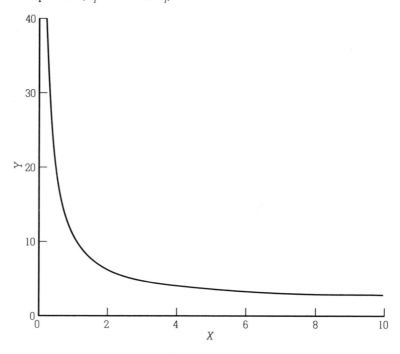

irrational number that is used as the base of natural logarithms ($\log_e$). Its approximate value is 2.71828.

These and other nonlinear functions can be brought into the conventional OLS estimation methods by transforming the predictor variables. The independent variable's values are changed to a new variable according to the desired functional form, then this new variable is entered into an OLS regression equation. For example, if X_i has both a linear and a quadratic relation with Y_i, the equation in population notation is $\hat{Y}_i = \alpha + \beta_1 X_i + \beta_2 X_i^2$. By creating a second variable that consists of the squared values of X, the equation is linear in terms of the *parameters* while remaining nonlinear in terms of the *variables*. Both X and X^2 may be entered into the same regression equation if they are not severely multicollinear (i.e., do not have a high correlation; see section 8.4.2 on page 294).

To illustrate this procedure, consider the relationship between persons' annual incomes (Y) and their ages (X). Although we

FIGURE 9.2C
Natural Logarithmic ($\hat{Y}_i = \log_e X_i$ and $\hat{Y}_i = 3 - \log_e X_i$)

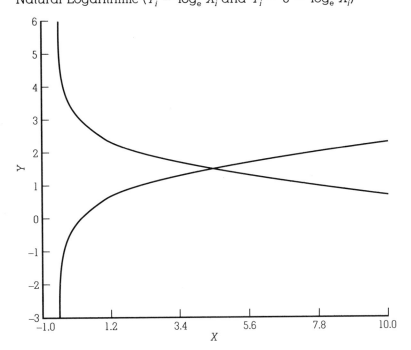

expect people's incomes to increase with age (in large measure through work experiences that increase their value to employers), we also do not expect their incomes to rise throughout the entire 40-year range of prime working ages. Rather, after an initial rise, incomes will tend to level off and may even fall as people near retirement age. Hence, a quadratic specification in sample notation seems plausible: $\hat{Y}_i = \alpha + \beta_1 X_i - \beta_2 X_i^2$, where Y is annual income in hundreds of dollars, X is age in years, and X^2 is age-squared. While β_1 has a positive sign, consistent with an hypothesized increase of income with age, the negative sign of β_2 reflects an hypothesized decrease of income with the square of age. Using the 366 currently working men in the 1991 GSS, the estimated OLS regression equation (with standard errors in parentheses) is:

$$\hat{Y}_i = -19{,}371 + 2{,}085\ X_i - 19\ X_i^2$$
$$\phantom{\hat{Y}_i = -}(9{,}701)\quad\ (469)\qquad (5)$$
$$R^2_{adj} = 0.101$$

FIGURE 9.2D
Exponential ($\hat{Y}_i = e^{.5 + .25X_i}$)

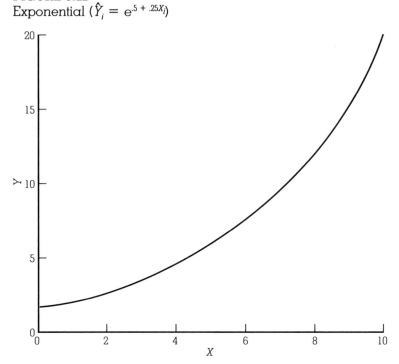

Both the linear and the quadratic coefficients differ significantly from zero at $\alpha = .05$. Each year of age increases a man's annual income by \$2,085, but the squared values of age decrease his income by \$19. To find where the peak earning age occurs, elementary differential calculus can be applied to determine the point on the age scale where the slope of the curve equals zero. Take the first derivative of the estimated equation with respect to X:

$$\frac{\delta Y}{\delta X} = 2{,}085 - (2)(19)X.$$ Set it equal to zero: $2{,}085 - 38X = 0$ then solve for $X = 54.9$ years.

The logarithmic function can also be estimated by transforming the predictor variable. Then an OLS regression using the transformed measure is linear in the estimated parameters while remaining logarithmic in terms of the variables. To illustrate, we specify a logarithmic function (base 10) between the number of children born to ever-married women and their ages at first marriage. The younger the age when a women first weds, the more children she is likely to bear. But we hypothesize that the total number of children born decreases in a negative logarithmic pattern the older a women is at her first marriage. Thus, an appropriate specification is $\hat{Y}_i = \alpha - \beta \log_{10} X_i$, where Y is the number of children born and $\log_{10} X$ is the logarithm (base 10) of age in years at first marriage. The β coefficient is shown with a negative sign, consistent with our hypothesis that women who marry later bear fewer children. Using the 713 ever-married women in the 1991 GSS, the OLS regression estimates (with standard errors in parentheses) are:

$$\hat{Y}_i = 11.30 - 6.75 \log_{10} X_i$$
$$(0.92) \quad (0.69)$$
$$R^2_{adj} = 0.116$$

As any nonlinear function implies, the expected number of children is not constant across the log-transformed age variable. For example, the equation predicts that a woman married at age 17 years ($\log_{10} = 1.23$) would have $11.30 - (6.75)(1.23) = 3.00$ children, while marriage at age 20 years ($\log_{10} = 1.30$) produces only $11.30 - (6.75)(1.30) = 2.53$ children, a difference of 0.47 children for the three-year delay. However, women married at ages 27 and 30 years are expected to bear 1.65 and 1.31 children, respectively, a difference of only 0.34 children for that three-year span. Clearly, how greatly a woman's marital history affects her childbearing is not constant, but depends significantly on the period of her life in which it occurs.

The exponential function shown in Figure 9.2D is just one of several alternative specifications. Another exponential form, often used to examine growth processes, is $\hat{Y}_i = \alpha X_i^{\beta}$. Here the intercept is separated from the regression parameter, which is an exponent for the predictor variable. An appropriate transformation that preserves linearity in the parameters takes natural logarithms of *both* sides of the estimated equation:

$$\log_e \hat{Y}_i = \log_e \alpha + \beta \log_e X_i$$

Unbiased estimates of β and $\log_e \alpha$ parameters can be obtained from an OLS regression of $\log_e Y$ on $\log_e X$. To recover the original α parameter value, take the antilog of the estimated $\log_e \alpha$. To illustrate, Figure 9.3A displays the population of the United States (in millions) at each decennial Census from 1790 to 1990. The pattern clearly implies accelerating growth over the two centuries (with a notable disruption during 1930–1940). But the plot in Figure 9.3B more closely approximates a straight line relationship. The estimated double-logged OLS equation (with standard errors in parentheses) is as follows:

$$\hat{\log_e \hat{Y}_i} = -.25 + 1.92 \, (\log_e X_i)$$
$$\quad\quad\quad (.08) \quad (.07)$$
$$R^2_{adj} = 0.972$$

where the values of X for decade time were recoded from $1790 = 2$ to $1990 = 22$. The R-square value shows that almost all the variation in logged population is captured by this specification (the linear regression of nonlogged population on decade time produces an $R^2 = 0.920$). The antilog$_e$ of the estimated intercept $(-.25)$ is 0.78. Thus, the estimated equation for the U.S. population's expo-

FIGURE 9.3A

U.S. Population by Census Year

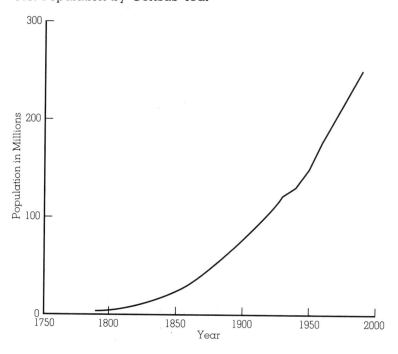

FIGURE 9.3B
U.S. Population (Log$_e$) by Census Year

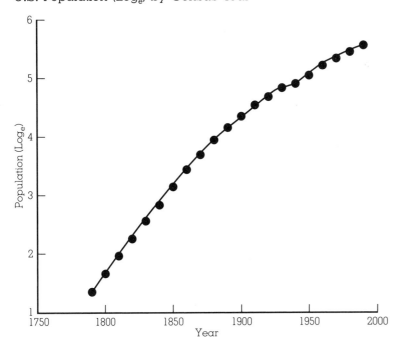

nential growth is $\hat{Y}_i = 0.78\ X_i^{1.92}$. The exponent 1.92 can be interpreted as the "elasticity" of the dependent variable with respect to the independent variable. That is, a 1% change in X is associated with an expected 1.92 percent change in the expected value of the dependent variable. Because 1% of two centuries under analysis is 2 years, the U.S. population grew on average by 1.92 percent every two years (i.e., 9.60% per decade). The derivative of the exponentiated double-log equation can also be used to calculate the expected value of the slope of the exponential growth line at any point X_i on the X-axis:

$$\frac{\delta Y}{\delta X} = \text{slope at } X_i = \alpha\ \beta\ X_i^{\beta-1}$$

$$= (0.78)(1.92)X_i^{1.92-1}$$

$$= 1.50X_i^{0.92}$$

An exponential slope changes nonlinearly, becoming increasingly larger as time goes by. For example, at the 9th Census (1860), the equation estimates the U.S. population to be growing by $(1.50)(9)^{0.92}$ = 11.3 million per decade, while by the 21st Census (1980) the expected slope value had more than doubled to $(1.50)(21)^{0.92}$ = 24.7 million additional Americans. The actual population increases were 8.4 million and 26.5 million, respectively. When the logarithmic equation is used to forecast growth in the decade A.D. 2090–2100 (32nd Census), a predicted $(1.50)(32)^{0.92}$ = 36.4 million new people would be added to the U.S. in 2090. Whether such heavy growth can actually be sustained over the coming century remains to be seen.

9.2 Dichotomous Dependent Variables

Until now, we have done regressions only with continuous dependent variables because they most closely approximate the best linear unbiased estimator (BLUE) criteria discussed in Box 8.2 (page 286). Nothing technically prevents us from analyzing dichotomous (1-0) or dummy dependent variables within an OLS framework. For example, 531 respondents in the 1991 GSS said they voted for George Bush (coded 1) and 354 reported voting for Michael Dukakis (coded 0) for president in 1988. The proportion voting for Bush is exactly .60. OLS regression of this dichotomy on four predictors yields the following unstandardized parameters (standard errors in parentheses):

$$\hat{Y}_i = \ .07 + .13\ X_{1i} + .04\ X_{2i} + .14\ X_{3i} - .01X_{4i}$$
$$\quad (.08)\quad (.01)\qquad (.01)\qquad (.04)\qquad (.004)$$
$$R^2_{adj} = 0.456$$

where $\hat{Y}$ is the expected vote for Bush; X_1 is the respondent's party identification (coded from 0 = strong Democrat to 6 = strong Republican); X_2 is his or her political views (1 = extremely liberal to 7 = extremely conservative); X_3 is a dummy variable for race (1 = white, 0 = other); and X_4 is education (0 to 20 years). (Four other predictors—occupational prestige, sex, Southern region, and Catholic religion—were included in an initial equation but were dropped from this specification because they did not have significant effects.) Because the dependent variable's range is confined between two choices, the equation can be interpreted as a **linear probability model** of the vote for Bush. For example, each point in

linear probability model— a linear regression model in which the dependent variable is confined between two choices

the Republican direction on the party identification increases the proportion a person voted for Bush by 0.13; whites are 0.14 more likely than nonwhites to vote for Bush; and so forth.

Two fundamental assumptions in regression analysis are violated by dichotomous dependent variables, making such linear probability models undesirable. First, the BLUE assumption that the error terms are normally distributed is not met. A regression error is the difference between an observed and a predicted score: $e_i = Y_i - \hat{Y}_i = Y_i - (\alpha + \Sigma \beta_{ji} X_{ji})$. However, because respondents can have observed scores of only 1 or 0, their error terms therefore can take only two values. For $Y_i = 1$, $e_i = 1 - \alpha - \Sigma \beta_{ji} X_{ji}$; while for $Y_i = 0$, $e_i = -\alpha - \Sigma \beta_{ji} X_{ji}$. Consequently, although the OLS parameter estimates of the β_js are unbiased, they are not the most efficient estimates (i.e., with the smallest possible sampling variances; see section 3.10 on page 112). Hypothesis tests using these estimated parameters and their standard errors can reach invalid conclusions, even for very large samples.

The second problem with dichotomous dependent variable regression is that some expected values may be nonsensical. Because the parameters depict multivariate linear relationships of the predictors to the dependent measure, the expected scores for some extreme combinations may fall outside the range from 0 to 1. Such results are meaningless because negative probabilities and chances greater than 1.00 are undefined. To illustrate, consider the expected score of a voter with the extreme values on the independent variables predisposing him or her to vote for Bush:

$$\hat{Y}_i = .07 + .13(6) + .04(7) + .14(1) - .01(0) = 1.27$$

A 1.27 probability of voting for Bush is impossible to comprehend. Similarly, persons with a contrasting configuration of independent values generate an expected Bush vote:

$$\hat{Y}_i = .07 + .13(0) + .04(1) + .14(0) - .01(20) = -0.09$$

This negative probability of voting for Bush cannot be imagined.

As these examples make clear, the linear probability version of OLS regression is unsatisfactory. We need an alternative approach that does not require unrealistic assumptions about probabilities that are linear functions of the predictor variables. Fortunately, such alternative nonlinear functional forms exist, for both dichotomous and nonordered discrete dependent variables, as discussed in the remainder of this chapter.

9.3   The Logistic Transformation and Its Properties

Percentages (%) and proportions (p) are not the only ways to measure a dichotomous response variable. The **logistic transformation of p** is a useful alternative with some insightful properties. Using the natural logarithm (that is, Euler's constant as the base), the logistic probability unit, or **logit,** for the ith observation is computed by forming the odds of p_i to its reciprocal, $1 - p_i$, and taking the $\log_e$ of this ratio (i.e., the logit is the natural log of an odds):

logistic transformation of p—a natural logarithmic change in the odds of a probability

logit—logistic probability unit

$$L_i = \log_e \left(\frac{p_i}{1 - p_i} \right)$$

The logit is symmetrically distributed around a central value. When $p_i = .50$, its reciprocal value is also $1 - .50 = .50$. Hence, the natural log of this ratio is $L_i = \log_e (.50/.50) = \log_e 1 = 0$. But as the dichotomy becomes more extreme in either direction, approaching 0 or 1, the logit values move further apart, as shown by these calculations:

p_i:	.10	.20	.30	.40	.50	.60	.70	.80	.90
$1 - p_i$:	.90	.80	.70	.60	.50	.40	.30	.20	.10
logit:	−2.20	−1.39	−.85	−.41	0.00	.41	.85	1.39	2.20

Although these probabilities have constant .10 intervals, their corresponding logits have increasingly wider intervals the farther they are from $p_i = .50$. Also note that, although no upper or lower limit exists for the logit, when p_i exactly equals 1.00 or 0.0, the logit is undefined. Figure 9.4 plots the continuous transformation of probabilities into their logits. It shows the cumulative probability distribution for the probability that $Y_i = 1$ (i.e., $p(Y_i = 1)$), where Y_i is a dichotomy, for values of the log odds that range from negative infinity to positive infinity. This S-shaped curve closely resembles the plot of the cumulative probability for the standardized normal distribution (Z scores). Within the range from $p_i = .25$ to .75, the

FIGURE 9.4

The Logistic Probability Form

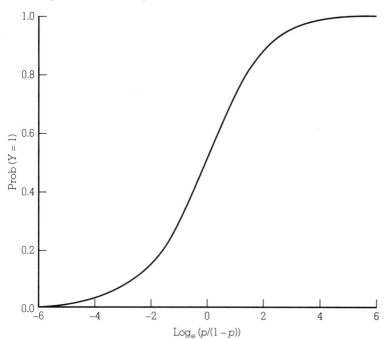

logistic transformation is nearly linear; consequently, the linear probability model gives results very similar to the logistic. However, as a dichotomy becomes more skewed in either direction, the nonlinearity of the logistic grows more pronounced. For very large L_i values in both the positive or negative direction, the probabilities for Y approach but never quite reach 1.00 and .00, respectively. Thus, even very extreme logit estimates can never be associated with expected probabilities that fall outside the meaningful 0-1 range. *This constraint on the expected values of the logistic transformation is its most important advantage over the linear probability form.*

Because they "stretch out" very high and low probabilities, logits are useful for making comparisons among proportions at differing levels. Table 9.1 shows the later school enrollments of four U.S. cohorts that entered the fifth grade at approximately four-year intervals between 1945 and 1960. The top panel displays the proportions of each cohort that subsequently entered the eighth grade, graduated from high school, and entered college. Over this

TABLE 9.1

Enrollments by Four Cohorts at Three Schooling Levels

Cohort Entering 5th Grade in	Subsequent Schooling		
	Entered 8th Grade	High School Graduation	Entered College
	Proportions		
1960	.967	.787	.452
1955	.948	.642	.343
1951	.921	.582	.308
1945	.858	.522	.234
	Odds		
1960	29.303	3.695	0.825
1955	18.231	1.793	0.522
1951	11.658	1.392	0.445
1945	6.042	1.092	0.305
	Logits		
1960	3.378	1.307	−0.193
1955	2.903	0.584	−0.650
1951	2.456	0.331	−0.809
1945	1.799	0.088	−1.186

Source: U.S. Census Bureau. (1975). *Historical Statistics of the United States: Colonial Times to 1970. Part 1.* Washington, DC: U.S. Government Printing Office. Series H587-597, p. 379.

period the rates rose for each successive cohort at all three schooling levels, but comparisons are complicated by the different initial rates of the three schooling levels. For example, comparing 1945 to 1960 proportions, the eighth grade enrollments were only .109 higher, while high school graduate and college attendance rates appear to have changed by more than twice as much, increasing .265 and .218, respectively. But, we could also assert that, relative to their 1945 proportions, the college entry rate almost doubled, the high school rate was 50% higher, but eighth grade attendance was up by only one-eighth over the 15-year period. Both these interpretations of the proportions suggest that school attendance changed at different rates between 1945–1960 across the three schooling levels. Because proportions and percentages are constrained to the interval between .00 and 1.00 (or 0% and 100%), such comparisons fail to adjust for "floor" and "ceiling" effects. That is, a 1% change in a 50% rate is not the same as a 1% change in a 98% rate.

Because of its symmetrical nature, the logistic transformation of an odds $(p_i/(1 - p_i))$ and an inverse odds $((1 - p_i)/p_i)$ result in equal but oppositely signed logits. For example, the proportions .75 and .25 correspond to odds of $.75/(1 - .75) = 3.000$ and inverse odds of $.25/(1 - .25) = 0.333$. Taking natural logs, these ratios yield logits of $+1.099$ and -1.099, respectively, indicating their fundamental equivalence. The second and third panels of Table 9.1 transform the school enrollment proportions, first into odds, then into logits. Figure 9.5 plots these logits, revealing the four cohorts' enrollment trends for the three schooling levels during this 15-year period. Each trend is roughly linear in the $\log_e$ odds, with the major deviation being a noticeable spurt in high school graduation by the 1960 cohort. We may reasonably conclude that the mid-century U.S. cohorts' school attendance grew at approximately constant rates at all three schooling levels.

The logit provides a suitable basis for an alternative to the unsatisfactory linear probability model. We can express the probability that the ith observation has a score of 1 on the dependent variable as a linear, additive function of K predictor variables. That is,

$$\text{Prob}(Y_i = 1) = p_i = \alpha + \sum_{j=1}^{K} \beta_j X_{ji}$$

Letting $Z = \alpha + \Sigma \beta_j X_{ji}$ to simplify the notation, the general functional form of a logistic equation is

$$F(Z) = \frac{e^Z}{1 + e^Z} = \frac{1}{1 + e^{-Z}}$$

FIGURE 9.5

Logits of Enrollments by Four Cohorts at Three Schooling Levels

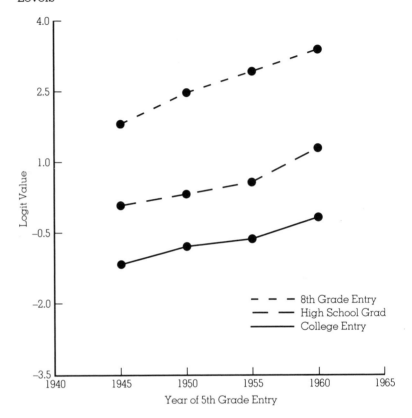

where e is Euler's constant (2.71828). By substituting the expression for Z, the probability that the ith case has a score of 1 on the dependent variable is as follows:

$$p_i = \frac{1}{1 + e^{-\alpha - \Sigma \beta_j X_{ji}}}$$

Because the logit (L_i) for the ith observation is computed by taking the natural logarithm of the odds,

$$L_i = \log_e \left(\frac{p_i}{1 - p_i} \right)$$
$$= \log_e (e^{\alpha + \Sigma \beta_j X_{ji}})$$
$$= \alpha + \Sigma \beta_j X_{ji}$$

Box 9.1 gives the details of this derivation. In the presidential voting example the odds of the probability of a vote for Bush relative to the probability of a vote for Dukakis is .60/(1 − .60) = .60/.40 = 1.50. The natural log of this number is .405. Figure 9.6 illustrates the

---

BOX 9.1   The Derivation of the Logit

First, to simplify notation, set $\alpha + \Sigma \beta_j X_{ji} = Z$. Given that the probability that the ith case has a score of 1 is $p_i = \dfrac{1}{1 + e^{-Z}}$, its reciprocal must be

$$1 - p_i = 1 - \frac{1}{1 + e^{-Z}} = \frac{1 + e^{-Z} - 1}{1 + e^{-Z}} = \frac{e^{-Z}}{1 + e^{-Z}}$$

Take the ratio of these reciprocal terms and simplify:

$$\frac{p_i}{1 - p_i} = \frac{1/(1 + e^{-Z})}{e^{-Z}/(1 + e^{-Z})} = \frac{1}{e^{-Z}} = e^Z$$

Next, take natural logarithms of the ratio:

$$\log_e \left(\frac{p_i}{1 - p_i} \right) = \log_e \left(\frac{1}{e^{-Z}} \right) = \log_e (e^Z) = Z$$

Finally, substituting for Z and defining the result as the logit L for the ith case:

$$\log_e \left(\frac{p_i}{1 - p_i} \right) = L_i = \alpha + \Sigma \beta_j X_{ji}$$

FIGURE 9.6
Linear Probability Compared to Logistic Regression

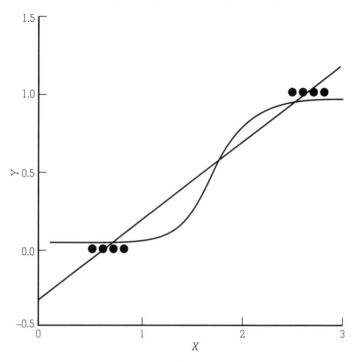

difference with hypothetical linear probability and logistic regression lines calculated using the same dichotomous sample data. The predicted linear probability is less than 0 and greater than 1 for extreme values of Z, but the logit never exceeds these limits for any value of Z.

Although the underlying probability is not a linear function of the predictors, the log-odds transformation makes the logit a linear additive function of the X_K independent variables. A dichotomous logit is directly interpretable as the (natural log of the) odds of the probability that $Y = 1$ to the probability that $Y = 0$. Given the symmetry of the logistic curve shown in Figure 9.4, when the probability that an observation has a score of 1 exactly equals .50, the logit equals 0 (i.e., $p_{Y=1}/p_{Y=0} = .50/.50 = 1.00$ and thus $\log_e 1.00 = 0.0$). When the probability that $Y = 1$ is greater than the probability that $Y = 0$, the logit is greater than 0. Finally, when the probability that $Y = 1$ is less than the probability that $Y = 0$, the logit is smaller than 0. The logit is undefined in the situation where the probability that $Y = 0$ is exactly zero: Division by zero in the denominator is mathematically impossible. But as the probability that $Y = 1$ approaches certainty (i.e., $p_{Y=1} \rightarrow 1.00$) and thus the probability that $Y = 0$ approaches zero (i.e., $p_{Y=0} \rightarrow 0$), their odds approaches infinity ($p_{Y=1}/p_{Y=0} \rightarrow \infty$) as does the logit of their ratio (see the right-hand side of Figure 9.4). In the opposite situation where the probability that $Y = 0$ approaches certainty and hence the probability that $Y = 1$ drops toward zero, both the odds and the logit of their ratio approach zero (see the left-hand side of Figure 9.4). These properties of the logit as the ratio of probabilities for the dichotomous case make it a very useful functional form for multivariate analysis.

9.4 Estimating and Testing Logistic Regression Equations

9.4.1 Parameter Estimates

Logistic regression parallels multiple regression analysis, with the dependent variable as the log odds of a dichotomy rather than a continuous measure. Just as in multiple regression, the independent or predictor variables in a logistic regression may be continuous measures, dichotomies, multicategory dummy variables, or interaction terms. The basic **dichotomous logistic regression equation** for K independent variables is as follows:

$$\hat{L}_i = \alpha + \beta_1 X_{1i} + \beta_2 X_{2i} + \ldots + \beta_K X_{Ki}$$

dichotomous logistic regression equation—a regression of the logit for a dichotomous dependent variable that is a linear function of the independent variables

The expected natural log (logit) of the ratio of the two probabilities, $p_i/(1 - p_i)$, is a linear function of the K predictors. Taking antilogs of the preceding equation (i.e., applying the principles that e ($\log_e W$) = W and e (Z) = e^Z), we can rewrite the basic dichotomous logistic regression equation to reveal how the independent variables affect the ratio of the probabilities:

$$e(\hat{L}_i) = e\left(\log_e \left(\frac{p_{Y=1}}{p_{Y=0}} \right) \right)$$

$$\frac{p_{Y=1}}{p_{Y=0}} = e^{\alpha + \beta_1 X_1 + \beta_2 X_2 + \ldots + \beta_K X_K}$$

The logistic regression equation resembles a linear, additive multiple regression equation, in that a β_j coefficient indicates by how much the log of the dependent variable's odds change when the corresponding predictor variable X_j changes by one unit.

Logistic regression parameters cannot be estimated using the OLS techniques that are suitable to multiple regression. Instead, a method called **maximum likelihood estimation (MLE)** is used. Briefly, MLE attempts a series of successive approximations to the unknown true population parameter values, α and the β_js. The goal is to use the sample data to make estimates of the parameters, a and b_js, that maximize the likelihoods of having obtained these observed sample values. In contrast to OLS regression, which uses a least-squares criterion (sum of squared differences) for judging the fit between observed and predicted values of Y, the MLE method calculates the probability of observing each sample Y_i if a given set of parameters is assumed to be true. The set that yields the highest probability comprises the maximum likelihood estimates.

maximum likelihood estimation— a method of estimating parameter values that chooses the set with the highest probability of generating the sample observations

Because MLE has no algebraic formulas similar to the normal equations used in OLS regression, its solution requires a computer program capable of examining many parameter sets until the best choice is identified. (Most computer programs use the Newton-Raphson method.) The procedure begins with an initial estimate (typically that all parameters equal 0). A series of *iterations*, or cycles, produces new estimates and compares them with the previous ones. The iterations continue until successive estimates differ from the preceding ones by less than a specified small amount. For large samples MLE parameter estimates are unbiased, efficient, and normally distributed, and thus allow significance tests using statistics we have previously examined.

Recall the example in section 9.2 from the 1991 GSS where four independent variables (party identification, liberal versus conservative political views, race, and education) were used to predict the expected vote for Bush versus Dukakis in the 1988 presidential election. These same predictors were used to estimate a logistic regression equation.[1] The estimated equation (standard errors in parentheses) is:

$$\hat{L}_i = -2.68 + .79\,X_{1i} + .33\,X_{2i} + .87\,X_{3i} - .08\,X_{4i}$$
$$\phantom{\hat{L}_i = }(.61)\quad(.05)\quad\quad(.08)\quad\quad(.33)\quad\quad(.03)$$

---

1. Estimation was done using the SPSS logistic regression routine.

The *t* ratios for the four predictor variables, which can be calculated by dividing the parameter estimates by their standard errors, are all statistically significant at $\alpha < .01$ or less.

Directly interpreting each effect is problematic because it requires thinking in terms of log odds, hardly a conventional framework. However, a positive or negative sign indicates how a predictor linearly increases or decreases the log odds. Thus, a coefficient can be interpreted similarly to a linear regression parameter, as long as you remember that the dependent variable is *not* a probability, but rather a logarithm of the odds of two probabilities. In the above example the positive coefficients mean that being a Republican (X_1), holding conservative political views (X_2), and being white (X_3) each increase the log odds of voting for Bush, while the negative coefficient means that being more educated (X_4) decreases the log odds of a Bush vote.

Calculating the confidence interval around a logistic regression coefficient point estimate resembles procedures used in OLS regression. For a large sample with a chosen level of α, the upper and lower confidence limits for the $(100)(1 - \alpha\%)$ interval around the estimate of b_j are given by

$$b_j \pm t_{\alpha/2}s_{b_j}$$

where

s_{b_j} is the standard error of the estimated b_j coefficient.

For example, the 95% confidence limits for the party identification (X_1) logistic coefficient are $.79 \pm (1.96)(.05)$, or LCL = .692 and UCL = .888.

A simple transformation allows one to interpret the net effect of a dichotomous *independent* variable (dummy variable) on the dependent variable's probability. Simply multiply the estimate, b_j, by the variance of the dependent dichotomy, which is $(p_i)(1 - p_i)$. The resulting value indicates the proportional effect of the predictor on the dependent variable's probability of occurring (evaluated at the sample mean) net of the other variables in the equation. Because the proportion voting for Bush is .60, its variance is $(.60)(1 - .60) = .24$. Therefore, the effect of being white on voting for Bush is $(.87)(.24) = .21$. That is, being white increases the chances of voting for Bush by 21% relative to being nonwhite.

We showed in section 9.2 that extreme values of independent variables may lead to out-of-bounds predictions (i.e., predictions not falling within the 0.00 to 1.00 range of probability) if a dichotomous dependent variable is estimated using OLS regression. Applying the same extreme combinations for a pro-Bush voter to the logistic regression equation yields the following:

$$\hat{L}_i = -2.68 + .79(6) + .33(7) + .87(1) - .08(0)$$
$$= -2.68 + 4.74 + 2.31 + 0.87 + 0.0 = 5.24$$

To translate 5.24 back into a probability, we make use of the basic logistic function $F(Z) = e^Z/(1 + e^Z)$ where $Z = \alpha + \Sigma b_j X_{ji}$. Thus, the expected probability of a Bush vote by a person having these extreme pro-Bush values on the four independent variables is

$$P_{Y=1} = \frac{e^{5.24}}{1 + e^{5.24}} = \frac{188.67}{1 + 188.67} = \frac{188.67}{189.67} = 0.9947$$

In other words, such persons are predicted to have a 99.5% chance of voting for Bush, not the absurd 127% chance predicted by the OLS model. Similarly, for voters with extreme pro-Dukakis predictor values, the logistic regression equation yields $Z = -3.95$, which translates into an expected probability of a Bush vote of .019, compared to the meaningless negative probability (-0.09) estimated by the linear probability model.

9.4.2.   Measuring Equation Fits

log likelihood ratio—a ratio that contrasts two nested logistic regression equations, where one equation is a restricted version of the other

Four procedures are available to assess the overall fit of a logistic regression equation to the data. The first, the **log likelihood ratio,** contrasts two nested logistic regression equations, where one equation is a restricted version of the other. If the less-restricted equation has K_1 independent variables and the more-restricted equation has K_0 independent variables, all of which also appear in the less-restricted equation, the null hypothesis states that none of the additional $K_1 - K_0$ logistic regression parameters differ significantly from zero in the population. That is, for all β_j where $j > K_0$, H_0: $\beta_{K_0+1} = \beta_{K_0+2} = \ldots = \beta_{K_1} = 0$. The alternative hypothesis is that at least one of the β_j parameters is significantly different from zero.

L_1 is the maximized likelihood for the less-restricted equation that has K_1 independent variables. It has $N - K_1 - 1$ degrees of freedom. L_0 is the likelihood for the more-restricted equation with K_0 predictors. It has $N - K_0 - 1$ degrees of freedom. The test statistic, (G^2), which compares the ratio of these two likelihoods, is distributed as a chi square with degrees of freedom equal to the difference in the number of predictors between the two equations, that is, $df = K_1 - K_0$. The formula for the test statistic is

$$G^2 = -2 \log_e \left(\frac{L_0}{L_1} \right) = (-2 \log_e L_0) - (-2 \log_e L_1)$$

The most common application of the log likelihood ratio test is that *all* the parameters in an equation equal zero, except the intercept α, which then equals the sample proportion coded 1 on the dependent variable. In the voting example the equation with only the intercept (i.e., $K_0 = 0$) yields $-2 \log_e L_0 = 1,191.2$.[2] The equation including all four predictors (i.e., $K_1 = 4$) has $-2\log_e L_1 = 712.1$. Hence, $G^2 = (-2 \log_e L_0) - (-2 \log_e L_1) = 1,191.2 - 712.1 = 479.1$, with $df = 4$. If we set $\alpha = .05$, Appendix B shows that the critical value equals 9.49. Therefore, we reject the null hypothesis that all four predictors have zero coefficients in favor of the alternative hypothesis that at least one parameter is probably nonzero.

Each of the logistic regression coefficients can also be tested using the log likelihood ratio. A set of K_1 more-restricted equations is estimated, each of which omits just one of the predictors. The differences between the log likelihood ratios for the full, less-restricted equation and each more-restricted equation are tested relative to the single degree of freedom difference (critical value = 3.84 for $\alpha = .05$). For example, when education is dropped from the full four-predictor equation, $-2 \log_e L = 718.2$, so $G^2 = 718.2 - 712.1 = 6.1$, which is significant at $p < .05$ but not at $p < .01$. Given that the $-2 \log_e Ls$ for the equation omitting party identification = 1,040.82; for omission of political views = 729.9; and for omission of race = 719.7; prove to yourself that each predictor significantly improves the equation's fit to the data for $\alpha = .05$.

A second test statistic, the **goodness of fit statistic,** uses the standardized residuals to compare the observed probabilities to those predicted by the equation. The goodness of fit statistic is the

goodness of fit statistic— a test statistic that uses standardized residuals to compare the observed probabilities to those predicted by the equation

---

2. This value is routinely calculated and printed out by standard logistic regression software packages.

sum of the squared ratio of a residual standardized by dividing its estimated standard deviation:

$$Z^2 = \sum_{i=1}^{N} \frac{(p_i - \hat{p}_i)^2}{(\hat{p}_i)(1 - \hat{p}_i)}$$

The closer each predicted probability comes to the observed probability, the better the fit and hence the smaller the Z^2 value. This statistic is distributed as a chi square with degrees of freedom approximately equal to $N - K_1 - 1$. In the four-predictor voting model the goodness of fit value is 871.6 for $df = 880$, leading to the same conclusion we reached above. That is, at least one of the four logistic regression coefficients differs significantly from zero.[3]

pseudo-R^2—a descriptive measure for logistic regression that indicates roughly the proportion of variation in the dependent variable accounted for by the predictors

A third procedure, **pseudo-R^2**, takes into account the fact that chi square distributions are proportional to sample size. It adjusts the log likelihood ratio for N and is a measure of the variance explained by the K independent variables:

$$\text{pseudo-}R^2 = \frac{-2 \log_e L}{N + (-2 \log_e L)}$$

The formula does not consider the degrees of freedom in the equation and no sampling distribution is available. Hence, a significance test for pseudo-R^2 does not exist and it is only a descriptive measure that indicates roughly the proportion of observed variation in the dependent variable accounted for by K predictors.

For the four-predictor voting model pseudo-R^2 = (712.1)/(885 + 712.1) = 0.45, meaning that slightly less than half the variation in voting choice is accounted for by these four independent variables.

Finally, a logistic regression equation can be used to classify each observation according to its most probable category on the dependent variable, given that observation's particular combination of values for its independent variables. These predicted values are then compared to the observed values for all N sample cases,

3. The goodness of fit statistic is routinely calculated and printed out by logistic regression software packages such as SPSS.

and the percentage of accurate classifications is used to judge how well the equation accounts for dichotomous outcomes. In the voting data the four-predictor logistic equation correctly identified 283 of the 354 Dukakis voters (80%) and 437 of the 531 Bush voters (82.3%), for an overall accuracy of 81.4% (720/885). This success rate is not as impressive as it seems; merely guessing that all GSS respondents voted for Bush would prove correct 60% of the time (the sample mean). However, the information on voters' party identification, political views, race, and education did lead to a reduction in errors of classification by more than half (from 40% incorrect to 18.6% incorrect).

9.5 Multicategory Dependent Variables

Logistic regression analysis of dichotomies is a special instance of a more general multicategory discrete dependent variable model. Natural dichotomies do not cover all measures of potential interest. For example, workers' employment status might be classified as working full-time, working part-time, unemployed, on layoff, and not in the labor force. Artificially forcing all observations into an employed-unemployed dichotomy could be more concealing than revealing. Fortunately, the logistic regression estimation techniques discussed above can be extended to analyze M nonordered categories in a **polychotomous logistic regression equation.** This can be illustrated by adding the 362 nonvoting GSS respondents to the 531 Bush voters and the 354 Dukakis voters previously analyzed, creating a trichotomy ($M = 3$) among $N = 1,247$ cases in the GSS electorate sample.[4]

polychotomous logistic regression equation— logistic regression with a dependent variable having more than two discrete, nonordered categories

The probability that the ith observation occurs in the jth category of a polychotomous dependent variable is designated p_{ij}. Thus, where nonvoters, Dukakis voters, and Bush voters are respectively labeled categories 1 through 3, these probabilities are symbolized p_{i1}, p_{i2}, and p_{i3}. Probabilities are defined as relative frequencies, so that their sum across the M polychotomous categories must always equal unity: $\sum_{j=1}^{M} p_{ij} = 1$. Thus, in our GSS electorate sample $p_{i1} + p_{i2} + p_{i3} = .290 + .426 + .284 = 1.00$.

---

4. These analyses were performed with the LIMDEP program of William Greene, because the SPSS logistic regression program did not have the capability of handling polychotomous dependent variables.

In a logistic regression equation the expected probabilities depend in nonlinear ways on the set of K independent variables that predict them. The relationship is given by a multivariate logistic distribution function:

$$p_{ij} = \frac{e^{\Sigma \alpha + \beta_{kj} X_{kji}}}{\sum\limits_{j=1}^{J} e^{\Sigma \alpha + \beta_{kj} X_{kji}}}$$

where

p_{ij} = The probability that the ith case is in the jth category of the dependent variable.

The triple subscripts on the X's indicate the ith observation on the kth predictor variable in the logistic equation for the jth category of the polychotomous dependent variable. To solve these equations for unique parameter estimates, a linear constraint must be placed on the set of βs pertaining to the kth predictor. A conventional constraint is that they sum to zero: $\sum\limits_{j=1}^{M} \beta_{kj} = 0$. Just as with dummy-variable predictors in a linear regression (see section 8.6 on page 303), the M categories of a polychotomous dependent variable have only $M - 1$ degrees of freedom. In addition to requiring that the βs for the K predictors sum to 1.00, we can also specify that all coefficients in the Mth equation equal zero. Then, each estimated coefficient β_{kj} reveals the effect of predictor X_k on the odds of respondent i being in the jth dependent variable category *relative to* the omitted category M. The dependent variable category that we designate as our reference, or baseline, group is arbitrary. For the dichotomous presidential voting example in section 9.4, we chose Dukakis voters as the omitted category; mirror-image results would have occurred if we had instead designated the Bush voters as our baseline. For a polychotomous logistic regression the nonlinear transformations cannot assure that the probabilities will add to 1.00. But as Box 9.2 demonstrates, the natural logarithms of the ratios of the probabilities for each category relative to the baseline category must sum to 1.00 as required.

Table 9.2 displays the parameter estimates for the trichotomous voting example, where nonvoters were the omitted baseline category. In addition to the four significant predictors used above, both Southern residence and occupational prestige had significant

BOX 9.2   Polychotomous Probabilities Relative to a Baseline Category

For $M \geq 2$ discrete nonordered categories of a dependent variable and $K \geq 1$ predictor variables, let any arbitrarily chosen baseline or reference category M have the logit probability

$$p(Y_i = M) = \frac{1}{1 + \sum\limits_{j=1}^{M-1} e^{Z_{im}}}$$

where Z_{im} represents $\alpha + \sum\limits_{k=1}^{K} \beta_{jk} X_{jki}$ for the $m = M - 1$ other

categories of the dependent variable (the subscript i stands for the ith individual observation).

Given an mth dependent variable category, its polychotomous logit relative to the Mth baseline category is

$$\log_e \left(\frac{p(Y_i = m)}{p(Y_i = M)} \right) = Z_{im}$$

Exponentiate this expression and rearrange as follows:

$$\frac{p(Y_i = m)}{p(Y_i = M)} = e^{Z_{im}}$$

Therefore, $p(Y_i = m) = (p(Y_i = M))\,(e^{Z_{im}})$

Now, substituting the first equation in this box into the immediately preceding equation and carrying out the multiplication results in the following equation for the probability that the ith observation falls into the mth category of the dependent variable:

$$p(Y_i = m) = \left(\frac{1}{1 + \sum\limits_{j=1}^{M-1} e^{Z_{im}}} \right) (e^{Z_{im}}) = \frac{e^{Z_{im}}}{1 + \sum\limits_{j=1}^{M-1} e^{Z_{im}}}$$

(Continued next page)

BOX 9.2   *(continued)*

Next, normalize the denominator of the preceding equation by setting α and all the βs in the Mth baseline equation equal to 0. Because in general $e^0 = 1$, so $e^{Z_{iM}} = 1$ when all the α and β parameters in the Mth equation are set to zero. Consequently, we can replace the 1 in the denominator with this exponential term:

$$p(Y_i = m) = \frac{e^{Z_{im}}}{1 + \sum\limits_{j=1}^{M-1} e^{Z_{im}}} = \frac{e^{Z_{im}}}{e^{Z_{iM}} + \sum\limits_{j=1}^{M-1} e^{Z_{im}}} = \frac{e^{Z_{im}}}{\sum\limits_{j=1}^{M} e^{Z_{im}}}$$

because the denominator now sums across all M equations. Thus, the probability that observation Y_i is in the mth polychotomous category is expressed relative to the sum over all M categories.

Finally, also apply the probability formula to the Mth category where all parameters were set to zero:

$$p(Y_i = M) = \frac{e^0}{e^0 + \sum\limits_{j=1}^{M-1} e^{Z_{im}}} = \frac{1}{1 + \sum\limits_{j=1}^{M-1} e^{Z_{im}}} = \frac{1}{\sum\limits_{j=1}^{M} e^{Z_{im}}}$$

When the probabilities for all M categories are added, their sum equals 1.00. That is,

$$\sum\limits_{j=1}^{M} p_i = \sum\limits_{j=1}^{M-1} \left(\frac{e^{Z_{im}}}{\sum\limits_{j=1}^{M} e^{Z_{im}}} \right) + \frac{1}{\sum\limits_{j=1}^{M} e^{Z_{im}}}$$

$$= \frac{\sum\limits_{j=1}^{M-1} e^{Z_{im}} + 1}{\sum\limits_{j=1}^{M} e^{Z_{im}}} = \frac{\sum\limits_{j=1}^{M} e^{Z_{im}}}{\sum\limits_{j=1}^{M} e^{Z_{im}}} = 1.00$$

TABLE 9.2

Additive Parameter Estimates for Polychotomous Logistic
Regression of the 1988 Presidential Election, Where Nonvoters
Are the Omitted Reference Category

Independent Variables	Logistic Coefficients	Standard Errors	t Ratio
Dukakis Voters:			
Intercept	−1.13	.55	−2.08*
Party Identification	−.65	.06	−11.70**
Political Views	−.09	.07	−1.31
Race	−.21	.24	−0.86
Southern	−.42	.18	−2.33*
Education	.19	.04	5.40**
Occupation	.02	.01	1.95
Bush Voters:			
Intercept	−4.53	.52	−8.68**
Party Identification	.26	.04	6.33**
Political Views	.21	.06	3.44**
Race	.68	.30	2.25*
Southern	−.22	.16	−1.38
Education	.12	.03	4.01**
Occupation	.02	.01	3.38**

* $p < .05$
** $p < .001$
$N = 1,247$
Missing data = 270
Source: 1991 General Social Survey

effects and are therefore included. Whereas the dichotomous
equation coefficients in section 9.4 indicate the chances of voting for
Bush relative to voting for Dukakis, the logistic regression coefficients in the upper panel of Table 9.2 indicate the effects of each
predictor on voting for Dukakis relative to nonvoting, while the
parameters in the lower panel indicate the effects on voting for
Bush relative to nonvoting. Logically enough, many of these
coefficients have opposite signs. For example, the +0.26 party
identification parameter for Bush voters means that Republican
identifiers were more likely to vote for him than to stay home, while
the −0.65 parameter for Dukakis voters means they were more likely
to stay home than to vote for the Democrat. Similarly, political
conservatives and whites were significantly more likely to vote for
Bush (0.21 and 0.68, respectively), but were less likely to support
Dukakis than not to vote (−0.09 and −0.21). The negative signs for

the South/non-South predictor in both equations indicates that people living in the South were more likely to be nonvoters than to vote for either candidate (although this parameter statistically is significant only in the Dukakis equation). By contrast, the positive signs for education and occupation in both equations mean that persons of higher status were more likely to vote for either candidate than not to vote.

For the polychotomous logistic equation with K_1 = six predictors, $-2 \log_e L = 1,026.3$. But for the equation that includes only the intercept ($K_0 = 0$), $-2 \log_e L = 1,346.8$. Therefore, the improvement in fit is $G^2 = 1346.8 - 1026.3 = 320.5$ for $df = 6 - 0 = 6$, a highly statistically significant improvement, since the critical value for $df = 6$ and $\alpha = .001$ is 22.46.

The rule for predicting outcomes in a polychotomous logistic regression equation is to classify the ith case as belonging in the jth category if p_j for that case has the highest predicted probability. Using this rule to classify the 1,247 respondents into the three dependent variable categories and comparing these predictions to the observed values, we find correct classifications for only 62.9% of the sample. But the success level varies across categories: 75.7% were correctly classified among the Bush voters, compared to 74% of the Dukakis voters. However, only 33.1% of the nonvoters were correctly classified. Clearly, the six predictors are much more useful in placing the voters' choices than in distinguishing who did not vote. Further research should concentrate on discovering additional predictors that better explain voter turnout, for example, the respondents' interests in political affairs.

9.6   Probit Analysis

The logit is not the only nonlinear functional form, although it is probably more widely available in packaged computer programs than any other form. Among the other possibilities, perhaps the next most common one is the cumulative normal distribution, or **probit** (probability unit), function. Its values are obtained by integrating the normal distribution (see section 3.4 on page 84); hence, it is sometimes called the standardized logistic distribution, or the "normit." Like the logit, the probit forms a symmetrical S-shaped

probit—probability unit for the cumulative normal distribution

curve ranging between 0 and 1 for values between $-\infty$ and $+\infty$. Thus, it also satisfies the 0-1 constraint on a dichotomous dependent variable without putting constraints on values of the predictor variables. The logit and probit curves are very similar, as Figure 9.6 shows. Both are approximately linear in the middle range and their estimates of probabilities differ by .02 or less. The probit approaches extreme values more slowly than the logit, but the differences are relatively small and statistically detectable only in very large samples.

The substantive results of nonlinear regressions for logits and probits are likely to be very similar, with their parameter estimates differing by a constant factor of proportionality that normalizes the standard deviations (approximately 1.75 in the voting example). Comparing the logit equation estimates for the dichotomous voting data in section 9.4 to the following probit equation estimates for the same data shows that one would come to the same substantive conclusions (standard errors in parentheses):

$$\text{Probit: } \hat{L}_i = -1.57 + .46\,X_{1i} + .19\,X_{2i} + .50\,X_{3i} - .04\,X_{4i}$$
$$\quad\quad\quad (.34)\quad (.03)\quad\quad (.04)\quad\quad (.18)\quad\quad (.02)$$
$$\text{Logit: } \hat{L}_i = -2.68 + .79\,X_{1i} + .33\,X_{2i} + .87\,X_{3i} - .08\,X_{4i}$$
$$\quad\quad\quad (.61)\quad (.05)\quad\quad (.05)\quad\quad (.33)\quad\quad (.03)$$

The logit coefficients are approximately 1.75 times larger than the corresponding probit parameters. The similarity of results can also be seen by comparing the two sets of t ratios:

	Intercept	X_1	X_2	X_3	X_4
Probit:	-4.62	15.33	4.75	2.78	-2.00
Logit:	-4.39	15.80	6.60	2.64	-2.67

The choice between these two nonlinear regression methods seems more a matter of taste and experience than anything else. Because both functions give essentially identical results for dichotomous dependent variables, and because only the logit also applies to polychotomous dependent measures, we prefer working with the logit specification for nonlinear multivariate analyses.

FIGURE 9.7

Logit and Probit Curves Compared

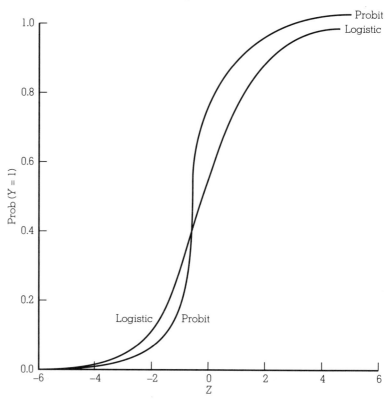

Review of Key Concepts and Symbols

These key concepts and symbols are listed in the order of appearance in this chapter. Combined with the definitions in the margins, they will help you to review the material and can serve as a self-test for mastery of the concepts.

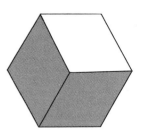

Euler's constant	dichotomous logistic regression
linear probability model	equation
logistic transformation of p	maximum likelihood estimation
logit	log likelihood ratio

goodness of fit statistic	L_i
pseudo-R^2	$\text{Prob}(Y_i = 1)$
polychotomous logistic regression equation	e^Z
	MLE
probit	K_0
e	K_1
$\log_e$	G^2
$\log_{10}$	Z^2

PROBLEMS

General Problems

1. The 1991 GSS respondents were asked "Generally speaking, would you say that most people can be trusted or that you can't be too careful in dealing with people?" A linear regression of 1,009 responses to this item on seven education categories yielded an $R^2 = 0.0575$, while a one-way analysis of variance for the same variables resulted in an $\hat{\eta}^2 = 0.0679$. Is there a significant nonlinear relationship between trust and education at $\alpha = .05$?

2. The following pairs of numbers represent, respectively, the per capita incomes and electricity usage per person for 10 nations:

   (1, 2) (2, 3) (3, 5) (4, 6) (5, 7) (6, 8) (15, 9) (18, 11) (24, 15) (30, 16)

   Plot these pairs on graph paper, with income on the Y-axis and electricity use on the X-axis, and interpret the shape of their relationship.

3. A regression of the occupational prestige scores for 1,411 respondents in the 1991 GSS on their education (X_i, measured in years) and the squared values of their education (X_i^2) produces the following equation (standard errors in parentheses):

$$\hat{Y}_i = 33.668 - 1.118\, X_i + 0.134\, X_i^2$$
$$\phantom{\hat{Y}_i = }(3.700) \quad (0.573) \quad\;\; (0.022)$$

   a. What is the expected prestige score of someone with 1 year of education?

b. What is the expected prestige score of someone with 12 years of education?

c. What is the expected prestige score of someone with 16 years of education?

d. At what amount of education does the minimum expected prestige score occur, and what is that score?

4. Regressing the 1991 GSS respondents' occupational prestige scores on the base 10 logarithm of their education yields this equation (standard errors in parentheses):

$$\hat{Y}_i = -19.556 + 56.684 \, (\log_{10} X_i)$$
$$\phantom{\hat{Y}_i = } (3.099) \quad (2.796)$$

a. What is the expected prestige score of someone with 1 year of education?

b. What is the expected prestige score of someone with 12 years of education?

c. What is the expected prestige score of someone with 16 years of education?

5. In the 1991 GSS 886 respondents were asked, "Do you believe there is a life after death?" A logistic regression of their dichotomous responses ($1 =$ yes, $0 =$ no) on age (X_1) and church attendance (X_2) produced the following equation (standard errors in parentheses):

$$\hat{L}_i = 0.812 - 0.005 \, X_{1i} + 0.224 \, X_{2i}$$
$$\phantom{\hat{L}_i = } (0.254) \quad (0.005) \quad\quad (0.035)$$

What effects do these predictors have on belief in an after life, using $\alpha = .05$?

6. Construct the 95% confidence intervals around the parameters in the equation in Problem 5.

7. Adding dummy variables for Catholic (X_3) and Jew (X_4) to the logistic regression in Problem 5, treating Protestant as the omitted category, the following equation results (standard errors in parentheses):

$$\hat{L}_i = 1.093 - 0.006 \, X_{1i} + 0.234 \, X_{2i} - 0.721 \, X_{3i} - 1.405 \, X_{4i}$$
$$\phantom{\hat{L}_i = } (0.268) \quad (0.005) \quad\quad (0.036) \quad\quad (0.192) \quad\quad (0.566)$$

Given that proportion of respondents believing there is life after death is 0.806, what are the net proportional effects of being Catholic and of being Jewish on belief in the afterlife, relative to Protestants?

8. In the equation shown in Problem 7, what are the probabilities that a person believes in a life after death who is (*a*) Catholic, 65 years old, and attends church nearly every week ($X_2 = 6$); (*b*) Protestant, 25 years old, and never attends church ($X_2 = 0$)?

9. The logistic regression equation in Problem 8 has a $-2 \log_e$ likelihood of 809.38, while an equation that has only the intercept yields a $-2 \log_e$ likelihood of 872.10. Calculate G^2 and test whether the model in Problem 8 is a significant improvement, using $\alpha = .001$. What is the pseudo-R^2 given that $N = 886$?

10. Below are polychotomous logistic regression equations, based on 844 women in the 1991 GSS. The omitted category of the dependent variable is women who keep house, the second category is women in the paid labor force, and the third category is retired women. The independent variables are married (X_1), any children at home (X_2), and age (X_3).

$$\hat{L}_{2i} = \underset{(0.408)}{4.091} - \underset{(0.172)}{0.339}\, X_{1i} - \underset{(0.209)}{0.886}\, X_{2i} - \underset{(0.007)}{0.065}\, X_{3i}$$

$$\hat{L}_{3i} = \underset{(0.944)}{-6.101} - \underset{(0.276)}{0.279}\, X_{1i} - \underset{(0.664)}{1.252}\, X_{2i} + \underset{(0.013)}{0.088}\, X_{3i}$$

Test each coefficient for significant, using $\alpha = .05$, and give a substantive interpretation.

Problems Requiring the 1991 General Social Survey

11. Does the number of hours of daily television viewing (TVHOURS) have a linear or nonlinear relationship with education (EDUC), as measured by seven categories? Test the difference between R^2 and η^2, setting $\alpha = .05$. [RECODE EDUC (0 THRU 7=1)(8=2)(9 THRU 11=3)(12=4)(13 THRU 15=5)(16=6)(17 THRU 20=7).]

12. Does occupational prestige (PRESTG80) vary significantly with both linear age (AGE) and with the square of age? Compute the squared age term and enter both predictors into a regression,

reporting the coefficient estimates and standard errors, and calculating the 99% confidence intervals for the parameters. What is the age at which expected occupational prestige peaks, and what is its value? [COMPUTE AGESQ=AGE*AGE.]

13. Are attitudes favorable to busing schoolchildren for racial integration (BUSING) a function of a person's race (RACE) and personal cross-racial contact (RACHOME). Perform a logistic regression, presenting the coefficient estimates, standard errors, and t ratios. Also give the $-2 \log_e$ likelihoods for this equation and a logistic regression where only the intercept is entered. What are the percentages of correctly predicted respondents favoring and opposing busing? SELECT IF (RACE NE 3). COMPUTE BUS=BUSING. RECODE BUS(2=0)(1=1)(ELSE =9). RECODE RACHOME(2=0)(1=1)(ELSE=9). MISSING VALUES BUS,RACHOME(9).

14. Respondents were asked, "Tell me if you agree or disagree with this statement: Most men are better suited emotionally for politics than are most women" (FEPOL). After recoding into a 1-0 dichotomy (eliminating the "not sure" responses), estimate a logistic regression equation with respondent's gender (SEX), age (AGE), and occupational prestige (PRESTG80) as predictors. Present the coefficient estimates, standard errors, and t ratios. Also give the $-2 \log_e$ likelihoods for this equation and a logistic regression where only the intercept is entered. What are the percentages of correctly predicted respondents who agree and disagree with the statement?

Problems Requiring Use of the U.S. States Data Set

15. Do states' crime rates have a nonlinear relationship with policing effort? Compute the square of the percent of local government budget spent on police (POLICEEX). Regress the number of serious crimes per 100,000 population (CRIMEPC) on both the squared and nonsquared police expenditure predictors. Present the coefficient estimates and standard errors. At what level of policing expenditure does expected serious crime reach its peak and what is that value? What is your interpretation?

16. Is the number of people who enter or leave a state a logarithmic function of the number of unemployed people? Regress

POPCHNG on the base 10 log of UNEMPLED, and present the coefficients and standard errors.

a. If a state had 30,000 unemployed, what is its predicted population change?

b. What is a state's predicted population change if it had 300,000 unemployed?

Statistics for
Social Data
Analysis

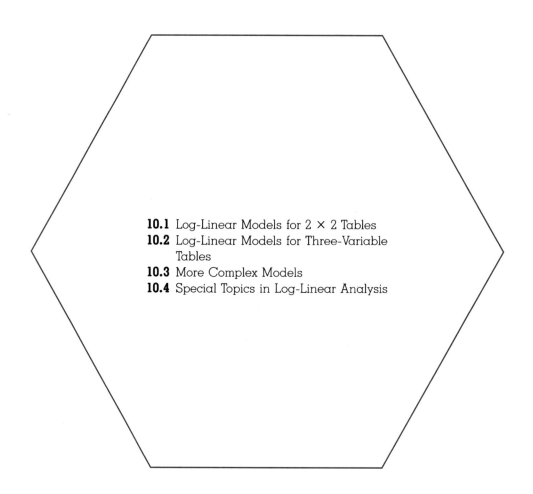

Log-Linear Analysis

10

The preceding chapters have presented multivariate statistical techniques suitable for continuous variables. In this chapter we offer some basic procedures for conducting **multivariate contingency table analysis,** that is, statistical analysis of data on three or more categorical variables. The technique for analyzing cross-classified data presented in this chapter is called **log-linear analysis.**

In examining the various aspects of crosstabulation between two categorical variables in chapter 5, we discussed measures of association and tests of significance for both discrete and ordered variables. Methods were presented to help determine whether two variables systematically covary and whether the covariation observed in sample data is likely to reflect the population from which the sample was drawn. As we pointed out in chapter 5, establishing that two variables, such as smoking and gender, significantly covary may be sufficient for some research purposes. But most researchers want to determine whether such bivariate relationships are affected by other factors (e.g., age, education, social class, health attitudes, etc.). In such cases the research problem changes from describing a two-variable relationship to considering three or more variables, as their relationships bear upon some theoretical issue.

multivariate contingency table analysis—the statistical analysis of data on three or more categorical variables

log-linear analysis— a technique for analyzing cross-classified data

361

10.1   Log-Linear Models for 2 × 2 Tables

To demonstrate log-linear analysis for tabular data, we analyze a specific substantive problem, white Americans' attitudes toward racial segregation. Despite the civil rights movement's success at tearing down formal *legal* subordination of minorities, a significant proportion of the white majority still favors restrictions on black Americans' rights to live, work, attend school, and marry as they choose. In the 1991 GSS respondents were asked the strength of their agreement or disagreement with the following statement:

> "White people have the right to keep blacks out of their neighborhoods if they want to, and blacks should respect that right."

For the frequency and percentage crosstabs displayed in Table 10.1, we collapsed the "agree strongly" and "agree slightly" categories and also the "disagree strongly" and "disagree slightly" categories to form a dichotomy. The row marginals show that 82.2% disagreed with residential racial segregation. As discussed in section 5.4 (on page 178), the odds of disagreeing with the item (i.e.,

TABLE 10.1

Frequency and Percentage Crosstabulations of Residential Racial Segregation Attitude by Education for Whites

Racial Segregation (S)	Education (E)		Total
	Noncollege	College	
Frequency Crosstabulation:			
Disagree	$f_{11} = 389$	$f_{12} = 403$	$f_{1.} = 792$
Agree	$f_{21} = 118$	$f_{22} = 53$	$f_{2.} = 171$
Total	$f_{.1} = 507$	$f_{.2} = 456$	$f_{..} = 963$
Percentage Crosstabulation:			
Disagree	76.7	88.4	82.2
No	23.3	11.6	17.8
Total	100.0%	100.0%	100.0%
(N)	(507)	(456)	(963)

Missing Data: 554 cases

Source: 1991 General Social Survey

supporting segregation) are 792/171 = 4.63. However, as the conditional odds in the two columns of Table 10.1 reveal, disagreement with the item depends on level of education: Among the college educated, the odds are 403/53 = 7.60, but among the noncollege educated, the odds of opposing segregation are much lower, 389/118 = 3.30. The odds ratio formed by these two conditional odds, a ratio that indicates the association of education with racial segregation attitude, is 7.60/3.30 = 2.30. In other words, the college educated are almost two and one-third times more likely to oppose racial segregation than are the noncollege educated. Because chi square is 22.3 for $df = 1$, this association is statistically significant, since for 1 *df* and $\alpha = .05$, the critical value is 3.84.

In the frequency crosstab of Figure 10.1, we denote the four cell frequencies by subscripts (f_{ij}), where the first subscript indexes the *i*th row and the second subscript indexes the *j*th column. In general, the odds ratio between two variables X and Y is the ratio of the two conditional odds:

$$\text{OR}^{YX} = (f_{12}/f_{22})/(f_{11}/f_{21})$$

Or, on rearrangement, the cross-product ratio for a 2×2 table of two variables X and Y is

$$\text{OR}^{YX} = (f_{12})(f_{21})/(f_{22})(f_{11})$$

FIGURE 10.1
Schematic Showing the Computation of a Conditional Log Odds

		X 1	X 2	
Y	1	f_{11}	f_{12}	$f_{.1}$
	2	f_{21}	f_{22}	$f_{.2}$
		$f_{.1}$	$f_{.2}$	$f_{..}$

The marginal frequencies for the row variable are designated by f_i. and those of the column variable by $f_{\cdot j}$ (see Figure 10.1).

10.1.1.   Expected Frequencies as Functions of Effect Parameters

A log-linear model expresses the *expected value* of the frequency in the *i,j*th cell (labeled F_{ij}) as a function of a set of parameters that represents the categoric effects of the variables and their relationships. In the log-linear notational system we use, the natural logarithmic ($\log_e$ or ln) of each expected cell frequency is the sum of four parameters:

$$\ln F_{ij} = \mu + \lambda_i^X + \lambda_j^Y + \lambda_{ij}^{XY}$$

and for the data in Table 10.1, $\ln F_{ij} = \mu + \lambda_i^S + \lambda_j^E + \lambda_{ij}^{SE}$. This particular model is called a **saturated model** because all possible effects among the variables are present (i.e., none are constrained *a priori* to equal zero). Because all possible effects are present, $F_{ij} = f_{ij}$ (i.e., the expected cell frequency equals the observed cell frequency). The format for these parameters makes clear that an expected logged cell frequency is a linear combination of the categoric effects of the variables, hence the name "log-linear analysis." Note the superficial resemblance of a log-linear equation to a multiple regression or logistic regression equation.

saturated model—a log-linear model in which all possible effects among variables are present

The μ (mu) is a constant that applies to every cell in the crosstab. Its presence is necessary to assure that the frequencies sum to the correct total. Although μ seems analogous to the intercept in a regression equation or to the grand mean in an ANOVA, it has no substantive interpretation. The λ (lambda) terms represent the effects of the crosstabulated variables on the expected logs of the cell frequencies. Each category of a variable has a unique lambda parameter associated with it, as do all combinations of categories. Positive lambda values increase the size of an expected logged cell frequency, negative lambdas decrease their magnitudes, and a $\lambda = 0$ indicates that a variable category has no effect on the tabled frequency, leaving the expected logged frequency unchanged. The superscripts attached to each lambda indicate to which variable or variables the effects occur. The λ_i^S capture the effects (one for each of the *i* categories of *S*) of an unequal marginal distribution of racial segregation attitude. Similarly, the λ_j^E (one for each of the *j* categories of *E*) capture the effects of unequal marginals for education. If the expected frequencies in both categories of a dichotomous variable are exactly equal, then the odds are $F_1./F_2. = 1$ and its lambda parameter is 0, because the natural logarithm of 1 is zero (i.e., because $e^0 = 1$ and $\ln 1 = 0$). In general, lambda for a single variable departs from 0 to the extent that category has either more or less than $1/K$th of the observations, where K is the number of categories for that variable.

The λ_{ij}^{SE} parameters (one for each of the i,j cells of the crosstab) reveal the extent to which the variables S and E are associated. If its value is 0, the two variables are unrelated, while a positive value indicates that both "high" categories are associated. A negative value means that the high category of one variable covaries with the low category of the other variable.

The nine log-linear effect parameters, associated with the 2×2 table frequencies in our example, are shown in Table 10.2. For dichotomies, such as segregation attitude and education, the two lambda effect parameters associated with a pair of categories are inverse values of one another:

$$\lambda_1^S = -\lambda_2^S = \lambda^S$$
$$\lambda_1^E = -\lambda_2^E = \lambda^E$$

Because the lambda effects for each pair of categories are inverses of one another, the effects for dichotomous variables are represented by nonsubscripted lambdas, in this case by λ^S and λ^E. In general, for a variable with K categories, only $K - 1$ unique parameter values exist, with the Kth category's value determined by the others. Thus, both education and segregation attitude have

TABLE 10.2

Expected Cell Frequencies for Saturated Model of Residential Racial Segregation Attitude by Education for Whites

Racial Segregation (S)	Education (E)	
	Noncollege	*College*
Disagree	$F_{11} = \mu + \lambda_1^S + \lambda_1^E + \lambda_{11}^{SE}$	$F_{12} = \mu + \lambda_1^S + \lambda_2^E + \lambda_{12}^{SE}$
Agree	$F_{21} = \mu + \lambda_2^S + \lambda_1^E + \lambda_{21}^{SE}$	$F_{22} = \mu + \lambda_2^S + \lambda_2^E + \lambda_{22}^{SE}$

only one independently determined lambda parameter, with the second parameter having the same value but opposite sign of the first parameter.

In similar fashion the four parameters representing the association between education and segregation attitude are not independent of one another:

$$\lambda_{11}^{SE} = \lambda_{22}^{SE} = -\lambda_{12}^{SE} = -\lambda_{21}^{SE} = \lambda^{SE}$$

Thus, instead of four unique values, any one joint parameter determines the values of the remaining three. In a saturated model for a 2 × 2 table, only four effect parameters are independent: one each for μ, S, E, and SE. These four values produce the four expected cell frequencies (the frequencies in Table 10.2), that exactly equal the observed cell frequencies. Other log-linear models that require fewer effect parameters to generate the expected cell frequencies thereby gain degrees of freedom for assessing the fit between these expected values and the observed cell frequencies. Section 10.2.2 discusses how to test the fit of log-linear models with tabulated data.

10.1.2.   Parameters as Functions of Expected Frequencies

Numerical values of the effect parameters for the saturated log-linear model applied to a 2 × 2 crosstab can be calculated as functions of the four expected frequencies. The estimate of the constant (μ) is the average of the natural logs of the four cells (recalling that observed and expected values are identical in the saturated model):

$$\hat{\mu} = \frac{\ln (F_{11}F_{12}F_{21}F_{22})}{4}$$

For the data in Table 10.1: $\hat{\mu} = [\ln (389) + \ln (403) + \ln (118) + \ln (53)]/4 = 5.176$, because the logarithm of a product equals the sum of the logarithms.

The λ_{ij}^{SE} effect parameters show the strength and direction of the association between the two categoric variables. First, consider the SE relationship as an odds ratio of expected frequencies:

$$E(OR^{SE}) = \frac{F_{12}F_{21}}{F_{11}F_{22}}$$

which is 2.30 for the education-racial segregation example. Next, take the natural logarithm of the right-hand side, and recalling that the logarithm of a ratio is the difference of logarithms:

$$\ln\left(\frac{F_{12}F_{21}}{F_{11}F_{22}}\right) = \ln F_{12} + \ln F_{21} - \ln F_{11} - \ln F_{22}$$

Now, replace each expected frequency with its equivalent equation (see Table 10.2):

$$\begin{aligned}\ln\left(\frac{F_{12}F_{21}}{F_{11}F_{22}}\right) = \quad &(\mu + \lambda_1^S + \lambda_2^E + \lambda_{12}^{SE})\\ &+ (\mu + \lambda_2^S + \lambda_1^E + \lambda_{21}^{SE})\\ &- (\mu + \lambda_1^S + \lambda_1^E + \lambda_{11}^{SE})\\ &- (\mu + \lambda_2^S + \lambda_2^E + \lambda_{22}^{SE})\end{aligned}$$

After simplification of terms,

$$\ln\left(\frac{F_{12}F_{21}}{F_{11}F_{22}}\right) = \lambda_{12}^{SE} + \lambda_{21}^{SE} - \lambda_{11}^{SE} - \lambda_{22}^{SE}$$

Thus, the OR depends only on the size and direction of the association between S and E and not on the marginal effects of either variable. Because we showed that the four individual effect parameters for this association are opposites of one another, we can rewrite this logged OR as a single parameter without subscripts:

$$\ln\left(\frac{F_{12}F_{21}}{F_{11}F_{22}}\right) = 4\,\lambda^{SE}$$

Dividing both sides by 4 and rearranging terms, the estimated parameter of the association between two variables in a saturated log-linear model for dichotomies is

$$\hat{\lambda}^{SE} = \frac{\ln \left[(F_{12}F_{21})/(F_{11}F_{22})\right]}{4}$$

Entering the numerical values from Table 10.1 (again recalling that the expected frequencies equal the observed frequencies in a saturated model), the estimated value of the λ^{SE} parameter is

$$\hat{\lambda}^{SE} = \frac{\ln \left[(403)(118)/(389)(53)\right]}{4} = 0.209$$

The positive value indicates that the "high" categories of the two variables covary (i.e., college education and disagreement with residential racial segregation).

Finally, the single super-scripted lambda parameters are derived for a saturated 2×2 log-linear model by a similar procedure. For S, begin with the product of the two conditional odds:

$$
\ln \left(\frac{F_{11}}{F_{21}}\right)\left(\frac{F_{12}}{F_{22}}\right) = \begin{aligned} & (\mu + \lambda_1^S + \lambda_1^E + \lambda_{11}^{SE}) \\ & + (\mu + \lambda_1^S + \lambda_2^E + \lambda_{12}^{SE}) \\ & - (\mu + \lambda_2^S + \lambda_1^E + \lambda_{21}^{SE}) \\ & - (\mu + \lambda_2^S + \lambda_2^E + \lambda_{22}^{SE}) \end{aligned}
$$

which simplifies to

$$\ln \left(\frac{F_{11}F_{12}}{F_{21}F_{22}}\right) = (\lambda_1^S + \lambda_1^S - \lambda_2^S - \lambda_2^S) = 4\,\lambda^S$$

Solving for λ^S, we find the estimate:

$$\hat{\lambda}^S = \frac{\ln \left[(F_{11}F_{12})/(F_{21}F_{22})\right]}{4}$$

The estimated value for the segregation parameter, λ^S, in our example is

$$\hat{\lambda}^S = \frac{\ln \left[(389)(403)/(118)(53)\right]}{4} = 0.805$$

Similarly, the estimated effect parameter for education is a function of its two conditional odds:

$$\hat{\lambda}^E = \frac{\ln\ [(F_{12}F_{22})/(F_{11}F_{21})]}{4}$$

which has the estimated numerical value

$$\hat{\lambda}^E = \frac{\ln\ [(403)(53)/(389)(118)]}{4} = -0.191$$

For dichotomous variables these last two parameters indicate how the observations are distributed. The farther a lambda is from 0, the more unevenly the cases are divided. The positive segregation parameter merely means that more respondents disagreed than agreed with the segregation item, while the negative education parameter means that a larger proportion of respondents fell into the noncollege-educated category than into the college-educated category.

The numerical estimates of the four effect parameters for a saturated model can be combined appropriately to calculate the logged values of the expected cell frequencies:

$$\ln F_{11} = 5.176 + 0.805 + 0.191 - 0.209 = 5.964$$

$$\ln F_{12} = 5.176 + 0.805 - 0.191 + 0.209 = 5.999$$

$$\ln F_{21} = 5.176 - 0.805 + 0.191 + 0.209 = 4.771$$

$$\ln F_{22} = 5.176 - 0.805 - 0.191 - 0.209 = 3.971$$

When antilogs of these values are computed, the results equal (within rounding error) the frequencies in the four cells of Table 10.1, as they must in any saturated model.

Because the saturated model always fits the data perfectly, it is not a substantively interesting model. Instead, its value is as a model against which to compare alternative models with fewer parameters, that is, nonsaturated models, a topic to which we turn in section 10.1.4.

10.1.3. Standard Errors for Parameters

The statistical significance of the lambda effect parameters for a saturated log-linear model can be computed by the following formula:

$$\hat{s}_\lambda = \sqrt{\frac{\sum\limits_{i}^{K_R} \sum\limits_{j}^{K_C} (1/F_{ij})}{[(K_R)(K_C)]^2}}$$

where K_R is the number of categories in the row variable and K_C is the number of categories in the column variable. For large samples, if the null hypothesis is that the population value of a lambda is zero, its significance can be assessed by a t test.

In our 2 × 2 example the estimated standard error is

$$\hat{s}_\lambda = \sqrt{\frac{\dfrac{1}{389} + \dfrac{1}{403} + \dfrac{1}{118} + \dfrac{1}{53}}{[(2)(2)]^2}} = 0.045$$

Dividing each of the three parameter estimates calculated above by this standard error yields t scores of $+17.89$ for racial segregation attitude, -4.24 for education, and $+4.64$ for the education-segregation association. All three ratios are significant at $\alpha = .05$ for a two-tailed test, given that sample $N = 963$, since the critical value is ± 1.96.

10.1.4. Nonsaturated Models

nonsaturated model—a log-linear model in which one or more of the lambda parameters equals 0

As pointed out in section 10.1.2, the expected frequencies in a saturated model always equal the observed frequencies. A less complex, but more interesting and important, **nonsaturated model** can be specified by setting one or more lambda parameters equal to 0. Estimates of the remaining parameters then may result in expected cell frequencies that do not exactly reproduce the observed frequencies.

The most obvious nonsaturated model for a 2 × 2 table sets the two-variable association parameter (λ^{SE}) equal to zero:

$$\ln F_{ij} = \mu + \lambda_i^S + \lambda_j^E$$

This model asserts that the conditional odds for either variable are identical to the marginal odds. In other words, the two variables are independent. The four expected cell frequencies are simply the sum of the constant plus the two marginal effects. For the data in Table 10.1, these are the parameter estimates:

$$\mu = 5.214$$

$$\lambda^S = +.766$$

$$\lambda^E = -.053$$

Setting $\lambda^{SE} = 0$, the model for independence implies that

$$F_{11} = \mu + \lambda^S + \lambda^E$$

$$F_{12} = \mu + \lambda^S - \lambda^E$$

$$F_{21} = \mu - \lambda^S + \lambda^E$$

$$F_{22} = \mu - \lambda^S - \lambda^E$$

For our data, the estimated values of $\ln F_{ij}$ are

$$\ln F_{11} = 5.214 + .766 + (-.053) = 5.927$$

$$\ln F_{12} = 5.214 + .766 - (-.053) = 6.033$$

$$\ln F_{21} = 5.214 - .766 + (-.053) = 4.395$$

$$\ln F_{22} = 5.214 - .766 - (-.053) = 4.501$$

Hence, taking antilogs:

$$F_{11} = 375.03 \text{ compared with } f_{11} = 389,$$

$$F_{12} = 416.96 \text{ compared with } f_{12} = 403,$$

$$F_{21} = 81.04 \text{ compared with } f_{22} = 118,$$

$$\text{and } F_{22} = 90.11 \text{ compared with } f_{22} = 53.$$

If the independence model fits the data, the difference between F_{ij} and f_{ij} should be so small that these differences can be attributed to sampling error alone.

These expected values are also the same as the expected frequencies computed for the chi-square significance test in section

5.2 (page 161). In fact, this log-linear model *is* equivalent to that independence hypothesis. The discrepancies between observed and expected frequencies can be tested for a statistically significant fit of the log-linear model to the data, using procedures described in the next section.

10.2 Log-Linear Models for Three-Variable Tables

In this section we consider log-linear models for three-variable tables, such as Table 10.3, where the original racial segregation by education crosstab has been split into two subtables according to respondents' ages (A, dichotomized at 50 years). The observed OR^{SE} for the original table was 2.30, but the **conditional odds ratios** for these two subtables are not identical. The relationship between education and segregation seems to be stronger among the younger group ($OR^{SE|A=1} = 2.45$) than among the older respondents ($OR^{SE|A=2} = 1.53$). The notation $OR^{SE|A=1}$ is read "the odds ratio for segregation by education given that age equals 1 (i.e., for persons 50 or younger). How would you read $OR^{SE|A=2}$? The important question is whether this difference in the sample odds ratios reflects an interaction among the three variables in the population from which the 1991 GSS was drawn. In other words, can we reject the null hypothesis that education and racial segregation covary the

conditional odds ratio— an odds ratio between two variables for a given category of a third variable

TABLE 10.3

Frequency Crosstabulation of Residential Racial Segregation Attitude by Education by Age for Whites

Age (A):	50 Years and Under			51 Years and Older		
	Education (E)			Education (E)		
Racial Segregation (S)	Noncollege	College	Total	Noncollege	College	Total
Disagree	234	318	552	155	85	240
Agree	54	30	84	64	23	87
Total	288	348	636	219	108	327

Missing Data: 554 cases

Source: 1991 General Social Survey

same within both age groups, with only a small probability of a Type I error? To answer this question, we must specify a log-linear model consistent with the null hypothesis of no interaction among the three measures, compute the expected frequencies, and compare them to the observed frequencies.

The class of models used to examine hypotheses of this sort are called **hierarchical log-linear models** because whenever a complex multivariate relationship is present, less complex relationships are also included. For example, if a model specifies a two-variable effect parameter between variables X and Y (i.e, λ^{XY}), it also includes both the single-variable effect parameters (λ^X and λ^Y). Similarly, any hierarchical model that includes a three-way effect parameter must also include all possible two-way effects involved in that three-way interaction, as well as the three single-variable effects. Thus, a hierarchical model that specifies λ^{XYZ} also must include six other parameters: λ^{XY}, λ^{XZ}, λ^{YZ}, λ^X, λ^Y, and λ^Z, as well as the constant, μ.

hierarchical log-linear model— a model in which the inclusion of multi-way effects also implies the inclusion of all less-complex effects

10.2.1. Standard Notation

The nested nature of hierarchical log-linear models provides researchers with a compact standard notational system for designating the parameters of a log-linear equation. This standard notation encloses within curly braces—{}—the combinations of capital letters representing variables whose relationships are hypothesized *not* to have zero lambdas. (The constant term is always present, even in a model with no other parameters.) All subsets of letters within braces are also understood to have nonzero effect parameters in the equation. For example, the saturated model described in section 10.1.1 was written in full equation form as

$$\ln F_{ij} = \mu + \lambda_i^S + \lambda_j^E + \lambda_{ij}^{SE}$$

and more compactly as simply {*SE*}. Because both S and E are included within the same pair of braces, we know that a lambda parameter for the association between these two is specified, as well as both the single-variable parameters. However, if the standard notation designates these two variables in separate braces—{*S*}{*E*}—we know that only λ^S and λ^E are included in the equation. In other words, model {*S*}{*E*} tells us that λ^{SE} is hypothesized to equal zero. (Note that model {*S*}{*E*} is the independence model for a two-variable crosstab, in which the pair has no significant association.) Because the model $\{SE\}$ contains not only λ^{SE}, but also λ^{S} and λ^{E}, we can say that model $\{S\}\{E\}$ is *nested within* model $\{SE\}$. Thus, hierarchical log-linear models are also **nested models.** One model is nested within a second model if every parameter in the first also appears in the second.

nested models— models in which every parameter included in one model also appears in another model

Consider some alternative hypothesized log-linear models for the three variables, S, E, and A. The model $\{SEA\}$ corresponds to the equation:

$$\ln F_{ijk} = \mu + \lambda_{ijk}^{SEA} + \lambda_{ij}^{SE} + \lambda_{ik}^{SA} + \lambda_{jk}^{EA} + \lambda_{i}^{S} + \lambda_{j}^{E} + \lambda_{k}^{A}$$

Clearly, the curly-brace notation system allows for great economy in expression! What are the equations designated by models $\{SE\}\{A\}$ and $\{SA\}\{SE\}$? Convince yourself that the model $\{SE\}\{A\}$ corresponds to the equation:

$$\ln F_{ijk} = \mu + \lambda_{ij}^{SE} + \lambda_{i}^{S} + \lambda_{j}^{E} + \lambda_{k}^{A} \ .$$

What equation corresponds to the model $\{SA\}\{SE\}$?

In addition to concise communication, the standard notational system also reveals an important aspect of the log-linear estimation method. The combinations of K variables enclosed within curly braces comprise the set of **marginal subtables**—or simply "the marginals"—that are necessary and sufficient to generate the expected cell frequencies of the full V-way crosstab under the hypothesized model (where V is the number of variables). That is, the expected frequencies generated by the model must exactly equal the observed frequencies of these marginal subtables. However, any relationships involving combinations of variables that do *not* appear within curly braces are constrained to have expected odds ratios equal to one (that is, lambda parameters equal to zero). Indeed, the discrepancies between the expected and observed frequencies among unspecified marginals become the basis for testing the statistical significance of a hypothesized model. Thus, the standard notation for a log-linear model is often referred to as the **fitted marginals** for that hypothesis. For example, we say that model $\{SA\}\{E\}$ "fits the marginals SA and E." This specification also assures that the expected odds ratios of the marginals $\{SE\}$, $\{EA\}$, and $\{SEA\}$ will equal exactly 1.00 (i.e., no association occurs among these combinations of variables), and hence $\lambda^{SE} = \lambda^{EA} = \lambda^{SEA} = 0.0$.

marginal subtable— a method to show the combinations of K variables that are necessary and sufficient to generate the expected cell frequencies of a full crosstab

fitted marginal— the standard notation for a log-linear model

Details of the computer algorithms for generating the expected cell frequencies (F_{ijk}s) from the fitted marginals are too complex to explain here. A bivariate crosstab (whether dichotomous or polychotomous) has simple formulas for directly estimating the expected frequencies for its nonsaturated models of the type used in section 10.1.2. But, for larger V-way tables most log-linear programs use either **iterative proportional fitting** procedures or **Newton-Raphson algorithms** since simple analytic (algebraic) solutions do not exist.[1] These methods proceed by successively refined estimates of the fitted marginal subtables hypothesized by the standard notation, until an arbitrarily small difference from one cycle to the next is met. The final expected cell frequencies are maximum likelihood estimates, which have such desirable statistical properties as consistency and efficiency. Once these F_{ijk}s have been obtained, they are used to calculate the lambda effect parameters for the hypothesized model, as was done in section 10.1.2.

iterative proportional fitting— a computer algorithm for successively approximating the expected frequencies in an unsaturated log-linear model

Newton-Raphson algorithm— an iterative proportional fitting procedure used in log-linear analysis

10.2.2.   Testing Models for Statistical Significance

To determine whether the hypothesized relationships among variables in a population of interest are supported by observed relationships in the sample, the cell frequencies expected under the hypothesis and generated by a log-linear equation are compared to the observed relationships. The fit between expected and observed frequencies can be assessed with the Pearson chi-square test statistic (χ^2), discussed in section 3.11 (page 115). However, the preferred test statistic is the **likelihood ratio** (L^2), because it is minimized by the maximum likelihood estimates of the expected frequencies. Its formula is as follows:

likelihood ratio— the preferred test statistic for testing the fit between expected and observed frequencies in an unsaturated log-linear model

$$L^2 = 2 \sum_{i=1}^{K} f_i \ln \left(\frac{f_i}{F_i} \right)$$

where the summation occurs over the K cells of the crosstab.

The L^2 test statistic is distributed approximately as a chi-square variable with degrees of freedom equal to the number of unique

---

1. Bishop, Yvonne M. M., Fienberg, Stephen E., and Holland, Paul W. (1975). *Discrete Multivariate Analysis: Theory and Practice.* Cambridge, MA: MIT Press, pp. 82–102; and Haberman, Shelby J. (1978). *Analysis of Qualitative Data. Volume 1: Introductory Topics.* New York: Academic Press.

lambda parameters that are set equal to zero. In general, if a variable X has C_X categories, then $C_X - 1$ of its parameters are free to vary. In our example crosstab, each dichotomous variable has $C = 2$ categories. Thus, the log-linear model specification $\{AE\}\{SE\}\{SA\}$ includes all parameters except the three-way interaction λ^{SEA}, which is hypothesized to equal to zero. This model has $(C_S - 1)(C_E - 1)(C_A - 1) = (2 - 1)(2 - 1)(2 - 1) = 1$ df for the likelihood ratio. One degree of freedom makes sense because one unique parameter was set to zero, λ^{SEA}.

Another important advantage in using the likelihood ratio is that it can be easily partitioned so that conditional independence tests can be carried out on multiway crosstabs. As indicated in section 10.2.1, a pair of hierarchical log-linear models applied to the same table is nested if one model consists only of a subset of the effect parameters found in the second model. For example, every parameter in model $\{SE\}\{A\}$ is also included in model $\{AE\}\{SE\}\{SA\}$. The difference in L^2 values for these nested models, relative to the difference in the degrees of freedom of the two models, is a test of significance. Thus, if model 2 is more inclusive than model 1,

$$\Delta L^2 = L_1^2 - L_2^2$$

and

$$\Delta df = df_1 - df_2$$

where Δ (delta) means difference.

Table 10.4 illustrates the application of these principles, showing likelihood ratios, dfs, and probabilities for six nested hierarchical

TABLE 10.4
Hierarchical Log-Linear Models for the Data in Table 10.2

Model	L^2	df	P
1. $\{E\}\{A\}\{S\}$	83.3	4	< .0001
2. $\{EA\}\{S\}$	41.9	3	< .0001
3. $\{EA\}\{SE\}$	19.1	2	< .001
4. $\{EA\}\{SA\}$	16.5	2	< .001
5. $\{EA\}\{SE\}\{SA\}$	1.6	1	.204
6. $\{SEA\}$	0.0	0	1.000

models estimated with the three-variable crosstab in Table 10.3. Model 1 is the least complex, fitting only the marginal distributions of the three variables. Because λ^{SA}, λ^{SE}, λ^{EA}, and λ^{SEA} have all been fixed to zero, model 1 has 4 *df*. With $L^2 = 83.3$ for $df = 4$, it also provides a terrible fit of the expected frequencies to the observed frequencies. Note that, in seeking to identify the "best fitting model" for a given sample crosstab, we ultimately want to find a hypothesized log-linear specification that *cannot* be rejected on statistical grounds. Thus, our goal is to find a model with a low likelihood ratio relative to its *df* that has a high probability of representing the relationships in the population.

The *p* values associated with a given model are to be interpreted as follows. "If Model A is true in the population, then the probability of observing this result is *p*." Thus, if Model 1 is the true model, we would expect the fit we observe to occur less than one in ten thousand. If we set $\alpha = .05$, we require that the observed *p* value be .05 *or greater* in order not to reject the hypothesis associated with the model. Hence, the *higher* the probability that the observed data could have been generated by a given model, the more plausible the model. Unlike standard hypothesis testing where support is provided for the alternative hypothesis by observing small *p* values, when you posit a nonnull model to which data are fit, support for that model is provided by observing high *p* values.

Model 2 adds the two-variable marginal $\{EA\}$ to the three single-variable marginals in model 1, at the cost of 1 *df;* that is, model 2 has 3 *df*. This price is well worth paying, as $\Delta L^2 = L_1^2 - L_2^2 = 83.3 - 41.9 = 41.4$ is a significant improvement in fit at $\alpha = .05$ for $\Delta df = df_1 - df_2 = 4 - 3 = 1$. Note that when testing for the difference between two competing models (models 1 and 2 in this case), we are back to traditional hypothesis testing. In this case the null hypothesis is $H_0: \Delta L^2 = 0$ and the alternative hypothesis is $H_1: \Delta L^2 > 0$. At $\alpha = .05$ the critical value for $L^2 = 3.84$ for $df = 1$. Since $\Delta L^2 = 41.4$, we are confident that $\Delta L^2 > 0$, and thus we reject H_0, concluding that $\{EA\}$ is necessary to fit the data. However, the overall fit of model 2 is still improbable since $p < .0001$, so we continue testing more-inclusive models. Model 2 is nested within both models 3 and 4, because each of the latter fits one of the other two-variable relationships. At $\alpha = .05$ both parameters significantly reduce the L^2 fit ($L_2^2 - L_3^2 = 41.9 - 19.1 = 22.8$ and $L_2^2 - L_4^2 = 41.9 - 16.5 = 25.4$) at the cost of 1 *df*.

Finally, model 5, which includes *both* {*SE*}{*AS*} makes a significant improvement in ΔL^2s compared to either model 4 or model 3. Furthermore, although the saturated model 6, which specifies the three-variable interaction parameter {*SEA*}, obviously reproduces the relationships perfectly (and has $p = 1.00$), importantly it is not a significant improvement over model 5. By giving up 1 *df* to estimate λ^{SEA}, we decrease L^2 by only 1.6, which is not significant at $\alpha = .05$. (Recall again that the critical value is 3.84.) Therefore, we conclude that model 5, which omits the three-variable interaction parameter but includes all three two-variable associations, offers the best fit to the data.

Importantly, just because model 5 fits the data best does not mean the model is true. We can never uncover truth by hypothesis testing. The best we can say is that the data are conformable with model 5. But other models with other variables might fit the data just as well. Again, the best we can say is that the data are conformable (or not conformable) with a given hypothesis (or model).

To aid in the substantive interpretation of model 5, Table 10.5 displays the expected cell frequencies, the actual observed frequencies, and the parameter estimates. Because the λ^{SEA} parameter was constrained to equal zero, the three-variable interaction observed in the original crosstab (see Table 10.3) has not been preserved. Instead, the two conditional odds have been constrained to equal one another:

$$OR^{(ES|A=1)} = \frac{(314.59)(50.59)}{(237.41)(33.41)} = 2.01$$

$$OR^{(ES|A=2)} = \frac{(88.41)(67.41)}{(151.59)(19.59)} = 2.01$$

And as a direct consequence of setting $\lambda^{SEA} = 0$, the odds ratio formed by these two conditional odds ratios is constrained to equal 1.00; that is,

$$OR^{(SE|A)} = \frac{OR^{(SE|A=1)}}{OR^{(SE|A=2)}} = \frac{2.01}{2.01} = 1.00$$

Under this constraint, the relationship between education and racial segregation attitude is the same regardless of respondents' ages. The odds that the college educated disagree with the segregation item is 9.42, the odds that the less educated disagree

TABLE 10.5

Expected Frequencies and Effect Parameters for Model {*EA*}{*SE*}{*SA*} Fitted to Residential Racial Segregation Attitude by Education by Age

Age (A):	50 Years and Under		51 Years and Older	
	Education (E)		Education (E)	
Racial Segregation (S)	Noncollege	College	Noncollege	College
Expected Frequencies:				
Disagree	237.41	314.59	151.59	88.41
No	50.59	33.41	67.41	19.59
Observed Frequencies:				
Disagree	234	318	155	85
No	54	30	64	23

Effect Parameters:

	Category	$\hat{\lambda}$	$\hat{s}_\lambda$	*t*
S	Disagree	.763	.046	16.59
E	College	−.239	.047	−5.09
A	Younger	.246	.045	5.47
AE	Younger-College	.205	.036	5.69
SA	Disagree-Younger	.184	.044	4.18
SE	Disagree-College	.174	.046	3.78

with the item is 4.69, and the odds ratio is (9.42/4.69) = 2.01. Because this model fits the data so well, we conclude that age does not condition the effect of education on racial attitude. An equivalent substantive conclusion could be drawn about the effect of age on attitude not varying by education, but we chose the former interpretation because our example began with the bivariate education-attitude relationship. The fact that both interpretations are consistent with the data makes the point that a good statistical fit does not imply that a model is necessarily the true one.

The parameter estimates tell a similar story. The single-variable effects show that more respondents disagree with segregation ($\hat{\lambda}^S = 0.763$), are less educated ($\hat{\lambda}^E = -0.239$), and are younger

($\hat{\lambda}^A = 0.246$) than fall into the opposite categories. Younger people are more likely to be college educated ($\hat{\lambda}^{AE} = 0.205$), while the younger respondents disagree with segregation ($\hat{\lambda}^{SA} = 0.184$) and the college educated are also more opposed to segregation ($\hat{\lambda}^{SE} = 0.174$) than the contrasting two-variable combinations. Finally, note that the expected frequencies are very close to the observed frequencies, further evidence that model 5 provides a good fit to the data.

Before moving on to the next section, it might be useful to review model-fitting strategies. In the example developed in this section, we followed a systematic forward-fitting strategy. That is, we began by examining the simplest, most concise model that contained only marginal distributions of the variables. We then added one of the two-variable associations to the three single-variable marginals, to see if the fit could be improved. It did improve significantly, suggesting that association should be retained in the model. If the fit had not improved, we would have dropped this term. We then developed two additional models, one for each of the remaining two-variable relationships. Again both parameters improved the model's fit over the previous model. As a result, all three two-variable association terms were retained in the model, representing not only an improvement in fit over the previous models, but also providing an acceptable fit to the data overall.

An alternative search strategy would begin with the model having all three two-variable associations, and then dropping these terms one at a time to see if the fit of the model deteriorated. Demonstrate to yourself that, for the example developed in this section, by following this backward-search strategy, you would have reached the same conclusion about which model produced the best fit.

A third way to test log-linear models is first to hypothesize a specific model in advance of looking at the data. Then, fit the data to that model and ask whether the probability that the model could have generated the model is greater than or equal to some chosen value for α.

10.2.3. Testing Models for Large Data Sets

The likelihood ratio is a useful test statistic for finding discrepancies between models and data when samples are moderate in size, such as GSS data sets ranging up to 1,500 cases. But with much larger samples, the L^2 is almost guaranteed to reject even a good model, because its value increases with the total sample size, N. A more appropriate test statistic for assessing log-linear models fitted to large-sample crosstabulations is the **BIC statistic,** which is approximated by:

$$BIC = L^2 - (df)(\ln N)$$

where $\ln N$ is the natural logarithm of the total sample size. In general, the more negative the BIC statistic's value, the better a model's fit to the data.

To illustrate applications of the BIC statistic for finding a good fit to a large data set, consider Table 10.6. This four-variable crosstabulation displays the number of U.S. scientists in three sectors of employment (industry, education, and government), broken down by three fields (physical science, engineering, and social science), year (1976 and 1981), and gender (men and women). The table $N =$ 30,029 (which is actually only 1% of the total scientist population). Table 10.7 reports a series of nested log-linear models fitted to the

BIC statistic— a test statistic for assessing log-linear models fit to large-sample crosstabulations

TABLE 10.6

Frequency Crosstabulation of Scientists' Sectors of Employment by Field, Gender, and Year (Hundreds of Scientists)

			Sector of Employment (S)		
Year (Y)	Gender (G)	Field (F)	Industry	Education	Government
1976	Men	Physical Science	911	420	174
1976	Men	Engineering	8,376	512	925
1976	Men	Social Science	383	745	192
1976	Women	Physical Science	95	63	16
1976	Women	Engineering	77	100	8
1976	Women	Social Science	59	160	50
1981	Men	Physical Science	1,085	504	171
1981	Men	Engineering	11,180	682	1,037
1981	Men	Social Science	457	635	189
1981	Women	Physical Science	135	80	24
1981	Women	Engineering	263	30	25
1981	Women	Social Science	79	177	100

Source: National Science Foundation. (1982). *Science Indicators 1982.* Washington, DC: United States Government Printing Office.

TABLE 10.7

Some Log-Linear Models for the Data in Table 10.6

Model	L^2	df	p	BIC
1. {FSY}{GFS}{GFY}{GSY}	1.50	4	.83	−39.74
2. {GFS}{GFY}{GSY}	14.97	8	.06	−67.51
3. {FSY}{GFY}{GSY}	32.26	8	.00	−50.22
4. {FSY}{GFS}{GSY}	26.54	6	.00	−35.32
5. {FSY}{GFS}{GFY}	6.36	6	.38	−55.50
6. {GFS}{GFY}{YS}	24.17	10	.01	−78.93
7. {GFY}{GS}{YS}{FS}	54.96	14	.00	−89.38
8. {GFS}{GY}{SY}{FY}	51.90	12	.00	−71.82
9. {GFY}{YS}{GS}	5269.23	18	.00	5,083.65
10. {GFY}{FS}{YS}	88.94	16	.00	−76.02
11. {GFY}{FS}{GS}	71.24	16	.00	−93.72
12. {GS}{GY}{GF}{SY}{FS}{FY}	82.87	16	.00	−82.09
13. {GFY}{GS}	5,324.29	20	.00	5,118.09
14. {GFY}{FS}	103.20	18	.00	−82.38

data. If the L^2 criterion for assessing fit is applied, we would conclude that the best fit is model 5, {FSY}{GFS}{GFY}, since $L^2 = 6.36$ for $df = 6$, $p = .38$. However, model 5 requires three of the four possible three-variable interaction terms, thus implying a complicated pattern of relationships. But applying the BIC formula to model 5 yields $(6.36) − (6)(\ln 30,029) = −55.50$. Several other models in Table 10.7 have BIC statistics that are more negative than model 5's BIC. In particular model 11 {GFY}{FS}{GS}, which fits only one of the three-variable interactions, has a large negative BIC statistic $71.24 − (16)(\ln 30,029) = −93.72$. If the {GFY} term is dropped from model 11 (compare model 12), the BIC statistic is less negative (−82.09), suggesting that retaining the {GFY} term is essential for a good fit. Further, if either of the two-variable effects in model 12 are dropped, their BIC statistics are also less negative (compare models 13 and 14 to model 11). Thus, we conclude that model 11 offers the best fit to the large cross-tabulation. One substantive interpretation of this model is that gender differences among fields changed during the five-year interval {GFY}, but the distributions of fields among sectors {FS} and of genders among sectors {GS} did not vary during that time.

10.3 More Complex Models

10.3.1. Interaction in a Four-Variable Crosstabulation

To demonstrate the complexity of analyses for large-dimensioned tables, we added a fourth dichotomous variable—region (R), split between southerners and nonsoutherners—to the three used in the racial segregation example above. Table 10.8 displays the observed frequencies. The eight conditional odds of disagreeing relative to agreeing with the racial segregation item vary markedly across combinations of the other three variables. In particular, the younger, college-educated respondents residing outside the South are especially likely to disagree ($OR^{(S|ERA)} = 13.29$). The series of log-linear models in Table 10.9 all include the fitted marginal $\{ARE\}$. The reason for including $\{ARE\}$ is that we assume these three variables are interrelated, and therefore we do not seek to test any hypotheses about their two- or three-variable associations. In other words, the causal relationships among these predictor variables are viewed as arising outside the scope of the model. Rather, we are interested in estimating how these three antecedent variables relate to the variable we consider to be dependent in this log-linear model, the racial segregation item.

TABLE 10.8

Frequency Crosstabulations of Residential Racial Segregation Attitude by Education, Age, and Region for Whites

Education	Region	Age	*Racial Segregation*		
			Disagree	*Agree*	*Odds*
Noncollege	North	Younger	153	24	6.38
Noncollege	North	Old	86	41	2.10
Noncollege	South	Younger	81	30	2.70
Noncollege	South	Old	69	23	3.00
College	North	Younger	226	17	13.29
College	North	Old	59	16	3.69
College	South	Younger	92	13	7.08
College	South	Old	26	7	3.71

TABLE 10.9

Some Log-Linear Models for the Data in Table 10.8

Model	L^2	df	p
1. {ARE}{S}	53.8	7	< .0001
2. {ARE}{SR}	49.1	6	< .0001
3. {ARE}{SE}	30.9	6	< .0001
4. {ARE}{SA}	28.4	6	< .0001
5. {ARE}{SR}{SE}	28.0	5	< .0001
6. {ARE}{SA}{SR}	24.4	5	< .0001
7. {ARE}{SA}{SE}	13.5	5	.02
8. {ARE}{SA}{SR}{SE}	10.8	4	.03
9. {ARE}{SER}{SA}	10.7	3	.01
10. {ARE}{SEA}{SR}	9.2	3	.03
11. {ARE}{SAR}{SE}	1.6	3	.65
12. {ARE}{SAR}	15.4	4	.004

Model 1 serves as a "baseline model" in the sense that it specifies none of these variables is related to racial attitude. As expected, this model produces a poor fit, with $L^2 = 53.8$ for $df = 7$. Comparing models 2, 3 and 4 to the baseline model 1, we see that each two-variable association between a predictor variable and the segregation item is statistically significant at the $\alpha = .05$ level. However, none of the models fit the data well, since in all cases $p < .0001$. To test whether all the two-variable associations are needed to fit the data, all three of the two-variable associations are included in model 8. Its fit is then compared against three models (5, 6, and 7) each of which contains two of the three two-variable associations, as well as {ARE}. The null hypothesis is that $\Delta L^2 = 0$ for each of the three comparisons, with $\alpha = .05$, that is, where the critical value is 3.84 for $df = 1$. $L_5 - L_8 = 28.0 - 10.8 = 17.2$, indicating that the segregation-by-age association is significant. Similarly, $L_6 - L_8 = 24.4 - 10.8 = 13.6$, indicating that the segregation-by-education association is also significant. However, $L_7 - L_8 = 13.5 - 10.8 = 2.7$, which indicates that the segregation-by-region association {SR} is not significant.

Both models 7 and 8 have poor fits to the four-way crosstab (i.e., $p < .05$ in both cases), implying that additional three-variable interactions may be present. We first ask whether adding the interaction among segregation, education, and region is significant, by comparing the fit of a model with that term (model 9) to one without (model 8). Because $\Delta L^2 = 10.8 - 10.7 = 0.1$ with $df = 1$, we conclude that the $\{SER\}$ relationship does not improve the model's fit. Similarly, the ΔL^2 comparison of models 8 and 10 ($\Delta L^2 = 10.8 - 9.2 = 1.6$) reveals a nonsignificant improvement due to the interaction among segregation, education, and age $\{SEA\}$. But the change in L^2 between model 11 (which includes the interaction among segregation, age, and region $\{SAR\}$), and model 8—$L_8^2 - L_{11}^2 = 10.8 - 1.6 = 9.2$, $df_8 - df_{11} = 4 - 3 = 1$—is highly significant. Further, the fit of model 11 is excellent ($p = .65$). As a comparison with model 12 shows, we cannot drop the $\{SE\}$ marginal without significantly worsening the fit, since $p = .004$ for model 12.

The $\{ARE\}\{SAR\}\{SE\}$ specification of model 11 clearly provides the best fit to the four-variable crosstab. Table 10.10 reports the lambda parameters, standard errors, and t ratios for each effect. Two values tell the essential story. The $\lambda^{SE} = .169$ parameter means that college-educated respondents disagree with racial segregation. Because the $\{SE\}$ marginal includes neither age nor region, this relationship is not conditional on those two variables. But the $\lambda^{SAR} = -.134$ parameter means that the age-segregation relation *is* conditional on region, though not on education. Specifically, the age-segregation association is much stronger among non-

TABLE 10.10

Effect Parameters for Model $\{ARE\}\{SAR\}\{SE\}$ Fitted to Residential Racial Segregation Attitude by Education by Age by Region

	Category	λ	s_λ	t
S	Disagree	.754	.047	16.04
E	College	−.266	.048	−5.54
A	Younger	.254	.047	5.40
R	South	−.256	.047	−5.45
AE	Younger-College	.212	.038	5.58
AR	Younger-South	.068	.047	1.45
RE	South-College	−.105	.038	−2.76
SA	Disagree-Younger	.159	.045	3.53
SE	Disagree-College	.169	.046	3.67
SR	Disagree-South	−.061	.045	−1.36
ARE	Younger-College-South	.028	.038	0.74
SAR	Disagree-Younger-South	−.134	.044	−3.05

southerners than it is among southerners. To illustrate this three-variable interaction, Figure 10.2 plots the odds of disagreeing relative to agreeing with the racial segregation item for the four age-region combinations. (These values were obtained from Table 10.8 by collapsing frequencies across the education category, then computing the four conditional odds. Recall that the {SAR} loglinear specification constrains the expected frequencies to equal the observed frequencies in this three-variable marginal.) Three of these conditional odds have approximately the same values: 1.43 for older southerners, 1.82 for younger southerners, and 2.54 for older nonsoutherners. But the odds for disagreement by young nonsoutherners (10.24) is four to seven times larger. Thus, substan-

FIGURE 10.2

Odds of Racial Segregation Disagreement by Age for Southerners and Nonsoutherners

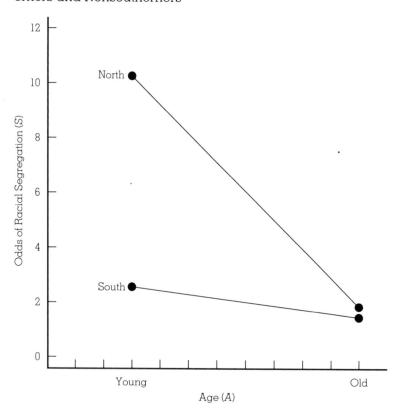

tial differences occur across pairs of odds ratios: for southerners, $OR^{(SA|R=2)} = (1.43/1.82) = .79$ while for nonsoutherners, $OR^{(SA|R=1)} = (2.54/10.24) = .25$. The different slopes of the lines connecting the two pairs of odds in Figure 10.2 exactly capture this regional disparity in the magnitude of the age-segregation relationship. If no interaction had been observed, then the lines would be parallel; but the significant $\{SAR\}$ term in the best-fitting log-linear model for the four-variable crosstab confirms that regional differences in white racial attitudes among age groups are substantial.

To summarize the strategy we used for finding a model that fits well to the observed four-variable crosstab, note that we again followed a forward stepwise fitting strategy, moving from less-complex to more-complex models. Alternatives would have been either to use a backward stepwise strategy, or to hypothesize a specific model and test its fit to the data.

10.3.2. The Logit Model

All the log-linear analyses up to this point used a general specification, one that does not distinguish between independent and dependent variables in the calculation of effect parameters. When one dichotomous variable is considered to be dependent on the other variables, a special type of log-linear model, the **logit model** is appropriate. A logit is simply the natural logarithm of an odds, that is, the ratio of two expected frequencies:

logit model— a log-linear model in which one dichotomous variable is considered to be dependent on the other variables

$$\text{logit } (F_1/F_2) = \ln (F_1/F_2) = \ln F_1 - \ln F_2$$

Thus, the parameters of a logit model are easily derived from a general log-linear model, as shown in Box 10.1. *Instead of predicting expected individual cell frequencies, the logit model predicts the log odds of the dependent variable.*

To illustrate the transformation, consider the logit equation for the log-odds of racial segregation disagreement from the three-variable analysis shown in Table 10.5. This equation is as follows:

$$\ln \left(\frac{F_{1jk}}{F_{2jk}} \right) = \beta^S + \beta_j^{SA} + \beta_k^{SE}$$

BOX 10.1   Deriving Logit Effect Parameters from General Log-Linear Parameters

The logit specification in log-linear analysis is analogous to the logistic regression equations in chapter 9, except that the predictor variables are categoric rather than continuous measures. Assume that variable Y is a dichotomous dependent variable and the variables X and Z are categoric predictors in a three-variable log-linear model $\{YX\}\{YZ\}\{XZ\}$ that yields the following equation for the expected frequency in the i,j,kth cell of the crosstab:

$$\ln F_{ijk} = \mu + \lambda_i^Y + \lambda_j^X + \lambda_k^Z + \lambda_{ij}^{YX} + \lambda_{ik}^{YZ} + \lambda_{jk}^{XZ}$$

Because $\ln (A/B) = \ln A - \ln B$, the logged ratio of expected frequencies for any pair of cells involving the dependent variable Y is

$$\begin{aligned}\ln \left(\frac{F_{1jk}}{F_{2jk}}\right) &= \ln F_{1jk} - \ln F_{2jk}\\ &= (\mu + \lambda_1^Y + \lambda_j^X + \lambda_k^Z + \lambda_{1j}^{YX} + \lambda_{1k}^{YZ} + \lambda_{jk}^{XZ})\\ &\quad - (\mu + \lambda_2^Y + \lambda_j^X + \lambda_k^Z + \lambda_{2j}^{YX} + \lambda_{2k}^{YZ} + \lambda_{jk}^{XZ})\end{aligned}$$

Collecting and canceling terms shows that

$$\ln \left(\frac{F_{1jk}}{F_{2jk}}\right) = \lambda_1^Y - \lambda_2^Y + \lambda_{1j}^{YX} - \lambda_{2j}^{YX} + \lambda_{1k}^{YZ} - \lambda_{2k}^{YZ}$$

But because for dichotomous variables $\lambda_1^Y = -\lambda_2^Y$, $\lambda_{1j}^{YX} = -\lambda_{2j}^{YX}$, and $\lambda_{1k}^{YZ} = -\lambda_{2k}^{YZ}$, the equation for the expected log odds of Y further simplifies to

$$\ln \left(\frac{F_{1jk}}{F_{2jk}}\right) = 2\lambda_1^Y + 2\lambda_{1j}^{YX} + 2\lambda_{1k}^{YZ}$$

To distinguish logit effect parameters from general log-linear parameters, we replace them in the equation above with appropriate subscripted and superscripted betas:

BOX 10.1   *(continued)*

$$\ln \left(\frac{F_{1jk}}{F_{2jk}} \right) = \beta_1^Y + \beta_{1j}^{YX} + \beta_{1k}^{YZ}$$

where $\beta_1^Y = 2\lambda_1^Y$, $\beta_{1j}^{YX} = 2\lambda_{1j}^{YX}$, and $\beta_{1k}^{YZ} = 2\lambda_{1k}^{YZ}$. Thus, the effect parameters for a logit equation are twice the corresponding lambdas parameters from the general log-linear equation.

The numerical values for these coefficients are obtained by doubling the corresponding lambdas. That is, $\beta^S = 2\lambda^S$ and $\beta^{SA} = 2\lambda^{SA}$. Positive betas indicate that an independent variable increases the expected log-odds for the dependent variable, while negative betas reveal that an independent variable decreases the log-odds. By changing the subscripts of the two independent variables, and thus changing the signs of their two beta parameters, we can estimate the log-odds on segregation attitude for all combinations of predictors. For example, the predicted log-odds of disapproving of segregation for respondents who are young and college educated is

$$\ln \left(\frac{F_{111}}{F_{211}} \right) = (2)(.763) + (2)(.184) + (2)(.174)$$
$$= 1.526 + .368 + .348 = 2.242$$

The expected log-odds of disapproving of segregation for the older college-educated respondents is

$$\ln \left(\frac{F_{111}}{F_{221}} \right) = 1.526 - .368 + .348 = 1.506$$

and for the older noncollege-educated respondents the log-odds is

$$\ln \left(\frac{F_{111}}{F_{222}} \right) = 1.526 - .368 - .348 = 0.810$$

Notice that the interpretation of results is identical to that of the log-linear analysis in section 10.2.

10.4   Special Topics in Log-Linear Analysis

Log-linear analysis is a powerful tool in the social researcher's tool kit, with applications to many substantive problems. Space limitations allow us to examine only a few special topics, whose comprehension requires a firm grasp of the fundamentals discussed in the preceding sections.

10.4.1.   Zero Cells

The log-linear analysis is potentially applicable to tables of very large dimensions, both in numbers of variables and numbers of categories. However, as these dimensions expand, the number of cells in the table increases relative to the number of observations, resulting in decreasing numbers of cases per cell. As a rule of thumb, a practical limit on crosstabulation analysis can arise with as few as five variables having only three categories apiece. Completely crossing such measures yields $3^5 = 243$ cells, which results in an average cell frequency of barely five observations for a typical survey with only 1,500 respondents. Many cells will have zero observed frequencies, particularly when variables are highly skewed. Rare combinations of variables may go unrepresented in a particular sample, (e.g., black female heads of major corporations). Because **random zeros** pose problems in defining odds ratios, researchers who seek to analyze such tables are well advised to add a small constant—typically 0.5—to *all* cell counts before fitting log-linear models. (Using 0.5 as the constant value concurs with the convention of rounding such fractional values arbitrarily up or down to the nearest integer.)

random zero— a combination of variables that is unrepresented in a sample

By contrast **structural zeros** arise because certain combinations of variable categories cannot logically occur. Teenage grandparents or women with prostate cancer are conditions that are not just unlikely, but impossible. Such structural zeros cannot be adjusted by adding a small constant, but must be treated as fixed-zero cells in log-linear analyses.

structural zero— a combination of variables that cannot logically occur

The top panel of Table 10.11 contains the observed frequencies for a crosstabulation for 1991 GSS respondents of five categories of their current marital status by previous widowhood. Because current widows were not asked this question, and because never-married respondents logically cannot have experienced widowhood, these two cells are structural zeros. However, the zero in the currently separated row is assumed to be a random zero, as it is

TABLE 10.11

Observed and Expected Frequencies in Crosstabulation of
Current Marital Status by Previous Widowhood

Current Status	Observed Frequencies		Independence Model		Quasi-Independence Model	
	Previously Widowed		Previously Widowed		Previously Widowed	
	Yes	*No*	*Yes*	*No*	*Yes*	*No*
Married	22	769	106.39	685.61	25.61	765.39
Divorced	9	159	22.70	145.30	5.47	163.53
Separated	0	43	5.91	38.09	1.42	42.58
Widowed	168	0*	22.70	146.30	168.50	0*
Never Married	0*	325	43.79	282.21	0*	325.50

* Structural zero

Missing Data: 22 cases

Source: 1991 General Social Survey

possible for such respondents to have been widowed before their current marriage (and these 43 respondents were asked this question). The second panel shows the expected cell frequencies when the independence model $\{M\}\{W\}$ is applied to the full 5×2 table. (We added .5 to the eight nonstructural-zero cell frequencies before analyzing the entries). This hypothesis is strongly rejected at the $\alpha = .10$ level, whose critical value is 7.78 for $df = 4$ since $L^2 = 886.10$. But it is clearly an absurd model because it generates large expected frequencies in both structural-zero cells.

The relevant model for a table with one or more structural-zeros is the **quasi-independence model,** which ignores the structural-zero cells and tests for independence only among the remaining entries. Most log-linear analysis computer programs have an option that allows an analyst to designate which cell entries must be fixed to zero. The degrees of freedom for a quasi-independence model are adjusted by subtracting one df for each fixed-zero cell. Thus, for a two-variable crosstab having R rows, C columns, and Z structural zeros, the df for the quasi-independence model is $(R - 1)(C - 1) - Z$.

quasi-independence model— a model that ignores structural-zero cells and tests for independence only among the remaining entries

The third panel of Table 10.11 displays the expected frequencies for the quasi-independence model, which has an excellent fit to the data ($L^2 = 3.76$, $df = [(5 - 1)(2 - 1) - 2] = 2$, $p = .152$). The expected odds of previous widowhood among the currently married, divorced, and separated respondents is .033. We conclude that current marital status is unrelated to the dissolution of a previous marriage through a spouse's death.

10.4.2. Symmetry

Many research problems concern relationships within a square crosstabulation, that is, where both variables have the same K categories in the same sequence. Such tables might be formed by remeasuring a variable for the same respondents at two time periods (so-called "turnover tables" produced by a panel survey with repeated measures). For example, a marketing researcher may ask consumers each month to report their current cereal purchases, in order to investigate brand-name loyalty and defection. Square tables may also be constructed by jointly classifying two partners in a social interaction, using the same set of categories. For example, pairs of workers and supervisors may be asked how much satisfaction they find in their relationship.

symmetry hypothesis—
an hypothesis that predicts
exactly equal frequencies
in inversely corresponding
cells of a $K \times K$
crosstabulation

marginal homogeneity—
corresponding row and
column marginal totals are
equal

The basic substantive hypotheses about $K \times K$ square tables are the patterns of stability and change over time (in panels) or agreement and difference (in interaction pairs). The **symmetry hypothesis** predicts exactly equal frequencies in the inversely corresponding cells; that is, $f_{ij} = f_{ji}$ for all $i \neq j$. The observed frequency in the ith row, jth column equals the observed frequency in the jth row, ith column for all nondiagonal cells. A symmetrical pattern also implies **marginal homogeneity,** that is, the corresponding row and column marginal totals are equal (i.e., $f_{i \cdot} = f_{\cdot j}$). However, the converse is not true; homogenous marginals do *not* imply symmetry within the body of the square crosstab because identical row and column totals can be produced in many ways.

Because the GSS is not a longitudinal survey, we illustrate symmetry with a cross-sectional assortative mating process. The top panel of Table 10.12 contains the observed frequency counts for a crosstab classifying married respondents (R) and their spouses (S) by their religions at age 16, using five broad groupings. (To adjust for the four random-zero cells, we added a constant .5 to each of the 25 cells, giving a total of 811.5 cases.) Clearly, we do not expect couples' religious affiliations to be independent, as the large

TABLE 10.12

Observed and Expected Frequencies in Crosstabulation of
Religious Affiliations of Respondents and Spouses at Age 16

Respondent's Religion	Spouse's Religion					Total
	Protestant	*Catholic*	*Jewish*	*None*	*Other*	*Total*
*Observed Frequencies:***						
Protestant	406.5	81.5	4.5	21.5	4.5	518.5
Catholic	73.5	152.5	2.5	5.5	1.5	235.5
Jewish	2.5	3.5	10.5	1.5	0.5	18.5
None	11.5	2.5	0.5	7.5	1.5	23.5
Other	5.5	2.5	0.5	0.5	6.5	15.5
Total	499.5	242.5	18.5	36.5	14.5	811.5
Expected Frequencies in Symmetry Model:						
Protestant	406.5*	77.5	3.5	16.5	5	509
Catholic	77.5	152.5*	3	4	2	239
Jewish	3.5	3	10.5*	1	.5	18.5
None	16.5	4	1	7.5*	1	30
Other	5	2	.5	1	6.5*	15
Total	509	239	18.5	30	15	811.5

* Cell frequencies were fixed with structural zeros.

** A constant .5 was added to each to correct for random zeros.

Missing Data: 718 cases

Source: 1991 General Social Survey

majority of Americans are known to marry primarily within their
own religious groups. Indeed, when the $\{R\}\{S\}$ independence
model (i.e., $\ln F_{ij} = \mu + \lambda_i^R + \lambda_j^S$) is fitted to the bivariate table, it
must be rejected at the $\alpha = .10$ level with 16 df (critical value is 23.54)
since $L^2 = 308.69$. Leaving aside the obvious clustering on the main
diagonal, do interfaith marriages tend to occur more in one
direction than the other? Such a pattern seems implausible given
that, for example, a person raised Catholic marrying a person
raised Protestant seems no more likely than a person raised
Protestant marrying a person raised Catholic. Furthermore, the
corresponding row and column marginals are very close. Thus, we
should expect that a symmetrical model would produce an excellent
fit to the $(5 \times 5) - 5 = 20$ off-diagonal cells in the $\{RS\}$ crosstab in
Table 10.12. That is, we seek to fit the model $\ln F_{ij} = \mu + \lambda_i^R + \lambda_j^S + \lambda_{ij}^{RS}$, taking into account the symmetrical choices of respondents
and their spouses.

Using log-linear analysis to test the symmetry hypothesis involves forming a three-dimensional crosstab from the observed frequencies in the original two-variable $\{RS\}$ table. First, we create a square $K \times K$ subtable **A** that is identical to the original observed frequencies (where K is the number of categories in the row and column variables):

$$
\mathbf{A} = \begin{pmatrix}
406.5 & 81.5 & 4.5 & 21.5 & 4.5 \\
73.5 & 152.5 & 2.5 & 5.5 & 1.5 \\
2.5 & 3.5 & 10.5 & 1.5 & 0.5 \\
11.5 & 2.5 & 0.5 & 7.5 & 1.5 \\
5.5 & 2.5 & 0.5 & 0.5 & 6.5
\end{pmatrix}
$$

Second, we transpose the rows and columns of **A** (i.e., we substitute f_{ij} with f_{ji} and vice versa for all i and j), creating a second $K \times K$ subtable **B:**

$$
\mathbf{B} = \begin{pmatrix}
406.5 & 73.5 & 2.5 & 11.5 & 5.5 \\
81.5 & 152.5 & 3.5 & 2.5 & 2.5 \\
4.5 & 2.5 & 10.5 & 0.5 & 0.5 \\
21.5 & 5.5 & 1.5 & 7.5 & 0.5 \\
4.5 & 1.5 & 0.5 & 1.5 & 6.5
\end{pmatrix}
$$

All paired off-diagonal cells are now located in corresponding positions across these two subtables. Third, we combine subtables **A** and **B** into a two-variable $2K \times K$ crosstab:

$$
\begin{pmatrix}
406.5 & 81.5 & 4.5 & 21.5 & 4.5 \\
73.5 & 152.5 & 2.5 & 5.5 & 1.5 \\
2.5 & 3.5 & 10.5 & 1.5 & 0.5 \\
11.5 & 2.5 & 0.5 & 7.5 & 1.5 \\
5.5 & 2.5 & 0.5 & 0.5 & 6.5 \\
406.5 & 73.5 & 2.5 & 11.5 & 5.5 \\
81.5 & 152.5 & 3.5 & 2.5 & 2.5 \\
4.5 & 2.5 & 10.5 & 0.5 & 0.5 \\
21.5 & 5.5 & 1.5 & 7.5 & 0.5 \\
4.5 & 1.5 & 0.5 & 1.5 & 6.5
\end{pmatrix}
$$

The subtable **A** has been "stacked" on top of subtable **B.** That is, the first five rows of the matrix contain the 5×5 subtable **A,** while the next five rows contain the subtable **B.** Hence, what appears above as a 10×5 matrix is just a compact representation of a $5 \times 5 \times 2$ crosstabulation.

Fourth, we enter this table into a log-linear analysis program and specify a **design matrix.** A design matrix has the same dimensions as the combined data table ($2K \times K$), but uses "0" and "1" entries to show which cells are fixed (structural zeros) and which cells are free to take on values according to the particular model being estimated. In the symmetry hypothesis all the diagonal cells and all the above-diagonal cells in both subtables of the design matrix are designated structural zeros:

design matrix— a matrix whose "0" and "1" entries show which cells are fixed (structural zeros) and which cells are free to take on values according to the particular log-linear model being estimated

$$
\begin{bmatrix}
0 & 0 & 0 & 0 & 0 \\
1 & 0 & 0 & 0 & 0 \\
1 & 1 & 0 & 0 & 0 \\
1 & 1 & 1 & 0 & 0 \\
1 & 1 & 1 & 1 & 0 \\
0 & 0 & 0 & 0 & 0 \\
1 & 0 & 0 & 0 & 0 \\
1 & 1 & 0 & 0 & 0 \\
1 & 1 & 1 & 0 & 0 \\
1 & 1 & 1 & 1 & 0
\end{bmatrix}
$$

Note that the first five rows of the design matrix correspond to the original subtable **A** and the second five rows to subtable **B.** In effect, this design matrix procedure forces the log-linear analysis program to fit observed values only in the paired *below-diagonal* cells.

The symmetry hypothesis is tested by fitting the $\{RS\}$ marginal table to the combined crosstabulation. The symmetry model forces the corresponding expected row and expected column marginals in the $R \times S$ crosstab to be equal. That is, $F_{i.} = F_{.i}$ even when the observed $f_{i.} \neq f_{.i}$. In particular, $F_{i.} = F_{.i} = (f_{i.} + f_{.i})/2$. The symmetry model's expected cell frequencies are calculated as an average of the observed paired off-diagonal entries (i.e., $F_{ij} = F_{ji} = (f_{ij} + f_{ji})/2$. Because the diagonal entries are structural zeros and the off-diagonal expected frequencies are symmetric (i.e., $F_{ij} = F_{ji}$), the symmetry model's $df = (K^2 - K)/2$.

For our example of assortative religious mating the symmetry model yields an excellent fit: $L^2 = 6.79$, $df = 10$, $p > .75$. The expected frequencies for this model are displayed in the bottom panel of Table 10.12. Note that the corresponding row and column marginals equal one another, but are not equal to the observed totals in the top panel. However, the dissimilarity is so small that the overall fit is acceptable. Since the model fits the data so well, we cannot reject the hypothesis that American marriages between the five broad religious groupings is basically a symmetrical process. People of various religions marry those of other religions in roughly the same proportions.

10.4.3. Quasi-Symmetry

When the row and column totals in a square table are not the same (i.e., are not homogeneous), the symmetry model cannot satisfactorily fit the data. A good example appears in Table 10.13, an intergenerational mobility table from father's (F) to offspring's (O) occupations, using five broad categories. (The convention in stratification and network research is to arrange the origin categories in the rows and the destination categories in the columns, ranging from highest status to lowest status. Thus, the upwardly mobile

TABLE 10.13

Observed and Expected Frequencies in Crosstabulation of Father's and Respondent's Occupations

| | Respondent's Occupation | | | | | |
Father's Occupation	Upper White-Collar	Lower White-Collar	Upper Blue-Collar	Lower Blue-Collar	Farm	Total
Observed Frequencies:						
Upper White-Collar	113	73	24	44	4	258
Lower White-Collar	50	58	13	37	3	161
Upper Blue-Collar	69	83	50	78	2	282
Lower Blue-Collar	53	83	32	93	2	263
Farm	45	33	20	90	22	210
Total	330	330	139	342	33	1,174
Expected Frequencies in Quasi-Symmetry Model:						
Upper White-Collar	113*	73	23	45.29	3.71	258
Lower White-Collar	50	58*	14	37.53	1.47	161
Upper Blue-Collar	70	82	50*	76.18	3.82	282
Lower Blue-Collar	51.71	82.47	33.82	93*	2	263
Farm	45.29	34.53	18.18	90	22*	210
Total	330	330	139	342	33	1,174

* Cell frequencies were fixed with structural zeros.

Missing Data: 343 cases

Source: 1991 General Social Survey

appear in the cells below the main diagonal, while the downwardly mobile are above the diagonal.) The now well-known historical shift in the American labor force is evident in the grossly unequal marginal distributions: The offspring generation has twice as many lower white-collar workers as their fathers' generation, but only half as many upper blue-collar workers and far fewer farmers. Although the independence hypothesis $\{F\}\{O\}$ is clearly rejected at $\alpha = .05$ ($df = 16$, critical value is 26.30) since $L^2 = 134.18$. The symmetry hypothesis $\{FO\}$ is also rejected ($L^2 = 317.59$, $df = 10$, critical value $\neq 15.99$ at $\alpha = .10$). The corresponding row and column totals differ too drastically to accommodate equivalent upward and downward intergenerational mobility flows.

Because symmetry is rejected, we know that the corresponding cell frequencies are not equal ($f_{ij} \neq f_{ji}$), and the corresponding row and column marginals are not homogeneous (i.e., $F_{i\cdot} \neq F_{\cdot i}$). We could stop the analysis here and conclude that symmetry is not present, but one option is to continue the analysis within the constraint of nonhomogeneous marginals, to see if a special type of symmetry can be detected. That is, we can estimate a **quasi-symmetry model** that preserves the inequality of the corresponding row and column marginals, but produces equal corresponding odds ratios among the off-diagonal cells. For the occupational mobility example the movement across pairs of occupations has the same magnitude whether the direction of movement is up or down. That is, the fathers' and the offsprings' occupational distributions are allowed to equal the observed values, rather than constrained to be identical. Only the paired off-diagonal frequencies are free to vary within these looser constraints.

As in the symmetry model (see section 10.4.2), we first stack the $K \times K$ mobility table on top of its transpose, creating a single $2K \times K$ data matrix:

$$\begin{bmatrix} 113 & 73 & 24 & 44 & 4 \\ 50 & 58 & 13 & 37 & 3 \\ 69 & 83 & 50 & 78 & 3 \\ 53 & 83 & 32 & 93 & 2 \\ 45 & 33 & 20 & 90 & 22 \\ 113 & 50 & 69 & 53 & 45 \\ 73 & 58 & 83 & 83 & 33 \\ 24 & 13 & 50 & 32 & 20 \\ 44 & 37 & 78 & 93 & 90 \\ 4 & 3 & 2 & 2 & 22 \end{bmatrix}$$

quasi-symmetry model — a special type of symmetry that preserves the inequality of the corresponding row and column marginals, but produces equal corresponding odds ratios among the off-diagonal cells

Next, we specify a corresponding design matrix having the same dimensions, which has 1s only in the lower off-diagonal cells and 0s in the diagonal and upper off-diagonal cells:

$$
\begin{bmatrix}
0 & 0 & 0 & 0 & 0 \\
1 & 0 & 0 & 0 & 0 \\
1 & 1 & 0 & 0 & 0 \\
1 & 1 & 1 & 0 & 0 \\
1 & 1 & 1 & 1 & 0 \\
0 & 0 & 0 & 0 & 0 \\
1 & 0 & 0 & 0 & 0 \\
1 & 1 & 0 & 0 & 0 \\
1 & 1 & 1 & 0 & 0 \\
1 & 1 & 1 & 1 & 0
\end{bmatrix}
$$

Note that both the data and design matrix are identical to those used in the symmetry model. However, the quasi-symmetry model is tested by fitting the marginals $\{FO\}\{FT\}\{OT\}$, where F is the father's occupation, O is the offspring's occupation, and T is a dichotomous variable that designates each off-diagonal cell as falling either into the upper triangle or the lower triangle of the partitioned design matrix (i.e., upward or downward mobility). For these data the quasi-symmetry model yields an excellent fit to the mobility table: $L^2 = 2.92$, $df = 3$, $p > .41$. Furthermore, we can test a marginal homogeneity hypothesis by taking the difference in fits between the symmetry and quasi-symmetry models. In this example marginal homogeneity is soundly rejected: $\Delta L^2 = L_S^2 - L_{QS}^2 = 317.59 - 2.92 = 314.67$, $\Delta df = df_S - df_{QS} = 10 - 3 = 7$, $p < .001$.

Taking into account the presence of marginal nonhomogeneity, upward and downward mobility across corresponding pairs of categories is symmetrical. For example, the odds that respondents with farm and lower blue-collar fathers who rose to upper and lower white-collar jobs is

$$\frac{(82.47)(45.29)}{(51.71)(34.53)} = 2.09$$

which is identical to the odds that the offspring of upper and lower white-collar fathers fell into the blue-collar and farm categories:

$$\frac{(3.71)(37.53)}{(45.29)(1.47)} = 2.09$$

We hope these examples illustrate that many useful applications of log-linear methods are available to social scientists. However, to benefit fully from these tools, much extended study is essential.

Review of Key Concepts and Symbols

These key concepts and symbols are listed in the order of appearance in this chapter. Combined with the definitions in the margins, they will help you to review the material and can serve as a self-test for mastery of the concepts.

multivariate contingency table analysis	symmetry hypothesis
log-linear analysis	marginal homogeneity
saturated model	design matrix
nonsaturated model	quasi-symmetry model
conditional odds ratio	OR^{YX}
hierarchical log-linear model	F_{ij}
nested models	$\ln F_{ij}$
marginal subtable	μ
fitted marginal	λ_{ij}^{XY}
iterative proportional fitting	$\hat{s}_{\lambda}$
Newton-Raphson algorithm	$OR^{(XY|Z=1)}$
likelihood ratio	$\{XY\}$
BIC statistic	L^2
logit model	ΔL^2
random zero	Δdf
structural zero	BIC
quasi-independence model	β^X

PROBLEMS

General Problems

1. Here is a 2 × 2 crosstabulation of response to the question "Please tell me whether or not *you* think it should be possible for a pregnant woman to obtain a *legal* abortion if she is not married and does not want to marry the man" by respondent's gender in the 1991 GSS:

	Abortion by Gender	
	Gender	
Should a single woman be able to obtain a legal abortion?	**Women**	**Men**
Yes	218	208
No	321	203

Missing data = 567

Source: 1991 General Social Survey

Calculate the odds in favor of abortion for the table as a whole and the conditional odds in favor for each gender. Calculate the odds ratio. What is the relationship of gender to abortion support?

2. For the 1991 GSS a saturated log-linear model fitted to a 2 × 2 crosstabulation of race (*R*, classified as white = 1 and black = 2) and response to a question about school busing for integration (*B*, with favor = 1 and oppose = 2), produced the following log-linear coefficient estimates (0.5 was added to each cell):

$$\mu = \quad 5.018 \qquad \lambda_1^R = +0.923$$

$$\lambda_1^B = -0.060 \qquad \lambda_{11}^{BR} = -0.315$$

Calculate the expected frequencies for the four cells of the table.

3. For the 1991 GSS responses to "Are there any situations that you can imagine in which you would approve an adult male

punching an adult male stranger?" (*P,* yes =1, no = 2) were crosstabulated with responses to "Have you ever been punched or beaten by another person?" (*B,* yes =1, no = 2), yielding the following observed frequencies:

Approval of Punching by Being Beaten		
	Ever been beaten? (B)	
Any situations in which you would approve punching? (P)	Yes	No
Yes	221	332
No	111	275

Missing data = 578

Source: 1991 General Social Survey

Estimate the log-linear effect parameters for the saturated model:

$$\ln F_{ij} = \mu + \lambda_i^P + \lambda_i^H + \lambda_{ij}^{PH}$$

4. Estimate the standard error of the lambda effect parameters in Problem 3 and calculate the three *t* scores.

5. When the independence log-linear model {*P*}{*H*} is fitted to the data in Problem 3, the following parameter estimates are found: $\mu = 5.398$; $\lambda_1^P = +0.180$; $\lambda_1^H = -0.302$.
   a. Calculate the four expected frequencies for the 2 × 2 table.
   b. Using these expected frequencies and the observed frequencies in Problem 3, calculate L^2 for the independence model and test whether the null hypothesis can be rejected at $\alpha = .01$.

6. For the 1991 GSS a three-variable crosstabulation of age (*A*) dichotomized at 44 and under, subjective social class (*C*), and satisfaction with family financial situation (*S*) produced the following observed frequencies:

		Satisfaction with Financial Situation (S)		
Age (A)	Subjective Class (C)	Satisfied	More or Less Satisfied	Not at All Satisfied
< 45 Years	Lower & Working	57	202	196
< 45 Years	Middle & Upper	114	200	77
≥ 45 Years	Lower & Working	63	127	81
≥ 45 Years	Middle & Upper	183	155	47

Financial Satisfaction by Age and Subjective Class

Missing data = 15

Source: 1991 General Social Survey

For each of the two age categories, calculate the conditional odds ratio of social class to the categories "satisfied" and "more or less satisfied," and the conditional odds ratio of class to the categories "satisfied" and "not at all satisfied." What is your interpretation?

7. Five log-linear models were fitted to the three-variable crosstabulation in Problem 6, with the following likelihood ratios:

Model	L^2	df	p
1. {A}{C}{S}	208.67	7	.000
2. {AC}{AS}	121.31	4	.000
3. {AC}{CS}	48.80	4	.000
4. {AS}{CS}	7.63	3	.054
5. {AC}{AS}{CS}	0.61	2	.739

Does model 5 produce a better fit to the observed data, testing for differences in L^2s with each of the other four models at $\alpha = .001$?

8. For the 1991 GSS a four-way crosstabulation was created using dichotomous 1988 presidential vote (V, Dukakis = 1, Bush = 2) by dichotomous party identification (P, Democrat or Independent = 1, Republican = 2), liberal-conservative self-placement

(*C*, liberal or moderate = 1, conservative = 2), and education (*E*, high school or less = 1, some college or more = 2). Log-linear models were fitted to the 913 cases in this table, producing the following likelihood ratios:

Model	L^2	df	p
1. {*PCE*}{*V*}	444.36	7	.000
2. {*PCE*}{*EV*}	443.88	6	.000
3. {*PCE*}{*CV*}	338.02	6	.000
4. {*PCE*}{*PV*}	12.68	6	.050
5. {*PCE*}{*EV*}{*CV*}	382.94	5	.000
6. {*PCE*}{*EV*}{*PV*}	10.35	5	.066
7. {*PCE*}{*CV*}{*PV*}	5.49	5	.359
8. {*PCE*}{*CV*}{*EV*}{*CV*}	3.55	4	.472

Calculate the BIC statistics for each model and decide which provides the best fit. Does your conclusion differ from that reached by testing for differences in model L^2s when $\alpha = .05$?

9. The effect parameters for model 7 in Problem 8 are as follows:

$$\mu = 3.528 \quad \lambda_1^P = 0.269 \quad \lambda_1^C = 0.398 \quad \lambda_1^E = -0.091$$
$$\lambda_1^V = -0.482 \quad \lambda_{11}^{PC} = 0.225 \quad \lambda_{11}^{PE} = 0.144 \quad \lambda_{11}^{VP} = 0.840$$
$$\lambda_{11}^{VC} = 0.136 \quad \lambda_{11}^{CE} = 0.011 \quad \lambda_{11}^{PCE} = -0.161$$

a. What is the expected frequency of cases having the first category on all four variables?

b. What is the expected frequency of cases having the first category on *V* and *C* and in the second category on *P* and *E*?

10. Using the effect parameters in Problem 9, calculate the expected logits of voting for Dukakis for respondents who are: (a) liberal (*C* = 1) and Democratic or Independent (*P* = 1); (b) conservative (*C* = 2) and Republican (*P* = 2).

Problems Requiring the 1991 General Social Survey

11. Crosstabulate happiness (HAPPY) and relative financial well-being (FINRELA). Report L^2 and the expected frequencies from

the independence model, which fits the $\{H\}\{F\}$ marginals. Can you reject this model at $\alpha = .001$?

12. In chapter 5 we examined the relationship between SMOKING and gender (SEX) (see Table 5.5 on page 165). Use the SPSS LOGLINEAR program to reanalyze this 2×2 table. Report L^2 for the independence model, which fits the $\{S\}\{G\}$ marginals. Can you reject this model at $\alpha = .01$? Report the effect parameters for the saturated model $\{SG\}$.

13. Fit a log-linear model having all two-way effects to the $2 \times 2 \times 2$ crosstabulation of gender (SEX), viewing an X-rated movie in the past year (XMOVIE), and belief that "sexual materials lead to breakdown of morals" (PORNMORL). Then successively test a series of models, each of which removes one of the two-variable effects. Report the L^2s and BIC statistics for each model and decide which provides the best fit.

14. Fit a log-linear model having all two-way effects to the $3 \times 2 \times 2$ crosstabulation of RELIG (Protestants, Catholics, and Jews only), AGE (dichotomized at 44 years and under versus 45 years and older), and approval or disapproval of the Supreme Court's ruling that "no state or local government may *require* the reading of the Lord's Prayer or Bible verses in public school" (PRAYER). Can you reject this model at $\alpha = .05$? Report the model's effect parameters and give an interpretation of the age and religion effects on approval of prayer decision.

Statistics for
Social Data
Analysis

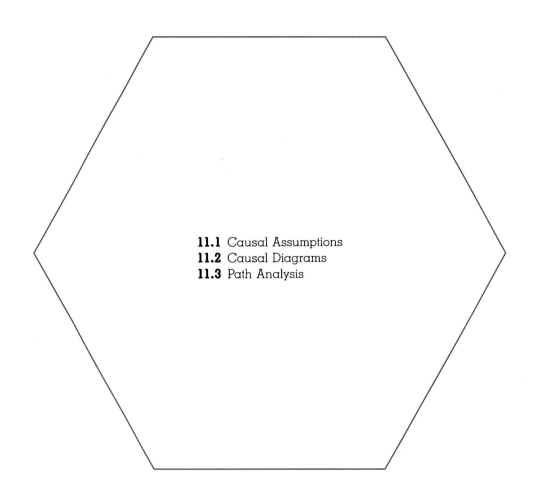

Causal Models and Path Analysis

11

Throughout this text we have stressed the idea that social research investigates two or more variables in an implicitly causal relationship. This chapter elaborates on the causal mode of thinking about social behavior and describes a basic technique—path analysis—for representing causal relations among quantitative variables. Causal reasoning dominates many areas of social research, but the foundations of these conceptualizations often are not carefully articulated. Considerable pseudo-philosophical mumbo jumbo may accompany efforts to explain social phenomena in cause-and-effect terms. The first section of this chapter states the basic assumptions that must be met before causal explanations can be seriously entertained.

11.1 Causal Assumptions

Hypotheses of the form "If A, then B," or "The higher the A, the higher (lower) the B," merely state an expectation that variables A and B are related. Such hypotheses are covariation statements that systematically relate differences or changes in one variable to differences or changes in a second variable. Often, the author of a research proposition clearly intends a causal effect to be present. For example, "The higher the level of test anxiety, the lower the performance on a course final exam," quite obviously means that test anxiety precedes and is a cause of poor scores. However, "The greater the practice of irrigation, the more centralized the state authority in early civilizations," is unclear about which variable— technology or political structure—is the cause and which is the effect. A genuinely causal hypothesis should explicitly state the researcher's expectations. Statements of the format, "An increase in variable A causes an increase (decrease) in variable B," leave no doubt as to the author's intentions.

A proposition in causal form is more informative than one that is only covariational. Causation is typically (but not necessarily) asymmetrical, in the sense that a change in the cause creates a change in the effect, whereas the reverse is not true—changing the dependent variable should leave the independent variable unaltered. Consider a causal hypothesis from agricultural economics: "Greater rainfall causes higher crop yields" (everything else being equal, which it seldom is). Because extensive experimental and observational data have been collected, the covariation of moisture and productivity is well established. Knowledge of plant physiology provides a sound basis for inferring which variable is cause and which is effect. A student who asserted that sowing more seeds per acre would increase a locality's rainfall would soon be laughed out of agriculture school. This trite but true hypothesis, therefore, is unambiguously causal in its intent and consequences.

Many theoretical statements in social research are not so clear. Sometimes theorists and researchers are simply confused about the "chicken-and-egg" sequence of the phenomena they study. More often, social reality is so incredibly complex that disentangling a causal process is almost impossible. Rarely does any interesting social behavior have a single cause that can be easily isolated. Rather, human activity is governed by a variety of influences, not the least of which is intentionality (purpose). For example, race riots in the United States may erupt from a complex interplay of police insensitivity, summer heat, poor housing, ghetto size, unemployment, black power ideology, white political incompetence, "outside" agitators (including mass media reports)—the list of potential causes is endless. To assert that a single variable has a discernible impact is a bold step that cannot be undertaken lightly.

As it has matured, social research has abandoned the simplistic monocausal thinking of the 19th century for the contemporary emphasis on multicausal theories or models. An important statistical development—path analysis—provides a way to cast hypotheses into explicit multicausal frameworks. Three basic conditions are necessary to establish causal priority among variables, none of which is sufficient by itself. The conditions of causality are covariation, time order, and nonspuriousness.

For a causal relationship to be present between a pair of variables, **covariation** between the independent and dependent variables must exist. Systematic changes or differences in one variable must accompany systematic changes or differences in the other. Covariation can take several forms: positive or negative linear association or several kinds of nonlinear relationships (see chapter 9).

covariation—joint variation, or association, between a pair of variables

The **time order** condition of causality is a metatheoretical assumption shared almost unconsciously by most Western peoples. For causality to occur, the change in the purported independent variable must precede in time the change in the alleged dependent measure. Temporal order helps to establish the essential asymmetry in a causal relationship. Causal research on social mobility and socioeconomic attainment developed rapidly by applying knowledge about the time sequences among parents' status and their offspring's occupational careers. Causal explanations of attitude structures, however, have been frustrated by an inability to determine temporal sequences among expressed attitudes recorded during a single interview. Researchers frequently assume that certain background characteristics of survey respondents—race, education, religion, or occupation, for example—were formed sufficiently prior to later behaviors—such as voting, drinking, marrying, or divorcing—and that these characteristics can safely be assumed to cause the behaviors.

time order—the necessary condition that changes in a purported independent variable must precede in time the change in the dependent measure, when a causal relationship between the two is assumed

Even if two variables covary, and a temporal order can be determined, a third condition must be satisfied before a causal relationship can be seriously considered to exist: The pattern of association between variables Y and X must not arise from other, common causal factors. The classic observation is that Dutch communities that have many storks nesting in chimneys have higher birth rates than communities where fewer storks nest. While covariation and temporal-order conditions reasonably can be met in this example, various "rival factors" might affect both the number of nesting storks and the number of human babies. The predominance of rural areas, pollution sanitation levels, community attitudes, and patterns of selective migration may all combine to produce a spurious correlation between the two variables.

nonspuriousness—
covariation between two
variables that is causal
and not due to the effects
of a third variable

Establishing **nonspuriousness** in a causal relationship is one of the most difficult problems to solve in social research. We cannot literally examine every possible alternative explanation for why two variables are related. Various research methods and statistical techniques have been developed that reduce much of the opportunity for spurious covariation to remain undetected. Controlled experiments represent the most effective way to control rival factors. When subjects are randomly assigned to various experimental and control conditions, all factors except the manipulated independent variable can be expected to be held constant. Nonexperimental research, such as field studies or systematic interviews, provide fewer means to control potential common causes. Hence, the conclusions drawn from nonexperimental research about causal relationships among variables are far more tentative.

11.2 Causal Diagrams

The three basic assumptions described in the preceding section (covariation, time order, and nonspuriousness) must be satisfied before causality can be imputed among variables. They are embedded graphically in a **causal diagram** that reveals the hypothesized cause-and-effect relationships. The conventions for causal diagrams are indispensable aids in thinking through problems of causal reasoning, as well as communicating your ideas to other researchers.

causal diagram—a
visual representation of the
cause-and-effect
relationships among
variables, using keyword
names and directed
arrows

In a causal diagram variables are represented by short names or letters. Annual household unit income might be labeled "Income" in a diagram. Scores on the Stanford-Binet intelligence test could be shortened to "IQ." Time order is conventionally organized from left to right, as in Western-culture reading and writing. Therefore, variables placed farther to the left in a diagram are considered temporally antecedent to those located farther to the right. Variables placed at the left-most side of the diagram are considered to be **exogenous variables,** or predetermined, because their causes remain unspecified, unanalyzed, and therefore outside the scope of the model. Each pair of predetermined variables is linked by a curved double-headed arrow, indicating that they are correlated but not causally connected within the diagram. Variables that are not exogenous are **endogenous variables;** that is, the causes of their variation are represented

exogenous variable—a
predetermined variable
whose causes remain
unexplained, unanalyzed,
and outside the scope of a
model

endogenous variable—a
variable whose cause(s) of
variation are represented
in a model

within the model. If a researcher posits a direct causal connection between two variables—either from a predetermined to an endogenous variable, or between two endogenous variables—it is represented by a single-headed straight arrow. The tail emerges from the causal variable and the arrowhead points at the effect variable. If two dependent variables are not hypothesized to have a direct causal connection, no arrow is drawn between the two. The direction of the causal effect between a pair of variables is indicated by placing signs along the arrow. A plus sign indicates positive causation: The higher the cause, the higher the effect. A negative sign indicates an inverse causal effect: The higher the cause, the lower the effect. Box 11.1 summarizes these rules.

Figure 11.1 displays some elementary types of causal diagrams using these diagrammatic conventions. Letters rather than substantive variable names are used. Figure 11.1A illustrates a bivariate pattern, showing a simple **direct effect,** or causal relationship, between *A* (the independent variable) and *B* (the dependent variable). By adding a third variable *C* in the temporal sequence, the simple causal chain in Figure 11.1B shows that increases in levels of *A* raise the value of *B,* and, in turn, a higher level of *B*

direct effect—a connecting path in a causal model between two variables without an intervening third variable

---

BOX 11.1   Rules for Constructing Causal Diagrams

1. Variable names are represented either by short keywords or letters.
2. Variables placed to the left in a diagram are assumed to be causally prior to those on the right.
3. Causal relationships between variables are represented by single-headed arrows.
4. Variables assumed to be correlated but not causally related are linked by a curved double-headed arrow.
5. Variables assumed to be correlated but not causally related should be at the same point on the horizontal axis of the causal diagram.
6. The causal effect presumed between two variables is indicated by placing + or − signs along the causal arrows to show how increases or decreases in one variable affect the other.

FIGURE 11.1

Some Elementary Causal Diagrams

A. Bivariate

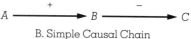

B. Simple Causal Chain

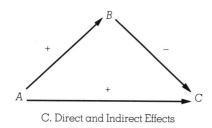

C. Direct and Indirect Effects

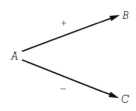

D. Spurious Common Cause

indirect effect—a compound path connecting two variables in a causal model through an intervening third variable

reduces the level of C. By inference, then, the higher the amount of A, the less the amount of C. The sign of this **indirect effect** of A on C via B can also be calculated by multiplying the signs of the two paths. A positive $(+)$ times a negative $(-)$ is a negative, so the indirect effect of A on C is negative.

Figure 11.1C, the direct-and-indirect-effects model, depicts A as having both types of impact on C, but opposite in sign. The indirect effect through B is still negative, while the direct effect—holding constant the contributions of B—is for A to raise the level of C. This diagram does not give enough information to determine whether the negative indirect effect or the positive direct effect is stronger. Later, in discussing path analysis, we will show how to estimate actual values of each causal effect, in order to answer this question.

The spurious common cause model, Figure 11.1D, shows how an observed covariation between B and C might arise without any direct causal link between these two variables. Variable A is a common cause of both, raising the level of B while lowering the magnitude of C, thereby generating an inverse covariation between both dependent variables. If B is the number of trucks at a fire and C is the amount of undamaged property, what variable might A be?

You now should have enough information about causal thinking and diagramming to begin to put it to use in your own social research. We will work through one simple example to show you how all these pieces fit together. This is a model of the development of political democracy among nations. Four causal propositions capture the verbal essentials:

P1: The greater a nation's economic wealth, the more likely it is to be a political democracy.

P2: The more militarized a nation, the less likely it is to be a political democracy.

P3: The more industrialized a nation, the greater its wealth.

P4: The more militarized a nation, the greater its wealth.

Figure 11.2 displays the hypothesized causal relations among these four variables. The double-headed curved arrow between Industrialization and Militarization indicates that no causal assumptions are made about this exogenous pair. Figure 11.2 also introduces another convention of causal diagrams: arrows to each dependent variable from unmeasured variables (e.g., to Democracy from U). Such unobserved factors, called **residual variables,** represents the belief that the variation in Democracy is not completely explained by the causal factors explicitly included in the model. Therefore, our model is **probabilistic,** or stochastic, rather than **deterministic.** Note also that a residual cause is shown as uncorrelated and not causally related to any independent or residual variables in the diagram.

The model in Figure 11.2 is also a **recursive model.** That is, all of the causal influences are assumed to be in one direction and one direction only. If X causes Y, then we do not allow for Y in return to cause X. Models that allow for bidirectional causality are said to be **nonrecursive models.** The estimation of nonrecursive models is complex, and the discussion in this chapter will be restricted to recursive models. The following section shows how the numerical values of the paths, as well as the values of the residual effects, are estimated.

residual variable—an unmeasured variable in a path model that is posited as causing the unexplained part of an observed variable

probabilistic—a causal relationship in which change in one variable produces change in another variable, with a certain probability of occurrence

deterministic—a causal relationship in which change in one variable always produces a constant change in another variable

recursive model—a model in which all the causal influences are assumed to be asymmetric (one-way)

nonrecursive model—a model in which causal influences between dependent variables may occur in both directions

FIGURE 11.2

Causal Diagram for Model of Political Democracy

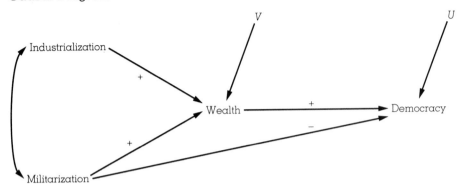

11.3.   Path Analysis

path analysis—a statistical method for analyzing quantitative data that yields empirical estimates of the effects of variables in an hypothesized causal system

Path analysis is a statistical method for analyzing quantitative data that yields empirical estimates of the effects of variables in an hypothesized causal system. Originally developed by the geneticist Sewell Wright, path analysis and its structural equation variants (see chapter 12) have gained wide currency among social researchers. The technique requires all the causal assumptions discussed above and it makes extensive use of diagrams to represent the cause-and-effect relationships among empirical variables. Moreover, before you can follow the discussion in this section, you must be familiar with standardized multiple regression equations, as described in section 8.2.2 (on page 272).

11.3.1.   An Example: Approval of Abortion

The example we use to illustrate path analytic principles is a simple four-variable causal system representing some hypothesized causes of respondents' approval of abortion if an unmarried woman does not want children, as shown in Figure 11.3. The pluses (+) and minuses (−) indicate the direction of the hypothesized relationships. The intensity of respondents' religious beliefs and their educational attainments are both posited as predetermined variables and thus are placed to the left in the diagram. The curved double-headed arrow indicates we are not interested in explaining the causal

FIGURE 11.3

Causal Diagram for Abortion Attitude Model

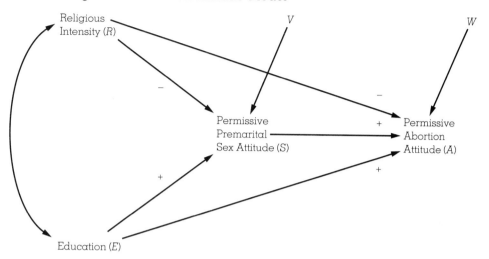

relationship between these two measures. Higher self-reported religiosity (*R*) is hypothesized to decrease permissive attitudes toward premarital sex relations (*S*), while more education (*E*) is expected to increase respondents' tolerance of premarital sex. Religiosity, education, and premarital sex attitude all are hypothesized to have direct causal impacts on approval of abortion for single women (*A*). The direct effect of religiosity is posited to be negative, but the direct effects of education and premarital sex attitude are posited to be positive. Both dependent variables in the diagram have arrows drawn from uncorrelated residual factors (*V* and *W*) to indicate effects from other unknown causes of abortion and premarital sex attitudes than those shown. The operationalization of these variables is described in section 11.3.6, where we also discuss how to estimate the model's coefficients.

11.3.2.   Structural Equations

Path analysis begins with a set of **structural equations** that represent the structure of interrelated hypotheses in a model. These equations bear a one-to-one relationship to a causal diagram such as Figure 11.3. Typically, the variables in a path analysis have been put in standardized, or *Z* score, form.

structural equation—a mathematical equation representing the structure of hypothesized relationships among variables in a social theory

The four relations among the variables—religious intensity (R), education (E), approval of premarital sex relations (S), and approval of abortion for unmarried women (A)—can be represented by two structural equations for the causes of the two endogenous variables. The first equation captures the hypothesized effects of religiosity and education on premarital sex attitudes, under the assumption that the two predetermined variables are linearly related to the endogenous variable. In general, if p_{IJ} represents a **path coefficient** to variable I from variable J, the equation linking premarital sex attitudes (S) to religious intensity (R) and education (E) is as follows:

path coefficient—a numerical estimate of the causal relationships between two variables in a path analysis

$$S = p_{SR}R + p_{SE}E + p_{SV}V$$

The path coefficient linking each causal variable to the effect variable is multiplied by the causal variable. Also, a path coefficient (p_{SV}) represents the causal link between the unobservable residual term, V, and the effect variable, S. The second structural equation depicts two exogenous variables (religiosity, R, and education, E) and one endogenous variable (premarital sex attitude, S) as causes of the second endogenous variable (approval of abortion, A):

$$A = p_{AR}R + p_{AE}E + p_{AS}S + p_{AW}W$$

Again a path coefficient is present for each direct cause of abortion attitude, plus a residual path from variable W. Figure 11.4 is the causal diagram that incorporates the two equations.

Path analysis has two major tasks:

1. Estimate numerical values of path coefficients.
2. Show that the correlations between all pairs of variables in the system are accounted for by the presumed causal population parameters.

These problems are considered in the next two subsections.

11.3.3.   Estimating Path Coefficients

To estimate numerical values of the path coefficients, we need only presume that the effect variables are linearly related to the causal variables in each equation. Then, one simply regresses each

FIGURE 11.4

Path Diagram with Coefficient Symbols for Abortion Attitude Model

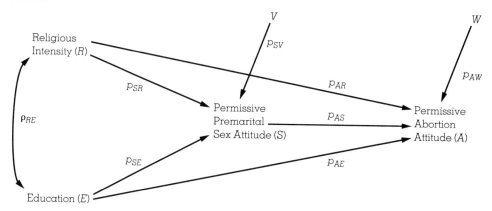

dependent variable on its predictors. Because all variables are in standardized form, the beta weights from the multiple regression are BLUE estimates of the path coefficients (see section 6.5 on page 220 and Box 8.2 on page 286). Thus, for the first structural equation:

$$\hat{p}_{SR} = \beta^{*}_{SR}$$
$$\hat{p}_{SE} = \beta^{*}_{SE}$$

The first subscript of a path coefficient is always the dependent variable, followed by the independent variable, just as the subscripts for R-square. The double subscripts SR and SE make clear which dependent variable is being predicted by religious intensity and education, because these two variables are also assumed to be causally linked to abortion attitude in the second equation. We state without proof that the residual path can be estimated by the following:

$$\hat{p}_{SV} = \sqrt{1 - R^{2}_{S \cdot RE}}$$

That is, the path coefficient from a residual variable to a dependent variable is simply the square root of the coefficient of nondetermination. The carets ($\hat{}$) above the path coefficients make clear that they are estimates of the population path coefficients parameters obtained from standardized regressions with sample data.

The estimated path coefficients for the second equation are similarly obtained by a multiple regression of abortion attitude on religiosity, education, and premarital sex attitude. Thus,

$$\hat{p}_{AR} = \beta^*_{AR}$$

$$\hat{p}_{AE} = \beta^*_{AE}$$

$$\hat{p}_{AS} = \beta^*_{AS}$$

$$\hat{p}_{AW} = \sqrt{1 - R^2_{A \cdot RES}}$$

11.3.4. Decomposing Implied Correlations into Causal Parameters

The solution to the second task, showing that the path coefficients imply or account for the correlations between pairs of variables, is less straightforward. It involves **decomposition,** or separation of a correlation coefficient into its components.

decomposition—the division of a correlation coefficient into its component parts, involving direct effects, indirect effects, and dependence on common causes

In this process the correlation is reexpressed in terms of path coefficients. Some algebra with which you may not be familiar is required. The theorem you need to know is: $\Sigma aX = a\Sigma X$, where a is a constant and X is a variable. That is, the sum of a times X equals a times the sum of X. You also need to know that $\Sigma(X + Y) = \Sigma X + \Sigma Y$. That is, the sum of variable X plus variable Y equals the sum of X plus the sum of Y. The details of these theorems are given in Appendix A as Rules 2 and 5.

Now consider the first equation given in section 11.3.2:

$$S = p_{SR}R + p_{SE}E + p_{SV}V$$

To find the correlation between religious intensity and premarital sex attitude, we first multiply both sides by R:

$$RS = R(p_{SR}R + p_{SE}E + p_{SV}V)$$

$$= p_{SR}R^2 + p_{SE}RE + p_{SV}RV$$

Then we take the sum of both sides:

$$\Sigma RS = \Sigma(p_{SR}R^2 + p_{SE}RE + p_{SV}RV)$$

$$= \Sigma p_{SR}R^2 + \Sigma p_{SE}RE + \Sigma p_{SV}RV$$

(This last step follows from Rule 5 in Appendix A.) Next, we divide both the left-hand and right-hand terms by N, and bring the ps outside the summation signs (i.e., apply Rule 2):

$$\frac{\Sigma RS}{N} = p_{SR}\frac{\Sigma R^2}{N} + p_{SE}\frac{\Sigma RE}{N} + p_{SV}\frac{\Sigma RV}{N}$$

As we showed in section 6.3.4 (on page 210), however, the sum of the product of two Z scores divided by $N - 1$ in the sample (or by N in the population, as here) just equals their correlation. That is,

$$\frac{\Sigma RS}{N} = \rho_{RS}$$

$$\frac{\Sigma RE}{N} = \rho_{RE}$$

$$\frac{\Sigma RV}{N} = \rho_{RV}$$

These terms appear in the equation below. Further, $\Sigma(R^2/N) = \rho_{RR}$. However, because the correlation of a variable with itself equals 1.0, $\rho_{RR} = 1$.

Substituting this information into the equation above yields:

$$\rho_{SR} = p_{SR} + p_{SE}\rho_{RE} + p_{SV}\rho_{RV}$$

In the correlation between religiosity and the residual term (ρ_{RV}), the V is an unobservable variable, so it cannot be measured. Thus, we have no way directly to estimate ρ_{RV}. Instead, consistent with the BLUE requirements (see Box 8.2 on page 286), the correlations between the residual variable and the independent variables in a given equation are *assumed* to be zero. That is, in the first equation, we assume that $p_{RV} = 0$.

Incorporating this assumption into the path equation above, we add a prime (') to make clear this correlation is implied by the model, and not necessarily equal to the correlation observed in the sample data:

$$\rho'_{SR} = p_{SR} + p_{SE}\rho_{RE}$$

That is, the implied correlation between R and S, ρ'_{SR}, is due to a direct path from religiosity to premarital sex attitude, p_{SR}, and the product of the path from education to premarital sex times the correlation between religiosity and education (i.e., $p_{SE}\rho_{RE}$).

In the same way we can also decompose the implied correlation between education and premarital sex attitude suggested by the causal model. We again begin with the first equation:

$$S = p_{SR}R + p_{SE}E + p_{SV}V$$

This time we multiply both sides by E (since we want to analyze p_{SE}):

$$ES = E(p_{SR}R + p_{SE}E + p_{SV}V)$$
$$= p_{SR}ER + p_{SE}E^2 + p_{SV}EV$$

Now, sum both sides and divide by N:

$$\Sigma ES = \Sigma(p_{SR}ER + p_{SE}E^2 + p_{SV}EV)$$
$$\frac{\Sigma ES}{N} = \Sigma p_{SR}\frac{ER}{N} + \Sigma p_{SE}\frac{E^2}{N} + \Sigma p_{SV}\frac{EV}{N}$$

Then bring the path coefficients outside the summation signs:

$$\frac{\Sigma ES}{N} = p_{SR}\frac{\Sigma ER}{N} + p_{SE}\frac{\Sigma E^2}{N} + p_{SV}\frac{\Sigma EV}{N}$$

Now, $\Sigma ES/N = \rho_{ES}$, $\Sigma ER/N = \rho_{ER}$, $\Sigma E^2/N = \rho_{EE}$, and $\Sigma EV/N = \rho_{EV}$. Recall from above that the correlation between a variable and itself is 1.0, that is, $\rho_{EE} = 1.0$. Furthermore, on the BLUE assumption that the independent variables in a given equation are uncorrelated with the residual variable, we assume $\rho_{EV} = 0$. Substituting these results into the equation above and rearranging terms yields:

$$\rho'_{SE} = p_{SR}\rho_{RE} + p_{SE}$$

$$= p_{SE} + p_{SR}\rho_{RE}$$

In words, the implied correlation between education and premarital sex attitude is composed of a direct path from education to premarital sex (p_{SE}) plus the product of the path from religiosity to premarital sex times the correlation between education and religiosity ($p_{SR}\rho_{ER}$).

The same procedures can decompose the bivariate correlations between the effect variable (A) and three causal variables (R, E, S) in the second equation, as implied by the hypothesized causal structure. In outline form, follow these steps for *each* causal variable:

1. Multiply the dependent variable by the causal variable and multiply each independent variable on the right-hand side of the equation by the causal variable.
2. Take sums of both sides of the equation, distributing the sum across all terms on the right-hand side of the equation.
3. Divide both sides of the equation by N in order to form correlations between the independent variable and all other variables in the equation.
4. Simplify the result, taking into account two assumptions:
   a. A variable correlated with itself is 1.0.
   b. The correlation between an independent variable and the residual variable is zero.
5. Repeat steps 1–4 for each causal variable in the equation.

As an exercise, you should be able to prove the following results:

$$\rho'_{SA} = p_{AS} + p_{AR}\rho_{SR} + p_{AE}\rho_{SE}$$

$$\rho'_{RA} = p_{AR} + p_{AS}\rho_{SR} + p_{AE}\rho_{RE}$$

$$\rho'_{EA} = p_{AE} + p_{AS}\rho_{SE} + p_{AR}\rho_{RE}$$

The five implied correlations that we derived above (two for the first structural equation and three for the second structural equation) are summarized in the **fundamental theorem of path analysis:**

$$\rho'_{ij} = \sum_{q=1}^{Q} p_{iq}\rho_{qj}$$

The fundamental theorem of path analysis states that the bivariate correlation between variables i and j implied by the hypothesized causal model is the sum of the products consisting of the path from variable q to variable i times the correlation between variable q and variable j. The sum of these products is formed over all Q variables that have direct paths to variable i. Convince yourself that the fundamental theorem of path analysis could have been used to decompose each of the five implied correlations above.

The three implied correlations with A as the endogenous variable each contain one or more correlations involving S. These correlations were themselves previously decomposed into path components in analyzing the first structural equation with S as the endogenous variable. In particular, as we saw above,

$$\rho'_{SR} = p_{SR} + p_{SE}\rho_{RE}$$
$$\rho'_{SE} = p_{SE} + p_{SR}\rho_{RE}$$

If we substitute these two quantities into the equation for ρ'_{SA} above, for ρ_{SR} and ρ_{SE} we obtain:

$$\rho'_{SA} = p_{AS} + p_{AR}(p_{SR} + p_{SE}\rho_{RE}) + p_{AE}(p_{SE} + p_{SR}\rho_{RE})$$
$$= p_{AS} + p_{AR}p_{SR} + p_{AR}p_{SE}\rho_{RE} + p_{AE}p_{SE} + p_{AE}p_{SR}\rho_{RE}$$

Similarly,

$$\rho'_{RA} = p_{AR} + p_{AS}(p_{SR} + p_{SE}\rho_{RE}) + p_{AE}\rho_{RE}$$
$$= p_{AR} + p_{AS}p_{SR} + p_{AS}p_{SE}\rho_{RE} + p_{AE}\rho_{RE}$$

and

$$\rho'_{EA} = p_{AE} + p_{AS}(p_{SE} + p_{SR}\rho_{RE}) + p_{AR}\rho_{RE}$$
$$= p_{AE} + p_{AS}p_{SE} + p_{AS}p_{SR}\rho_{RE} + p_{AR}\rho_{RE}$$

We recognize that these results are somewhat complex. Bear in mind that we have expressed the implied correlations between the causal variables and the effect variables as a function of the hypothesized path coefficients. Notice, too, that the right side of each of the final versions of the equations contains only path coefficients and the correlation between the two exogenous variables, religiosity and education (p_{RE}). As a general principle of the fundamental theorem, *the end result of decomposing an implied bivariate correlation contains only path coefficients and the correlations among the predetermined variables.*

11.3.5. Decomposing Implied Correlations by Tracing Paths

We can also obtain the decompositions for the five implied correlations by *tracing paths* in the diagram itself. In stating the following rules, which summarize how to trace paths to obtain decompositions, we assume that variable j is causally prior to variable i. The steps are as follows:

1. Beginning with a particular endogenous variable i, trace backward along the arrow that comes from variable j, if such a path exists. This is the simple *direct path coefficient*, p_{ij}. To its value should be added all the *compound paths* found by applying the following steps.

2. If other arrows come to variable i from third variables, q, trace all the connections between i and j that involve each q, multiplying the values of the path coefficients for these compound paths. In general, two kinds of compound linkages will occur:

   a. Variable q sends arrows to both i and j (either directly or through still other intervening variables). In this case trace backward along the paths from i to q, then forward along the paths from q to j, multiplying coefficient values as you go. If more than one distinct compound pathway exists for a given q, treat each separately.

    b. Variable *j* sends an arrow to variable *q,* which in turn sends an arrow to variable *i* (either in two steps or through yet other intervening variables). In this case simply trace backward from *i,* through *q* to *j,* multiplying path values as you go. If more than one distinct compound pathway back to *j* exists, treat each separately.

3. The following rules must be observed during tracing:

    a. You may trace backward along a series of arrows (from arrow head to arrow tail) for as many links as necessary to reach variable *q.* But once the direction has been changed in order to trace forward from *q* to *j* (from arrow tail to arrow head, as allowed in rule 2a), no subsequent reversals of direction are allowed.

    b. A particular double-headed curved arrow (for the correlation between two predetermined variables) can be traversed only once during the tracing of a given compound path. And only one double-headed arrow can be traversed during any given compound linkage. Note that a traverse of a double-headed arrow always results in a change of direction, from backward to forward tracing. A traverse of a double-headed arrow results in a multiplication of the compound path by that correlation coefficient.

    c. All the legitimate compound paths presented in the path diagram must be traced and their values multiplied to determine the magnitude and sign of the compound effects.

4. When all direct and compound path values have been calculated, add them together to obtain the correlation between *i* and *j* implied by the causal model (ρ'_{ij}).

To illustrate the use of tracing procedures, we will show how to decompose the correlation between abortion attitude (*A*) and education (*E*), ρ_{AE}. Referring to Figure 11.4 we can see that, applying rule 1, the direct path between education (*E*) and abortion attitude (*A*) is:

$$p_{AE}$$

Using rule 2, we see that there are two q variables, religious intensity (R) and premarital sex attitude (S), with direct paths to abortion attitude. Therefore, these variables must provide indirect links with education. Under rules 2a and 3b, we trace backward from abortion to religiosity (p_{AR}), and traverse the double-headed arrow to reach education (ρ_{RE}). This compound path will be added to the equation for decomposing ρ'_{AE} into direct and indirect effects:

$$p_{AR}\rho_{RE}$$

Notice that we *cannot* trace a compound path via premarital sex, such as $p_{AR}p_{SR}p_{SE}$, because it violates rule 3a about changing directions more than once. However, a second compound path connecting abortion attitude to education through religiosity is permissible:

$$p_{AS}\,p_{SR}\rho_{RE}$$

Because no other compound paths via religiosity occur, we next turn to the indirect connections involving premarital sex. One of these paths, also involving religiosity, has just been noted. The only remaining compound path allowed by rule 2b is

$$p_{AS}\,p_{SE}$$

Putting these four direct and indirect paths together, and reordering terms, we arrive at the final dissection of the implied correlation between abortion attitude and education:

$$\rho'_{AE} = p_{AE} + p_{AS}\,p_{SE} + p_{AS}p_{SR}\rho_{RE} + p_{AR}\,\rho_{RE}$$

which is the same result obtained with algebraic methods at the end of section 11.3.4. Notice that the basic theorem did not permit any indirect pathways involving the paths from the residual factors, V and W. As stated above, one assumption of path analysis is that residual variables are uncorrelated with the independent variables in the model, and, hence, no compound paths involve these residuals.

Table 11.1 shows how the entire correlation matrix can be rewritten in terms of path equations. (The results have been rearranged slightly compared to those derived earlier.) As a check

TABLE 11.1

Decomposition of Correlations in Path Model Shown in Figure 11.4

	Education (E)	Religious Intensity (R)	Premarital Sex Attitude (S)
Religious Intensity (R)	ρ_{RE}		
Premarital Sex Attitude (S)	$p_{SE} + p_{SR}\rho_{RE}$	$p_{SR} + p_{SE}\rho_{RE}$	
Abortion Attitude (A)	$p_{AE} + p_{AS}p_{SE} + p_{AR}\rho_{RE}$ $+ p_{AS}p_{SR}\rho_{RE}$	$p_{AR} + p_{AS}p_{SR} + p_{AE}\rho_{RE}$ $+ p_{AS}p_{SE}\rho_{RE}$	$p_{AS} + p_{AE}p_{SE} + p_{AR}p_{SR}$ $+ p_{AE}\rho_{RE}p_{SR}$ $+ p_{AR}\rho_{RE}p_{SE}$

of your understanding of the basic path theorem, you should derive these decompositions yourself, using the tracing rules presented above, and compare them to the table. Since the results can be obtained using either algebra or the tracing method, the technique you choose is immaterial.

11.3.6.   Estimating the Abortion Attitude Model

We now have all the tools we need to estimate the model shown in Figure 11.4. To do this, we use data from the 1991 GSS. Respondent's education is coded in number of years of schooling completed (from 0 to 20). Religious intensity is a follow-up question to respondent's affiliation (e.g., Catholic, Baptist, Lutheran, Jew, etc.): "Do you consider yourself a strong (preference named) or a not very strong (preference named)?" The three response categories are recoded "strong" = 3, "somewhat strong" = 2 (a volunteered response), and "not very strong" = 1. The premarital sex relations item asks: "If a man and woman have sex relations before marriage, do you think it is always wrong, almost always wrong, wrong only sometimes, or not wrong at all?" Responses were coded from "always wrong" = 1 to "not wrong at all" = 4. Finally, abortion attitude comes from responses to a battery of seven questions asking whether the respondent believes "it should be possible for a pregnant woman to obtain a *legal* abortion if . . . " a variety of conditions exist. In our analysis we chose only the responses to the condition " . . . if she is not married and doesn't want to marry the man." A "yes" response was coded 1 and a "no" response coded 0. The matrix of observed correlations among these four variables, using pairwise deletion of cases with missing values, appears in Table 11.2. Only 401 of the 1,517 GSS cases had complete data, because the two attitude items were restricted to a third of the sample, according to the GSS's questionnaire design.

The results of the regression analysis appear in Table 11.3. Because path analysis uses only standardized regression coefficients, metric (unstandardized) coefficients are not tabled. For a recursive model the estimated path coefficients are simply the beta

TABLE 11.2

Correlation Matrix of Variables in Abortion Attitude Path Analysis

	Religious Intensity	*Education*	*Premarital Sex Attitude*	*Abortion Attitude*
Religious Intensity (R)	1.00			
Education (E)	−.026	1.00		
Premarital Sex Attitude (S)	−.298	.186	1.00	
Abortion Attitude (A)	−.191	.292	.405	1.00

$N = 401$

Missing data = 1,116

Source: 1991 General Social Survey

TABLE 11.3

Standardized Regression Coefficients (Beta Weights) for Premarital Sex and Abortion Attitude Equations

Independent Variables	*Premarital Sex Attitude*	*Abortion Attitude*
Religious Intensity	−0.293***	−0.084*
Education	0.178***	0.227***
Premarital Sex Attitude	—	0.338***
Coefficient of Determination (R^2)	.120***	.219***

* $p < .05$

*** $p < .001$

$N = 401$

Missing data = 1,116

Source: 1991 General Social Survey

weights, and a residual path is just the square root of 1 minus the coefficient of determination (see section 11.3.3). The path coefficients for this example appear on the path diagram in Figure 11.5.

Because path coefficients are standardized values, the interpretation of causal effects must be made in terms of standard deviation (Z score) units. For example, $\hat{p}_{AS} = 0.338$ means that a 1 standard deviation increase in permissive premarital sex attitude leads to about a one-third standard deviation increase in approval of abortion for unmarried women. And since all path coefficients are standardized, comparison between the direct effects of causal variables is straightforward, as it is in multiple regression. Thus, we see that the direct causal impacts of religiosity and of education on a permissive abortion attitude are opposite in direction, with more-religious respondents less favorable to abortion ($\hat{p}_{AR} = -0.084$), but more-educated people approving abortion for single women ($\hat{p}_{AE} = 0.227$). We also find that both variables have much smaller effects on abortion attitude than does premarital sex attitude. The diagram also shows that more-religious respondents hold less permissive premarital sex attitudes ($\hat{p}_{SR} = -0.293$), while

FIGURE 11.5
Path Diagram with Numerical Estimates of Path Coefficients, Abortion Attitude Model

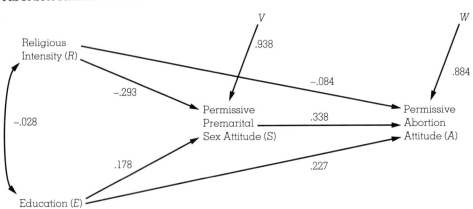

more-educated respondents express more permissive premarital sex attitudes ($\hat{p}_{SE} = 0.178$).

Path coefficients also permit the calculation of indirect causal effects through the multiplication of path values of compound paths connecting two variables via intervening variables. As section 11.3.4 showed, the sample estimates are:

$$r'_{AR} = \hat{p}_{AR} + \hat{p}_{AS}\hat{p}_{SR} + \hat{p}_{AS}\hat{p}_{SE}r_{RE} + \hat{p}_{AE}r_{RE}$$

The first term on the right is, of course, the estimated direct effect ($\hat{p}_{AR} = -0.084$). The second term—$\hat{p}_{AS}\hat{p}_{SR}$—is the estimated indirect causal effect, which shows the effect of religiosity on abortion attitude via premarital sex attitude. Note that the estimated indirect effect of religiosity lies in the same direction as the direct effect, $(0.338)(-0.293) = -0.099$, and it has roughly the same numerical value.

By adding together the direct and indirect causal effects, and comparing the sum to the observed correlation in Table 11.2, we can see how much of the covariation is due to the correlated effects involving education. Thus, the observed religious intensity-abortion attitude correlation is -0.191, the direct effect is -0.084, and the indirect effect is -0.099, which leaves only -0.008 of the observed correlation due to their dependency on education. This effect is small because religiosity and education have a correlation very close to zero, as can be seen in the final two terms of the decomposition. These are the **correlated effects,** since their values depend on the correlation between R and E: $\hat{p}_{AS}\hat{p}_{SE}r_{RE} + \hat{p}_{AE}r_{RE} = (0.338)(0.178)(-0.026) + (0.227)(-0.026) = -0.0075$. As an exercise, you should determine how much of the correlation between abortion attitude and education (r_{AE}) is due to a direct effect, to an indirect effect, and to the correlation of education with religious intensity.

correlated effect—a component in the decomposition of a correlation coefficient that is due to a correlation among predetermined variables

By squaring the path coefficients from the residual variables, we can discover how much of the variance in the endogenous variables remains unexplained by the hypothesized causal process. Both values are very large: 88.0% of the variance in premarital sex attitude and 78.1% of abortion attitude cannot be explained by the causal structure. Clearly, this simple example does not come close to containing all the important social and psychological causes of these two attitudes. If we were to pursue this research, we would want to specify more elaborate models, including additional possible sources of abortion attitude.

Fully recursive path models—in which all possible one-way arrows between variables are present—will always exactly reproduce the observed correlations when the basic path theorem is applied. Because the causal sequence among variables can be arbitrarily reordered, the empirical estimates of path coefficients generally provide no definitive answer to the question of whether a causal model is valid. For example, if the locations of premarital sex attitude and abortion attitude were switched in Figure 11.3, we could still derive path coefficients for each arrow. Or, even more drastically, we could switch the places between the two predetermined variables and the two dependent measures and still generate path coefficients that would add up to the observed correlations. Clearly, the credibility of a path model cannot be based on statistical criteria alone.

A causal model must justify its specifications on nonstatistical grounds. In this text we have stressed the importance of theoretical understanding of social behavior in guiding empirical research. In organizing a causal model for path analysis, all the researcher's knowledge of social relationships, past empirical research, and logical deduction must be brought to bear. In specifying a causal sequence among variables, understanding their temporal order is often indispensable. For example, given that people's formal schooling is typically completed many years before the survey interview, we can plausibly treat this variable as temporally antecedent to the two current attitudes. Unless a causal analysis is firmly grounded in basic principles of social behavior, the resulting path model estimates can be no firmer than the foundation of a house built on sand.

11.3.7.   A Chain Path Model Example

We stated above that full recursive path models offer no statistical basis for their own rejection. Path models that are not fully recursive—that is, those in which some possible arrows are not present—do offer limited grounds for deciding whether a specific model fits the data. When some possible causal paths are hypothesized to be zero, the implied correlations (r'_{ij}) from the path model do not necessarily and often will not equal the observed correlations (r_{ij}). When such discrepancies occur, the analyst may conclude that the model was incorrectly specified as a representation of the causal process, unless the discrepancy is small enough to be caused by sampling fluctuation.

To illustrate, we will use data from the 1972-1974-1976 Survey Research Center's (SRC) panel study of American voters. A sample of voters was reinterviewed at two-year intervals about various issues and activities. One item asked respondents to rate their position on a seven-point scale from favoring school busing for racial integration to opposing busing. Among the simplest models of attitude causation through time is the chain model, where responses at time t depend solely on responses at the immediately preceding time, $t - 1$. (This property is called the **Markovian principle,** which maintains that history prior to time $t - 1$ has no causal impact on the present.)

Markovian principle— variables measured prior to time $t - 1$ have no causal impact on variables measured at time t

In path diagrammatic terms a **chain path model** for school busing attitude is shown in Figure 11.6. We assume that attitude toward busing in 1976 (Y_3) is caused by attitude toward busing in 1974 (Y_2) but not by attitude toward busing in 1972 (Y_1). And busing attitude in 1974 (Y_2) is assumed to be caused only by busing attitude in 1972. Figure 11.6 implies two structural equations:

chain path model— a causal model in which variables measured on the same sample at three or more times are depicted as the causes of their own subsequent values

$$Y_2 = p_{21}Y_1 + p_{2V}V$$
$$Y_3 = p_{32}Y_2 + p_{3U}U$$

FIGURE 11.6

Causal Diagram of Busing Attitudes, 1972–1976, with Estimated Path Coefficients

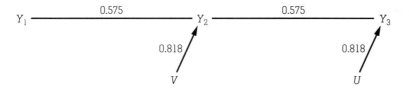

Y_1 = Attitude toward busing in 1972
Y_2 = Attitude toward busing in 1974
Y_3 = Attitude toward busing in 1976
Source: Survey Research Center, University of Michigan's panel study of American voters

Because these two equations are recursive, they can be estimated by the two beta coefficients obtained by regressing Y_2 on Y_1 and by regressing Y_3 on Y_2:

$$\hat{p}_{21} = \beta^*_{21}$$

$$\hat{p}_{2V} = \sqrt{1 - R^2_{2 \cdot 1}}$$

$$\hat{p}_{32} = \beta^*_{32}$$

$$\hat{p}_{3U} = \sqrt{1 - R^2_{3 \cdot 2}}$$

Table 11.4 shows the correlations among the three variables. Because beta weights are zero-order correlations in the case of a single independent variable, we have $\hat{p}_{21} = 0.575$, $\hat{p}_{2V} = 0.818$, $\hat{p}_{32} = 0.575$, and $\hat{p}_{3U} = 0.818$. Now we want to test whether the correlation implied between Y_1 and Y_3 equals the observed correlation (0.535). To determine the implied correlation, we follow the method used in section 11.3.4. We begin with

$$Y_3 = p_{32}Y_2 + p_{3U}U$$

Then we multiply this equation by Y_1, yielding:

$$Y_1Y_3 = p_{32}Y_1Y_2 + p_{3U}Y_1U$$

We sum both sides, distribute the summation, and divide by N:

$$\frac{\Sigma Y_1Y_3}{N} = \frac{p_{32}\Sigma Y_1Y_2}{N} + \frac{p_{3U}\Sigma Y_1U}{N}$$

TABLE 11.4

Correlation Matrix of Attitudes Toward Busing 1972–1976

	Y_1	Y_2	Y_3
Y_1: Attitude in 1972	1.000	0.575	0.535
Y_2: Attitude in 1974		1.000	0.575
Y_3: Attitude in 1976			1.000

Source: Survey Research Center, University of Michigan's panel study of American voters

Because we assume that $p_{Y_1U} = 0$, we have $\rho'_{13} = p_{32}\rho_{21} + 0 = p_{32}p_{21}$, because $p_{21} = \beta^*_{21} = \rho_{21}$. That is, the correlation between Y_1 and Y_3 implied by the causal model equals the product of the two paths, p_{32} and p_{21}. Now convince yourself that you get the same results by tracing paths between Y_3 and Y_1.

In the SRC data

$$r'_{13} = (0.575)(0.575) = 0.331$$

But as seen in Table 11.4, the actual observed correlation is 0.535. Hence, the large discrepancy between observed and implied correlations, $r_{13} - r'_{13} = 0.204$, suggests a **misspecification** of the causal model.

misspecification—a condition in which a structural equation or path model includes incorrect variables or excludes correct variables

A plausible alternative model for these three variables is shown in Figure 11.7. Here we assume a **lagged causal effect** from 1972 to 1976 attitude. (A lagged causal effect is also the same as a direct effect.) The two structural equations in this case are as follows:

lagged causal effect— direct effect of a variable measured prior to time $t -$ 1 on a variable measured at time t

$$Y_2 = p_{21}Y_1 + p_{2V}V$$
$$Y_3 = p_{31}Y_1 + p_{32}Y_2 + p_{3U}U$$

FIGURE 11.7
Causal Diagram of an Alternative Set of Relations Among Busing Attitudes, 1972–1976

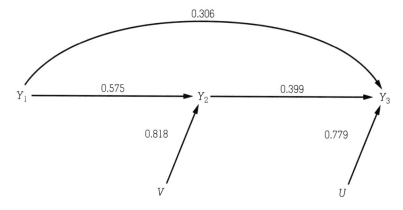

The estimates of the path coefficients are as follows:

$$\hat{p}_{21} = \beta^{*}_{21}$$

$$\hat{p}_{2V} = \sqrt{1 - R^{2}_{2\cdot1}}$$

$$\hat{p}_{31} = \beta^{*}_{31}$$

$$\hat{p}_{32} = \beta^{*}_{32}$$

$$\hat{p}_{3U} = \sqrt{1 - R^{2}_{3\cdot21}}$$

Using the data from Table 11.4, these estimates are shown in Figure 11.7. While the estimates look plausible, this model fits the observed correlations perfectly, because all three possible one-way paths are present.

This alternative is only one of several possible causal models that might account for the pattern of correlations over time. Other models could include additional independent variables, with correlated residual variables and measurement errors. Some of these techniques are considered in chapter 12, but here we have demonstrated that the simple causal chain must be rejected as the explanation of the observed pattern of covariation.

This chapter introduced the bare essentials of path analysis. We hope we have convinced you that causal inferences can be drawn from nonexperimental data if you have strong theoretical propositions. When you cannot conduct experiments, path models can be very useful for estimating presumed causal processes. As we suggested above, however, to avoid nonsensical results, you must pay close attention to meeting the assumptions of the model.

In the next and final chapter, we generalize the principles of path analysis to more general structural equation models, introducing techniques that allow for evaluating the goodness of fit of hypothesized models to observed variances and covariances.

Review of Key Concepts and Symbols

These key concepts and symbols are listed in the order of appearance in this chapter. Combined with the definitions in the margins, they will help you to review the material and can serve as a self-test for mastery of the concepts.

covariation
time order
nonspuriousness
causal diagram
exogenous variable
endogenous variable
direct effect
indirect effect
residual variable
probabilistic
deterministic
recursive model
nonrecursive model
path analysis

structural equation
path coefficient
decomposition
fundamental theorem of path
   analysis
correlated effect
Markovian principle
chain path model
misspecification
lagged causal effect
p_{ij}
$\hat{p}_{ij}$
ρ'_{ij}
r'_{ij}

PROBLEMS

General Problems

1. Rewrite this statement as a causal proposition: "Whenever an advanced industrial economy enters a period of economic recession of more than 6 months' duration within a year of a national election, the voters punish the party in control of the government by increasing their electoral support for the party out of power."

2. Diagram the causal process implied by these hypotheses:
   a. The higher a person's rank in a group, the greater that person's centrality.
   b. The more central a person is to a group, the greater that person's conformity to group norms.

c. The more central a person is to a group, the more influence that person has on group decisions.

d. The greater the conformity to group norms, the more influence a person has on group decisions.

3. In the following path equations, A, B, C, and D are observations and U and V are unobservables:

$$D = p_{DC}C + p_{DA}A + p_{DV}V$$
$$C = p_{CB}B + p_{CA}A + p_{CU}U$$

a. Derive the formula for the correlation between B and D in terms of path coefficients and correlations.

b. What are the direct effects of B on D?

4. Here is a path diagram in which H is the grade point average, J is teacher's encouragement, K is parental social status, and L is student's IQ:

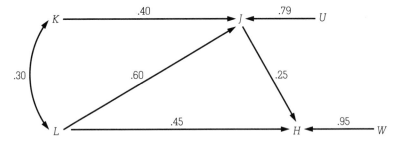

a. Does K or L have a larger indirect causal effect on H?

b. How much variance in J is explained by the linear combination of K and L?

5. Consider the following path diagram:

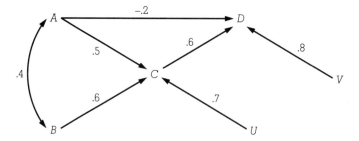

a. Does A or B have a larger indirect causal effect on D?

b. How much variance in D is explained by A, B, and C?

6. In a chain model where

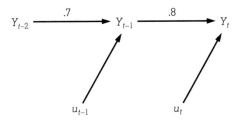

what is $r'_{t,t-2}$?

7. In the following causal diagram A is age at which respondent was first married, B is the social status of the family, C is current financial security, and D is marital happiness:

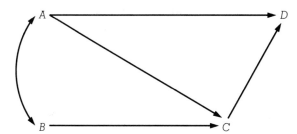

Write an equation in symbolic terms for the correlation between marital happiness and family social status, designating the portion that arises from causal connections and the portion due to mutual dependency.

8. Consider the following causal diagram:

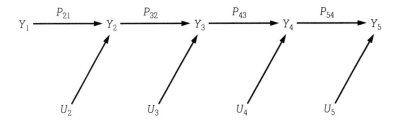

Assuming that all p_{ij} = 0.50, generate the matrix of correlations implied among the five variables.

9. For the causal relations in Problem 7, what is the correlation between B and D if the following values occur: r_{AB} = +0.44; p_{CB} = +0.60; p_{CA} = −0.10; p_{DC} = +0.35; and p_{DA} = +0.50? What is the correlation between A and D?

10. Consider the following causal diagram:

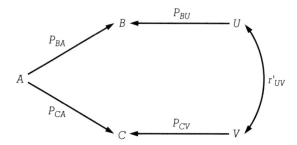

a. Prove that r'_{UV} = $r_{BC \cdot A}$ (i.e., the partial correlation between U and V, controlling for A).

b. If p_{BA} = 0.40, p_{CA} = 0.30, and r_{BC} = 0.15, what does r'_{UV} equal?

Problems Requiring the 1991 General Social Survey

11. Some political sociologists have argued that lower social status produces greater rigidity and intolerance in political thought and behavior. Test this idea by using an index of intolerance (INTOL) towards those opposed to churches and religion, created by summing responses to SPKATH (should not be allowed to make speeches), COLATH (should not be allowed to teach in a college), and LIBATH (book written by an atheist should be removed from public library). The path model to be estimated is as follows:

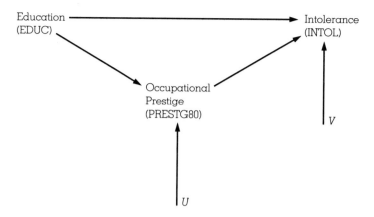

12. Estimate the following path model as an explanation of personal happiness:

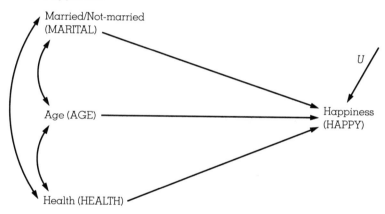

In estimating this model use the following recodes:
RECODE MARITAL (1=1)(ELSE=0).
RECODE HAPPY(1=3)(3=1).
RECODE HEALTH(1=4)(2=3)(3=2)(4=1).

13. Estimate the path coefficients of this causal model of status attainment among working persons:

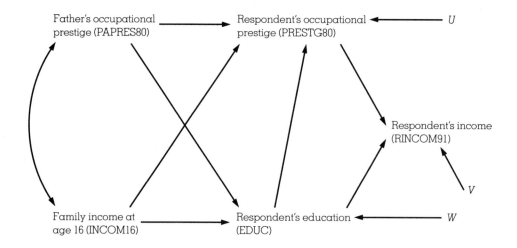

In estimating this model use the following recode:
RECODE RINCOM91(1=.5)(2=2)(3=3.5)(4=4.5)(5=5.5)(6=6.5)
(7=7.5)(8=9)(9=11.25)(10=13.75)(11=16.25)(12=18.75)(13=21.25)
(14=23.75)(15=27.5)(16=32.5)(17=37.5)(18=45)(19=55)(20=67.5)
(21=85)(0,22=99).

Problems Requiring Use of the U.S. States Data Set

14. Estimate the path coefficients for the following model:

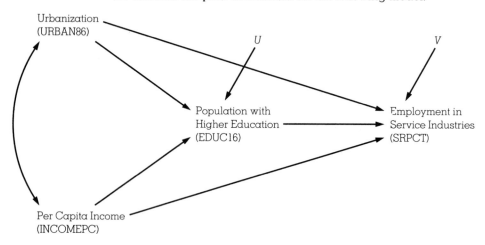

15. Estimate the path coefficients for the following model:

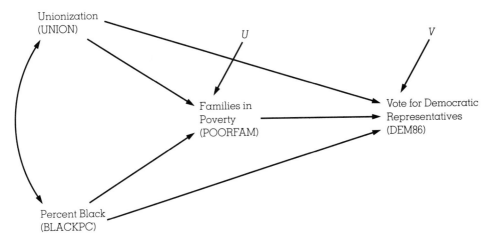

Statistics for Social Data Analysis

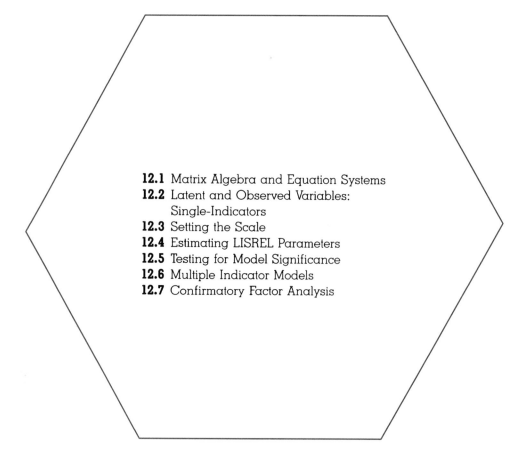

Structural Equation Models: LISREL

12

T his chapter concludes our presentation of statistics for social data analysis with an introduction to structural equation modeling and estimation. The techniques for analyzing multivariate relationships among systems of equations build directly on the path analysis methods of chapter 11. But they are far more comprehensive and flexible in their ability to link multiple, observed indicators to unmeasured causes; to make quantitative estimates of model parameters and their standard errors; to assess the overall fit of a model to data; and even to determine the equivalences of model parameters across several samples. Although these methods can be applied to even more complex problems, such as nonrecursive models that estimate reciprocal causal effects, this book's space constraints allow us only to explore a basic set of applications.

The particular structural equation method we examine is LISREL (LInear Structural RELations). It has been developed continuously since the 1960s by the Swedish statisticians Karl Jöreskog and Dag Sörbom and was most recently added as a special package to the mainframe version of SPSS. All our applications were performed with a personal computer version directly marketed by Jöreskog and Sörbom. Although other structural equation analysis programs are available, such as EQS, the widespread familiarity of the LISREL notation system definitely gives it the edge in preference.

443

Our presentation begins with a causal model that you now recognize as a recursive path diagram. As shown in the two diagrams in Figure 12.1, socioeconomic status and family status are

FIGURE 12.1A
Causal Model in Path Analysis Notation

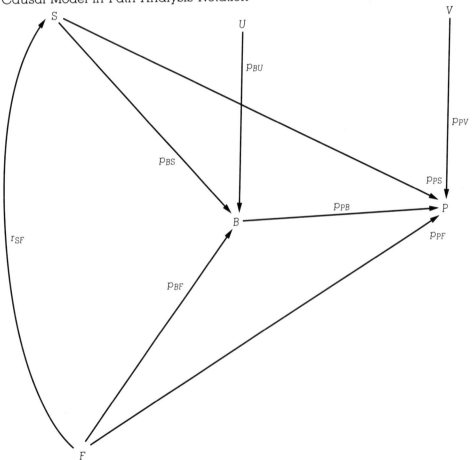

S = Socioeconomic Status
F = Family Status
B = Religious Belief
P = Religious Participation

FIGURE 12.1B

Structural Model in LISREL Notation

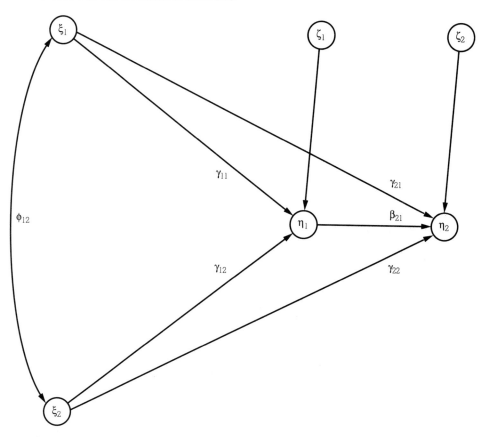

ξ_1 = Socioeconomic Status
ξ_2 = Family Status
η_1 = Religious Belief
η_2 = Religious Participation

predetermined causes of people's religious belief, with all three variables causing religious participation. This structural equation system is displayed both in path model notation (12.1A) and in the LISREL notation (12.1B). The specific example's notation is explained in detail in the next paragraph, while Box 12.1 summarizes all the LISREL symbols and gives their phonetic pronunciations. As

BOX 12.1   The LISREL Notation System

The following list gives the Greek and Roman character symbols, their pronunciations, and their uses in the LISREL system. Capitalized letters are designated by spelling their pronunciations in CAPITAL LETTERS:

Symbol	Name	Use
β	beta	Structural parameter linking endogenous variables
$\mathbf{B}$	BETA	Matrix of structural parameters linking endogenous variables
γ	gamma	Structural parameter linking exogenous to endogenous variables
Γ	GAMMA	Matrix of structural parameters linking exogenous to endogenous variables
δ	delta	Error term for exogenous structural variable indicator
ϵ	epsilon	Error term for endogenous structural variable indicator
ζ	zeta	Error term for endogenous structural variable
η	eta	Endogenous structural variable
Θ_δ	THETA-delta	Matrix of covariances among errors in exogenous variable indicators
Θ_ϵ	THETA-epsilon	Matrix of covariances among errors in endogenous variable indicators
λ	lambda	Factor loading for structural variable indicators
Λ_x	LAMBDA-x	Matrix of factor loadings for exogenous indicators
Λ_y	LAMBDA-y	Matrix of factor loadings for endogenous indicators
ξ	xi (ksi)	Exogenous structural variable
Σ	SIGMA	Matrix of expected covariances among observable indicators
ϕ	phi	Covariance among exogenous structural variables
Φ	PHI	Matrix of covariances among exogenous structural variables
ψ	psi	Covariance among error terms of endogenous structural variables
Ψ	PSI	Matrix of covariance among error terms of endogenous structural variables
$\mathbf{I}$	EYE	Identity matrix
$\mathbf{R}$	ARE	Matrix of residuals
$\mathbf{S}$	ESS	Matrix of observed covariances among observable indicators
x	eks	Observed indicator of exogenous structural variable
y	why	Observed indicator of endogenous structural variable

we proceed, this basic model will be elaborated, first using only single indicators of each variable, then considering multiple indicators.

In both path analysis and LISREL notation, a structural parameter has a double subscript that uniquely identifies the effect (first subscript) and the cause (second subscript) linked by an arrow. Unlike path analysis, LISREL notation clearly distinguishes between variables that are predetermined (exogenous), symbolized by xi (ξ_i), and variables that are determined within the model (endogenous), symbolized by eta (η_i). Consequently, the parameters attached to the causal arrows are of two types: a structural effect from exogenous variable j to endogenous variable i is denoted γ_{ij}, while an effect from one endogenous to a second endogenous variable is denoted β_{ij}. The correlation between a pair of exogenous variables is symbolized by phi (ϕ_{ij}). A residual variable is symbolized by zeta (ζ_i); but, unlike path analysis residual paths, LISREL has no notation for the effect of a zeta on an eta.

12.1 Matrix Algebra and Equation Systems

A LISREL structural equation system represents multivariate relations at two distinct levels of analysis: the conceptual model, considered in this section, and the measurement model, discussed in section 12.2. A **conceptual model** depicts causal relations among abstract terms that are not directly observable. Conceptual model equations can be written in two distinct formats. The first format, parallel to the path equations in chapter 11, presents each equation on a separate line. A dependent variable appears on the left-hand side of the equal sign, while the linear combinations of parameters and predictor variables appear on the right-hand side. Using this format, the causal model in Figure 12.1B is written in LISREL notation as follows:

conceptual model—a model that depicts causal relations among abstract terms that are not directly observable

$$\eta_1 = \gamma_{11}\xi_1 + \gamma_{12}\xi_2 + \zeta_1$$
$$\eta_2 = \beta_{21}\eta_1 + \gamma_{21}\xi_1 + \gamma_{22}\xi_2 + \zeta_2$$

Note that the endogenous variable η_1 appears both as an independent and as a dependent variable in separate equations. In fact, a complete representation of this system requires including *all* endogenous variables on the right-hand sides of both equations, with certain β_{ij}s set equal to 0 to show that they are hypothesized as fixed zero values:

$$\eta_1 = \phantom{\beta_{21}}0\eta_1 + 0\eta_2 + \gamma_{11}\xi_1 + \gamma_{12}\xi_2 + \zeta_1$$
$$\eta_2 = \beta_{21}\eta_1 + 0\eta_2 + \gamma_{21}\xi_1 + \gamma_{22}\xi_2 + \zeta_2$$

matrix algebra—algebra whose elements are matrices and whose operations include addition and multiplication of matrices

matrix—a rectangular array of mathematical elements in rows and columns that can be combined with other matrices or scalar values using ordinary arithmetic operations

An alternative representation of an equation system uses **matrix algebra.** Because instructions to the LISREL computer program use this format, you must become familiar with some basic matrix algebra principles. A **matrix** is a rectangular array of mathematical elements in rows and columns that can be combined with other matrices or scalar values using ordinary arithmetic operations, especially addition and multiplication. A full matrix contains elements inside brackets.

$$\begin{bmatrix} 7 & -2 & 6 \\ -3 & 22 & 8 \end{bmatrix}$$

If the matrix elements are symbols rather than numbers, then double subscripts identify each element's row and column location:

$$\begin{bmatrix} x_{11} & x_{12} & x_{13} \\ x_{21} & x_{22} & x_{23} \end{bmatrix}$$

More simply, an entire matrix is symbolized by a single capital letter in boldface type: **X.**

A given matrix has a specific **order,** reflecting the number of its rows and columns. A matrix with R rows and C columns has "order $R \times C$" (read "R by C"). Thus, matrix **X** above has order 2×3. The number of rows and columns is important, as this 3×2 matrix **Y** clearly reveals:

$$\begin{bmatrix} y_{11} & y_{12} \\ y_{21} & y_{22} \\ y_{31} & y_{32} \end{bmatrix}$$

vector—a special type of matrix that has only one row or column

One special type of matrix is a **vector,** which either has only a single row or a single column. Matrix **A** is a 1×4 row vector, while matrix **B** is a 4×1 column vector:

$$\mathbf{A} = [1\ 3\ 8\ 2] \qquad \mathbf{B} = \begin{bmatrix} 5 \\ -3 \\ 7 \\ 14 \end{bmatrix}$$

Another special matrix is a **square matrix,** with order $N \times N$. Matrix $\mathbf{C}$ is a square matrix of order 3×3:

square matrix—a matrix with an equal number of rows and columns

$$\mathbf{C} = \begin{bmatrix} 3 & 4 & 4 \\ 7 & 3 & 1 \\ 2 & 6 & 5 \end{bmatrix}$$

The **diagonal** of a square matrix consists of those elements whose row and column subscripts are the same. In matrix $\mathbf{C}$, the three diagonal elements are 3, 3, and 5. The **trace** of a matrix (symbolized by "tr") is the sum of the diagonal elements. Thus, $\mathrm{tr}(\mathbf{C})$ = 11. An **identity matrix** (symbolized $\mathbf{I}$) is a square matrix with ones in the diagonal and zeros in the off-diagonal. An $N \times N$ identity matrix has trace equal to N (i.e., the number of rows or columns). What is the trace of this 4×4 identity matrix $\mathbf{I}$?

diagonal—in a square matrix, those elements whose row and column subscripts are the same

trace—the sum of the diagonal elements in a square matrix

identity matrix—a square matrix with ones in the diagonal and zeros in the off-diagonal

$$\begin{bmatrix} 1 & 0 & 0 & 0 \\ 0 & 1 & 0 & 0 \\ 0 & 0 & 1 & 0 \\ 0 & 0 & 0 & 1 \end{bmatrix}$$

The **transpose** of a matrix is a matrix whose rows and columns have been interchanged, and hence its order is inverted. The transpose of $\mathbf{C}$ is indicated by a prime following the matrix symbol:

transpose—a matrix whose rows and columns have been interchanged (inverted order)

$$\mathbf{C}' = \begin{bmatrix} 3 & 7 & 2 \\ 4 & 3 & 6 \\ 4 & 1 & 5 \end{bmatrix}$$

Notice that the diagonal elements remain unchanged. In effect, transposition rotates the off-diagonal elements around a fixed diagonal axis.

Two matrices can be added if they have **conformability,** that is, have identical orders. Addition takes place element-wise, with each element of the resultant matrix as the sum of the corresponding pairs of elements in the original matrices. For example, $\mathbf{A} + \mathbf{B} = \mathbf{C}$:

conformability—a property of two matrices in which their orders are suitable for addition and/or for multiplication

$$\begin{bmatrix} 1 & 3 & 0 \\ -2 & 4 & 5 \\ 8 & 7 & -6 \end{bmatrix} + \begin{bmatrix} 2 & 1 & 3 \\ 2 & -6 & 0 \\ -3 & 1 & 4 \end{bmatrix} = \begin{bmatrix} 3 & 4 & 3 \\ 0 & -2 & 5 \\ 5 & 8 & -2 \end{bmatrix}$$

Two matrices are conformable for multiplication if the number of columns in the first matrix equals the number of rows in the second matrix. The order of the product matrix has the number of rows of the first matrix and the number of columns of the second matrix. Thus, if **X** is order 3 × 5 and **Y** is order 5 × 2, then the **XY** multiplication can be performed—the product has order 3 × 2. But, the **YX** multiplication cannot be performed. Matrix multiplication takes place element-wise as follows:

1. To find the element in the ith row, jth column of the product matrix, select the vector in the ith row of the first matrix and the vector in the jth column of the second matrix.
2. Next, multiply the corresponding pairs of elements in these two vectors (e.g., the first element of the row vector times the first element of the column vector; the second elements of both vectors; etc.).
3. Finally, sum these vector products. The result is the i,jth element of the product matrix.
4. Repeat steps 1–3 for every combination of i rows and j columns in the two matrices. Each product-sum is an element of the product matrix.

To illustrate, consider the following matrix multiplication:

$$\begin{bmatrix} 1 & 0 & -2 \\ 3 & 4 & 5 \end{bmatrix} \begin{bmatrix} 1 & 0 \\ 6 & -3 \\ 2 & 4 \end{bmatrix} =$$

$$\begin{bmatrix} (1)(1) + (0)(6) + (-2)(2) & (1)(0) + (0)(-3) + (-2)(4) \\ (3)(1) + (4)(6) + (5)(2) & (3)(0) + (4)(-3) + (5)(4) \end{bmatrix} = \begin{bmatrix} -3 & -8 \\ 37 & 8 \end{bmatrix}$$

Multiplying a matrix by a conformable identity matrix leaves the first matrix unchanged: **XI** = **X** and **IX** = **X**. The transpose of a product matrix equals the product of the transposes of the original matrices, in reverse order: **(AB)′** = **B′A′**.

The final matrix algebra feature that is important for LISREL is the concept of an **inverse** for a square matrix (i.e., with order

inverse—a matrix, when multiplied with another matrix, that produces the identity matrix

$N \times N$). The inverse of square matrix **Y** is symbolized by **Y**$^{-1}$ and has the property that their product, in either order, is an identity matrix: **YY**$^{-1}$ = **I** and **Y**$^{-1}$**Y** = **I**. For example:

$$\mathbf{YY^{-1}} = \begin{bmatrix} 2 & 0 & 0 \\ -4 & 1 & 0 \\ 5 & 0 & 1 \end{bmatrix} \begin{bmatrix} 0.5 & 0 & 0 \\ 2 & 1 & 0 \\ -2.5 & 0 & 1 \end{bmatrix} = \begin{bmatrix} 1 & 0 & 0 \\ 0 & 1 & 0 \\ 0 & 0 & 1 \end{bmatrix}$$

$$\mathbf{Y^{-1}Y} = \begin{bmatrix} 0.5 & 0 & 0 \\ 2 & 1 & 0 \\ -2.5 & 0 & 1 \end{bmatrix} \begin{bmatrix} 2 & 0 & 0 \\ -4 & 1 & 0 \\ 5 & 0 & 1 \end{bmatrix} = \begin{bmatrix} 1 & 0 & 0 \\ 0 & 1 & 0 \\ 0 & 0 & 1 \end{bmatrix}$$

Finding a matrix's inverse is a complex process that involves computing another matrix function called the determinant of a matrix. To indicate a matrix's determinant, its symbol is enclosed between vertical lines: $|Q|$. The procedures for computing determinants and inverses are not worth describing here. Whenever matrix inverses and determinants are required, the LISREL program calculates them.

These basic matrix algebra principles allow us to express any equation system for a causal model. Five matrices or vectors of parameters and variables are required for every LISREL **structural equation system.** For a system of M equations, the **eta vector (η)** is an $M \times 1$ vector of endogenous variables. The $M \times M$ **beta matrix (β)** contains the causal parameters linking all pairs of endogenous variables. The **xi vector (ξ)** is a $K \times 1$ vector, where K is the number of exogenous variables. The $M \times K$ **gamma matrix (Γ)** contains the causal parameters that link endogenous variables to exogenous variables. And the $M \times 1$ **zeta vector (ζ)** contains the error terms for each endogenous variable. The general structural equation that combines these five matrices is as follows:

$$\eta = \beta\eta + \Gamma\xi + \zeta$$

To write the matrix algebra equation system for a specific model, two sets of restrictions must be placed on this general equation. First, the orders of all five fundamental matrices and vectors must be conformable for multiplication and addition in the sequence shown by the general equation. Second, each effect parameter in the β and Γ matrices must either be set to zero (indicating that its value is not to be estimated) or designated by a subscripted Greek

structural equation system—five matrices or vectors of parameters and variables that are required for LISREL

eta vector—the $M \times 1$ vector of endogenous variables

beta matrix—matrix containing the causal parameters that link all pairs of endogenous variables

xi vector—the $K \times 1$ vector, where K is the number of exogenous variables

gamma matrix—matrix containing the causal parameters that link endogenous variables to exogenous variables

zeta vector—the $M \times 1$ vector of error terms for each endogenous variable

letter (indicating that LISREL is to estimate its value). For the two-equation causal system in Figure 12.1B, where $M = 2$ and $K = 2$, the specific restrictions yield the following matrix algebra equation:

$$\begin{bmatrix} \eta_1 \\ \eta_2 \end{bmatrix} = \begin{bmatrix} 0 & 0 \\ \beta_{21} & 0 \end{bmatrix} \begin{bmatrix} \eta_1 \\ \eta_2 \end{bmatrix} + \begin{bmatrix} \gamma_{11} & \gamma_{12} \\ \gamma_{21} & \gamma_{22} \end{bmatrix} \begin{bmatrix} \xi_1 \\ \xi_2 \end{bmatrix} + \begin{bmatrix} \zeta_1 \\ \zeta_2 \end{bmatrix}$$

When these multiplications and additions are carried out, the result is identical to the pair of equations at the beginning of this section:

$$\eta_1 = 0\eta_1 + 0\eta_2 + \gamma_{11}\xi_1 + \gamma_{12}\xi_2 + \zeta_1$$
$$\eta_2 = \beta_{21}\eta_1 + 0\eta_2 + \gamma_{21}\xi_1 + \gamma_{22}\xi_2 + \zeta_2$$

Two other matrices are important for LISREL structural equations. Consider the errors in the etas, the ζs. When the $M \times 1$ zeta vector is multiplied by its $1 \times M$ transpose, the result is a square $M \times M$ **psi matrix** (Ψ) containing the variances of each error term (in the diagonal elements) and their covariances (in the off-diagonal elements). In general matrix algebra notation,

psi matrix—matrix containing the variances of each error term (in the diagonal elements) and their covariances (in the off-diagonal elements)

$$\zeta\zeta' = \Psi$$

Figure 12.1B shows that the two errors are uncorrelated (i.e., no curved double-headed arrow connects ζ_1 to ζ_2, consistent with BLUE assumptions). Therefore, the 2×1 zeta vector multiplied by its 1×2 transpose produces a 2×2 psi matrix, whose values are as follows:

$$\begin{bmatrix} \zeta_1 \\ \zeta_2 \end{bmatrix} \begin{bmatrix} \zeta'_1 & \zeta'_2 \end{bmatrix} = \begin{bmatrix} \zeta_1\zeta'_1 & \zeta_1\zeta'_2 \\ \zeta_2\zeta'_1 & \zeta_2\zeta'_2 \end{bmatrix} = \begin{bmatrix} \Psi_{11} & \Psi_{12} \\ \Psi_{21} & \Psi_{22} \end{bmatrix} = \begin{bmatrix} \Psi_{11} & 0 \\ 0 & \Psi_{22} \end{bmatrix}$$

A second important matrix at the structural level shows the variances and covariances among the K predetermined variables, the xis. When the $K \times 1$ xi vector is multiplied by its $1 \times K$ transpose, it produces a $K \times K$ **phi matrix** (Φ) containing the variances (diagonal elements) and covariances (off-diagonal elements). In general matrix algebra notation,

phi matrix—matrix containing the variances of the exogenous variables in the diagonal elements and the covariances in the off-diagonal elements

$$\xi\xi' = \Phi$$

In the example,

$$\begin{bmatrix} \xi_1 \\ \xi_2 \end{bmatrix} [\xi_1' \ \xi_2'] = \begin{bmatrix} \phi_{11} & \phi_{12} \\ \phi_{21} & \phi_{21} \end{bmatrix}$$

Because Figure 12.1B shows that ξ_1 and ξ_2 are correlated, the off-diagonal elements are not constrained to equal zero. But, since the covariance of variables A and B equals the covariance of B and A, the Φ matrix actually has only $(K^2 + K)/2$ unique parameters. Thus, for our two-equation system, the elements in the phi matrix can be written to reflect its symmetry around the diagonal:

$$\begin{bmatrix} \phi_{11} & \phi_{12} \\ \phi_{12} & \phi_{21} \end{bmatrix}$$

This section has shown how the structural relations among variables in a causal model can be expressed in diagrams, by sets of equations, and with matrix algebra. The central importance of the matrix algebra format is that the LISREL computer program only understands instructions given to it in this notation, as will become apparent in the following sections.

12.2 Latent and Observed Variables: Single-Indicators

The conceptual model discussed in section 12.1 comprises only half the LISREL approach to structural equations. Those variables and parameters refer to an abstract level of analysis that cannot be directly observed and measured. Therefore, in order to estimate the numerical values of the parameters from empirical data, we must link the unobserved conceptual variables to observable indicators. An example may make clearer this distinction between conceptually abstract and observable levels of analysis. In the conceptual causal model in Figure 12.1A, we depict a person's religious belief as intervening between the two predetermined variables, socioeconomic status and family status, and the ultimate dependent variable, religious participation. We really cannot directly observe and measure anyone's "true values" on these four concepts, which are presumably hidden from external view (and, indeed, may not even be fully accessible to the subject). Rather, we can only measure overt behaviors or verbal utterances that may more or less accurately reflect the unobservable construct. Further, our measuring instruments themselves are subject to errors, such as faulty respondent memory or inaccurate interviewer recording of responses to survey questions.

The 1987 GSS collected data from 840 respondents that provide plausible empirical indicators for each concept. (The 1991 GSS did not ask all the items used in this example.) Religious belief is operationalized by, "Which comes closest to describing your feelings about the Bible?" Responses offered were 3 = "The Bible is the actual Word of God and is to be taken literally, word for word"; 2 = "The Bible is the inspired Word of God but not every word should be taken literally, word for word"; and 1 = "The Bible is an ancient book of fables, legends, history, and moral precepts recorded by man." Socioeconomic status is operationalized by education in completed years of formal schooling, ranging from 0 to 20. Respondent's family status is operationalized by the number of children ever born, ranging from 0 to 8 or more. Religious participation is measured as church attendance by, "How often do you attend religious services?" Responses are recorded on a nine-point scale from 0 = "never" to 8 = "several times a week." Below, we consider other similar indicators, but we initially analyze each item as the sole indicator of an unobserved concept.

The top panel of Table 12.1 displays a square matrix of sample correlations and standard deviations for these four indicators. Because LISREL bases its analysis on **S,** a matrix of variances and covariances among the observed variables, the bottom panel of Table 12.1 contains these values. They were calculated from the correlations and standard deviations, using the formula in section 6.3.3 (on page 209): $s_{XY} = r_{XY}s_Xs_Y$. LISREL can also convert a correlation matrix and vector of standard deviations into a matrix of covariations. Note that the covariances on the diagonal are actually each variable's variances (i.e., squared standard deviations), because $r_{XX} = 1.00$. Thus, such an **S** matrix is often called the observed **variance-covariance matrix.**

variance-covariance matrix—a square matrix containing the variances (on the diagonal) and covariances (off the diagonal) of the observed indicators in a LISREL model

Measurement theory depicts the observed responses as arising from two sources, neither directly observable: the respondent's "true" score and an error component. In causal diagram and equation form, respondent i's measured score on variable X is the sum of these two components:

$$\text{True}_i \rightarrow X_i \leftarrow \text{Error}_i$$
$$X_i = T_i + e_i$$

TABLE 12.1

Correlation and Covariance Matrices Among Four Observed Variables ($N = 840$)

	x_1	x_2	y_1	y_2
Correlation Matrix				
x_1 Education	1.00	−.31	−.36	.03
x_2 Children Ever Born	−.31	1.00	.18	.17
y_1 Bible Belief	−.36	.18	1.00	.31
y_2 Church Attendance	.03	.17	.31	1.00
Standard Deviation	3.12	1.81	.69	2.56
Covariance Matrix				
x_1 Education	9.71	−1.71	−.77	.20
x_2 Children Ever Born	−1.72	3.26	.23	.80
y_1 Bible Belief	−.77	.23	.48	.54
y_2 Church Attendance	.20	.80	.54	6.53

Source: 1987 General Social Survey

Across repeated measurements of variable X for a single respondent, the errors are assumed to be normally distributed around a mean of zero. In other words, while some measured scores are higher than the true score and some are below, these deviations around the true score should cancel one another out. Therefore, the expected value (mean) of the measured scores equals respondent i's true score, that is, $E(X_i) = \overline{X}_i = T_i$. Further, because an error term is assumed to be uncorrelated with its true score, both components make unique contributions to the variance of the observed scores in a population:

$$\sigma_X^2 = \sigma_T^2 + \sigma_e^2$$

These basic principles of measurement theory are embedded in the LISREL approach to structural equation modeling. Two sets of equations comprising the **measurement model** link each observed indicator to the unobserved variables in the structural model. An indicator of the ith endogenous variable (eta) is assigned the symbol y_i. In general matrix algebra notation, the measurement equation is

measurement model—
two sets of equations that link each observed indicator to the unobserved variables in the structural model

$$Y = \Lambda_y \eta + \epsilon$$

lambda-y matrix—matrix containing parameters for ys that show how strongly each y_i indicator is affected by unobserved etas

epsilon vector—vector containing the unique error terms for each observed y_i indicator

The **lambda-y matrix** (Λ_y) for the ys contains parameters that show how strongly each y_i indicator is affected by unobserved etas. The **epsilon vector** (ϵ) contains the unique error terms for each observed y_i indicator. In our example, which has only a single indicator for each endogenous variable:

$$\begin{bmatrix} y_1 \\ y_2 \end{bmatrix} = \begin{bmatrix} \lambda_{11} & 0 \\ 0 & \lambda_{22} \end{bmatrix} \begin{bmatrix} \eta_1 \\ \eta_2 \end{bmatrix} + \begin{bmatrix} \epsilon_1 \\ \epsilon_2 \end{bmatrix}$$

Each y_i indicator "loads" on only one of the two etas and also has a unique epsilon error term. Thus, y_1, belief in the Bible as God's Word, is the indicator of η_1, religious belief and λ_{11} is the parameter that links the empirical indicator to the abstract concept.

The second set of measurement equations is constructed in parallel fashion. An indicator of the ith exogenous variable (xi) is assigned the symbol x_i. In general matrix algebra notation, the measurement equation is

$$X = \Lambda_x \xi + \delta$$

lambda-x matrix—matrix containing parameters for xs that show how strongly each x_i indicator is affected by unobserved xis

delta vector—vector containing the unique error terms for each observed x_i indicator

The **lambda-x matrix** (Λ_x) for the xs contains parameters that show how strongly each x_i indicator is affected by the unobserved xis. The **delta vector** (δ) contains the unique error terms for each observed x_i indicator. Because our example uses only a single indicator for each exogenous variable,

$$\begin{bmatrix} x_1 \\ x_2 \end{bmatrix} = \begin{bmatrix} \lambda_{11} & 0 \\ 0 & \lambda_{22} \end{bmatrix} \begin{bmatrix} \xi_1 \\ \xi_2 \end{bmatrix} + \begin{bmatrix} \delta_1 \\ \delta_2 \end{bmatrix}$$

For example, x_2, respondent's family status, is linked via λ_{22} to ξ_2, the unobservable family status concept, with error term δ_2. Each x_i indicator loads on only one of the two xis and has a unique delta error term. To avoid confusion, we do not superscript the individual lambda coefficients with x or y in the two sets of measurement equations, but the distinction between lambda-x and lambda-y should be clear in each context.

theta delta matrix—matrix containing the errors of the xs

If the two $M \times 1$ error term vectors are each multiplied by their transposes, two resultant $M \times M$ matrices contain the variances (on the diagonal) and covariances (off-diagonal elements) of the measurement model errors. The **theta delta matrix** (Θ_δ) contains the errors of the *x*s, and the **theta epsilon matrix** ($\mathbf{\Theta}_\epsilon$) shows the errors of the *y*s. In general matrix algebra terms,

theta epsilon matrix— matrix containing the errors of the *y*s

$$\mathbf{\delta\delta'} = \mathbf{\Theta}_\delta \text{ and } \mathbf{\epsilon\epsilon'} = \mathbf{\Theta}_\epsilon$$

In our example, which does not allow the pairs of exogenous and endogenous error terms to be correlated, these two error matrices are as follows:

$$\mathbf{\Theta}_\delta = \begin{bmatrix} \theta_{\delta_1} & 0 \\ 0 & \theta_{\delta_2} \end{bmatrix} \text{ and } \mathbf{\Theta}_\epsilon = \begin{bmatrix} \theta_{\epsilon_1} & 0 \\ 0 & \theta_{\epsilon_2} \end{bmatrix}$$

Figure 12.2 combines both the conceptual model and measurement model into a single causal diagram. The unobservable conceptual variables are represented inside circles and the four observable empirical indicators are shown inside squares. A version of the fundamental path theorem presented in section 11.3.4 (on page 422) can be applied to the eight fundamental LISREL parameter matrices—$\mathbf{\Lambda}_x$, $\mathbf{\Lambda}_y$, $\mathbf{\Phi}$, $\mathbf{\Psi}$, $\mathbf{\beta}$, $\mathbf{\Gamma}$, $\mathbf{\Theta}_\delta$, and $\mathbf{\Theta}_\epsilon$—to compute the **sigma matrix** ($\mathbf{\Sigma}$), showing the implied variances and covariances among the *y*s and the *x*s for any LISREL model. If the indicators are ordered from y_1 to y_p followed by x_1 to x_q, then the $\mathbf{\Sigma}$ matrix consists of four submatrices (quadrants) showing the expected relationships among the *y*s, among the *x*s, and of the *y*s with the *x*s:

sigma matrix— matrix showing the implied variances and covariances among the *y*s and *x*s for a LISREL model

$$\mathbf{\Sigma} = \begin{bmatrix} \text{Covariances among the } ys & \text{Covariances between the } ys \text{ and the } xs \\ \text{Covariances between the } xs \text{ and the } ys & \text{Covariances among the } xs \end{bmatrix}$$

Given the symmetric nature of variance-covariance matrices, the lower-left and upper-right quadrants are transposes of one another. For *p* indicators of the *y*s and *q* indicators of the *x*s, $\mathbf{\Sigma}$ has exactly $((p + q)^2 + p + q)/2$ independent pieces of information from which to estimate the model's parameters. Thus, with $y = 2$ and $x = 2$, Table 12.1 contains $(2 + 2)^2 + 2 + 2)/2 = 10$ unique variances and covariances.

Without going into the details of $\mathbf{\Sigma}$'s derivation, the general formulas in each submatrix show how the expected variances and

FIGURE 12.2
Structural and Measurement Models in LISREL Notation

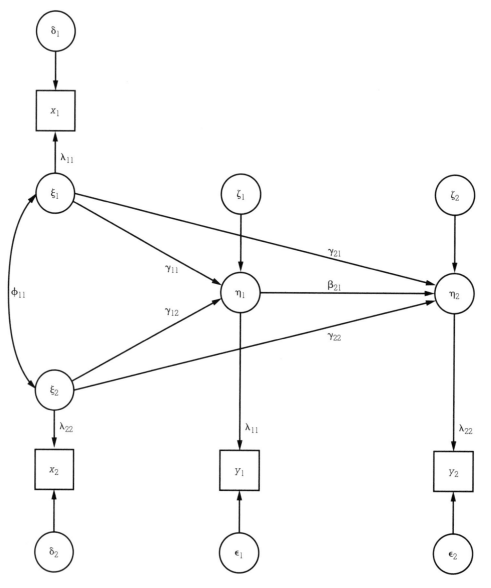

ξ_1 = Socioeconomic Status x_1 = Education
ξ_2 = Family Status x_2 = Children Born
η_1 = Religious Belief y_1 = Belief in Bible
η_2 = Religious Participation y_2 = Church Attendance

covariances are decomposed into the eight fundamental LISREL parameter matrices:

$$\Sigma = \left[\begin{array}{c|c} \Lambda_y[(I - B)^{-1}(\Gamma\Phi\Gamma' + \Psi)(I - B')^{-1}]\Lambda'_y + \Theta_\epsilon & \Lambda_y(I - B)^{-1}\Gamma\Phi\Lambda'_x \\ \hline \Lambda_x\Phi\Gamma'(I - B')^{-1}\Lambda'_y & \Lambda_x\Phi\Lambda'_x + \Theta_\delta \end{array} \right]$$

Fortunately, the LISREL computer program takes care of all calculations necessary to solve this formidable set of equations! In section 12.4 we will discuss how LISREL uses the observed variance-covariance matrix, **S,** and the eight fundamental parameter matrices for a specific model to compute an expected variance-covariance matrix, **Σ.** These two matrices are then compared to assess the accuracy of the model's fit to the observed data. But we must first describe how to set a metric scale for the unobserved variables in the conceptual model.

12.3   Setting the Scale

Although both the *xs* and *ys* in the measurement model have scales whose units are determined by the procedures used to collect the data, neither the xis nor the etas in the conceptual model have definite scales. As a result, efforts to solve the LISREL equations for parameter estimates will not yield solutions. Indeed, the LISREL program will reject any effort to analyze the data unless the researcher provides scales for all conceptual variables. Two approaches to setting the metrics are possible:

1. Assume that each xi and eta is standardized (i.e., has zero mean and unit variance).
2. Assume that each unobserved variable has the same scale as one of its indicators.

The first scaling approach requires instructing LISREL to set the diagonal entries in the **Φ** matrix (i.e., their variances) and ηs equal to 1.00. This procedures poses no problems for the ϕ_{ii} values. But section 12.1 showed that the expected values of the η_{ii} are functions of both the beta and gamma parameters to be estimated from the data and, hence, they cannot be given arbitrary values. Therefore, the second approach is preferred to setting measurement units for both types of unobserved concepts. The most convenient way is to fix a single indicator of each xi and eta to have unit value. That is, one λ-x or λ-y for each xi or eta, respectively, is set equal to 1.00. Thus, each xi or eta is given the same scale as its fixed indicator. If every xi and eta has only a single indicator, as is the case in our example, then all unobserved variables in the conceptual model will be identical to their indicators in the measurement model. However, as discussed later in section 12.6, when several indicators are available for each unobserved variable, only one λ-x or λ-y is set equal to 1.00 in order to fix the metric, leaving the other indicators free to be estimated.

In our four-indicator example each λ-x parameter is fixed to 1.00, resulting in a Λ_x matrix that is an identity matrix:

$$\begin{bmatrix} y_1 \\ y_2 \end{bmatrix} = \begin{bmatrix} 1 & 0 \\ 0 & 1 \end{bmatrix} \begin{bmatrix} \eta_1 \\ \eta_2 \end{bmatrix} + \begin{bmatrix} \epsilon_1 \\ \epsilon_2 \end{bmatrix}$$

Similarly, fixing each λ-y parameter to 1.00 results in an identity matrix for Λ_y:

$$\begin{bmatrix} x_1 \\ x_2 \end{bmatrix} = \begin{bmatrix} 1 & 0 \\ 0 & 1 \end{bmatrix} \begin{bmatrix} \xi_1 \\ \xi_2 \end{bmatrix} + \begin{bmatrix} \delta_1 \\ \delta_2 \end{bmatrix}$$

Because the variances of an unobserved variable and its single indicator are equal ($\sigma^2_{x_i} = \sigma^2_{\xi_i}$ and $\sigma^2_{y_i} = \sigma^2_{\eta_i}$), then the error variances in the four equations above must each be zero. That is, for the xs and the ξs:

$$\sigma^2_{x_i} = \sigma^2_{\xi_i} + \sigma^2_{\delta_i}$$
$$\sigma^2_{x_i} - \sigma^2_{\xi_i} = \sigma^2_{\delta_i}$$

$$0 = \sigma^2_{\delta_i}$$

Similarly, for the ys and the ηs:

$$\sigma^2_{y_i} = \sigma^2_{\eta_i} + \sigma^2_{\epsilon_i}$$
$$\sigma^2_{y_i} - \sigma^2_{\eta_i} = \sigma^2_{\epsilon_i}$$
$$0 = \sigma^2_{\epsilon_i}$$

Thus, the conceptual model and the measurement model are identical when each unobserved concept is represented by a single, perfectly measured, indicator. Only when we examine multiple-indicator models will this identity between LISREL's two levels of analysis break down.

12.4   Estimating LISREL Parameters

We have presented enough of the general LISREL approach and our specific example to turn next to the methods for estimating model parameters. We do not present a detailed description of the LISREL instructions necessary to generate the computer output. Jöreskog and Sörbom's *LISREL 7: A Guide to the Program and Applications* (1989) offers a wealth of detail that we cannot summarize here. Instead, we give a nontechnical overview of the LISREL estimation procedures, model identification, and the results for our example.

12.4.1.   Iterative Routines

A researcher inputs the sample variance-covariance matrix (**S**) for the observed indicators and instructs the LISREL program about which parameters are fixed and which are to be estimated. LISREL has several estimation **algorithms,** or computer routines, available depending on various characteristics of the data and model to be estimated. The most commonly used algorithm is the maximum likelihood estimation (MLE), which chapter 9 described for logistic regression (see page 342). MLE assumes multivariate normality, that is, the kth parameter in the model has a normalized sampling distribution at all values of the other parameters. Taking the input **S,** LISREL's MLE routine proceeds iteratively, that is, through a series of successively improved approximations, to generate estimates for the eight fundamental parameter matrices that make the expected variance-covariance matrix Σ as close to **S** as possible. When improvement on a successive step is smaller than a specified amount, the estimation routine stops and LISREL prints the results.

algorithm — computer routine

A **residual matrix** (**R**) reveals how closely the model's estimated parameters reproduce the variances and covariances among the observed x and y indicators:

$$\mathbf{R} = \mathbf{S} - \Sigma$$

residual matrix — matrix that reveals how closely a LISREL model's estimated parameters reproduce the variances and covariances among the x and y indicators

fitting function—function
that compares the
observed to the expected
variance-covariance
matrices

The MLE algorithm finds the best available solution to the
LISREL equations by minimizing a **fitting function (F).** The formula
for this function, which compares the observed to the expected
variance-covariance matrices, uses the logs of matrix determinants
and traces:

$$F(\mathbf{S},\mathbf{\Sigma}) = \log|\mathbf{\Sigma}| + \text{tr}\,(\mathbf{S}\mathbf{\Sigma}^{-1}) - \log|\mathbf{S}| + (p + q)$$

where p is the number of x indicators and q is the number of y
indicators (i.e., $p + q$ equals the number of rows or columns in the
variance-covariance matrix). If the model's $\mathbf{\Sigma}$ exactly reproduces
the input $\mathbf{S}$, then the value of F equals zero (because the trace of an
identity matrix equals the number of its rows or columns). More
typically, a model's parameters will not perfectly reproduce the
observed data, so F is some positive value. The smaller the F, the
better the fit that the expected parameters make to the observed
variances and covariances. Section 12.5 discusses some
procedures for assessing how close is the fit between the $\mathbf{S}$ and $\mathbf{\Sigma}$.

12.4.2   Identification of Models

identified—unique
parameter values in a
structural equation model

For a LISREL model to be estimated, all of its specified parameters
must be **identified,** that is, their values must be unique. Although
one set of values for the eight fundamental parameter matrices may
generate a given expected variance-covariance matrix, a different
set of parameter estimates may also produce the same $\mathbf{\Sigma}$. In such a
situation, these two sets of parameters are said to be *equivalent*,
and hence at least some of the model parameters are not identified.
In any given LISREL analysis the status of different parameters
may vary. Some may be identified while others may not be
identified. But, for the entire model to be identified, all parameters
must be identified. As long as a single parameter is not identified,
the entire model remains not identified and no unique solution is
possible.

The *necessary* condition for identification is easily stated: Given
p indicators of the xis and q indicators of the etas, a model may not
specify more than $t = \dfrac{1}{2}(p + q)(p + q + 1)$ free parameters to be
estimated. Thus, in our four-indicator example (two xs and two ys),
at most 10 parameters are free to vary. All other parameters must be
given fixed values by the researcher (for example, by instructing
LISREL to set them equal to 0 or to 1).

However, the necessary condition cannot be met with just any arbitrary set of *t* free parameters. Only a proper combination of free and fixed values that meets a *sufficiency condition* will enable LISREL to generate meaningful estimates for a specific model. Earlier approaches to model identification advocated that, before submitting instructions to the LISREL program, a researcher should ascertain by laborious hand calculations whether the sufficient conditions for identification of every parameter were met. And, whenever even a small change in model specification was made, the identification status of all model parameters should then be reestablished. But this goal proved unattainable except for some special classes of LISREL models. And, as Jöreskog and Sörbom commented, " . . . the conditions that have been proposed are almost impossible to verify in practice" (1989, p. 17).

Current practice among researchers is to work interactively with LISREL to produce identifiable models. Most researchers begin their analyses by specifying a model for their data that restricts many more parameters than the minimum required by the necessary conditions. LISREL then checks the so-called **information matrix** (a second-order derivative of the fitting function) to determine whether a specification meets identification criteria. If a model is poorly conditioned, the information matrix will be *singular* and LISREL will not generate any parameter estimates. However, if a model is identified, the information matrix will almost certainly have a *positive definite* condition. By tinkering on successive computer runs with a model's fixed and free parameters, a researcher usually can find a version that is identified. Then using other LISREL-generated information, particularly the *modification indices*, previously fixed parameters can be freed and the model reestimated to improve its fit to the observed data. One fortunate aspect of all single-indicator recursive models, such as our initial example, is that they are always exactly identified. Hence, we proceed directly in the next subsection to show its parameter estimates.

information matrix—a second-order derivative of the fitting function

12.4.3. Standardizing Parameters

In our discussions of bivariate and multivariate regression (section 6.4 and section 8.1) and path analysis (section 11.3), we pointed out that the effects of the independent variables on a dependent variable could be measured in two forms: metric and standardized coefficients. LISREL solutions also can represent predictor variables' effects in both standardized and unstandardized forms. Because a model consists of both structural and measurement equations, standardization may be done separately at both levels of analysis. In an unstandardized maximum likelihood solution, each unobserved η or ξ variable obtains its metric scale from that observed indicator whose λ is set equal to 1.0 (see section 12.3). Hence, an unstandardized solution yields beta and gamma parameter estimates that can only be interpreted in terms of the indicator scale units. A γ_{ij} parameter means that a one-unit difference in exogenous variable ξ_j produces a γ_{ij}-unit change in endogenous variable η_i, holding other variables in the equation constant. Similarly, a β_{kl} indicates that a one-unit difference in the endogenous variable η_l produces a β_{kl}-unit change in endogenous variable η_k.

Comparing effects among unstandardized variables is difficult when the various indicators have different scales, for example, education measured on a 20-year scale and belief in the Bible with a three-point scale. Standardized LISREL solutions facilitate judgments about the relative importance of predictor variables by using a common scale based on standard deviations units. Three standardization procedures are available:

1. Standardizing only the observed x- and y-indicators
2. Standardizing only the unobserved η and ξ variables
3. Standardizing *both* the indicators and the latent variables.

The easiest way to standardize only the x- and y-indicators is to omit the vector of standard deviations from the **S** matrix that is submitted to the LISREL program, preventing it from creating a variance-covariance matrix. That is, only a matrix of correlations among the indicators is analyzed, which are the products of pairs of standardized variables (Z scores), as demonstrated in Section 6.3.4 (on page 210). The problem with standardizing only the indicators is that no scale is provided for the unobserved variables, so the beta and gamma coefficients cannot easily be interpreted.

Standardizing only the unobserved η and ξ variables involves rescaling the etas and xis to have unit variances (i.e., $\sigma_\eta^2 = \sigma_\xi^2 = 1.0$), while leaving the indicators still in their original metrics. A **standardized solution** can be computed only after obtaining the initial unstandardized LISREL solution to a model, because ele-

standardized solution— etas and xis have unit variances, while the indicators are still in their original metrics

ments from the computed Σ matrix rather than the observed S matrix are used. First, estimated standard deviations for the β, Γ, Φ, and Ψ matrices are calculated. Then, each unstandardized coefficient is transformed to its standardized value by multiplying by the ratio of that independent variable's standard deviation to the dependent variable's standard deviation. For example, in Figure 12.3, the unstandardized beta coefficient for religious belief's effect on religious participation is 1.29. The estimated standard deviations for religious belief and religious participation are 0.69 and 2.56, respectively. Hence, the standardized beta coefficient is

$$\beta_{ij}^* = \beta_{ij}\left(\frac{\sigma_j}{\sigma_i}\right) = 1.29\left(\frac{.69}{2.56}\right) = 0.35$$

The third approach to standardization, the **completely standardized solution,** involves additional transformations of the initial LISREL solution. First, the standard deviations for the Λ_x, Λ_y, Θ_δ, and Θ_ϵ matrices are also calculated. Then, these standard deviations or their reciprocals are used as scale factors to compute the standardized values of the lambda-*x*, lambda-*y*, theta-epsilon, and theta-delta parameters. Thus, both latent concepts and observable indicators are standardized, and all parameters can readily be interpreted in terms of the effects of standard units of one variable on another. In the case where each unobserved variable in the structural equation model is represented by a single observable indicator in the measurement model, the completely standardized solution is identical to the standardized solution. However, in the multiple-indicator case considered in section 12.6, these two standardization procedures do not yield identical results. Because of the ease with which LISREL parameters from the completely standardized solution can be interpreted at both levels of analysis, we recommend using these values to the exclusion of the other two standardization methods.

completely standardized solution—all observed and unobserved variables are standardized and parameters are expressed in standard deviation units

Figure 12.3 displays both the unstandardized metric estimates and the completely standardized coefficients for our causal model with single indicators. All effects are significant at the $\alpha = .05$ level or lower. Higher socioeconomic status decreases religious belief (the standardized γ_{11} value is -0.34 standard deviation units), while family status increases religious belief ($\gamma_{12} = 0.08$). In turn, higher religious belief raises the level of religious participation ($\beta_{21} = 0.35$), as do the direct effects of socioeconomic status ($\gamma_{21} = 0.20$) and family status ($\gamma_{22} = 0.17$). However, a substantial negative indirect

FIGURE 12.3
Parameters Estimates for Model in Figure 12.2

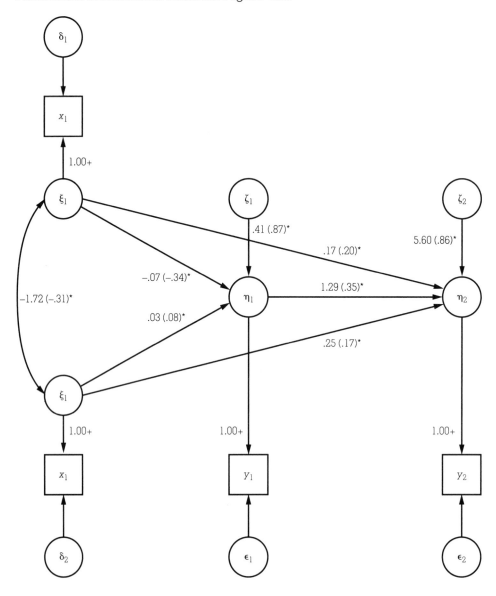

+ = Fixed Coefficient
*$p < .05$
Completely standardized values in parentheses

causal effect of socioeconomic status on religious participation operates through religious belief (i.e., $\gamma_{11}\beta_{21} = (-0.34)(0.35) = -0.12$). Socioeconomic status also has an inverse covariation with religious participation that arises from its negative correlation with family status (i.e., $\gamma_{22}\phi_{21} + \beta_{21}\gamma_{12}\phi_{21} = (0.25)(-0.31) + (0.35)(0.08)(-0.31) = -0.09$). Thus, higher socioeconomic status both increases and decreases religious participation.

The direct effect of family status on religious belief is small but significant ($\gamma_{12} = 0.08$), while the direct effect of family status on religious participation is twice as large ($\gamma_{22} = 0.17$). The largest direct cause of religious participation is religious belief ($\beta_{21} = 0.35$), about twice as large as the direct effects from socioeconomic status and family status. The hypothesized causal structure accounts for a little more than 10% of the variation in both endogenous variables, as shown by the residual paths from the two zetas.

12.5 Testing for Model Significance

The parameter estimates for a specified LISREL model generate the expected variance-covariance matrix, Σ, which can be compared to the observed variance-covariance matrix, S, to determine how closely the model reproduces the data. Several indices are available to summarize the overall model fit, while other detailed statistics test for the significance of individual model parameters.

12.5.1. Overall Fit Indices

Because the maximum likelihood estimator minimizes the fitting function, $F(S,\Sigma)$, this numerical value can be used to assess how well the whole model fits to the data. If the sample size is large, multiplying the minimum value of the fit function by $N - 1$ yields a measure that is distributed as a chi-square test statistic, with the following degrees of freedom:

$$df = \frac{1}{2}(p + q)(p + q + 1) - t$$

where p is the number of exogenous (x) indicators, q is the number of endogenous (y) indicators, and t is the total number of independent parameters to be estimated in the model. In other words, the number of independent elements in the beta, gamma, phi, and psi matrices is subtracted from the number of independent elements in $\boldsymbol{\Sigma}$. The null hypothesis tested with the χ^2 statistic is that the hypothesized causal model generated the observed variance-covariance matrix $\boldsymbol{S}$. The alternative hypothesis is that the variance-covariance matrix is unrestricted (i.e., a perfectly fitting model). The larger the differences between $\boldsymbol{\Sigma}$ and $\boldsymbol{S}$, the larger the chi-square, and hence, the worse the fit of the hypothesized model to the data. If the probability of the calculated χ^2 for the df is *greater* than the critical value for a given α-level (for example, at $\alpha = .05$), the hypothesized model is rejected as not true for the population from which the sample data were drawn.

As with the significance tests for log-linear models in chapter 10, our substantive research goal is *not to reject* the specified model. Thus, we always try to specify an hypothesized model that will yield a good fit to the data, that is, one with a small chi-square value relative to its degrees of freedom. If a small value of χ^2 occurs, then the differences between $\boldsymbol{S}$ and $\boldsymbol{\Sigma}$ can be attributed to chance sampling fluctuations, rather than to real effects in the population that are not represented in the model. Unfortunately, chi-square values are proportional to sample size and sensitive to departures from multivariate normality. Thus, a sufficiently large sample size can produce a test statistic requiring rejection of the null hypothesis. For this reason, Jöreskog and Sörbom (1989, p. 43–44) argue that χ^2 is better regarded as a goodness-of-fit statistic rather than as a test statistic. That is, a large chi-square value corresponds to a poor fit between model and data, while a small chi-square value reflects a good fit. Given that our example has $N = 840$ respondents, obtaining poor model fits is a distinct possibility.

Instead of performing tests of a specific model's overall fit, two nested models—which differ only in a particular parameter—can be compared by testing the differences in their χ^2s relative to the differences in their dfs. A large change in chi-square, compared to the change in degrees of freedom, indicates that the parameter makes a real improvement in model fit, whereas an insignificant change means that including the parameter results is no real advancement in model accuracy. The LISREL model shown in Figure 12.3 is equivalent to a fully recursive path diagram: the 10 parameters to be estimated (5 causal effects, 2 endogenous error terms, and 3 exogenous variances and covariances) exactly equal the 10 unique elements in the observed $\boldsymbol{S}$ matrix. Hence, this model has no degrees of freedom and $\chi^2 = 0$, a perfect fit. However, if one additional parameter is constrained to equal zero, a degree of freedom allows a test of the improved fit for this simpler model. The γ_{12} causal effect of family status on religious belief is a good candidate for restriction, as it has a small standardized value. When this model is run, it produces a chi-square of 5.30 for 1 *df*, which can be rejected at $\alpha = .05$ (critical value is 3.84). The difference in the two models' χ^2s ($5.30 - 0 = 5.30$) is likewise significant for the difference in *df*s ($1 - 0 = 1$). Hence, we can conclude that the causal effect of family status on religious belief is probably not zero in the population. Consequently, we conclude that a model specifying that this parameter equals zero results in a poorer fit between the expected and the observed variance-covariance matrices.

LISREL generates three other indices that can be useful in assessing overall model fit. The **goodness-of-fit index (GFI)** expresses the ratio between the minimum of the fitting function after the model is fitted to the fitting function before any model is fitted:

$$GFI = 1 - \frac{(s - \hat{\sigma})' \, \mathbf{W}^{-1} (s - \hat{\sigma})}{s' \, \mathbf{W}^{-1} s}$$

goodness-of-fit index— the ratio between the minimum of the fitting function after the model is fitted to the fitting function before any model is fitted

where $\mathbf{W}^{-1}$ is the inverse of a weight matrix that gives consistent estimates of the model parameters. The closer the GFI is to 1.00, the better the fit; a value of 1.00 means that the hypothesized model exactly reproduces the observed data, since each expected covariance ($\hat{\sigma}$) exactly equals the corresponding observed covariance (s).

An **adjusted goodness-of-fit index (AGFI)** reexpresses the GFI in terms of the numbers of degrees of freedom used in fitting the model:

$$AGFI = 1 - \left[\frac{(p + q)(p + q + 1)}{2d} \right](1 - GFI)$$

adjusted goodness-of-fit index— the reexpression of the GFI in terms of the numbers of degrees of freedom used in fitting the model

where $p + q$ is the sum of the number of *x*- and *y*-indicators, and *d* is the model degrees of freedom.

Finally, the **root mean squared residual index (RMSR)** measures the average of the fitted residuals:

root mean squared residual index— the average of the fitted residuals

$$\text{RMSR} = \sqrt{2 \sum_{i=1}^{p+q} \sum_{j=1}^{i} \frac{(s_{ij} - \hat{\sigma}_{ij})^2}{(p+q)(p+q+1)}}$$

The closer that the RMSR is to zero, the better the fit, in the sense that the differences between observed and expected variances and covariances are small. The RMSR is meaningful only when all observed variables are standardized (i.e., analyses are performed with an **S** that is a correlation matrix).

In our preceding example model, which set the path from family status to religious belief to zero, GFI = .997, AGFI = .969, and RMSR = .024. These three values suggest an extremely good overall fit between the model and the data, with little room for improvement. Because none of these fit indices have known sampling distributions, no probabilities can be attached to their descriptive values.

12.5.2. Testing Model Parameters

A LISREL model may be judged to have an overall good fit by the measures described above, yet one or more parameters within the model may be poorly determined. Further, if the model produces a poor overall fit, the indices do not reveal precisely where the model fails. The LISREL program produces two measures that help to pinpoint possible sources of poor fits that can be improved in subsequent model respecification and reestimation.

The most useful test statistics are the individual parameters' standard errors, used to calculate the t ratios according to the formula presented in section 6.4.3 (on page 217). For a two-tailed null hypothesis that a causal parameter equals zero in the population, the critical value is ± 1.96 for $\alpha = .05$ for a large sample. For example, in the recursive model with all paths present (see Figure 12.3), the unstandardized effect of socioeconomic status on religious participation (0.17) had a small standard error (0.029), resulting in a highly significant $t = +5.86$ ($p < .001$). The unstandardized 0.03 gamma from family status to religious belief had a standard error of 0.013, yielding a $t = +2.31$ for $df = 839$, which is significant at $\alpha < .05$. We previously demonstrated the importance of retaining this parameter by examining the change in chi-square values between a pair of nested models.

The impact of parameters that are fixed to zero or otherwise constrained within a model can be assessed by examining the so-called **modification indices** produced by LISREL. For each such parameter, the program computes how much the chi-square measure of overall fit would decrease by relaxing that constraint and reestimating the model, thus picking up a single *df*. Although the model with a modification index value above the critical minimum (i.e., 3.84 for $\alpha = .05$) will typically improve the overall fit, this procedure should be used only if relaxing that constrained parameter makes substantive sense within the hypothesized causal model.

modification indices— LISREL estimates of the change in model chi-square if a constraint is relaxed

12.6   Multiple Indicator Models

This section elaborates on the basic single-indicator LISREL model to consider models where one or more latent variables are represented by several indicators. First, we consider how the item reliability concept is embedded in a multiple-indicator approach to unobserved variables. Then, we examine several increasingly complex LISREL models that use multiple indicators of the endogenous and exogenous variables. These models are illustrated with examples that use the 1987 GSS data. To the four items used above, we add another four, creating pairs of indicators for each latent construct: (1) for socioeconomic status: years of education and occupational prestige; (2) for family status: children ever born and respondents' current marital status (0 = never married or divorced, 1 = married, separated, or widowed); (3) for religious belief: belief in the Bible and self-reported fundamentalism (1 = liberal, 2 = moderate, 3 = fundamentalist); and (4) for religious participation: church attendance and frequency of praying (from 1 = never to 6 = several times a day). Table 12.2 displays the correlations, standard deviations, and variance-covariances used in the analyses.

12.6.1.   Item Reliability

Section 12.2 introduced the concept of an observed variable composed of both true score and error components. We now generalize this approach to consider the case where a specific unobserved variable has three indicators, as shown in Figure 12.4. Here we focus on endogenous η_j and its y_i indicators, but the same analysis applies to an exogenous ξ_j and its x_i indicators. As in classical measurement theory, two types of uncorrelated causes produce variation in each indicator:

TABLE 12.2

Correlation and Covariance Matrices Among Eight Observed Variables ($N = 840$)

	x_1	x_2	x_3	x_4	y_1	y_2	y_3	y_4
Correlation Matrix								
x_1 Education	1.00	.52	−.31	−.10	−.36	−.23	.03	−.16
x_2 Occupational Prestige	.52	1.00	−.10	.04	−.23	−.17	.04	−.08
x_3 Children Ever Born	−.31	−.10	1.00	.38	.18	.13	.17	.20
x_4 Marital Status	−.10	.04	.38	1.00	.07	.03	.21	.14
y_1 Bible Belief	−.36	−.23	.18	.07	1.00	.30	.31	.35
y_2 Fundamentalism	−.23	−.17	.13	.03	.30	1.00	.21	.24
y_3 Church Attendance	.03	.04	.17	.21	.31	.21	1.00	.49
y_4 Prayer	−.16	−.08	.20	.14	.35	.24	.49	1.00
Standard Deviation	3.12	13.97	1.81	0.46	0.69	0.78	2.56	1.48
Covariance Matrix								
x_1 Education	9.71	22.56	−1.72	−.15	−.77	−.55	.20	−.73
x_2 Occupational Prestige	22.56	195.27	−2.57	.23	−2.23	−1.85	1.54	−1.70
x_3 Children Ever Born	−1.72	−2.57	3.26	.31	.23	.19	.80	.54
x_4 Marital Status	−.15	.23	.31	.21	.02	.01	.25	.09
y_1 Bible Belief	−.77	−2.23	.23	.02	.48	.16	.54	.36
y_2 Fundamentalism	−.55	−1.85	.19	.01	.16	.61	.42	.27
y_3 Church Attendance	.20	1.54	.80	.25	.54	.42	6.53	1.85
y_4 Prayer	−.73	−1.70	.54	.09	.36	.27	1.85	2.19

Source: 1987 General Social Survey

1. The unobserved factor (eta) is a common source of variation in every indicator, with its differential effects represented by the λ_{ij} "factor loadings."
2. Each y_i observable measure also has a unique source of variation, represented by its error term, ϵ_i.

Thus, for the *i*th indicator:

$$y_i = \lambda_{ij}\eta_j + \epsilon_i$$

Because true score and error terms are uncorrelated (a BLUE assumption), when both sides are squared and averaged across all cases, the result shows the decomposition of each indicator's variance into two components:

$$\sigma_{y_i}^2 = \lambda_{ij}^2\sigma_{\eta_j}^2 + \sigma_{\epsilon_i}^2$$

FIGURE 12.4
Sources of Variation in Multiple Indicators of a Single Unobservable Variable

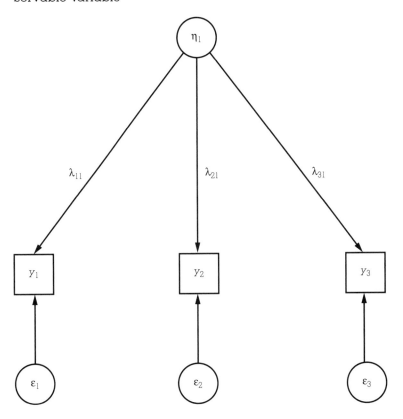

Rearranging the terms to isolate the squared loading:

$$\lambda_{ij}^2 = \frac{\sigma_{y_i}^2 - \sigma_{\epsilon_i}^2}{\sigma_{\eta_j}^2}$$

A squared lambda coefficient measures the **reliability** of the *i*th indicator. As shown in Box 12.2, an item's reliability is just the square of its correlation with the unobserved cause. Therefore, reliability is the proportion of an observed variable's variance that is attributable to the effect of the unobserved variable, that is, the proportion that is not due to unique sources (error). The higher the variance of an indicator's error term (ϵ_i), the lower its reliability. If

reliability—the proportion of an item's variance that is attributable to the unobserved cause

BOX 12.2 Item Reliability

Assume that all variables are measured as deviations about their means. Begin with the decomposition of the y_i variable according to the basic LISREL measurement equation:

$$y_i = \lambda_{ij}\eta_j + \epsilon_i$$

Multiply both sides of the equation by η_j and sum across the N observations:

$$\Sigma\frac{\eta_j y_i}{N} = \lambda_{ij}\Sigma\frac{\eta_j^2}{N} + \Sigma\frac{\eta_j \epsilon_i}{N}$$

$$\mathrm{Cov}\,(\eta_j y_i) = \lambda_{ij}\mathrm{Var}\,(\eta_j) + 0$$

$$s_{\eta_j y_i} = \lambda_{ij}\phi_{jj}$$

because the error term is uncorrelated with the unobserved variable. Thus, the covariance between an unobserved factor and its indicator is the product of the item loading times the factor variance.

Define the reliability of an observed indicator as the square of its correlation with the unobserved cause. Recall from Section 6.3.3 (page 209) that a correlation coefficient is the ratio of the covariance of two variables to the product of their standard deviations:

$$r_{XY} = \frac{s_{XY}}{s_X s_Y}$$

The correlation between an indicator and its unobserved cause is

$$r_{\eta_j y_i} = \frac{s_{\eta_j y_i}}{s_{\eta_j} s_{y_i}} = \frac{\lambda_{ij}\phi_{jj}}{s_{n_j} s_{y_i}}$$

and the item reliability is the squared correlation:

$$\mathrm{REL}\,y_i = \frac{\lambda_{ij}^2\phi_{jj}^2}{s_{n_j}^2 s_{y_i}^2}$$

BOX 12.2   *continued*

Thus, in a completely standardized LISREL solution, where the variances of all indicators and unobserved variables equal 1.00, the item-reliability formula reduces simply to the square of the factor loading:

$$\text{REL } y_i = \lambda_{ij}^2$$

---

the $\sigma_{\epsilon_i}^2$ error component is zero, then $\lambda_{ij}^2 = 1.00$, meaning that the observed measure is a perfectly reliable indicator of the unobserved variable. When we set each lambda-*y* and lambda-*x* equal to 1.0 in the single-indicator LISREL models above, we not only set the metric scales for these unobserved variables, but we implicitly asserted that each item was a perfectly reliable indicator of its corresponding construct.

   Given multiple indicators for an unobserved variable, as in Figure 12.4, the relative sizes of each lambda will very likely differ. Some items may better represent the latent concept than do other items; hence, their higher reliabilities should be reflected in larger estimated lambdas. To obtain a LISREL solution, we still must set the lambda for one of the y_i indicators equal to 1.0 in the unstandardized solution, in order to fix the unmeasured η_is scale. However, that constraint does not mean we conceive this indicator to be a perfectly reliable measure. Rather, that y_i indicator now serves as a yardstick against which the other indicators will be scaled. If its reliability is higher than the others, then it will have the highest factor loading in a completely standardized solution. If one of the other indicators has a higher reliability than the y_i whose lambda we chose to set equal to 1.0, then the latter indicator's lambda loading in the completely standardized solution will have a smaller estimated value than the lambda of the more reliable indicator.

12.6.2.   The MIMIC Model

Perhaps the simplest multiple-indicator LISREL causal model is the **MIMIC** or *M*ultiple-*I*ndicator and *M*ult*i*ple *C*ause **model.** At the structural equation level, variation in a single dependent variable is directly caused by several predetermined variables. At the mea-

MIMIC model—
multiple-indicator and multiple-cause model in which variation in a single dependent variable with two or more indicators is directly caused by several predetermined variables, each of which has only a single indicator

surement equation level, each ξ_j has a single, perfectly measured x_i indicator, but the η_j has two or more y_j indicators. The λ for each x-indicator is set equal to 1.0 to fix the scale of its corresponding ξ_j. But only one of the y-indicators' λ is set to 1.00 to fix the η_j scale; the factor loadings of the remaining y_js are free parameters whose estimated values reflect their reliabilities relative to the reliability of the fixed y-indicator.

Figure 12.5 shows the metric and the standardized coefficients for a MIMIC model where four predetermined variables cause religious belief. For the two indicators of religious belief, we fixed the coefficient for belief in the Bible to 1.00 and let the parameter for fundamentalism be free. In matrix algebra notation the two sets of measurement equations are as follows:

$$\begin{bmatrix} x_1 \\ x_2 \\ x_3 \\ x_4 \end{bmatrix} = \begin{bmatrix} 1 & 0 & 0 & 0 \\ 0 & 1 & 0 & 0 \\ 0 & 0 & 1 & 0 \\ 0 & 0 & 0 & 1 \end{bmatrix} \begin{bmatrix} \xi_1 \\ \xi_2 \\ \xi_3 \\ \xi_4 \end{bmatrix} + \begin{bmatrix} \delta_1 \\ \delta_2 \\ \delta_3 \\ \delta_4 \end{bmatrix}$$

$$\begin{bmatrix} y_1 \\ y_2 \end{bmatrix} = \begin{bmatrix} 1 \\ \lambda_{21} \end{bmatrix} \begin{bmatrix} \eta_1 \end{bmatrix} + \begin{bmatrix} \epsilon_1 \\ \epsilon_2 \end{bmatrix}$$

This model produces a very good fit to the data ($\chi^2 = 1.35$, $df = 3$, $p > .70$), with a GFI of .999 implying little room for improvement.

The factor loadings in the completely standardized solution reveal that belief in the Bible is a more reliable indicator ($.68^2 = .462$) than is self-reported fundamentalism ($.44^2 = .194$), although both items fall considerably short of perfect reliability. Three of the four gamma coefficients from the predetermined variables to the unobserved religious belief factor are statistically significant. Higher education and higher occupational prestige decrease religiosity, while respondents with more children have stronger religious belief. But marital status is not significantly related to religiosity. Education clearly has the greatest causal effect, with religious belief decreasing by -0.43 standard deviations for each one-standard unit increase in education. Altogether, the four exogenous variables account for 29.4% of the variance in religious belief (i.e., $R^2 = 1 - \Psi_{11}^2 = 1 - (.84)^2 = .294$).

Because the standardized LISREL coefficients are also path coefficients, the fundamental theorem of path analysis (see section 11.3.4 on page 422) can be applied to compute the implied

FIGURE 12.5
MIMIC Model

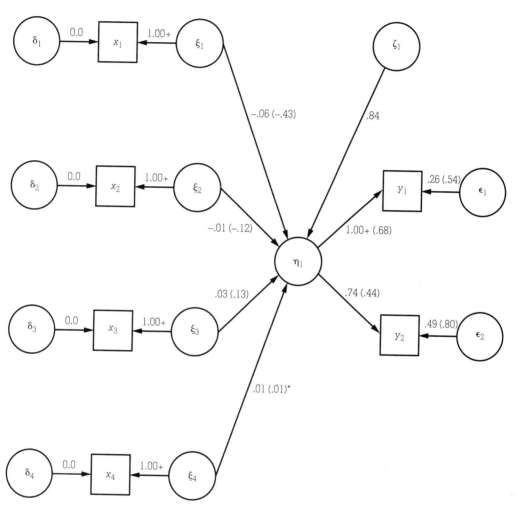

+ = Fixed Coefficient
* p > .05
Completely standardized values in parentheses. Covariations among exogenous variables not shown.

ξ_1 = Education
ξ_2 = Occupational Prestige
ξ_3 = Children Born
ξ_4 = Marital Status
η_1 = Religious Belief
x_1 = Education

x_2 = Occupational Prestige
x_3 = Children Born
x_4 = Marital Status
y_1 = Belief in Bible
y_2 = Fundamentalism

correlation between any pair of observed variables. For example, the implied correlation between the two religious belief indicators is just product of their standardized lambda loadings: $r'_{y_1 y_2} = \lambda^y_{11} \lambda^y_{21} =$ (0.68)(0.44) = 0.299. (We superscript the lambda-parameters to make clear to which set of indicators they refer.) Similarly, the implied correlation between education and fundamentalism is $r'_{x_1 y_2} = \lambda^x_{11} \lambda^y_{21}$ = (−0.43)(0.44) = −0.189. What is the expected correlation between occupational prestige and belief in the Bible?

12.6.3. Single-Link Causal Chains

single-link causal chain—a LISREL model in which one exogenous variable causes variation in one endogenous variable, both of which have multiple indicators

A slightly more complex LISREL model is a **single-link causal chain** in which one exogenous variable causes variation in one endogenous variable, both of which have multiple indicators. Again, to fix the metric scale of the unobserved variables, one indicator in each set must be set equal to 1.00. Figure 12.6 shows such a model in which religious belief causes religious participation, with both unobserved variables having two indicators. Here we constrained the factor loadings for fundamentalism and church attendance to equal 1.0, while belief in the Bible and prayer were freely estimated parameters. The two sets of LISREL measurement equations are as follows:

$$
\begin{bmatrix} x_1 \\ x_2 \end{bmatrix} = \begin{bmatrix} \lambda_{11} \\ 1 \end{bmatrix} \begin{bmatrix} \xi_1 \end{bmatrix} + \begin{bmatrix} \delta_1 \\ \delta_2 \end{bmatrix}
$$

$$
\begin{bmatrix} y_1 \\ y_2 \end{bmatrix} = \begin{bmatrix} \lambda_{11} \\ 1 \end{bmatrix} \begin{bmatrix} \eta_1 \end{bmatrix} + \begin{bmatrix} \epsilon_1 \\ \epsilon_2 \end{bmatrix}
$$

This model yields an excellent fit to the data ($\chi^2 = 0.01$, $df = 1$, $p > .90$, and AGFI = 1.00). At the structural equation level of analysis, religious belief causes approximately half the variance in religious participation (e.g., $\beta^2_{11} = (0.71)^2 = .504$). As before, the completely standardized solution shows that belief in the Bible is a more reliable indicator of religious belief ($\lambda^2_{11} = 0.66^2 = 0.436$) than is fundamentalism ($\lambda^2_{21} = 0.45^2 = 0.203$). However, the two factor loadings for prayer and church attendance suggest roughly comparable reliabilities as indicators of religious participation ($\lambda^2_{11} = 0.66^2 = 0.436$ and $\lambda^2_{12} = 0.75^2 = 0.563$). Indeed, when both these loadings are constrained to be equal, a LISREL model fits very well ($\chi^2 = 1.68$, $df = 2$, p > .40, and AGFI = .995). The two constrained parameters are estimated to be $\lambda_{11} = \lambda_{12} = 0.70$. The 1.67 increase in

FIGURE 12.6
Single-Link Causal Chain

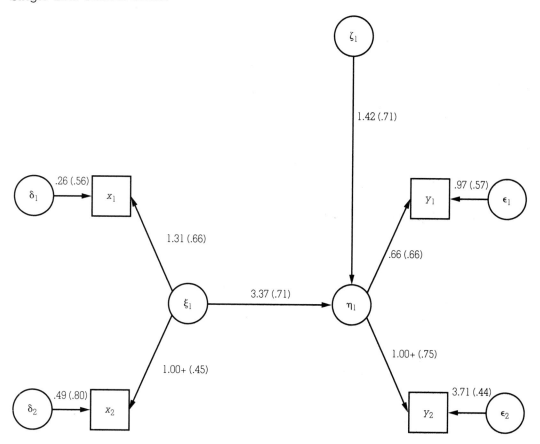

+ = Fixed Parameter
Completely standardized values in parentheses
ξ_1 = Religious Belief
η_1 = Religious Participation
x_1 = Belief in Bible
x_2 = Fundamentalism
y_1 = Prayer
y_2 = Church Attendance

this constrained model's chi-square over the unconstrained model's chi-square is not significant for the additional degree of freedom, meaning that we cannot reject the model in which the two loadings of η_1 are constrained to equality.

Applying the fundamental theorem of path analysis to a causal chain allows us to compute the implied correlation between any pair of indicators. For example, the implied correlation between prayer and church attendance is product of their standardized lambda loadings: $r'_{y_1 y_2} = \lambda^y_{11} \lambda^y_{21} = (0.66)(0.75) = 0.495$. Similarly, the implied correlation between belief in the Bible and church attendance is $r'_{x_1 y_2} = \lambda^x_{11} \beta_{12} \lambda^y_{21} = (0.66)(0.71)(0.75) = 0.351$. What is the expected correlation between fundamentalism and prayer?

12.6.4. Multiple-Indicator, Multiple-Structural Variable Models

The final model we consider has several exogenous and several endogenous variables at the structural level, each of which has multiple indicators. As ever, one indicator of each unobserved factor is set equal to 1.00 to fix the scale, while the remaining indicators are free parameters. Figure 12.7 reports the metric and completely standardized parameter estimates for a model involving four unmeasured variables and eight observed variables. The measurement equations for the ys are as follows:

$$
\begin{bmatrix} y_1 \\ y_2 \\ y_3 \\ y_4 \end{bmatrix} = \begin{bmatrix} 1 & 0 \\ \lambda_{21} & 0 \\ 0 & 1 \\ 0 & \lambda_{42} \end{bmatrix} \begin{bmatrix} \eta_1 \\ \eta_2 \end{bmatrix} + \begin{bmatrix} \epsilon_1 \\ \epsilon_2 \\ \epsilon_3 \\ \epsilon_4 \end{bmatrix}
$$

The chi-square value for this model is too high to be acceptable ($\chi^2 = 72.85$, $df = 16$, $p < .001$), but the large sample size ($N = 840$) exaggerates the discrepancies between Σ and S. The other descriptive measures of model fit all imply better congruence: GFI = .979, AGFI = .952, and RMSR = .04. All five structural equation causal parameters are significant at $\alpha < .05$ or lower. Socioeconomic status decreases religious belief, but family status increases it. Religious belief, with a completely standardized coefficient of 0.88, is the strongest predictor of religious participation, but both socioeconomic status and family status also increase religious involvement, by 0.42 and 0.16 standard units, respectively. The structural equations account for 29.4% of the variance on religious belief and 61.6% of the variance in religious participation. Among

FIGURE 12.7

Multiple-Indicator, Multiple-Structural Variable Model

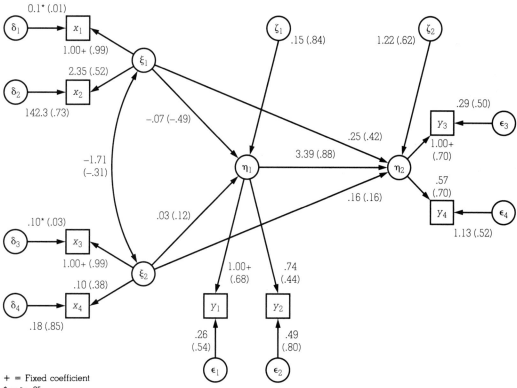

+ = Fixed coefficient
* p > .05
ξ_1 = Socioeconomic Status
ξ_2 = Family Status
η_1 = Religious Belief
η_2 = Religious Participation
x_1 = Education
x_2 = Occupational Prestige
x_3 = Children Born
x_4 = Marital Status
y_1 = Belief in Bible
y_2 = Fundamentalism
y_3 = Church Attendance
y_4 = Prayer

the four pairs of observed measures, education, children ever born, and belief in the Bible are more reliable indicators of their respective concepts than are occupational prestige, marital status, and fundamentalism. The completely standardized factor loadings for the church attendance and prayer indicators are estimated to have identical values (0.70), although this analysis did not constrain them to equality.

The LISREL modification indices for this analysis (not shown here) suggested that the prayer measure is also a very good indicator of unobserved religious belief. If another model specifying free loadings of the prayer item on *both* endogenous variables is estimated, its overall fit is $\chi^2 = 44.67$, $df = 15$, $p < .001$ (and AGFI = .968). This model significantly reduces the chi-square while costing only one degree of freedom. In this latter model the prayer measure has a much higher loading on the religious belief variable ($\lambda = 0.98$) than on the participation variable ($\lambda = 0.29$). Clearly, a more reliable second indicator of religious participation would be desirable.

12.7   Confirmatory Factor Analysis

confirmatory factor analysis—a structural equation model, with one or more unobserved variables having multiple indicators, in which the research specifies the pattern of indicator loadings

The final topic in our introduction to structural equation modeling is a special case of LISREL that has no dependent variable. Instead, the researcher's concern is to represent the covariations among one or more exogenous factors having multiple indicators. A **confirmatory factor analysis (CFA)** resembles the measurement model depicted in Figure 12.3, in which each indicator has both common and unique sources of variation. The confirmation aspect comes from the analyst's ability to specify the J number of factors and the x_i indicators' patterns of loadings on each factor (λ_{ij}s), in contrast to so-called exploratory factor analysis methods in which a computer program decides the number of factors and the pattern of item loadings.

To illustrate how a confirmatory factor analysis strategy can use LISREL to uncover the covariance structure of among items, we examine responses to five questions about ways of spending social evenings by 1,011 respondents in the 1991 GSS. Respondents were asked how often they spent such evenings with (1) relatives; (2) parents; (3) a brother or sister; (4) "someone who lives in your neighborhood"; and (5) "friends who live outside the neighborhood." They were offered seven response categories ranging from "never" to "almost every day" (coded 1 to 7, respectively). The correlation and variance-covariance matrices appear in Table 12.3, but, to save space, we present only the completely standardized solutions for the CFA models estimated below.

Because CFA requires only the x-indicators, its structural and measurement equations are much simpler than the full LISREL approach. Four of the basic matrices are not required ($\mathbf{B}$, $\mathbf{\Gamma}$, $\mathbf{\Lambda}_y$, $\mathbf{\Theta}_\epsilon$). The formula for the expected correlations uses only three basic matrices:

$$\mathbf{\Sigma} = \mathbf{\Lambda}_x \mathbf{\Phi} \mathbf{\Lambda}_x' + \mathbf{\Theta}_\delta$$

and two other basic matrices are necessary to represent the observed variables:

$$\mathbf{X} = \mathbf{\Lambda}_x \mathbf{\xi} + \mathbf{\Theta}_\delta$$

As in all LISREL analyses, a chi-square statistic tests a CFA model's fit of the $\mathbf{\Sigma}$ matrix to the $\mathbf{S}$ matrix. If the data consist of q indicators (x-variables), the maximum degrees of freedom available for the

TABLE 12.3

Correlation and Variance-Covariance Matrices Among Five Observed Variables ($N = 1{,}011$)

	x_1	x_2	x_3	x_4	x_5
Correlation:					
x_1 Relatives	1.00	.33	.38	.08	.23
x_2 Parents	.33	1.00	.34	.01	.20
x_3 Siblings	.38	.34	1.00	.07	.17
x_4 Neighbors	.08	.01	.07	1.00	.15
x_5 Friends	.23	.20	.17	.15	1.00
Standard Deviation	1.63	2.41	1.91	2.06	1.66
Variance-Covariance:					
x_1 Relatives	2.64	1.28	1.17	.27	.62
x_2 Parents	1.28	5.79	1.55	.04	.79
x_3 Siblings	1.17	1.55	3.65	.26	.55
x_4 Neighbors	.27	.04	.26	4.24	.51
x_5 Friends	.62	.79	.55	.51	2.77

Source: 1991 General Social Survey

test statistic are $(q^2 - q)/2$. Each model parameter that an analyst specifies to be freely estimated reduces the degrees of freedom by one. For example, with five indicators, the maximum available degrees of freedom are $(5^2 - 5)/2 = 10$. If a CFA model specifies that all five items load on a single unobserved factor, the five λ_{i1} factor loadings use five degrees of freedom. In addition, the variance of ξ_1 (i.e., ϕ_{11}^2) also uses one degree of freedom. However, these six parameters cannot all be free within the CFA model: In order to establish a scale for the unobserved xi-variable, either one lambda coefficient must be fixed, or the variance of ξ_1 must be fixed (in the models estimated below, we chose the latter option, which allows all the lambdas to vary freely). Either choice increases the degrees of freedom by one for testing the model fit. Hence, a chi-square statistic for a one-factor, five-indicator CFA model always has $10 - 5 = 5\ df$.

Figure 12.8 shows the parameter estimates for the single-factor CFA model. This specification produces a fairly good fit to the data: $\chi^2 = 22.2$, $df = 5$, $p < .001$, with GFI = .991, AGFI = .974, and RMSR = .126. However, inspection of the lambdas indicates that the three family variables have high loadings (0.62, 0.54, and 0.60 for relatives, parents, and siblings, respectively), but the loadings for neighbors and friends are much smaller (0.12 and 0.35, respectively). This pattern suggests that people may segregate their visiting patterns between family and nonfamily members.

An alternative CFA model, shown in Figure 12.9, specifies two unobserved variables, and allows the three family items to load only on the first factor and the two nonfamily items to have nonzero loadings only on the second factor. In the measurement model the matrix of free factor loadings linking the five indicators to the two unobserved variables is as follows:

$$\Lambda_x = \begin{bmatrix} \lambda_{11} & 0 \\ \lambda_{21} & 0 \\ \lambda_{31} & 0 \\ 0 & \lambda_{42} \\ 0 & \lambda_{52} \end{bmatrix}$$

To set the metric scales for the two unmeasured variables, we fix the variances of the two xis, $\sigma_{\xi_1}^2 = \sigma_{\xi_2}^2 = 1.00$. Thus, the phi matrix of variances and covariances among the two xis is

FIGURE 12.8

Confirmatory Factor Analysis Model of Social Evening with One Factor

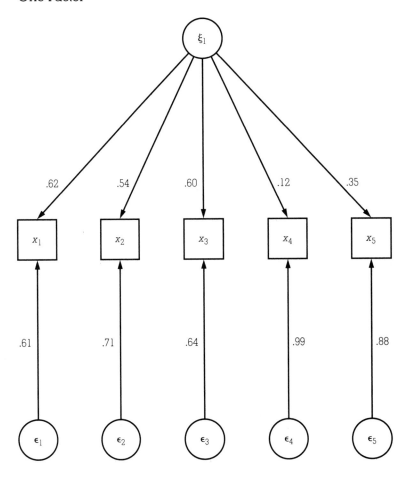

ξ_1 = General Social Evening Scale
x_1 = Relatives
x_2 = Parents
x_3 = Siblings
x_4 = Neighbors
x_5 = Friends

FIGURE 12.9

Confirmatory Factor Analysis Model of Social Evenings with Two Factors

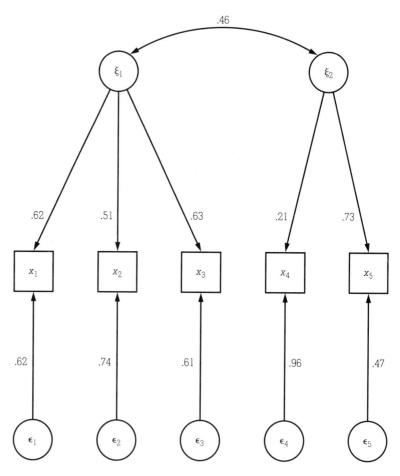

ξ_1 = Family Factor
ξ_2 = Nonfamily Factor
x_1 = Relatives
x_2 = Parents
x_3 = Siblings
x_4 = Neighbors
x_5 = Friends

$$\Phi = \begin{bmatrix} 1 & \phi_{12} \\ \phi_{12} & 1 \end{bmatrix}$$

The data still consist of the same 10 covariances that we had for the one-factor model. Because the two-factor model specifies that the five lambdas and one phi are free parameters, we have $10 - 6 = 4$ *df* to test its fit to the data. The model yields a chi-square of 7.1, which is not only a very good fit ($p < .13$), but also a significant improvement over the fit of the one-factor model. The difference in $\chi^2 = 22.2 - 7.1 = 15.1$ for a difference in $df = 5 - 4 = 1$, $p < .001$. The three descriptive fit measures also have very good values: GFI = .997, AGFI = .990, and RMSR = .068. As shown in Figure 12.9, the two unobserved factors are moderately correlated ($\phi_{11} = .46$). However, the magnitudes of the five items' factor loadings vary considerably, indicating reliabilities for the three family indicators that range between 0.260 and 0.396, and for the two nonfamily items between 0.044 (neighbors) and 0.533 (friends).

The final CFA models we estimated for these data are two-factor models that have the same pattern of item loadings, but specify that two or more of the λ_{ij} values are equal. An option in LISREL allows such constraints to be placed on a model, with each such constraint yielding an additional degree of freedom to test whether the deterioration in chi-square is too great to be tolerated. For example, a model in which the two nonfamily items were forced to have the same lambdas on the second factor yielded a $\chi^2 = 21.6$, $df = 5$, which is significantly worse than the preceding model in which all five parameters have unique values. However, a model in which the lambdas for the relatives and siblings items (λ_{11} and λ_{31}) are constrained to be equal, yielded a $\chi^2 = 8.6$, $df = 5$, which is not significantly worse than the model with all free lambdas ($\Delta\chi^2 = 8.6 - 7.1 = 1.5$, $\Delta df = 6 - 5 = 1$, $p < .05$). However, constraining the loading for the parental item to equal the other two family visitation items could not be accepted ($\Delta\chi^2 = 13.2 - 8.6 = 4.6$, $\Delta df = 7 - 6 = 1$, $p > .05$). Hence, we conclude that the best-fitting model for the underlying factor structure of the five social visiting items is that shown in Figure 12.10.

FIGURE 12.10

Confirmatory Factor Analysis Model of Social Evenings with Two Factors, and Two Loadings Constrained to Equality

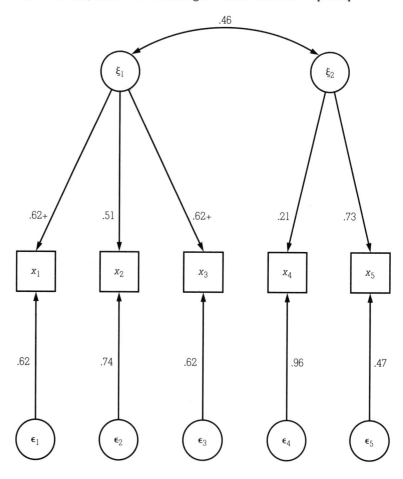

+ = Loadings Constrained to Be Equal
ξ_1 = Family Factor
ξ_2 = Nonfamily Factor
x_1 = Relatives
x_2 = Parents
x_3 = Siblings
x_4 = Neighbors
x_5 = Friends

Review of Key Concepts and Symbols

These key concepts and symbols are listed in the order of appearance in this chapter. Combined with the definitions in the margins, they will help you to review the material and can serve as a self-test for mastery of the concepts.

conceptual model	standardized solution
matrix algebra	completely standardized
matrix	solution
order	goodness-of-fit index
vector	adjusted goodness-of-fit index
square matrix	root mean squared residual
diagonal	index
trace	modification indices
identity matrix	reliability
transpose	MIMIC model
conformability	single-link causal chain
inverse	confirmatory factor analysis
structural equation system	ξ
eta vector	η
beta matrix	γ
xi vector	$\boldsymbol{\Gamma}$
gamma matrix	β
zeta vector	$\mathbf{B}$
psi matrix	ϕ
phi matrix	$\boldsymbol{\Phi}$
variance-covariance matrix	ζ
measurement model	$\boldsymbol{\Psi}$
lambda-y matrix	$\mathbf{I}$
epsilon vector	$\text{tr}(\mathbf{A})$
lambda-x matrix	$\mathbf{A}'$
delta vector	$|A|$
theta delta matrix	$\mathbf{S}$
theta epsilon matrix	T
sigma matrix	$\boldsymbol{\Lambda}_y$
algorithm	$\boldsymbol{\Lambda}_x$
residual matrix	ϵ
fitting function	δ
identified	$\boldsymbol{\Theta}_\delta$
information matrix	

$\boldsymbol{\Theta}_\epsilon$ AGFI
$\boldsymbol{\Sigma}$ RMSR
$\mathbf{S}$ λ_{ij}^2
$\mathbf{R}$ λ^y
$F(\mathbf{S},\boldsymbol{\Sigma})$ λ^x
GFI

PROBLEMS

General Problems

1. Write in LISREL notation the equations that correspond to this conceptual model:

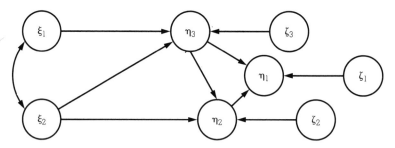

2. Given these matrices:

$$\mathbf{P} = \begin{bmatrix} 1 & 4 & 3 \\ -2 & 1 & 6 \end{bmatrix} \quad \mathbf{Q} = \begin{bmatrix} 6 & 1 \\ 2 & -4 \\ -3 & 5 \end{bmatrix} \quad \mathbf{R} = \begin{bmatrix} 2 & 1 & 3 \\ -2 & -1 & -3 \\ 2 & 1 & 3 \end{bmatrix}$$

Calculate the following:
a. $\mathbf{P}'$ d. $\mathbf{RQ}$
b. $\mathbf{P} + \mathbf{Q}'$ e. $\mathbf{IR}$
c. $\mathbf{Q}'\mathbf{P}$ f. $\mathbf{R}^{-1}\mathbf{R}$

3. Use these LISREL matrices to write the full structural equations and diagram the conceptual model of a causal system:

$$\mathbf{B} = \begin{bmatrix} 0 & 0 \\ \beta_{21} & 0 \end{bmatrix} \quad \boldsymbol{\Gamma} = \begin{bmatrix} \gamma_{11} & \gamma_{12} & \gamma_{13} \\ 0 & 0 & \gamma_{23} \end{bmatrix}$$

4. Write in LISREL notation the lambda matrices that correspond to the measurement portions of the following causal diagram.

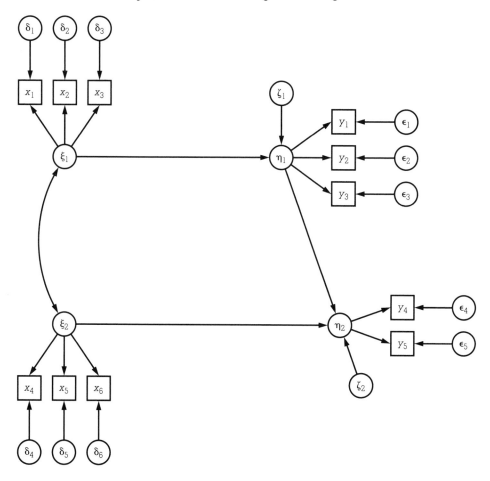

5. Given the following LISREL matrices, write the full LISREL equations for the measurement portion of the causal model:

$$
\Lambda_y = \begin{bmatrix} 1 & 0 \\ y_{21} & 0 \\ 0 & y_{32} \\ 0 & 1 \end{bmatrix} \quad \Lambda_x = \begin{bmatrix} 1 & 0 & 0 \\ x_{21} & 0 & 0 \\ 0 & 1 & 0 \\ 0 & x_{42} & 0 \\ 0 & 0 & 1 \\ 0 & 0 & x_{63} \end{bmatrix}
$$

6. Here are LISREL estimates for a completely standardized solution to a MIMIC model. Give a substantive interpretation of this model.

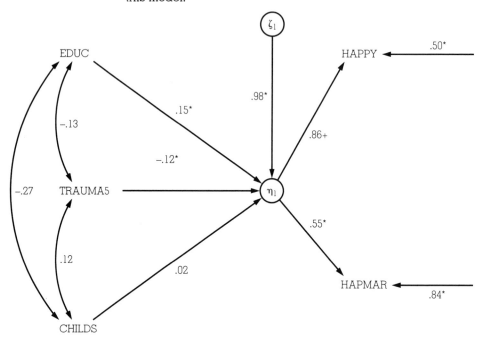

$\chi^2 = 11.69$, $df = 2$, $p = .003$; GFI $= .991$; AGFI $= .935$.
* $p < .05$
+ fixed coefficient

7. Here are estimates from a completely standardized solution to a simple chain model. Calculate the expected correlations among the four indicators and their reliabilities.

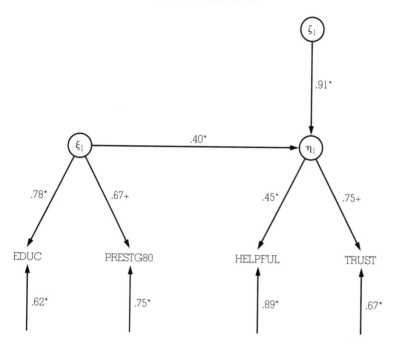

$\chi^2 = 0.40$, $df = 1$, $p = .53$; GFI = 1.00; AGFI = .996.
* $p < .05$
+ fixed coefficient

8. Here is the completely standardized solution to a LISREL model. Give a substantive interpretation and calculate the expected correlations $r_{\xi_1 \eta_1}$ and $r_{\xi_2 \eta_1}$.

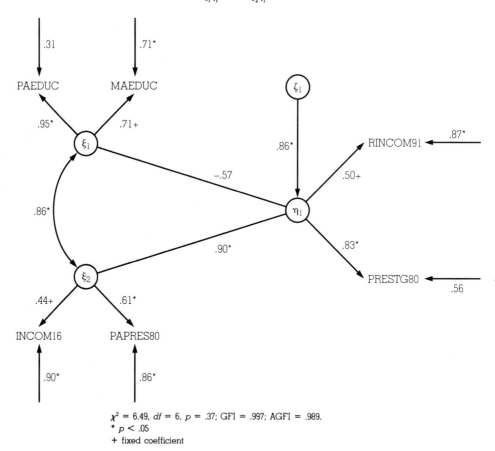

$\chi^2 = 6.49$, $df = 6$, $p = .37$; GFI $= .997$; AGFI $= .989$.
* $p < .05$
+ fixed coefficient

9. Here is the completely standardized solution to a LISREL model. Give a substantive interpretation and calculate the expected correlations $r_{\xi_1\eta_1}$ and $r_{\xi_2\eta_1}$.

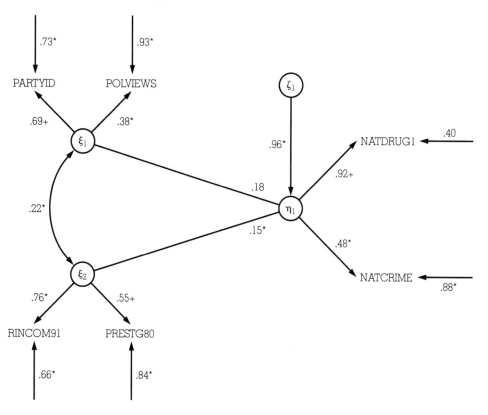

$\chi^2 = 3.39$, $df = 6$, $p = .76$; GFI $= .997$; AGFI $= .990$.
* $p < .05$
+ fixed coefficient

10. Here is the completely standardized solution from a confirmatory factor analysis model for seven indicators of confidence in U.S. institutions. Give a substantive interpretation of this model:

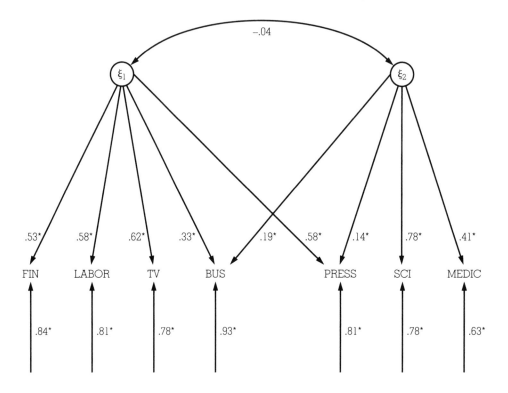

$\chi^2 = 20.1$, $df = 11$, $p = .04$; GFI = .993; AGFI = .983.
* $p < .05$

Problems Requiring the 1991 General Social Survey

11. Does education mediate the effects of age and race on attitudes toward racial segregation? Select respondents whose race is either white or black and estimate the completely standardized solution for the LISREL model below, where each indicator is a single perfect measure of its concept.

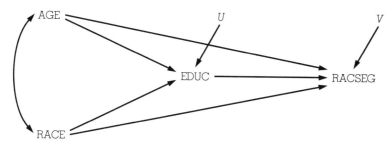

12. Below is a MIMIC model with two indicators of how much is being spent on national problems. Estimate a LISREL model, report the completely standardized solution and all model fit statistics.

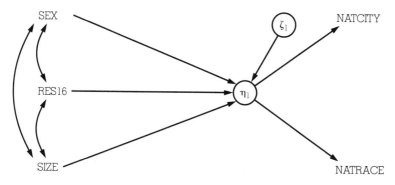

13. Does women's socioeconomic status affect their sex-role attitudes? For the simple chain model below estimate a completely
standardized LISREL solution and report all model fit statistics.

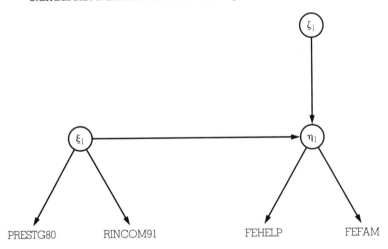

Note: Use this recode for respondent's income:
RECODE
RINCOM91(1=.5)(2=2)(3=3.5)(4=4.5)(5=5.5)(6=6.5)(7=7.5)
(8=9)(9=11.25)(10=13.75)(11=16.25)(12=18.75)(13=21.25)(14=23.75)
(15=27.5)(16=32.5)(17=37.5)(18=45)(19=55)(20=67.5)(21=85)
(0,22=99).

14. Among women, is satisfaction with work and finances affected more by socioeconomic status or by sex-role attitudes? Estimate the completely standardized LISREL solution for this multiple indicator model and report all fit statistics.

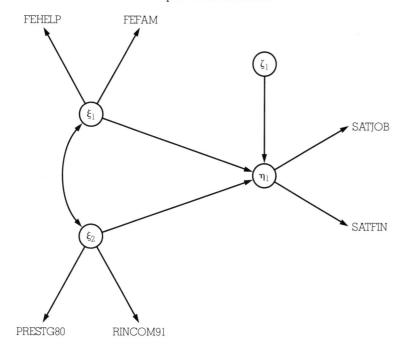

FEHELP   FEFAM

ζ_1

ξ_1

SATJOB

η_1

SATFIN

ξ_2

PRESTG80   RINCOM91

Note: In addition to the income recode in Problem 13, use these recodes:
RECODE SATJOB(4=1)(3=2)(2=3)(1=4).
RECODE SATFIN(3=1)(1=3).

15. Using the six scales for liking of RUSSIA, JAPAN, CANADA, CHINA, ISRAEL, and EGYPT, determine whether a single-factor or a two-factor confirmatory factor analysis model best represents the covariations among the scales. For the latter, determine which lambda coefficients for each unobserved ξ_i can be set to zero without significantly worsening the fit. Report the completely standardized LISREL solutions for both models and report all fit statistics.

The Use of Summations

Appendix A

1. Variables and Subscripts

In this text we use the letters X, Y, and Z to stand for *variables*. Variables have outcomes that can be kept track of through the use of *subscripts*. If we have N individuals, then X_i denotes the particular value or outcome observed for individuals, i. For example, if we have four persons in a sample, then the four outcomes associated with them are represented by X_1, X_2, X_3, and X_4.

2. Sums

Many of the statistical techniques used in this text depend on the *sum* of observations across the N individuals in the sample. The summation sign, denoted by the Greek symbol sigma (Σ), is used to stand for the sum of the values that immediately follow the summation sign. An index value written under the Σ indicates the lowest value the subscript will take, and an index value written above Σ indicates the highest value the subscript will take in the summation. Therefore,

$$\sum_{i=1}^{N} X_i$$

is read as "the sum of the N outcomes of X_i from X_1 to X_N," or

$$\sum_{i=1}^{N} X_i = X_1 + X_2 + X_3 + \ldots + X_N$$

Suppose we observe four individuals (i.e., $N = 4$) and the four outcomes are $X_1 = 2$, $X_2 = 6$, $X_3 = 0$, $X_4 = 3$. Then,

$$\sum_{i=1}^{4} X_i = 2 + 6 + 0 + 3 = 11$$

The simplest use of the summation is in computing the *mean,* the average value of a set of observations. As you probably know, an average of this sort is computed by adding all the outcomes and then dividing the total by the number of observations. In summation notation, the mean is simply

$$\frac{\sum_{i=1}^{N} X_i}{N}$$

or, in the example above, the mean is

$$\frac{\sum_{i=1}^{4} X_i}{4} = \frac{11}{4} = 2.75$$

After you become familiar with the use of Σ and it becomes clear from the context that we are summing across all observations, we may use either $\Sigma_i X_i$ or ΣX_i, instead of the longer $\sum_{i=1}^{N} X_i$ notation.

Sometimes variables are represented by more than a single subscript. Multiple subscripts will be used for two situations. The first use is when we wish to represent not only an individual, i, but also a group, j, to which the person belongs (e.g., sex or religious identification). In this case the notation is X_{ij}. If the last observation in group j is notated by n_j, then the sum across the n_j individuals in group j is

$$\sum_{i=1}^{n_j} X_{ij}$$

Written out, this is

$$\sum_{i=1}^{n_j} X_{ij} = X_{1j} + X_{2j} + X_{3j} + \ldots + X_{n_j}$$

If we wish to sum across all J groups of n_j individuals, this is symbolized by

$$\sum_{j=1}^{J} \sum_{i=1}^{n_j} X_{ij}$$

When written out, it is

$$\sum_{j=1}^{J} \sum_{i=1}^{n_j} X_{ij} = (X_{11} + X_{21} + \ldots + X_{n_1 1})$$
$$+ (X_{12} + X_{22} + \ldots + X_{n_2 2})$$
$$+ (X_{1J} + X_{2J} + \ldots + X_{n_J J})$$

As an example, suppose we have three political groups where 1 = Republican, 2 = Democrat, and 3 = Other, and there are four Republicans, three Democrats, and two Others in the groups. We observe the following nine outcomes:

$$
\begin{array}{c c}
 & i= \\
 & 1\ 2\ 3\ 4 \\
\hline
1 & 3\ 4\ 2\ 3 \\
j = 2 & 2\ 0\ 1 \\
3 & 2\ 4 \\
\end{array}
$$

Now if we want to sum the values of the Republicans (where $i = 1$), we have

$$\sum_{i=1}^{4} X_{i1} = 3 + 4 + 2 + 3 = 12$$

The sum of the others is

$$\sum_{i=1}^{2} X_{i3} = 2 + 4 = 6$$

Or, summing *all* observations across all groups

$$\sum_{j=1}^{3}\sum_{i=1}^{n_j} X_{ij} = (3 + 4 + 2 + 3) + (2 + 0 + 1) + (2 + 4)$$

$$= 12 + 3 + 6 = 21$$

Where there is no ambiguity about the groups and individuals being summed across, we will also use $\sum_{j}\sum_{i} X_{ij}$ or $\sum\sum X_{ij}$, instead of the more cumbersome $\sum_{j=1}^{J}\sum_{i=1}^{n_j} X_{ij}$.

The second use of double subscripts is applied when we want to distinguish the same individual on two different variables. For example, we may have two variables, X_1 and X_2. In this case X_{1i} and X_{2i} symbolize the ith individual's outcomes on the two variables, and

$$\sum_{i=1}^{N} X_{1i} = X_{11} + X_{12} + \ldots + X_{1N}$$

3.   Rules of Summation

There are a few simple rules of summation that you should learn. If you do so, you should have no difficulty with the few derivations presented in this book.

> *Rule 1:* The sum over a constant for N observations equals N times the constant. That is, if a is a constant, then
>
> $$\sum_{i=1}^{N} a = Na$$

This may not seem intuitively obvious, but an example should make the rule clear. Suppose we have $N = 4$ observations, and each observation equals 5. Then $a = 5$ and

$$\sum_{i=1}^{4} a = (5 + 5 + 5 + 5) = (4)(5) = 20$$

We can also extend this rule, as shown below.

> *Rule 2:* If each observation is multiplied times a constant, the sum of the constant times the observations equals the constant times the sum of the observations. That is,

$$\sum_{i=1}^{N} aX_i = a\sum_{i=1}^{N} X_i$$

For example, consider $a = 4$ and $X_1 = 2$, $X_2 = 6$, and $X_3 = 1$. Then,

$$\sum_{i=1}^{3} 4X_i = (4)(2) + (4)(6) + (4)(1)$$

$$= 4(2 + 6 + 1)$$

$$= 4\sum_{i=1}^{3} X_i = 36$$

This rule can also be applied to double sums. That is,

$$\sum_{j=1}^{J}\sum_{i=1}^{n_j} aX_{ij} = a\sum_{j=1}^{J}\sum_{i=1}^{n_j} X_{ij}$$

> *Rule 3:* If the only operation to be carried out before a summation is itself a sum, the summation can be distributed.

This rule sounds more complex than it is. Consider the following example:

$$\sum_{i=1}^{3} (X_i + 2) = (X_1 + 2) + (X_2 + 2) + (X_3 + 2)$$

$$= (X_1 + X_2 + X_3) + (2 + 2 + 2)$$

$$= \sum_{i=1}^{3} X_i + \sum_{i=1}^{3} 2$$

$$= \sum_{i=1}^{3} X_i + (3)(2)$$

$$= \sum_{i=1}^{3} X_i + 6$$

A more general expression of this double summation rule is as follows:

$$\sum_{i=1}^{N}(X_i \pm a) = \sum_{i=1}^{N} X_i \pm \sum_{i=1}^{N} a = \sum_{i=1}^{N} X_i \pm Na$$

This last step, that $\sum_{i=1}^{N} a = Na$, follows from Rule 1. Note, however, that

$$\sum_{i=1}^{N} = (X_i + a)^2 \neq \sum_{i=1}^{N} X_{i1}^2 + \sum a^2$$

We can only distribute the summation sign when the term within the parentheses is itself a simple sum or difference.

If we expand the term $(X_i + a)^2$, then we can distribute the sum. Now it follows from Rules 1 and 2 that we can simplify this expression even further as follows:

$$\Sigma(X_i + a)^2 = \Sigma(X_i^2 + 2aX_i + a^2)$$

$$= \Sigma X_i^2 + \Sigma 2aX_i + \Sigma a^2$$

$$\Sigma X_i^2 + 2a\Sigma X_i + Na^2$$

4. Sums of Two or More Variables

Sometimes we will want to examine sums of two or more variables at once. Suppose we ask what is the sum of a product of two variables across N observations.

> *Rule 4:* If each observation has a score on two variables, X_i and Y_i, then
>
> $$\sum_{i=1}^{n} X_i Y_i = X_1 Y_1 + X_2 Y_2 + \ldots + X_N Y_N$$

Suppose we have observations on two variables, X and Y, for each of three persons. The observations are

$$
\begin{array}{c|rr}
 & X_i\ Y_i \\
\hline
1 & 2\ \ \ 1 \\
i = 2 & \ \ 4\ -2 \\
3 & 2\ -3 \\
\end{array}
$$

Then

$$\sum_{i=1}^{3} X_i Y_i = (2)(1) + (4)(-2) + (2)(-3) = -12$$

Convince yourself, using this last example, that, in general,

$$\sum_{i=1}^{N} X_i Y_i \neq \Sigma\, X_i\, \Sigma\, Y_i$$

Thus, we *cannot* distribute a summation sign across products. But Rule 2 *does* apply to products. That is,

$$\Sigma a X_i Y_i = a \Sigma X_i Y_i$$

This relationship can be seen using the data from the example immediately above. If $a = 3$, then

$$\sum_{i=1}^{3} 3 X_i Y_i = 3(2)(1) + 3(4)(-2) + 3(2)(-3)$$

$$= 3[(2)(1) + (4)(-2) + (2)(-3)] = (3)(-12) = -36$$

$$= 3 \sum_{i=1}^{3} X_i Y_i$$

Rule 5: The sum of two or more variables equals the sum of the sums of the variables. That is,

$$\Sigma_i (X_{1i} + X_{2i} + \ldots + X_{ki})$$

$$= \Sigma_i X_{1i} + \Sigma_i X_{2i} + \ldots + \Sigma_i X_{ki}$$

where
$$X_1, X_2, \ldots X_k = k \text{ different variables.}$$

A special case of this rule follows:

$$\sum_i (X_i + Y_i) = \sum_i X_i + \sum_i Y_i$$

Again using the data from the example above, we can show this rule as follows:

$$\sum_{i=1}^{3} (X_i + Y_i) = (2 + 1) + [4 + (-2)] + [2 + (-3)]$$

$$= (2 + 4 + 2) + [1 + (-2) + (-3)] = 4$$

$$= \sum_i^{3} X_i + \sum_{i=1}^{3} Y_i$$

Rule 6: For constants a and b,

$$\sum_i (aX_i + bY_i) = a\sum_i X_i + b\sum_i Y_i$$

Rule 6 is really a derivative from Rules 2 and 5. Rule 5 states that we can distribute the summation sign across sums of variables, and Rule 2 states that we can pull a constant out in front of a sum.

Again using the example data above, let $a = 2$ and $b = 4$. Then

$$\sum_{i=1}^{3} (2X_i + 4Y_i) = [(2)(2) + (4)(1)] + [(2)(4) + (4)(-2)] + [(2)(2) + (4)(-3)]$$

$$= 2(2 + 4 + 2) + 4(1 - 2 - 3)$$

$$= 0$$

$$= 2\sum_{i=1}^{3} X_i + 4\sum_{i=1}^{3} Y_i$$

With this set of rules you should be able to follow the algebra used in this text. Our one piece of advice is not to be overwhelmed by sums. When in doubt about an equivalence, for example, try writing out the sums. They usually are not as complex as they seem.

Critical Values of Chi Square

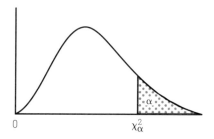

Level of Significance (α)

df	.100	.050	.025	.010	.005	0.001
1	2.7055	3.8414	5.0238	6.6349	7.8794	10.828
2	4.6051	5.9914	7.3777	9.2103	10.5966	13.816
3	6.2513	7.8147	9.3484	11.3449	12.8381	16.266
4	7.7794	9.4877	11.1433	13.2767	14.8602	18.467
5	9.2363	11.0705	12.8325	15.0863	16.7496	20.515
6	10.6446	12.5916	14.4494	16.8119	18.5476	22.458
7	12.0170	14.0671	16.0128	18.4753	20.2777	24.322
8	13.3616	15.5073	17.5346	20.0902	21.9550	26.125
9	14.6837	16.9190	19.0228	21.6660	23.5893	27.877
10	15.9871	18.3070	20.4831	23.2093	25.1882	29.588
11	17.2750	19.6751	21.9200	24.7250	26.7569	31.264
12	18.5494	21.0261	23.3367	26.2170	28.2995	32.909
13	19.8119	22.3621	24.7356	27.6883	29.8194	34.528
14	21.0642	23.6848	26.1190	29.1413	31.3193	36.123
15	22.3072	24.9958	27.4884	30.5779	32.8013	37.697
16	23.5418	26.2962	28.8454	31.9999	34.2672	39.252
17	24.7690	27.5871	30.1910	33.4087	35.7185	40.790
18	25.9894	28.8693	31.5264	34.8058	37.1564	42.312
19	27.2036	30.1435	32.8523	36.1908	38.5822	43.820

continued

Source: Abridged from Table IV of Fisher and Yates: *Statistical Tables for Biological, Agricultural, and Medical Research*, 6th ed. (London: Longman Group Ltd., 1974). Previously published by Oliver & Boyd Ltd. (Edinburgh) and by permission of the authors and publishers.

Critical Values of Chi Square (Cont.)

df	*Level of Significance (α)*					
	.100	*.050*	*.025*	*.010*	*.005*	*0.001*
20	28.4120	31.4104	34.1696	37.5662	39.9968	45.315
21	29.6151	32.6705	35.4789	38.9321	41.4010	46.797
22	30.8133	33.9244	36.7807	40.2894	42.7956	48.268
23	32.0069	35.1725	38.0757	41.6384	44.1813	49.728
24	33.1963	36.4151	39.3641	42.9798	45.5585	51.179
25	34.3816	37.6525	40.6465	44.3141	46.9278	52.620
26	35.5631	38.8852	41.9232	45.6417	48.2899	54.052
27	36.7412	40.1133	43.1944	46.9680	49.6449	55.476
28	37.9159	41.3372	44.4607	48.2782	50.9933	56.892
29	39.0875	42.5569	45.7222	49.5879	52.3356	58.302
30	40.2560	43.7729	46.9792	50.8922	53.6720	59.703
40	51.8050	55.7585	59.3417	63.6907	66.7659	73.402
50	63.1671	67.5048	71.4202	76.1539	79.4900	86.661
60	74.3970	79.0819	83.2976	88.3794	91.9517	99.607
70	85.5271	90.5312	95.0231	100.425	104.215	112.317
80	96.5782	101.879	106.629	112.329	116.321	124.839
90	107.565	113.145	118.136	124.116	128.299	137.208
100	118.498	124.342	129.561	135.807	140.169	149.449

Area Under the Normal Curve

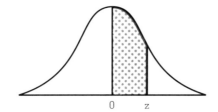

z	.00	.01	.02	.03	.04	.05	.06	.07	.08	.09
0.0	.0000	.0040	.0080	.0120	.0160	.0199	.0239	.0279	.0319	.0359
0.1	.0398	.0438	.0478	.0517	.0557	.0596	.0636	.0675	.0714	.0753
0.2	.0793	.0832	.0871	.0910	.0948	.0987	.1026	.1064	.1103	.1141
0.3	.1179	.1217	.1255	.1293	.1331	.1368	.1406	.1443	.1480	.1517
0.4	.1554	.1591	.1628	.1664	.1700	.1736	.1772	.1808	.1844	.1879
0.5	.1915	.1950	.1985	.2019	.2054	.2088	.2123	.2157	.2190	.2224
0.6	.2257	.2291	.2324	.2357	.2389	.2422	.2454	.2486	.2517	.2549
0.7	.2580	.2611	.2642	.2673	.2704	.2734	.2764	.2794	.2823	.2852
0.8	.2881	.2910	.2939	.2967	.2995	.3023	.3051	.3078	.3106	.3133
0.9	.3159	.3186	.3212	.3238	.3264	.3289	.3315	.3340	.3365	.3389
1.0	.3413	.3438	.3461	.3485	.3508	.3531	.3554	.3577	.3599	.3621
1.1	.3643	.3665	.3686	.3708	.3729	.3749	.3770	.3790	.3810	.3830
1.2	.3849	.3869	.3888	.3907	.3925	.3944	.3962	.3980	.3997	.4015
1.3	.4032	.4049	.4066	.4082	.4099	.4115	.4131	.4147	.4162	.4177
1.4	.4192	.4207	.4222	.4236	.4251	.4265	.4279	.4292	.4306	.4319
1.5	.4332	.4345	.4357	.4370	.4382	.4394	.4406	.4418	.4429	.4441
1.6	.4452	.4463	.4474	.4484	.4495	.4505	.4515	.4525	.4535	.4545
1.7	.4554	.4564	.4573	.4582	.4591	.4599	.4608	.4616	.4625	.4633
1.8	.4641	.4649	.4656	.4664	.4671	.4678	.4686	.4693	.4699	.4706
1.9	.4713	.4719	.4726	.4732	.4738	.4744	.4750	.4756	.4761	.4767
2.0	.4772	.4778	.4783	.4788	.4793	.4798	.4803	.4808	.4812	.4817
2.1	.4821	.4826	.4830	.4834	.4838	.4842	.4846	.4850	.4854	.4857
2.2	.4861	.4864	.4868	.4871	.4875	.4878	.4881	.4884	.4887	.4890
2.3	.4893	.4896	.4898	.4901	.4904	.4906	.4909	.4911	.4913	.4916
2.4	.4918	.4920	.4922	.4925	.4927	.4929	.4931	.4932	.4934	.4936
2.5	.4938	.4940	.4941	.4943	.4945	.4946	.4948	.4949	.4951	.4952
2.6	.4953	.4955	.4956	.4957	.4959	.4960	.4961	.4962	.4963	.4964
2.7	.4965	.4966	.4967	.4968	.4969	.4970	.4971	.4972	.4973	.4974
2.8	.4974	.4975	.4976	.4977	.4977	.4978	.4979	.4979	.4980	.4981
2.9	.4981	.4982	.4982	.4983	.4984	.4984	.4985	.4985	.4986	.4986
3.0	.4987	.4987	.4987	.4988	.4988	.4989	.4989	.4989	.4990	.4990

Source: Abridged from Table I of *Statistical Tables and Formulas,* by A. Hald (New York: John Wiley & Sons, Inc., 1952). Reproduced by permission of A. Hald and the publishers, John Wiley & Sons, Inc.

Student's *t* Distribution

A. Two-Tailed

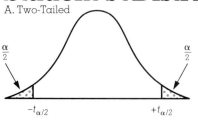

B. One-Tailed

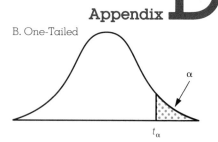

Level of Significance for:

	df	.20	.10	.05	.025	.01	.001
Two-Tailed Test		.20	.10	.05	.025	.01	.001
One-Tailed Test		.10	.05	.025	.01	.005	.0005
	1	3.078	6.314	12.706	31.821	63.657	636.619
	2	1.886	2.920	4.303	6.965	9.925	31.598
	3	1.638	2.353	3.182	4.541	5.841	12.941
	4	1.533	2.132	2.776	3.747	4.604	8.610
	5	1.476	2.015	2.571	3.365	4.032	6.859
	6	1.440	1.943	2.447	3.143	3.707	5.959
	7	1.415	1.895	2.365	2.998	3.499	5.405
	8	1.397	1.860	2.306	2.896	3.355	5.041
	9	1.383	1.833	2.262	2.821	3.250	4.781
	10	1.372	1.812	2.228	2.764	3.169	4.587
	11	1.363	1.796	2.201	2.718	3.106	4.437
	12	1.356	1.782	2.179	2.681	3.055	4.318
	13	1.350	1.771	2.160	2.650	3.012	4.221
	14	1.345	1.761	2.145	2.624	2.977	4.140
	15	1.341	1.753	2.131	2.602	2.947	4.073
	16	1.337	1.746	2.120	2.583	2.921	4.015
	17	1.333	1.740	2.110	2.567	2.898	3.965
	18	1.330	1.734	2.101	2.552	2.878	3.922
	19	1.328	1.729	2.093	2.539	2.861	3.883
	20	1.325	1.725	2.086	2.528	2.845	3.850
	21	1.323	1.721	2.080	2.518	2.831	3.819
	22	1.321	1.717	2.074	2.508	2.819	3.792
	23	1.319	1.714	2.069	2.500	2.807	3.767
	24	1.318	1.711	2.064	2.492	2.797	3.745
	25	1.316	1.708	2.060	2.485	2.787	3.725
	26	1.315	1.706	2.056	2.479	2.779	3.707
	27	1.314	1.703	2.052	2.473	2.771	3.690
	28	1.313	1.701	2.048	2.467	2.763	3.674
	29	1.311	1.699	2.045	2.462	2.756	3.659
	30	1.310	1.697	2.042	2.457	2.750	3.646
	40	1.303	1.684	2.021	2.423	2.704	3.551
	60	1.296	1.671	2.000	2.390	2.660	3.460
	120	1.289	1.658	1.980	2.358	2.617	3.373
	∞	1.282	1.645	1.960	2.326	2.576	3.291

Source: Adapted from Table III of Fisher and Yates: *Statistical Tables for Biological, Agricultural and Medical Research*, 6th ed. (London: Longman Group Ltd., 1974). Previously published by Oliver & Boyd Ltd. (Edinburgh) and by permission of the authors and publishers.

F Distribution

The *F* distribution table consists of three parts, for $\alpha = .05$, $\alpha = .01$, and $\alpha = .001$. These tables appear on the next three pages.

$\alpha = .05$

v_2 \ v_1	1	2	3	4	5	6	7	8	9	10	12	15	20	24	30	40	60	120	∞
1	161.4	199.5	215.7	224.6	230.2	234.0	236.8	238.9	240.5	241.9	243.9	245.9	248.0	249.1	250.1	251.1	252.2	253.3	254.3
2	18.51	19.00	19.16	19.25	19.30	19.33	19.35	19.37	19.38	19.40	19.41	19.43	19.45	19.45	19.46	19.47	19.48	19.49	19.50
3	10.13	9.55	9.28	9.12	9.01	8.94	8.89	8.85	8.81	8.79	8.74	8.70	8.66	8.64	8.62	8.59	8.57	8.55	8.53
4	7.71	6.94	6.59	6.39	6.26	6.16	6.09	6.04	6.00	5.96	5.91	5.86	5.80	5.77	5.75	5.72	5.69	5.66	5.63
5	6.61	5.79	5.41	5.19	5.05	4.95	4.88	4.82	4.77	4.74	4.68	4.62	4.56	4.53	4.50	4.46	4.43	4.40	4.36
6	5.99	5.14	4.76	4.53	4.39	4.28	4.21	4.15	4.10	4.06	4.00	3.94	3.87	3.84	3.81	3.77	3.74	3.70	3.67
7	5.59	4.74	4.35	4.12	3.97	3.87	3.79	3.73	3.68	3.64	3.57	3.51	3.44	3.41	3.38	3.34	3.30	3.27	3.23
8	5.32	4.46	4.07	3.84	3.69	3.58	3.50	3.44	3.39	3.35	3.28	3.22	3.15	3.12	3.08	3.04	3.01	2.97	2.93
9	5.12	4.26	3.86	3.63	3.48	3.37	3.29	3.23	3.18	3.14	3.07	3.01	2.94	2.90	2.86	2.83	2.79	2.75	2.71
10	4.96	4.10	3.71	3.48	3.33	3.22	3.14	3.07	3.02	2.98	2.91	2.85	2.77	2.74	2.70	2.66	2.62	2.58	2.54
11	4.84	3.98	3.59	3.36	3.20	3.09	3.01	2.95	2.90	2.85	2.79	2.72	2.65	2.61	2.57	2.53	2.49	2.45	2.40
12	4.75	3.89	3.49	3.26	3.11	3.00	2.91	2.85	2.80	2.75	2.69	2.62	2.54	2.51	2.47	2.43	2.38	2.34	2.30
13	4.67	3.81	3.41	3.18	3.03	2.92	2.83	2.77	2.71	2.67	2.60	2.53	2.46	2.42	2.38	2.34	2.30	2.25	2.21
14	4.60	3.74	3.34	3.11	2.96	2.85	2.76	2.70	2.65	2.60	2.53	2.46	2.39	2.35	2.31	2.27	2.22	2.18	2.13
15	4.54	3.68	3.29	3.06	2.90	2.79	2.71	2.64	2.59	2.54	2.48	2.40	2.33	2.29	2.25	2.20	2.16	2.11	2.07
16	4.49	3.63	3.24	3.01	2.85	2.74	2.66	2.59	2.54	2.49	2.42	2.35	2.28	2.24	2.19	2.15	2.11	2.06	2.01
17	4.45	3.59	3.20	2.96	2.81	2.70	2.61	2.55	2.49	2.45	2.38	2.31	2.23	2.19	2.15	2.10	2.06	2.01	1.96
18	4.41	3.55	3.16	2.93	2.77	2.66	2.58	2.51	2.46	2.41	2.34	2.27	2.19	2.15	2.11	2.06	2.02	1.97	1.92
19	4.38	3.52	3.13	2.90	2.74	2.63	2.54	2.48	2.42	2.38	2.31	2.23	2.16	2.11	2.07	2.03	1.98	1.93	1.88
20	4.35	3.49	3.10	2.87	2.71	2.60	2.51	2.45	2.39	2.35	2.28	2.20	2.12	2.08	2.04	1.99	1.95	1.90	1.84
21	4.32	3.47	3.07	2.84	2.68	2.57	2.49	2.42	2.37	2.32	2.25	2.18	2.10	2.05	2.01	1.96	1.92	1.87	1.81
22	4.30	3.44	3.05	2.82	2.66	2.55	2.46	2.40	2.34	2.30	2.23	2.15	2.07	2.03	1.98	1.94	1.89	1.84	1.78
23	4.28	3.42	3.03	2.80	2.64	2.53	2.44	2.37	2.32	2.27	2.20	2.13	2.05	2.01	1.96	1.91	1.86	1.81	1.76
24	4.26	3.40	3.01	2.78	2.62	2.51	2.42	2.36	2.30	2.25	2.18	2.11	2.03	1.98	1.94	1.89	1.84	1.79	1.73
25	4.24	3.39	2.99	2.76	2.60	2.49	2.40	2.34	2.28	2.24	2.16	2.09	2.01	1.96	1.92	1.87	1.82	1.77	1.71
26	4.23	3.37	2.98	2.74	2.59	2.47	2.39	2.32	2.27	2.22	2.15	2.07	1.99	1.95	1.90	1.85	1.80	1.75	1.69
27	4.21	3.35	2.96	2.73	2.57	2.46	2.37	2.31	2.25	2.20	2.13	2.06	1.97	1.93	1.88	1.84	1.79	1.73	1.67
28	4.20	3.34	2.95	2.71	2.56	2.45	2.36	2.29	2.24	2.19	2.12	2.04	1.96	1.91	1.87	1.82	1.77	1.71	1.65
29	4.18	3.33	2.93	2.70	2.55	2.43	2.35	2.28	2.22	2.18	2.10	2.03	1.94	1.90	1.85	1.81	1.75	1.70	1.64
30	4.17	3.32	2.92	2.69	2.53	2.42	2.33	2.27	2.21	2.16	2.09	2.01	1.93	1.89	1.84	1.79	1.74	1.68	1.62
40	4.08	3.23	2.84	2.61	2.45	2.34	2.25	2.18	2.12	2.08	2.00	1.92	1.84	1.79	1.74	1.69	1.64	1.58	1.51
60	4.00	3.15	2.76	2.53	2.37	2.25	2.17	2.10	2.04	1.99	1.92	1.84	1.75	1.70	1.65	1.59	1.53	1.47	1.39
120	3.92	3.07	2.68	2.45	2.29	2.17	2.09	2.02	1.96	1.91	1.83	1.75	1.66	1.61	1.55	1.50	1.43	1.35	1.25
∞	3.84	3.00	2.60	2.37	2.21	2.10	2.01	1.94	1.88	1.83	1.75	1.67	1.57	1.52	1.46	1.39	1.32	1.22	1.00

Source: Adapted from E. S. Pearson and H. O. Hartley: *Biometrika Tables for Statisticians,* 2nd ed. (Cambridge: Cambridge University Press, 1962).

F Distribution (Cont.)

$\alpha = .01$

v_2 \ v_1	1	2	3	4	5	6	7	8	9	10	12	15	20	24	30	40	60	120	∞
1	4052	4999.5	5403	5625	5764	5859	5928	5982	6022	6056	6106	6157	6209	6235	6261	6287	6313	6339	6366
2	98.50	99.00	99.17	99.25	99.30	99.33	99.36	99.37	99.39	99.40	99.42	99.43	99.45	99.46	99.47	99.47	99.48	99.49	99.50
3	34.12	30.82	29.46	28.71	28.24	27.91	27.67	27.49	27.35	27.23	27.05	26.87	26.69	26.60	26.50	26.41	26.32	26.22	26.13
4	21.20	18.00	16.69	15.98	15.52	15.21	14.98	14.80	14.66	14.55	14.37	14.20	14.02	13.93	13.84	13.75	13.65	13.56	13.46
5	16.26	13.27	12.06	11.39	10.97	10.67	10.46	10.29	10.16	10.05	9.89	9.72	9.55	9.47	9.38	9.29	9.20	9.11	9.02
6	13.75	10.92	9.78	9.15	8.75	8.47	8.26	8.10	7.98	7.87	7.72	7.56	7.40	7.31	7.23	7.14	7.06	6.97	6.88
7	12.25	9.55	8.45	7.85	7.46	7.19	6.99	6.84	6.72	6.62	6.47	6.31	6.16	6.07	5.99	5.91	5.82	5.74	5.65
8	11.26	8.65	7.59	7.01	6.63	6.37	6.18	6.03	5.91	5.81	5.67	5.52	5.36	5.28	5.20	5.12	5.03	4.95	4.86
9	10.56	8.02	6.99	6.42	6.06	5.80	5.61	5.47	5.35	5.26	5.11	4.96	4.81	4.73	4.65	4.57	4.48	4.40	4.31
10	10.04	7.56	6.55	5.99	5.64	5.39	5.20	5.06	4.94	4.85	4.71	4.56	4.41	4.33	4.25	4.17	4.08	4.00	3.91
11	9.65	7.21	6.22	5.67	5.32	5.07	4.89	4.74	4.63	4.54	4.40	4.25	4.10	4.02	3.94	3.86	3.78	3.69	3.60
12	9.33	6.93	5.95	5.41	5.06	4.82	4.64	4.50	4.39	4.30	4.16	4.01	3.86	3.78	3.70	3.62	3.54	3.45	3.36
13	9.07	6.70	5.74	5.21	4.86	4.62	4.44	4.30	4.19	4.10	3.96	3.82	3.66	3.59	3.51	3.43	3.34	3.25	3.17
14	8.86	6.51	5.56	5.04	4.69	4.46	4.28	4.14	4.03	3.94	3.80	3.66	3.51	3.43	3.35	3.27	3.18	3.09	3.00
15	8.68	6.36	5.42	4.89	4.56	4.32	4.14	4.00	3.89	3.80	3.67	3.52	3.37	3.29	3.21	3.13	3.05	2.96	2.87
16	8.53	6.23	5.29	4.77	4.44	4.20	4.03	3.89	3.78	3.69	3.55	3.41	3.26	3.18	3.10	3.02	2.93	2.84	2.75
17	8.40	6.11	5.18	4.67	4.34	4.10	3.93	3.79	3.68	3.59	3.46	3.31	3.16	3.08	3.00	2.92	2.83	2.75	2.65
18	8.29	6.01	5.09	4.58	4.25	4.01	3.84	3.71	3.60	3.51	3.37	3.23	3.08	3.00	2.92	2.84	2.75	2.66	2.57
19	8.18	5.93	5.01	4.50	4.17	3.94	3.77	3.63	3.52	3.43	3.30	3.15	3.00	2.92	2.84	2.76	2.67	2.58	2.49
20	8.10	5.85	4.94	4.43	4.10	3.87	3.70	3.56	3.46	3.37	3.23	3.09	2.94	2.86	2.78	2.69	2.61	2.52	2.42
21	8.02	5.78	4.87	4.37	4.04	3.81	3.64	3.51	3.40	3.31	3.17	3.03	2.88	2.80	2.72	2.64	2.55	2.46	2.36
22	7.95	5.72	4.82	4.31	3.99	3.76	3.59	3.45	3.35	3.26	3.12	2.98	2.83	2.75	2.67	2.58	2.50	2.40	2.31
23	7.88	5.66	4.76	4.26	3.94	3.71	3.54	3.41	3.30	3.21	3.07	2.93	2.78	2.70	2.62	2.54	2.45	2.35	2.26
24	7.82	5.61	4.72	4.22	3.90	3.67	3.50	3.36	3.26	3.17	3.03	2.89	2.74	2.66	2.58	2.49	2.40	2.31	2.21
25	7.77	5.57	4.68	4.18	3.85	3.63	3.46	3.32	3.22	3.13	2.99	2.85	2.70	2.62	2.54	2.45	2.36	2.27	2.17
26	7.72	5.53	4.64	4.14	3.82	3.59	3.42	3.29	3.18	3.09	2.96	2.81	2.66	2.58	2.50	2.42	2.33	2.23	2.13
27	7.68	5.49	4.60	4.11	3.78	3.56	3.39	3.26	3.15	3.06	2.93	2.78	2.63	2.55	2.47	2.38	2.29	2.20	2.10
28	7.64	5.45	4.57	4.07	3.75	3.53	3.36	3.23	3.12	3.03	2.90	2.75	2.60	2.52	2.44	2.35	2.26	2.17	2.06
29	7.60	5.42	4.54	4.04	3.73	3.50	3.33	3.20	3.09	3.00	2.87	2.73	2.57	2.49	2.41	2.33	2.23	2.14	2.03
30	7.56	5.39	4.51	4.02	3.70	3.47	3.30	3.17	3.07	2.98	2.84	2.70	2.55	2.47	2.39	2.30	2.21	2.11	2.01
40	7.31	5.18	4.31	3.83	3.51	3.29	3.12	2.99	2.89	2.80	2.66	2.52	2.37	2.29	2.20	2.11	2.02	1.92	1.80
60	7.08	4.98	4.13	3.65	3.34	3.12	2.95	2.82	2.72	2.63	2.50	2.35	2.20	2.12	2.03	1.94	1.84	1.73	1.60
120	6.85	4.79	3.95	3.48	3.17	2.96	2.79	2.66	2.56	2.47	2.34	2.19	2.03	1.95	1.86	1.76	1.66	1.53	1.38
∞	6.63	4.61	3.78	3.32	3.02	2.80	2.64	2.51	2.41	2.32	2.18	2.04	1.88	1.79	1.70	1.59	1.47	1.32	1.00

F Distribution (Cont.)

$\alpha = .001$

ν_2 \ ν_1	1	2	3	4	5	6	7	8	9	10	12	15	20	24	30	40	60	120	∞
1	4053*	5000*	5404*	5625*	5764*	5859*	5929*	5981*	6023*	6056*	6107*	6158*	6209*	6235*	6261*	6287*	6313*	6340*	6366*
2	998.5	999.0	999.2	999.2	999.3	999.3	999.4	999.4	999.4	999.4	999.4	999.4	999.4	999.5	999.5	999.5	999.5	999.5	999.5
3	167.0	148.5	141.1	137.1	134.6	132.8	131.6	130.6	129.9	129.2	128.3	127.4	126.4	125.9	125.4	125.0	124.5	124.0	123.5
4	74.14	61.25	56.18	53.44	51.71	50.53	49.66	49.00	48.47	48.05	47.41	46.76	46.10	45.77	45.43	45.09	44.75	44.40	44.05
5	47.18	37.12	33.20	31.09	29.75	28.84	28.16	27.64	27.24	26.92	26.42	25.91	25.39	25.14	24.87	24.60	24.33	24.06	23.79
6	35.51	27.00	23.70	21.92	20.81	20.03	19.46	19.03	18.69	18.41	17.99	17.56	17.12	16.89	16.67	16.44	16.21	15.99	15.75
7	29.25	21.69	18.77	17.19	16.21	15.52	15.02	14.63	14.33	14.08	13.71	13.32	12.93	12.73	12.53	12.33	12.12	11.91	11.70
8	25.42	18.49	15.83	14.39	13.49	12.86	12.40	12.04	11.77	11.54	11.19	10.84	10.48	10.30	10.11	9.92	9.73	9.53	9.33
9	22.86	16.39	13.90	12.56	11.71	11.13	10.70	10.37	10.11	9.89	9.57	9.24	8.90	8.72	8.55	8.37	8.19	8.00	7.81
10	21.04	14.91	12.55	11.28	10.48	9.92	9.52	9.20	8.96	8.75	8.45	8.13	7.80	7.64	7.47	7.30	7.12	6.94	6.76
11	19.69	13.81	11.56	10.35	9.58	9.05	8.66	8.35	8.12	7.92	7.63	7.32	7.01	6.85	6.68	6.52	6.35	6.17	6.00
12	18.64	12.97	10.80	9.63	8.89	8.38	8.00	7.71	7.48	7.29	7.00	6.71	6.40	6.25	6.09	5.93	5.76	5.59	5.42
13	17.81	12.31	10.21	9.07	8.35	7.86	7.49	7.21	6.98	6.80	6.52	6.23	5.93	5.78	5.63	5.47	5.30	5.14	4.97
14	17.14	11.78	9.73	8.62	7.92	7.43	7.08	6.80	6.58	6.40	6.13	5.85	5.56	5.41	5.25	5.10	4.94	4.77	4.60
15	16.59	11.34	9.34	8.25	7.57	7.09	6.74	6.47	6.26	6.08	5.81	5.54	5.25	5.10	4.95	4.80	4.64	4.47	4.31
16	16.12	10.97	9.00	7.94	7.27	6.81	6.46	6.19	5.98	5.81	5.55	5.27	4.99	4.85	4.70	4.54	4.39	4.23	4.06
17	15.72	10.66	8.73	7.68	7.02	6.56	6.22	5.96	5.75	5.58	5.32	5.05	4.78	4.63	4.48	4.33	4.18	4.02	3.85
18	15.38	10.39	8.49	7.46	6.81	6.35	6.02	5.76	5.56	5.39	5.13	4.87	4.59	4.45	4.30	4.15	4.00	3.84	3.67
19	15.08	10.16	8.28	7.26	6.62	6.18	5.85	5.59	5.39	5.22	4.97	4.70	4.43	4.29	4.14	3.99	3.84	3.68	3.51
20	14.82	9.95	8.10	7.10	6.46	6.02	5.69	5.44	5.24	5.08	4.82	4.56	4.29	4.15	4.00	3.86	3.70	3.54	3.38
21	14.59	9.77	7.94	6.95	6.32	5.88	5.56	5.31	5.11	4.95	4.70	4.44	4.17	4.03	3.88	3.74	3.58	3.42	3.26
22	14.38	9.61	7.80	6.81	6.19	5.76	5.44	5.19	4.99	4.83	4.58	4.33	4.06	3.92	3.78	3.63	3.48	3.32	3.15
23	14.19	9.47	7.67	6.69	6.08	5.65	5.33	5.09	4.89	4.73	4.48	4.23	3.96	3.82	3.68	3.53	3.38	3.22	3.05
24	14.03	9.34	7.55	6.59	5.98	5.55	5.23	4.99	4.80	4.64	4.39	4.14	3.87	3.74	3.59	3.45	3.29	3.14	2.97
25	13.88	9.22	7.45	6.49	5.88	5.46	5.15	4.91	4.71	4.56	4.31	4.06	3.79	3.66	3.52	3.37	3.22	3.06	2.89
26	13.74	9.12	7.36	6.41	5.80	5.38	5.07	4.83	4.64	4.48	4.24	3.99	3.72	3.59	3.44	3.30	3.15	2.99	2.82
27	13.61	9.02	7.27	6.33	5.73	5.31	5.00	4.76	4.57	4.41	4.17	3.92	3.66	3.52	3.38	3.23	3.08	2.92	2.75
28	13.50	8.93	7.19	6.25	5.66	5.24	4.93	4.69	4.50	4.35	4.11	3.86	3.60	3.46	3.32	3.18	3.02	2.86	2.69
29	13.39	8.85	7.12	6.19	5.59	5.18	4.87	4.64	4.45	4.29	4.05	3.80	3.54	3.41	3.27	3.12	2.97	2.81	2.64
30	13.29	8.77	7.05	6.12	5.53	5.12	4.82	4.58	4.39	4.24	4.00	3.75	3.49	3.36	3.22	3.07	2.92	2.76	2.59
40	12.61	8.25	6.60	5.70	5.13	4.73	4.44	4.21	4.02	3.87	3.64	3.40	3.15	3.01	2.87	2.73	2.57	2.41	2.23
60	11.97	7.76	6.17	5.31	4.76	4.37	4.09	3.87	3.69	3.54	3.31	3.08	2.83	2.69	2.55	2.41	2.25	2.08	1.89
120	11.38	7.32	5.79	4.95	4.42	4.04	3.77	3.55	3.38	3.24	3.02	2.78	2.53	2.40	2.26	2.11	1.95	1.76	1.54
∞	10.83	6.91	5.42	4.62	4.10	3.74	3.47	3.27	3.10	2.96	2.74	2.51	2.27	2.13	1.99	1.84	1.66	1.45	1.00

Fisher's r-to-Z Transformation

r	z	r	z	r	z	r	z	r	z
.000	.000	.200	.203	.400	.424	.600	.693	.800	1.099
.005	.005	.205	.208	.405	.430	.605	.701	.805	1.113
.010	.010	.210	.213	.410	.436	.610	.709	.810	1.127
.015	.015	.215	.218	.415	.442	.615	.717	.815	1.142
.020	.020	.220	.224	.420	.448	.620	.725	.820	1.157
.025	.025	.225	.229	.425	.454	.625	.733	.825	1.172
.030	.030	.230	.234	.430	.460	.630	.741	.830	1.188
.035	.035	.235	.239	.435	.466	.635	.750	.835	1.204
.040	.040	.240	.245	.440	.472	.640	.758	.840	1.221
.045	.045	.245	.250	.445	.478	.645	.767	.845	1.238
.050	.050	.250	.255	.450	.485	.650	.775	.850	1.256
.055	.055	.255	.261	.455	.491	.655	.784	.855	1.274
.060	.060	.260	.266	.460	.497	.660	.793	.860	1.293
.065	.065	.265	.271	.465	.504	.665	.802	.865	1.313
.070	.070	.270	.277	.470	.510	.670	.811	.870	1.333
.075	.075	.275	.282	.475	.517	.675	.820	.875	1.354
.080	.080	.280	.288	.480	.523	.680	.829	.880	1.376
.085	.085	.285	.293	.485	.530	.685	.838	.885	1.398
.090	.090	.290	.299	.490	.536	.690	.848	.890	1.422
.095	.095	.295	.304	.495	.543	.695	.858	.895	1.447
.100	.100	.300	.310	.500	.549	.700	.867	.900	1.472
.105	.105	.305	.315	.505	.556	.705	.877	.905	1.499
.110	.110	.310	.321	.510	.563	.710	.887	.910	1.528
.115	.116	.315	.326	.515	.570	.715	.897	.915	1.557
.120	.121	.320	.332	.520	.576	.720	.908	.920	1.589
.125	.126	.325	.337	.525	.583	.725	.918	.925	1.623
.130	.131	.330	.343	.530	.590	.730	.929	.930	1.658
.135	.136	.335	.348	.535	.597	.735	.940	.935	1.697
.140	.141	.340	.354	.540	.604	.740	.950	.940	1.738
.145	.146	.345	.360	.545	.611	.745	.962	.945	1.783
.150	.151	.350	.365	.550	.618	.750	.973	.950	1.832
.155	.156	.355	.371	.555	.626	.755	.984	.955	1.886
.160	.161	.360	.377	.560	.633	.760	.996	.960	1.946
.165	.167	.365	.383	.565	.640	.765	1.008	.965	2.014
.170	.172	.370	.388	.570	.648	.770	1.020	.970	2.092
.175	.177	.375	.394	.575	.655	.775	1.033	.975	2.185
.180	.182	.380	.400	.580	.662	.780	1.045	.980	2.298
.185	.187	.385	.406	.585	.670	.785	1.058	.985	2.443
.190	.192	.390	.412	.590	.678	.790	1.071	.990	2.647
.195	.198	.395	.418	.595	.685	.795	1.085	.995	2.994

Glossary

A

Adjusted coefficient of determination. A coefficient of determination that takes into account the number of independent variables relative to the number of observations.

Adjusted goodness-of-fit index. The re-expression of the GFI in terms of the numbers of degrees of freedom used in the fitting model.

Algorithm. Computer routine.

Alpha area. The area in the tail of a normal distribution that is cut off by a given Z_α.

Alternative hypothesis. A secondary hypothesis about the value of a population parameter that often reverses the research or operation hypothesis. Symbolized H_1.

Analysis of covariance (ANCOVA). A multiple regression equation including one or more dummy variables, with a continuous independent variable and no interaction terms.

Analysis of variance. A statistical test of the difference of means for two or more groups.

ANOVA summary table. A tabular display summarizing the results of an analysis of variance.

Applied research. Research that attempts to explain social phenomena with immediate public policy implications.

Average absolute deviation. The mean of the absolute value of the difference between a set of continuous measures and their mean.

B

Bar chart. A type of diagram for discrete variables in which the numbers or percentages of cases in each outcome are displayed.

Basic research. Research that examines the validity of general statements about relationships involving fundamental social processes.

Best linear and unbiased estimate (BLUE). An estimator for population regression parameters that assumes a linear relationship, no measurement error, and normally distributed error terms.

Beta coefficient (beta weight). A standardized regression coefficient indicating the amount of net change, in standard deviation units, of the dependent variable for an independent variable change of one standard deviation.

Beta matrix. Matrix containing the causal parameters that link all pairs of endogenous variables.

Between sum of squares. A value obtained by subtracting the grand mean from each group mean, squaring these differences for all individuals, and summing them.

BIC statistic. A test statistic for assessing log-linear models fit to large-sample crosstabulations.

Bivariate crosstabulation (joint contingency table). A tabular display of the simultaneous outcomes of observations on two discrete variables.

Bivariate linear relationship (bivariate regression). A regression of *Y* on *X*.

Bivariate regression coefficient. A parameter estimate of a bivariate regression equation that measures the amount of increase or decrease in the dependent variable for a one-unit difference in the independent variable.

Box-and-whisker (boxplot). A type of graph for discrete and continuous variables in which boxes and lines represent central tendency, variability, and shape of a distribution of observed data.

C

Causal diagram. A visual representation of the cause-and-effect relationships among variables, using keyword names and directed arrows.

Cell. The intersection of a row and a column in a crosstabulation of two or more variables. Numerical values contained within cells may be cell frequencies, cell proportions, or cell percentages.

Central limit theorem. If all possible random samples of *N* observations are drawn from any population with mean μ_Y and variance σ_Y^2, then as *N* grows large, these sample means approach a normal distribution, with mean μ_Y and variance σ_Y^2/N.

Central tendency. Average value of a set of scores.

Chain path model. A causal model in which variables measured on the same sample at three or more times are depicted as the causes of their own subsequent values.

Chebycheff's inequality theorem. The probability a variable differs absolutely from the mean by *k* or more standard deviations is *always* less than or equal to the ratio of 1 to k^2 (for all *k* greater than 1.0).

Chi-square distribution. A family of distributions, each of which has different degrees of freedom, on which the chi-square test statistic is based.

Chi-square test. A test of statistical significance based on a comparison of the observed cell frequencies of a joint contingency table with frequencies that would be expected under the null hypothesis of no relationship.

Chow test. A test of statistical significance for the differences in multiple regression coefficients for a pair of identically specified equations.

Codebook. A complete record of all coding decisions.

Coefficient difference test. A statistical test to determine whether two correlation coefficients differ in the population.

Coefficient of determination. A PRE statistic for linear regression that expresses the amount of variation in the dependent variable explained or accounted for by the independent variable(s) in a regression equation.

Coefficient of nondetermination. A statistic that expresses the amount of variation in a dependent variable that is left *unexplained* by the independent variable(s) in a regression equation.

Column marginals. The frequency distribution of the variable shown across the columns of a crosstabulation.

Completely standardized solution. All observed and unobserved variables are standardized and parameters are exposed in standard deviation units.

Computing formula for b. Easy-to-use formula for calculating the bivariate regression coefficient.

Concept. A precisely defined object, behavior, perception (of self or others), or phenomenon that is relevant to the particular theoretical concerns at hand.

Conceptual model. A model that depicts causal relations among abstract terms that are not directly observable.

Concordant pair. In a crosstabulation of two orderable discrete variables, one observation has a higher rank on both variables than does the other member of the pair.

Conditional correlation coefficients. Correlation coefficients calculated between two crosstabulated continuous variables within each category of a third variable.

Conditional mean. The expected average score on the dependent variable, Y, for a given value of the independent variable, X.

Conditional odds. The chance of being in one category of a variable relative to the remaining categories of that variable, within a specific category of a second variable.

Conditional odds ratio. An odds ratio between two variables for a given category of a third variable.

Confidence interval. A range of values constructed around a point estimate that makes it possible to state that an interval contains the population parameter between its upper and lower confidence limits.

Confidence interval for mean differences. An interval constructed around the point estimate of the difference between two means.

Confirmatory factor analysis. A structural equation model, with one or more unobserved variables having multiple indicators, in which the research specifies the pattern of indicator loadings.

Conformability. A property of two matrices in which their orders are suitable for addition and/or multiplication.

Consistent estimator. An estimator of a population parameter that approximates the parameter more closely as N gets large.

Constant. A value that does not change.

Construct. Unobserved concept used by social scientists to explain observations.

Continuous probability distribution. A probability distribution for a continuous variable, with no interruptions or spaces between the outcomes of the variable.

Continuous variable. A variable that, in theory, can take on all possible numerical values in a given interval.

Contrast. A set of weighted population means that sum to zero, used in making post hoc comparisons of treatment groups.

Correlated effect. A component in the decomposition of a correlation coefficient that is due to a correlation among predetermined variables.

Correlation coefficient. A measure of association between two continuous variables that estimates the direction and strength of linear relationship.

Correlation ratio (eta-squared). A measure of nonlinear covariation between a discrete and continuous variable, the ratio of SS_{BETWEEN} to SS_{TOTAL}.

Covariance. The sum of the product of deviations of the *X*s and *Y*s about their respective means, divided by $N - 1$ in the sample and *N* in the population.

Covariate. A continuous variable in an analysis of covariance.

Covariation. Joint variation, or association, between a pair of variables.

Critical value. The minimum value of *Z* necessary to designate an alpha area.

Cronbach's alpha. A measure of internal reliability for multi-item summed indexes.

Cumulative frequency. For a given score or outcome of a variable, the total number of cases in a distribution at or below that value.

Cumulative frequency distribution. A distribution of scores showing the number of cases at or below each outcome of the variable being displayed in the distribution.

Cumulative percentage. For a given score or outcome of a variable, the percentage of cases in a distribution at or below that value.

Cumulative percentage distribution. A distribution of scores showing the percentage of cases at or below each outcome of the variable being displayed in the distribution.

D

Data collection. The activity of constructing primary data records for a given sample or population of observations.

Data file. The entire set of numerical values for each variable for every case.

Deciles. The values of a number scale that divide a set of observations into 10 groups of equal size.

Decomposition. The division of a correlation coefficient into its component parts, involving direct effects, indirect effects, and dependence on common causes.

Degrees of freedom. The number of values free to vary when computing a statistic.

Delta vector. Vector containing the unique error terms for each observed x_i indicator.

Dependent variable. A variable that has a consequent, or affected, role in relation to the independent variable.

Descriptive statistics. Statistics concerned with summarizing the properties of a sample of observations.

Design matrix. A matrix whose "0" and "1" entries show which cells are fixed (structural zeros) and which cells are free to take on values according to the particular log-linear model being estimated.

Deterministic. A causal relationship in which change in one variable always produces a constant change in another variable.

Diagonal. In a square matrix, those elements whose row and column subscripts are the same.

Diagram (graph). A visual representation of a set of data.

Dichotomous logistic regression equation. A regression of the logit for a dichotomous dependent variable that is a linear function of the independent variables.

Dichotomous variable. A discrete measure with two categories that may or may not be ordered. A variable having only two categories.

Direct effect. A connecting path in a causal model between two variables without an intervening third variable.

Discordant pair. In a crosstabulation of two orderable discrete variables, one member of a pair of observations ranks higher than the other member on one variable, but ranks lower on the second variable.

Discrete variable. A variable that classifies persons, objects, or events according to the kind or quality of their attributes.

Dummy variable. A variable coded 1 to indicate the presence of an attribute and 0 in its absence.

E

Effect. The impact of the classification variable on the dependent variable.

Efficient estimator. The estimator of a population parameter among all possible estimators that has the smallest sampling variance.

Endogenous variable. A variable whose cause(s) of variation are represented in a model.

Epistemic relationship. The relationship between abstract, theoretical (unobserved) concepts and their corresponding operational (observed) measurements.

Epsilon vector. Vector containing the unique error terms for each observed y_i indicator.

Error sum of squares. A numerical value obtained in linear regression by subtracting the regression sum of squares from the total sum of squares.

Error term. In ANOVA, that part of the observed score that cannot be attributed to either the common component or the group component. The difference be-

tween an observed score and a score predicted by the model.

Eta vector. The $M \times 1$ vector of endogenous variables.

Euler's constant. An irrational number that is used as the base of natural logarithms.

Exhaustive. Every case must receive a code for each variable, even if only a missing value can be assigned.

Exogenous variable. A predetermined variable whose causes remain unexplained, unanalyzed, and outside of the scope of a model.

Expected frequency. In a chi-square test, the value that cell frequencies are expected to take, given the hypothesis under study (ordinarily, the null hypothesis).

Expected value. The single number that best describes a probability distribution of discrete scores.

Explanation (interpretation) of association. Covariation between two variables due to an intervening third variable.

Exploratory data analysis. Methods for displaying distributions of continuous variables.

F

F distribution. A theoretical probability distribution for one of a family of F ratios having ν_1 and ν_2 df in the numerator and denominator, respectively.

First-order table. A subtable containing the crosstabulation or covariation between two variables, given a single outcome of a third, control variable.

Fitted marginal. The standard notation for a log-linear model.

Fitting function. Function that compares the observed to the expected variance-covariance matrices.

Frequency distribution. A table of outcomes, or response categories, of a variable and the number of times each outcome is observed.

Fundamental theorem of path analysis. An equation stating that the bivariate correlation between variables *i* and *j* implied by the hypothesized causal model is the sum of the products consisting of the path from variable *q* to variable *i* times the correlation between variable *q* and variable *j*. The sum of these products is formed over all *Q* variables that have direct paths to variable *i*.

G

Gamma. A symmetric measure of association suitable not only to crosstabs of two dichotomies, but also to tables whose variables are both ordered discrete measures with more than two categories.

Gamma matrix. Matrix containing the causal parameters that link endogenous variables to exogenous variables.

General linear model. A model that assumes the relationships among independent and dependent measures basically vary according to straight-line patterns.

Goodness-of-fit index. The ratio between the minimum of the fitting function after the model is fitted to the fitting function before any model is fitted.

Goodness of fit statistic. A test statistic that uses standardized residuals to compare the observed probabilities to those predicted by the equation.

Grand mean. In analysis of variance, the mean of all observations.

Grouped data. Data that have been collapsed into a smaller number of categories.

H

Hierarchical log-linear model. A model in which the inclusion of multi-way effects also implies the inclusion of all less-complex effects.

Histogram. A type of diagram that uses bars to represent the frequency, proportion, or percentage of cases associated with each outcome or interval of outcomes of a variable.

Hinge spread (H-spread). The difference between the upper and lower hinges, i.e., $H_2 - H_1$. Symbolized by *HS*.

Homoscedasticity. A condition in which the variances of the prediction errors are equal at every outcome of the predictor variable.

I

Identified. Unique parameter values in a structural equation model.

Identity matrix. A square matrix with ones in the diagonal and zeros in the off-diagonal.

Independent variable. A variable that has an antecedent or causal role, usually appearing first in the hypothesis.

Index. A variable that is a summed composite of other variables that are assumed to reflect some underlying construct.

Index of diversity. Measures whether two observations selected randomly from a population are likely to fall into the same or into different categories.

Index of qualitative variation. A measure of variation for discrete variables. A standardized version of the index of diversity.

Indicator. Observable measure of underlying unobservable theoretical construct.

Indirect effect. A compound path connecting two variables in a causal model through an intervening third variable.

Inference. A generalization or conclusion about some attribute of a population based on the data in a sample. The process of making generalizations or drawing conclusions about the attributes of a population from evidence contained in a sample.

Inferential statistics. Statistics that apply the mathematical theory of probability to make decisions about the likely properties of populations based on sample evidence.

Information matrix. A second-order derivative of the fitting function.

Interaction effect. The association between two variables in each partial table differs when controlling for a third variable. Differences in the relationship between two variables within categories of a third variable.

Intercept. A constant value in a regression equation showing the point at which the regression line crosses the Y axis when values of X equal 0.

Inverse. A matrix, when multiplied with another matrix, that produces the identity matrix.

Iterative proportional fitting. A computer algorithm for successively approximating the expected frequencies in an unsaturated log-linear model.

L

Lagged causal effect. Direct effect of a variable measured prior to time $t - 1$ on a variable measured at time t.

Lambda-x matrix. Matrix containing parameters for xs that show how strongly each x_i indicator is affected by unobserved xis.

Lambda-y matrix. Matrix containing parameters for ys that show how strongly each y_i indicator is affected by unobserved etas.

Latent variable. A variable that cannot be observed and can only be measured indirectly.

Likelihood ratio. The preferred test statistic for testing the fit between expected and observed frequencies in an unsaturated log-linear model.

Linearity. The amount of change (increase or decrease) in one concept caused by a change in another concept is constant across its range.

Linear probability model. A linear regression model in which the dependent variable is confined between two choices.

Linear regression model. A model that takes into account deviations from the linear prediction by showing the linear relationship between a continuous dependent variable and one or more independent variables, plus an error term.

Linear relationship. Covariation in which the value of the dependent variable is proportional to the value of the independent variable.

Listwise deletion. In multiple regression analysis the removal of all cases that have missing values on any of the variables.

Logistic transformation of p. A natural logarithmic change in the odds of a probability.

Logit. Logistic probability unit.

Logit model. A log-linear model in which one dichotomous variable is considered to be dependent on the other variables.

Log likelihood ratio. A ratio that contrasts two nested logistic regression equations, where one equation is a restricted version of the other.

Log-linear analysis. A technique for analyzing cross-classified data.

Lower confidence limit. The lowest value of a confidence interval.

Lower hinge. The value of the observation that divides the lower quartile from the upper three-quarters of an ordered distribution. Symbolized by H_1.

Lower inner fence. That part of an ordered distribution below which an observation is considered an outlier. Symbolized by LIF.

M

Manifest variable. A variable that can be observed.

Marginal distributions. The frequency distributions of each of two crosstabulated variables.

Marginal homogeneity. Corresponding row and column marginal totals are equal.

Marginal subtable. A method to show the combinations of k variables that are necessary and sufficient to generate the expected cell frequencies of a full crosstab.

Markovian principle. Variables measured prior to time $t - 1$ have no causal impact on variables measured at time t.

Matrix. A rectangular array of mathematical elements in rows and columns that can be combined with other matrices or scalar values using ordinary arithmetic operations.

Matrix algebra. Algebra whose elements are matrices and whose operations include addition and multiplication of matrices.

Maximum likelihood estimation. A method of estimating parameter values that chooses the set with the highest probability of generating the sample observations.

Mean. The arithmetic average of a set of data in which the values of all observations are added together and divided by the number of observations.

Mean difference hypothesis test. A statistical test of a hypothesis about the difference between two population means.

Mean of a probability distribution. The expected value of a population of scores.

Mean square. Estimate of variance used in the analysis of variance. Estimate of variance in a linear regression.

Mean square between. A value in ANOVA obtained by dividing the between sum of squares by its degrees of freedom.

Mean square error. A value in linear regression obtained by dividing the error sum of squares by its degrees of freedom.

Mean square regression. A value in linear regression obtained by dividing the regression sum of squares by its degrees of freedom.

Mean square within. A value in ANOVA obtained by dividing the within sum of squares by its degrees of freedom.

Measurement. The process of assigning numbers to observations according to a set or rules.

Measurement interval (measurement class). A grouping of observations that is treated equally.

Measurement model. Two sets of equations that link each observed indicator to the unobserved variables in the structural model.

Measures of association. Statistics that show the direction and/or magnitude of a relationship between pairs of discrete variables.

Median. The outcome that divides an ordered distribution exactly into halves.

Midpoint. A number exactly halfway between the true upper and lower limits of a measurement class or interval, obtained by adding the upper and lower limits and dividing by 2.

MIMIC model. Multiple-indicator and multiple-cause model in which variation in a single dependent variable with two or more indicators is directly caused by several predetermined variables, each of which has only a single indicator.

Missing data. No meaningful information for a given observation on a particular variable.

Misspecification. A condition in which a structural equation or path model includes incorrect variables or excludes correct variables.

Mode. The single category among the K categories in a distribution with the largest number (or highest percentage) of observations.

Modification indices. LISREL estimates of the change in model chi-square if a constraint is relaxed.

Multicollinearity. A condition of high or near perfect correlation among the independent variables in a multiple regression equation.

Multiple causation. The view that social behavior is caused by more than one factor.

Multiple correlation coefficient. The coefficient for a multiple regression equation, which, when squared, equals the ratio of the sum of squares due to regression to the total sum of squares.

Multiple regression analysis. A statistical technique for estimating the relationship between a continuous dependent variable and two or more continuous or discrete independent, or predictor, variables.

Multiple regression coefficient. A measure of association showing the amount of increase or decrease in a continuous dependent variable for a one-unit difference in the independent variable, controlling for the other independent variable(s).

Multivariate contingency analysis. Statistical techniques for analyzing relationships among three or more discrete variables.

Multivariate contingency table analysis. The statistical analysis of data on three or more categorical variables.

Mutually exclusive. Each observation must receive one and only one code on a given variable.

N

Negative skew. The tail of a skewed distribution is to the left of the median (median greater than mean).

Nested models. Models in which every parameter included on one model also appears in another model.

Nested regression equations. Regression equations where independent variables are successively added to an equation to observe changes in the predictors' relationships to the dependent variable.

Newton-Raphson algorithm. An iterative proportional fitting procedure used in log-linear analysis.

Nonorderable discrete variable. A discrete measure in which the sequence of categories cannot be meaningfully ordered.

Nonrecursive model. A model in which causal influences between dependent variables may occur in both directions.

Nonsaturated model. A log-linear model in which one or more of the lambda parameters equals 0.

Nonspuriousness. Covariation between two variables that is causal and not due to the effects of a third variable.

Normal distribution. A smooth, bell-shaped theoretical probability distribution for continuous variables that can be generated from a formula.

Null hypothesis. A statistical hypothesis that one usually expects to reject. Symbolized H_0.

O

Odds. The frequency of being in one category relative to the frequency of not being in that category.

Odds ratio (cross-product ratio). The ratio formed by dividing one conditional odds by another conditional odds.

One-tailed hypothesis test. A hypothesis test in which the alternative is stated in such a way that the probability of making a Type I error is entirely in one tail of a probability distribution.

Operational hypothesis. A proposition in which observable, concrete referents or terms are restated to replace abstract concepts.

Order. The number of rows and columns in a matrix.

Orderable discrete variable. A discrete measure that can be meaningfully arranged into an ascending or descending sequence.

Ordinary least squares. A method for obtaining estimates of regression equation coefficients that minimizes the error sum of squares.

Outcome. A response category of a variable.

Outlier. An observed value that is so extreme (either large or small) that it seems to stand apart from the rest of the distribution.

P

Pairwise deletion. In multiple regression analysis the removal of a case from the calculation of a correlation coefficient only if it has missing values for one of the variables.

Part correlation. A measure of the proportion of variance in a dependent variable that an independent variable can explain, when squared, after controlling for the other independent variable in a multiple regression equation.

Partial correlation coefficient. A measure of association for continuous variables that shows that magnitude and direction of covariation between two variables that remains after the effects of a control variable have been held constant.

Partial regression coefficient. The effect of regressing a dependent variable on an independent variable, controlling for one or more other independent variables.

Path analysis. A statistical method for analyzing quantitative data that yields empirical estimates of the effects of variables in an hypothesized causal system.

Path coefficient. A numerical estimate of the causal relationships between two variables in a path analysis.

Percentage. A number created by multiplying a proportion by 100.

Percentage distribution. A distribution of relative frequencies or proportions in which each entry has been multiplied by 100.

Percentile. The outcome or score below which a given percentage of the observations in a distribution falls.

Phi. A symmetric measure of association for 2×2 crosstabulations.

Phi adjusted. A symmetric measure of association for a 2×2 crosstabulation in which phi is divided by phi maximum to take into account the largest covariation possible, given the marginals.

Phi matrix. Matrix containing the variances of the exogenous variables in the diagonal elements and the covariances in the off-diagonal elements.

Phi maximum. The largest value that phi can attain for a given 2×2 crosstabulation; used in adjusting phi for its marginals.

Planned comparison. Hypothesis test of differences between and among population means carried out before doing an analysis of variance.

Point estimate. A sample statistic used to estimate a population parameter.

Point estimate for mean differences. The difference between the sample means used to estimate the difference between two population means.

Polychotomous logistic regression equation. Logistic regression with a dependent variable having more than two discrete, nonordered categories.

Polygon. A diagram constructed by connecting the midpoints of a histogram with a straight line.

Population. The entire set of persons, objects, or events that have at least one common characteristic of interest to the researcher.

Population parameter. A descriptive characteristic of a population, such as mean, standard deviation, or variance. Symbolized by θ.

Population regression equation. A regression equation for a population rather than a sample.

Population regression model. A regression model for a population in which K independent variables are each hypothesized to affect a dependent, continuous variable in a linear, additive manner.

Positive skew. The tail of a skewed distribution is to the right of the median (mean greater than median).

Post hoc comparison. Hypothesis test of the differences among population means carried out following an analysis of variance.

Power of the test. The probability of correctly rejecting H_0 when H_0 is false.

Prediction equation. A regression equation without the error term, useful for predicting the score on the dependent variable from the independent variable(s).

Predictor variable. Independent variable in a regression analysis.

Probabilistic. A causal relationship in which change in one variable produces change in another variable, with a certain probability of occurrence.

Probability (alpha) level. The probability selected for rejection of a null hypothesis, which is the likelihood of making a Type I error.

Probability distribution. a set of outcomes, each of which has an associated probability of occurrence.

Probit. Probability unit for the cumulative normal distribution.

Proposition. A statement about the relationship between abstract concepts.

Pseudo-R^2. A descriptive measure for logistic regression that indicates roughly the proportion of variation in the dependent variable accounted for by the predictors.

Psi matrix. Matrix containing the variances of each error term (in the diagonal elements) and their covariances (in the off-diagonal elements).

Q

Quantile. A division of observations into groups with known proportions in each group.

Quartiles. The values of a number scale that divide a set of observations into four groups of equal size.

Quasi-independence model. A model that ignores structural-zero cells and tests for independence only among the remaining entries.

Quasi-symmetry model. A special type of symmetry that preserves the inequality of the corresponding row and column marginals, but produces equal corresponding odds ratios among the off-diagonal cells.

Quintiles. The values of a number scale that divide a set of observations into five groups of equal size.

R

Random assignment. In an experiment the assignment of subjects to treatment levels on a chance basis.

Random sample. A sample whose cases or elements are selected at random from a population.

Random sampling. A procedure for selecting a set of representative observations from a population, in which each observation has an equal chance of being selected for the sample.

Random zero. A combination of variables that is unrepresented in a sample.

Range. The difference between the largest and smallest scores in a distribution.

Recode. The process of changing the codes established for a variable.

Recoding. The process of grouping continuous variables from many initial values into fewer categories.

Recursive model. A model in which all the causal influences are assumed to be asymmetric (one-way).

Regression different test. A statistical test to determine whether two regression coefficients differ in the population.

Regression line. A line that is the best fit to the points in a scatterplot, computed by ordinary least squares regression.

Regression sum of squares. A number obtained in linear regression by subtracting the mean of a set of scores from the value predicted by linear regression, squaring, and summing these values.

Regression toward the mean. A condition demonstrated when the predicted scores on the dependent variable show less variability about the mean than the observed scores do, due to the imperfect correlation between two variables.

Relative frequency (proportion). The number of cases in an outcome divided by the total number of cases.

Relative frequency distribution. A distribution of outcomes of a variable in which the number of times each outcome is observed has been divided by the total number of cases.

Reliability. The extent to which different operationalizations of the same concept produce consistent results. The proportion of an item's variance that is attributable to the unobserved cause.

Representativeness. The selection of units of analysis whose characteristics accurately stand for the larger population from which the sample was drawn.

Research hypothesis. A substantive hypothesis that one usually does not expect to reject.

Residual. The amount that remains after subtracting the prediction equation from the linear regression model.

Residual matrix. Matrix that reveals how closely a LISREL model's estimated parameters reproduce the variances and covariances among the *x* and *y* indicators.

Residual variable. An unmeasured variable in a path model that is posited as causing the unexplained part of an observed variable.

Robust. Methods used in which violating assumptions will seldom produce wrong conclusions.

Root mean squared residual index. The average of the fitted residuals.

Rounding. Expressing digits in more convenient and interpretable units, such as tens, hundreds, or thousands, by applying an explicit rule.

Row marginals. The frequency distribution of the variable shown across the rows of a crosstabulation.

r-to-Z transformation. A natural logarithm transformation in the value of the correlation coefficient to a *Z* score, to test the probability of observing *r* under the null hypothesis.

S

Sample. A subset of cases or elements selected from a population.

Sampling distribution of sample means. A distribution consisting of the mean of all samples of size *N* that could be formed from a given population.

Saturated model. A log-linear model in which all possible effects among variables are present.

Scale construction. The creation of new variables from multiple items.

Scatterplot. A type of diagram that displays the covariation of two continuous variables as a set of points on a Cartesian coordinate system.

Scheffé test. One form of post hoc comparison of differences in group means.

Scientific research. The effort to reduce uncertainty about some aspect of the world by systematically examining the relationships among its parts.

Scope (boundary conditions). The times, places, or activities under which the propositions of a social theory are expected to be valid.

Sigma matrix. Matrix showing the implied variances and covariances among the *y*s and *x*s for a LISREL model.

Significance testing with proportions. Using statistical tests to determine whether the observed difference between sample proportions could occur by chance in the populations from which the samples were selected.

Single-link causal chain. A LISREL model in which one exogenous variable causes variation in one endogenous variable, both of which have multiple indicators.

Skewed distribution. A distribution that is nonsymmetric about its median value, having many categories with small frequencies at one end.

Social theory. A set of two or more propositions in which concepts referring to certain social phenomena are assumed to be causally related.

Somers's d_{yx}. An asymmetric PRE measure of association for discrete ordered variables that counts not only the number of concordant and discordant untied pairs, but also the number of tied pairs of a certain type.

Spuriousness. Covariation between two variables due only to the effect of a third variable.

Square matrix. A matrix with an equal number of rows and columns.

Standard deviation. The positive square root of the variance.

Standard error. The standard deviation of a sampling distribution.

Standardized solution. Etas and xis have unit variances, while the indicators are still in their original metrics.

Standard scores (Z scores). A transformation of the scores of a continuous frequency distribution by subtracting the mean from each outcome and dividing by the standard deviation.

Statistical significance test. A test of inference that conclusions based on a sample of observations also hold true for the population from which the sample was selected.

Statistically independent. A condition of no relationship between variables in a population.

Statistic table. A numerical display that either summarizes data or presents the results of a data analysis.

Status variable. A variable whose outcomes cannot be manipulated.

Stem-and-leaf diagram. A type of graph that displays the observed values and frequency counts of a frequency distribution.

Structural equation. A mathematical equation representing the structure of hypothesized relationships among variables in a social theory.

Structural equation system. Five matrices or vectors of parameters and variables that are required for LISREL.

Structural zero. A combination of variables that cannot logically occur.

Sufficient estimator. An estimator of a population parameter that cannot be improved by adding information.

Suspending judgment. A position taken by a researcher when the results of a statistical test permit neither clear rejection nor clear acceptance of the null hypothesis and alternative hypothesis.

Symmetry hypothesis. An hypothesis that predicts exactly equal frequencies in inversely corresponding cells of a $k \times k$ crosstabulation.

Systematic sampling interval. The number of cases between sample elements in a list used for a systematic random sample.

System file. A data file created by a computer software statistics package.

T

Tally. A count of the frequency of outcomes observed for a variable or the frequency of joint outcomes of several variables.

Tau c. A non–PRE-type measure of association that uses information about the number of concordant and discordant untied pairs in a crosstab of two discrete ordered variables.

t distribution. One of a family of test statistics used with small samples selected from a normally distributed population or, for large samples, drawn from a population with any shape.

Theta delta matrix. Matrix containing the errors of the *x*s.

Theta epsilon matrix. Matrix containing the errors of the *y*s.

Tied pair. A pair in which both cases have the same value on at least one of the variables.

Time order. The necessary condition that changes in a purported independent variable must precede in time the change in the dependent measure, when a causal relationship between the two is assumed.

Total sum of squares. A number obtained by subtracting the scores of a distribution from their mean, squaring, and summing these values. The total of regression and error sums of squares.

Trace. The sum of the diagonal elements in a square matrix.

Transpose. A matrix whose rows and columns have been interchanged (inverted order).

Treatment level. A term in experimental research to indicate the experimental group to which a subject has been assigned.

True limits. The exact lower and upper bounds of numerical values that could be rounded into the category.

t test. A test of significance for continuous variables where the population variance is unknown and the sample is assumed to have been drawn from a normally distributed population.

t variable (t score). A transformation of the scores of a continuous frequency distribution derived by subtracting the mean and dividing by the estimated standard error.

2 × 2 table. A crosstabulation of a pair of dichotomies.

Two-tailed hypothesis test. A hypothesis test in which the region of rejection falls equally within both tails of the sampling distribution.

Type I error (false rejection error). A statistical decision error that occurs when a true null hypothesis is rejected; its probability is alpha.

Type II error (false acceptance error). A statistical decision error that occurs when a false null hypothesis is not rejected; its probability is beta.

U

Unbiased estimator. An estimator of a population parameter whose expected value equals the parameter.

Unit of analysis. An object for observation.

Upper confidence limit. The highest value of a confidence interval.

Upper hinge. The value of the observation that divides the upper quartile from the lower three-quarters of an ordered distribution. Symbolized by H_2.

Upper inner fence. That part of an ordered distribution above which an observation is considered to be an outlier. Symbolized by UIF.

V

Validity. The degree to which a variable's operationalization accurately reflects the concept it is intended to measure.

Variable. Any characteristic or attribute of persons, objects, or events that can take on different numerical values.

Variance. The mean square deviation of a continuous distribution.

Variance-covariance matrix. A square matrix containing the variances (on the diagonal) and covariances (off the diagonal) of the observed indicators in a LISREL model.

Variance of probability distribution. The expected spread or dispersion of a population of scores.

Variation. The spread or dispersion of a set of scores around some central value.

Vector. A special type of matrix that has only one row or column.

Venn diagram. A type of graph that uses overlapping shaded circles to demonstrate relationships or covariation among a set of variables.

W

Within sum of squares. A value obtained by subtracting each subgroup mean from each observed score, squaring, and summing.

X

xi vector. The $K \times 1$ vector, where K is the number of exogenous variables.

Y

Yule's Q. A symmetric measure of association for 2×2 crosstabulations.

Z

Zero-order table. A crosstabulation of two variables in which no additional variables have been controlled.

Zeta vector. The $M \times 1$ vector of error terms for each endogenous variable.

List of Mathematical and Statistical Symbols

A′	Transpose of matrix **A.**
$|A|$	Determinant of A.
AAD	Average absolute deviation.
AGFI	Adjusted goodness-of-fit index.
a	1. The point at which a line intercepts the Y-axis ($X = 0$).
	2. Intercept term in a regression equation for sample data.
α	1. Greek lowercase letter *alpha*.
	2. Alpha area.
	3. Probability level of committing a Type I error.
	4. Population regression intercept.
α_j	The effect of the jth group.
$\alpha/2$	Alpha area of only one tail of a distribution.
BIC	A test statistic for assessing log-linear models fitted to large-scale crosstabulations.
b	Bivariate regression coefficient for a sample.
β	1. Greek lowercase letter *beta*.
	2. Probability of committing a Type II error.
	3. Structural parameter linking endogenous variables.
	4. Population regression coefficient.
B	Greek uppercase letter *beta*.

$\mathbf{B}$	Matrix of structural parameters linking endogenous variables.
β_j	Regression coefficient for the jth predictor.
β_j^*	Standardized regression coefficient for the jth predictor.
β^X	Logit effect parameters for variable X.
β_{YX}	Population parameter for the regression of Y on X.
β_{YX}^*	1. Beta coefficient.
	2. Standardized regression coefficient for a population.
b_{YX}	Regression coefficient of Y on X in a sample.
cf	Cumulative frequency distribution.
c_j	Weights under the constraint that $c_1 + c_2 + \ldots + c_j = 0$.
$c\%$	Cumulative percentage.
D	1. Index of diversity.
	2. Dummy variable.
δ	1. Greek lowercase letter *delta*.
	2. Error term for exogenous structural variable indicator.
df	Degrees of freedom.
Δdf	Change in degrees of freedom.
df_{ERROR}	Error degrees of freedom.
$df_{\text{REGRESSION}}$	Regression degrees of freedom.
df_{TOTAL}	Total degrees of freedom.
D_i	Score of the ith decile.
d_i	Deviation (distance) of a score from the mean.
d_{yx}	Somers's d_{yx}, a measure of association.
e	1. Euler's constant.
	2. Base for natural logarithm.
e_i	Error term for the ith observation.
e_{ij}	The error score unique to the ith case in the jth group.
ϵ	1. Greek lowercase letter *epsilon*.
	2. Error term for endogenous structural variable indicator.
η	1. Greek lowercase letter eta.
	2. Endogenous structural variable.
η^2	Correlation ratio for a population.
$\hat{\eta}^2$	Sample estimate of the correlation ratio.
$f(Y)$	A function of Y.

F_{ij} The expected value of the frequency in the i,jth cell.

$\ln F_{ij}$ Natural logarithm of the expected cell frequency.

f_{ij} The observed frequency in the i,jth cell.

$E(Y)$ Expected value of a probability distribution.

F F distribution.

$F(\mathbf{S},\mathbf{\Sigma})$ Fitting function for determining the fit closeness between $\mathbf{S}$ and $\mathbf{\Sigma}$.

f_i Frequency associated with the ith outcome category of a variable.

G Gamma, a measure of association.

G^2 Test statistic that compares the ratio of two likelihoods.

GFI   Goodness-of-fit index.

γ 1. Greek lowercase letter *gamma*.
            2. Population parameter that G estimates.
            3. Structural parameter linking exogenous to endogenous variables.

Γ Greek uppercase letter *gamma*.

Γ Matrix of structural parameters linking exogenous to endogenous variables.

$g(Y)$ A function of Y.

H_0 Null hypothesis.

H_1 1. Lower hinge.
          2. Alternative hypothesis.

H_2 Upper hinge.

HS H-spread.

$\mathbf{I}$ Identity matrix.

IQV   Index of qualitative variation.

K_i Score the ith quintile.

K_0 More-restricted equation.

K_1 Less-restricted equation.

$\boldsymbol{\lambda}_x$ Factor loadings for x (exogenous) indicators.

$\boldsymbol{\lambda}_y$ Factor loadings for y (endogenous) indicators.

$\boldsymbol{\Lambda}_x$ Matrix of factor loadings for exogenous indicators.

$\boldsymbol{\Lambda}_y$ Matrix of factor loadings for endogenous indicators.

λ_{ij}^{XY} The effect of association between variables on the expected logs of crosstabulated cell frequencies.

λ_{ij}^2	Squared factor loading of structural variable indicators.
L_i	1. Logit.
	2. Natural log of an odds.
L^2	Likelihood ratio.
ΔL^2	The difference in L^2 values in nested models.
LIF	Lower inner fence.
$\log_e$	Natural logarithm.
$\log_{10}$	Base 10 logarithm.
m	The smaller of R rows and C columns.
Mdn	Median.
MLE	Maximum likelihood estimation.
MS_{BETWEEN}	Mean square between.
MS_{ERROR}	Mean square error.
$MS_{\text{REGRESSION}}$	Mean square regression.
MS_{WITHIN}	Mean square within.
μ	1. Greek lowercase letter *mu*.
	2. Constant applied to every cell of a crosstab in log-linear analysis.
μ_Y	Mean of a population.
$\mu_{\bar{Y}}$	Mean of the sampling distribution of means for variable Y.
$\mu_{(\bar{Y}_1 - \bar{Y}_2)}$	Mean difference between the means of variables Y_1 and Y_2 in two populations.
N	Total sample size.
n_d	Number of discordant pairs.
n_s	Number of concordant pairs.
ν	1. Greek lowercase letter *nu*.
	2. Degrees of freedom in a *t* distribution.
ν_1, ν_2	Number of degrees of freedom in an F distribution.
OR^{XY}	The odds ratio of variables X and Y.
$OR^{(XY|Z=1)}$	Conditional odds ratio.
$1 - \beta$	Power of the test.
ϕ	1. Greek lowercase letter *phi*.
	2. A measure of association.
	3. Covariance among exogenous structural variables.
Φ	Greek uppercase letter *phi*.
Φ	Matrix of covariances among exogenous structural variables.
ϕ_{adj}	Phi adjusted.

ϕ_{max}	Phi maximum.
P_i	Score of the ith percentile.
p_i	Proportion of cases in the ith outcome of a variable.
p_{ij}	Path coefficient to variable i from variable j.
$\hat{p}_{ij}$	Estimate of population path coefficient parameter.
ψ	1. Greek lowercase letter *psi*. 2. Contrast between population means.
Ψ	Greek uppercase letter *psi*.
$\boldsymbol{\Psi}$	Matrix of covariances among error terms of endogenous structural variables.
PRE	Proportionate reduction in error.
$\text{Prob}(Y_i = 1)$	Probability that the ith observation of variable Y has a score of 1.
$p(Y_i)$	Probability of the ith outcome of variable Y.
Q	Yule's Q, a measure of association.
Q_i	Score of the ith quartile.
ρ_{YX}	Correlation of variables X and Y in a population.
$\rho^2_{Y \cdot X}$	Coefficient of determination in a population.
r'_{ij}	Estimated correlation of variables i and j.
$\mathbf{R}$	Residual matrix.
RMSR	Root mean squared residual index.
R^2_{adj}	Adjusted coefficient of determination.
R^2_{YX}	1. R-square. 2. Coefficient of determination in a sample.
$R^2_{Y \cdot X}$	Coefficient of determination in a sample.
$R^2_{Y \cdot X_1 X_2 \ldots X_K}$	Multiple regression coefficient of determination for an equation with K predictors.
$r_{XY \cdot W}$	The partial correlation between X and Y, controlling for (or in the presence of) W.
$r_{YX_j \cdot X_i}$	Partial correlation coefficient.
r_{YX}	Correlation coefficient in a sample.
$r_{Z_X Z_Y}$	Correlation of two Z scores in a sample.
$\mathbf{S}$	1. Variance-covariance matrix. 2. Matrix of observed covariances among observable indicators.
$\hat{s}_\lambda$	The standard error of a lambda effect parameter in a saturated log-linear model.
s_b	Standard error of a regression coefficient in a sample.

s_{b_j}	Standard error of a regression coefficient for the jth predictor in a sample.
$s_{b_1-b_2}$	Standard error of the difference in regression coefficients in a sample.
Σ	Greek uppercase letter *sigma.*
$\mathbf{\Sigma}$	Matrix of expected covariances among observable indicators.
$\hat{\sigma}_\Psi^2$	Estimated variance of a contrast.
$\hat{\sigma}_Z^2$	Estimated variance of a standardized variable
σ_e^2	1. Standard error of estimate in a population. 2. Variance of regression prediction errors.
σ_Y	Standard deviation of variable Y in a population.
$\hat{\sigma}_{\bar{Y}}$	Estimated standard error for a population.
σ_Y^2	Variance of variable Y in a population.
σ_b^2	Squared standard error of a regression coefficient in a population.
$\sigma_{(\bar{Y}_1-\bar{Y}_2)}$	Standard error of the sampling distribution for the difference between the means of variables Y_1 and Y_2 in two populations.
$\hat{\sigma}_{(\bar{Y}_1-\bar{Y}_2)}$	Estimated standard error of the sampling distribution for the difference between the means of variables Y_2 and Y_1 in two populations.
$\hat{\sigma}_{\tau_c}$	Standard error of the sampling distribution for tau c.
$\hat{\sigma}_{d_{yx}}$	Standard error of the sampling distribution for Somers's d_{yx}.
s_p	Standard error of a sampling distribution of proportions in a sample.
s^2	Variance of a sample.
$s_{Z_Y}^2$	Variance of estimated Z scores for variable Y.
s_{YX}	Covariance of variables X and Y in a sample.
s_Y^2	Variance of variable Y in a sample.
SS_{BETWEEN}	Between sum of squares.
SS_{ERROR}	Error sum of squares.
$SS_{\text{REGRESSION}}$	Regression sum of squares.
SS_{TOTAL}	Total sum of squares.
SS_{WITHIN}	Within sum of squares.
t	1. t variable. 2. t score.

t_α	Critical value of t for a one-tailed test.
$t_{\alpha/2}$	Critical value of t for a two-tailed test.
τ_c	Tau c, a measure of association.
θ	1. Greek lowercase letter *theta*.
	2. Population parameter.
Θ	Greek uppercase letter *theta*.
$\mathbf{\Theta}_\delta$	Matrix of covariances among errors in exogenous variable indicators.
$\mathbf{\Theta}_\epsilon$	Matrix of covariances among errors in endogenous variable indicators.
T	True score on a variable.
T_r	The number of ties associated with the row variable.
$\mathrm{tr}(\mathbf{A})$	Trace of matrix $\mathbf{A}$.
UIF	Upper inner fence.
$\{XY\}$	Fitted marginal table for variables X and Y in a log-linear analysis.
$\bar{Y}$	Mean of variable Y in a sample.
$\hat{Y}_i$	Predicted or expected value of variable Y for the ith observation.
χ^2	Chi-square distribution.
ξ	1. Greek lowercase letter *xi*.
	2. Exogenous structural variable.
ζ	1. Greek lowercase letter *zeta*.
	2. Error term for endogenous structural variable.
Z^2	Goodness of fit statistic.
Z_α	Critical value of Z for a one-tailed test.
$Z_{\alpha/2}$	Critical value of Z for a two-tailed test.
Z_i	Standardized score for the ith observation.
$\hat{Z}_Y$	Estimated Z score for variable Y.

Answers to Problems

Answers to Chapter 1 Problems

1. For example, the number of full- and part-time employees whose contracts were involuntarily terminated in the past 12 months.

2. P1: The higher the female labor force participation, the higher the family income. P2: The higher the number of children, the lower the divorce rate.

3. The theory is probably restricted to rural Latin Americans in the modern era.

4. Respondents are more likely to report that they donated to a community charity if a friend or relative had mentioned that people in their social group were supposed to contribute.

5. *a.* Race is independent, annual income is dependent.
   b. International competition is independent, profit levels are dependent.
   c. Deinstitutionalization is independent, homelessness is dependent.

6. *a.* Variable   *d.* Variable
   b. Constant   *e.* Variable
   c. Variable   *f.* Constant

7. Using a systematic sampling interval of $k = 200$ will yield 750 residents, of whom 500 would be expected to be of voting age.

8. *a.* These six categories are neither mutually exclusive nor exhaustive.
   b. First, decide whether region, state, or city is the level of residence desired; then include every possible category of that type in the response set. For example, list all 50 states.

9. *a.* Continuous   *e.* Dichotomous
   b. Dichotomous   *f.* Nonorderable discrete
   c. Orderable discrete   *g.* Continuous
   d. Continuous   *h.* Orderable discrete

10. *a.* Scientific research
    b. Applied researchers
    c. valid
    d. epistemic relationship
    e. representative, randomly
    f. Measurement
    g. the general linear model

Answers to Chapter 2 Problems

1.

VARIABLE	TALLY	f
0	||||	4
1	||	2
2	|||	3
3	⊬⊦	5
4	|||	3
5	||	2

($N = 19$)

2. National origins:

VARIABLE	f	p	%
F	4	.200	20.0
G	2	.100	10.0
E	5	.250	25.0
I	4	.200	20.0
R	3	.150	15.0
O	2	.100	10.0
Total		1.000	100.0%
($N = 20$)			

3. Men's suit prices:

PRICES	cf	c%
$99 & under	1	9.1
$100–199	5	45.5
$200–299	8	72.7
$300–399	11	100.0
Total	11	100.0

4. (a) 7; (b) 7; (c) 2; (d) 4; (e) 14; (f) 7.

5. Graphs not shown.

6. (a) 2.1; (b) 2; (c) 2.

7. (a) 12; (b) 3.6; (c) 22.5; (d) 4.74.

8. (a) 7; (b) 9; (c) 6.5; (d) 6.57; (e) 2.56; (f) 0.59.

9. .248.

10. (a) +2.00; (b) −0.33; (c) +1.67.

11. The range is from 0 to 26 brothers and sisters. The modal frequency is two siblings (18.2% of the sample), while the mean is 3.93 and median is 3.00. The standard deviation is 3.05 siblings.

12. (a) 2; (b) 2.00; (c) 8 or more; (d) 2.84; (e) 2.54; (f) 1.60; and (g) $Z =$ +0.73.

13. Percentage distributions of family incomes:

RELATIVE INCOME	FAMILY AGE 16	CURRENT FAMILY
Far below average	8.5	5.1
Below average	23.3	23.1
Average	49.3	50.3
Above Average	16.9	19.0
Far Above Average	1.9	1.8
Total	100.0%	100.0%
(N)	(1,492)	(1,497)

The mode and median are "average" for both variables. Although there is a slight improvement in perceived incomes from earlier to later family, the distributions differ by only 2% or 3%.

14. Confidence in American institutions:

AMOUNT OF CONFIDENCE	PRESS	EXECUTIVE BRANCH
A great deal	.336	.375
Some	.420	.378
Hardly any	.244	.247
Total	1.000	1.000
(*N*)	(993)	(990)

Confidence in the press and in the executive branch have almost identical distributions, with respective means of 1.91 and 1.87 and standard deviations of .76 and .78.

15. *(a)* 35; *(b)* 4.1; *(c)* 4.1; *(d)* 6.6; and *(e)* 6.9.

16. *(a)* 52.1; *(b)* 49.9; *(c)* 55.8; *(d)* 47.3; *(e)* 104.7; *(f)* 10.2; *(g)* $Z = -0.42$.

17. The mean for all states is 4,836.4 serious crimes per 100,000 residents and the standard deviation is 1,344.5. Because New York's Z score is $+0.53$, it is more typical than Iowa with a Z score of -0.66.

Answers to Chapter 3 Problems

1. *(a)* 30.0; *(b)* 37.5.

2. At least .75.

3. *(a)* 20; *(b)* 10; *(c)* 4.

4. *(a)* 1.88; *(b)* 1.04; *(c)* 2.06; *(d)* ± 2.33; *(e)* ± 1.28; *(f)* ± 3.08.

5. *(a)* $\mu_{\bar{Y}} = 12.5$, $\sigma_{\bar{Y}} = .89$; *(b)* $\mu_{\bar{Y}} = 40$, $\sigma_{\bar{Y}} = 1.00$; *(c)* $\mu_{\bar{Y}} = 0$, $\sigma_{\bar{Y}} = .45$; *(d)* $\mu_{\bar{Y}} = 14$, $\sigma_{\bar{Y}} = 1.41$; *(e)* $\mu_{\bar{Y}} = 200$, $\sigma_{\bar{Y}} = 1.00$.

6. *(a)* 1.699; *(b)* ± 2.756.

7. *(a)* LCL = 16, UCL = 24; *(b)* LCL = 14.68, UCL = 25.32.

8. (a) −2.492; (b) 24; (c) −2.25; (d) do not reject the null hypothesis.

9. (a) ±2.021; (b) 48; (c) +2.50; (d) reject the null hypothesis.

10. With $df = 14$, the critical value for t at $\alpha = .01$, one-tailed, is +2.624. The observed value of $t_{14} = +3.87$, so reject the null hypothesis. The reading-readiness test scores of pupils taking the new curriculum is above the minimum level for first grade entry.

11. The empirical probability of a first marriage after age 30 among GSS respondents who ever marry is .064.

12. $Z = +7.77$, so reject null hypothesis that mean on SOCFREND scale equals 3.50.

13. $t_{133} = -11.11$, so reject null hypothesis that blacks' mean on HELPBLK scale equals 3.00.

14. $t_{123} = +1.41$, so do not reject null hypothesis that women working part-time averaged 20 hours at work last week.

15. $t_{50} = -33.93$, so reject the null hypothesis that mean expectancy for men is the same as for women.

16. $t_{50} = +17.58$, so the probability is less than .001 that any state has an average of more than three persons per household.

17. $t_{50} = +3.70$, so reject the null hypothesis that mean state labor force in manufacturing fell by 5% or more.

Answers to Chapter 4 Problems

1. $H_0: \mu_D = \mu_I = \mu_R;\ H_1: \mu_D > \mu_I > \mu_R.$

2. $\alpha_{city} = -8.5;\ \alpha_{rural} = -4.2;\ \alpha_{suburb} = 10.6.$

3. $\alpha_{educ} = -0.94;\ \alpha_{art} = +1.83;\ \alpha_{engin} = -0.33.$

4. (a) $F_{1,28} = 4.20$; (b) $F_{1,298} = 6.63$; (c) $F_{5,54} = 4.76$; (d) $F_{19,580} = 2.37.$

5. (a) $F_{1,15} = 4.54$; (b) $F_{2,30} = 5.39$; (c) $F_{2,57} = 7.76$; (d) $F_{3,56} = 6.17.$

6. 13 minutes.

7. $MS_{BETWEEN} = 22.25.$

8. $\hat{\eta}^2 = 0.13$; $F_{2,48} = 2.34$, less than the critical value of 2.84, so do not reject H_0 that the four auto plant population means are equal.

9. $\alpha_{\text{None}} = -0.73$, $\alpha_{\text{Alone}} = -0.13$, $\alpha_{\text{Together}} = +0.87$.

SOURCE	SS	df	MS	F
Between	6.53	2	3.27	1.26
Within	31.20	12	2.60	
Total	37.73	14		

Since the c.v. = 3.89 for α = .05, do not reject the null hypothesis. $\hat{\eta}^2$ = 0.17. That is, only 17% of the variation in test scores can be explained by the type of studying.

10. $\hat{\Psi}$ = 1.30; $\hat{\sigma}^2_{\hat{\Psi}}$ = 0.78; t = +1.47; since c.v. = 2.79, do not reject H_0.

11. $F_{8,954}$ = 3.22, $p < .001$, $\hat{\eta}^2$ = 0.026. Trust in people is highest in the South Atlantic, East South Central, and West South Central states, lowest in the other five regions, but less than 3% of the variation is explained by region.

12. $F_{5,1501}$ = 71.32, $p < .001$, $\hat{\eta}^2$ = 0.192. The number of children ever born is curvilinear, increasing from 0.70 to respondents under 30 years, to a maximum of 3.02 for those aged 50–59, and falling off to 2.39 for those 70 and older. Age explains almost one-fifth the variation in number of children ever born.

13. $F_{5,658}$ = 1.82, not significant at p = .05, $\hat{\eta}^2$ = 0.014. Size of place is unrelated to preferences for spending on the cities.

14. $F_{1,49}$ = 20.64, $p < .05$, $\hat{\eta}^2$ = 0.296. The 13 Mountain and Pacific states had mean growth rates of 12.98%, but the other states grew only 4.42%.

15. $F_{1,49}$ = 5.62, $p < .05$, $\hat{\eta}^2$ = 0.103. The poorest half of states had only 120.5 persons on AFDC per 1,000 population, while the richest states had 309.3 persons per 1,000.

Answers to Chapter 5 Problems

1. χ^2 = 12.84, df = 1, $p < .001$; Yule's Q = 0.238. This falls between a weak and almost no relationship, with men more likely than women to vote for Bush.

2. $\chi^2 = 22.77$, $df = 1$, $p < .001$; Yule's $Q = -0.304$. This is a weak relationship, with women more likely than men to expect a war in the next 10 years.

3. $\chi^2 = 34.77$, $df = 1$, $p < .001$; $\phi = 0.185$, $\phi_{max} = 0.696$, $\phi_{adj} = 0.266$. The less-educated respondents are more likely to abstain from alcoholic beverages than are the more-educated respondents.

4. The odds favoring the least educated $= 1.40$, the middle educated $= 3.66$, and the most educated $= 5.38$.

5. The odds in favor for men $= 3.90$, the odds in favor for women $= 2.09$; the odds ratio $= 1.86$, indicating that men are about 1.86 times more favorable than women to allowing an atheist to speak.

6. The odds in favor for the more educated $= 6.45$, odds in favor for the less educated $= 1.52$; the odds ratio $= 4.25$, indicating the more educated are over four times more likely to favor an atheist speaking.

7. $\chi^2 = 110.34$, $df = 4$, $p < .001$; gamma $= -0.34$, $t_c = -0.18$. TV watching and confidence in the press covary inversely.

8. $\chi^2 = 29.16$, $df = 3$, $p < .001$; gamma $= -0.32$, $t_c = -0.15$. There is an inverse relationship between traditional sex-role attitude and expectations of having more children. That is, persons holding more traditional attitudes expect to have fewer additional children, perhaps because they tend to be older and past their childbearing years.

9. $\chi^2 = 108.25$, $df = 9$, $p < .001$; Somers's $d_{yx} = 0.29$ with premarital sex dependent. Persons holding traditional sex-role attitudes are more likely to say premarital sexual relations are always wrong.

10. $\chi^2 = 59.33$, $df = 6$, $p < .001$; Somers's $d_{yx} = -0.19$ with homosexuality dependent. Less-educated persons are more likely to say homosexual relations are always wrong.

11. $\chi^2 = 7.56$, $df = 1$, $p < .01$; phi $= 0.09$. Whites are more willing than blacks to allow an atheist to speak.

12. $\chi^2 = 20.56$, $df = 2$, $p < .001$; gamma $= -0.25$; $t_c = -0.13$; Somers's $d_{yx} = -0.11$ with smoking dependent. Less-educated people are more likely to smoke than better-educated people.

13. $\chi^2 = 54.55$, $df = 2$, $p < .001$; gamma $= 0.38$; $t_c = 0.20$; Somers's $d_{yx} = 0.17$ with drinking dependent. Better-educated people are more likely to drink alcoholic beverages than less-educated people.

14. $\chi^2 = 1.69$, $df = 1$, $p > .05$; phi $= -0.22$; gamma $= -0.45$; $t_c = -0.21$; Somers's $d_{yx} = -0.21$ with income rank dependent. No relationship.

15. $\chi^2 = 19.92$, $df = 1$, $p < .001$; phi $= 0.67$; gamma $= 0.96$; $t_c = 0.63$; Somers's $d_{yx} = 0.71$ with turnout dependent. Non-Southern states have higher turnout than Southern states.

Answers to Chapter 6 Problems

1. Scatterplot not shown. Relationship is that with higher education, greater interest in politics.

2. $\hat{Y}_i = 1,230 - 20\, X_i$, $R_{YX}^2 = .444$. Each increase of 1% in export-sector dependency reduces per capita income by $20. The equation accounts for 44.4% of the variance in per capita income.

3. (a) 3.7 new jobs; (b) 413.6 vacancies; (c) 933,514 students.

4. (a) 17,132; (b) 26.25; (c) 808.7; (d) 418.27.

5. $R_{YX}^2 = 0.240$.

SOURCE	SS	df	MS	F
Regression	2,050	1	2,050	17.66*
Error	6,500	56	116.07	
Total	8,550	57		

* Significant for $\alpha = .001$

Reject the null hypothesis of no linear relationship between wives' marital happiness and husbands' participation in household chores.

6. $r_{XY} = .75$ and $R_{XY}^2 = .5625$.

7. $t_{30} = 2.27$, reject H_0 at $\alpha = .05$.

8. *(a)* $F_{1,28} = 3.11$, not reject H_0; *(b)* $F_{1,59} = 25.29$, reject H_0; *(c)* $F_{1,98} = 5.16$, do not reject H_0.

9. LCL = 0.32, UCL = 3.68.

10. *(a)* 0.19; *(b)* −0.56; *(c)* 0.35.

11. $t_{1,1455} = 5.50$, reject H_0.

12. $R^2_{YX} = .174$, $F_{1,1336} = 281.16$, $p < .01$.

13. $\hat{Z}_{Y_i} = -0.07\ Z_i$, $t_{979} = -2.10$, reject H_0.

14. $\hat{Y}_i = 1.49 + .024\ X_i$, $F_{1,662} = 5.97$, $p > .01$, do not reject H_0.

15. $t_{49} = 1.41$, do not reject H_0.

16. $R^2_{YX} = .267$, $F_{1,49} = 17.82$, $p < .01$, reject H_0.

17. $\hat{Y}_i = 10.58 - .016\ X_i$, $F_{1,49} = 2.60$, $p > .05$, $t_{49} = -1.61$, do not reject H_0.

Answers to Chapter 7 Problems

1. These hypotheses suggest a causal sequence in which level of supervision interprets the relationship between family status (disruption) and illegal actions by male children. Diagram not shown.

2. Married women with fewer or no children probably participate in the paid labor force more than women with many children. In marriages with no or fewer children, the financial and emotional capability of dissolving a poor marriage is greater than where many children are present. If these assumptions are correct, holding constant the number of children would cause the correlation between labor force participation and divorce to fall to zero. Diagram not shown.

3. Examples of such relationships include the following: (a) Dependency on a single raw export product makes a nation's economy prone to periodic price depressions that result in civil unrest, and thus the armed forces step in to restore order. (b) Dependency on single products encourages multinational corporations to invest heavily in the economy, but these foreign investors feel secure only when a military strongman is in control. (c) Single-product dependency makes a nation suscep-

tible to guerrilla insurgencies supported by the poor, whose repression ultimately incites a military takeover. Many other intervening variables are plausible candidates to interpret the causal relation. Diagrams not shown.

4. The correlation in the zero-order table is $r_{XY} = -0.23$, with women having lower wages. Controlling for work status provides a partial explanation for this relationship, since it is reduced to $r_{XY} = -0.21$ for full-time work and $r_{XY} = -0.12$ for part-time work. The odds ratios show the same pattern. In the zero-order table the odds ratio is 2.14, whereas it is 2.50 for full-time work and 1.67 for part-time work. These results also suggest an interaction effect: the relationship between gender and wages is stronger for full-time workers than for part-time workers.

5. The correlation for the zero-order table is $r_{XY} = -0.21$, with fewer women than men watching X-rated movies. But controlling for belief that sexual materials lead to moral breakdown, the gender differences in attendance and the gender differences in viewing remains unchanged among those seeing no breakdown ($r_{XY} = -0.21$), but the partial correlation is much smaller for gender and viewing among those seeing a moral breakdown ($r_{XY} = -0.13$). The odds ratios confirm the results from the correlational analysis: the zero-order table odds ratio is 0.38, while for "no" and "yes" levels of the control variable, the odds ratios are 0.42 and 0.49, respectively. Thus, holding constant the third variable provides a partial explanation of the original gender difference in viewing sexual materials.

6. Age and opinion zero-order $r_{XY} = -0.07$; highly religious subtable $r_{XY} = -0.01$; not highly religious subtable (not shown) $r_{XY} = -0.33$. Similarly, the odds ratios for the zero-order table are 0.75, 0.97 for the highly religious, and 0.22 for those not highly religious. This interaction effect shows that the relationship is strongest among persons who are not highly religious.

7. The zero-order $r_{XY} = -0.18$ (odds ratio = 0.45) does not disappear in the subtables, as it would if attitude completely explained the relationship between proximity and behavior. Instead, an absence of explanation occurs, with $r_{XY} = -0.13$ (odds ratio = 0.45) among those who say there is too much spending on the problems of blacks, and $r_{XY} = -0.17$ (odds ratio = 0.46) among those who say the amount of spending is too little or about right.

8. *(a)* 0.03; *(b)* −0.41; *(c)* 0.46; *(d)* −0.90.

9. *(a)* (1) 0.42; (2) 0.26 and 0.65; (3) 0.40; (4) $t_{252} = 6.93$, reject H_0 that $\rho_{YX \cdot W} = 00$; *(b)* interaction effect; the relationship is stronger in rural than in urban areas.

10. *(a)* −0.28; *(b)* −0.43 for teens, −0.13 for later; *(c)* −0.23; *(d)* $t_{302} = 4.16$, reject H_0.

11. The more educated are slightly more conservative (37.5%) than the less educated (29.1%), $r_{XY} = 0.08$. Holding age constant, the POLVIEWS–EDUC correlation is virtually the same among the younger ($r_{XY} = 0.08$) and among the older ($r_{XY} = 0.09$) respondents.

12. Zero order $r_{XY} = -0.19$; Protestant $r_{XY} = -0.15$; Catholic $r_{XY} = -0.30$. The correlation of religious intensity and attitude toward abortion for a poor woman is stronger among Catholics than among Protestants.

13. Zero order $r_{XY} = 0.05$; partial, controlling for education $r_{XY} = 0.03$.

14. Zero order $r_{XY} = -0.33$; states with low population change $r_{XY} = -0.51$; states with high population change $r_{XY} = -0.15$. The covariation between state wealth and generous AFDC payments is much stronger in states experiencing lower population change than in states with higher growth rates.

15. Zero order $r_{XY} = 0.36$; partial, controlling for physicians per capita $r_{XY} = 0.34$.

Answers to Chapter 8 Problems

1. $a = 39.232$; $b_1 = 2.952$; $b_2 = -1.190$.

2. $\hat{Y}_i = 0.738 Z_{X_1} - 0.595 Z_{X_2}$

3. For $N = 65$, $F_{8,56} = 0.55$; critical value for $\alpha = .05$ is 2.02, so do not reject H_0. But for $N = 650$, $F_{8,641} = 6.31$; critical value for $\alpha = .05$ is 1.94, so reject H_0.

4. $t_{b_1} = 2.31$, $df = 397$; critical value for $\alpha = .01$ one-tailed is 2.326, so do not reject H_0; $t_{b_2} = -1.85$, $df = 397$, so do not reject H_0.

5. $t_{b_1} = 3.375$, $df = 193$; critical value for $\alpha = .001$ is 3.291, so reject H_0.

6. $LCL_{95} = 1.455$, $UCL_{95} = 5.485$; $UCL_{99} = 0.822$; $UCL_{99} = 6.118$.

7. For each $10,000 of annual income, monthly social evenings increase by 0.161; each year of marriage decreases evenings by 0.034 per week; and having young children decreases monthly evenings by 0.562.

8.

CATEGORY	D_1	D_2	D_3	D_4	D_5	D_6
Married, living together	1	0	0	0	0	0
Partner, living together	0	1	0	0	0	0
Married, living apart	0	0	1	0	0	0
Partner, living apart	0	0	0	1	0	0
Not married, no partner	0	0	0	0	1	0
No answer	0	0	0	0	0	1

9. Equation 1: $\hat{Y} = a + b_N D_N + b_S D_S + b_E D_E + b_1 X_1$
   Equation 2: $\hat{Y} = a + b_N D_N + b_S D_S + b_E D_E + b_1 X_1$
   $+ b_2 X_1 D_N + b_3 X_1 D_S + b_4 X_1 D_E$

10. *a.* $F_{1,633} = 15.46$; c.v. $= 100.83$, so reject H_0.
    b. $\hat{Y} = 3.28 - 0.42(1) - 0.003(25) + 0.12(25) = 3.086$ hours.

11. *a.*

VARIABLE	b_i	t_i	β_i
Education	.076	4.81*	.153
Age	−.010	−3.86*	−.122
Constant	4.803	17.90*	

* Significant beyond $p < .001$, given critical value $= \pm 2.58$ for two-tailed test.

b. $R^2 = 0.0477$; $F_{2,1005} = 25.19$. Since critical value $= 6.91$, reject H_0.
c. The higher one's education (net of age), the greater the satisfaction with one's health. The older one is, the less the health satisfaction. The standardized effects of education and age have almost the same magnitude.

12. *a.* Separated $= -0.281$; Divorced $= -0.164$; Widowed $= -0.158$; Married $= +0.088$.
    b. $F_{4,1001} = 1.37$; c.v. $= 2.37$, so do not reject H_0.

13. *a.* $R^2 = 0.1077$; $F_{4,1485} = 44.82$; c.v. $= 2.37$; reject H_0.
    b. $R^2 = 0.1145$; $F_{7,1482} = 27.39$; c.v. $= 2.01$; reject H_0.
    c. Difference in $R^2 = 0.0068$; $F_{3,1482} = 3.79$; c.v. $= 2.60$; reject H_0.

14. *a.*

REGION	μ_j	β_j
New England	.246	.505
Middle Atlantic	−.047	.212
East North Central	.024	.283
West North Central	.023	.282
South Atlantic	−.011	.248
East South Central	.140	.399
West South Central	.214	.473
Mountain	−.061	.198
Pacific	−.259	—
Mean/Intercept	4.088	3.829

b. $\beta_j - 0.259 = \alpha_j.$

c.

SOURCE	SS	df	MS	F
Between	28.401	8	3.550	2.02*
Within	2,549.194	1,450	1.758	
Total	2,574.595	1,458		

* Significant at α = .005, since c.v. = 1.94.

15. $R^2 = 0.1286$; $F_{2,48} = 3.54$; since c.v. = 3.15, reject H_0. For AGE3, $t_b = 0.32$, $df = 48$; since c.v. = 2.00, two-tailed, do not reject H_0. For HHMDNINC, $t_b = 2.51$, $df = 48$; since c.v. = 2.00, two-tailed, reject H_0.

16. For POORPCT, $UCL_{95} = 0.915$, $LCL_{95} = 17.467$. For FEMLFP, $UCL_{95} = 2.340$, $LCL_{95} = 14.828$. For UNION, $UCL_{95} = -0.426$, $LCL_{95} = 6.686$.

17. *a.* $R^2 = 0.0645$; $F_{2,48} = 1.66$; since c.v. = 3.15, do not reject H_0. Neither regression coefficient is significant at α = .005, two-tailed.

   b. Change in $R^2 = 0.6129$; $F_{3,47} = 89.31$; since c.v. = 3.15, do not reject H_0. With MARRYPC in the equation, all three regression coefficients are significant at α = .05. States' divorce rates increase with the marriage rate and the net migration rate, but decrease with the percentage urbanized.

Answers to Chapter 9 Problems

1. Because $F_{5,1002} = 2.24$ and c.v. $= 2.21$ for $\alpha = .05$, reject the null hypothesis. Trust in people deviates significantly from a linear relationship with education.

2. Graph not shown. The plotted values suggest a logarithmic relationship between per-capita income and electricity consumption.

3. *a.* 32.684 prestige score.
   b. 39.548 prestige score.
   c. 50.084 prestige score.
   d. 4.172 years of education and 31.336 prestige score.

4. *a.* 37.128 prestige score.
   b. 41.616 prestige score.
   c. 48.698 prestige score.

5. Age decreases the log odds of belief in an afterlife, but not significantly, while higher church attendance significantly raises the log odds.

6. *a. For a:* $UCL_{95} = 1.310$; $LCL_{95} = 0.314$.
   b. For b_1: $UCL_{95} = 0.005$; $LCL_{95} = -0.015$.
   c. For b_2: $UCL_{95} = 0.293$; $LCL_{95} = 0.155$.

7. Being Catholic reduces the log odds by 11.2%, being Jewish reduces the log odds by 21.9%, relative to Protestant.

8. *a.* 0.800.
   b. 0.720.

9. $G^2 = 62.72$, $df = 4$. Since c.v. $= 18.467$, reject the null hypothesis. At least one coefficient is significantly different from zero. Pseudo $R^2 = 0.447$.

10. For women in the paid labor force, *a:* $t = 10.03$, $p < .001$; X_1: $t = -1.97$, $p < .05$; X_2: $t = -4.24$, $p < .001$; $X_3 = -9.29$, $p < .001$. For retired women, *a:* $t = -6.46$, $p < .001$; X_1: $t = -1.01$, $p > .05$; X_2: $t = -1.89$, $p > .05$; $X_3 = 6.77$, $p < .001$. Relative to women keeping house, women in the paid labor force are less likely to be married, to have children at home, and to be older. Retired women are more likely to be older.

11. The difference between R-squared and eta-squared, $F_{5,1005} = 1.91$. Since c.v. $= 2.21$, do not reject the null hypothesis of linearity.

12. $\hat{Y}_i = 31.822 + 0.498\ X_i - 0.005\ X_i^2$
    (2.751) (0.119) (0.001)
    For age: $UCL_{95} = 0.805$; $LCL_{95} = 0.191$.
    For age squared: $UCL_{95} = -0.002$; $LCL_{95} = -0.008$.
    At the age of 49.8 years, occupational prestige is predicted to reach a maximum value of 44.2 prestige points.

13. $\hat{L}_i = -2.619 + 1.611X_{1i} + 0.357X_{2i}$
    s.e. $= (0.380)\ (0.324)\ (0.221)$
    $t = (-6.89)\ (4.97)\ (1.62)$
    Equation -2 log likelihood $= 542.51$; constant only -2 log likelihood $= 573.67$; $G^2 = 31.16$, $df = 2$, $p < .001$. Correct predictions: 94.7% against busing, 22.1% for busing.

14. $\hat{L}_i = -1.352 - 0.049\ X_{1i} + 0.023\ X_{2i} - 0.018\ X_{3i}$
    s.e. $= (0.342)\ (0.157)\ (0.004)\ (0.006)$
    $t = (-3.95)\ (-0.31)\ (5.75)\ (-3.00)$
    Equation -2 log likelihood $= 1,008.60$; constant only -2 log likelihood $= 1,044.36$; $G^2 = 35.76$, $df = 3$, $p < .001$. Correct predictions: 99.7% disagree, 0.9% agree.

15. $\hat{Y}_i = -763.114 + 1490.870\ X_i - 71.116\ X_i^2$
    (1201.278) (329.182) (18.192)
    The maximum crime rate is 7,050.5 per 100,000 population when policing expenditures are 10.48% of local government budgets. Policing effort initially rises with crime rate, but decreases at the highest levels.

16. $\hat{Y}_i = -2,835,900 + 627,048\ (\log_{10} X_i)$
    (808,251) (161,722)
    a. 28,530 people would leave the state.
    b. 598,518 people would enter the state.

Answers to Chapter 10 Problems

1. Odds in favor for entire table $= 0.81$; odds for women $= 0.68$; odds for men $= 1.02$; odds ratio $= 0.66$. Women are only about two-thirds as likely as men to support abortion in the case of a single woman.

2.

	BUSING BY RACE	

		RACE	
SUPPORT FOR SCHOOL BUSING FOR INTEGRATION		WHITE	BLACK
Favor		261.4	77.5
Oppose		553.4	46.5

3. $\hat{\mu} = 5.382$; $\hat{\lambda}_1^P = 0.219$, $\hat{\lambda}_1^B = -0.329$; $\hat{\lambda}_{11}^{PB} = 0.125$.

4. $\hat{s}_\lambda = 0.0355$; $t_{\lambda P} = +6.17$; $t_{\lambda H} = -9.27$; $t_{\lambda PH} = -3.52$.

5. *a.* $\hat{F}_{11} = 195.59$; $\hat{F}_{12} = 357.81$; $\hat{F}_{21} = 136.46$; $\hat{F}_{22} = 249.64$.

   b. $L^2 = 11.64$; reject null hypothesis since c.v. = 6.63 for $\alpha = .01$.

6. The conditional odds ratio of class to satisfied and more or less satisfied = $+2.02$ for persons under 45 years and = $+2.38$ for persons 45 years and older. The conditional odds ratio of class to satisfied & not at all satisfied = $+5.09$ for persons under 45 years and = $+5.01$ for persons 45 years and older. The effects of class are almost identical in each age group, but the effects are much stronger on no satisfaction than on some satisfaction, relative to those who are satisfied.

7. Model 5 fits better than models 1–3, but model 5 does not fit better than model 4 since $L_4^2 - L_5^2 = 7.63 - 0.61 = 7.02$ for $df_4 - df_5 = 3 - 2 = 1$, while c.v. = 10.83 at $\alpha = .001$.

8. The smallest BIC statistics are for model 4 (BIC = -28.22) and model 7 (BIC = -28.59). Testing for the differences in model L^2s, with $\alpha = .05$, model 7 fits significantly better than model 4 ($L_7^2 - L_4^2 = 12.68 - 5.49 = 7.19$; $df_7 - df_4 = 6 - 5 = 1$). Hence, both the {CV} and {PV} effects seem essential to fit the data, but the {EV} parameter is not required.

9. *(a)* 123.59; *(b)* 10.06.

10. *(a)* $+0.988$; *(b)* -2.916.

11. For the independence model, $L^2 = 94.14$, $df = 8$; reject null hypothesis because c.v. = 26.13 at $\alpha = .001$. The expected frequencies are as follows:

	HAPPY		
FINRELA	VERY HAPPY	PRETTY HAPPY	NOT TOO HAPPY
Far Below Average	23.55	44.03	8.43
Below Average	105.96	198.12	37.92
Average	235.46	440.27	84.27
Above Average	87.68	163.94	31.38
Far Above Average	8.36	15.64	2.99

12. For the independence model, $L^2 = 8.08$, $df = 1$; reject null hypothesis because c.v. $= 6.63$ at $\alpha = .01$. For the saturated model, $\hat{\mu} = 5.450$; $\hat{\lambda}_1^S = -0.376$; $\hat{\lambda}_1^G = -0.144$; $\hat{\lambda}_{11}^{SG} = +0.097$.

13. The models' statistics, where G = SEX, P = PORNMORL, X = XMOVIE, are

MODEL	L^2	df	p	BIC
1. {GP}{GX}{PX}	0.20	1	.655	−6.65
2. {GP}{GX}	17.81	2	.000	4.11
3. {GP}{PX}	24.65	2	.000	10.95
4. {GX}{PX}	53.63	2	.000	39.93

Both the L^2 and BIC statistic identify model 1 as the best fit.

14. The model containing all two-variable effects is the best fit, because it has $L^2 = 3.68$, $df = 2$, $p = .16$, and no model deleting any two-variable effect has ΔL^2 that is not significant at $\alpha = .05$. The effects parameters are

$$\mu = 3.411 \qquad \lambda_1^P = +0.189 \qquad \lambda_1^{Rp} = +1.582 \qquad \lambda_1^{Rc} = +0.698$$
$$\lambda_1^A = +0.109 \qquad \lambda_{11}^{ARp} = +0.014 \qquad \lambda_{11}^{ARc} = +0.130$$
$$\lambda_{11}^{PA} = +0.222 \qquad \lambda_{11}^{PRp} = -0.564 \qquad \lambda_{11}^{PRc} = -0.380$$

Younger persons are more likely than older people to approve the prayer decision, Protestants are the least likely to approve the decision, followed by Catholics and Jews. The absence of a significant three-variable effect means that the age effect is the same for each denomination (or, the denomination effect is the same for both age groups).

Answers to Chapter 11 Problems

1. An example: "A prolonged economic recession causes voters to cast ballots for the opposition party."

2.

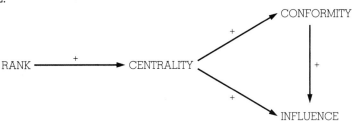

3. (a) $r'_{BD} = p_{DC}p_{CB} + p_{DC}p_{CA}r_{BA} + p_{DA}r_{BA}$
   (b) There are none.

4. (a) L has a larger indirect causal effect on H (0.15) than does K (0.10); (b) 37.6% of the variance in J is explained by L and K.

5. (a) B has the larger indirect on D; (b) 36% of the variance in D is explained.

6. $r'_{t,t-2} = 0.56$.

7. $r'_{DB} = p_{DC}p_{CB} + p_{DC}p_{CA}r_{AB} + p_{DA}r_{AB}$; the first term is causal and the last two terms are correlated effects.

8.

	Y_1	Y_2	Y_3	Y_4	Y_5
Y_1	1.00	0.50	0.25	0.13	0.06
Y_2		1.00	0.50	0.25	0.13
Y_3			1.00	0.50	0.25
Y_4				1.00	0.50
Y_5					1.00

9. (a) $r'_{BD} = 0.415$; (b) $r'_{AD} = 0.557$.

10. (a) proof not shown; (b) $r'_{UV} = 0.034$.

11.

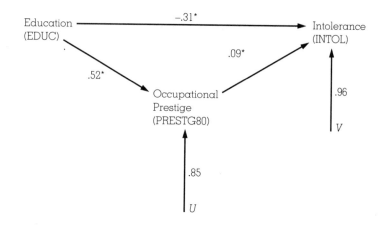

* Significant beyond α = .05.

12.

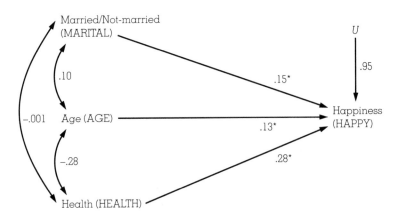

* Significant beyond α = .001.

13.

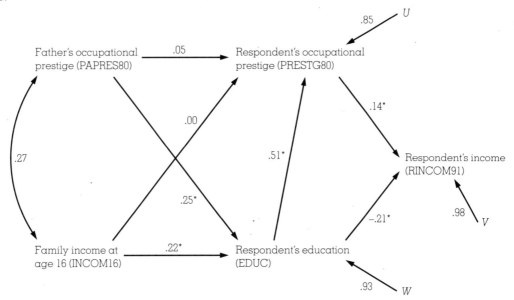

* Significant beyond α = .001.

14.

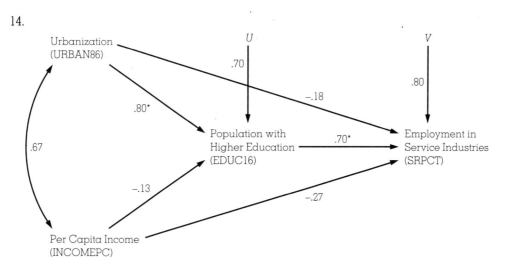

* Significant beyond α = .05.

15.

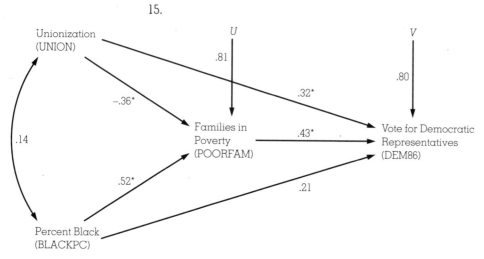

* Significant beyond $\alpha = .05$.

Answers to Chapter 12 Problems

1. $\eta_1 = \beta_{12}\eta_2 + \beta_{13}\eta_3 + \zeta_1$
   $\eta_2 = \beta_{23}\eta_3 + \gamma_{22}\xi_2 + \zeta_2$
   $\eta_3 = \gamma_{31}\xi_1 + \gamma_{32}\xi_2 + \zeta_3$

2. (a) $\mathbf{P'} = \begin{pmatrix} 1 & -2 \\ 4 & 1 \\ 3 & 6 \end{pmatrix}$ (b) $\mathbf{P} + \mathbf{Q'} = \begin{pmatrix} 7 & 6 & 0 \\ -1 & -3 & 11 \end{pmatrix}$

(c) $\mathbf{Q'P}$ is not conformable for multiplication.

(d) $\mathbf{RQ} = \begin{pmatrix} 5 & 13 \\ -5 & -13 \\ 5 & 13 \end{pmatrix}$ (e) $\mathbf{IR} = \begin{pmatrix} 2 & 1 & 3 \\ -2 & -1 & -3 \\ 2 & 1 & 3 \end{pmatrix}$

(f) $\mathbf{R^{-1}\,R} = \begin{pmatrix} 1 & 0 & 0 \\ 0 & 1 & 0 \\ 0 & 0 & 1 \end{pmatrix}$

3. $\eta_1 = \gamma_{11}\xi_2 + \gamma_{12}\xi_2 + \gamma_{13}\xi_3 + \zeta_1$
   $\eta_2 = \beta_{21}\eta_1 + \gamma_{23}\xi_3 + \zeta_2$

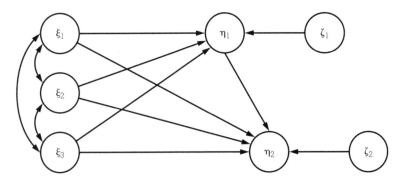

4.

$$\Lambda_y = \begin{pmatrix} \lambda_{11} & 0 \\ \lambda_{21} & 0 \\ \lambda_{31} & 0 \\ 0 & \lambda_{42} \\ 0 & \lambda_{52} \end{pmatrix} \qquad \Lambda_x = \begin{bmatrix} \lambda_{11} & 0 \\ \lambda_{21} & 0 \\ \lambda_{31} & 0 \\ 0 & \lambda_{42} \\ 0 & \lambda_{52} \\ 0 & \lambda_{62} \end{bmatrix}$$

5.

$$y_1 = \eta_1 + \epsilon_1$$
$$y_2 = \lambda_{21}\eta_1 + \epsilon_2$$
$$y_3 = \lambda_{32}\eta_2 + \epsilon_3$$
$$y_4 = \eta_2 + \epsilon_4$$

$$x_1 = \xi_1 + \delta_1$$
$$x_2 = \lambda_{21}\xi_1 + \delta_2$$
$$x_3 = \xi_2 + \delta_3$$
$$x_4 = \lambda_{42}\xi_2 + \delta_4$$
$$x_5 = \xi_3 + \delta_5$$
$$x_6 = \lambda_{63}\xi_3 + \delta_6$$

6. HAPPY and HAPMAR are both significant indicators of unobserved happiness. The reliability of HAPPY (0.74) is greater than the reliability of HAPMAR (0.30). Education has a significant positive effect on happiness, the number of traumas has a significant negative effect, but the number of children does not affect happiness.

7. Expected correlations:

	EDUC	PRESTG80	TRUST	HELPFUL
EDUC	1.00			
PRESTG80	.52	1.00		
TRUST	.23	.20	1.00	
HELPFUL	.14	.12	.34	1.00

Reliabilities:
EDUC = .61; PRESTG80 = .45; TRUST = .56; HELPFUL = .20.

8. Parental socioeconomic status, measured by income and occupational prestige, is a significant cause of offsprings' socioeconomic status, but parental education, measured by father's and mother's education, is not significant. $r_{\xi_1 \eta_1} = .20$ and $r_{\xi_2 \eta_1} = .41$.

9. Socioeconomic status, measured by income and occupational prestige, significantly increases spending preferences, measured by NATDRUG and NATCRIME, but political preference, measured by PARTYID and POLVIEWS, has no significant effect on spending preferences. $r_{\xi_1 \eta_1} = .21$ and $r_{\xi_2 \eta_1} = .19$.

10. Two uncorrelated factors exist: (1) a science-medicine factor and (2) a media-business-labor factor. The CONBUS and CONPRESS indicators load significantly on both factors.

11.

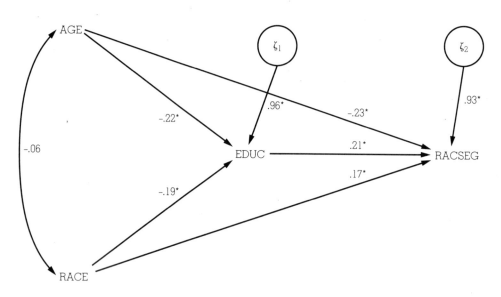

$^*\, p < .05$

12.

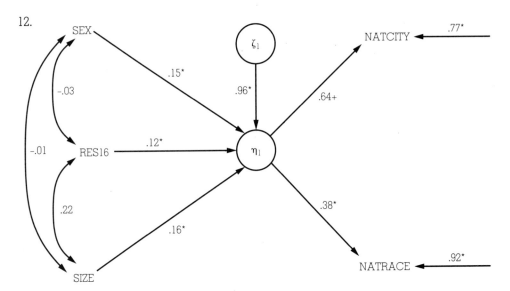

$\chi^2 = 3.76$, $df = 2$, $p = .15$; GFI = .998; AGFI = .988.
* $p < .05$
+ fixed coefficient

13.

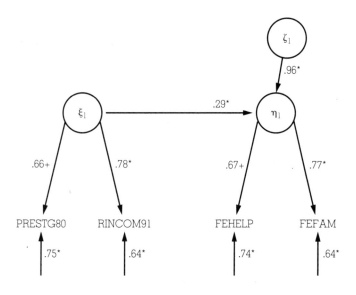

$\chi^2 = 0.02$, $df = 1$, $p = .89$; GFI = 1.00; AGFI = 1.00.
* $p < .05$
+ fixed coefficient

14.

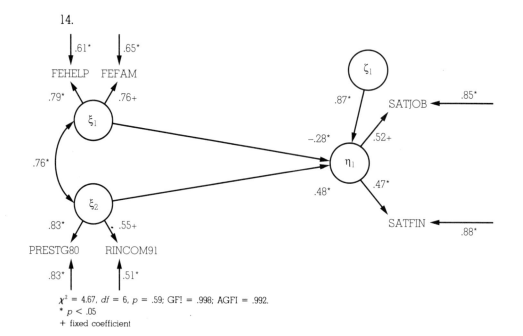

$\chi^2 = 4.67$, $df = 6$, $p = .59$; GF! = .998; AGFI = .992.
* $p < .05$
+ fixed coefficient

15. A single-factor model produced a poor fit ($\chi^2 = 227.5$; $df = 9$; $p = .00$; GFI = .910; AGFI = .789). A two-factor model, with the same lambdas set to zero, produced a better fit:

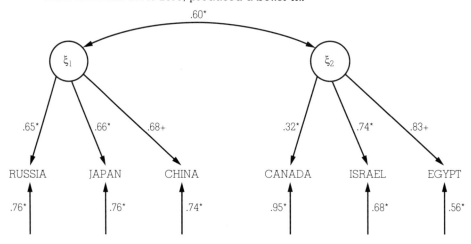

$\chi^2 = 29.7$, $df = 8$, $p = .00$; GFI = .989; AGFI = .972.
* $p < .05$
+ fixed coefficient

INDEX

THE BOOK'S MANUFACTURE

Statistics for Social Data Analysis, Third
Edition, was edited by Caryl Wenzel of
Publishers Services, Inc. Design and
production tasks, including typesetting, were
performed by the staff of Publishers Services,
Inc. The book was printed on 50 lb finch by
Arcata Graphics.